IN DOCTOR LUKE'S S

A Pupil's and Teacher's Guide to St. Luke

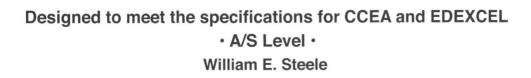

Designed to meet the specifications for CCEA and EDEXCEL
· A/S Level ·
William E. Steele

Copyright:

William E. Steele and Sunkleros Education

2007

Designed by: Martin McGilton and Kris Acheson

Printed by GPS Colour Graphics Ltd

ISBN 978-0-9555673-0-8

Except where otherwise stated, the Scripture quotations contained here in are from the Revised Version of the Bible, © 1952 by the Division of Christian Education of the National Council of the Churches of Christ in the United States of America, Centre Column References © and used by permission.

Other quotations from The New Revised Standard Version of the Bible, Anglicized Edition, ©1989, 1995 by the Division of the Division of Christian Education of the National Council of the Churches of Christ in the United States of America. All rights reserved.

Cover picture:
Cambridge University Library from the manuscript LL.1.10 of symbol of Luke's Gospel from the Book of Cerne.

Sunkleros Education

16 Coniston Road,

Bangor,

County Down,

Northern Ireland

BT20 4QQ

Tel: (028) 91463175

E-mail: billyandsheila@btopenworld.com

The purpose of this book is to provide a resource for teachers and activities for pupils preparing for A/S Lower-Sixth examinations CCEA and Edexcel Examining Boards. Some of the material e.g. women in Luke's Gospel will also be appropriate for A2 Upper Sixth pupils (CCEA). At the end of this chapter suitable pupils' activities have been designed mainly for revision purposes. This book came as a cry from the heart from some Secondary teachers who identified the need for a resource based upon the specifications laid down by the two Examining Boards. Schools were having to spend considerable amounts of money "dipping into" numerous commentaries when a book designed to cover the entire specification was required. This book has been written using recent research, contemporary scholarship and up to date commentaries on Luke's Gospel. I am hopeful that Volume Two for A2 pupils will follow this book in the future.

The contents have been thoroughly researched at Tyndale House, Cambridge where I had the use of a rented desk and all the facilities of the library. I should like to thank the staff at Tyndale House for all their hospitality, for the wonderful selection of journals, books and commentaries on Luke's Gospel, and in particular Dr. Bruce Winter for providing my wife, family and myself with the accommodation. Thanks are also due to Dr. David Instone Brewer for his technical support for my computer. Luke's emphasis on universality became a basic reality when at Tyndale I was privileged to meet Christian researchers authors, missionaries and lecturers from all over the world. I am deeply indebted to Dr. R. Jennings, Principal of Slemish Integrated College, Ballymena for his painstaking editorial comments, helpful suggestions and encouragement when I was preparing the book. My thanks are also due to Mr. Martin McGilton for the first drafts of the document in "InDesign," to Tatch Design for the completed document before going to press and finally to Mr. David Barr (BELB) who rescued my computer when I experienced technical difficulties.

This book could not have been written without the support and continual encouragement from my wife Sheila and daughters: Claire and her husband Gary for all their help when my computer failed, Katy for her meticulous care of the house and Sarah for her frequent visits to Cambridge and present of a commentary on Luke's Gospel. My thanks are also due to Dr. Chris. Wright, International Ministries Director of the Langham Trust International for his comments of the Passion Narrative and O.T. connections and to Mr. David McKnight former Principal of Cliftonville Primary School for the final editorial comments. Thanks are also due also to my former religious adviser colleagues Frances, Paul, Philip, John, and Bill from the five Education and Library Boards for their continual support and encouragement. My final thanks again to those religious education teachers who read some of my earlier attempts and gave me invaluable advice and editorial comments regarding suitability.

I trust that Luke's Gospel will come alive to pupils as they study its contents and that Luke will prove to be for them "a most beautiful book." It is also to be hoped that this resource will encourage and inspire some of our pupils to do further biblical studies study, join the ranks of those from Northern Ireland who are presently lecturing in this area and produce books and commentaries in biblical, textual studies. Scripture quotes are from the RSV unless otherwise stated. Specific targets and outcomes have been used to introduce and conclude each chapter to correspond with the self-evalution exercise.

First published Spring 2007 (William E. Steele) This book is gratefully dedicated to my wife Sheila for all the happy years at Sunkleros and the pleasant autumn months spent in Tyndale House Cambridge. © **W.E. Steele**

William E. Steele • 16 Coniston Road • Bangor • Co. Down • Northern Ireland • BT20 4QQ

[e] billyandsheila@btopenworld.com **[t]** 028 9146 3175

Acknowledgements:

Cambridge University Library from the manuscript LL.1.10 of symbol of Luke's Gospel from the Book of Cerne.

Mrs H. Mahood (London) for the use of the graphics on Sufferings in the Passion Narrative.

Symbol for Luke's Gospel in the Book of Kells,

Streams in the Desert, No. 9 Jesus' Boats in the Sea of Galilee, Israel: Photo by H.J. Mears.

Student's self-evaluation sheet based upon Ch.12: Parables   Please tick in the box.

1. I can identify at least six different types of parable in Luke's Gospel. ☐

2. I can classify the parables in Luke's Gospel in five different ways. ☐

3. I would need to do more work on the following related issues: metaphor, similitude, synedoche, monarchic parables, monadic, dyadic and triadic parables. (A/2) ☐

4. I can identify different parables of mercy. ☐

5. I understand the connection between Jesus as a compassionate teacher and the parables of mercy. ☐

6. I can construct a spidergram on Jesus as a compassionate teacher. ☐

7 I can summarise the key points in the mercy parables which relate to Jesus as a compassionate teacher. ☐

8. I can now define the word "parable" in different ways and give examples of each definition. ☐

9. I can differentiate between a parable and a similitude. ☐

10. I can recognise the different types of responses to the ministry of Jesus as seen in the parables. ☐

11. I would need to do more work on the purposes of the parables. ☐

12. I have found the use of "the chiasmus" as a teaching aid for recall to be useful, helpful, confusing. ☐

13. As an aid to memory, I can summarise the parables in the journey narrative as a chaismus. ☐

14. I can summarise the three parables on "lostness." ☐

15. I can differentiate between the different kinds of "lostness" in these parables. ☐

16. I know and understand the teaching of Jesus about forgiveness from my detailed study of the Good Samaritan and the parable of the two debtors. ☐

17. In the parable of the Sower, I know, understand and can interpret the parable in terms of the "Great Commandment" in Deuteronomy Ch.6. ☐

18. I understand the significance of "joy" in the parables on "lostness". ☐

19. I now understand the meaning of the term "advent parable." (A/2) ☐

20. From the classification of parables I can identify the parables of the kingdom, crisis and discipleship (A/2) and mercy (A/S) ☐

21. This study of the parables in Luke's Gospel has whetted my appetite to go on to do Religious Studies at A/2 level in Upper-Sixth. ☐

Total ☐

CCEA A/S + Edexcel A/S Level

Targets:
- Identify the key issues relating to the authorship of the Third Gospel, e.g. the identity of the author. (CCEA A/S)
- Identify the other contemporary writings at that time and their link with the Third Gospel.
- Recognise the terms and concepts in the prologue relating to the authorship, for example narrative, eyewitnesses, sources, "investigated closely," "we passages" and orderly account. (CCEA A/S)
- Recognise the significance of internal and external evidence relating to authorship.
- Recognise the significance of the link between authorship and understanding of the Third Gospel. (Edexcel A/S)
- Identify the views of scholars about the authorship. (Edexcel A/S)
- Recognise the importance of knowing who wrote the Third Gospel. (CCEA A/S)

---

[1] The Authorship of the Third Gospel in Relationship to the Prologue (Read 1:1-4.)

Introduction: Let us imagine the writer of the Third Gospel is explaining his prologue and giving us hidden clues about himself. This is what he might have said.

Dear Theophilus,

As I have hinted in my prologue (1:1-4), I didn't want to do a repeat of Mark and Matthew but rather to paint a different portrait of the life of Jesus with a variety of hues and colours. You will note in (1:1-2) that I was particularly dependent upon some others before me who wrote a similar account. "The many" from whom I received much useful written material (1:1) include some of the following sources: the Septuagint version otherwise known as the (LXX) **(1)**, Mark and "Q" **(2)** and to help identify with my Jewish readers, I have used portions of the O.T. (1 Kgs.17-21; Deut.1-26). The (LXX) went down particularly well with my Gentile readership. I am also highlighting the idea that "the things that have been accomplished among us" are the things promised, performed and "fulfilled" by God (1:1; 9:51; parts of Chs.7-10; 22-24). To identify further with my Gentile readers, I have used the word "teacher" (Gk. didaskalos) as a title for Jesus rather than "rabbi" (9:38; 10:25; 11:45; 12:13; 18:18). Although Aramaic is not my language (Acts 1:19) my knowledge of the O.T. in Greek (LXX) more than makes up for this.

My reference to "those who from the beginning were eyewitnesses and ministers of the word" (1:2) is a reference to those who preached the gospel. I liked the idea of summing up the content of the message as the word: the word of God which means the word preached as God's authoritative message. These ministers served the cause of God's message. Look out for this expression "word" (Gk. logos meaning Jesus' message enshrined in His words and deeds) as you read the rest of the Gospel; I have used it twenty-three times in my Gospel for example 1:20; 3:4; 4:22; 4:32; 11:28; 24:19,44. Later, I go on to show the importance of preaching as the purpose of Jesus' ministry (4:43). I myself was not an eyewitness but I became very indebted to those who provided me with their own oral accounts. My mentors were not academic historians but people who lived by the word, which they preached. "From the beginning" (1:2) means going back to the ministry of John the Baptist as I wanted to go back to the roots of the faith. "As they were delivered to us" covers both the oral and written traditions of the word (1:2).

This means I have used three types of sources: **(1)** actual events, "Things that have been accomplished among us." (1:1) **(2)** spoken or passed on oral reports, "Just as they were delivered to us by those who from the beginning were eyewitnesses." (1:2) **(3)** written reports, "Many people have done their best to write a report of these things." (1:1) It seemed good to me to write my own "orderly account." (1:3) By this I mean I like precise order and accuracy, which reflects my Greek background and culture. Even though I was not an eyewitness of the actual life of Jesus, I have "followed all things closely," in that I have been able to track down and investigate all things thoroughly or, as your margin reading says, I "followed all things accurately." (1:3 RSV) My information has been thoroughly researched in that I traced this story right from its roots "from the very first." (1:1 AV)

I also wanted you Theophilus, to be absolutely certain about the truth of the gospel. As I pointed out (1:4), in my own culture I have had the privilege of meeting citizens from Rome, people steeped in Jewish culture and others with a good Greek background and in-depth interest in literature. I can boast of having friends from Gentile and Jewish backgrounds. I really wanted you my dear friend Theophilus, as someone who genuinely loves God to be at home with your newly found Christian friends from whatever background they come. I can speak from experience, as I am a Gentile and the majority of my church community come from a Jewish culture and we were great friends with Peter, James and John and the other disciples. I have counted it a great privilege to get to know Paul through our travels together and our missionary journeys in the Mediterranean. The reference to "my" (1:3) is designed to show my zeal and enthusiasm for my subject. I hope that you will also read Volume Two, the Acts of the Apostles, and that you will be pleased to see your name in the introduction. I trust that you will recognise God's Big Picture, His purpose and plan for the world. Best wishes for the present. I will write again later.

Your loving friend,

Luke

Pupil's Activity: One

a) Read 1:1-4.

"It [Luke's Gospel] is the most beautiful book in the world which brings health to body and soul." (Renan) (3)

b) What insights do the above imaginary writing give us into Luke as an author?

Pupil's Activity: Two

a) Consider what makes these openings of the following books so effective.

1) "It is a truth, universally acknowledged, that a single man in possession of a good fortune, must be in want of a wife." Pride and Prejudice by Jane Austen.

2) "It was the best of times, it was the worst of times, it was the age of wisdom, it was the age of foolishness." A Tale of Two Cities by Charles Dickens.

3) "Mr. and Mrs. Dursley of number 4 Privet Drive were proud to say that they were perfectly normal thank you very much. They were the last people you'd expect to be involved in anything strange or mysterious because they didn't hold with such nonsense." Harry Potter and the Philosopher's Stone by J.K. Rowling.

b) How does the writer of the Third Gospel gain the attention of his readers in his prologue? [See Ch.3: Theories of Source Criticism.]

[2] The prologue of the Third Gospel compared with other writers at that time

This Gospel has a preface (1:1-4) which is quite unique in the New Testament. The author uses the word "account" to describe his narrative of the life of Jesus (1:3). His introduction to the Third Gospel is a long, carefully constructed sentence in the tradition of the finest historical works in Greek literature. (Liefeld) (4) It is like the the "jacket" precis of a modern book: the first sentence was crucial, saying to the reader read on. All Greek historical writers explained their work in a preface. Here are three examples compared with the Third Gospel:-

1) The letter of Aristeas (285-247 B.C.) to Philocrates (5) states, **"Inasmuch as the account** of our deputation to Eleazar, the high priest of the Jews is worth narrating, Philocrates, and because you set a **high value,** as you constantly remind me, on hearing the purposes of our mission, I have endeavoured to set **the matter forth clearly."**

Comment: notice the similarity of the words and expressions used by Aristeas and Luke, "to set down an orderly account"(1:1)(NIV). Aristeas' narratee is Philocrates.

2) Ben Sirach, (190 B.C.) (6) the writer of Ecclesiaticus 50:27, the author's postscript and signature states, **"In this book I have written lessons of good sense and understanding**, I, Jesus son of Sirach, of Jerusalem, whose mind was a fountain of wisdom."

Comment : this was a common style by authors at this time and has similarities with Luke in the way he broke with the traditional anonymity of biblical writers. Both authors present themselves as characters within the story even though the author of the Third Gospel does not present himself in that writing.

3) Josephus (A.D. 94) (7) writes, "In my history of our Antiquities, **most excellent Epaphroditus,** I think I have made clear..... the extreme antiquity of our Jewish race...... Since however I observe, that a considerable number of persons discredit the statements in my history..... I consider it my duty **to devote the truth (historical truth)** concerning the antiquity of our race. As witness of my statements, I propose to call the writers who, in the estimation of the Greeks are **the most trustworthy authorities as a whole."**

Comment: Luke's style of writing in the preface is also like that of Josephus. He identifies his narratee (the one to whom the work is issued and dedicated) as Theophilus even though he has a wider audience (1:3). Josephus identifies his narratee as Epaphroditus.

4) The prologue to the Third Gospel (Read 1:1-4.)

"Inasmuch as many have undertaken to compile a narrative of the things **which have been accomplished among us,"** (1:1) just as they were delivered to us by those who from the beginning were eyewitnesses and **ministers** of the word (1:2), it seemed **good to me** also, having followed all things closely (accurately) [RSV margin] **for some time past, to write an orderly account for you, most excellent Theophilus (1:3), that you may know the truth concerning the things of which you have been informed."** (1:4)

Comment : notice the similarity of the words, style and expressions used by Luke, Aristeas, Ben Sirach and Josephus. Of all the Gospel writers, Luke's style of writing, his words and expressions come closest to that of the great Classical Greek writers like Aristeas. He uses the Greek word "logos" meaning the message of the gospel embodied in the words and deeds of Jesus (1:2). Ancient writers tended to match words with appropriate deeds. Acts 1:1 combines "doing" and "teaching" in the author's description of Jesus' ministry. This is important for the fulfilment of Scripture (1:1). (Liefeld) (8)

Pupil's Activity: Three

a) Compare the start of Third Gospel with those of Ben Sirach and Josephus and Aristeas.

b) Look for the similarities in style and wording between the four writers.

We know that this is the only Gospel writer to use the personal pronoun "I", "It seemed good to me also." (1:3) In the ancient world it was a regular thing to attach books to famous names; no one thought it wrong. But Luke was never one of the famous figures of the early Church. If he had not written the Gospel no one would have attached it to his name." (Barclay) **(11)**

[3] Comments on the prologue of the Third Gospel which tell us about the author
(Read 1:1-4.) (pp. 35, 59)

1. A "narrative" is an account which can be either oral or written (1:1). For Luke narrative is proclamation. He uses history to present a convincing account of Jesus' earthly ministry. It is significant that he says he "set down an orderly account" (1:1) (NIV) and makes the parallel point when he says that "he writes an orderly account." (1:3) (NIV) (Green) **(9)**

2. "Many have undertaken" means literally to "set one's hand to." (1:1)

3. The narrative starts with the word (Gk.epeideper) (AV) "forasmuch as" (RSV) "inasmuch as" is a Classical word used only here in the N.T. but is common with major writers as Thucydides, Philo and Josephus (1:1). This Greek style is contrast to the Hebrew colloquial expression in 1:5 "there was" (Gk.egeneto). (Liefeld) **(10)**

4. The people referred to have two roles: they are "eyewitnesses" and "ministers or servants of the word." These were Jesus' apostles who saw at first hand the life of Jesus and His ministry (1:2).

5. "Delivered to us" means handed down with care. Luke started at the very beginning, with John the Baptist who points to Jesus (1:2). Luke tells us four things about his work:
• He has investigated the story and followed it closely (1:3).
• He takes a long careful look at it developing his story in a very precise way (1:3).
• He was thorough in having examined and investigated everything even though he was not an eyewitness (1:2b). About thirty percent of his Gospel is found nowhere else and forty-nine percent of the journey narrative (9:51-19:48) contains material unique to Luke. [See pp.28, 80.]

6. We know that this is the only Gospel writer to use the personal pronoun "I", "It seemed good to me also." (1:3) In the ancient world it was a regular thing to attach books to famous names; no one thought it wrong. But Luke was never one of the famous figures of the early Church. If he had not written the Gospel no one would have attached his name to it." (Barclay) **(11)**

7. His orderly account is told in a very clear style (1:3). "Orderly" here could mean "broadly in chronological order" (Marshall) **(12)** or "systematic in his presentation." (Fitzmyer) **(13)**

8. Luke's purpose is to assure Theophilus that he may know the certainty of the things he had been taught and he was probably a new Gentile believer. Luke tries to assure him that he is very welcome into his new racially mixed community group of believers (1:4).

9. "The Gospel according to St. Luke is part of the two-volume publication that includes Acts." (Danker) **(14)**

10. His use of the first person singular in the openings of both Luke and Acts supports the "we passages" in Acts and shows that the author took a personal interest in what he was writing. (CMM) **(15)**

11. The final "we passage" Acts 27:1-28:16 places the author in Rome during the time when Paul was in prison, so that the author is one of those named as being with Paul at that time and is probably not mentioned in Acts. This leaves us with Titus, Demas, Crescens (2 Tim. 4:10), Jesus called Justus, Epaphroditus and Luke (Col. 4:10-14). Luke is the only one of these early Christians identified as the author of Luke/Acts. (CMM) **(16)**

12. His style is like that of Josephus **(17)** quoted above. This statement shows that the preface of the Third Gospel is like a secular writer of his time and the signature to the book of Ecclesiasticus is also similar. The author of the preface of the Third Gospel (1:1-4) comes closest to the style of the Greek classical writers for example the letter of Aristeas to Philocrates **(18)**, "Inasmuch as the account of our deputation to Eleazar, the high priest of the Jews is worth narrating, Philocrates, and because you set a high value, as you constantly remind me, on hearing the purposes of our mission, I have endeavoured to set the matter forth clearly."

13. A key feature of the author's style is his frequent use of the vocabulary of the Septuagint version of the O.T. (LXX) (1:1; Hab.1:5). (Evans) **(19)** The word "account" (Gk. diegesis) can literally mean a "narrative" as used later by Luke in Acts 2:17; 13:41 and shows his use of a Semitic expression in the prologue. This sensitivity to the Jews shows his concern to identify with both cultural groups. He was not an eyewitness of the ministry of Jesus but he does make careful inquiries (1:2).

A key feature of the author's style is his frequent use of the vocabulary of the Septuagint version of the O.T. (LXX) (1:1; Hab.1:5). (Evans) **(19)**

14. The author set out to write two volumes, his Gospel and Acts. He wants to show that the God of Abraham has kept His promise to bless all nations through his family and keep His promise (1:54-55). The good news is for Jews as well as Gentiles, like Theophilus.

Pupil's Activity: Four
What insights do the key words in the prologue tell us about the author of the Third Gospel?

Pupil's Activity: Five
a) Comment on the statement that this Gospel succeeds in presenting "an orderly account" of the Good News.
b) Justify your answer. (CCEA A/S 2001)   [15 marks]

[4] The authorship of the Third Gospel in relation to external and internal evidence

This authorship was never disputed until the second half of the nineteenth century. As the author of the Third Gospel does not identify himself, it is important to look at (1) the external evidence (2) internal evidence and come to our own conclusions as to who wrote the book. (3) The "we passages" in Acts help to identfy the author. It is equally important to see how the tradition of the early Church was consistent in attributing the Third Gospel to Luke. Evidence for the authorship comes basically from three key areas: external (church tradition) internal and the "we passages" of Acts.

A) The external evidence based upon church tradition

The following writings from outside the New Testament, mainly from the second century, help to provide evidence that Luke was the author of the Acts of the Apostles.

1. Clement of Alexandria (A.D. 150-215) **(20)** alludes to "the Gospel of Luke."

2. Justin Martyr (A.D. 160) in his book "Memoirs of Jesus" refers to Luke as a "follower of Paul."

3. The Muratorian Canon (A.D.170-180) attributes the Gospel to Luke saying, "Luke a doctor, who is Paul's companion." Marcion the heretic has also identified Luke as the author.

4. The Anti-Marcionite Prologue (A.D.175) describes Luke as "a native of Antioch in Syria, lived to an age of eighty-four, was a doctor, unmarried, childless, wrote in Achaia and died in Boeotia." The statement about Luke coming from Syria is generally accepted.

5. Irenaeus attributes the Gospel to Luke. **(21)** "Luke the follower of Paul, recorded in a book, the gospel that was preached by him." He cites the "we passages" in Acts, "we came to Troas" and calls him "the Syrian from Antioch and the inseparable companion of Paul."

6. Tertullian (A.D.160-225) **(22)** in the early third-century calls this Gospel a "digest of Paul's Gospel."

7. The oldest manuscript of Luke, Bodman papyrus p75 (A.D.175-225) **(23)** ascribes the book to Luke.

8. Eusebius (A.D.260-340) **(24)** says that Luke was "from Antioch, a companion to Paul and author of the Gospel and Acts."

9. Jerome (A.D. 345-440) **(25)** also claimed that Luke was the author.

Summary

• All of these quotes help us to identify the Third Gospel with Luke and some also make the connection between Paul and Luke.

• There is uniform agreement from the external evidence that Luke is the author. "The fact that Luke was a non-apostolic man of no prominence, is universally held in antiquity to have been the author and must be given weight." Morris **(26)**

• The main evidence for saying that Luke was the author of Luke/Acts comes from this external evidence.

• No one in the early church disputed the identification of Luke as the author.

• While we must not equate tradition with truth, we should not reject such tradition because of a dislike for anything traditional. Unless there is good reason to reject the ancient tradition it should be accepted. This is particularly true when tradition names a minor figure in the early church and a non-apostle as the author of over a quarter of the entire N.T.

B) The Internal Evidence

The internal arguments concentrate on two points.

a) Evidence within the Gospel itself: the author was not an eyewitness to most of the events in his two volumes, particularly those linked to the ministry of Jesus, rather he has relied upon "the eyewitnesses and servants of the word." (1:2) This would suggest that the author was a second generation Christian who was able to investigate the ministry of Jesus.

1. **Query:** How did the author of the Third Gospel receive his information about the ministry of Jesus if he was not an eyewitness? Possibly Luke received some of this material when he stayed with Paul for two years in Caesarea before going on to Rome (Acts 24:27; 27:1). Stott **(27)** suggests that Luke received his details of the birth narratives at this time from Mary. Luke tells Mary's story and he may well have spent two years when Paul was imprisoned in Caesarea (Acts 21:17; 24:27), occupying his time interviewing eyewitnesses like Mary (now in her later years) and visiting sacred places.

2. The apostle Paul refers to Luke as the "beloved physician." (Col. 4:14)

3. Paul makes a clear distinction between "Mark, Jesus called Justus who are the only Jews (the only men of the circumcision) among my fellow workers." It can be implied from Col.4:10-14 that Luke was one of those fellow workers who is "one of the circumcision and he was a Gentile. Later Paul links Luke with Demas in sending greetings, which would suggest that Luke was among the Gentile believers. "Luke the beloved physician and Demas greet you." (Col. 4:14) On the basis of this, Luke is generally thought to be the Gentile Christian, Paul refers to in Col. 4:10-14 although he does not explicitly state this. Some have argued that Luke was a Jewish Christian and he is known to have had a long involvement with the church

One of Luke's distinctive features is his use of the Greek word for lawyer 'nomikos' instead of the Hebrew word scribe 'grammateus' to emphasise Jesus' practical teaching in Chs. 12 and 16 on wealth and finance. (Liefeld) (28)

at Antioch in Syria (Acts 11:19-20; 13:1-4; 14:26-28; 15:1-3; 13-40; 18:22-23).

4. The shortened form of Luke's name Loukas, a Greek form of a Latin name is also used here (Col. 4:14a).

5. Some passages in the Third Gospel speak of a medical interest:

• "high fever" (4:38) while (Matt. 8:14; Mk. 1:30) speak of "a fever".

• "a man full of leprosy." (5:12)

• "a woman with a flow of blood for twelve years." (8:43-44)

• Healings are also described from a medical viewpoint. "When the demon had thrown him down in the midst, he came out of him, having done him no harm." (4:35)

• "A woman who had a spirit of infirmity for eighteen years; she was bent over and could not fully straighten herself." (13:11)

6. The author appears to be speaking to a pagan world, "a light for revelation to the Gentiles;" and also to the Jewish world, "for glory to your people Israel." (2:32)

7. One of Luke's distinctive features is his use of the Greek word for lawyer 'nomikos' instead of the Hebrew word scribe 'grammateus' to emphasise Jesus' practical teaching in Chs. 12 and 16 (10:25,11:45, 46, 52;14:3) on wealth and finance. (Liefeld) **(28)**

8. He writes good Greek. In Acts 1:19 he refers to "their language"; Aramaic was not his language. (CMM) **(29)**

C) Luke presents himself as Paul's companion in those parts of Acts called the "we passages."
(Read Acts 16:10-17; 20:5-16; 21:1-18; 27:1-28.)

1. While some scholars question the reliability of the "we passages," they do help to limit the options about the author's identity, e.g. Haenchen argued that the "we passages" are only a literary device or journey notes picked up by the author and are not genuine. **(30)** The "we passages" seem to come from a diary by one of Paul's companions. The writer stayed in Caesarea with Philip the evangelist and his four daughters (Acts 21:8). "We entered the house in Caesarea and stayed with the evangelist, one of the seven." The style of the "we passages" is similar to that of the rest of the book of Acts.

2. Query: How well did the author of the Third Gospel know Paul?

Some say not very well as the picture presented of Paul in Acts does not quite fit his self-portrait in the Pauline letters and Luke fails to use Paul's letters to describe his work and to use his position as an apostle. Examples of the difference in these self-portraits are:

• the different attitude of Paul to Jewish law over the circumcision of Timothy (Acts 16:3).

• Paul's undertaking of a Jewish vow in Acts 21:21. Some scholars argue that the real Paul would not have acted in this way of opposing the doctrine of the law as set out in Acts and therefore could not have been a companion of Luke. Both of these examples can be reinterpreted in different ways in that Paul becomes "all things to all men" depending upon the cultural context in which he finds himself (1 Cor. 9:22).

3. A strong objection to Luke as the author of the Third Gospel comes from Vielhauer (31) who says that Luke could not have been Paul's companion as his theology is quite different from Paul in a number of places, for example in the Areopagus address, Paul uses the Stoic idea of natural theology (Acts 17:25). "Nor is He served by human hands, as though he needed anything, since He Himself gives to all men life and breath and everything." The human race is capable of a natural knowledge of God and of ethics and has immediate access to God. Paul in this context does not appear to use the "word of the cross." However, some hearers did come to a saving knowledge of Christ in Athens after this speech and as Moule **(32)** says it is highly likely that there would be differences between a speaker's presentation of the Gospel in public and the way he might have addressed them when they came to faith. This objection only proves Luke wrote independently of Paul." (Morris) **(33)** Luke is not a diluted form of Paul. Vielhauer **(34)** does not give sufficient weight to that part of Paul's teaching (1 Cor. 9:20) "To the Jews I became a Jew, that I might win the Jews."

Fitzmyer **(35)** says Luke may only have been a "junior companion" of Paul rather than being "inseparable from him" as Ireneaus said. **(36)** Others scholars defend the compatibility of the two portraits of Paul. (Bruce) **(37)**

4. Internal evidence in both Luke and Acts tends to suggest that the author knew Paul. Paul's letters give many examples of people who travelled with him: Mark, Aristarchus, Demas, and Luke (Philemon 24; Col. 4:14). Despite the wide selection of possibilities, church tradition gives only one name as the author of Luke/Acts and that is Luke. Luke was not making any attempt to tell all that he knew ; he omits certain chronological and geographical features.

Conclusion

Both the external and internal evidence point strongly to Luke, the doctor, Paul's "close friend" as the author (Col.4:14). (CMM) **(38)**

[5] What is the link between the Third Gospel and Acts?

1. We know that Luke and Acts are both dedicated to Theophilus.

2. Acts talks of the "first book" thought to be the Third Gospel (Acts 1:1).

3. Luke and Acts have a similar style of language and interests for example Gentiles "on earth peace among men" (2:14) and the issue of Gentile inclusion at the council of Jerusalem (Acts 15).

4. Women feature in both books: Anna (2:36-38), Lydia (Acts 16:14-16) and in the resurrection appearances the women from Galilee (24:8-9).

5. Scholars who disagree with the link are Kummel, Conzelmann and Wilder who say that the end of Luke and the start of Acts are interpolations (additions to the text). However the evidence is strong for linking both volumes as the work of one person and few dispute this today.

6. Virtually all scholars today agree that the same person wrote Luke and Acts, and most find a considerable degree of thematic unity. (CMM) (39)

Virtually all scholars today agree that the same person wrote Luke and Acts, and most find a considerable degree of thematic unity. (CMM) (39)

[6] Was Luke a Gentile?

1. Luke is generally thought to be the Gentile Christian to whom Paul refers (Col. 4:10-14).

2. "Mark, Jesus called Justus are the only Jews (the only men of the circumcision) among my fellow workers." (Col. 4: 11)

3. Later in the passage Paul sends greetings from Luke, which would put Luke among the Gentile believers. "Luke the beloved physician and Demas greet you." (Col. 4 :14)

4. The shortened form of Luke's name (Loukas), a Greek form of a Latin name is used in this verse (Col. 4: 14a).

5. Fitzmyer (40) says that church tradition links Luke with Antioch in Syria and suggests he was a former "God-fearer" or Jewish proselyte and was not just someone who interviewed the real author and used him as a source.

6. It is unclear whether his cultural background was Semitic. He probably had a religious background with Judaism before coming to faith. (Bock) (41)

Summary of Luke as a Gentile

• It seems very likely that Luke was a Gentile though it is unclear whether his cultural background was Semitic. He probably had a religious background with Judaism before coming to faith. (Bock)(42) Fitzmyer (35) says he may well have been Paul's junior companion. Luke uses the (LXX) and Semitic expressions. [See p. 7.] This would suggest that he had contact with Judaism in his earlier life.

• "Luke is regarded as one of the great theologians of the early church. He is usually held to have been a Gentile Christian." (CMM) (43)

• One of Luke's distinctive features is his use of the Greek word for lawyer 'nomikos' instead of the Hebrew word scribe 'grammateus' to emphasise Jesus' practical teaching in Chs.12 and 14; 10:25. (Liefeld)(44)

• Somehow of all the Gospel writers, one would like to meet Luke best of all, for this gentle doctor with the tremendous vision of the infinite sweep of the love of God must have been a lovely soul." (Barclay) (45)

• It seems likely he was a Gentile and possibly from Syria. (Bock) (46)

[7] Was Luke a doctor?

1. The fact that he uses medical language does not prove that he was a doctor but it does indicate that he was a literary person, well-educated.

2. He is Paul's "sometime companion, likely to be a medical doctor, possibly from Antioch in Syria which is not Jewish, and tradition indicates he had a long life. It is uncertain whether he is Syrian or Greco-Roman." (Bock) (47)

3. Luke is very well-educated especially in his use of Greek and particularly in the preface. He says he composed his narrative (1:1). He wrote as a "litterateur of the Roman period." (Fitzmyer) (48): he wrote well and his style was varied with good structure and distinctive theological terms (Fitzmyer). (49) The rest of Chs.1-2 have a Hebrew style in the use of many Semitic/Hebraic expressions for example "the time of her birth being full" meaning the time of fulfilment has come for Elizabeth (1:57; Gen.25:24). This expression is repeated again for Mary in (2:6). However, the introduction has a Classical style like that of contemporary Greek and Roman writers (1:1-4). "This versatility points to a writer of no mean competence." (CMM) (50)

4. While the use of medical language does not actually prove that the author was a doctor, it does indicate that his descriptions of ailments and cures is in keeping with ancient tradition that the author was a doctor.

5. Luke says "the field was called in their language Akeldama, that is field of blood."By this he was referring to Aramaic, a language which he did not speak (Acts 1:19).

> "Somehow of all the Gospel writers, one would like to meet Luke best of all, for this gentle doctor with the tremendous vision of the infinite sweep of the love of God must have been a lovely soul." (Barclay) (45)

Summary

• Those scholars who say that Luke is the author are not only in the majority but come from a wide spectrum of theological opinion.

• While neither the Third Gospel nor Acts names its author both the external and internal evidence suggest that Luke was the author. Morris says that no suitable alternative to Luke as the author has been suggested. (51)

• The prologue makes it clear that the author was not an eyewitness: that makes at least two Gospel writers who were not eyewitnesses, Mark and Luke. Mark was very dependent upon Peter for his material.

• The author shows a great interest in Gentiles and this may point to a Gentile author.

• He was well-educated, writes good Greek and is regarded as one of the great theologians of the early church. (CMM)(52)

• While 1-4 has a Classical style, the rest of the book is good Hellenistic Greek which reminds the reader of the (LXX).

Pupil's Activity: Six

Do an investigative study supporting Luke as a doctor. Look up some of these instances in which Luke describes illnesses:

• How does he describe the illness of Peter's mother-in law (4:38)?

• How is the leper's condition described (5:13)?

• Why does he omit to say that the woman with the issue of blood had spent her savings going to the doctor and was not cured (8:43 RSV margin)?

• Which expression in this verse suggests someone with a professional view of medicine (9:11)?

Pupil's Activity: Seven

By way of revision draw a spidergram giving the external and internal evidence to show that Luke was the author of the Third Gospel.

Pupil's Activity: Eight

Here are some more facts about the characteristics of the author Luke. See if you can make them into an acrostic to help you with your revision.

1. A **clever** man – he was a Gentile and is the only writer in the bible who is not a Jew.
2. An **adventurous man** – he travelled with Paul and describes shipwrecks in Acts 27. His use of technical nautical terms is quite accurate.
3. An **earnest** and **sincere** man – he was probably a Christian when he met Paul.
4. A **loyal** man who never gave up (2 Tim. 4:10-11; Hebrews 13:5-6).

Pupil's Activity: Nine

a) Identify and examine the evidence concerning the authorship and date of Luke's Gospel.
(Edexcel A/S 2001/2003)   [14 marks]
b) How far is an accurate knowledge of the authorship and date necessary for an understanding of Luke's Gospel?
(Edexcel A/S 2001)   [6 marks]

Pupil's Activity: Ten

a) Outline the evidence concerning the authorship of the Gospel according to Luke.
(Edexcel A/S 2002/2004/2006)   [14 marks]
b) To what extent is it important to know the authorship and date of the Gospel of Luke in order to understand it?
(Edexcel A/S 2002)   [6 marks]

Pupil's Activity: Eleven

a) Outline your knowledge and understanding of the authorship of Luke's Gospel.
(CCEA A/S 2002/2004 Resit)   [30 marks]
b) Explore the claim that it is possible to identify the author of Luke's Gospel with certainty. Justify your answer.
(CCEA A/S 2005 Resit)   [15 marks]

Pupil's Activity: Twelve

a) Examine the view of scholars concerning the authorship and date of Luke's Gospel.
(Edexcel A/S 2005)   [14 marks]
b) To what extent is it important to know who the author of the Gospel was, and when it was written, in order to understand it? (Edexcel A/S 2005)   [6 marks]

Outcomes

Students should have a knowledge and understanding of:

• the key issues relating to the authorship of the Third Gospel, for example his identity.(CCEA A/S)

• other contemporary writings at that time e.g. Ben Sirach, Josephus, Aristeas.

• terms and concepts in the prologue relating to the authorship, for example narrative, eyewitnesses, investigated closely, orderly account and the "we passages" (CCEA A/S)

Students should be able to provide evidence for:

• the internal and external evidence relating to authorship.

• a link between the Third Gospel and Acts and how it impinges upon authorship. (Edexcel A/S)

• the importance of knowing who wrote the Third Gospel and how this helps in understanding the contents. (Edexcel A/S)

Notes on Ch. 1: The Authorship of The Third Gospel

1. The Septuagint version was the Greek translation of the O.T. Hebrew Bible otherwise known as the LXX. It was produced by seventy scholars in seventy–days, by Greek speaking Jews, in Alexandria and completed by 132 B.C.

2. "Q" is a hypothetical document containing the sayings of Jesus, which are common to Matthew and Luke. It comes from the German word "Quelle" meaning source and is thought to contain 230 verses. It originated with J. Weiss in 1890. [See Ch.3: Sources.]

3. E. Renan, Les Evangiles, Paris, (1877) p. 25.

4. Walter Liefeld, Commentary on Luke's Gospel, EBC. NIV. (1984) p.821.

5. Letter of Aristeas to Philocrates 1:1-12 cited in Marshall (See below.) p.39.

6. Ben Sirach, Ecclus. 50:27 , cited in J.N. Snaith in NEB Cambridge Bible Commentary, (1974) p.255.

7. Josephus, (A.D.37-100) "Against Apion", (A.D. 94), 1:1-4.

8. Walter Liefeld, op. cit.p, 822.

9. Joel Green, op. cit. pp 34-36.

10. Walter Liefeld, op. cit.p, 821.

11. William Barclay, The Daily Study Bible (Revised Edition), The Gospel of Luke, St. Andrew Press, (1975) p.6.

12. I. Howard Marshall, The Gospel of Luke, Paternoster (1979) p.43.*

13. Joseph A. Fitzmyer, Anchor Bible : The Gospel According to St. Luke, N.Y. : Doubleday (1985) p.296. *

14. Fredrick W. Danker, Jesus and the New Age, Fortress Press (1988) p.1.

15. Donald Carson, Douglas Moo and Leon Morris, An Introduction to the New Testament : Apollos Press, First Edition (1992) p. 114. *

16. CMM (First edition) (ibid.)

17. Josephus, "Against Apion" (1:1-4).

18 Aristeas, (ibid.)

19. Craig A. Evans, Luke, NIBC, Hendrickson Press, (1990) p.19.*

20. Clement of Alexandria, (A.D.95-96) Stromateis, 5,12 (1 Clement 13.2; 48.4/2 Clement 13.4).

21. Irenaeus, (A.D.175-195) in his book Against Heresies (3.1:1; 3.14.1) argued that the orthodox churches were superior to the heretical ones because they recognised the authors of the Gospels and names Luke as author of the Third Gospel.

22. Tertullian, Against Marcion, (iv.2).

23. Bodman Papyrus p75 (A.D.175-225) - the oldest manuscript of Luke.

24. Eusebius, (early fourth century) Historia Ecclesiastica 3,4.2.

25. Jerome, (A.D.345- 420) De viris illustribus cited in note 7 above.

26. Leon Morris, Luke, TNTC, (First edition), IVP (1974) p.15.*

27. John Stott, The Incomparable Jesus , IVP, (2001) p.31.

28. Walter Liefeld, op. cit p.798.*

29. CMM (Second edition) op.cit. p.204.

30. E. Haenchen, The Acts of the Apostles, Oxford, (1971) p.85.

31. Philip Vielhauer, cited in Morris p.24. Vielhauer follows Leander E. Keck and J. Louis Martyn, Studies in Luke/Acts, SLA (1966) p.37. Firstly, he argued that Luke made Paul (Acts 17) present a Stoic idea of natural theology and that there is no mention of the word of the cross in Paul's Areopagus Speech. Secondly, he said in Acts, Paul is a Jewish Christian who is utterly loyal to the law. He circumcises Timothy (Acts 16:3) and conforms to the law (Acts 21:21ff.) in shaving his head to keep a Nazarite vow and pays the costs of the sacrifice of the four men who were under the vow. After 7 days Paul fulfils the conditions of the vow. (Acts 21:26) Thirdly, Paul circumcises Timothy (16:3) to indicate that he keeps the law. Fourthly, in Acts the doctrine of the Person of Christ is adoptionistic [Jesus was an ordinary man who was adopted into Divine Sonship at his baptism and is therefore pre-Pauline.] Fifthly, in Acts the doctrine of the last things has been removed from the centre of Paul's faith to the end and has become a section on the last things.

32. C.F. D. Moule, cites SLA (ibid.)*

33. Leon Morris, op. cit. p. 24.

34. Philip Vielhauer, (ibid.) p. 24.

35. Joseph A. Fitzmyer, op. cit. p.53.

36. Ireneaus, Against Heresies, (ibid.)

37. Frederick F. Bruce, Is the Paul of Acts the real Paul? Bulletin of John Rylands University Library of Manchester: 58:282-305, (1975) p.76.

38. CMM, (ibid.)

39. CMM, (Second Edition)(2005) op. cit. p.203.

40. Joseph A. Fitzmyer, op. cit. p.53.

41. Darrell L. Bock, ECNT: Luke, Vol. 1 (1996) pp. 6-7.

42. Darrell L. Bock, (ibid.)

43. CMM, (First Edition) (1992) op. cit. p.115.

44. Walter Liefeld, (ibid.)

45. William Barclay, op. cit. p.1.

46. Darrell L. Bock, (ibid.)

47. Darrell L. Bock, op. cit. p.7.

48. Joseph A. Fitzmyer, op. cit. p.92.

49. Joseph A. Fitzmyer, (ibid.)

50. CMM, (First Edition) op. cit. p. 115.

51. Leon Morris, op. cit. p.24.

52. CMM, cited in note 43.

*These books are highly recommended.

CCEA A/S and Edexcel A/IS Level

> **Targets:**
> • **Identify three main possible views on the date of Luke's Gospel.**
> • **Have a knowledge and understanding of the issues in the dating of Luke's Gospel (CCEA).**
> • **Recognise why a knowledge of the date helps in understanding the text of this Gospel (CCEA).**
> • **Evaluate the reliability of the evidence (Edexcel).**
> • **Recognise the views of scholars regarding the dating of Luke's Gospel (Edexcel).**
> • **Recognise the key concepts: the multi-ethnic nature of the early Church, "desolating sacrilege", Gentile inclusion, early Catholic theology, table fellowship, "vaticinium ex eventu" and the Hellenists.**

The Date of Luke's Gospel

Introduction

A) Here is another imaginary letter from Luke to Theophilus regarding the dating of his Gospel.

Dear Theophilus,

         Scholars have often speculated about the dating and the circumstances in which I wrote my Gospel. This is one of my best kept secrets. As you are fully aware, I wrote two separate books: my Gospel Volume One and Acts Volume Two, both bearing your illustrious name (1:3; Acts 1:1). It is worth noting even if it is somewhat trite to say that Volume Two followed on from Volume One, quite soon afterwards. I deemed it wiser and urgent to put my material on a scroll approx. thirty-forty feet long for each volume. I also wrote because some of our close friends had already lost their lives and Paul and I could be next on the hit list. You would not be too far out to suggest that I started to collect my material for my Gospel during my stay in Palestine and when Paul was imprisoned in Caesarea (A.D.57-59). I was inspired to write about the details of the birth of Our Lord which Mary had passed on to me again during my stay at Caesarea. It proved to be a very fruitful, prolific and inspirational time for me as a would-be author. Look out for external and internal clues, which helps scholars pinpoint my date of writing and in turn to establish the outside limits.

         Best wishes in your research,

            Your loving friend,

               Luke

B) The dating of Luke's Gospel has been greatly disputed by scholars but there are certain limits for discussion. The outside limits for the dating of Luke's Gospel can be established by four factors. Firstly, the last event in Acts, the Apostle Paul's two-year house arrest, took place in A.D.62 which is the earliest possible date for Volume Two. (CMM) **(1)** "Luke's Second Volume cannot be earlier than Volume One." (Bock) **(2)** Secondly, since Irenaeus **(3)** quotes from Luke, (A.D.170) is the latest possible date for Luke's Gospel. Thirdly, the dating of Luke's Gospel "the former treatise" should also be considered alongside the date of Acts. [See above.] Fourthly, some conservative scholars date Mark's Gospel as in the early 60s; it is also thought that Luke follows Mark. It is probable that Luke obtained a copy of Mark's Gospel quite early as Mark and Luke were in the group associated with Paul. Therefore Luke must be later than A.D. 62. Other considerations are the reference to the destruction of Jerusalem (Ch.21) and the theological and church tone of Luke/Acts. From these arguments it has been suggested that the earliest possible date for the writing of the Third Gospel would be after the final event of Acts 28, after Paul's arrest.

C) As an aid to the background to the dating of the Third Gospel here is a fact file.

Suggested dates for some N.T. Books and key events (Figure 1)

N.T. books and events	Approx. dates of the Gospels, Acts and other key events
Paul's imprisonment in Caesarea	A.D. 57-59 (Acts 23:35-26:32; 24:27)
Paul's Letters	A.D. 50s-early 60s
Paul's two-year house imprisonment in Rome	A.D. 60-62 (Acts 28:20)
Mark	A.D. 62 + or late 50s (Some scholars argue for a date after A.D.70)
Luke	A.D. 62 + (Some scholars argue for a date after A.D.70 and others first-century.)
Acts	A.D. 62-64
The Fire of Rome under Nero	A.D. 64 July (Tacitus, Annals, 15, 44)
Nero's persecution	A.D. 62-65
Deaths of Peter and Paul by Nero	A.D. 64-66 is more common (Traditional date 29th June A.D.67.) This is a late date.
Matthew	A.D. 60-70 (Some scholars argue for a date after A.D.70)
Fall of Jerusalem	A.D. 70

No event after A.D. 62 is described in Acts. Paul's two-year imprisonment in Rome is in Acts 28:20.

There are three possibilities for the dating of Luke's Gospel.

[1] An early date in the early sixties.

A) Luke, in Volume Two, The Acts of the Apostles, makes no mention of three main events:

• the Emperor Nero's persecution of the Early Church in A.D. 62.

• the deaths of the apostles James A.D. 62 and Paul in A.D. 64-66, even though Paul's arrest, his imprisonment and trials are included over eight chapters. There is no account in Acts of the outcome of his appeal to Caesar and no mention of his martyrdom. Why did Luke not tell his readers what happened to Paul?

• Acts is silent on the Fall of Jerusalem in A.D. 70. This argument would require a date for Luke's Gospel before the book of Acts and no later than about A.D. 62, since Acts would have been written immediately after the event it records. These three omissions, conservative scholars argue, point to an early date for Luke's Gospel.

1. No event after A.D. 62 is described in Acts. Paul's two-year imprisonment in Rome is in Acts 28:20.

2. Time also must be allowed for Luke to have received a copy of Mark's Gospel and to be able to make use of it (1:1).

B) It has been assumed by the scholar Kummel (4) (who opposed the conservative date) that Luke deliberately changed Mark 13:14, "the desolating sacrilege" to "Jerusalem surrounded by armies." (21:20) (Figure 2)

1. "But when you see the desolating sacrilege set where it ought not to be (let the reader understand), then let those who are in Judea flee to the mountains;" Kummel argued that by the time of writing, Luke knew exactly what had happened to Jerusalem. Jesus' prophecy regarding the Fall of Jerusalem by implication in Luke 21:20, had taken place as it is not mentioned in Luke's Gospel. "But when you see Jerusalem surrounded by armies, then know that its desolation has come near." (21:20) (Kummel) **(5)** Kummel rejected the authenticity of the prediction of "the Son of Man coming in clouds." (21:27) It can also be inferred from 13:34-35 that Jerusalem has not fallen. "O, Jerusalem, Jerusalem, killing the prophets and stoning those who are sent to you! How often would I have gathered your children together as a hen gathers her brood under her wings, and you would not!" (13:34)

2. The silence about the fulfilment of the prophecy regarding the destruction of Jerusalem is deafening in Luke/Acts and Paul in his visit to Jerusalem in Acts Chs.21-23, does not mention it.

3. Luke 21:20 is evidence of an early date, "Jerusalem surrounded by armies."

The multi-ethnic nature of the Church in Acts and the inclusion of the Gentiles suggests an early date for the Third Gospel. (Bock) (6)

C) The multi-ethnic nature of the Church in Acts and the inclusion of the Gentiles suggests an early date (Bock) **(6)** for example issues relating to law, "table fellowship"(sitting down to meals together) and offending practices. Evidence for these issues can be seen in:

1. Acts 6:1-6 the Grecian Jews (Hellenists) who spoke the Greek language but came from outside Palestine. Their widows had not received gifts at the daily handouts and they felt they were neglected by the Hebraic Jews who spoke Aramaic and/or Hebrew.

2. Acts 10-11 is the story of the Gentile Roman centurion called Cornelius.

3. Simon, the tanner's trade would have been despised by the Jews.

4. Acts 15-abstaining from food that had been offered to idols. When sharing a meal sometimes called "table fellowship", Peter withdrew from eating with Gentiles and argued that Gentiles should become Jews.

5. The Jewish/Gentile relations in Luke-Acts are much in keeping with Paul's letters, which have similar tensions.

D) There is no mention of any of Paul's letters in the Acts of the Apostles, yet the early Church treasured these letters. This would suggest that Luke's Gospel and his book of the Acts of the Apostles were written before Paul's letters were widely circulated. [We know that by A.D.110, Ignatius wrote about Paul's letters and we can conclude that Paul's letters were widely circulated by A.D.110; Luke/Acts was written before this date.]

E) It is unlikely that a Christian writer would give such a friendly picture of Rome as in Luke/Acts after Nero's persecution (A.D. 62-65).

F) Luke collected much of his special material when staying in Caesarea. He had spent some time in Palestine while Paul was imprisoned at Caesarea. It is reasonable to conjecture that Luke collected much of his special material at this time and would have written his Gospel soon after his time in Palestine. (Guthrie) **(7)**

> "Given that the Third Gospel would have preceded Acts, a mid-sixties date is slightly more likely." (Bock) (16)

[2] A Second possible date A.D.75-85 after the Fall of Jerusalem in A.D.70

A) The discourses on the future events in Luke's Gospel assume a post-A.D.70 date. (Read 13:35a; 19:41-44; 21: 20-24.)

Some scholars say that it is self-evident from 19:43 that the Fall of Jerusalem preceded the writing of this Gospel because of the details of the description of that Fall.

1. Jesus could not have predicted the Fall of Jerusalem as he did not have the gift of prophecy and Luke's doctrine of the last things (eschatology) assumes a date after A.D. 70. "For the days shall come upon you, when your enemies will cast up a bank about you and surround you, and hem you in on every side, and dash to the ground, you and your children within you, and they will not leave one stone upon another in you; because you did not know the time of your visitation." (19:43)

"But when you see Jerusalem surrounded by armies, then know that it's desolation has come near." (21:20)

"They will fall by the edge of the sword, and be led captive among all nations; and Jerusalem will be trodden down by the Gentiles, until the times of the Gentiles be fulfilled." (21:24)

2. Many scholars say that the language in these three passages suggest that the siege of Jerusalem had already taken place.

3. These scholars argue that Luke altered Mark's Gospel and added to it because by the time of Luke's writing the Third Gospel, he knew what happened. This explanation would require a date for Luke after A.D. 70. The basis for this view is called a "vaticinium ex eventu"- prophesying from an outcome which would require Jesus to be prophesying about the Fall of Jerusalem after the event had taken place.

4. However, CMM **(8)** argue that (21:20), "Jerusalem surrounded by armies" and (19:43) "building an embankment" are ordinary references to siege techniques and are not prophecies after the event.

5. By the same token in (21:27), CMM argue that we cannot say that, "the Son of Man coming in a cloud with power and great glory," also happened after the event. **(9)** This verse was rejected by Kummel. The early Church took these words seriously when they fled from Jerusalem to Pella as the Romans approached (21:21).

6. Throughout his Gospel Luke sees Jerusalem as a city of destiny.

B) If Luke used Mark this would mean Luke's Gospel being written well into the 70s after Mark's Gospel.
Both Mark and Luke were closely associated with Paul and it is probable that Luke received a copy of Mark's Gospel quite early. It is also possible that the two Gospel writers were in direct contact with each other. (Reicke) **(10)** [See p.37.]

C) The picture of Paul as the "great apostle" with hero status needed time to emerge. However it is not apparent that Paul had to be a hero figure before he could be a major character in the early Church.

D) Luke's writings reflect an "early Catholic" theology and would indicate a more structured church and this would place the Third Gospel towards the end of the first-century. Marshall questions this view by saying that "the church of Luke cannot dispense salvation by means of the sacraments. The Lord's Supper is not in Luke a means of salvation but a fellowship meal in which the Lord's death is remembered." (Marshall) **(11)**

E) As Luke used Mark it would have taken Mark's Gospel considerable time to circulate. If Mark is mid-to-late sixties then Luke must be much later. Luke says that "many" had written before him (1:1). It is more likely that these writings were much earlier than A.D. 70. (Morris) **(12)** [See pp. 15, 35.]

[3] A second-century date

> Luke's style in writing is like that of the first-century authors such as Jerome, Marcion and the apologist Justin Martyr. (O' Neill) (13)

A) Luke's style in writing is like that of the first-century authors such as Jerome, Marcion and the apologist Justin Martyr. Acts is said to reflect a theological climate and church situation non-existent in A.D. 60-70. There is little knowledge of Paul in Acts. Luke and Justin are apologists with the same theological outlook and therefore belong to the same period of time. This is the view of O'Neill. **(13)** Luke however had a very positive attitude to state rulers and it is generally agreed that by A.D. 125 to profess Christ required automatic punishment by death as in Pliny's letter to the Emperor Trajan (A.D. 112-3). Luke in his writings does not appear to see the state as the arch-enemy of the Christians. The tone of the book of Acts does not reflect that of other second-century writings such as Clement (A.D. 95) and Ignatius (A.D.110). This date is less probable since we know that by A.D.140, Marcion used part of Luke's Gospel in drawing up his canon of scripture. This would suggest that by A.D.140, Luke's Gospel was regarded as a document having authority. People who agree on theological issues do not always belong to the same era.

B) Hans Conzelmann argued that Luke used the Jewish historian Josephus' writings "The Antiquities" published in A.D.94. This would require a second-century date. However there is little in Josephus which would have been of use to Luke.

Conclusion

• Acts suggests a racially mixed community in dealing with matters of law and sharing meals together. Gentile inclusion suggests an earlier rather than a later date.

• The fact that Paul's death is not recorded in Acts may be an indication that the work was completed in the early to mid-sixties. Time would have to be permitted for the other sources "many have undertaken to compile a narrative of the things which have been accomplished among us" referred to in (1:1) and Mark or Matthew. Bock **(14)** however concludes that, "Luke may have left the end of Paul's career open-ended because that is where matters stood when Luke wrote."

• Both Luke and Acts are tied together by the Ascension which concludes Luke's Gospel and begins Acts. It is hard to be specific but a mid-sixties date is more likely due to the inclusion of parts of Mark in Luke's Gospel. **(15)**[See Ch.3:p. 27.]

• The last event in Acts is dated A.D. 62 and, seeing that Luke seems to relate closely to Acts, the two volumes would have followed closely after each other. Luke should only precede Acts slightly in the time of writing. The simplest explanation is to say that Acts ended suddenly when Paul had been in Rome for two years in A.D. 62 according to the probable chronology of Harnack and Rackham. **(16)**

• Were the predictions regarding Jerusalem genuine predictions about the future? The answer to this question depends upon one's view of the authority of scripture and whether Jesus was a prophet. Luke often presents Jesus as a prophet and it seems feasible to claim that Jesus could have made predictions of the kind in (21:20), "Jerusalem surrounded by armies." There is no convincing argument for a date in the eighties. The evidence for an early date seems more convincing than that for a later date.

• Given that the Third Gospel would have preceded Acts, a mid-sixties date is slightly more likely. (Bock) **(17)**

• In the sayings after the final events Luke 19 and 21:20 there is no direct reference to the Fall of Jerusalem. It can only be inferred. Why is there silence about this? Luke does not update his remarks about the Fall of Jerusalem; he only reports that when the Temple collapses so also does the city. A date in the 80s seems unlikely. A date around A.D. 62-64 is possible.

Pupil's Activity: One

Construct your own time line for the dating of Luke's Gospel to include some of the following events:
the death of Jesus A.D. 33, death of James A.D. 33, Paul's house arrest in Rome A.D. 60-62 the last incident in Acts, the death of Paul A.D.64, the flight of the Christians to Pella A.D.70, The Council of Jamnia (Jabneh), A.D.90 (O.T. Canon agreed by the Jews), the earliest surviving document of the Gospels (P5 P Eger 2) A.D.125, Marcion's Canon A.D.140, Irenaeus Against Heresies A.D.170, the earliest surviving document of Luke (P75) A.D. 200.

Pupil's Activity: Two

Plot this against the political and topical events of the Roman Empire: the Romans invade Britain A.D.43, the revolt by Boudicca in Britain A.D.60, the Great Fire of Rome A.D.64, the siege of Jerusalem A.D.66, the Fall of Jerusalem A.D.70, Mount Vesuvius erupts A.D.79, Domitian's persecution of the Christians A.D.80-96, Josephus wrote his book "The Antiquities" A.D.94, Hadrian's Wall built between England and Scotland in A.D.122, Fall of Jerusalem to the Gentiles A.D.172.

(Figure 2) The destruction of Jerusalem

Mark 13:14 The abomination of desolation	Luke 21:20-21 Jerusalem surrounded by armies
1. "But when you see **the desolating sacrilege** set where it ought not to be (let the reader understand),then let those who are in Judea flee to the mountains." Mark sees Jerusalem at risk. Those present are to," flee to the mountains." Note that the reader is meant to understand the warning. This verse could refer to the desecration of the Temple (167 B.C.) (1Macc.1:54-59) or the city and Temple in the events of A.D. 66-70.	**1.** "But when you see **Jerusalem surrounded by armies**, then know that its **desolation** has come near. Then let those who are in Judea flee to the mountains, and let those who are inside the city depart, and let not those who are out in the country enter it." Judgement on the city reflects O.T. and N.T. promises to judge unfaithfulness (Jer.7:7-14; 22:5; Mic.3:12). Luke changes Mark to read "Jerusalem...surrounded by armies" describing the siege of Jerusalem by the Romans.
2. In Mark, Jesus alludes to the "abomination that causes the desolation."	**2. In Luke** it is very explicit that Jesus has the destruction of Jerusalem in mind. "Jerusalem will be surrounded by armies."
3. Mark says Jesus predicted a terrible calamity which would take place. Jesus speaks about the "desolating sacrilege set up where it ought not to be." At the Fall of Jerusalem 1.1 million Jews were killed, 97,000 were taken captive by the Romans and children were cooked for food. (Fitzmyer) **(18)** Luke focuses on the Fall of Jerusalem rather than the Fall at the end of the ages. It is just as likely that he saw the writing on the wall for Jerusalem in the 60s just as Jesus did.	**3. Luke** rewrites this verse in Mark to read, "When you see Jerusalem surrounded by armies." Some scholars say that Luke interprets Mark in terms of the Fall of Jerusalem A.D.70. Likewise in (19:43) the prediction about Jerusalem, "For the days shall come upon you, when your enemies will cast up a bank about you and surround you and hem you in on every side." Some scholars conclude that Luke wrote after the siege of Jerusalem, which started in A.D.66 and ended A.D.70. For Luke the nation of Israel is to blame for its rejection of Jesus (19:14). Unique to Luke is the reference to people falling by the sword (21:24a). **Did Luke invent these sayings after the fact and after the Fall of Jerusalem (21:20,24)?**

Pupil's Activity: Three
What factors should be taken into consideration in discussing when Luke wrote his Gospel?

Pupil's Activity: Four
Outline your knowledge and understanding of the dating of Luke's Gospel. (CCEA A/S 2005 Resit) [15 marks]

Pupil's Activity: Five
a) Examine carefully the differences between the parallel passages in Luke 21:20-21 and Mark 13:14.
b) How do they provide insights into the dating of Luke's Gospel?

Pupil's Activity: Six
Some scholars suggest that Luke does not use the actual words of Jesus but makes a prophecy after the event a "vaticinium ex eventum." Discuss this statement in the context of the date of Luke's Gospel.

Pupil's Activity: Seven
For revision purposes prepare a summary of the three main positions regarding the dating of Luke's Gospel.

(Figure 3) A summary of the three main positions regarding the dating of Luke's Gospel

Pre-A.D.70	Post-A.D.70	Second-Century
1.	1.	1.
2.	2.	2.
3.	3.	3.
4.	4.	4.
5.	5.	

(Figure 4) The views of scholars regarding the three possible dates for Luke's Gospel

First view-Pre-A.D.70 Late 60s Conservative View	Second View-Post A.D.70 (80-90) Moderate Liberal View	Third View-Second-Century Extreme Liberal View
C. Blomberg A.D. 64 (2000)	F. Bovon A.D. 80-90 (1989)	H. Conzelmann A.D. 96 + (1960)
D. Bock A.D. 65-66 (1994)	G. Caird A.D. 75 (1963)	J. Knox A.D.130-35 (1942)
E. M. Blaiklock A.D. 62 (1959)	F. Danker A.D. 80-90 (1988)	J. O'Neill A.D.115-130 (1970)
F. F. Bruce A.D. 61 (1951-76)	P. F. Esler A.D. 80-90 (1987)	J.T. Townsend A.D. 80-90 (1984)
E.Ellis A.D.61-65 (1974)	C. F. Evans A.D.80-90 (1990)	G.Vermes A.D. 70-110 (2000)
G.Geldenhuys A.D. 66 (1950)	J. Fitzmyer A.D. 80-90 (1985)	
D. Guthrie A.D. 63 (1970)	W.G.Kummel A.D.80-90 (1967)	
C.J.Hemer A.D. 62 (1989)	A. M. Hunter A.D. 80 (1945)	
H. Marshall A.D. 69 (1978)	L. Johnson A.D. 80-90 (1991)	
L.Morris A.D. 63 (1988)	G. Stanton A.D. 80-85 (2002)	
D.P. Moessner A.D. 64 (1989)	R. Stein A.D. 70-90 (1992)	
B. Reicke pre-A.D. 62 (1972)	C.H.Talbert A.D. 80-90 (1982)	
J.A.T. Robinson A.D. pre-62 (1964)	V.Taylor A.D. 80-85 (1960)	
D.Wenham A.D. 58 (1972)	C.Tuckett A.D. 80-90 (1996)	

Pupil's Activity: Eight
Identify the following places on the map. (p. 21)
1) Britain   2) Caesarea   3) Hadrian's Wall   4) Jamnia (Javneh)   5) Jerusalem   6) Rome   7) Mount Vesuvius   8) Syria

Pupil's Activity: Nine   **[For Edexcel students]**
Discuss the pattern of the views expressed in Figure 4.

Pupil's Activity: Ten
Examine the views of scholars concerning the possible date of the writing of the Gospel of Luke.
(Edexcel A/S 2002/2005)   [7 marks]

Pupil's Activity: Eleven
a) How far is an accurate knowledge of the authorship and date necessary for an understanding of Luke's Gospel?
(Edexcel A/S 2001)   [6 marks]
b) To what extent is it important to know the authorship and date of the Gospel in order to understand it?
(Edexcel A/S 2002)   [6 marks]
c) To what extent is the evidence concerning the date of Luke's Gospel reliable?
(Edexcel A/S 2002)   [6 marks]

Pupil's Activity: Twelve
a) Identify and examine the evidence concerning the authorship and date of Luke's Gospel.
(Edexcel A/S 2001 and 2004)   [14 marks]
b) Explore the view that the dating of this Gospel is a problem. Justify your answer.
(CCEA A/S 2003)   [15 marks]

Outcomes
Students should have a knowledge and understanding of:
- **the three main possible views for the dating of Luke's Gospel.**
- **the dating of Luke's Gospel.**
- **why it is important to know the date of Luke's Gospel and how it helps to understand this Gospel. (CCEA)**
- **the reliability of the evidence for the dating of Luke's Gospel. (Edexcel)**
- **the views of scholars regarding the dating of Luke's Gospel. (Edexcel)**
- **key concepts: the multi-ethnic nature of the early Church, "desolating sacrilege", Gentile inclusion, "early Catholic" theology, table fellowship, "vaticinium ex eventu" and the Hellenists.**

Notes on Chapter 2: The Date of Luke's Gospel
1. Donald A. Carson, Douglas J. Moo and Leon Morris, Apollos Press, (1992); this view is based upon Rackham and Harnack's chronology of Paul cited in CMM, p.192.
2. Darrell Bock, Article on the Gospel of Luke, D.J.G. IVP, (1992) p. 498.*
3. Irenaeus, "Against Heresies", 3.13.3; 3.15.1.
4. W.G. Kummel, Introduction to the N.T. London, (1965) p.132.
5. W.G. Kummel, op. cit. p.105.
6. Darrell Bock, Vol.1, Luke, op.cit. p.18.
7. Donald Guthrie, New Testament Introduction, IVP, (1965) p.109.
8. Carson, Moo and Morris, op. cit. p.116.
9. Carson, Moo and Morris, (ibid.)
10. Bo Reicke, The Roots of the Synoptic Gospels, Philadelphia: Fortress Press, (1986) quoted in Bock NTCS. IVP, (1994) p.17.
11. Howard Marshall, op.cit. p. 213.
12. Leon Morris, op. cit. pp. 23-24.
13. J.O' Neill, The Theology of Acts, London: (1970) SLA, p.287.
14. Darrell Bock, op. cit. p.500.
15. Darrell Bock, op. cit. pp.499-500.
16. Harnack and Rackham, cited in CMM, op. cit. p.192.
17. Darrell Bock, op. cit. p.509.
*This article is highly recommended.

Map of the Roman Empire

Map of The Roman Empire from 146 B.C. to A.D. 117

North Sea

Atlantic Ocean

Belgica

Germania

Italy

Macedonia

Black Sea

Mediterranean Sea

Cyrene

Cyrenia

Egypt

Red Sea

N.Africa

Carthage

CCEA A/S

Targets:
- Identify the main sources used by Luke.
- Recognise the main source theories, for example Griesbach's Hypothesis, Holtzmann's Two–Source Theory.
- Identify issues in the prologue (1:1-4) which relate to the sources of Luke's Gospel.
- Identify the key words and concepts:- orderly account (1:3), eyewitnesses (1:2), LXX, oral tradition, written source, Synoptic problem, Synoptic, "Q", (M), (L), Source Criticism, multiple attestation, double and triple tradition, One-Source Theory, Four-Document Theory, parataxis, asyndeton, literary dependence, catechesis and doublet.

The Sources of Luke's Gospel

Introduction

In order to determine Luke's sources, one needs to look at the Synoptic Problem and Source Criticism. Criticism does not mean being destructive and rationalistic about the bible. The word "criticism" comes from "krites" meaning a judge who assesses and evaluates a text. Source Criticism is a method of study of the Gospel stories, which tries to find the sources used by the evangelists and to discover if they are historically reliable. It works on the theory that, if similar matter occurs in one or more evangelists, it is due to their common use of one or more written sources. Source Criticism has been likened to four or five roads which begin in a common place or the loop of a railway system or the branch of a tree. (Taylor) **(1)** "It is a study of ordinary human means of writing, which God's Spirit superintended to ensure the final product was what God had wanted." (Achtemeier) **(2)** A basic principle of Synoptic Criticism says that similarities can only be accounted for on the basis of literary dependence. (Guthrie) **(3)** There are three major issues in Source Criticism today:
- The priority of Mark,
- The nature and existence of "Q",
- The priority of Matthew,

"Another basic principle of Source Criticism is that of 'multiple attestation', which works on the premise that several witnesses are better than one and, if a teaching of Jesus is witnessed to in Mark, "Q", (M), (L) and John, then we have five different sources which witness to its reliability." (Stein) **(4)** It is worth noting that a source does not necessarily mean a written source; it can be either an oral or a written tradition. A document in Source Criticism means a written source as distinct from an oral one. In Source Criticism a "doublet" is thought to be one event in two versions, for example the feeding of the five thousand and four thousand (Mk. 8:1-10). [See pp.25,33.] John's Gospel is excluded from Source Criticism.

[1] The Synoptic Problem is the explanation given regarding the similarities and the distinctive differences between Matthew, Mark and Luke.

Do they contradict each other and what is their literary relationship? Why do Matthew, Mark and Luke seem to be alike and yet they are different? What do they have in common?

Their commonality is the same: a) general scheme b) passages c) words d) O.T. quotations e) parenthesis.

Model 1: A synopsis (Similar passages set out in parallel form next to each other in columns to compare the wording.)

A) Same scheme and order in all three Gospels

Matthew	Mark	Luke
a. Jesus' ministry in Galilee, b. Journey to Jerusalem followed by the Passion.	a. Jesus' ministry in Galilee, b. Journey to Jerusalem followed by the Passion.	a. Jesus' ministry in Galilee, b. Journey to Jerusalem followed by the Passion.

B) Same passages in two Gospels

Matthew 3:7-10 and Luke 3:7-9 are the same. But when he saw many of the Pharisees and Sadducees coming for baptism he said to them, "You brood of vipers! Who warned you to flee the wrath to come? Bear fruit that befits repentance and do not presume to say to yourself, 'We have Abraham as our father'; for I tell you God is able from these stones to raise up children to Abraham. Even now the axe is laid to the root of the trees; every tree that does not bear good fruit is cut down and thrown into the fire."	These verses are absent in Mark, who in 1:2-8 describes the baptism of Jesus.	Luke 3:7-9 and Matthew 3:7-10 similar. He said to the multitudes that came out to be baptised by him, "You brood of vipers! Who warned you to flee the wrath to come? Bear fruit that befits repentance and do not begin to say to yourselves, 'We have Abraham as our father'; for I tell you, God is able from these stones to raise up children to Abraham. Even now the axe is laid to the root the trees; every tree that does not bear good fruit is cut down and thrown into the fire."

C) Same words in all three Gospels   Model 1 (cont'd)

Matthew 19:13 Then children were brought to Him that He might lay hands on them and pray. The disciples rebuked the people.	**Mark 10:13** And they were bringing children to Jesus, that He might touch them; and the disciples rebuked them.	**Luke 18:15** Now they were bringing even infants to Him that He might touch them; and when the disciples saw it, they rebuked them.

D) Same O.T. quotes in all three Gospels

Matthew 3:3 For this is He who was spoken of by the prophet Isaiah when he said, "The voice of one crying in the wilderness: Prepare the way of the Lord, make His paths straight."	**Mark 1:2** As it is written in Isaiah the prophet, "Behold, I send my messenger before your face, who shall prepare your way; the voice of one crying in the wilderness: Prepare the way of the Lord, make His paths straight."	**Luke 3:4** As it is written in the book of the words of Isaiah the prophet, "The voice of one crying in the wilderness: Prepare the way of the Lord, make His paths straight." The (LXX) has 'paths of our God' which Stein says Luke and the other Synoptics do not include. Liefeld concludes that Luke and the other Synoptics make it easier to understand the words "the Lord" refer to Christ.

Luke's distinctiveness: Luke continues the quotation (Is.4:3) to show that the gospel is for everyone. "Every valley shall be filled, and every mountain and hill brought low, and the crooked shall be made straight, and the rough ways shall be made smooth; **and all flesh shall see the salvation of God." (3:6)** Both Liefeld and Morris note that Luke's addition follows the (LXX). This shows Luke's own universal concern and his central message of salvation. Luke omits "the appearance of God's glory." (Is.40:5) He does stress the glory of God elsewhere (2:14) but not in this context.

E) Same parenthesis in all three Gospels

Matthew 9:6 (He then said to the paralytic.)	**Mark 2:10** (He said to the paralytic.)	**Luke 5:24** (He said to the man who was paralysed.)

Source critics came to the conclusion that agreement in these five areas indicated a common source; a common oral tradition existed but this does not explain the same editorial comments, for example "let the reader understand." (Matt. 24:15; Mk. 13:14) One literary explanation was to say that all three writers wrote independently of each other but this does not explain 1:1-2 which refers to predecessors, "as many have undertaken to compile a narrative." Some scholars concluded from this that Mark was the first Gospel to be written. There is considerable agreement between the three Gospels. The Holy Spirit guided the three authors and helped them to recall everything (Jn. 14:26). The agreement between the Gospels is too close to be explained as the accidental convergence of independent accounts. Either we say there is a common source or there is mutual dependence. Only 31 verses in Mark have no parallel in Matthew and Luke.

The number of verses in Matt. Mk. and Lk.

Model 2

Matthew 1068 verses
(M) 308 verses 29% approx.

"Q" 250 verses in Matt. and Lk.

Mark 523 verses

Mark 661 verses

31 verses unique to Mark

Luke 1149 verses

(L) 475 verses 30% approx.

"Q" 250 verses in Matt. and Lk.

95 reflected verses of Mark

325 verses of Mark

F) Theories of Source Criticism
Model 3

The following theories have been given and all of them have a connection with the sources of Luke's Gospel:

The Priority of Matthew	Priority of Matt/Rejection of "Q" Source	Priority of Mark + "Q" Source
1 A) Augustine of Hippo the earliest and the Traditional View (5) (Figure 2)	**2 A) J. J. Griesbach's Hypothesis (11)** (1774) A "Two-Gospel" Theory (Figure 4)	**3 A) H.J.Holtzmann (1863) (14)** A "Two-Document" Theory: two basic documents underlie the Synoptics, Mark's Gospel and "Q". (Figure 5)
1 B) B.C.Butler (7) and J.Chapman **(8)** **(1951)** (Figure 3) and J.Wenham **(6)** **(1991)** **1 C) L.Vaganay (1954) (10)**	**2 B) W.R.Farmer (1964) (12)** A "Two-Gospel" Theory **2 C) B.Orchard (1989)**	**3 B) B.H.Streeter (1924)** (Figure 7) **(15)** A Four-Document/Source Theory **3 C) Proto-Luke Hypothesis (1921)** (A2 level CCEA) **(18)** **3 D) Farrer's Hypothesis (1955) (19)**
	2 D) M. Goulder: A One-Source (13) Theory (Figure 6)	

The Priority of Matthew	Priority of Matt./Rejection of "Q"	Priority of Mark + "Q"
1A) Augustine (A.D. 410) **(5)** argued: 1) Matthew was the first Gospel to be written, 2) Mark used Matthew, 3) Luke used Mark, 4) This was also the view of the early church, 5) It was the order in the N.T. canon of Scripture, 6) The priority of Matthew is still the official position of the Roman Catholic Church. This view is based on the fact that Matthew was the only apostle among the Synoptic writers. It is also the view of Wenham. **(6)** 7) Matthew also wrote for the Jews as most of the Christians had a Jewish background. Some of the Gospel writers were aware of the work of others. **1B) B.C.Butler (1951) (7) and J.Chapman (8)** said: 1) Matthew wrote his Gospel in Aramaic. 2) Peter used this in his preaching which included eyewitness accounts. 3) At some stage, Matthew was translated into Greek and Luke produced his Gospel using a Greek Matthew and Mark. 4) Some passages in Matthew appear more original than Mark. 5) Only Mark is medial to Matthew and Luke: therefore Mark used Matthew and Luke used Matthew and Mark.	**2A) J.J.Griesbach (1783)** in his Two-Gospel theory also suggested that: **(11)** 1) Matthew was the first to write a Gospel. 2) Luke was the second to write and used Matthew. 3) Mark was the last to write and used Matthew and Luke. It fitted with the traditional view and with the order in the N.T. canon of Scripture. It suggests that Mark copied first from Matthew and then from Luke and wanted to keep a balance between them. 4) This view is also based upon Church tradition. 5) Matt. + Luke = Mark 6) There is no need for a hypothetical "Q". **2 B) W.R.Farmer (1964)(12) and B. Orchard (1910-2006)** a Two-Gospel theory 1. In the last twenty-five years there has been a renewed interest in this theory due to the writings of Farmer. 2. He argued for the priority of Matthew. 3. Mark was the last Gospel to be written. 4. Luke used Matthew. 5. Farmer also argued if this theory of the priority of Matthew is wrong then Mark was the first to be written.	**3A) H.J.Holtzmann (1863)** in his Two-Source theory argued that: **(14)** 1) Mark was the first Gospel to be written and was the main source for Matthew and Luke. 2) Matthew used Mark. 3) Luke used Mark. 4) Matthew and Luke used a common source called "Q" from the German word "Quelle" meaning source. This was to explain why Matthew and Luke used another common source. 5) "Q" is thought to be the written sayings of Jesus which are peculiar to Matt. and Luke and not in Mark. Mark did not use "Q". 6) There are reckoned to be over two hundred of these verses with identical language. (Model 2) 7) Matthew and Luke both improved Mark's rough Greek style and tightened up his theology. Mark has an eyewitness style "after sunset" (1:32) and the "green grass". (6:39) In his grammar and style, he omits conjunctions, has a fondness for asyndeton (omitting conjunctions) and parataxis only using "and" when he wants to connect clauses. Of the 92 passages Mark shares with Luke, Mark is longer 71 times. 8) Mark uses Aramaic words for example Boanerges (3:7); "Talitha cumi" (5:41) ; Abba (14:36). 9) This view upholds the priority of "Q".
The weakness of this view 1) However, it is hard to explain the contents of Mark as a summarising Gospel without appealing to its use of Luke. (Bock) **(9)** 2) The early Church traditionally claimed that Matthew was the first Gospel to be written and Mark was thought to be an abridged version of Matthew. 3) The priority of Matthew was assumed. **1C) L.Vaganay (1954) (10)** (A modified form of Matthew's priority and Butler's Theory.) 1. Vaganay supposed that Luke used Mark and that Luke used a "Sayings Source" in Greek as did Matthew .	**The weakness of this view** 1) This view agrees with church tradition that Matthew was the first Gospel to be written. 2) It was based upon the old Tubingen theory of thesis, antithesis and synthesis. It is like going from two extremes to a middle view, for example from Arctic-Antartic-Equator. 3) It argues that Mark conflates the two other sources which explains the repeated phrase in Mark 1:32. "When evening came and the sun was setting" and why Mark seems to use Matt. 8: 16, "That evening they brought to Him many who were possessed of demons; and He cast out the spirits with a word, and healed all who were sick." (Matt. 8:16) "Now when the sun was setting all those with various diseases brought them to Him." (Lk. 4:42)	**The weakness of this view** 1) This theory has become the basis for modern source criticism of the Synoptic Gospels. However, it does not explain why Matthew and Luke have unique material. 2) In many places Matthew and Luke agree against Mark and this would show that Luke knew Matthew or alternatively Matthew knew Luke directly. 3) The Arguments for "Q" a) The similarities between Matthew and Luke indicate that each of them have 235 verses in common with each other and with identical language. These are mostly the sayings of Jesus. [See p. 23.] b) "Q" consists of the sayings of Jesus. (Manson) **(20)** [See p.32.] c) The purpose seems to have been for the early Church to have a manual of moral instruction for new converts. d) Matthew and Luke did not know and did not use each other.

The priority of Matthew	Priority of Matt./rejection of "Q"	The priority of Mark + "Q"
2. He started with the Aramaic version of Matthew as the first Gospel to be written. 3. Mark was written second using a shorter edition of Matthew. 4. Luke was the Third Gospel to be written. 5. Luke also used a Sayings Source in Greek which was also used by Matthew.	4) It also explains all the Gospel agreements but not why two agree against one. 5) If Mark came last why did he deliberately omit the Sermon on the Plain, the Lord's Prayer, the Infancy Stories, and the Resurrection appearances? It would be more logical to say that Mark wrote first and Matthew and Luke added this material from other sources.	**Model 3** Matt. 3: 7-10 | Luke 3: 7-9 Matt. 11: 25-27 | Luke 10: 21-22 e) There is a common order to Matthew and Luke in the non-Markan material and therefore a single written source. [See pp. 25-27.] below to see Luke's "scattered" use of "Q" in 6:20-8:3; 9:51-18:14.]

f) Three examples of comparisons between Matthew and Luke as a reason for "Q"

Matthew	Luke
Matthew 7: 7-8 First example: Ask, and it shall be given you; seek, and you will find; knock and it will be opened to you. For everyone who asks receives, and he who seeks finds, and to him who knocks it will be opened.	**Luke 11:9-10** Ask, and it will be given you; seek, and will find; knock and it will be opened to you. For everyone who asks receives, and he who seeks finds, and to him who knocks it will be opened.
Second example of "Q" : a comparison between Matthew 5-7 the Sermon on the Mount and the Sermon on the Plain in Luke 6:20-49. Jesus says in the Sermon on the Mount the best gifts are righteousness, sincerity, humility, piety and love (7:8).	**Luke 6:20-49 Sermon on the Plain and the Sermon on the Mount** in Matthew are comparable in content and have double accounts of the same incidents. These are called "doublets" by scholars. But it could be argued they are separate occasions and two different sermons.
Comment Thirty-eight of the words are identical in Matthew and Luke hence the argument for "Q."	**What was the Form of Q?** 1) a single written source? 2) several written sources? 3) a common oral tradition? a) CMM **(11)** favour a Two-Source Theory. b) "Q" is the best explanation of the agreements between Matt. and Luke and a substantial portion of "Q" was in written form. c) There may have been other written sources and oral traditions.
Third example of "Q": a comparison between Matthew 10:37-38 and Luke 14:26 "He who loves Father or mother more than me is not worthy of me; and he who loves son or daughter more than me is not worthy of me." (Matt. 10:37-38) Matthew helps us to interpret Luke. Where Luke uses "hatred," Matthew uses "love." Jesus does not desire hatred of one's parents which would contradict Ex. 20:12 but he uses exaggeration to show that love for Jesus must outweigh all other loyalties.	**Luke 14:26** "If anyone comes to me and does not hate his own father and mother and wife and children and brothers and sisters, yes, and even his own life, he cannot be my disciple." **Conclusion** a) By understanding how Matthew and Luke used Mark and "Q", we can understand their own theological emphasis and comprehend their meaning. However, "Q" has never been found and is purely hypothetical. b) There is little agreement about the contents of "Q", its order or its purpose and some scholars today see it as a combination of a shorter and/or an oral source rather than one big definite document.

Prior-ity of Matt.	Priority of Mark/rejection of "Q"	Priority of Mark + "Q" Sayings
	2 D) Goulder's Theory (1989) is a form of the Two-Gospel theory. **(14)** 1. Goulder's order is Mark-Matthew-Luke. 2. The priority of Mark, 3. There is no "Q". 4. Luke used Matthew and rewrote much of it. **Weakness** 1. How do you account for the unique infancy material in Luke and Luke's omission of the birth stories in Matthew? 2. Matthew re-organises Luke's central material. [See below Figure 1 p. 27.] 3. What about Luke's distinctive use of the eschatological discourses? 4. What about the recasting of some of Matthew's parables e.g. the pounds, the lost sheep and the Beatitudes/Sermon on the Mount in Matthew/Sermon on the Plain in Luke? 5. Goulder's view denies Luke 1:1-4 with its appeal to the two Gospels and "the many predecessors" or "many have undertaken" in (1:1) and Goulder's Two-Sources are also not "the many". Goulder says that the only reliable documents Luke used were Matthew, Mark and "the many." The rest are not authoritative. 6. Luke never has the number of triple tradition material as Matthew has.	**3 B) Streeter's Four-Source Theory** 1. Streeter argued that in addition to Mark and "Q" both Matthew and Luke had written sources of their own on which they drew their own material "M" and "L". **(15)** 2. Scholars who follow this view today are Fitzmyer (1981) **(16)** and Tuckett. (1983) **(17)** 3. This Four-Source Theory identifies the sources of Matthew and Luke as they rely on Mark. 4. Mark is the source of Matthew and Luke. 5. This theory examines the inter-relationship between the sources. 6. Mark was the earliest and the shortest Gospel. 7. Matthew and Luke copied Mark word for word and added their own selections "Q" and "L" for Luke and "Q" and "M" for Matthew. 8. Scholars who support this view say that Luke's "Great Omission:" Mk. 6:45-8:26;9;41-10:12 has passages which contain "doublet" events, which Luke left out rather than repeat. **3 C) Streeter's Proto-Luke Theory (18)** 1. Streeter said that Luke wrote a first draft called "Proto–Luke", before he saw a copy of Mark and then revised it after reading Mark. This would account for larger blocks of non-Markan–non "Q" material in Luke than in Matthew e.g. Nearly all of the material in Luke 9:51-18:14 is from "Q"+"L". [See Figure 1 p.27.] This theory will be explored in depth at A2 level (CCEA).
3 D) Farrer's Hypothesis Four-Source Theory (1955) (19) • Rejects "Q". • Luke used Matthew. • Priority of Matthew • Matt.+ Mk.+(M)= Luke		

[3A] The contents of "Q" viewed in topics Model 4

Topic	Luke	Content
1. John the Baptist and Jesus	3:7-9	**Warning of God's judgement and a call to repentance:** the rebuke which warns about judgement (3:7), make fruit worthy of repentance (3:8a), do not rely on ancestry (3:8b), a reminder about judgement (3:9).
	3:16-17	The promise of a greater baptism
	4:1-13	Messianic Preparation – the Temptations
	6:20-49	The Sermon on the Plain: the four beatitudes (6:20-23), the four woes (6:24-26), the call to love and mercy (6:27-38), judge and you will be judged by how you judge (6:38), the call to righteousness, foolish and wise building (6:39-49).
	7:1-10	The faith of a centurion
	7:18-35	Questions about John the Baptist
2. Jesus and His disciples	9:57-62	Warning about discipleship
	10:21-24	Jesus gives thanks to the Father (10:21-22). Jesus blesses the disciples (10:23-24).
	*11:1-4	Jesus' teaching on prayer: the setting and the example prayer (11:2-4)
	11:9-13	Trust a gracious Father (9-13).

3. Jesus and His opponents	11:14-26	Controversy: the meaning of the healings (11:14-23) and the parable of the returning spirits (11:24-26)
	11:29-36	The sign of Jonah (11:29-30), sayings about light (11:33), the light in a person (11:34-36)
	11:42-52	Jesus rebukes the Pharisees and Scribes.
	12:2-3	Promise: all that is done in secret will be exposed.
	12:4-12	Fear God and not human beings.
	12:22-34	Avoid anxiety.
4. The future	12:35-59	Be ready and be faithful stewards: the parable of the faithful and unfaithful servants (12:35-48), Jesus as the cause of division (12:49-53), Jesus brings division in families (12:51-53); reading the times like the weather (12: 54-56), settling accounts with your accuser (12:57-59).
	13:18-21	Parables of the mustard seed and the leaven
	13:22-30	The narrow door
	13:34-35	Lament over Jerusalem
	16:13	Serve God and not mammon.
	16:16-18	The law and the kingdom-the standard of the heart and divorce.
	17:22-37	The quick coming of the kingdom and the accompanying judgement
	*19:11-27	Parable of stewardship
	* 22:24-30	Greatness comes in service: appointment to authority over Israel
5. Other sayings	14:1-6	Sabbath healing and silence
	14:7-12	Lessons on humility and generosity
	17:1-2	Warning about false teaching
	17:3-4	Confronting the sinner and forgiving the penitent
	17:5-6	Request for faith (17:5): the power of a little genuine faith (17:6)
	18:14	The justified man (18:14a): God honours humility (18:14b).

* Added by Kloppenborg in 1988 **(22)**

[3B] The structure of Luke showing sections of Mark, "Q" and (L).

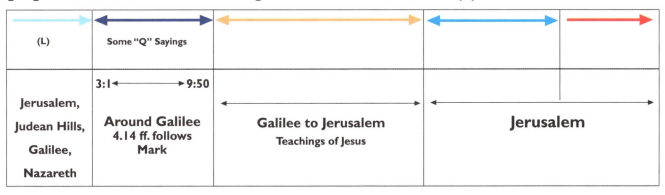

(Figure 2)

I A) The Augustinian View (5)

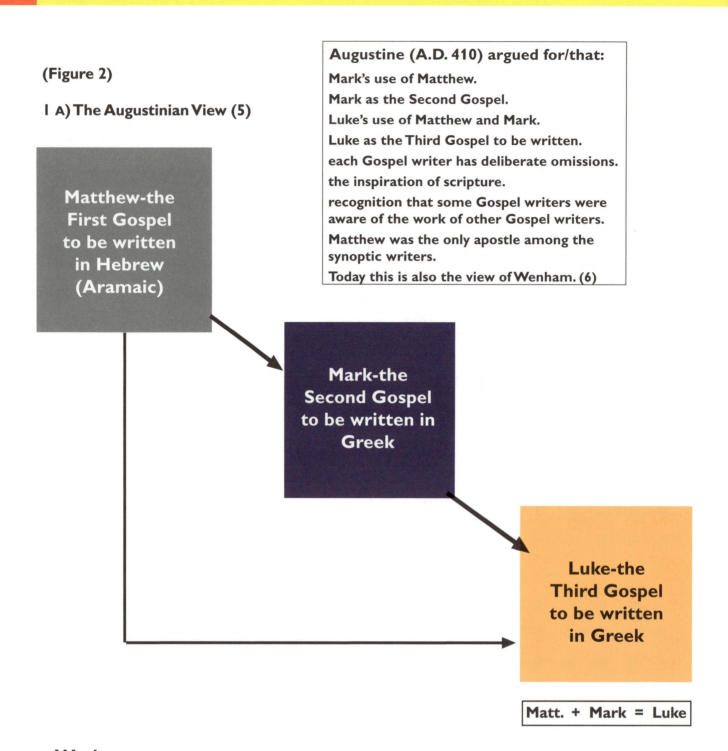

Augustine (A.D. 410) argued for/that:

Mark's use of Matthew.

Mark as the Second Gospel.

Luke's use of Matthew and Mark.

Luke as the Third Gospel to be written.

each Gospel writer has deliberate omissions.

the inspiration of scripture.

recognition that some Gospel writers were aware of the work of other Gospel writers.

Matthew was the only apostle among the synoptic writers.

Today this is also the view of Wenham. (6)

Matthew-the First Gospel to be written in Hebrew (Aramaic)

Mark-the Second Gospel to be written in Greek

Luke-the Third Gospel to be written in Greek

Matt. + Mark = Luke

Weakness

■ This was the traditional view of the early Church using the canonical order.

■ The early Church assumed the priority of Matthew.

■ If Luke is the Third Gospel why does Mark summarise Luke and not show his use of Luke?

■ Mark is either the most used of the three Gospels (Luke has 420 verses of Mark and Matt. has 523 verses of Mark, 51 verses are unique to Mark) or he has the least amount of independent material. (See p. 23.)

■ Mark uses "verbal redundancies" of which there are 213 examples, e.g. "when evening came, as the sun was setting" (1:32, 42; 2:25; 4:21; 15:24).

(Figure 3)

1 B) Butler's Theory (7)

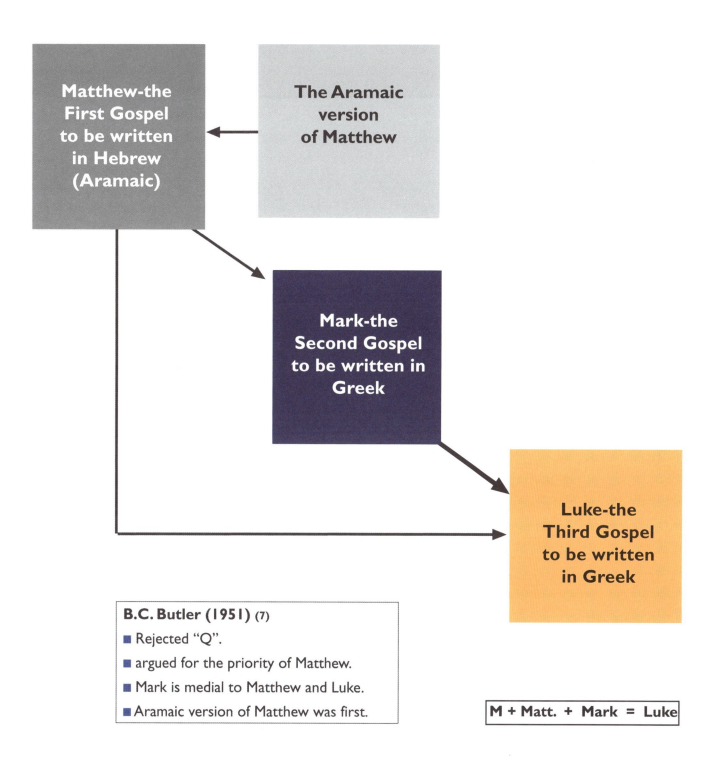

Matthew-the First Gospel to be written in Hebrew (Aramaic)

The Aramaic version of Matthew

Mark-the Second Gospel to be written in Greek

Luke-the Third Gospel to be written in Greek

B.C. Butler (1951) (7)
- Rejected "Q".
- argued for the priority of Matthew.
- Mark is medial to Matthew and Luke.
- Aramaic version of Matthew was first.

M + Matt. + Mark = Luke

(Figure 4)

2 A) Griesbach's Two-Gospel Theory (11) (1783) omits "Q".

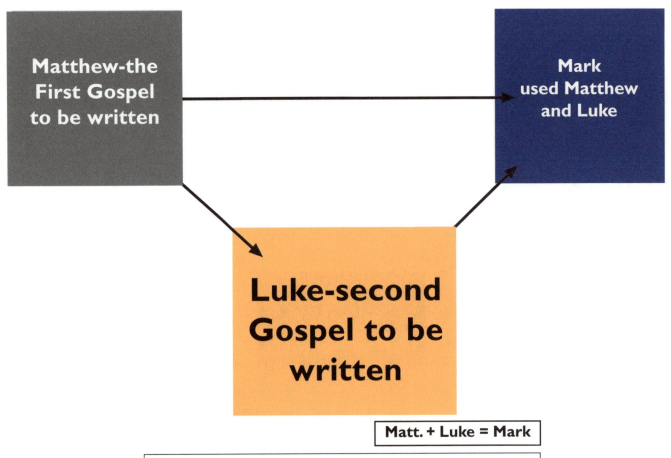

Matthew-the First Gospel to be written

Mark used Matthew and Luke

Luke-second Gospel to be written

Matt. + Luke = Mark

Griesbach (1783) said:
- the order is Matthew, Luke and Mark,
- no "Q",
- Mark copied from Matthew and then from Luke,
- This view has been developed by Farmer (1964) **(12)** who said that Luke used Matthew.

Weakness:
- It is hard to see if Mark used Matthew and Luke why did Mark omit the infancy narratives, the Post-Resurrection appearances and the beatitudes (Matt.5:3-12)?
- It is hard to justify Mark as the lead Gospel to be written as it is Mark's ambiguities which are smoothed out in Matt. and Luke.
- In the triple tradition material it is Mark's ambiguities which are smoothed out in Matt, and Luke.
- Why does Mark not summarise the 200-250 verses shared by Matt. and Luke?

Figure 5   **2B) W. R. Farmer (1964) [See Pupil's Activity.]**
                2C) B. Orchard (1987)
                2D) M. Goulder (1989) One-Source Theory, Two-Gospel Theory (13)

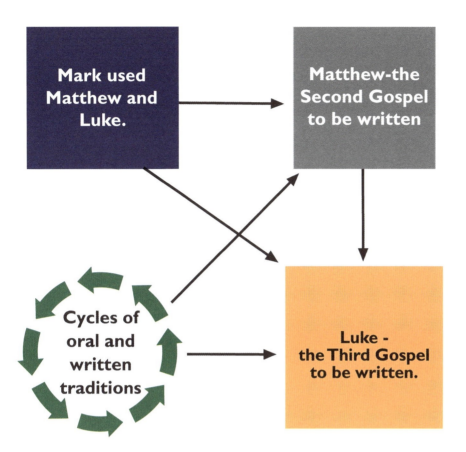

M. Goulder's Theory (1984):

- Mark first,
- Matthew second,
- Luke third,
- no "Q",
- assumes that Luke used Matthew and
  cycles of oral and written traditions .

Goulder:
- Goulder rejects the reference in Luke 1:1-4 which refers to many predecessors, he later argued that other predecessors were not authoritative. (Goulder 1989)
- Luke rewrote much of Matthew.
- little of Luke comes from a source but it reflects his emphasis.
- a variation of The Two-Gospel Theory.

(Figure 6)
3 A) Two-Source-Document Theory (Holtzmann) (14)

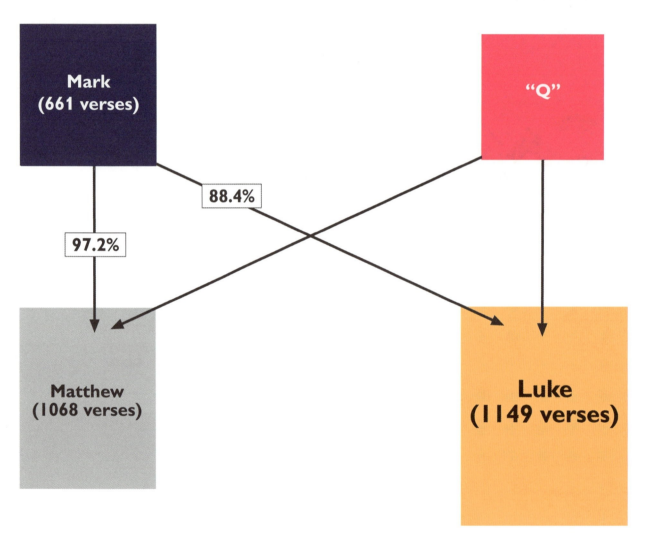

"Q" is thought to be sayings about:
- Jesus and John the Baptist,
- Jesus and His disciples,
- Jesus and His opponents,
- Jesus' sayings about the future,
- other sayings.

Mark
(661 verses)

"Q"

88.4%

97.2%

Matthew
(1068 verses)

Luke
(1149 verses)

Holtzmann (1863) said:
- Mark was first.
- Matthew and Luke used Mark independently.
- Matthew and Luke used a common source "Q".

Weakness
- There is little agreement about the contents of "Q" its order or its purpose.
- Was it a combined, shorter and an oral source?
- "Q" is purely hypothetical.
- There is no clear evidence for "Q".

Mark. + "Q" = Luke

Figure 7

3 B) The Four-Document Theory (Streeter) (15)

> **(L) has over one third of Luke's Gospel and includes:**
>
> (a) **fourteen unique parables**: eg. the Good Samaritan, the Rich Fool, the Unjust Judge, the Two Debtors (7:48-50),
>
> (b) **various Sayings eg**. the Lord's Prayer (11:1-4), Herod that fox (13:31-33),
>
> (c) **narratives**: the scene at Nazareth (Ch. 4), the call of Simon (5:1-11), the choice of "The Twelve." (6:1-11)

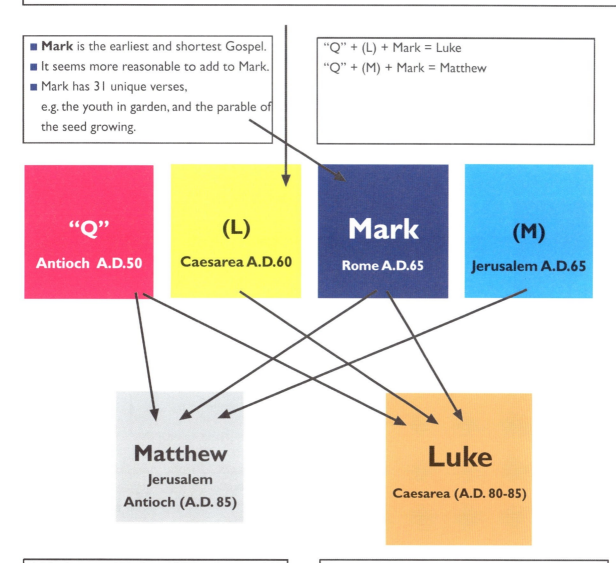

> - **Mark** is the earliest and shortest Gospel.
> - It seems more reasonable to add to Mark.
> - Mark has 31 unique verses,
>   e.g. the youth in garden, and the parable of the seed growing.

> "Q" + (L) + Mark = Luke
> "Q" + (M) + Mark = Matthew

"Q"   Antioch A.D.50

(L)   Caesarea A.D.60

Mark   Rome A.D.65

(M)   Jerusalem A.D.65

Matthew   Jerusalem Antioch (A.D. 85)

Luke   Caesarea (A.D. 80-85)

1. Matthew used Mark and "Q" and a special M.
2. **Luke used Mark and "Q" and** another source L.
3. The material from **(M) and (L)** comes from an **oral tradition.**

Streeter (15) said:
- Mark's Gospel originated in Rome A.D.65.
- "Q" probably came from Antioch A.D.50.
- (M) represented a Jerusalem source.
- (L) represented Caesarea(A.D.60) and was probably oral in character.
- Streeter dates Luke (A.D.80 - 85).
- Each source was linked to a particular community of Jesus.

> **Weakness:**
> - What about Luke's "Great Omission" of Mk.6:45-8:26? Streeter saw these incidents as doublets and therefore Luke omitted them, e.g. the feeding of the 4,000. (Mk.8:1-10) This was thought to be a doublet of the feeding of the 5,000. A doublet is one event in two versions.
> - This view questions the historicity of the feeding of the 4,000. The so-called doublets are "mirror" miracles which reproduce earlier scenes, yet they show that little has changed by way of response to Jesus.

Figure 8

3 C) Proto-Luke Theory (15)

(A2 only CCEA)

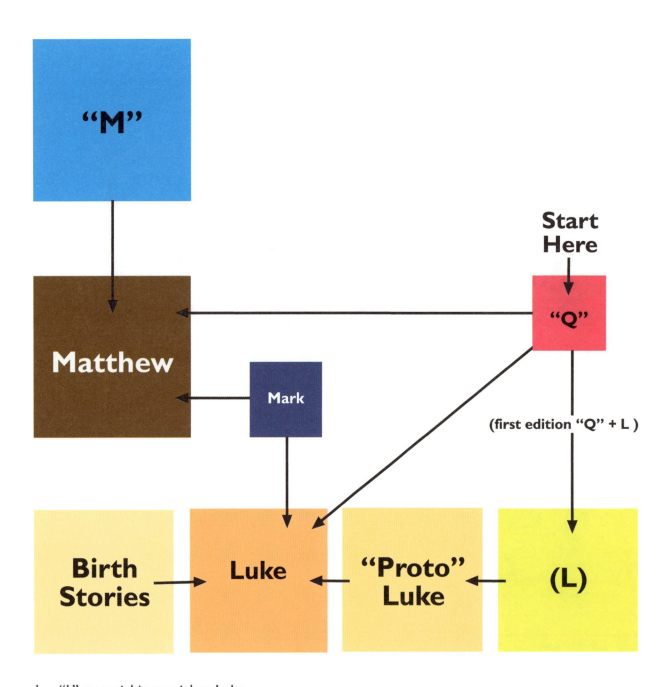

1. "L" material is special to Luke.
2. Luke has a tendency to do his own thing even when the material is shared with Matthew and Luke as in the Passion Narrative.
3. Use of material from Mark in blocks and yet he omits Mark 6:45-8:10. and 9:41-10:12.
4. His first edition was ("Q" + L).
5. Proto-Luke passages are mainly in the Central Section.
6. Proto-Luke existed before Matthew and Mark.
7. Luke uses words like "the Lord" rather than Jesus.
8. This theory omits the Infancy Narratives. [Chs. 1-2]

[4] The prologue (1:1-4) and the sources of the Third Gospel [See pp. 9, 59, 68.]

In the prologue Luke anticipates three divisions of study in the formation of the Gospel.

A) He speaks of "the things that have been accomplished among us." (1:1)

1) "Among us" refers to those who experienced the effects of Jesus' presence up to the time of Luke's writing (1:1). These were the first generation of believing Christians who witnessed the salvation history.

2) "The things fulfilled" could be the events which fulfilled O.T. prophecies "words which will be fulfilled in their time;" (1:20) "the time came" (2:6) and "when the time came." (2:21-22) [See also 4: 21; 9:31; 21:22; 24:24, 44-47.] "Accomplished" (Gk. peplerophoremenon) means fulfilled (NIV) as Luke tends to use it in this sense (1:1b). (Bock) **(23)** The O.T. prophecies were brought to completion (1:1b).

3) "They were delivered to us by those who were eyewitnesses and ministers of the word (Gk. huperetai tou logou)." (1:2) The Greek word for eyewitness here is "autoptai" and from this our word "autopsy" is derived. These eyewitnesses reported all the events of the Jesus they saw. There could have been a two-step process here (1) the tradition passed on to the eyewitnesses and then (2) on to the ministers of the word.

4) The credibility of the sources can be seen in the fact they were "handed down"(Gk. paredosan) (1:2).

5) Luke went back to the beginning (Gk.anothen) (1:2b). This could refer to Luke starting his story with John the Baptist or the birth stories which he could have received from Mary.

6) "Even as" (Gk.kathos) (RSV) "just as they were delivered to us." (1:2a) This indicates the reliable basis on which the accounts rested.

> Luke says that he looked at "everything" (Gk.pasan). While his content is not comprehensive, he has really done his homework, for example Luke's "Great Omission" of Mk.6:45-8:26; 9:41-10:12 describes Jesus walking on the water, crossing the lake and going on His way to Bethsaida (Mk.6:45-52).

B) "Many" have undertaken to draw up a narrative or an account (Gk.diegesis) of these things (1:1a).

The many (Gk. polloi) (where our "hoi polloi" comes from) could be a reference to the oldest Gospels or Gospel sources, his literary or oral predecessors or both. [See: Source theories.]

1) "Have undertaken" (Gk. epecheiresan) describes the work of Luke's predecessors (1:1). The word means literally "to set their hand to" and suggests the presence of either written materials or oral reports. This word is also used for composing accounts. At this time in history there was no printed page. The predecessors could be Mark and "Q", a source thought to include the "sayings of Jesus." Those who accept "Q" tend to say that Mark was written first. Others say Matthew was written first and tend to reject "Q". What is clear is that:

a) Luke was not the first to write a Gospel.

b) Luke does not name his sources.

c) Luke appears to recognise other sources and had them in his presence.

d) These other sources had tried to give an account of the ministry of Jesus and had access to similar sources or traditions as Luke.

e) These accounts have their roots in the testimony of the eyewitnesses or in the roots of the other accounts (Acts 20:35; 1 Clement 46:7).This is an example of a saying of Jesus not in the Gospels. "It is more blessed to give than to receive."

f) "The many" could be a reference to (1) oral accounts (2) eyewitnesses (3) written accounts. 2) Luke feels that he has something worthwhile to contribute, "It seemed good to me also." (1:3a)

2) He says that he looked at "everything" (Gk.pasin) and, while his content is not comprehensive, he has really done his homework. Consider Luke's Great Omissions of Mk. 6:45-8:26; 9:41-10:12, Jesus walking on the water and crossing the lake going on His way to Bethsaida (Mk.6:45-52).After Jesus healed the Syro-phoenician woman's daughter, He left Tyre and came into the region of Decapolis (Mk. 7:24-30) where He healed the deaf and dumb mute (Mk. 7: 31-37).After feeding the 4,000, Jesus went on the way to Dalmanutha/Magdala (Mk. 8:1-10); the Pharisees looked for a sign at Dalmanutha on the western shore of Galilee (Mk.7:11-13). Mark omits the geographical reasons. [See p. 45.]

3) Luke says that he went back to the very beginning (1:2).

C) Luke the "careful historian" writes an "orderly (Gk.kathezes) account." (1:3)

1) Luke tells us that he is a careful historian who wants to write his own special account to commend the truth of the gospel (1:3a). It is not a mystery story, a novel, a comedy, a fiction or a non-fiction.

2) Marshall **(24)** says "orderly account" (1:3b) means "broadly chronological." Schneider **(25)** calls it "a salvation–history". Fitzmyer sees it as "a literary systematic presentation." **(26)** Bock **(27)** says it is "a combination of all three ideas.Therefore Luke is not writing in strict chronological order but in a more general order." Bock also recognises a general geographical arrangement in Luke and sees Luke as really describing his clear emphasis.

3) He writes "carefully" (Gk.akribos) and develops his story in a very precise way; he tells us how he wrote his Gospel (1:3b). [See p. 59.]

4) He provides his own theological reason for writing, "that Theophilus might know the truth about the ministry of Jesus, the things of which Theophilus had been informed (Gk.katechethesis) or was instructed." (1:4) Our words "catechesis" and "catechism" originate from this word. It can mean either informed or instructed. "The truth" (Gk.asphaleian) here can be:
• the correctness of the message,
• its reliability,
• giving certainty to the reader. Bock says it means reliability and assurance. Nearly half of this Gospel is not in any of the others. **(28)**
5) He investigated (Gk. parekolouthekoti) thoroughly for his Gospel, even though he was not an eyewitness and would have travelled the country trying to gather information (1:3a).
6) "It seemed good to me also," (Gk.edoxekamoi) indicates that Luke identified with his predecessors and greatly appreciated their work (1:3a). [See p. 37.]

[5] Summary of the prologue and the sources of Luke's Gospel
• Luke's preface is important for discovering the method used by Gospel writers as all followed a similar course.
• In Luke's time the compiling of written narratives was common.
• These writings came from the reports of eyewitnesses and ministers of the word; each writer would select from eyewitness accounts materials most relevant to his purpose (1:2b).
• Guthrie **(29)** says the "predecessors" would have had similarities and divergencies as in the Synoptics with large agreement but different verbal expressions in the narrative.
• Luke in the preface seems to suggest that he is writing an independent account. He mentions the earlier attempts but does not say that he used them. His own investigations have been thoroughly made.
• Source theory has suggested that Luke's quest for authentic material was mainly based upon his own (L) material.
• Luke's predecessors could have been Mark or even Matthew but he emphasises his own careful investigations (1:3).
• Luke does not tell us who the "ministers of the word" were but points out clearly that it was these people and the "eyewitnesses", who delivered "the traditions" (Gk.paredosan). If this group existed the tradition would have been handed on in set forms with the approval of the apostles. The eyewitnesses and ministers of the word could have been the same group and also apostles (1:1-4). The tradition then would have had the authority of the apostles. (Guthrie) **(30)**

The style and structure of the prologue: **(Figure 8)**
• reflects a Greek style.
• has parallelism for aesthetic purposes and to be culturally friendly.
• has balanced phrases:
"Many have undertaken .... I too decided to set down an orderly account.
the events that have been fulfilled among us .... everything from the beginning.
just as they were handed to us .... so that you might know."
• has a rhyme pattern.
• There is a balance in the pattern between 1:1-2 and 1:3-4,
(A) "Inasmuch as many have undertaken   (1:1a)
(B) to compile an account of the things   (1:1b),
(C) even to those.......... delivered to us   (1:2),
(A) it seemed good to me........   (1:3a),
(B) to write an orderly account for you   (1:3b),
(C) that you might know certainty........   (1:4)."

---

[6] Can the Synoptic Problem be solved?
Due to a lack of sufficient data, the Synoptic problem has remained largely unsolved but some issues are valid.
A) The written Gospels were accepted as authoritative at an early period.
1. Why were Luke's "predecessors" not given an authoritative position (1:1)?
2. Why did the Gospels not have inherent authority even though their contents were authentic? Guthrie **(31)** says that "as the Gospels are about a unique Person, they have a literary uniqueness." There is a two-step process described here; the nature of the sources guarantees the quality." (Bock) **(32)** By two-steps Bock means the eyewitness accounts (oral traditions) and those of the servants (ministers of the word) (1:32).

B) Jesus promised to teach His disciples all things and bring all things to their remembrance (Jn. 14:26).

1. The Holy Spirit controlled the traditions.

2. Transmission was during the pre-literary period.

3. The tradition bearers were men of the Spirit and sensitive to the Spirit's promptings. Literary and historical criticism may shed light on the external circumstances of the period but it cannot comment upon the preservation of the Gospel traditions during that period. The Spirit controlled selection and helped the memory.

4. Many more traditions could have been included. "Jesus did many other signs in the presence of the disciples, which are not written in this book." (Jn. 20:30) "But there are many other things which Jesus did; were everyone of them to be written, I suppose that the world itself could not contain the books that would be written." (Jn. 21:25)

5. Under the control of the Spirit, the authors had to select from either eyewitnesses, oral accounts or written accounts.

6. Source Criticism has tended to omit the work of the Holy Spirit and to provide a mechanistic and rigid interpretation of Gospel authorship. (Guthrie) **(33)**

7. A more moderate approach which caters for oral tradition is more in keeping with the N.T. concept of the early Church as men of the Spirit.

8. "The Gospels came as a result of a purposeful selective process keeping in touch with the Spirit and not due to editorial ingenuity." (Guthrie) **(34)**

> **Under the control of the Spirit, the authors had to select from either eyewitnesses, oral accounts or written accounts.**

[7] A possible theory of the origin of the Synoptic Gospels (adopted from Guthrie's outline) (35)

Stage 1 - the apostles using the passion narrative
The apostolic preachers used the passion material, but could not present the material in isolation. Peter gave connected accounts of Jesus as in Acts 10:39 and this may have been a standard pattern.

Stage 2 - catechetical instruction
New converts received catechetical instruction and careful arrangement was required. This would have consisted of the sayings of Jesus in oral form, or entirely written as in "Q", or a mixture of both. This type of early catechesis could have been linked to Matthew which existed in its early Aramaic form.

Stage 3 - preparation for writing Mark's Gospel
Mark was closely linked with Peter and reduced the content of Peter's preaching to writing. Mark could have written notes during his links with Peter and used them later to write his Gospel. After Peter left Rome, Mark would have written his recollections.

Stage 4 - Mark's Gospel is written.
Mark's Gospel was produced at Rome. Matthew came across it and added catechesis and other material from personal memoirs. Sayings materials would have been in discourses and were used by Matthew to dovetail the teaching into Mark's framework. [See p. 15.]

Stage 5 - Luke's careful account is written.
Luke knew Mark personally and had a plan to write a careful account of the events "from the beginning" (1:2) for example the birth of Jesus. He studied all the material he could lay hands upon and all the eyewitness reports given to him orally. Luke seems to have had a copy of Mark but he did not possess it until after his first draft of teaching material (Proto-Luke) plus narrative material. Most of the teaching material would have been transmitted by catechesis which Mark would have picked up when Luke was in Caesarea. Luke may have had access to some written tract and possibly a copy of Matthew. The catechesis available to Luke would have shorter discourses of Jesus than those available to Matthew and this would help to explain the differences in the order of the sayings material in Matthew and Luke. The peculiarities of Matthew and Luke can be accounted for more easily if Luke did not use Matthew as a source and if both Luke and Matthew drew independently from the catechetical material. [See pp. 15, 36.]

Stage 6 - Luke gathered material from Joanna and Susanna (8:2) regarding the Galilean Ministry and Journey Narrative and received the birth narratives from Mary in Caesarea.
Probably churches at first used only one of the three Gospels as authoritative, as all three would not have been circulated in the same area. Through these six stages the three Synoptics may have reached us.

Pupil's Activity: One
a) Outline your knowledge and understanding of the main sources used by the writer of the Third Gospel.
(CCEA   2001/2003   A/S)   [30 marks]
b) Outline your knowledge and understanding of the sources of Luke's Gospel
(CCEA   2006 A/S)   [30 marks]
c) Comment upon the statement that this Gospel succeeds in presenting an "orderly account" of the Good News.
Justify your answer. (CCEA   2001 A/S)   [15 marks]

Pupil's Activity: Two
"Inasmuch as many have undertaken to compile a narrative of the things which have been accomplished among us, just as were delivered to us by eyewitnesses and ministers of the word". (1:1-2) Comment upon this statement and show how it gives us insights into the sources of the Third Gospel.

Pupil's Activity: Three
Here is a poem to help you recall one source theory based upon the priority of Mark.

> **There was a young doctor called Luke.**
> **Ideas from Mark he first took.**
> **From hypothetical "Q",**
> **Or so they argue,**
> **To write his "most beautiful book."**

a) Which Source theory about the Third Gospel does this limerick best describe?
b) Outline your knowledge and understanding of this particular theory.

Pupil's Activity: Four
As an aid to memory compose your own limerick, acrostic or mnemonic on some of the other source theories in Luke's Gospel.

Pupil's Activity: Five
Give an outline of how you think the Third Gospel was written using insights from (1:1-4) and ideas from Source Criticism.

Pupil's Activity: Six
a) Which source theory of the Third Gospel is presented in this formula: Luke = Mark + "Q" + (L)?
b) What are the strengths and weaknesses of this theory?

Pupil's Activitiy: Seven
In Luke 1:1-4 find four characteristics which show Luke's approach in writing his Gospel.

Pupil's Activity: Eight
"In Luke 1:1-2 Luke is still discussing the early accounts here, not his own study, which he will describe in 1:1-3."
(Bock) **(36)** Discuss this statement in the light of the main sources of the Third Gospel and what does it tells about the way in which Luke wrote his Gospel.

Pupil's Activity: Nine
As a revision exercise compete the grid below and link the sources to each theory. (Figure 9) [See p. 39.]

Pupil's Activity: Ten
Draw a spidergram to show the sources of Luke's Gospel and their connection with the prologue.

Pupil's Activity: Eleven
Produce your own diagram and formula for Farmer's theory of the sources of Luke from the information supplied. [See Theories of Source Criticism Model 2B.] [See p. 24.]

Outcomes
Students should have have a knowledge and understanding of:
- **the main sources used by Luke.**
- **source theory.**
- **key words and concepts in 1:1-4 and how they impinge upon Source Criticism.**
- **related key concepts such as :"orderly account," LXX, oral tradition, written source, Synoptic Problem, "Q," (L) , Source Criticism, multiple attestation, double and triple tradition, the priority of Matthew and the priority of Mark, Griesbach's Hypothesis, parataxis, asyndeton, literary dependence, catechesis and doublet.**

(Figure 9) Sources of the Third Gospel

Theorists	Matt. in Aramaic	Matt. in Greek	(M)	Mark	Luke	(L)	A sayings source in Greek.	"Q"	Oral and written tradition.
1a Augustine	Matthew			Mark	Luke				
1b Butler, Chapman and Wenham									
1c L. Vaganay									
2a J. Griesbach									
2b W. Farmer									
2c M. Goulder									
3a H.J. Holtzmann									
3b B. Streeter									
3c A. Farrer									
Total									

Notes on Ch. 3: Source Criticism

1. Vincent Taylor, The Gospels: A Short Introduction, Epworth Press, (1960) p.34.
2. Paul J. Achtemeier, Joel B. Green, Marianne Meye Thompson, Introducing the New Testament its Literature and Theology, Eerdmans Publishing, (2001) p.81.*
3. Donald Guthrie, New Testament Introduction: Gospels and Acts, IVP, (1970) p. 125.
4. Robert H. Stein, Article on the Synoptic Problem, DJG, IVP. (1992) p. 792. *
5. Augustine of Hippo, Orchard and Riley, The Order of the Synoptics: Why Three Synoptic Gospels? Mercer U. Press, (1987) pp.212-213.
6. John Wenham, Redating Matthew, Mark and Luke: A Fresh Assault on the Synoptic Problem, London: Hodder and Stoughton (1991).
7. B.C. Butler, The Originality of St. Matthew, Cambridge Press (1951).
8. John Chapman, Matthew, Mark and Luke, London: Longmans, Green, (1937).
9. Darrell L. Bock, Vol. 1, Luke, (Baker Press) (1999) p.7.*
10. L. Vaganay, The Synoptic Problem, Paris, (1954).
11. Henry Owen, Observations on the Four Gospels, Analysis of Griesbach's Theory, (1764).
12. William R. Farmer, The Synoptic Problem: A Critical Analysis, New York: Macmillan (1964).
13. Michael D. Goulder, Luke a new Paradigm, JSNT, Sheffield: JSOT (1989).
14. H.J. Holtzmann, The Synoptic Gosoels, Leipzig: W. Engelmann, (1863).
15. Brian H. Streeter, The Four Gospels, London: Macmillan (1930).
16. Joseph A. Fitzmyer, The Gospel According to Luke, Vol. 1, Anchor Bible, Doubleday Press, (1985) pp.63-106.*
17. Christopher M. Tuckett, The Revival of the Griesbach Hypothesis, Cambridge Univ. Press, Monograph 44 (1983).
18. Brian H. Streeter, The Four Gospels, Proto-Luke, London: Macmillan (1930).
19. Austen Farrer, "On dispensing with Q": Studies in the Gospels, Ed. by D.E. Nineham, OUP, (1955) pp.55-86.
20. Thomas W. Manson, The Sayings of Jesus, London, SCM, (1957). C. Blomberg says there are approx. 250 verses in "Q" in Matt. and Lk. cited in The Historical Reliability of the Gospels, Apollos, IVP (1987) p.15.
21. Donald Carson, Douglas Moo and Leon Morris, An Introduction to the N.T., Apollos Press, (1992) p.36.*
22. John S. Kloppenburg, Q Parallels: Synopsis, Critical Notes, and Concordances, (Sonoma California) (1988) 31-33, cited in Bock (b) Studying the Historical Jesus : A Guide to Sources and Methods, Apollos (2002) p.175.
23. Darrell L. Bock, op. cit. p.56.
24. Ian Howard Marshall, op. cit. pp.40, 43.*
25. Gerd Schneider, ZNW 68 (1977) (b) pp. 128-131.
26. Joseph A. Fitzmyer, op. cit. pp. 298-299. *
27. Darrell L. Bock, op. cit. p.62.
28. Darrell L. Bock, op. cit. p.65.
29. Donald Guthrie, op .cit. p. 202.
30. Donald Guthrie, op. cit. p. 204.
31. Donald Guthrie, op.cit. p. 205.
32. Darrell L. Bock, op. cit. p. 57.
33. Donald Guthrie, op. cit. p. 208.
34. Donald Guthrie, (ibid.)
35. Donald Guthrie, op. cit. pp. 209-220.
36. Darrell L. Bock, (ibid.)
* These books are highly recommended.

CCEA A/S and Edexcel A2

> **Targets:**
> • Identify the six main purposes of Luke's Gospel. (CCEA A/S)
> • Recognise the views of different scholars regarding the purposes of Luke's Gospel. (Edexcel only)
> • Identify key concepts, for example apologetics, catechetical, eschatological, evangelistic, final consummation, pluralistic, sociological, primary and secondary purposes.

The Purposes of the Gospel of Luke

Introduction

Luke shows that he had a very definite purpose in mind when he wrote his Gospel wanting people to accept the message which was so vital for him. His book is like a portrait of the life of Jesus in which he carefully selects his material to speak to a particular group of people. As can be seen from the structure of Luke's Gospel [See Ch.7: Structure.] the author had a very comprehensive agenda, which shows a variety of purposes.

[1] Evangelistic: to "convince his readers about the 'truthfulness' of what they had been informed." (Stein) (1) This evangelistic purpose shows that Luke wants to share his faith. (O'Neill) (2)

A) He writes as a "historian" compiling a narrative (Gk. diegesin) or "orderly account" which should be taken seriously (1:4). For Luke "narrative" means proclaiming, setting forth a persuasive, narrative, interpretation of God's work in Jesus. (Green) (3) He has examined all the facts with great care and his purpose is to write a historical account in which he presents the progress of Jesus from Galilee to Jerusalem and the prominence of Jerusalem in the birth and the resurrection accounts. He wants his readers to be certain of the traditions which they had been taught. He is also concerned to show that God is guiding the events and refers to God (Gk. Theos) one hundred and twenty-two times.

B) Luke wants Theophilus to know the truth and certainty (Gk. asphaleilan) meaning certainty or assurance of the facts, which had been transmitted to him. "Luke stresses the accuracy of the historical facts which formed part of the early Christian teaching." (1:4) (Marshall) (4) [See Ch.3: Sources.] Luck (5) says that Luke was only presenting acts of God not transmitting facts. Marshall however argues that this ignores words like "eyewitnesses" (1:2), "accurately" (1:3), and "orderly". (1:3) (Marshall) (6) Theophilus, having been linked to the Church, may be wondering if he really does belong to a racially mixed and persecuted community of the Church, calling him to be a faithful follower. Luke is offering general assurance to all Gentiles who may feel out of place in an original Jewish movement. The theme of salvation, the frequent preaching of the Good News based upon eyewitnesses, the historical references (1:2), all help to make the evangelism of non-christians a possible purpose for Luke/Acts. The eyewitness reference helps to confirm the factual basis for faith.

C) The fulfilment of prophecy was from angels (1:14-17), prophets (2:32) "a light for revelation to the Gentiles and for glory to your people Israel," (Is. 42:6 ; 49:6) and from God (2:26). "And it had been revealed to him [Simeon] by the Holy Spirit that he would not see death before he had seen the Lord's Christ." (2:25-28)

D) There is evidence from the miracles that Jesus is the expected Messiah. Jesus is the answer to John the Baptist's question, "Are you the one who is to come?" (7:20) "As Jonah became a sign to the men of Nineveh, so will be the Son of Man to this generation." The sign of Jonah is the supreme miracle which proves the claim of Jesus and the Christian message (11:30). The demons regognised Jesus as the Son of God as did the Gerasene demoniac demon (4:44; 8:28). The Sanhedrin asked Jesus if he was the Son of God and he replied, "You have said so." (22:70)

E) How can Theophilus and a wider audience from the Gentile dominated Churches of Greece and Asia Minor be sure that they are part of God's people and are doing His will? Luke felt that Theophilus needed a "life" of Christ which would appeal to the cultivated taste of a high Roman official (compared with Mark's account which was written in less sophisticated Greek), that he [Theophilus] might know the "solid truth" of the religion they had embraced (1:4). (Hunter) (7) Luke tells a story of God's mighty acts "among us" (1:1) not only accomplished in Jesus' story but also "among us", showing his readers how they stand at the crest of God's plan for redemption. (de Silva) (8)

[2] Catechetical: to instruct Theophilus in the Christian faith. [See pp. 37, 59.]

A) Creed (9) argued that Luke had a "catechetical" purpose in mind in his use of the word (Gk. katechethes) meaning instruction in (1:4). Creed saw this as instruction in the Christian faith and therefore Theophilus must have been a Christian. It is more probable that instruction means Christian instruction (like attending a course today on Christian Discipleship) and therefore Theophilus would have been a professed Christian of good standing. If, however, Theophilus was an outsider then the Gospel would have been written for everyone in the non-Christian world, who was averse to Christianity and who wanted a historical account of its origins (like some one attending an Alpha or Christianity Explored Course today).

B) Luke includes Theophilus in the new community, calling him to remain faithful, even in the middle of Jewish rejection. (Bock) (10)

C) The book is dedicated to Theophilus who is referred to as "most excellent" (Gk. kratiste) (1:3) which could indicate social rank. "Concerning the things about which you have been informed," suggests the Third Gospel was designed for all in the non-Christian world who were open to Christianity and who wanted a historical account of its origin. (Guthrie)(11)

> **Luke is offering general assurance to all Gentiles who may feel out of place in an original Jewish movement.**

[3] Apologetic: to make clear the Christian's own understanding of the gospel despite opposition. This apologetic purpose provided a rational defence of Christianity by giving a reason for the hope which lies within.

A) Was Luke writing a polemic against Gnosticism which minimised the importance of Jesus' real historical and early life? (Talbert) **(12)** The Gnostics challenged the Resurrection and the Person of Jesus. Luke replies to these opponents by assuring Theophilus that the gospel narrative is historically true and by showing who Jesus is.

B) Was Luke responding to Jewish opposition? Luke was trying to draw authentic Jews to Christianity. (Brawley) **(13)** Despite the rejection of Jesus' Person and Teaching by the majority of Israel, the Christian faith for Luke is based upon the O.T. The early church consists of faithful Israel and those Gentiles who had joined them in faith. Rejection of their Messiah by the Jews has not negated the coming of the Kingdom. Their unbelief has caused them to reject and crucify God's Son. However, it is believing Israel who take the gospel to the Gentiles and judgement would come upon unbelieving Israel.

C) For Luke, Jerusalem and the Temple represented the Jews and showed how God had visited His people to fulfil the O.T. promises. What happened to Israel was due to their unbelief (9:27). (Maddox) **(14)** Three times, Luke repeats the majority of Israel's rejection of the fulfilment of the hopes of their fathers accomplished in Jesus and the subsequent mission to the Gentiles (Acts 13:46; 18:6; 28:28). "There are some standing here who will not taste of death before they see the Kingdom of God." Those disciples who witnessed the Transfiguration as well as those who experienced Pentecost had a "sneak preview" of the coming kingdom before they died. "The days are coming when you [the disciples] will desire to see one of the days of the Son of Man and you will not see it." (17:22) This could refer to the disciples longing for the end so that they might avoid the suffering of the present. Therefore, they might be attracted by obscure reports of the appearances of the Son of Man. However, the return of Jesus will be like lightning that lights up the entire sky, prominent and pervasive (17:24). The disciples represent Jewish believers in the Kingdom.

D) (Green) **(15)** and Tiede **(16)** argued that Luke's purpose was to present a "theodicy of God's faithfulness:" God was in control despite the existence of evil.

E) Is Theophilus' belief also an issue? Caird **(17)** argued that the dedication to Theophilus is too formal for Theophilus to be a believer, therefore Luke's purpose was apologetic or a defence of the gospel. This argument is not convincing as classical prologues are usually formal in style and purposely have a literary character. (Bock) **(18)** The fact that this Gospel is dedicated to Theophilus does not mean that Luke intended his Gospel to be written exclusively for Theophilus. Other ancient writers such as Aristeas dedicated their works to individuals knowing that they were writing for a wider audience. [See Ch.1 : Authorship.]

> **Luke has an inclusive purpose indicating that the gospel is for everyone.**

[4] Inclusive: to confirm the word and message of salvation to readers irrespective of race, nationality, rank, sex, need or age. (Marshall, O'Toole and van Unnik) **(19) This inclusive purpose indicates that the gospel is for everyone.**
Luke shows that the Third Gospel was written for:-
A) the whole world - all who want and need it and not just for Jews.
B) women as well as for men. Luke uses the word for woman (Gk.gune) twenty-one times (3:6). This usage is as often as Matthew and Mark put together and shows Jesus' concern for women even though they were despised by the Scribes and Pharisees, for example the Widow of Nain, the Virgin Mary, Anna, Martha and Mary Magdalene. [See Ch. 15: Women.]
C) children as well as grown ups. Luke alone records the birth and boyhood of Jesus and John the Baptist.
D) the poor as well as the well-off. Luke points out how much God cares for the needs of the poor and how much He values their simple gifts, for example the widow's mite (21:1-4).
E) the bad as well as the **good**. The prodigal returns (15:11-24) as does Zacchaeus (19:1-10) and the thief on the cross (23:40-43). Today, we have to take at full value what Luke says about his method in the preface to the Gospel. It is neither myth nor midrash (Jewish interpretation of the law) but historical truth. The events have been handed down by eyewitnesses so that the reader may know the certainty of what they had been taught and believed (1:1-4). (Stott) **(20)** Luke's aim is to tell Mary's story and he may have picked up the information during his two-year stay at Caesarea (Acts 21:27-24:27). He could have interviewed Mary, who at that time would have been quite elderly. Luke is the only Gospel writer to quote Is. 40:3-5 in (3:6) "and all flesh shall see the salvation of God." His purpose is to bring good news of salvation to everyone. Luke, a Gentile, wanted everybody particularly, the poor and marginalized to know, the good news of Jesus. [See Ch. 5: Characteristics – universalism.] [See p. 45.]

[5] Eschatological: to clarify Jesus' teaching about the end times. (Stein) **(21)** This eschatological **purpose provides coping strategies for Christians in a time of persecution.**

A) Luke tries to allay the fears of the early Church regarding the expectations of Christ's return. Because Luke found himself in the "third period" of Conzelmann's period of time [See Ch.6: Luke the Historian.], Luke emphasised that the "Kingdom is present."

B) Luke also taught that the Kingdom was also future. For Luke there is a present joy and a future hope of the final consummation. "Blessed are you when men hate you, and when they exclude you and revile you, and cast out your name as evil, on account of the Son of Man!" (6:22-27) "You will be delivered up even by parents and brothers and kinsmen and friends, and some of you, they will put to death; you will be hated by all for my name's sake." (21:16-17) The length of the interval until the Second Coming was of less importance to Luke. Generally there is little teaching in Luke on the Second Coming: therefore it is difficult to agree with Conzelmann that Luke's purpose is to explain why Jesus had not returned. (Marshall) **(22)**

[6] Sociological: to ensure that the Gentiles were fully accepted into complete fellowship.
This sociological purpose indicates that everyone should be included in the fellowship of the Church especially the marginalized and shows that they were not a threat to the state. (Stein) **(23)** (Esler) **(24)**

A) Luke was providing a defence for the new community of believers and showing that they were not unfaithful to Rome. He was trying to convince the Romans that the Christians were not trouble makers. To assure his readers that Rome was not a threat, Luke points out in the Passion Narrative (Chs. 22-23) that Herod said, "I did not find this man guilty of any of your charges." (23:15) Pilate and the Roman centurion both pronounced that Jesus was innocent but that He was also crucified due to Roman pressure (23:4, 14-16, 22). "Of all the Gospels it is the most pluralistic. We see Jesus living in the middle of a world, which did not understand God." (Bock) **(25)** Jesus models how disciples are to live, for as disciples they are called to follow after Him.

B) "Render to Caesar the things that are Caesar's, and to God the things that are God's." This indicates that Christians were not a threat but an asset to the Empire (20:25). Luke is anxious to assure Christians that if they follow Jesus they have nothing to fear from Rome. They have only to fear God." (12:4-5) "I tell you, my friends, do not fear those who kill the body and after that have no more that they can do. But....... fear Him who, after he has killed, has power to cast into hell." Persecution is more likely to come from the home and family than from the empire.

C) Luke makes a point of showing up the Romans in good light. Jesus praises the faith of the Roman centurion who loves our people and who built a synagogue for us (7:1-10) and Luke records the Roman soldier who said, "This man is innocent." (23:47)

> **"Of all the Gospels it is the most pluralistic. We see Jesus living in the middle of a world which did not understand God." (Bock) (25)**

Conclusion
• Luke did not write for one person but for anyone who felt tension or any Gentile feeling out of place and anyone from an originally Jewish movement, could benefit from Luke's words of reassurance.
• He was also writing for any Jew or Jewish Christian troubled by the lack of Jewish response to the Gospel or by Gentile openness; they could see that God was in control and that He provided many opportunities to join in God's renewal work. Christianity was forced out of Judaism and these seeds of rejection of Jesus are evident in "the Journey" (Chs.9-13) and Passion Narratives (Chs.22-23).
• The new community is broad in its extension of blessing. Jesus reaches out to all kinds of people in need so that all may benefit from His power to heal (5:32).
• The question has been asked by the Tubingen School, has the history in Luke's Gospel been conformed to the theology? Luke it was argued that Acts was an an example of Hegel's philosophy of thesis, anthesis and synthesis. Luke was trying to reconcile opposing groups of supporters of Paul and Peter and the historical account was controlled by this tendency. While differences did exist as at the Council of Jerusalem these differences were resolved. Luke presents the theological significance of the history in the prominence he gives to Jerusalem and Jesus going to die there. He presents the main movements of Jesus from Galilee to Jerusalem with the ultimate aim of Jesus going up to Jerusalem to die.
• Did Luke have a multi-purpose aim or did he have a primary/secondary aim in writing his Gospel? If the latter is true then the prologue (1:1-4) could be the primary purpose, and the rest supplements the instruction Theophilus already received, to confirm him in his faith. Luke could have fulfilled his purpose in Vol. One and then continued the story of "all that Jesus began to do and to teach" in Vol. 2 (Acts 1:1) to accomplish further objectives. Luke brings together all these purposes to further the cause of Jesus throughout the world. (Liefeld) **(26)** He is writing for a variety of cultures.

Pupil's Activity: One

"There is no single purpose for Luke but it may be more accurate to speak of various purposes." Stein **(27)** Discuss this statement in the light of your understanding of the purposes of Luke's Gospel, for example (12:4-5).

Pupil's Activity: Two

Divide the class into six groups giving each group one purpose which Luke may have had for writing the Third Gospel with appropriate references. Bring all six groups together for a class presentation on the purposes of Luke's Gospel either by Powerpoint or OHP (size 14).

Group One: Evangelistic Purpose: look up (1:1-4) to find evidence that Luke wanted to tell others about his faith.

Group Two: Catechetical purpose: look up (1:4) to find evidence to instruct people in the Christian faith.

Group Three: Apologetic purpose: find evidence to show that Luke wanted people to have a deeper understanding of the Christian faith.

Group Four: An inclusive purpose: find evidence to show that Jesus wanted to include everyone especially the marginalized. Find references to salvation for all people and other relevant issues.

Group Five: Eschatological purpose: find evidence to show that the Kingdom is both past and present and that Christians needed coping strategies in the face of persecutions.

Group Six: Sociological purpose: find evidence to show that Luke wanted people to know that Christianity was not just for Israel. Also find evidence to show that Luke wanted the Romans to know that Christians were not out to cause trouble.

Pupil's Activity: Three

For revision purposes complete the grid to provide an overview of the purposes Luke had in writing his Gospel. For Edexcel A/2 students, complete the second and third columns to Figure 1 to show the views of the different scholars. CCEA students should complete only column three.

(Figure 1) Summary of Luke's purposes

Luke's purposes	Views of scholars [Edexcel]	Comment on the evidence of Luke's purposes
1. Evangelistic : wanting to tell others about his faith.	e.g. O'Neill	1:1-4; 2:26,32; 11:29-30; 18:23
2.Catechetical : instructing others in the faith.		1:1-4
3. Apologetic : giving a reason for the Christian hope within.		1:1, 20; 2:6; 9:27; 17:22
4. Inclusivity : wanting to show that Christianity was not just for the Jews.		3:6; 5:32; 15:11-24; 19:1-10; 21:1-4; 23:40-43
5. Eschatological : providing coping strategies to help Christians deal with persecution and the end events.		6:22-27; 21:16-17, 20-24
6. Sociological : wanting everyone to be made welcome in the church including the marginalised and to reassure the Romans that the Christians were not a threat to the state.		7:1-10; 23:4-5,14-16,22; 23:15, 47

Pupil's Activity: Four

a) What were Luke's purposes in writing his Gospel? (CCEA A/S Resit 2002)   [30 marks]

b) Outline your knowledge and understanding of the main purposes of the writer of Luke's Gospel.
   (CCEA A/S 2004/2006 Resit)   [30 marks]

Pupil's Activity: Five

a) Examine the views of scholars concerning the possible purposes of Luke's Gospel.
   (Edexcel A/2 2001/2004)   [12 marks]

b) To what extent does the internal evidence of the Gospel support these views.
   (Edexcel A/2 2004)   [8 marks]

Pupil's Activity: Six

"The Gospel was written to prove to non-believers that Jesus Christ is the Son of God," Examine and consider critically this view of the purpose of the author of Luke's Gospel. (Edexcel A/2 2005)   [20 marks]

Outcomes

Students should have a knowledge and understanding of:

• **the six main purposes of Luke's Gospel, (CCEA A/S)**

• **the key concepts such as apologetic, catechetical, eschatological, evangelistic, final consummation, pluralistic, sociological, primary and secondary purposes.**

Students should be able to discuss and critically evaluate:

• **the views of scholars regarding the purposes of Luke's Gospel. (Edexcel A2)**

• **events and sayings which prove to non-believers that Jesus is the Son of God. (Edexcel A/2)**

Notes on Ch.4: The purposes of the Gospel of Luke

1. Robert H. Stein, The New American Commentary Series: Vol. 24, Luke: Broadman Press, (1992) p.35.
2. J. C. O' Neill, The Theology of Acts , SPCK, Second edition (1970): cited in Guthrie, First Edition p. 88.
3. Joel Green, New Testament Theology, Cambridge University Press, (1995) p.19.*
4. Howard Marshall, Historian and Theologian, Paternoster Press, (1997) p.37.*
5. U. Luck, cited in Marshall, (H and T) p.38.
6. Howard Marshall, op. cit. p.36.
7. Alan M. Hunter, Introducing the N.T. , SCM Press, (1961) p.51.
8. David A. de Silva, An Introduction to the N.T., Apollos, (2004) p.310.
9. J. M. Creed, The Gospel According to St. Luke, Macmillan Press, (1930) p.75.
10. Darrell L. Bock, D J G in the Article, The Gospel of Luke, I V P, (1992), p.498.*
11. Donald Guthrie, New Testament Introduction, IV P, (1965) p.90.
12. Charles H. Talbert, Literary Patterns, Theological Themes and the Genre of Luke-Acts, Missoula: (1974) cited in DJG as above Brawley, Luke-Acts and the Jews, Atlanta (1987) p.155, [See also Jacob Jervell, Luke and the People of God. Augsburg, (1972)]
13. Robert L. Brawley, (ibid.)
14. Robert Maddox, The Purpose of Luke-Acts, Edinburgh: T. and T. Clark, (1982) pp.183-187.
15. Joel Green, The Gospel of Luke, The New International Commentary on the N.T., Eerdmans, (1997) p.633.*
16. David L. Tiede, Luke: Augsburg, Commentary on the N.T. Minniepolis: Augsburg (1988) cited in DJG as above.
17. George Caird, op. cit. p. 44.
18. Darrell Bock, Vol.1, op. cit. p.64.
19. Marshall, O'Toole and van Unnik, cited in Article : Gospel of Luke, DJG, IVP, (1992) p.498.
20. John Stott, The Incomparable Jesus, IVP, (2001) p.31.
21. Robert H. Stein, op. cit. p.12.
22. Howard Marshall, Historian and Theologian op. cit. pp.77-88, 107-115.
23. Robert H. Stein, op. cit. p.44.
24. Philip Francis Esler, Community and Gospel in Luke-Acts, Monograph 57, CUP (1987) cited in DJG as above.
25. Darrell L. Bock, IVP New Testament Commentary, Series (3) IVP, (1994) p.20.*
26. Walter Liefeld, op. cit. p.802.
27. Robert H. Stein, op. cit. p.35.
* These books and articles are highly recommended.

CCEA A/S + Edexcel A/S (2007 ff.)   **The outline of Luke's Gospel is from Galilee to Jerusalem.**

> **Target:**
> • Identify the main characteristics of Luke's Gospel.
> • Identify the key concepts of Luke's characteristics: comprehensive history of Jesus, universalistic approach, interest in people including individuals, women, children, social relationships, poverty and wealth, a special interest in prayer, the Holy Spirit, joyfulness and praise.
> • Identify the use of the texts in Luke's Gospel to exemplify all of these characteristics.

The Characteristics of Luke's Gospel

Introduction

There are many characteristics and themes of the Gospel of Luke which distinguish it from the other Gospels. Some of these show Jesus' humanity and compassion for the marginalised and outsiders in society and His coming for everyone to shape a restored community of believers consisting of Jews, Samaritans and Gentiles. These characteristics also indicate that the followers of Jesus were not the enemies of the Roman Empire. Overarching all the special themes in Luke's Gospel is the universal relevance of the gospel.

[1] Luke's well-ordered comprehensive history of Jesus

A) This Gospel, which starts with the annunciation of the births of John the Baptist and Jesus, has the fullest birth narratives (Chs.1-2) and ends with the Ascension (24:50-53). It is the longest of the Synoptic Gospels and provides a very detailed account of the last journey of Jesus to Jerusalem (9:51-19:48). The outline of Luke's Gospel is from Galilee to Jerusalem. It is also the longest book in the N.T. and no other N.T. book provides such a comprehensive history of Jesus.

B) Luke says that "it seemed good to me also, having followed all things closely for some time past, to write a comprehensive orderly account for Theophilus." (1:3) The word "orderly" can mean a "complete presentation" Klein **(1)** or a "continuous series." (Volkel) **(2)** Luke could have included many more events in the ministry of Jesus but all the books of the world could not have contained them (Jn.21:25). Luke looked at everything (Gk.pasin) (1:30). Luke's Gospel is a full comprehensive account of the story of Jesus but it is not an exhaustive presentation. It does have some gaps for example the Great Omission of Mark 6:45-8:26 and Matthew's birth stories. [See p. 35.]

C) Luke presents a close link between O.T. and N.T. periods. Scripture is fulfilled as the audience listens to the message (4:21). From 4:14ff, he shows how Jesus through word and deed revealed Himself more and more as the Son of God and Almighty Saviour (2:11). Mary calls Jesus, "God my Saviour." (1:47) Salvation has been identified as the main theme of this Gospel.

D) God's divine plan in history is evident in the use of key words like "it is necessary," (17:25) "to determine," (22:22) "it is accomplished." (12:50) God controls the agenda of the story which is so designed that it fulfils the O.T. prophecies. "Today this scripture has been fulfilled in your hearing." (4:21)

E) Luke's infancy stories are more detailed than Matthew's and he puts great emphasis on the birth of John the Baptist. He provides a detailed account of the Galilean ministry of Jesus (4:14-9:50). Like Mark, he has a deep interest in the passion of Jesus (19:45-24:53). He shows how Jesus predicted His passion, "Jesus set His face steadfastly to go to Jerusalem." (9:51) Jesus sees His own death in the light of Isaiah's Suffering Servant (22:37; Is.53:12). Luke concludes with a note of joy and victory and shows great devotion to God who brought about such a wonderful salvation (24:52-53).

F) He sums up the life of Jesus in three parts linking each of them to the O.T. . Firstly, Jesus must die; secondly, He must be raised from the dead on the third day; and thirdly, repentance for the forgiveness of sins must be preached in His name to all nations beginning in Jerusalem (24:44-49).

It is also the longest book in the N.T. and no other N.T. book provides such a comprehensive history of Jesus.

Pupil's Activity: One

Play as a background music selections from Handel's Messiah which bring out the idea in Luke that the gospel is for everyone (1) And the Glory of the Lord...; and all flesh shall see it together (Is.40:5). (2) Glory to God in the highest and peace on earth (2:14). (3) Rejoice greatly, O daughter of Zion!...He shall speak unto the heathen (Zech.9: 9-10).

[2] Luke's universalism [See p. 41.]

Throughout his Gospel Luke shows that the ultimate scope of the gospel includes the Gentiles (2:14,32; 3:6). The gospel is for those who respond to the coming of Jesus. Jesus comes for all (2:10) but not all wish to receive Him (2:16).

A) The evidence for this is in (2:14) where the angels' good will message is directed to everyone, "and on earth peace among men." Simeon predicts Jesus to be the light for revelation to the Gentiles. The Gentiles are attracted by the brightness of the glory and the light (2:32). John the Baptist is referred to as a voice crying in the wilderness and Luke goes on to say, "all flesh shall see the salvation of God." (3:6; Is.40:3-5) Luke extends this quotation from Isaiah to include the Gentiles. God's salvation is for everyone. At the start of the Messianic period the call for repentance and preparing for the Messiah is not just for Jews. "The crooked shall be made straight, and the rough ways shall be made smooth;" (3:5) are the people who have already undergone repentance. (Green) **(3)**

B) The Samaritans are treated equally with the Jews. Jesus rebukes James and John for wanting to bring fire down from heaven upon the Samaritans because they rejected Jesus (9:54). "But a Samaritan, who saw the man who had been attacked in the parable, had compassion, bound up his wounds, poured in oil and wine, brought him to an inn, and took care of him." (10:33) The Samaritan leper fell on his face at the feet of Jesus giving thanks (17:16).

C) Two examples from the O.T. are recorded in Luke's Gospel featuring non-Israelites: the widow of Zarephath (4:25-26) and Naaman the Syrian (4:27) (L).

D) To the saying about those who come from the east and the west, and sit down in the Kingdom of God, Luke adds "the north and the south." (13:29) (L)

E) In the parable of the Great Supper, Luke is the only Gospel writer to say "the servants were sent into the hedges to constrain more people to come to the feast." (14:23) (L)

F) As in Matthew 28:19 the great commission is for all nations."That repentance and forgiveness of sins should be preached in His name to all nations (Gk.ta ethne)." (24:47) Here Gentile inclusion is explicitly commanded.

G) Particularism in seen in the healing of the woman with the bent back (13:16)."Ought not this woman, a daughter of Abraham whom Satan has bound for eighteen years, be loosed from this bond on the Sabbath day?" Gentile inclusion is apparent in the occasional contact between Jesus and those outside Israel for example the Roman centurion (7:1-10), the Samaritan leper (17:11-19) and explicit in 24:47.

[3] Interest in people [See p. 68.]

A) **As individuals:** most of the parables in Luke centre on people. Jesus' high regard for the individual greatly impressed Luke, who himself, is attracted to people. Some examples are Elizabeth, Mary and Martha, Zacchaeus, and a sorrowful Cleopas. Interest in social outcasts: Luke more than any other Synoptic writer shows Jesus' deep concern for the social outcasts.

1. In the house of Simon the Pharisee, Jesus is anointed by a prostitute (7:36). Zacchaeus is transformed by the grace of God (19:8ff). In both of these interactions at the table and in His healing ministry, Jesus communicates Himself as divine salvation for the needy. He is "good news for the poor."(4:18-19)

2. One thief who repents says, "Jesus, remember me when you come in your kingly power." (23:42)

3. There are three parables dealing with mercy: the Prodigal Son (15:11-32)(L), the Two Debtors (7:41-50) (L) and the Pharisee and the Publican (18:9-14)(L).

4. Jesus does not make the way easy for His disciples; there is the cost of discipleship. "If any one comes to me and does not hate His own father and mother and wife and children and brothers and sisters, yes, and even his own life, He cannot be my disciple." (14:26) Jesus requires His followers to distance themselves from materialistic attachments; possessions are to be renounced. All the disciples are to be prepared for this although it will not become a reality for all (14:23). Jesus told the parable of the dutiful servant to teach that, as always with a servant the Master's wishes come first. He raises the issue, will the dutiful servant who comes in from fields after a day's work, prepare the meal for the slave or will the slave prepare it for the master? The slave has to prepare the chores out of a sense of duty (17:7-9).

B) **Women have rights**

Luke makes special reference to thirteen women not mentioned in the other Gospels including two in the parables;

• the women in the birth stories Elizabeth, Mary and Anna (Chs.1-2),

• the widow of Nain (7:11-15) and the immoral woman (7:36),

• some women who had been healed of evil spirits and diseases: Mary Magdalene, Joanna and Susanna and many other women who supported Jesus and the disciples with their gifts (8:2-3),

• Martha who was distracted by much serving. Mary in listening to the words of Jesus is an example of someone who knows that, "man does not live by bread alone but everything that proceeds from the mouth of God." (10:38; Deut.8:3a)

• the woman with the spirit of infirmity (13:10).

• the women lamenting for Jesus on the way to the cross (23:27).

• at the cross " the women who had followed Him from Galilee, stood at a distance and saw these things." (23:49)

• the women who had come from Galilee, saw the tomb and watched how the body was laid. They returned home and prepared spices (Gk. aroma) and a variety of perfumes (Gk. muron) to anoint the body of Jesus after the Sabbath. These spices would help to slow down the decomposition. These women honour the Jewish law by resting on the Sabbath (23:55-56a; Ex.20:10; Deut.5:12-15; m.Sab.23.5). [See Ch.15: Women in Luke's Gospel.]

• the women in the resurrection narratives, "It was Mary Magdalene, Joanna and Mary the mother of James and the other women with them, who told this to the apostles." (24:11)

Luke was very concerned to emphasise Jesus' positive attitude to women and to raise their status. [See Ch. 16: Outcasts.]

C) **Interest in children**

The childhood of John the Baptist and the birth stories of Jesus are (L). On three occasions he mentions "only" children.

1. The widow of Nain's son is referred to as the "only" son (7:12) and Jesus in healing the son says, "Young man, I say to you arise." (7:14)

2. Jairus begged Jesus to come to his house because his "only daughter" of twelve years of age was dying (8:42).

3. After the Transfiguration, a man from the crowd said, "Look upon my son, for he is my only child; and a spirit seizes him."(9:38) The infant children in arms (Gk. brephe) were brought to Jesus that He might touch them (18:15).

4. Only Luke uses this word for the very young children. God's 'favour' (Gk. eudokia) rests upon the little children to whom God reveals truth according to His great treasure (10:21). (Liefeld) **(4)** [See p. 244.]

D) Social relationships

Luke uses **three examples of Jesus dining with the Pharisees**: [See pp. 273-4.]

1. Jesus is anointed by a prostitute in the house of Simon the Pharisee (7:36-50).
2. A Pharisee is amazed to see Jesus did not wash before a meal in the house of one the Pharisees (11:37-44).
3. One Sabbath Jesus went to dine in the house of a ruler who belonged to the Pharisees (14: 1-4).

Other examples of social relationships: [See p. 273.]

1. Jesus' social relationships at the home of Mary and Martha (10:38-42).
2. Jesus goes to the house of Zacchaeus for a meal (19: 1-10).
3. Jesus dines at Emmaus after the resurrection (24:13-32).

Social interaction in the parables: [See p. 52.]

Social interaction takes place in the parables of:

1. the lost coin (15:8-10);
2. the woman who found the lost coin calls together her friends and neighbours and says, "Rejoice with me, for I have found the coin which I had lost." (15:9b)
3. the father in the parable of the prodigal son says, "Let us eat and make merry." (15:22) Feasting and rejoicing is appropriate. Thanksgiving is offered to God for bringing the prodigal back from death to life (15:23). All three parables on the lost end in celebration.

> **Luke presents a close link between the O.T. and N.T. periods.**

[4] Poverty and wealth

Money matters as in the parables of the two debtors, the rich fool, the tower builder the lost coin, the unjust steward, the rich man and Lazarus and the pounds.

1. Mary's Song the Magnificat: "He has filled the hungry with good things and the rich he has sent empty away." (1:53) John the Baptist warns the tax collectors against extortion and soldiers should be content with their wages (3:13).
2. At Nazareth, Jesus proclaims "good news to the poor." (4:17-21)
3. The poor and the humble are the objects of Jesus' mercy. "Blessed are you poor, for yours is the kingdom of God." (6:20) " The Gospels do not confer blessings; they express congratulations." (Talbert) **(5)** "Congratulations to....someone ...because." They celebrate someone's success. The Greek word "makarioi" can also mean happy. Jesus addresses and blesses the poor whereas in Matthew (5:3) he says "poor in spirit." The Sermon on the Plain "But woe (alas, pity) to you who are rich, for you have received your consolation (Gk. paraklesin)." They will receive a loser's trophy in the eternal future. The poor will reap their benefit from their commitment to God and share in His eternal kingdom (6:24), "When you have a feast, invite the poor, the maimed and the lame." (14:21) The Pharisees are called "lovers of money." (16:1)
4. Zacchaeus volunteers to gives up half of his money by way of restitution (19:1-10). Christians are encouraged to give their wealth to the needy (1:33; 14:33).

Pupil's Activity: Two

a) Explore in particular the claim that the writer had a special interest in the downtrodden and oppressed. Justify your answer. (CCEA A/S 2002) [15 marks]

[5] Special emphasis

A) Prayer in the birth narratives

The terms "prayer" and "pray" are used twenty-one times in Luke's Gospel, thirteen times in Mark and seventeen times in Matthew's Gospel: prayer is a key theme and characteristic of Luke's Gospel.

1. Elizabeth and Zechariah [See p. 82.]

a. When John the Baptist's birth was announced God's people had gathered outside the Temple for corporate prayer (Gk. proseuchomenon) at the hour of incense (1:10). This was not normal practice. (Lacks) **(6)** In Luke's Gospel major events are associated with prayer.

b. In the middle of the worship the angel Gabriel appears (1:10-11). Zechariah is not to be afraid because his prayer (Gk. deesis means a specific petition) that God would bless him and his wife with a child, has been answered. Another possibility is that he was praying for God to send the Messiah to deliver Israel. This prayer would be answered in a way the couple never dreamt of. Both prayers would be answered in the one event because their son would prepare the way for the Messiah (1:13). Gabriel appears at the ninth hour which was the hour of prayer and evening sacrifice. Luke represents the Temple as a house of prayer (1:10; 18:9-14; 19:46; Is. 56:7).

2. Mary

a. Mary offers praise to God in the words of the Magnificat which means Hymn of praise. (1:46-55)(L) She expresses this praise in a loud voice which shows an inspired utterance (1:42)(L). [See also Ch. 8: Infancy narratives p. 85.]

b. She glorifies God (1:46)(L) and her spirit rejoices in God her Saviour (1:47)(L). She thanks God for all the mighty things He has done for her (1:49).

3) Anna

A) Anna worshipped (Gk.latreuousa) meaning she served God through prayer, she also prayed (Gk.deesis) meaning a specific petition; she was also fasting (Gk.nesteiais) all day long, night and day, which was the Jewish way of reckoning time from sunset. This does not mean that she prayed twenty-four hours every day because women were not allowed to stay in the Temple during the night. She was there all day long (2:37). (Stein) **(7)** She responds to God's grace and His act of salvation by giving thanks to God and telling others what she had discovered (2:38). [See p. 95.]

B) The example of Jesus: Jesus' prayer life continued througout His ministry. [See pp. 50-51.]

In Luke, there are nine prayers of Jesus, which are spread at regular intervals throughout the Gospel, two of which are in the other gospels. In Luke/Acts prayer preceded every major crisis in the life of Jesus and the early church. (Stein) **(8)**

1. Prayer is linked to events at the baptism. When Jesus prays, something of real significance happens, "When Jesus also had been baptised and was praying (Gk. proseuchomenou) the heaven was opened." (3:21)(L) As Jesus prayed at His baptism the Holy spirit descended upon him. This is the first of several events in Jesus' life which took place when He prayed (3:21). As a result He had a true vision of the Deity as did Stephen (Acts 7:56) and Peter (Acts 10:11). At the Transfiguration as Jesus was praying, the disciples were enveloped by a cloud and, although they heard God speaking, their vision was of Jesus, Moses and Elijah, the heavenly visitors from God in heaven. In Luke/Acts prayer is often mentioned in the context of revelation and commission or empowerment (1:19-20; 2:37-38; Acts 4:23-31). (Crump) **(9)** [See p. 201.]

2. Jesus likes to begin the new day by going to "a lonely or quiet place" (4:42) to pray as Mk 1:35,45 indicates. Despite Luke's great interest in prayer, he omits to say that Jesus went specifically to pray on this occasion. We can assume from the parallel account (Mk.1:35) that Jesus did go out to pray.

3. After a day of miracles, "When crowds came to hear and be healed, He [Jesus] withdrew to the wilderness and prayed." (5:16) Jesus was heading for a series of conflicts in the events that followed.

4. Before Jesus got into trouble, He spent time praying to God. Before selecting the disciples, He went into the hills to pray and all night continued in prayer to God (6:12; Matt.14:13; Mk.1:35; Jn.11:54). This was following on from Sabbath controversies and complaints against Him by the Pharisees (5:30) and the selection of "the Twelve." Jesus prayed that God's purpose would come to fruition. Jesus predicts His passion and rejection by the elders.

5. "As He [Jesus] was praying (Gk.proseuchomenon) alone, the disciples were with Him and Jesus asked them, "Who do people say I am?" (9:18-22) Unique to Luke is the prayer setting which precedes this question (9:18). Jesus strengthens His relationship with God and receives and empowerment from God. Again prayer is the setting for Divine disclosure.

6. Jesus took Peter, James and John up the mountain to pray (9:28). When Jesus prays something significantly happens. "As He was praying (Gk. proseuchesthai), He was transfigured" (9:29). This reference to prayer is unique to Luke.

7. When the seventy(two) returned from their mission, Jesus thanks the Father (Gk. Pater) for having revealed things to them (10:17-21; Matt.11:25-26).

8. Luke makes the point that, despite the large crowds, Jesus withdrew to the wilderness to pray. He drew apart and took the disciples to a city called Bethsaida (9:10).

9. At the end of Jesus' final discourse on Mt. Olivet He tells the disciples to live faithfully watch and pray until He returns (21:36). He then goes out at night and lodges (Gk. aulizomai) spending the night either in a home or sleeping outside on the Mount of Olives (21:37).

10. Jesus prays specifically (Gk.edeethen) for Peter that his faith may not fail. Satan fails to destroy Peter because Jesus prays for him (22:31-33). (L) In predicting that Peter would betray Him, nonetheless Jesus assures Peter, "I have prayed for you, Simon, that your faith may not fail."

11. Upon arriving at the Mt. of Olives (22:39), Jesus kneels down and he prays (Gk. proseuchesthe) that the disciples may not enter into temptation (22:40) and He continues to pray for Himself. He warns the disciples to pray before He departs. Through prayer believers are able to keep from falling into temptation (22:40). Satan is trying to get the disciples to defect but Jesus' prayer will help them to be faithful. Unique also to Luke is the reference to Jesus praying a stone's throw from the disciples and to His kneeling in prayer (Gk. proseucheto)(22:41). Kneeling in prayer was not a general custom in Jesus' time, standing was the usual practice.

12. The theme of prayer and temptation is common in Luke. "Father (Gk. Pater), if you are willing, let this cup pass from me." (22:42) Luke omits reference to Gethsemane because he often lacks Semitic terms (Matt.26: 36; Mk.14:32). (Marshall) **(10)** Jesus rises up from prayer and goes on to repeat the call to pray and not come into temptation (22:40,46). This is a general word for prayer. Jesus is concerned to do His Father's will. "If you are willing." (22:45)

13. On the cross, Jesus prays for His enemies, "Father (Gk. Pater), forgive them; they do not know what they do." (23:34) This prayer is unique to Luke. It is a prayer for all those who had a role in the killing of Jesus. Then He prays for Himself. Jesus crying symth a loud voice said, "Father (Gk. Pater), into your hands I commit my spirit." Jesus is handing his spirit to God's care. His prayer is one of trust and submission to the will of God. This prayer is also unique to Luke (23:46). Through prayer, believers are able to keep from falling into temptation (22:40). The theme of prayer and temptation is common in Luke.

C) Jesus' teaching on prayer through parables

1. Two special parables on prayer: (1) the Friend at midnight (11:5-13) is an encouragement to pray. (2) The unrighteous judge (18:1-8) is to encourage the disciples to pray. [See also Ch. 14: Discipleship p.222.]

2. A parable on the wrong type of prayer The Pharisee and the Publican (18:9-14). Beware of the pretext of the scribes who make long prayers and give the appearance of piety but are not pious because they treat others callously (11:42; 20:47a).

Summary of Jesus' praying in Luke's Gospel

• Luke's Gospel is one of prayer; in it God's will is regularly revealed through prayer.

• For Luke individual and corporate prayer are an essential part of the life of the Christian. (Trites) **(11)**

• Prayer in Luke is a prelude to divine revelation: God hears, speaks and acts (1:8-23; 3:21; 9:28-36; 22:39-46). (Green) **(12)** Unique also to Luke is the reference to Jesus praying a stone's throw from the disciples and to His kneeling in prayer (Gk. proseucheto) (22:41).

Pupil's Activity: Three

a) Explore the claim that Luke presents Mary as a model of trust and prayer in the account leading up to the birth of Jesus. Justify your answer. (CCEA A/S 2001)   [15 marks]

b) Explore the view that Luke presents Jesus as praying at key moments during His ministry. Justify your answer. (CCEA A/S 2003 Resit)   [30 marks]

Pupil's Activity: Four

a) Outline your knowledge and understanding of Jesus' teaching on prayer as recorded in Luke's Gospel. (CCEA A/S 2004)   [30 marks]

b) Explore the claim that the Jesus of Luke's Gospel is a man of compassion and prayer. Justify your answer. (CCEA A/S 2004)   [15 marks]

D) Prayer in the life of the disciples: community prayer [See pp. 125-6, 222.]

1. Before teaching His disciples to pray, Jesus prays Himself. The disciples wait for Him to stop praying (11:1) (L), before asking Him to teach them to pray. "Lord (Gk.Kurie) teach us now to pray as John taught his disciples." (Arndt) **(13)** The disciples appear to want their own distinctive community prayer just like the other groups of disciples (11:1). Jesus then goes on to teach the disciples' prayer. This was a request by the disciples to share a common prayer (Gk. proseuchesthe). (11:1-4). Jesus uses the Greek word "Pater" for Father (11:2) Luke presents the Lord's prayer as "a badge designed to mark out the disciples of Jesus from those of John and "Father" can be "Dear Father." (Dunn) **(14)** The disciples' prayer should be compared with Jewish "Short Prayer" rather than the "Eighteen Benedictions." (Lachs) **(15)** "Perform your will in heaven and bestow satisfaction on earth upon those who revere you." (Berakoth 3,2) [See pp.126, 222.]

2. Through prayer (Gk. proseuchesthai), the disciples are able to persevere and not lose heart (18:1).

3. Jesus prays (Gk. edeethen) for Peter that that his faith may not fail. Satan fails to destroy Peter because Jesus prays for him (22:31-33) (L). [See p. 51.]

4. Upon arriving at the Mount of Olives, (22:39) Jesus kneels down and he prays (Gk. proseuchesthe) that the disciples may not enter into temptation (22:40) (L) and He continues to pray for Himself. He warns the disciples to pray before He departs (22:40). Satan is trying to get the disciples to defect but Jesus' prayer will help them to be faithful. Unique to Luke is Jesus' praying a stone's throw from the disciples and to His kneeling in prayer (Gk.proseucheto) (22:41) (L).

5. "Father(Gk.Pater), if you are willing, let this cup pass from me."(22:42) Luke omits reference to Gethsemane because he often lacks Semitic terms (Matt. 26:36; Mk.14:32). (Marshall) **(16)** Jesus goes on to repeat the call to pray and not come into temptation (22:40, 46).

Pupil's Activity: Five

As a revision exercise draw a spidergram to show the characteristics of the Gospel of Luke.

Pupil's Activity: Six

a) Outline your knowledge and understanding of the main characteristics of Luke's Gospel. (CCEA A/S 2003 Resit)   [30 marks

b) Comment on the claim that Luke offers a full story of Jesus. Justify your answer. (CCEA A/S 2004 Resit)   [15 marks]

Pupil's Activity: Seven

a) Explore the view that Luke presents Jesus as praying at key moments during His ministry. Justify your answer. (CCEA A/S 2003 Resit)   [30 marks]

b) Outline your knowledge and understanding of Jesus' teaching on prayer as recorded in Luke's Gospel. (CCEA A/S 2004)   [30 marks]

c) Explore the claim that the Jesus of Luke's Gospel is a man of compassion and prayer. Justify your answer. (CCEA A/S 2004)   [15 marks]

Summary of the examples of Jesus praying at key moments in His Ministry (Figure 1)

Key events in Jesus' prayer ministry	Ref.	Comment
1 Jesus was anointed by the Holy Spirit after **His baptism.** This is the first event in the life of Jesus which took place after He prayed (Gk. proseuchomenon). This is the word for general prayer. "When Jesus had been baptised and was praying, the heaven was opened." This is a relational prayer.	3:21 -22	Prayer precedes every decision or crisis in Jesus' life. As a result of His baptism Jesus was anointed and empowered for His ministry. Jesus has a true vision of the deity at his baptism. The heavens are opened and a voice says, "You are My Beloved Son; with You I am well pleased." There is divine disclosure here. God speaks and He acts. Here is obedience, commissioning and revelation.
2 At the **start of the Galilean ministry** when Jesus' popularity was widespread people came to hear and to be healed. After the healing of the leper, Jesus withdrew to the wilderness and prayed. Fast and pray.	5:15-16 5:33	Jesus prayed after a day of miracles. His popularity threatened to sideline Him from His mission. He refused to be thwarted in His mission through continued prayer. This is a relational prayer.
3 He prays following on from the Sabbath healing of the man with the withered hand which provoked a **great controversy with the Pharisees** and before selecting the Twelve (Gk. proseuxasthai).	6:12 -13	Jesus prayed all night to God following on from the first controversy with the Pharisees. As soon as morning comes, He appoints the Twelve apostles. Prayer precedes the discerning of God's will. He prays that God's purpose will come to fruition.
4 Before Peter confesses Jesus as Christ, Son of the living God at **Caesarea Philippi,** "Jesus was praying alone."	9:18	Before predicting His passion and rejection by the Jewish leaders and death and resurrection, Jesus prays (9:21-22). Here is obedience.
5 At the **Transfiguration,** Jesus took Peter, James and John up a mountain to pray and as He was praying, He was transfigured.	9:28 -29	Jesus' prayer to God is the setting for a divine disclosure; it is the prelude to divine revelation. God speaks, "This is my Beloved Son; listen to Him." And God acts. Here is obedience, revelation and commissioning.
6 When **the 70(2) returned from their mission** Jesus rejoices in the Holy Spirit. This incident points to the power of God and His control of history. "Lord of heaven and earth." (10:25) The content of the prayer points to Jesus as the Son who has become the ultimate revelation of God. "All things have been committed to me by my Father ....and no one knows the Father except the Son and those to whom the Son chooses to reveal him." (10:22) (Pao) **(17)** "Father" is Jesus' favourite word for addressing God. Jesus calls God "Father" sixty times in the Gospels and sixteen times in Luke's Gospel. This is a prayer of adoration and thanks.	10:21 -24 (Q)	After the Transfiguration He calls God "Father." Jesus is directed by the Holy Spirit. The Holy Spirit is the source of Jesus' joy (10:21). Again Jesus thanks the "Father" (Gk. Pater) for revealing these things to the disciples after their mission. Five times, He calls God His "Father" and once as "Lord of Heaven and earth," and Himself as "Son" three times. Jesus uses the Greek word "exomologoumai" which means "praise" or "thanks." (10:21) This is a common use of the word in the LXX (Dan.9:4, 20). This is a public acknowledgement of the mighty and faithful God. (Pao) **(18)** Jesus is the centre of the thanksgiving as He has become the focus to which all thanksgiving, remembering and proclamation should be directed (10:22; Jn 11:41-42).
7 Jesus teaches His disciples to pray. This is another "Pater" prayer. Jesus is the first person to make the Fatherhood of God so essential to prayer.	11:1-2	The disciples wait until Jesus stops praying. Through this prayer the disciples are able to persevere and not lose heart (18:1).
8 Jesus' teaching on prayer (Gk. deomenoi)/specific prayer: He warns His disciples to be continually watchful as the time of the return of the Son of Man is unknown.	21:36	"But watch at all times, praying that you may have strength to escape all these things that will take place, and to stand before the Son of Man." Watchfulness and wakefulness are in the context of prayer. (Pao) **(19)**

Key events in Jesus' prayer ministry	Ref.	Comment
9 Jesus prays for Peter that his faith may not fail and that He might be delivered from the Evil One.	22:31 -33(L)	Satan fails to destroy Peter because Jesus prays (Gk. edetheen) a specific prayer for Peter. [Petitionary]
10 On arrival at the Mt. of Olives, Jesus kneels down to pray that the disciples may not enter into temptation.	22:39 -41 (L)	Jesus' prayer helps the disciples to be faithful.
11 Jesus prays (Gk.proseucheto) at the Mt. of Olives, "Father (Gk. Pater), if you are willing remove this cup from me; nevertheless not my will but yours be done." When we overhear Jesus pray in the Gospels He always addresses God as "Father." (10:21) This is petitionary prayer .	22:42 -46	Prayer and temptation are common themes in Luke. Here again prayer is the prelude to divine disclosure. Jesus continues the call to prayer and not to enter temptation. Jesus is concerned to do God's will. God's will for Jesus to go to the cross is revealed through prayer. Here obedience and revelation are key aspects in the prayer life of Jesus.
12 On the cross Jesus prays for His enemies, "Father, (Gk. Pater) forgive them they do not know what they do." Luke omits the reference to "Golgotha" as it would neither mean anything to his Gentile readers nor was it in the source he was using.	23:34 (L)	Jesus was asking His Father to forgive those who nailed Him to the cross and those involved in His death. There is no attempt to justify anti-Semitism. (Stein) **(20)** Jesus in His prayer exemplifies the instructions He gave to his disciples, "Pray for those who abuse you." (6:27-28)
13 On the cross Jesus finally prays, "Father, into your hands I commit my spirit." Jesus borrows His prayer from Ps.31:5 in which the suffering righteous one entrusts himself to God's care. Jesus prayed that His death would not be in vain, that the Father would deliver Him from death and Satan. His prayer was answered when God raised Him from the dead, turning Satan's apparent triumph into bitter defeat.	23:46 (L)	Jesus hands His spirit to God's care. Jesus knowing He had completed His exodus (9:31) committed His spirit/ life into His Father's hands, in order to enter His glory; Jesus is a model for His followers (Acts 7:59). Jesus. voluntarily gave up His life to death. Through prayer in His death He was in control; Jesus was Master even in His death. In this prayer we see Jesus' faith in the God who raises from the dead. (Crump) **(21)**

[6] The Holy Spirit

Luke refers to the Holy Spirit at least seventeen times as well as reference to the Spirit as "power" or "promise."

A) The Holy Spirit is active in the birth of John the Baptist and Jesus.

• John is filled with the Spirit right from conception (1:15). Elizabeth, being filled with the Spirit extends a blessing to Mary and Mary's child (1:41-42). "The Holy Spirit will come upon you [Mary] (1:35), the child to be born will be called holy, the Son of God." Zechariah, being filled with the Spirit and to honour the birth of his son, prophesies in the words of the Benedictus (1:67-79). [See Ch. 8: Infancy Narratives.]

• The Holy Spirit is active in Mary's conception, "therefore the child to be born will be called holy, the Son of God." The Holy Spirit will come upon Zechariah's son (1:15), upon Zechariah at the birth of his son (1:67) and Jesus' birth (2:25-27).

B) The Holy Spirit in the ministry of Jesus: the Holy Spirit is present at Jesus' baptism in which He was anointed and empowered for His ministry. The Holy Spirit descended upon him (3:22).

• At the temptations Jesus is described as "full of the Holy Spirit and is led by the Spirit into the wilderness." (4:1)

• He starts His ministry in the power of the Spirit (4:14). Jesus announced that Isaiah's prophecy was about being anointed by the Holy Spirit has been fulfilled in Him.

• Jesus' rejoicing is directed by the Holy Spirit, when offering the prayer, "I thank You, Father (Pater), Lord (Gk. Kurie) of heaven and earth. "This means that He was aware of His sense of Sonship." (10:21) The Holy Spirit inspires prayer and praise. The only occasion in Luke when the Holy Spirit is the teacher is in 12:12.

• The disciples wait for the empowering of the Spirit (24: 29). Tuckett **(22)** seems to ignore this verse when he says that Luke is so silent about the Spirit's activity after 4:14 and finds this verse an enigma. [See also Ch. 8: Birth Narratives.]

[7] Joyfulness [See p. 148.]

Luke uses words like "rejoice" and "praise" to express joy and show that something jubilant has happened. The words "rejoice" and "praise" are more common in Luke than any other book in the N.T. He uses seven different words for joy. Theses are used thirty -six times. [See p.166,177.]

A) A message of joy: Rejoicing is tied to fulfilment, "And you will have joy and gladness, and many will rejoice at His birth." (1:14) Elizabeth said to Mary, "The babe in my womb leaped for joy." (1:44)

• Mary in the Magnificat said, "And my spirit rejoices in God my Saviour." (1:47) (RSV "rejoiced" is a better translation.)
• Elizabeth's relations and neighbours rejoice at the Lord's great mercy and kindness to her and at the birth of her son (1:58, 2:20). [See p. 92.]
• In the Sermon on the Plain, Jesus gave his followers words of encouragement when they would face persecution, "Rejoice in that day, and leap for joy, for behold, your reward is great in heaven;" (6:23)
• The Third Gospel begins and ends with rejoicing "and my spirit (Gk.psuche) rejoices in God my Saviour." (1:47) "And they returned to Jerusalem with great joy," when Jesus gave the disciples His final blessing (24:52-53).
• In the story of the Prodigal Son the father says, "let us eat and make merry; for this my son was dead but is alive again; he was lost and is found." (15:23) "And they began to make merry." (15:32). There is a joyous note in the three parables when the lost are found. The father restores the son's privileges. [See p. 47.]
• Zacchaeus came down quickly from the tree and received Jesus joyfully (19:6). A distinctive feature of Luke's Gospel is the sense of "joy and praise to God for His saving and healing work. (Liefeld) **(22)**
B) Jesus Himself rejoices (10:21) and the disciples rejoice when He enters Jerusalem (19:37-38).
C) The eschatological joy of the new age has come (4:18; 6:6-11;10:17; 24:41, 52, Is.61:1). The disciples are joyous at their success in casting out demons (10:17). [See pp.180-181,203-204.]

[8] Praise
A) Doxology (Praise to God)
Luke uses different words for praise and worship:(Gk.doxazo) glorify, (Gk. aineo) praise, (Gk. eulogeo) bless and (Gk. latreuo) (1:74; 2:36) a general word for worship. [See Figure 3 p. 53.]

1) The word "glory" is appropriate as there is a sense of ascribing glory to God, throughout this Gospel. The prominence of the Ascension in Luke contributes to his "theology of glory." Luke emphasises the resurrection, ascension and vindication of Christ. This includes the early chapters of Acts. Those who benefit from Jesus' healing power are filled with wonder and bring glory (Gk.doxazo) to God (5:25-26). Both the paralysed man and the crowd glorify God. This idea of praising God for a healing is unique to Luke. (L) Praise is offered by the one who is the object of God's power and by the witness of that power. (Stein) **(23)**

B) Praising and blessing [See p. 86.]
Examples of praising and blessing God are Mary's song the Magnificat (1:45-56), Zechariah's song the Benedictus (1:68-79) (L); the angels' doxology "Glory to God in the highest" (2:13-14), the shepherds "return glorifying (Gk.doxazo) and praising (Gk.ainounton) God." (2:20) This expression "praising God" is the believer's proper response and that of all of God's creation (Ps.148:1-4). Mary gives two reasons for her praise (1:47,48): declarative praise. [See Ch.8 p.85-6.]

C) "Praising" is a favourite word of Luke. It is used eight times in the N.T. and six of these are in Luke/Acts.
(1) Simeon took the child in his arms and praised (Gk. eulogeo) God in the words of the Nunc Dimittis (2:28-32).
(2) The paralysed man returned home praising God (Gk.doxazo). The people were amazed and all glorified God and were filled with awe in Capernaum (5:25).
(3) The people praised literally "glorified" God after the raising of the widow's son and the "news" (Gk. logos) of Jesus spread (7:16).

D) The Holy Spirit in Luke is often portrayed as inspiring prayer/praise and speech; this is the role of the Spirit in (10:21-24). God has concealed these from some and revealed them to others.

E) Praising God after a miracle: the beggar man and the people give praise to God after the miracle (18:43) (L); only the Samaritan leper returned to give praise to God (17:18) (L). When Jesus entered Jerusalem it was the whole crowd of disciples and not the people from Jerusalem who began to rejoice and praise (Gk.aineo) God in loud voices for all the miracles they had witnessed saying, "Blessed (Gk.eulogemenos) is the King who comes in the name of the Lord! Peace in heaven and glory in the highest." (19:37-38) Luke closes his Gospel with the theme of "joy." His theme of doxology also appears at the end as the disciples are last seen "praising" (Gk. aiounountes) God (24:53). They also continually blessed (Gk.eulogountes) God in the Temple. This is an appropriate way for Luke to conclude his Gospel as the believer has to live a life of praise as he/she waits for the return of the ascended Lord.

F) Rejoicing and praising
It is significant that the words "rejoice" and "praise" are more common in Luke than any other book in the N.T. In the O.T. concern for God's glory produces joy and stability (Ps.57:7). Luke uses the word "doxazo" fourteen times for glorify (five in Acts and five in (L) material; Matthew uses it four times and Mark only once. [See p. 56.]

G) Luke alone uses the word (Gk.aineo) "praise." [See Figure 3 p. 53.]

H) Summary of incidents of praise and blessing in Luke's Gospel   (Figure 3)

Examples of praise and blessing	Ref.	Comment
1. Mary praises and blesses (Gk.eulogeo) God in the words of the Magnificat. At least twelve people and groups give praise to God in Luke's Gospel.	1:42, 45-56) (L)	"My soul magnifies the Lord and my spirit rejoiced in God my Saviour." "Praising and blessing" are combined. She calls him "Lord" and "God my Saviour."
2. Zechariah in his song, the Benedictus, praises God for remembering His holy covenant.	1:63, 68-74 (L)	"Blessed be the Lord God of Israel for He has visited His people." Praising and blessing again are combined. God is praised for coming to redeem His people. Jesus' role in salvation is praised. He is the "horn of salvation." (1:69b)
3. The angels' song, the doxology: heaven tells the earth about the significance of Jesus' birth. The Gk. word "aineo" is unique to Luke. Luke uses it five times in Luke/Acts. This praise is repeated by the shepherds (2:20) and the crowd of disciples when Jesus entered Jerusalem (19:37-38).	2:13-14(L)	A multitude of the heavenly angels praised (Gk. ainonton) God. "Glory (Gk. doxa) to God in the highest and on earth peace among men with whom He is pleased." In this context "glory" is used to ascribe praise to God. Later in 2:9 it is an attribute of God. Praising and glorifying are combined.
4. God is praised (Gk.aineo) by the shepherds for the birth of Jesus. This word is unique to Luke's Gospel. The shepherds repeat the praise of the choir of angels.	2:20 (L)	The shepherds returned glorifying (Gk.doxazontes) and praising (Gk.ainountes) God. The response of the shepherds is one in which glorifying and praising are combined.
5. Simeon praises God in his Psalm of Praise the Nunc Dimittis. He praises God for the universal scope of work of Jesus. Anna served/worshipped God (Gk. latreuo) daily in the Temple (2:37; 1:74; 4:18).	2:26-32, 34 (L)	The Holy Spirit reveals to Simeon that he will not see death until he sees the promised Messiah. The Holy Spirit directed him into the Temple at the right time to meet Mary and Joseph (2:28).
6. In the synagogue at Nazareth Jesus was glorified by all the people when He taught. Jesus is given honour (Gk. doxazo) by all the people in Galilee (4:15).	4:15 (L)	The people respond to Jesus in the synagogue by glorifying Jesus for His teaching. Luke uses "glorify" of Jesus and his work. Luke could be drawing the reader into a sense of interest and excitement in Jesus.
7. The healing of the paralysed man - everyone glorifed (Gk.doxazo) God when the paralysed man was healed immediately. The healed man also praised (Gk.doxazo) glorified God.	5:25-26	He returned home glorifying God and all the people were filled with awe, amazement seized them and they glorified God. The people said, "We have seen strange things today." (5:25-26) This is conjoint praise.
8. After the raising of the widow's son and the news of Jesus spread fast, the people praised "glorified" God.	7:16 (L)	Fear gripped the crowd and they glorified God (Gk. doxazo) saying, "a great Prophet has risen among us!" and "God has visited His people!"
9. In the same way as the Twelve returned from their mission, Jesus rejoiced in the Spirit (10:21).	10:21-24	The Holy Spirit inspires prayer and praise and speech. Jesus rejoices in the Holy Spirit. This rejoicing is directed by the Spirit. The Holy Spirit is the source of the joy.
10. The woman with the bent back praised God (Gk.edoxazo) when she was healed at once.	13:13-17 (L)	The people were delighted at the wonderful things Jesus was doing.
11. The Samaritan leper returned to give praise (Gk. ainon) and thanks. "Rise and go your faith has made you well." (17:19) To offer thanks is to acknowledge God's act of healing and is a favourite expression in Luke. The leper falls at the feet of Jesus giving Him thanks: a sign of respect, giving Him (Jesus) His thanks. The leper praises God in a loud voice (Gk. megales doxazon). This is praise and thanks.	17:11-19 (L)	This "praise" is offered by the leper after the healing. Praise and giving thanks (Gk.euchariston) are combined (17:15-16). Real faith and genuine worship involves giving glory (Gk.doxa) to God. Thanksgiving is understood as an act of faith. It becomes an "expression of faith" as it remembers what God has done for us in Christ. (Pao) **(24)** This is praise in response to God's salvation.

Examples of praise and thankfulness	Ref.	Comment
12. Blind Bartimaeus - the people praised/glorified God (Gk. edoken) and praised (Gk.ainon) Him. This is Luke's unique use of the word praise (Gk. aineo).	18:43	Bartimaeus glorifies(Gk.doxazo) God for receiving his sight and all the people responded by praising God. Praise and giving thanks are combined.
13. When Jesus entered Jerusalem the crowd of disciples praised (Gk. eulogemenos) God "with a loud voice" for all the miracles they had seen (19:38). The shepherds' praise (2:13,20) at Jesus' birth now resumes as He enters Jerusalem. Joy,praise and blessing are all combined.	19:37-38 (L)	"Blessed be the King who comes in the name of the Lord! Peace in heaven and glory (Gk.doxa)in the highest!" Praise and blessing are combined. Ps.118:26 is quoted to accomplish Jesus' final act of deliverance to fulfil the covenant hope of Israel."In loud voices" is a favourite expression in Luke (4:33; 8:28; 23:46). The object of worship is the One who can be trusted. (Pao) **(25)** It is the song from Ps.118 recorded in all four Gospels of Jesus' entry into Jerusalem to accomplish the final act of deliverance in fulfilment of the covenant hope of Israel.
14. Jesus at the Last Supper said, "The power of the cross would be fully manifest in the Messianic banquet." (22:16) The centurion praised God when he saw what happened at the death of Jesus.	22:16-19 23:47	Jesus gives thanks/blessses (Gk. eucharistesas) for the cup and the bread. Our word eucharist comes from this word. A Gentile gives the final comment that Jesus was a righteous man.
15. Luke's Gospel ends with a doxology. This is a common theme in Luke's Gospel for glorifying (Gk. eulogountes) God (24:53). There is some textual evidence for "praising (Gk.ainoutes) and blessing (Gk. eulogoutes)."	24:30, 50, 51, 53 (L)	The apostles were continually (Gk. proskuneo) bowing in worship in the Temple blessing God. Blessing and joy are combined in this final event in this Gospel. Worship is a human response to a gracious God and needs to be put in this context to be properly understood. (Marshall)**(26)**

The Characteristics of Luke's Gospel cont'd Group: 4

[6] The Holy Spirit   **OHP**   [See p.51.]

 In different ways the Holy Spirit is linked with the life and ministries of Jesus and John the Baptist:

1] The Holy Spirit fills human beings so that they can convey God's messages.

• John the Baptist is filled with the Spirit right from conception (1:15). Elizabeth, being filled with the Spirit (1:41) extends a blessing to Mary and Mary's child (1:42).

• Zechariah, being filled with the Spirit and to honour the birth of his son, prophesies in the words of the Benedictus (1:67-79).

2] Jesus: The Holy Spirit is active in Mary's conception (1:35).

• The birth takes place because the Holy Spirit came upon Mary.

• The Spirit was on Simeon and revealed that Simeon would see the Lord's Christ (2:25-27).

• John the Baptist said that Jesus would baptise the people with the Holy Spirit and with fire (3:16).

• The Holy Spirit does not come upon Jesus until His baptism (3:22).

• Jesus is full of the Holy Spirit after His baptism (3:22), and is led by the Spirit into the wilderness to be tempted by the devil (4:1).

• At His baptism, the Holy Spirit descended upon Jesus in bodily form like a dove. In Luke and Matthew this is a public experience, in Mark it is in private (Mk.3:22, Matt.3:21-22, Lk.3:22). In John's Gospel the two experiences are tied together; the experience was private but it was revealed and explained publicly (Jn.1:32). Jesus also has the power and authority to bestow the Spirit like God Himself (Jn.1:33).

• Jesus starts His public ministry in Galilee in the power of the Spirit (4:14).

• Jesus, in the synagogue at Nazareth reads from Is.61:1-2. "The Spirit of the Lord is upon me." (4:18) Jesus claims to be directed by God to speak. [He is not supporting class struggle in this situation (4:18).]

• Jesus promises the Holy Spirit as an answer to prayer (11:13).

• His Spirit would give His followers all they needed to say (12:12).

Jesus taught that the Father gives the Spirit to those who ask him (11:13). Jesus rejoiced in the Holy Spirit and thanks God that the Father has revealed things to little children, rather than to the wise (10:21).

• What did the disciples wait for? (24:49) "To be clothed with power from on high" meant to receive the Holy Spirit.

Pupil's Activity: Eight

a) Divide the class into nine groups giving each a characteristic of Luke's Gospel.

b) Arrange for each group to do a five-minute presentation either by OHP (size 14) or powerpoint. Mount each group activity on card. Part of the Group 4 activity on the Holy Spirit has been completed for you.

c) As an aid to memory arrange the titles as an acrostic.

[1] Luke's comprehensive history of Jesus: Group: 1

a) What are the main features of Luke's comprehensive history of Jesus?

b) What do you think is the main theme of Luke's Gospel? Give your reasons.

c) How does Luke provide a close link between the O.T. and N.T. (4:18, 21)?

d) What key expressions does Luke use to show God's divine plan in history.

e) Show how Luke has a great interest in the passion of Jesus. [See.p .45.]

[2] Gospel for all: Group: 2

• The message of the angels, "Goodwill to all men". (2:14)

• Simeon's message: "salvation's preparation is in the sight of all people, a light for revelation to the Gentiles." (2:31-32)

• Quotation from Isa. 40:3-5 in (3:4-6), "all flesh shall see the salvation of God."

• The Samaritans are placed on a level with the Jews (9:54; 10:33; 17:16).

• Great interest in people who are not Jews; Look up evidence for this (4:25-27; 10:30-37; 17:16).

• "People of this world and people of the light." (10:14) Find out the meaning of this expression.

• People will come from all round the world to sit in the kingdom of God (13:29).

• As in Matthew's Gospel the great commission is for all nations (24:47). [See pp.45-6.]

[3] Luke's interest in people as individuals:

(a) social outcasts   Group: 3

• The sinful woman who anoints Jesus (7:36ff)

• Zacchaeus (19:8)

• The Good Samaritan (10:29-37)

• The thief on the cross (22:39)

Find out about other marginalized people in Luke's Gospel. Why are they outcasts? [See pp.144-6.]

Luke's interest in people:

(b) women   Group: 3

• What part did the women play in the Passion events leading up to the cross (23:27), the cross (23:49), at the tomb (23:55) and the resurrection (24:11)?

• Identify the thirteen women who are mentioned only in Luke's Gospel.

• How did some of the women serve Jesus and show that they were followers (8:1-3)?

Jesus taught women as well as men even though the rabbis thought it was a sin to teach a woman. In Luke's Gospel, women have a key role in God's plan as seen in the birth narratives. What was their role? [See pp.46,81,83-6, 94-6.]

(c) children   Group: 3

• The widow's son (7:12)

• Jairus' daughter (8:42)

• Boy with the unclean spirit (9:38)

• The children brought to Jesus (18:15)

• What is the significance of "only children" in Luke's Gospel?

• How does Luke show Jesus' love for children?

[4] Concern for the poor   Group: 3

• "Blessed are you poor......" (6:20). Here Jesus addresses and blesses the poor. Matthew has "poor in spirit." (Matt.5:3)

• "Give to him who begs from you......" (6:30)

• "When you have a feast invite the poor......." (14:13) Complete these verses for your presentation.

• How does Jesus show his concern for the poor and humble and what is His attitude to the abuse of money and wealth (4:17-21; 16:14)? [See p.47,243,249-250.]

[5] Luke's special emphasis:

(a) Events relating to prayer: Group: 4

• On what occasions did Jesus pray (3: 21; 5: 15-16; 6: 12; 9: 18-22, 29; 11:1; 22: 29-46)?

• In what way was prayer important in the birth of John the Baptist (1:10-11,13)? [See p.48-51.]

(b) Jesus' teaching on prayer in parables   **Group: 4**

• Name two parables Jesus told about prayer in Luke's Gospel in which the people of God are to ask Him to supply their needs (1) 11:5 (2) 18:8.

(c) Prayer for His enemies

Jesus prays for His enemies (23: 24).

• On what occasions did Jesus teach His disciples to pray for their enemies (6-28-36; 11:4)?

• Name an occasion when Jesus prayed for Himself (22:42).

• Name two occasions when Jesus prayed for Himself (23:42, 46).

[6] Holy Spirit [See OHP]   Group: 4

[7] Joyfulness [See pp. 51-2.]   Group: 4

• Look up these references to joy (1:14; 1:44; 1:47).

• Look up these references to joy in the parables (15:1-24).

• Find evidence to show that Luke begins and ends his Gospel on a note of joy.

• Luke 10:17-24 is bound together by the words "happy", "glad", "joyful".

a) The seventy/two returned with joy (10:17).

b) Jesus told the seventy/two when they returned to rejoice (Gk. chairete) constantly. Rejoice in the fact that their names are written in heaven rather than their ability to cast out demons (10:20).

c) Jesus rejoiced in the Holy Spirit and thanks God that the Father has revealed things to little children (Gk. nepiois) rather than to the wise (10:21).

• Find references to joy in the hymns of praise in the Birth Narratives of Luke Chs.1-2.

• Which two words are more common in Luke than any other Gospel?

[8] Praise and thanks [See pp. 52-4.]   Group: 4

• Identify occasions when people gave glory or praise to God.

• What are the different words used by Luke for worship? How would you distinguish between them?

• Identify events in Luke's Gospel where praise and blessing are combined? What is the significance of this?

• What does Mary thank God for in the Magnificat? What three divine attributes does Mary extol (1:49-50)?

• In the Benedictus what four things does Zechariah thank God for?

• What can we learn from the angels' message and the rejoicing of the heavenly host about the importance of Jesus' birth?

Outcomes

Students should have a knowledge and understanding of:

• **the main characteristics of Luke's Gospel.**

• **the key concepts of Luke's characteristics e.g. comprehensive history of Jesus, universalistic approach, interest in people including individuals, women and their rights, children, social relationships, poverty and wealth.**

• **special emphasis on prayer, the Holy Spirit, praise and joyfulness.**

Notes on Chapter 5: The Characteristics of Luke's Gospel

1. G.Klein, Luke 1:1-4 Redaction Criticism on Luke's Gospel, Zeit and Geschichte, Tubingen: Mohr (1974) pp.194-196.

2. M.Volkel, NTS, (1973-74) 20: pp.289-99.

3. Joel Green, NICET, op. cit. p.17.

4. Walter Liefeld, op. cit. p.849.

5. Charles H. Talbert, Reading Luke: A Literary and Theological Commentary on the Third Gospel. New York: Crossroad (1982) p.70.

6. Samuel Tobiah Lacks, A Rabbinic Commentary on the NT: The Gospels of Matthew, Mark and Luke. New York: Ktav, (1987) p.17.

7. Robert Stein, op. cit. p.118.

8. Robert Stein, op. cit. p.192.

9. David Crump, Jesus the Intercessor: Prayer and Christology in Luke/Acts. WUNT 2:49. Tubingen: JCBMohr (Paul Siebeck) (1992), Jesus the Intercessor.

10. Howard Marshall, op. cit. p.830.

11. Allison Trites, The Prayer Motif in Luke-Acts, In perspectives on Luke-Acts, edited by C.H. Talbert, 168-86. Edinburgh: T and T Clark, (1978). "Prayer Motif."

12. Joel Green, op. cit. p.258.

13. W.F. Arndt, op. cit. (1956) p.294 on 11:1 "Teach us now to pray is an Aorist Imperative which has a sense of urgency in the request.

14. G.D.G. Dunn, Article on Prayer, DJG, IVP, (1992) p.619.

15. Samuel T. Lachs, (ibid.)

16. Howard Marshall, (ibid.)

17. David Pao, Thanksgiving, NSBT, IVP, (2002) pp.64,70.*

18. David Pao, op.cit. p.70.

19. David Pao, (ibid.)

20. Robert Stein, op. cit. p.589.

21. David Crump, op.cit. p.89-90.

22. Walter Liefeld, op. cit p.842.

23. Robert Stein, (ibid.)

24. David Pao, op.cit. p.142.

25. David Pao, op. cit. p.64.

26. Howard Marshall, op. cit. p.830.

*This book is highly recommended.

CCEA A/S

> Targets:
> • Identify the main issues relating to Luke the historian, theologian, teacher and pastor.
> • Identify ancient history and historiography, different types of history, for example narrative history, 'empire history', theological history and synchronic dating.

The Role of Luke as a Historian

Introduction

Ancient history is said to entertain, instruct and to provide a concise summary of history. As a background pupils should have familiarity with some of the main events in the Roman Empire and especially in Palestine at this time. A possible time scale based upon Hoehner's Chronology **(1)** is provided.

(Figure 1) A chart of the key dates in the life of Jesus

No.	Event	Date	Ref. in Luke	Comment
1	The first phase in the completion of the Jewish Temple in Jerusalem when the Inner court was begun. [See A.D. 63 for final completion.]	18-17 B.C.	2:8	Herod came to power in 40 B.C. and died in 4 B.C. The Temple was built by Herod the Great, (an Edomite Jew) in one and a half years. He was declared "King of the Jews" (40-37 B.C.) by the Roman senate.
2	The census date of Quirinius	6-4 B.C.	2:1	The Romans took a census before the death of Herod the Great.
3	The births of John and Jesus	(Dec.-Jan.) 5-4 B.C. (John) (July) (Jesus)?	1:5	Jesus and John were born just before the death of Herod the Great.
4	The death of Herod the Great was recorded in Josephus.	Mar. – April 4 B.C.	Matt. 2:15	"In the days of Herod, King of Judaea"
5	Jesus goes to the Temple aged twelve.	A.D. 8	2:41-45	"Now His parents went to Jerusalem every year at the feast of the Passover."
6	Year of Jubilee in Palestine	A.D. 27-28	4:14-30	Jesus preaches in the synagogue in Nazareth.
7	The start of John the Baptist's ministry	A.D. 28-29	3:1-3	In the fifteenth year of Tiberias Caesar
8	The start of Jesus' ministry	A.D. 29	3:23	Jesus when He began His ministry, was about thirty (Gk. hosei) years of age.
9	The Death of Jesus	A.D. 33 Friday 3rd April?	23:26-54	Jesus was crucified and buried on Friday, April 3, A.D.33.
10	The Resurrection of Jesus	A.D. 33 Sunday 5th April?	24:1-35	Jesus rose from the dead on Sunday 5th April.
11	The Ascension of Jesus	A.D. 33 May 14?	24:50-53; Acts 1: 6-11	Luke refers to the Ascension at Bethany.

Pupil's Activity: One based upon Figures 1 and 2

Construct a timeline to show some of the main events in the life of Jesus in Luke's Gospel.

Pupil's Activity: Two based upon Figure 2

Construct a timeline to show some of the main events in the Roman Empire and Palestine from the time of Herod the Great 37 B.C to the fall of Jerusalem A.D.70.

(Figure 2) Key events in the Roman Empire around the time of Jesus

• 63 B.C. Pompeii conquered Palestine. The Romans kept a careful eye on Palestine but gave the Jews a fair degree of self-government.

• 37 B.C. Herod the Great was appointed King by the Romans.

• 31 B.C. The Romans captured Egypt.

• 31 B.C. - A.D.14 Caesar Augustus became Emperor of Rome.

• 31 B.C. Augustus declared himself on his coins to be "the saviour of the world".

• 19 B.C. Herod the Great built new foundation walls and enlarged the Temple area to 400 by 500 yards which was twice the size of the previous one built by Zerubbabel. (Ellis) **(2)**

• 18-17 B.C. The inner court of the Temple was completed in one and a half years.

• 8-7 B.C. Herod the Great falls out with Rome.

• 5-4 B.C. The Birth of Jesus/The Roman census 6-4 B.C. (1:5) "In the days of Herod King of Judea, the angel of the Lord appeared to Zechariah." (1:8) "A decree went out from Caesar Augustus." (2:1) The birth of Jesus is thought to be in the summer of 5 B.C. (Hoehner)

• A.D. 6-15 Annas becomes high priest.

• A.D. 4 The death of Herod the Great, Philip, the Tetrarch ruled Ituraea and Trachonitis up to A.D.34.

• A.D. 14 Tiberias becomes the sole Roman Emperor.

• A.D. 15 Annas ceases to be the high priest.

• A.D. 18 Caiaphas becomes the high priest in Jerusalem.

• A.D. 26 Pilate becomes the governor or prefect of Judea. He kept the peace for the Romans and collected taxes for them. This is thought to be the Jewish Jubilee Year - every fifty years debts were cancelled (4:19; Lev. 25:10). This was "the acceptable year". (Marshall) **(3)**

• A.D. 28 This is the start of John the Baptist's ministry, in the fifteenth year of Tiberias Caesar (3:1-2). John announces the coming of Jesus and when Herod Antipas was tetrarch of Galilee.

• A.D. 29 The start of Jesus' ministry in the reign of Tiberias Caesar (3:23)

• A.D. 30 Jesus' first Passover (Jn.2:13) April (1st. visit)

• A.D. 31 Jesus' second Passover (Jn. 5:1) April (2nd visit)?

• A.D. 31 Jesus at the Feast of Tabernacles (Jn.5:1) October (3rd. visit)

• A.D. 32 Jesus' third Passover (Jn.6:4) April (4th visit)

• A.D. 32 Jesus at Feast of Tabernacles (Jn.7:2,10) September - October (5th. visit)

• A.D. 32 Jesus at Feast of Dedication (Jn.10: 22-39) December (6th. visit)

• A.D. 33 The Death [Friday April 3rd] and Resurrection of Jesus [Sunday April 5th]

• A.D. 33 The Ascension [May 14th] (Luke 24; Acts 1)

• A.D. 33 The Day of Pentecost [May 24th](Acts 2)

• A.D. 34 The death of Philip the Tetrarch of Idumea and Trachonitis.

• A.D. 36 Paul's conversion and the end of Pilate's rule as governor of Judaea

> Histories in the ancient world had three main functions:
> • to entertain,
> • instruct and
> • provide a concise summary of the history being presented.

• A.D. 37-41 Caligula becomes the Emperor of Rome after the death of Tiberias Caesar A.D.37.

• A.D. 41 Caligula tries to erect a statute of himself in the Temple of Jerusalem. Before the Jews could protest, Caligula died.

• A.D. 44 Death of Herod Agrippa I (Acts 12)

• A.D. 41-54 Claudius becomes Emperor of Rome. In the late 40s in the time of Claudius there was a severe famine in the empire and particularly in Judaea (Acts 11:27-30, 2 Cor. 8-9).

• A.D. 49 The Jews are expelled from Rome by Claudius. Aquila and Priscilla are also expelled at this time (Acts 18:2).

• A.D. 54-68 Nero becomes the Emperor.

• A.D. 61 Tensions were growing between the Jews and the Romans in Judaea.

• A.D. 63 All of the area of the Jewish Temple in Jerusalem was completed.

• A.D. 64 The fire of Rome takes place in July and burns for a week. (Tacitus Annals,15,44.)

• A.D. 66-70 The Jews revolt against the Romans, when the Jews take to the streets because of the military, religious and socio-economic actions against them.

• A.D.70 The flight of the Christians to Pella

• A.D.70 The city of Jerusalem was captured and destroyed by the Roman general Titus and the Temple was also destroyed. Various parts of the city were burnt and many Jews were taken to Rome as prisoners of war. (Carson) **(4)** Never were the Jews to become a credible political and economic force until today.

• A.D. 135 After another revolt Jerusalem becomes a Gentile city and remains so until recently. The city is named Aelia Capitolina.

[1] Luke as a writer of narrative history-the author's intention (1:1-4) [See pp. 9, 35.]

A) What is ancient History?

Histories in the ancient world had three main functions: to entertain, instruct and provide a concise summary of the history being presented. In the Third Gospel the author's intention is to explain the roots of the new movement called "the Way", the story of its founder and shows His links with God's promised redemption (1:1-4). Luke tells us about "His-Story"- God's acts in history through Jesus. It is also our story of how God makes outsiders into insiders and how we can trust the Gospel as we read it, as it has been carefully written and God's promises are true. The issue of Luke as a historian has led some scholars to say that Luke's Gospel is "the storm centre of New Testament studies." (van Unnick) **(5)** Luke in writing to Theophilus says of himself that he was a "careful" researcher of his material, followed all things closely, and wrote an "orderly account." (1:1-4) Luke indicates that he was not an eyewitness of the events but, nevertheless, uses the following key words and phrases to describe his account:

1. What investigative skills did he use? He will be "**thorough**" (Gk. parekolouthekoti) meaning having followed all things closely (1:3). He will leave no stone unturned, wanting to consolidate the knowledge of those in "the Way" and will give them instruction. About thirty percent of Luke's material is unique to him.

2. Where does his Gospel start? "From the beginning" (Gk. anothen) can also mean "for a long time," (1:2) showing Luke went back and starts with John the Baptist.

3. What did he study? Having looked at "**everything**" (Gk. pasin) means he studied all the events and sources going back to the time of Jesus (1:3). These could have been written or oral sources. He also uses O.T. ideas.

4. How did Luke write his Gospel? He wrote in an "orderly" way or "carefully" (Gk. akribos) (1:3): a word which tells us about Luke's investigation. His detail is meticulous. He presents his material in an orderly way, meaning a logical and topical form of presentation. It can mean geographically orderly or a literary/logical way with one main theme, the "way". He writes that Theophilus might know the truth about the ministry of Jesus, "the things of which Theophilus had been informed (Gk.katechethes)." Today the word "catechesis" is used for teaching and instruction in some churches. The word "catechism" is also derived from this word. The word katechethes can mean either "as taught" (NIV and AV have "instructed") or "as informed" (RSV). This would suggest that Luke had a teaching role and purpose in writing his Gospel for Christians. His readers have been taught the gospel traditions and Luke expected them to understand the meaning of expressions like "Son of Man" and the "kingdom of God", which he does not explain. However, he does include various teachings, for example "watchfulness and faithfulness" (12:35-48), being a shrewd manager (16:1-9 esp.8-9), the disciples' service for God in a life of obedience (17:7-10), worship materials in the Lord's Prayer (11:1-4) and Lord's Supper (22:14-23); these are specific teachings for Christians. [See p. 40.]

5. What is apprehended? He presents his material accurately because he wants his readers to be certain of the truth (Gk.asphaleian) of the gospel (1:4). "A close investigation into his descriptions of settings, customs and localities reveal a consistent concern for accuracy." (Hengel and Hammer) **(6)** In his use of his sources Luke is very accurate with his material. In using these key expressions, Luke is at pains to show his readers how seriously he takes his research and writing of historical narrative. It is reasonable to say that Luke is a narrative historian and is not writing a fiction story, a comedy, a myth or a Greek tragedy.

> **About 30% of Luke's material is unique to him.**

B) Are there different kinds of historians ?

1. "Luke is a historian of the first rank." (Ramsay) **(7)** Bock agrees, "Luke is a first-class ancient historian, and most good ancient historians understand their task well." **(8)** Like us today, the ancients knew the difference between fact and fiction as shown in A.D.39-40 when Lucian wrote a book entitled "How to Write History!" (Ramsay) **(9)**

2. Luke places the start of the adult life of John and Jesus in historical context and from the perspective of the world scene and that of the Roman Empire. For user friendliness, he starts with the word of God coming to Zechariah and not with the baptism of Jesus. Luke dates the emergence of John the Baptist's ministry using six contemporary datings referred to by Blomberg **(10)** as "empire history." [See Figure 4 p.62.]

C) Is the Gospel of Luke historically reliable?

The rejection of Jesus in Nazareth (4:16-30) is placed at the start of the ministry in Galilee because Luke wants to show the type of rejection which Jesus had experienced from His own people. Mark has placed it after the raising of Jairus' daughter and well into the ministry of Jesus (Mk. 6:1-6).

1. Why do some events appear in a different chronological order?

Often the events are placed in a different order for Luke's own editorial purpose in keeping with a theme. He reverses the order of the second and the third temptations of Jesus to build up to a climax, with Jesus in the Temple in Jerusalem as a key theme in the book (4:1-13; Mk. 4:1-11).

2. Matt. 10:37 appears to correct the source of Luke in (14:26), "Hate your parents." The word "hate" in Luke means to love less (Gen. 29:30-31; Deut. 21:15-17). In case there is a misunderstanding, Matthew seems to soften the word in Luke and speaks of loving the family more.

3. In Luke's account of the trial of Jesus before the Sanhedrin, Luke telescopes Mark's account (22:66-71; Mk.14:53-15:1). This is a very common literary device used by the ancient historians. (Lucian) **(11)** The passion account is both history and narrative. Jesus' claim about Himself is what sends Him to death and is the major feature of the trial. Jesus, in claiming to be the Son of God, claims the right to go into the presence of God and be seated with Him in heaven. To the Jews this was blasphemy as it was worse than trying to reside permanently in the "Holy of Holies." (22:69-71)

4. The two anointings of Jesus (7:36-50; Mk.14:3-9) appear as doublets but the details show they are two events. The settings and the anointings are quite different. In this incident a different order in the events does not indicate unreliability and there are significant differences in the setting.

(Figure 3) A comparison between the anointing of Jesus in the house of Simon the Pharisee and that of Simon the Leper

The anointing of Jesus in Simon the leper's House (Mark 14:3-9)	The anointing of Jesus in Simon the Pharisee's House (Luke 7:36-50)
Jesus is in Bethany in the house of Simon the leper, when a woman anoints His head with an alabaster box of precious ointment.	In the house of Simon the Pharisee, Jesus' feet are anointed from an alabaster flask of ointment by a sinful woman.

D) Can we trust Luke as a historian if there is no extra-biblical evidence?

Luke 13:1-5 is unique to the Third Gospel and refers to two different tragic events which had taken place:

a) A national tragedy, the Temple massacre of the Galileans whose blood Pilate had mixed with Jewish sacrifices. Will God exercise a special judgement upon them?

b) A natural disaster, when the tower of Siloam had collapsed killing eighteen people. Did God judge them for excessive sin? The Seminar Group of scholars in their book "The Five Gospels" say Jesus never engaged in confrontation or talk of judgement and therefore it follows that this event is not rooted in His actual teaching. They argue that Jesus never challenged anyone other than to call for love and tolerance. He was a wise sage, a religious genius and a social revolutionary!

1. If Jesus were only a wise sage who went round making witty sayings, He would not have been threatening enough to have been crucified during the Passover when surrounded by hundreds who liked Him.

2. If Jesus were a religious genius who helped people to be kind, compassionate and gentle, He would not have been crucified.

3. If Jesus were a social revolutionary He would have been crucified but it is unlikely that He would have given birth to the Church. (McKnight) **(12)**

From a historical perspective there is much evidence from Josephus to show that Pilate had alienated the Jews. While Josephus does not record the gruesome events in Luke 13:1-5, he does describe three similar events. Pilate installed military standards and shields in Jerusalem with images of the Roman Empire which broke the second commandment. He took money from the Temple treasury to build an aquaduct. He suppressed an uprising of the Samaritans. The gruesome event of Luke 13:1-3 is not recorded in detail in Luke but similar events are to be found in Josephus. These events are in keeping with the image of Pilate as a ruthless ruler whose actions were recorded by Josephus and help to show that the material unique to Luke is both authentic and historical. "To be a Roman governor, at this time, was not a great privilege, but was like being between a rock and a hard place." (Blomberg) **(13)**

Pupil's Activity: Three

Luke, in writing to Theophilus, says of himself that he was a careful researcher of his material, followed all things closely, and wrote an orderly account (1:1-4). From your understanding of (1:1-4) show how Luke had a keen interest in history and was careful with his material.

Pupil's Activity: Four

a) How do we know that Luke was anchored in history and was not a myth?

b) Provide evidence of this from the birth narratives and material unique to Luke.

c) Name three incidents, unique to Luke, showing why you think Luke included these in his Gospel.

d) Write a detailed account of one of them indicating that it is historically reliable.

Luke in writing to Theophilus says of himself that he was a careful researcher of his material, followed all things closely, and wrote an orderly account. (1:1-4)

[2] Luke as a writer of "empire history"

Luke places the roots of the New Movement in "empire history." He begins his story by giving the historical setting for the births of Jesus and John in the reign of Herod the Great (B.C. 37-A.D. 4). (Hoehner) **(14)** On at least three occasions Luke ties his story in with "empire history" in:-

A) Luke 1:5

"In the days of Herod, king of Judea," (near the end of Herod the Great's reign) (5-4 B.C.), the angel appears to a priest Zechariah, of the division of Abijah. Luke tells us that the setting (1:10) was one of two times of daily prayer in the Temple (9 am sunrise or 3 pm dusk): the time of "perpetual offering" which was the name for the evening offering in first century Judaism (Exod. 29:38-42). (Schurer) **(15)** The preparation of the offering was about 2.30pm and it was taken to the altar an hour later. This offering coincided with the evening prayer in the Temple; hence the crowd mentioned in (1:10).

B) Luke 2:1

"In those days a decree went out from Caesar Augustus, when Quirinius was governor of Syria." [See Ch.8: p. 90.] The first enrolment (Gk. prote) "first" [our word proto comes from this] could refer to the first census when Quirinius was governor of Syria rather than to an earlier census. This remark could imply more than one census. Luke could also mean the later census of A.D.6 and Luke 2:2 cannot be relegated to historical error. Bock **(16)** says "to do this is premature and erroneous." Joseph went up from Galilee to be enrolled with his espoused wife (2:4-5).

C) Luke 3:1-2

Luke again uses "empire history." This technique is like putting a picture in a beautiful frame. In the fifteenth year of the reign of Tiberius Caesar, Pontius Pilate was the governor of Judea, Herod was tetrarch of Galilee, His brother Philip was tetrarch of Ituraea and Trachonitis, Lysanias was the tetrarch of Abilene, (N.W. Damascus given to the Jewish Herods in A.D.54). Schurer **(17)** shows that there was a second Lysanias during the time of Tiberius. [See map Ch.9.] In the high priesthood of Annas and Caiaphas, the word of the Lord came to John, son of Zechariah (Is.38:4). In these incidents the narrative comes between the historical context and that of the word as in the O.T. prophets (Jer.1: 1-2). In giving the setting to John's ministry Luke uses seven political and spiritual rulers. This is called "synchronic dating," as in the O.T. where the prophet's call is put beside the rulers who governed his ministry (Hos. 1:1). [See p.62.] Luke, in presenting his facts, is the only Gospel writer to name those who were in political and spiritual power when John appeared. Luke shows that the story of Jesus continues the long history of God's dealing with His people and that the life of Jesus is a major event in God's "salvation history." Secular events and people are used to undergird the relevance of Jesus for the world.

Pupil's Activity: Five

a) What reasons does the third Evangelist give for emphasizing the historical context of the Third Gospel?
b) As an aid to revision complete the synchronic dating as a diagram (3:1-2). [See Figure 4.]

Pupil's Activity: Six

a) Outline your knowledge and understanding of "empire history" as used by Luke in the Third Gospel.
b) What is "synchronic dating"? Show how and why Luke makes use of this technique.
c) How do we know that Luke enjoyed history and wrote like a historian?

Pupil's Activity: Seven

a) Explore the claim that in writing this Gospel, Luke was faithful in his role as a historian.
Justify your answer. (CCEA A/S 2003 Resit) [15 marks]
b) Comment on the claim that Luke is both a teacher and a historian. Justify your answer.
(CCEA A/S 2003/2004) [15 marks]

D) (Figure 4)   Empire History: "synchronic dating" (3:1-2) [See p. 67.]

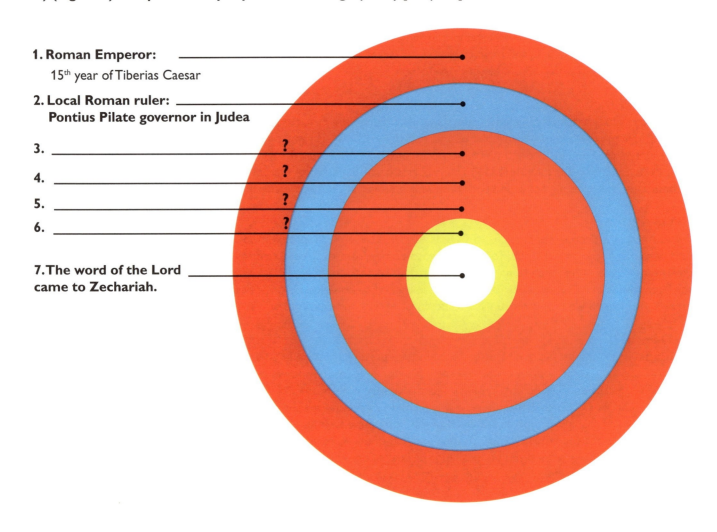

1. Roman Emperor:

     15th year of Tiberias Caesar

2. Local Roman ruler:
    Pontius Pilate governor in Judea

3. _____ **?**

4. _____ **?**

5. _____ **?**

6. _____ **?**

**7. The word of the Lord
came to Zechariah.**

[3A] Luke as a writer of "Salvation History" [See Vol. 2 (A2)]

This is an expression used by Hans Conzelmann **(18)** who saw Luke as the first "Christian Historian": the first to tell the history of Jesus and the history of God's dealing with His people. Conzelmann sees God's action in Jesus as God's main event in the affairs of people.

Pupil's Activity: Eight

a) See later Ch: 13: the Miracles of Jesus where there are some named cities and towns which Jesus visited and are recorded in Luke's Gospel. [p.218]

b) Divide the class into six groups (one group for each section of Luke) or give one geographical location to each pupil and complete the appropriate comment section in Figure 5.

c) Bring the six groups together to provide a class presentation on the geographical locations in Luke's Gospel and based upon the structure of Luke's Gospel

Group (A) The birth stories

Group (B) Introduction to the Ministry of Jesus

Group (C) Jesus in Galilee

Group (D) Journey narrative

Group (E) Jerusalem.

Group (F) Passion and resurrection

                                          "Luke is a historian of the first rank." (Ramsay) (7)

d) Do you think that Luke had an interest in geography? Justify your answer.

e) Does any particular pattern emerge from your class research?

B) Geographical locations in Luke's Gospel   (Figure 5)

	Place	Refs.	Comments
A	**The birth Narratives**	**1:5-2:52**	
1	"Joseph also went up from **Galilee,** from the **city of Nazareth**, to **Judea,** to the city of David, which is called **Bethlehem**."	2:4	Jesus' birth takes place in **Bethlehem** in a stable and not "along the way" as the apocryphal Psalm of Matthew 13 says or "in a cave" as the Protevangelium of James 17. 3 - 18 suggests.
2	"When the time came for their purification, Mary and Joseph brought him to **Jerusalem** to present him to the Lord."	2:22	Which social groupings did Luke include in his birth narratives and why did he include them? Which three Jewish ceremonies were combined here? Do you agree with Fitzmyer **(19)** that Luke was imprecise when he says "their purification"? How can a plural reference to the law apply only to women?
3	"They returned into **Galilee**, to their **own city, Nazareth.**"	2:39-40	What was the original home of Mary (1:26)?
4	"His parents went every year to **Jerusalem** at the Passover." [Jewish men were required to go to Jerusalem for three festivals: Passover, Pentecost and Tabernacles/Feast of Unleavened Bread but not women.] For a woman to go was a sign of deep spirituality. (Josephus)**(20)** (SB); **(21)**; (Preisker) **(22)** "But supposing Him to be in the company, they went a day's journey."	2:41-42 2:44-46	As whole villages travelled together in company/caravan (Gk. synodia), His parents would not have been worried about Jesus as villages travelled together (SB).**(23)** How long would it take to go from Nazareth to Jerusalem? See map p. 213 to see if they would have to by-pass Samaria! Where does the birth narrative end and what is the significance of this? Where in the Temple area was Jesus found? Some scholars say it would it have been the outer court, Solomon's Portico (Acts 3:11) or the house of instruction? (Rengstorf) **(24)**
B	**Introduction to the Ministry of Jesus**	**3:1-4:13**	
5	"The word of God came to John in the wilderness. John went into all the region **about the Jordan.**"	3:2,3	Only Luke mentions the Jordan but he is not specific about where in the desert John started his ministry. The entire Jordan area is meant (3:3).
6	"Jesus, full of the Holy Spirit, returned **from the Jordan**, and was led by the Spirit, for forty days in the wilderness."	4:1-2	Does return mean a) return to Galilee? or b) withdraw from the Jordan? Again Luke does not specify which part of the wilderness.

Pupil's Activity: Nine
Do you agree that Luke was the "first Christian historian"? Give reasons for or against this assertion.

Pupil's Activity: Ten
a) Sir William Ramsay says that the qualities of a good historian are: "Statements of fact are trustworthy, he is possessed of a good historic sense, he fixes his mind on the idea and plan that rules in the evolution of history and portions the scale of his treatment to the importance of each incident."
b) How far does Luke as a historian measure up to this definition?

Pupil's Acivity: Eleven
Find these places on the map [See p. 110.] and link them to events in Luke's Gospel:- Abilene, Bethlehem, Decapolis, Region of Galilee, Lake Gennesaret, the Country of the Gerasenes, Iturea, Jericho, Jerusalem, the Jordan region, the Mount of Olives, Nain, Nazareth, Perea, Samaria and Trachonitis.

	Place	Refs.	Comments
7	"Jesus began His ministry full of the Spirit in Galiee and a report concerning Him went out through all the surrounding country."	4:14	a) Where one passage flows into another it is called a "bridge passage" (Marshall) **(25)**: this is the first summary note in the Gospel which introduces a geographical shift. Was this the start of the Galilean ministry? Why does the Nazareth incident follow this? b) How does Luke use geographical details for editorial purposes? Jesus' fame (Gk. pheme) went everywhere. Our word "fame" comes from this Greek word. The grapevine soon got to work about Jesus. Luke makes a summary point regarding the honeymoon period which greeted a great preacher.
8	He taught in their **synagogues**, being glorified by all.	4:15	a) He introduces Jesus' ministry by showing the positive aspects. He records the people's response (Gk. doxazamenos) "being glorified." This is the only time Luke uses it of Jesus as it is usually used of God. b) God is praised for Jesus and His work in 2:13, 20, 28; 7:16. Luke intends the reader to be drawn into a sense of interest and excitement about Jesus.
9	In **Nazareth,** Jesus is rejected by His own people. "And they arose and put Him out of the city and led to the brow of a hill on which the city was built."	4:16-30	Is this the start of the Galilean ministry or is it in 4:14? The word "Nazara" is used only here and in Matt. 4:13 and is not the usual word (Nazareth). It could be a Semitic spelling or reflect an original Aramaic source. (Bock) **(26)**
10	And He went to **Capernaum, a city in Galilee.** And reports of Him went out into every place in the surrounding region.	4:31, 37	Jesus approached the city gate (Gk. pule). The people of Nazareth had noticed Jesus' work in **Capernaum**. Where was the centre of Jesus' ministry in Galilee?
C	**Jesus in Galilee**	4:1-9:50	
11	Jesus calls and commissions Peter by the **lake of Gennesaret.**	5:1	This is the only time Luke refers to lake (Gk.limne) **Gennesaret**. Peter would become a great fisherman of people and would rescue them from dangerous waters by the grace of God.
12	After He had ended all these sayings in the hearing of the people, He entered **Capernaum.** (Jesus heals a Roman centurion's servant in **Capernaum.**)	7:1-9	What is the setting of this incident of the centurion? Is it a transitional verse as in 4:30, 37,44, 5:1, 5:16, 5:26, 6:11, 6:17? Note: a centurion earned between 3,700 denarii and 7,500 a year. (Wegner) **(27)**
13	Jesus raises the only son of a widow in the city of **Nain in Galilee.**	7:11-17	This is the only time the city of Nain is mentioned in the Bible.
14	Jesus calms a storm on the **lake of Galilee.**	8: 22-25	The word for lake here is unique to Luke. [See above.]
15	Jesus heals the demon-possessed man in the **country of the Gerasenes.** Luke uses the word Gerasene rather the Gadarene (Mt. 8: 28; Mk.5:1).	8: 26	The region of the **Gerasenes** was opposite **Galilee** and **Decapolis** was 20 miles south east of the **Sea of Galilee**. [See map p.213.]

Geographical locations in Luke's Gospel

(Figure 5

D	Journey Narrative	9:51-19:48	Comments
16	"Jesus set His face to go to **Jerusalem**."	9:51	This is the start of the travel narrative because it seems like a journey from Galilee to Jerusalem. For the first time **Jerusalem** is seen as the goal of Jesus' movements. Jesus is not thinking of geographical progress from Galilee to Jerusalem.
17	And He is kept out of a **Samaritan village**.	9:53	It is the only time in the Gospels where Samaritan hostility is shown to Jesus and it is Luke who records it.
18	"Now as they went on their way, He entered a village… ."	10:38-42	Jesus was two miles outside Jerusalem in Bethany at the home of Mary and Martha but Luke **omits Bethany**. Why does Luke not give the location?
19	"On the way to Jerusalem, Jesus was passing along between **Samaria and Galilee**. And as He entered a village, He was met by ten lepers." [See map Ch.9.]	17:11-19	This indicates the extent of Jesus' ministry. Jesus does not take a straight line journey but a journey with a purpose. Why does Luke draw attention to the idea of a journey? Jesus moves from east to west along the boundary between **Samaria and Galilee**.
20	As Jesus **drew near to Jericho** (RSV), He heals a blind man. The disciples express their opposition, show their lack of understanding and tell the blind man to be silent. **Jerusalem** is the first city to be mentioned in the "journey narrative". There are more detailed locations in this last part of the journey narrative which could be a literary device to show that a key moment draws near. Other references to localities are: 1) 19:1 Jesus enters **Jericho** and was passing through. 2) 19:29 "When He drew near to **Bethphage and Bethany**." 3) 19:37 "As He was drawing near, at the descent of the **Mount of Olives**…" 4) 19:41 And when **He drew near** and saw the city He wept over it. 5) 19:45 And He entered the **Temple** and began to drive out those who sold. 6) 19:1 Luke says Jesus entered **Jericho** and was passing through. In Jericho Jesus meets Zacchaeus and goes to stay at his house. Jericho was also the centre of the balsam trade. Other journey references are 18 :31,35; 19:1,4, 5, 7, 9, 10.	18:35-43 19:1-9 19:29 19:37 19:41	This incident is part of the travel narrative and is a climax in the ministry of Jesus. Luke is telling us that Jesus is on a journey. Do you think that this incident is a "personal legend"? Dibelius **(28)** says, "the material is full of anecdotes which are important for the narrative." Mark and Matthew have the healing of blind Bartimaeus as Jesus leaves Jericho but Luke has it on entering. Mk. 10:46 says that Jesus came to Jericho and as He was **leaving Jericho**, He heals blind Bartimaeus but in Luke 19:1 He entered and was passing through Jericho. This could be a literary device to show that Jesus was on His way to Jerusalem. Another approach is to translate "draw near" (Gk.engizo) as "to be in the vicinity of" rather than "to draw near to". [18:35] The NIV has approached, "As Jesus approached Jericho, a blind man was sitting by the roadside begging."(18:35) (NIV) (Porter) **(29)** Another solution is the possibility of two Jerichos though we only know of one in the first-century. Matthew has two blind men healed (Matt.9:27). This could be due to the fact he was writing for Jews who required two witnesses. Luke was writing for Gentiles therefore he includes one witness (18:35). Jericho was approx. twenty kilometres away from Jerusalem and it was an important customs station for travellers between Judea and lands east of the Jordan. [See map p.110.]
21	Near to **Bethphage and Bethany** Jesus tells his disciples to go to a nearby village and prepare for His entry into Jerusalem.	19:28-30	Both villages were two miles east of Jerusalem. Jesus starts to direct events as He nears Jerusalem. These events are part of God's plan and Jesus is the centre of that plan. What was the destruction that came upon Jerusalem which Jesus had predicted?

	Place	Ref.	Comment
E	**Jesus' ministry around Jerusalem**		
22	And as He spoke of the **Temple** how it was adorned with noble stones and offerings, He said, "As for these things the time (Gk.kairos) will come when there will not be left here one stone upon another that shall not be thrown down."	21:5-38	The building of the **Temple** had started in 30 B.C. and continued until A.D. 63-64. The building programme would have been well under way in A.D.33 when Jesus spoke. (Tacitus) **(30)**
23	a) "The days will come" is an expression unique to Luke and indicates a prediction.	21:6	The "time" (Gk. kairos) is a key part of God's plan.
	b) "Do not be led astray;" by Messianic pretenders who say, 'I am He!' and, 'the time (Gk. kairos) is at hand!' "Do not go after them."	21:8	The disciples will need discernment not to be taken in by false Messianic claims.
	c) Great distress will come upon **Jerusalem** as it is besieged. God's judgement will continue upon Israel until the times (Gk. kairoi) of the Gentiles are fulfilled.	21:24	Jerusalem remains trodden until the "a special time of visitation and a period of Gentile rule. "
F	**Passion, Death and Resurrection**	**Chs. 22-24**	
24	Jesus is crucified in **Jerusalem** at a place called **The Skull**.	23:33	**At the place of the skull** (Gk.Kranion Topos) Jesus is crucified. Why was it given this name? Luke does not use the Semitic name Golgotha as in Mk.15:22.
25	The women, who came **from Galilee,** on going to the tomb to take the prepared spices, discover that the **tomb in Jerusalem** is empty.	24:3	Since the women were from Galilee why does Luke not have resurrection appearances in Galilee?
26	Jesus appears to two people on the way to **Emmaus** a village seven miles from Jerusalem.	24:13	Where does Luke end his Gospel and what is the significance of this?

[4] Luke as a historiographer: a study of the writing of history.

A) Luke shows in the prologue that he is interested in events rather than in a person or people "the things of which you (Theophilus) have been informed." (1:4)

B) He uses records based upon genealogy (3:23-38). Luke's use of this approach was also common among Greek and Jewish historians and there is evidence from remote tribes in China today.(Hattaway) **(31)** Luke records Jesus' ancestors and shows that Jesus' age at the start of His ministry was "about thirty years." (3:23) Luke presents this as a legal line and also shows that Jesus' "regal right" as heir to rule goes back to King David and he goes back to Adam who represents all humanity and shows Jesus' national promise and hope.

C) He uses speeches and drama as in Jesus' rejection at Nazareth (4:16-30) and uses meals to instruct (5:27-39; 14:1-24; 22:14-28). He uses travel narratives (9:51-19:48) and provides chronological notes about the pregnancy of Elizabeth.

- Elizabeth remained in seclusion in her **fifth month** (1:24).
- The angel Gabriel was sent to Elizabeth in her **sixth month** (1:26).
- Mary stayed with Elizabeth for about **three months** (1:56).
- **After eight days,** Luke points that Jesus was circumcised (2:21).

D) All these points show that Luke is concerned about historical detail and has an interest in chronology in the infancy narratives.

Pupil's Activity: Twelve

What is historiography? What evidence is there to suggest that Luke had an interest in historiography?

Luke was the Evangelist with the interest in theology and history. (Marshall) (32)

[5] Luke as a writer of "Theological History"

A) Luke was the evangelist with the interest in theology and history. (Marshall) **(32)** says in the use of his sources "we find him **trustworthy**." He uses a word like truth (1:4) (Gk.asphaleian) truth or trustworthiness. This word in Greek appears at the end of the sentence for emphasis. Luke wants Theophilus to be certain of the **truth** of the teaching. (Bock)**(33)**

B) He rearranges his material for **emphasis** and **summarises** events in his own language. He writes as a **theologian** and **pastor** but is influenced by the history that preceded him. (Bock)**(34)**

C) He is **both a historian and a theologian** and the best term to describe him is "an evangelist" which includes both of these. (Marshall)**(35)** Marshall goes on to say that Luke was not recording facts from the past for their own sake nor did he re-write theological facts in the guise of history but he wanted to show that the message about Jesus was based upon historical fact. Luke used his history to serve his theology.

D) "We cannot see Jesus as He was but only as Matthew Mark and Luke etc. saw Him." "Gospel writers had a great regard for history and theology." (Morris) **(36)** There is widespread recognition that Luke is a reliable historian. His theological purpose is real and his theology does not run away with his history. "To underemphasize any element in the Lucan effort, whether pastoral, theological, or historical, is to underestimate the depth of his account." (Bock) **(37)**

E) He writes very good Greek and was very familiar with all the great figures of the early Church through his close association with the apostle Paul. While imprisoned in Caesarea, he took the opportunity to redeem the time by study and research (1:1).[See p.10.] Barratt **(38)** sees Luke "not as a historian of the modern scientific kind.... but a historian of the Hellenistic Age": interested in things other than facts. "He gives more than the human testimony to Jesus. This is not carelessness with the truth but that the facts are given in fulfilment of their own religious and theological purpose." (Morris) **(39)** "Efforts to argue that Luke is exclusively either a theologian or a historian, with many opting to give history a lesser place, underplay the evidence in sources that show Luke is careful with his material. He is not careless nor is he a fabricator of events." (Bock) **(40)**

F) The historical situation in John's time   (3:1-2a) [See p. 58.]   **(Figure 6)**

• It is possible to date the start of John's ministry to A.D. 28-29 as it was in the 15th year of Tiberius Caesar, who ruled from a distance, while the real governors were those under him and took over from Augustus his stepfather in A.D.14.

• Pontius Pilate was the governor of Judea and Herod was the tetrarch of Galilee and came under the control of the senate in Rome. Pilate was only a prefect of lesser rank than a legate who ruled over a larger area of Herod's empire.

• Philip his brother was the tetrarch of Ituraea and Trachonitis (3:2).

• Lysanias was the tetrarch of Abilene. Did Luke make a historical blunder? There is evidence to show today that there was more than one Lysanias e.g. one who lived in the time of Tiberias. (Marshall) **(41)**

• The singular is used for priesthood (Gk.archiereos) to denote power sharing between Annas and Caiaphas, with Annas having more clout behind the scenes. Caiaphas was the formal high priest at this time and Annas had been high priest from 6-15 A.D. but now he is patriarch to the high priest. (Josephus)**(42)** Religious authority was shared between the two men with Annas exercising great power. The title high priest could be an official title for life or life peer like a Lord in the House of Lords today at Westminster. Luke gives us an insight to the religious power structure in Jerusalem and in Judaism at that time.

• This is the use of synchronic dating: these are events which are significantly related but with no causal connection. (Bock) **(43)** [See p.62.]

• The data shows Luke's concern for history and we can place the date as A.D.29 when the word of God came to the prophet John the son of Zechariah (3:2).

• The historical setting in Luke also shows the author's universal outlook.

• It is probably that Luke used a Roman or Julian calendar approach in figuring the 15th year of Tiberias' reign dating it from the 1st of January. * The period August –1st January 15 would be an accession year and not the actual year of Tiberias' reign therefore John came to public view from sometime in late summer to the autumn of A.D. 29 when he was thirty years of age (3:23). "When John began his ministry, he was about thirty years of age." It would seem that the ministry of John and that of Jesus spanned about a five-year period. (Bock) **(44)**

* Note: the Romans reckoned regnal years from the 1st January.

G) John the Baptist's ministry   (3:3b)   **(Figure 7)**

He [John] went into all the region about the Jordan, preaching a baptism of repentance for the forgiveness of sins.

H) Old Testament hope: an O.T. example of synchronic dating 3: 4-6   **(Figure 8)**
The use of O.T. dating is used: the call of the prophet is put alongside the rulers who governed at this time (Jer. 1:1-3; Is. 1:1; Amos 1:1). "The words of Amos, who was among the shepherds of Tekoa, which he saw concerning Israel in the days of Uzziah king of Judah and in the days of Jeroboam son of Joash, king of Israel, two years before the earthquake."

[6A] Summary of Luke as a teacher [See pp. 35-36.]
•He wrote to instruct Christians in their faith, intending his readers to comprehend key expressions like Son of Man, Kingdom of God the meaning of which he does not explain.
•He includes teaching words like "instruct" (NIV; AV) or inform (RSV) (Gk.katechethes) in which Theophilus had been taught the faith (1:4). It could mean formal church teaching (1:1NRSV; Gal. 6:6). This would suggest Luke had a teaching role as a purpose in writing his Gospel. He uses other teaching words such as "watchfulness" and "faithfulness" in the parable of the shrewd manager and "the children of this generation have more understanding than the children of light." (16:1-10) He uses meals "to instruct". Jesus dines with Levi (5:27-39); Jesus dines with a Pharisee (14:1-24); Luke was aware of Greco-Roman culture which encouraged an open "Symposia" tradition, a drinking and talking party which followed a formal banquet. Jesus reclines at a table of the Pharisees (14:7-11). [See p.240.] At the Lord's Supper (22:14-28) Jesus has specific instructions for believers, "Do this in remembrance of me." (22:19 margin)
• The life of the disciple is to be one of obedience (17:7-10). Luke recognised Jesus as Lord (11:39).
• He speaks of "wisdom's children." (7:35) Luke has a fondness for fours (14:12-14).
• Luke wanted Theophilus to be certain about the truth of the Gospel (1:4).
• Luke wrote in an "orderly" way with a key theme "the way." (1:3) His detail is meticulous.

B) Luke as a pastor
• He is like a pastor comforting a believer under siege by the world, so Luke wishes to encourage his readers.
• Theophilus may well be asking, "Is Christianity what I believed it to be, a religion sent from God?"
• Whether it is internal doubt, persecution or racial tension with the Jews that has caused this question to be raised, Luke invites his readers to consider the story of Jesus again and know that these indeed were events that "have been fulfilled among us." (1:1)

• He wants people to recognise what Theophilus already knows; namely that this Jesus is the Son of God, the Saviour of the world, the fulfilment of all God's purposes for the world He made (1:32,47).
• As a pastor, Theophilus could be experiencing doubts whether he belongs to this racially mixed and greatly persecuted community.
• He has a deep concern for individuals. [See p. 46.]
• Luke does not write specifically for Theophilus but for any one who shared the tension between Jew and Gentile. Any Jew or Jewish Christian troubled by the lack of Jewish response to the gospel or the openness with which the Gentiles were welcomed into it, could see how God had given the nation many invitations to join His renewed work.
• In 6:18, Luke shows his sympathy and compassion: people are "distressed with evil spirits." This is Luke's unique description (L). [See pp. 46, 189.]

C) Luke as a historian [See pp. 5, 36, 59.]
• He wants his readers to be certain about the truth of the gospel teachings the readers had been taught.
• He uses such terms as "carefully", "everything", "from the beginning", and "orderly account" to describe Luke's qualities as any historian would be proud to have included in an assessment of their work (1:1-4).
• He argues for the accuracy of his work by pointing to the direct link between his Gospel and the testimony of the eyewitnesses (1:2) and by referring to his investigation of various written accounts (1:2). This can be seen in the description of the settings, customs and locales which show a concern for accuracy.
• Luke establishes his credentials as a historian in his prologue by showing his care and expertise in writing.
• To underemphasize any element in Luke's enterprise whether pastoral, theological or historical is to underestimate the depth of his writing. Luke uses summary notes as a "bridge passage" (4:14-15). [See p.64.]

Pupil's Activity: Thirteen
a) How does Luke show that he has a keen interest in history and theology?
b) How does Luke show that the message of Jesus was based upon historical fact?
c) Comment on the claim that Luke is both a teacher and a historian. Justify your answer.
(CCEA A/S 2003/2004) [15 marks]
d) Explore the claim that in writing this Gospel, Luke was faithful in his role as a historian. (CCEA A/S 2003 Resit) [15 marks]

Pupil's Activity: Fourteen
From the example below (Figure 4) show how Luke placed John the Baptist's ministry "like a beautiful frame bracketed

Outcomes

Students should have a knowledge and understanding of:
- **Luke the historian, theologian, evangelist, teacher and pastor.**
- **ancient history and historiography regarding Luke as a writer.**
- **different types of history such as narrative history, 'empire history', theological history as exemplified in Luke's Gospel.**

Notes on Ch.6: The Role of Luke as a Historian

1. H.W. Hoehner, Article on Chronology, DJB, IVP, (1992) p.122.

2. Earle. E. Ellis, The Gospel of Luke, New Century Bible, MMS, (1974) p. 243.

3. Howard Marshall, H and T, Paternoster Press, (1970) p.184.

4. Donald A. Carson, The Expositor's Bible, Vol. 8: Matthew, Grand Rapids: Zondervan (1984) p.5. "There have been greater number of deaths – six millions in the Nazi death camps, mainly Jews, and an estimated twenty million under Stalin, but never so high a percentage of a great city's population so thoroughly and painfully exterminated and enslaved as during the Fall of Jerusalem."

5. W .C. van Unnick, Studies in Luke/Acts pp. 15-32 cited in Marshall, H and T, Paternoster Press, (1970) p.13.

6. Hengel and Hammer, cited in Bock, Article: Gospel Luke in DJG, IVP, (1992) p.498.

7. Sir William M. Ramsay, A Study on the Credibility of Luke: London, Hodder and Stoughton, (1898) p.222.

8. Darrell L. Bock, op. cit. Vol. 1, p.13.

9. Sir William Ramsay quotes from Lucian "How to write history." p.56.

10. Craig Blomberg, Jesus and the Gospels, "empire history", Apollos, IVP, (1997) p.142.*

11. Lucian, (ibid.) Sir William M. Ramsay op. cit.p.56.

12. Scot McKnight, Who is Jesus? An Introduction to Jesus : Studies in Jesus under Fire, pp.61-62.

13. Craig Blomberg, op. cit. p.294 cites Josephus, Jewish Antiquities , 18.3.1-2; 18.4. 1-2.

14. H.W. Hoehner, op. cit.p.122.

15. E. Schurer, A History of the Jewish People, 170 B.C.-A.D.135 Edinburgh: Clarke (Revised 1973-87) (2.301-303).

16. Darrell Bock, op. cit. Vol. 1, Excursus 2, p. 909.

17. E. Schurer, op. cit. History 1.567-569.

18. Hans Conzelmann, The Theology of Saint Luke, Fortress Press, (1961).

19. Joseph A. Fitzmyer, op. cit. p. 424.

20. Josephus, Life, op. cit 65¶354.

21. Strack and Billerbeck, Commentary on N.T. with Talmud and Midrash, KNT aus Talmud und Midrash, 2 (1922-28) 2:141-42

22. W. Preisker, TDNT, 2: 273.

23. Strack and Billerbeck, op. cit. pp. 148-49.

24. Karl Heinrich Rengstorf, TDNT, 4:435.

25. Howard Marshall, op. cit. p.175.

26. Darrell Bock, op. cit. Vol. 1 p. 421.

27. U. Wegner, Luke 7:1-10, WUZNT, 2/14, Tubingen: Mohr, p. 63.

28. Martin Dibelius, Studies in Acts, SCM Press, (1956) p.115 .

29. Stanley E. Porter, "In the Vicinity of Jericho: Luke 18:35 Bulletin for Biblical Research 2: (1992) pp. 91-104.

30. Tacitus, Annals, History 5.8.1. describes the Temple in Jerusalem as "a snow clad mountain looming over the city."

31. Paul Hattaway, Operation China, OM. (1999) p. 133 e.g. The Enipu who cannot read but can recite their genealogies and family trees, consider it a disgrace to make mistakes in one's genealogy and an insult to do it in another person's genealogy.

32. Howard Marshall, Historian and Theologian, cited in Vol. 1, Bock, p.13.

33. Darrell Bock, Luke, ECNT, Vol. 1, Baker, (1993) p.64.

34. Darrell Bock, op. cit. p. 498.

35. Howard Marshall, Historian and Theologian, op. cit. p.18.

36. Leon Morris, Luke, TNTC, IVP, (1970) p.30.

37. Darrell Bock, op. cit. p.14.

38. Charles Kingsley Barrett, cited in Morris p.34.

39. Leon Morris, op. cit. TNTC, p.35.

40. Darren Bock, op. cit. Vol. 1, p. 13.

41. Howard Marshall, H. and T. op. cit. p.134.

42. Josephus, Antiquities, 18.2.1 par 16. He also recorded the death of Herod the Great in 4 B.C. March-April. Ant.17,167,191; 14.487-490.

43. Darrell Bock, op. cit. Vol. 1 pp. 283-4.

44. Darrell Bock, op. cit. Vol. 1 p. 913.

* This book is highly recommended.

CCEA A/S and Edexcel A/S and aspects of A2

Luke uses words like "it is necessary" (4:43), "will be accomplished" (10:42) and "to determine" (22:22) to show God's design.

Targets:
• Identify the main sections of Luke's Gospel as in the narratives of infancy, Galilean ministry, journey, passion and resurrection.
• Recognise and identify the sub-themes within these sections, for example the titles for Jesus and His identity, Galilean ministry (nine sub-groups).
• Identify the general aspects of the structure of Luke's Gospel, for example an orderly, geographical and formal structure, time, place and movement as a basis for structure, a structure which follows sections of the O.T. (CCEA A/S).
• Identify the main events which relate to the Pharisees and Scribes, prayer and the Sabbath, (the nature of the Kingdom and praise Edexcel A/S).
• Identify key concepts, for example middle or central section, journey narrative, predictions of suffering, and chiastic patterns.

The General Structure of Luke's Gospel
Introduction
A general structure is like examining the framework of the human body to see how the bones and sections of the human skeleton fit together or like using a camera with a panoramic view to provide a bird's eye view of the scenery. Here is a diagram of Luke's Gospel showing the framework or a general structure to give a bird's eye view of the contents.

[1] Structure of Luke's Gospel: a bird's eye view of Luke's Gospel   (Figure 1)

The Beginning		Galilean ministry	From Galilee to Judea	Jesus in Jerusalem	Passion/ Resurrection
Birth and early years	Baptism and temptation	• Call of the disciples (Ch.5) • Early ministry in Galilee and teaching • Sermon on Plain (Ch.6) • Missions, miracles, Peter's confession (Chs.7- 9)	• Mission of the 70 (72) • Sayings and events • Parables /discipleship	• Arrest and trials	• Passion Narrative • Resurrection Narratives in Jerusalem
30 years		(3-5 years) →	Middle-Central	End (1 week)	End (3 days)
Section 1	Section 2	Section 3	Section 4	Section 5	Section 6
Chs.1-2	Chs. 3:1-4:13	Chs. 4:14-9:50	Chs.9: 51-19:48	Chs.20 -21:38	Chs. 22-24
Birth Narratives	Introduction to the Ministry of Jesus	Jesus in Galilee	Journey Narrative to Jerusalem	Jesus' Ministry around Jerusalem	Passion Narratives and Resurrection

A) General aspects of the structure of Luke's Gospel: the Third Gospel like most other books has a beginning (thirty years), a middle (three years or five?) and an ending (one week). Like Mark and Matthew, Luke's order of events is broadly the same. As noted in the sources section, Luke follows Mark's sequence more faithfully than does Matthew. Even though Luke has the same general framework as Matthew and Mark, he has his own characteristic variations, for example he has a preference for pairs: Elizabeth and Mary, Simeon and Anna, Jesus and John the Baptist. Luke has given much thought to the shape of his Gospel and his events have a special order with selected stories, events and sayings from the life of Jesus, aimed at showing who Jesus really is. [See p. 229.]

B) Orderly structure: Luke divides his Gospel into small thematic units and each section divides into many smaller units. Unlike the other Gospel writers, Luke also wrote a sequel to his Gospel: The Acts of the Apostles. He says that his purpose was to write an "orderly account" so we (the readers) can anticipate a narrative written in an orderly structure (1:3).

C) Expressions used to provide a structure: a number of passages in Luke include the expression "it is necessary", "I must", "ought". "I must be in my Father's house." (2:49)
• "I must preach the good news of the kingdom to the other cities." (4:43)
• "The Son of Man must suffer many things and be rejected by the elders." (9:22)
• Jesus said to the ruler of the synagogue, "Ought not this woman, a daughter of Abraham whom Satan had bound for eighteen years, be loosed from this bond on the Sabbath day?" Here the healing of the Jewess with the bent back is a moral necessity: in the same way as helping a trapped animal on the Sabbath (13:16). Does this show Jewish priority?

- Jesus said to the disciples, "This scripture must be fulfilled in me." and "He was numbered with the transgressors."
- "That the Son of Man must be delivered into the hands of sinful men, and be crucified and on the third day rise." (24:7)
- "Everything written about me in the law of Moses, and the prophets and the psalms must be fulfilled." Jesus comprehensively fulfils the O.T. law, prophets and writings (24:44).

> **Luke's infancy stories are much more detailed than Matthew's and he places particular significance upon the birth of John the Baptist.**

D) Other words used by Luke to show purpose and design: Luke uses other words to show God's design-"purpose" and "to determine" and "finish".
a) Jesus said to the Pharisees, "Go and tell that fox, 'Behold I cast out demons and perform cures today and tomorrow and the third day, I finish my course.' " (13:32)
b) "For the Son of Man goes as it has been determined," (Gk. horizo) and from which our word horizon comes (22:22). God's plan is at work and the events are destined (A.G.T.). **(1)**

[2A] Luke's more detailed account

1) His infancy stories are much more detailed than Matthew's and he places particular significance upon the birth of John the Baptist. John the Baptist is given a prominent position because his public ministry is linked with that of Jesus. All the events are part of a divine revelation; Luke presents John's birth and that of Jesus as miraculous.
2) God is at work in the history of Jesus and Luke links the two ministries of Jesus and John in his use of a six-fold dating (3:1). [See p. 62: the role of Luke as a historian.] Guthrie **(2)** suggests that the middle section should not in effect be called a journey as Luke may have fitted in material between the Galilean and the Judean ministries and prefers the title "From GalileSe to Judea." "Journey," as Guthrie says, tends to suggest a detailed route.
3) Luke in the Mary and Martha incident (10:38-42) gives us very little indication about the location of the event. He says that this incident takes place in the village and in the home of Mary and Martha but there is no reference to Bethany as Luke is not interested in giving detailed aspects of geography in this section (10:38). [See p. 65.]

B) A formal structure to Luke's Gospel: the views of scholars
There is considerable agreement among scholars that the structure of the overall Ministry of Jesus should be seen geographically. In recent years, interest has been shown in theories, which indicate a formal structure for the Third Gospel; items which have been included to mirror each other as in a "chiastic pattern" and those which follow the sections of the O.T. or comment on sections of the O.T. (Beck) **(3)** Beck is not happy with these conclusions and notes Luke's style of highlighting **time, place and movement** and the indication of **change in audience.**"
1) "In the meantime, when so many thousands of the multitudes had gathered together that they trod upon one another, He began to say to His disciples... ." (12:1)
2) One of the multitude said to Him, "Teacher, bid my brother divide the inheritance with me." (12:13)
3) Some expressions tie the two incidents together with a note of **time, sequence and audience:**
"In the same hour He rejoiced in the Holy Spirit." (10:21) Jesus' rejoicing is directed by the Holy Spirit. "While He was speaking, a Pharisee asked Him to dine with Him." (11:37)
4) A unit is sometimes introduced in a way which explains and gives guidance for interpretation. "As the people were in **expectation,** and all men questioned in their hearts concerning John, whether He was the Christ." This expression is used to introduce John's ministry (3:15). The people were "expecting" (Gk. prosdokaw) is a common expression in Luke and denotes a high level of expectancy about an event drawing near (1:21; 7:19-20; 8:40; 12:46).
5) Luke links two consecutive passages (5:30,33). The Pharisees and their scribes murmured against His disciples saying, "Why do you eat and drink with tax collectors and sinners?" (5:30) And they said to Him, "The disciples of John fast and offer prayers, and so do the disciples of the Pharisees, but yours eat and drink." Luke assumes that those who ask Jesus about praying and fasting in (5:33) are the same as those who grumble about His association with the marginalized, the tax collectors and sinners (5:30).

> **Luke divides his Gospel into small thematic units and each unit sub-divides into smaller units.**

Pupil's Activity: One
a) Compare the birth stories of John the Baptist with that of Jesus in Luke's Gospel.
b) What are the significant differences (Figure 2)?
c) Why do they follow a similar pattern?

> **Jesus' ministry around Galilee divides into nine sections : controversies, discipleship, obedience, journey, Jesus' identity, miracles, preaching and teaching, suffering and authority (4:14-9:50). (Blomberg) (14)**

Pupil's Activity: Two
For revision purposes draw a spidergram to show the general structure of Luke's Gospel.

C) Luke's preference for pairs: a comparison between the births of John the Baptist and Jesus (Figure 2)

The birth of John the Baptist	The birth of Jesus
1. Annunciation of birth in the Temple (1:5-25) a) Compare Zechariah's reception of the angel's message with that of Mary. b) What was Zechariah's response?	**1. Annunciation of the birth in Nazareth (1:26-38)** Mary's response: she is the faithful one (1:38). She sees the events and ponders their significance. She wrestles to comprehend the events. She is deeply familiar with the events, yet she struggles to understand their meaning.
2. Mary's visit to Elizabeth (1:39-45) a) Why did Mary leave in haste? b) How does Elizabeth interpret the significance of the movement of the foetus in her womb? "The fruit of the womb" is a Hebrew expression in which children were seen as a blessing from God and was related to faithful obedience to Him (Deut. 7:13; Lam. 2:20).	**2. Elizabeth greets and blesses Mary (1:39-45)** a) What aspects of Mary's character are revealed in this song? b) What can we learn from her example? c) How do we know that God was in control?
3. Birth (1:57-58) a) How does Luke draw attention to the time of birth (1:57)? b) What expression is used by Luke to show that God is performing His word (1:57)? "The time came for her to be delivered or the time of her birth being full," is an O.T. expression (Gen. 25:24). This is an example of a Semitic expression in the birth narratives (cf. 2:7). c) What were the circumstances of the birth of John? d) How does God magnify His mercy or show His mercy to Elizabeth (1:58)?	**3. Birth (2:1-7, 8-20)** a) In what ways did Mary and Joseph fulfil the Jewish laws (1:23, 57, 59; 2:22; Gen.17:11-12; Lev.12:3)? b) What similar expression is used in 2:6? c) What were the circumstances of Jesus' birth? d) What does the angel's message and the rejoicing of the heavenly host teach us? Luke shows how Jesus grew in developmental stages. 1) babe (RSV) (2:16) (Gk.brephos) 2) little child" though (RSV) has "child" (2:40) (Gk.paidion) 3) child (2:43) (Gk. pais) 4) The name Jesus (2:52)(Plummer) **(5)** [See also Ch.5: Characteristics-Children pp. 46-47.]

Pupil's Activity: Three [See p. 83.]
a) Complete the grid (Figure 2) based upon some suggestions by Lieu **(4)** by filling in the spaces and answering the questions.
b) Divide the class into five groups for a class presentation in powerpoint/acetate entitled "The births of Jesus and John", allowing five minutes for each presentation.
c) Provide a joint concluding slide. Number one has been completed for you.

> **The Journey Narrative, Galilee to Jerusalem has fourteen sub-divisions (9:51-19:48). (Marshall) (15) (Blomberg, Bock)**

Pupil's Activity: Four
a) What are some of the key themes which undergird Luke's Gospel?
b) Comment on the claim that Luke offers a full life story of Jesus. Justify your answer. [See Ch. 5: Characteristics of Luke's Gospel pp. 46-47.] (CCEA A/S Resit 2004)　　　[30 marks]

Pupil's Activity: Five
a) What is the "Journey Narrative"?
b) Identify the predictions about the sufferings of Jesus in the "Journey Narrative".
c) See if you can identify from the general outline a particular pattern towards the end of the "Journey Narrative".
d) Create a diagram to show the twelve different sub-sections in the "Journey Narrative".
[See Nos. 1-16 middle section pp. 77-78]

Pupil's Activity: Six
"The structure of the ministry of Jesus should be viewed geographically." Do you agree with this statement? Justify your answer.

The birth of John the Baptist	The birth of Jesus
4. Circumcision and naming of the child (1:59-66) This was in keeping with the Jewish law (Lev.12:3). a) How do we know that God was with John? b) What major role did John's parents play in this event (1:66)? All who heard about the events had a strong emotional reaction to them. "They laid them up in their hearts" is a Hebrew expression meaning "to take to heart" or put to memory and one which leaves a lasting impression upon them (1 Sam. 21:12; 2 Sam. 13:20; Mal. 2:2). The concern of the people is the role which John will have in God's plan. c) What (Gk.ti) then will this child be (1:66)? : what will John come to be?	**4. Circumcision and naming of the child (2:21)** a) Why do you think Jesus' parents are not mentioned? (Brown) **(6)** Compare "Mary she kept these things and pondered (Gk.sumballousa) them" means she "put the thoughts together as an understandable whole in her heart." (Bock) **(7)** She "mulled these matters" over in her mind: the revelation of God in Jesus (2:19, 51). b) How do the following people respond: (1) Mary (2:19)? (2) the people (2:17-18)? (3) the shepherds (2:20)? (4) What effect did it have on the shepherds (2:18)?
5. Inspired prophecy regarding the future of John in the Temple (1:68-79) a) According to Zechariah's song, what is the purpose of salvation?	**5. Inspired prophecy about Jesus' future in the Temple (2:25, 29-32, 38)** a) What was the effect of the coming of Jesus upon the different classes of people? b) What does the rise and fall of many in Israel mean (2:34)?
6. Growth (1:80) a) How did John grow up? b) Does this refer to human spirit? c) Why is John's growth recorded only once while that of Jesus is recorded on at least two occasions? **[See also Ch.8: Infancy Narratives.]**	**6. Growth (2:39-40)** a) Name four ways in which Jesus grew up. b) How did Jesus grow up in perception of God's will (2:41-52)? c) How does the story of (2:41-51) illustrate the truths of (2:40; 52)? d) Why does Luke provide additional events about Jesus compared with John? e) How far does Jesus later show a self-understanding of Himself as Messiah-Servant and the Son of God (2:41—50)?

Pupil's Activity: Seven

a) Explain the teaching of Jesus concerning Prayer and the Sabbath in Luke's Gospel.

(Edexcel A/2 2002)   [12 marks]   [See Ch. 5: Charactistics pp.47-51.]

b) "Jesus' teaching on prayer and the Sabbath was a radical departure from Jewish teaching at that time." Examine and evaluate this claim. (Edexcel A/2 2004 and 2005)   [20 marks]

c) Analyse the relationship between Jesus and the Religious Authorities as presented in Luke's Gospel.

(Edexcel A/2 2002)   [12 marks]

Occasions when Jesus dined and socialised with people

1 Jesus dines with Levi a tax collector   (5:29-32).

2 Jesus dines with a Pharisee (7:36-50).

3 Jesus dines with a Pharisee (9:10-17). '

4 Jesus stays with Mary and Martha (10:38-42).

5 Jesus dines with a Pharisee (11:37-54).

6 Jesus dines with a Pharisee (14:1-24).

7 Jesus dines with a chief tax collector (19:1-10).

8 Jesus dines with His disciples (22:7-38).

9 Jesus dines with two people on the road to Emmaus (24:29-32, 41-43).

Conclusion

• For Luke the key figure is the child, Jesus Christ the Lord, and not the powerful Roman ruler even though the event is set in Roman history (1:5; 2:1-2; 3:1-2).

• Jesus is superior to John (1:31-33).

• Heaven testifies to the shepherds who respond by going to see the child (2:10-12, 13-14, 17-18).

• Bystanders marvel at the event when Zechariah was writing the name John (1:63).

• Through the birth and in the person of Jesus, heaven (2:13-14) and earth come together (2:20).

• God is in control and His word has come to pass (1:15, 17, 38; 2:29; 3:2).

• Jesus' life is introduced by three titles:

1) Saviour, which means deliverer (1:47; 1:69; 2:11).

2) Messiah, which shows He is the promised anointed one of God 1:32,47, a Saviour who is Christ the Lord (2:11).

3) Lord, which shows his sovereign authority (2:11).

Key titles for Jesus in the Third Gospel (Figure 7) [See pp.140-1, 178-9.]

Titles	Meaning	Related biblical texts and comment
David's Son	This title denotes Jesus' Royal lineage and humanity. His destiny will be to receive from God the throne of His ancestor David.	"He will be great and will be called the Son of the Most High." (1:32) "He has raised up a horn of salvation for us in the house of his servant David (1:69; 18:38).
Lord	This is a **title** for Jesus. It was used to translate the O.T. name Yahweh for God: it means Sovereign Authority. This term is also used as a respectful way of addressing a person who is superior in wealth, position or authority. From 7:13ff it is Luke's way of referring to Jesus' main **character** (1:43, 76). This title is used 95 times out of 166 times in the Synoptics Gospels. It is used three times in the birth narratives. Jesus is "Lord" is His full deity (2:11; 2:26; Phil.2:11).	"For to you is born this day in the city of David a Saviour, who is Christ the Lord." (2:11) Peter calls Jesus "Lord," "Depart from me, for I am a sinful man O Lord." (5:8) "The Son of Man is Lord of the Sabbath." (6:5; 7:6-7,13,16) Throughout Luke/Acts there is a pervasive ambiguity in the use of the word "Lord" (Gk.Kurios) for God and Jesus, so that there is an identity between the bearers of the title that points in a Trinitarian direction. (Rowe) **(9)**
Messiah	This **title** refers to Jesus' office as God's Promised, Anointed One – Christ and it is a key thread running through Luke's Gospel. This title also denotes royalty (24:26,46).	Luke sees Jesus' Messiahship as a function of God's Son, rather than seeing Sonship as an aspect of Messiahship (1;32b-33,68-75; 2:11; 2:26; 3:15; 9:18-20; 23:2, 35,39). (Liefeld) **(10)**
Prophet	"The One who comes;" (3:15,17) Jesus is a counterpart to Elijah and Elisha. His activity fulfills the prophecies of the coming age of God's blessing (7:22; Is.35); Jesus' **role** can be seen as that of the end-time prophet like Moses, a messianic type of person. Hence Simon the Pharisee is wondering if Jesus is a prophet (7:39). (Marshall) **(8)**	"Truly I say to you no prophet is acceptable in his own country." (4:24) "A great prophet has risen among us!", "and God has visited his people!" (7:1, 22) "It cannot be that a prophet should perish away from Jerusalem." (13:33; 24:19,51) "Concerning Jesus of Nazareth who was a great prophet in word and deed before God and all the people." (24:19,51)
Saviour	This **title** means Deliverer from physical and spiritual danger. It sums up Jesus' humanity and compassion. It tells us about His **nature** (1:69 NRSV).	Mary sang, "My spirit rejoiced in God my Saviour." (1:47) "For to you is born this day in the city of David a Saviour, who is Christ the Lord." (2:11)
Son of God	Jesus, the Beloved Son is in a special Filial relationship with His heavenly Father. As the Divine Son He has Eternal Sovereignty with His Father. This **title** emphasises Jesus' **role** and His **nature**. He is the Son of the most High God. The title "Son of the Most High God" also shows His true nature. Jesus claims to be the Son of God. "You say that I am." (22:70) In the parable of the wicked tenants the owner of the vineyard said, "I will send my beloved son; it may be they will respect him." (20:13)[RSV] Sometimes Jesus is called "the Holy One of God." A voice from heaven said, "This is my Son, my Beloved; listen to Him (9:35 RSV marg. ; 22:66-70)!"	"The Holy One to be born will be called Son of God." This title is used proleptically; full revelation will be in the future. His Sonship relates to His Divine origin (1:32-35). His function as Son is that of a Messianic vocation. In 2:49, the expression "Father" expresses His Filial consciousness. In the temptations Satan says to him, "If you are the Son of God." Jesus is uniquely aware that God is His Father. He is "Son of the most High God." (8:28) (3:22; 4:3, 9, 41)
Son of Man	He is Divine and human with full authority. He is the One who serves, will suffer, and is exalted. At times this is Jesus' self-designated **title** for Himself, up until 7:34.	From 22:67, Jesus is the Son of Man who will be seated at the Father's right hand and on David's throne (22:69). From 12:8ff onwards this **title** is used of a Person who has a **role** in the last judgement.
Servant	This idea is found in (22:37) where Is.53:12 is quoted. "He was reckoned with the transgressors."	Jesus saw Himself in the **role** of the Servant, fulfilling this scripture.

[3] Aspects of Luke's Gospel seen as a chiasmus [See p. 89.]

A) The Temple visit viewed as a chiasmus.

Three key themes of Sonship, wisdom and infancy are presented as a chiasmus. This is the view of C.H. Talbert **(11)** who followed H. de Jonge. **(12) (Figure 3)**

A. Mary and Joseph go from Nazareth in Galilee to the Temple in Jerusalem (2:39, 41-2). (infancy)
    B. Jesus stays in Jerusalem unnoticed (2:43). (sonship)
        C. Jesus' parents seek and find Him (2:44-46a).
            D. Jesus among the teachers (2:46b-47) (wisdom)
        C. Jesus' parents show their annoyance and reproach Him (2:48). (wisdom)
    B. Jesus' reaction which is not understood (2:49-50) (sonship)
A. Mary, Joseph and Jesus return to Nazareth (2:51a) (infancy)

B) The Benedictus as a chiasmus (1:68-79):

part 1 A B C D - the Messiah (1:68-71)
the centre E-the mercy promised to our forefathers (1:72-73) and
part 2 D C B A - the child John. (1:76-79) [See Ch. 8: Infancy Narratives p.89.]
Stein **(13)** and Brown **(14)** divide the Benedictus into four parts: [See pp. 88-89.]
(1) narrative introduction (1:67)
(2) the opening praise (1:68a)
(3) the hymn itself (68b-79) divided into two parts (1:68b-75, 76-79)
(4) the conclusion (1:80)

C) The structure of Luke/Acts viewed as a chiasmus (Wolfe) (15)
The contrast by parallelism is in reverse order. (Figure 4)

A. The Birth of Jesus seen in the context of world history and Roman rule (Chs. 1-3).
    B. Jesus in Galilee (Luke Chs. 4-9)
        C. Jesus in Samaria and Judea (Luke Chs. 9-18)
            D. Jesus in Jerusalem (Luke Chs.19-23)
                E. Resurrection and Ascension (Luke Chs. 24)
            D. Church in Jerusalem (Acts Chs.1-7)
        C. In Judea and Samaria (Acts Chs.8-12)
    B. Throughout the Gentile world (Acts Chs. 12-28)
A. Paul preaches the gospel as far as Rome (Acts Ch.28).

D) Liefeld's view of key events in the Journey Narrative (9:51-19:48) as a chiasmus (Figure 5)

A. Eternal life-the lawyer asks Jesus about eternal life, "Teacher, what must I do to inherit eternal life?"	(10:25-42)
B. The disciples' prayer –"Lord teach us to pray!"	(11:1-4)
C. Healing miracle-a mute man possessed of an evil spirit	(11:14-23)
D. Hypocrisy of the Pharisees-controversy over washing before a meal	(11:37-41)
E. Money-the parable of the rich fool	(12:10)
F. Repentance-an unforgiven sin	(13:1-9)
G. Rejection of Israel and invitation to the outcasts-the crippled women	(13:10-17)
G. Rejection of Israel and invitation to the outcasts-the man with dropsy	(14:1-6)
F. Repentance-Pharisees object to Jesus receiving sinners - three parables on God's love	(15:1-2,3-32)
E. Money- the parable of the unjust or crafty steward	(16:1-9)
D. Hypocrisy of the Pharisees who were lovers of money (16:14)	(16:14-31)
C. Healing miracle- the ten lepers – the Samaritan leper who returned to give thanks	(17:11-19)
B. Prayer- the parable of the tax collector and the Pharisee	(18:9-14)
A. Eternal life - the rich ruler, "Good teacher, what shall I do to inherit eternal life?"	(18:18-30)

Pupil's Activity: Seven

As an aid to memory set out the Benedictus as a chiasmus. Check your answer in Ch. 8: Infancy Narrative. [See p.89.]

Pupil's Activity: Eight

On the map provided find the following places and write two sentences to explain their significance: [See map Ch.9 John the Baptist.] Bethany, Gergesa, Galilee, Nazareth, Capernaum, Nain and Caesarea Philippi.

Pupil's Activity: Nine

a) What is the journey narrative?
b) Identify the predictions about the sufferings of Jesus in the journey narrative.
c) Create a diagram to show the different sub-sections in the journey narrative.

[4] A detailed outline of the structure of Luke's Gospel   (Figure 6)

The Beginning Section [1]	Beginning Section [2]	Beginning Section [3]

The Beginning Section [1]

[1A] Preface (1:1-4)
Other accounts (1:1)
Sources of the accounts (1:2)
Luke's method of composition (1:3)
Luke's purpose in writing (1:4)

[1B] Infancy Narratives:
forerunner and fulfilment (1:5 – 2:52)
Introduction to John the Baptist and Jesus (Ch.1)

a. John the Baptist's birth foretold in Jerusalem (1:5-25) - the angel's announcement to Zechariah (1:11-25)

b. The announcement to Mary in Nazareth (1:26-38)

c. Mary's visit to Elizabeth in the Judean Hills (1:39-56).

d. Mary praises God -The Magnificat (1:46-56)

e. The birth of John (1:57-66) John's birth accompanied by joy (1:57-66); circumcision (1:59-66)

f. Zechariah praises God – The Benedictus (1:67-79)

g. Praise for Messianic deliverance (1:67-75)

h. Prophecy about Jesus and John (1:76-79)

i. John's birth in Judea (1:57-80) John's growth (1:80)

[1C] Birth of Jesus (2:1-2:52)

a. Reaction to the birth of Jesus (2:8-21)

b. Jesus' birth in Bethlehem. (2:1-20) The angels' Song (2:13-14)

c. The presentation of Jesus in the Temple in Jerusalem: (2:21-40), Simeon's Song (2:28-29), the return to Nazareth in Galilee (2:39-40), the witness of Anna (2:36-38).

[1D] Jesus' revelation of his self-understanding
Jesus in Jerusalem aged twelve. (2: 41-52)

Beginning Section [2]

[2] Introduction to Jesus' Ministry and Preparation for Jesus' Ministry: anointed by God (3:1-4:13).

[2A] John the Baptist-the forerunner (3:1-20)

a. John's ministry (3:1-6)

b. The preaching of John (3:7-14)
 - judgement and a call to repentance (3:7-9)
 - the genuine fruit of repentance (3:10-14)
 - for the crowd (3:10-14)
 - for the tax collectors (3:12-13)
 - for the soldiers (3:14)

c. The promise of John the Baptist (3:15-18)

d. John preaches the good news (3:18).

e. The imprisonment of John (3:19-20)

[2B] Jesus the one who comes after (3:21-4:13)

a. The baptism of Jesus (3:21-22)

b. The genealogy of Jesus: son of Adam, son of God (3:23-38).

c. Messianic preparation: resistance of Satan, the temptations (4:1-12), Satan departs (4:13).
1. The setting (4:1-2)
2. Temptation of bread and God's care (4:3-4)
3. Temptation of rule and false worship 4:5-8
4. Temptation to test God's protection 4:9-12

Beginning Section [3]

[3] Jesus' ministry around Galilee divided into 9 sections (4:14-9:50).

1) Mission and Journey (4:14-44)
a. Galilean ministry (summary) (4:14-15)

a. Nazareth preaching (4:16-30)
b. Teaching in the synagogue at Capernaum on the Sabbath (4:31-32).

2) Healings in Capernaum(4:31-44)
a. The 1st miracle in Galilee : the possessed man on the Sabbath (4:33-37).
b. The 2 miracle in Galilee: Peter's mother-in-law (4:38-39)
c. The first summary of the miracles (4:40-41)
d. Departure from Capernaum (4:42-43)
e. Preaching in Judea (summary) (4:44)

3) The calling of the first disciples
Peter is commissioned (5:1-11)
a. The 3rd miracle : the catch of fish (5:1-11)

b. The 4th miracle: the leper on the Sabbath (5:12-16)
c. The 5th miracle: healing the paralysed man

4) Controversies with the Jewish leaders over eating and drinking with sinners, fasting, Sabbath, healing on the Sabbath, Jesus dines with Levi (27-28)
a. Jesus is Lord of the Sabbath (5:29-6:11).
b. The unshrunk cloth/wine skins (5:33-39)

5) The formal call to discipleship (6:12-49) a. calling the Twelve (6:12-16)
b. Sermon on the Plain (6:17-49)
c. The parable of the two builders (6:47-49)
d. The second summary of the miracles (6:17-19)

6) Focus on the identity of Jesus:
a. (7:1-8:3) a. the Centurion's servant b. the widow's son c. envoys from John (7:18-23)
d. The third summary of the miracles, (7:18-23)
e. The Pharisees reject God's purpose for themselves, (7:30) f) Jesus dines with Simon the Pharisee/ a woman anoints His head. (7:36-50)
f. The parable of the complaining children (7:41ff)
g. The parable of the two debtors (7:41-43)
h. The fourth summary of the miracles (8:2-3)
i. The women who ministered to Jesus (8:1-3)

7) Obedience: hearing the word of God correctly (8:4-21)
a) the parable of the sower, (8:4-15)
b) call to respond to the light (8:16-18),
c) the true family of Jesus (8:19-21).

8) The authority of Jesus (8:22-56)
a. **Authority** over nature, stilling the storm (8: 22-25)
b. **Authority** over demons/Gerasene demoniac (8:26-ff)
c. **Authority** over disease and death – the woman with the flow of blood and Jairus' daughter (8:40-56)

9) The climax as to who is Jesus (9:1-50):
a. commissioned authority revealed (9:1-50),
b. the Twelve, discipleship, mission (9:1-9),
c. **Authority** to provide: feeding the 5,000 (9:10-17),
d. Peter's confession (9:18-20),
e. the Transfiguration (9:28-36),
f. the demon possessed boy (9:37-43).

The Beginning Section [1]	Beginning Section [2]	Beginning Section [3]
Comments on the infancy narratives (1:5- 2:52):	**Comments on the introduction to Jesus' Ministry (3:1-4:13)**	**Comments on Jesus' Ministry around Galilee (4:14-9:50)**
• Luke writes an "orderly account". (1:3)	**This section presents Jesus as:**	Ellis (16) says this section (4:31-9:50) has twenty episodes arranged in groups of six. Blomberg arranges them in nine groups as above. (17)
• he brings out the miraculous aspect of the birth of Jesus.	• God's intervention in history (3:10-14) and in (3:6) "All flesh shall see the salvation of God." This quote from Is. 61:1-2 is found only in Luke's Gospel.	• Trying to subdivide Luke's Gospel is more difficult than it first seems. It is likely that Luke grouped his material in small themes. [See colour code.]
• John the Baptist acts as the forerunner while Jesus is the fulfilment of the Old Testament prophecies .	• God's anointed,	• There are two predictons of the passion of Jesus in this section.
• John is like Elijah while Jesus has more of a Davidic role.	• a representative of humanity,	
• John is great as a prophet but Jesus is the Great Messiah, Servant, Son, the promised Davidic ruler.	• One who is faithful to God,	**First prediction of Jesus' suffering, rejection, by the elders and predicton of His death and resurrection (9:21-22)**
• the superiority of Jesus to John the Baptist is seen in Luke Chs. 1-2.	• John and Jesus remain side by side as Jesus prepares for his Ministry.	**Second prediction of His suffering and the betrayal (9:43b-44) - the disciples fail to understand (9:45).**
• He has a unique link with the Father	• John is "the one who goes before" 3:1-6 and Jesus is "the One who comes." (3: 15-17)	
• He will cause pain to Mary (2:35).	• John baptises Jesus.	• Jesus' Ministry is funded by some "well heeled" women who travelled with Him and His disciples! (8:1-3)
• He is Sovereign (2:49).	• in the genealogy (3:23-28), Jesus is presented as the Son of Adam and Son of God.	• This section emphasises: the activity and power of Jesus, O.T. fulfilment, teaching and miracles to answer the question, "Who is Jesus?" The answer is in Peter's reply to Jesus. He is the Promised Messiah who has power over nature, demons, disease and death and has been called to suffer (9:20).
• the four hymns sung by Mary, Zechariah, the angels, and Simeon are like four Christmas carols.	• He overcomes temptation which the first Adam failed to do.	
• In Luke the birth stories are told from Mary's perspective.	• Abraham's seed points to the promise made to Abraham.	
	• salvation is the product of God's design and the object of His plans.	
The two themes of these two chapters are:-	• the key names in Jesus' genealogy are David, Abraham, Adam, Son of God.	
1. Old Testament fulfilment and 2. God in control. These ideas continue throughout the Gospel	• Jesus is identified with the human race in His genealogy in the title Son of Adam.	• For the disciples there is no glory without suffering and to follow Jesus means rejection by others. The disciples are to love their enemies, pray for them and serve others. v.27
	• in His baptism, Jesus is confirmed as the Messiah-Servant.	• Jewish opposition to Jesus' claims arise from:
	• Jesus possesses the correct roots to be the promised agent of God.	1. His power to forgive sins (5:24).
(Continued in the next column 3:1) [See page 76.]		2. His association with sinners (7:37).
	(Continued in the next column 4:14) [See page 76.]	3. His claim to be God's anointed (9:20).
		4. His claim to have divine authority. These claims were too much for the Jewish leaders.
		(Continued in the column below 9:51) [See page 78.]

Colour Code for the sections and sub-sections based upon nine themes in Luke's Gospel in the Galilean Ministry (4:14-9:50) **(Figure 6)**

1. Controversies		4. Journey		7. Preaching and teaching	
2. Discipleship		5. Jesus' Identity		8. Suffering	
3. Obedience		6. Miracles		9. Authority	

Middle or Central Section [4]	End Section [5]	End Section [6]
[4] Journey narrative Galilee to Jerusalem (9:51-19:48) Jerusalem journey/Jesus' teaching on the way to Jerusalem-The theme - "listen to Jesus"/ discipleship with fourteen subdivisions (Marshall, **(18)** Blomberg and Bock. [Bock] **(19)**	**[5] The final week in Jerusalem (20:1-21:38) A] Jesus' teaching during the final week in the Temple (20:1-21:4)**	**[6] Passion, death and resurrection (22:1-24:53)**
1. Discipleship, eyeing the cross (9:51-62) a) Jesus and the Samaritans – the cost of discipleship (9:54-10:37)	**Five controversies between Jesus and the Jewish leaders: (20:1-44) 1. Authority challenged, the source of Jesus' authority (20:1-8)**	**A] The Passover (22:1-71)** a. The preparation for the last supper (22:1-13)
The Journey idea (9:51, 53, 58)	**2. Parable of the wicked husbandmen: warning about rejecting the Son of Man (20:9-19)**	b. The last supper (22:14-20)
2. Mission of the seventy (two) (10:1-24)	**3. The Pharisees raise the question of tribute to Caesar. (20:20-26)**	c. Betrayal (22:21-23)
3. Double love command: a) love, God and your neighbour (10:25-42). b. Good Samaritan (10:25-57) c. God the Gracious Father	**4. The Sadducees raise a trick question about the resurrection and seven husbands "levirate marriage" (20:28,28-33). Jesus' authority is questioned (20:27-40). Jesus' teaching about the resurrection (20:34-38)**	d. The disciples dispute greatness. True greatness is in service (22:24-30).

e. Prediction of Peter's denial (22: 31-34). |
4. Prayer and meditation (10:38-11:1) Fatherhood of God, a. Mary and Martha b. Lord's prayer, c. Friend at midnight.		f. The two swords (22:35-38)
	5. Jesus' question about the interpretation of Ps. 110:1 - The question of the Messiah - How can the Christ be David's Son? As David's Son how can He be the Lord? David's Son-His authority is questioned (20:41-44)	**Eighth prediction about His death, which must fulfil the O.T. (22:37)**
5. Controversies with the Pharisees and scribes (11:14-54): a. the authority of Jesus, healing the dumb man (11:14-23),		g. Near the Mt. of Olives (22:39-46) Arrest – Jesus prays and shows by example the trust the disciples must have in the face of rejection (22:47).
b. Binding the strong man (11:21-23) c. Return of the unclean spirit (11:24-26)		h. Healing the ear of the high priest's servant (22:51)
d. Jesus dines with a Pharisee (11:37-41), e. Jesus rebukes the Pharisees four times (11:39-44), f. Jesus rebukes the Scribes three times (11:46-52). g. The Pharisees try to trap Jesus (11:53). h. Warning about the leaven of the Pharisees (12:1).	**B] Warnings and commendations (20:45-21:4):**	**B] Crucifixion (23:1-56): a) Trial, before Pilate (23:1-5)**

b) Trial before Herod (23:6-12) |
	1. Jesus condemns the Scribes. There will be a greater judgement for the Scribes because of their self-centredness (20:45-47).	**c) Sentencing by Pilate and the release of Barabbas (23:13-25)**
6. Preparation for judgement (12:1-13:9) a. Advice to disciples-possessions, preparedness and repentance, b. Discipleship, trusting God. (12:13-21) Seek the kingdom (12:22-34),	**2.** Counter example: the widow who gave all. Jesus commends her for her sacrificial giving (21:1-4).	**d) Cross (23:23-56) three sayings from the cross (23:34, 43, 46): 'Father, forgive them' (23:34), implied forgiveness, 'remember me' (23:42)**
c. The parable of the rich fool (12:13-21)	**C] On Mt. Olivet, Jesus predicts the Fall of Jerusalem and His final return (21:5-38).** Jesus predicts the Fall of the Temple (21:5-6). Jesus replies to the disciples in three steps about the timing of the final events.	**e) the death of Jesus (23:44-49) f) Burial (23:50-56)**
d. Knowing the nature of the time: Israel turns away but blessings still come (12:49ff).	**Step a.** Events which do not foreshadow the Fall of Jerusalem (21:8-11). **Step b.** Incidents which precede these events (21:12-19). **Step c.** Events which describe the Fall of Jerusalem. Time for mission and an interim step before the end with great persecution and the Fall of Jerusalem to the nations (the Gentiles) (21:20-24).	**C] The Resurrection appearances, Exaltation of Jesus (24:1-49)** a. The empty tomb and the resurrection discovered (24: 1-10).
The third prediction about the suffering and rejection of Jesus (12:49-50)		**Ninth prediction about His death and resurrection is fulfilled. (24:7)**
e. The signs of the times (12:54-59) f. Repentance (13:1-9)		b. The response and report - The news of the excited women is met with doubt. The response of Peter (24:11-12) c. The experience on the Emmaus road (24:13-35) d. The appearance to the disciples-Jesus the Messiah fulfills God's plan and promise. Commission and promise (24:36-49).
(Continued in the column below 13:10) [See page 79.]	**(Continued in the column below 21:25) [See page 79.]**	**(Continued in the column below 24:36) [See page 79.]**

Middle or Central Section [4] Journey Narrative cont'd	End Section [5] Discourse on Mount Olivet cont'd	End Section [6] Resurrection cont'd
7. Kingdom reversals (13:10-14:24)	**D] Signs which precede the coming of the Son of Man in splendour (21:25-28).**	e) Jesus reassures the group with a call to touch his resurrected body (24:36-43).
a. Healing the bent woman on the Sabbath (13:10-17)	a. Awareness of these signs will help people know when the key moments of God's plan are near (21:25-28).	f) "All has happened according to God's plan." (24:44)
b. Who will take part in God's Kingdom (13:18-27)?		- The commission to wait (24:49)
c. The parables of the mustard seed and the leaven (18-21)		- The promises contained in the law, prophets and the psalms have been fulfilled (24:44).
d. Kingdom of God (13:28-30)	b. The parable of the fig tree (21:29-33)	- Repentance and forgiveness to be preached to all nations (24:47).
e. The Pharisees warn Jesus about Herod's plot to kill Him - Herod that fox (31-33).	c. How to prepare for the coming of the Son of Man (21:34-36)!	
f. The fourth prediction about His suffering in Jerusalem (13:32-33)	**E] The people listen to Jesus, daily teaching in the Temple, lodging at the Mt. of Olives (21:37-38).**	**D] The Ascension (24:50-53) Jesus' blessing and departure at Bethany (24:50).**
g. Jesus laments for Jerusalem/ prophets perish in Jerusalem "The third day I finish my course." (13:33, 31-35)	**Summary of the ministry of Jesus in Jerusalem (21:38)** [See page 78.]	**The threefold response of the disciples:**
h. Jesus dines with another Pharisee (14:1-24).	(Continued in the next column 22:1-24:53)	a) they are filled with "great joy" rather than grief (24:52).
i. The parable of the excuses (14:15-24)		b) they worship (Gk.proskunew) and bless God in thankful praise. This is the first time Luke refers to worship being offered to Jesus. (Marshall) (20) (24 :53)
Journey reference (13:22; 31-35; 17-11)		
8. Cost of discipleship (14:25-35): a. discipleship in the face of rejection - warning about destruction (14:25-35)		c) they return to Jerusalem Jesus' blessing and remain continually in the temple blessing God (24:53). They are like Anna who worshipped, fasted and prayed every day in the Temple (2:37).
b. The tower builders/The warring King (14:28-30,31-33)		
9. Pursuit of sinners: a. heaven's examples (15:1-32) [Mercy]		**(Continued in the column below general comment)** [See page 80.]
b. Parables-lost and found (15:1-32)		
10. Generosity: handling money and possessions (16:1-31)		
a. The shrewd manager (16:1-10)Rich man/Lazarus (16:1-10;19-31)		
b. The Pharisees as lovers of money (16:14-15)		
11. Teachings on faith, forgiveness and service (17:1-19):		
a. Humble servant (17:7-10)		
b. The ten lepers (17:11-19)		
12. How the kingdom will come (17:20-18:8): a. faithfulness in looking for the king b. the kingdom and the kingdom's consummation (17:11-18:8)		
c. Suffering and rejection predicted a fifth time (17:20b-25)		
d. two parables on prayer (18:1-14)		
13. How to enter the kingdom (18:9-30):		
a. Parable: the Pharisee and the Publican (18:9-14)		
b. humbly entrusting all to the Father, (18:9-30) c. the rich ruler. (18:18-30)		
Journey refs. (18:31-32; 19:11, 28-29, 41-44)		
c. Prediction about sufferings (sixth time) and also the Second Coming (18:32-33)		
(Cont'd in the column below 18:31-34) [See page 80.]		

Middle or Central Section [4]

14. Conclusion and transition: (18:31-34)

Turning to Jerusalem, Messianic power, personal transformation, warning of responsibility, and entry with mourning (18:31-19:48).

a. Healing the blind beggar of Jericho (18:31-43)

Suffering predicted a seventh time (19:27)

15. Jesus in Judea:
a) from Jericho to Jerusalem (18:35-19:27),
1) a blind man is healed (18:35-43),
2) Zacchaeus (19:1-10),
3) the parable of the pounds (19:11-27),
(Many scholars finish here. [See Ch.9: Journey Narrative.]
b) the entry into Jerusalem and Jesus' controversial approach to Jerusalem (19:24-27).

16. Jesus in Jerusalem:
a. Jesus enters Jerusalem (19:28-48).

b. The Pharisees urge Jesus not to approve of the disciples' exaggerated claims and to restrain their excessive zeal (19:39-40).

c. The eighth prediction about the Fall of Jerusalem and Jesus weeping for the city (19:41-44)

d. Jesus drives out the sellers in the Temple court to show His displeasure with the Jewish leaders (19:45-46).
e. Jewish leaders plot against Jesus (19:47-48). (Cont'd in the next column)
[See page 78.]

General comments: Middle or Central Section (4) (9:51-19:48)

•Approx. 44% of this material is (L)
•It is not in chronological order and is not a straight-line journey. The journey is part of God's "necessary" plan.
•Luke's material focuses on Jerusalem to prepare for the Passover.
•Manson calls this section "The sayings and doings of Jesus." Guthrie calls it "From Galilee to Judea."
•Jesus' journey lay via Jerusalem but the goal of His journey was "being received up" at His Ascension. The key emphasis is Jesus' teaching to three groups: followers, crowds and opponents with the backdrop of what will happen in Jerusalem.

General comments: End Section (5) (20:1-21:38)

In the Olivet Discourse, the reference to Jerusalem surrounded by armies and the times of the Gentiles is (L) (21:24). Luke is very explicit about the events regarding the destruction of Jerusalem (21:20,24). There will be a period of Jewish captivity and dispersion and the Gentiles will overrun the city. Luke sees these events happening after the Fall of Jerusalem. The end times compares the coming destruction of the Temple with the return of the Son of Man. Luke includes a series of controversies in Jerusalem to show how different Jesus is from the official leaders.

General comments: End Section (6) (22:1-24:53) (L)

•These resurrection appearances are (L). They all take place in or near to Jerusalem. There are no references to the Galilean appearances in Luke.
• Do not expect reciprocity for the good deeds you do. "But I am among you as one who serves." (22:24-25)
• Jesus fulfils the prediction of His exaltation at the trial. "From now on the Son of Man shall be seated at the right hand of the power of God." (22:69)

1. Discipleship		6. Preparing for judgement		11. Teachings on faith and forgiveness	
2. Mission		7. Kingdom reversals		12. How the Kingdom will come	
3. Teaching on love		8. Cost of discipleship		13. How to enter the Kingdom	
4. Prayer and meditation		9. Pursuit of sinners		14. Conclusion and transition	
5. Controversies		10. Generosity		15. Mission in Judea	
Colour code for the fourteen thematic sub-sections in the Journey Narrative. (Figure 5)				16. Journey	
				17. Predicted sufferings	

Outcomes

Students should have a knowledge and understanding of the:
• the main sections of Luke's Gospel as in the infancy, Galilean ministry, journey, passion and resurrection narratives.
• the sub-themes within these sections e.g. Galilean ministry (nine sub-themes), central section (fourteen sub-themes).
• general aspects of the structure of Luke's Gospel, for example an orderly, geographical and formal structure, time, place and movement as a basis for structure, a structure which follows sections of the O.T. (CCEA A/S).
• key concepts, for example middle or central section, journey narrative, predictions of suffering, and chiastic patterns.
• Students should have a critical understanding of: the main controversies and events which relate to the Pharisees and Scribes, prayer, the Sabbath and the nature of the Kingdom (Edexcel A2).

Notes on Ch. 7: Structure of Luke's Gospel

1. Paul Achtemeier, Joel Green, M. Meyer Thompson, op. cit. p. 150.
2. Donald Guthrie, New Testament Introduction: Gospels and Acts, Vol. 1, IVP, 1965) p.9.
3. Brian Beck, Christian Character in the Gospel of Luke, Epworth Press, (1989) p.144.
4. Judith Lieu, The Gospel of Luke based upon the Revised English Bible, Epworth Press, (1997).
5. Alfred Plummer, A Critical and Exegetical commentary on the Gospel according to Luke: ICC, T. and T. Clark, Edinburgh, (1896) p.78.
6. Raymond E. Brown, Luke's Method in the Annunciation Narrative, Perspectives in Luke–Acts, T. and T. Clark, (1978) p. 431.
7. Darrell L. Bock, Luke : Vol. 1, ECNT, Baker Press, (1996) p.223.
8. Howard Marshall, New Testament Theology, Luke-Acts: The Former Treatise, IVP, (2004) pp.146-7.*
9. C. Kavin Rowe, Luke and the Trinity: An essay in Ecclesial Biblical Theology, SJT 56 (2003):1-26.
10. Walter Liefeld, op. cit, p.831.
11. Charles H. Talbert, Reading Luke: A Literary and Theological Commentary on the Third Gospel based upon the RSV, Crossroad Press, (1984), SPCK, (1990) p.37.
12. Hank J. de Jonge, Sonship, Wisdom and Infancy in Luke 2:41-51a: New Testament Studies 24: (1978) pp.317-54.
13. Robert Stein, op. cit. p.96.
14. Raymond Brown, op. cit. pp.380-92.
15. Kenneth Wolfe, "The Chiastic Structure of Luke/Acts and some Implications for Worship", SWJT 22 (1980) pp. 60-71.
16. Earle E. Ellis, op. cit. pp.31-33, 98-99.
17. Craig Blomberg, op. cit. p. 144.
18. Howard Marshall, Luke, op. cit. p. 9.
19. Darrell L. Bock, follows Marshall and Blomberg, Vol. 2, op. cit. p. 963.
20. Howard Marshall, (ibid.)
*This book is highly recommended.

CCEA A/S and Edexcel A/S

Targets:
- Identify the main events in the Infancy Narratives in Luke's Gospel.
- Recognise the main features of these events in the Infancy Narratives.
- Recognise the Infancy Narratives as symbolic. (Edexcel)
- Identify key characters, for example Mary as a model of trust and prayer. (CCEA)
- Identify the mission of Jesus and that of John the Baptist in the Infancy Narratives. (Edexcel)
- Identify the events regarding the humanity and divinity of Jesus in the Infancy Narratives. (Edexcel)
- Recognise Luke's special interest in the early years of Jesus.
- Identify key concepts, for example the presence and power of the Holy Spirit, Saviour, salvation, angelophany, and universalistic message.

The Infancy Narratives

Introduction

Chapter one divides into four events:-

1. John the Baptist's birth is foretold in the Temple in Jerusalem.	1:5-25
2. The announcement to Mary in Nazareth	1:26-38
3. Mary's visit to Elizabeth in the unknown hill country in Judea	1:39-56
4. John's birth in the unknown hill country in Judea	1:57-80

Chapter two divides into three events:-

5. Jesus' birth in Bethlehem	2:1-20
6. The presentation of Jesus in the Temple in Jerusalem	2:21-40
7. Jesus in Jerusalem aged twelve	2:41-52

> **The Holy Spirit will come upon Mary (1:35). She is a model in obedience in accepting God's will for the birth of Jesus (1:38).**

Pupil's Activity: One

Read 1:5-14 and, based upon Wiebe's **(1)** criteria for assessing visions/miracles find out how many of these take place in the angel's visit to Zechariah. Complete the grids. **(Figure 1)**

Wiebe's criteria for assessing visions	Yes	No
1. eyes open		
2. private eye		
3. by touch		
4. body sensation		
5. use of hearing		

> **At the start of Luke's Gospel there is an emphasis upon God's people praying together here; a crowd of worshippers had assembled to pray outside the Temple (1:10).**

a) Discuss your findings.
b) Do you think that this was a real vision?
c) Do real visions happen today?
d) Why do you think that this incident is called an "angelophany"?

[1] John the Baptist's birth is foretold in the Temple in Jerusalem. (Read 1:5-25.)

A) John's background and family situation (Read 1:5-7.)

Oriental kings usually had a special herald to prepare for their coming. God planned that the Messiah's forerunner would be human and born of humble stock. Zechariah was a rural priest doing his half yearly stint of duty in the Temple in Jerusalem when he discovered that the lot fell upon him to offer incense. He won the "lottery". This only happened once in a lifetime. Each rotation involved four to nine priestly families. (Jeremias) **(2)** Zechariah was a very devout man and he and his wife Elizabeth were greatly respected for their integrity and sincerity. His name means, "The Lord has remembered" and this fits in with the account of John's unusual conception and calling. Elizabeth was also of priestly stock as she was a daughter of Aaron (1:5) and her name can mean "my God is the one by whom I swear" or "my God is fortune." (Fitzmyer)**(3)** Both ideas suggest trust in God. They kept the commandments and lived them out in their lives, "walking in all the commandments and ordinances of the Lord blameless." (1:6) Despite their prayers over many years, they had no children and society tended to look down upon them and treat them with contempt. At this point there is no evidence of Zechariah's lack of faith. In Ch.1 all the references to the Temple refer to the Inner Court; in Ch.2 the references to the Temple are to the Outer Court. [See p. 227.]

Pupil's Activity: Two

a) What are dormant prayers?
b) Do you think God answers dormant prayers? Give reasons.

Zechariah was a very devout man and he and his wife Elizabeth were greatly respected for their integrity and sincerity, "walking in all the commandments and ordinances of the Lord blameless." (1:6; 1 Kgs.9:4)

B) The vision (Read 1:8-11.)

Zechariah was alone in the Holy Place (Gk.naon) (1:9) (Fitzmyer) **(4)** in front of the altar of incense, when he became aware of another presence. It was not a fellow priest as only the chosen representative would dare enter. His task was to put incense on the heated altar and prostrate himself in prayer. Standing by the right of the altar was a heavenly visitor, Gabriel, the angel of the Lord (1:11). Zechariah was overcome in the face of mysteries. On seeing the angel Zechariah was terrified (Gk.etarachthe) and perplexed (1:12) as Mary was (1:29). He was taken aback by the angel's appearance which caused him deep anxiety; fear gripped him until the angel spoke (1:13). He had heard of similar heavenly appearances happening to John Hyrcanus, the high priest who, when he was burning incense, heard God's voice telling of his son's victory, but Zechariah wondered why this visit had happened to him? (Josephus) **(5)** At the start of Luke's Gospel there is an emphasis upon God's people praying together; here a crowd of worshippers had assembled to pray outside the Temple (1:10). [See Ch. 5: Characteristics-Prayer.]

C) What Zechariah heard! (Read 1:12-17.)

He was not to be afraid because his prayer for a son was to be answered and the son was to be called John (1:13). God relieves the anxiety that the encounter with God's angel has produced. (Bock) **(6)** He was surprised at this, as his wife was too old to bear a son and Jewish custom required him to call the son after his father. He questioned this unexpected announcement. The message was not specific about the part Zechariah's son would play in heralding the Messiah, but it told him about the characteristics of the child to be born. His coming would be like that of the Messiah; it would be an occasion of great joy to his parents and many others (1:14). The angel describes John's character and his ministry: this promised son of Zechariah would be great before the Lord (1:15).

God had answered his specific prayer (Gk.deesis) (1:13).

John's mission would be mainly evangelistic. Zechariah knew that many people had strayed from God. "He will turn (Gk. epistrepsei) meaning bring back many of the sons of Israel to the Lord their God." (1:16)

Conclusion

• No father could ask for anything nobler than a son.
• This was a heart warming prospect for godly parents-to-be.
• Some of the child's greatness would be reflected glory.
• The pre-natal announcement of John's coming greatness must have cheered the ageing priest who may not see the greatness for himself. This event marks the start of the Messianic age; this was the beginning of the things God had fulfilled among His people.

D) The prospect for John (Read 1:15-23.)

1) Aspects of John's greatness

a) **Personal**:- He would be a lifelong Nazarite with strict self-discipline (1:15). The reference here is more to his ascetic life style which for him was a special dedication not to take intoxicating drink made from grapes or beer from barley (1:15b). He would be set apart by God to be a prophet and his birth was part of God's plan. Having been filled with the Holy Spirit before birth, his greatness would not be of his own making: the presence of the Holy Spirit before the birth indicates God's sovereign choice of one to serve Him (1:15c). When human beings are God's agents, the Holy Spirit fills them so that they convey God's message (1:15, 67). God revealed His message to Simeon by the Holy Spirit (2:25).

b) His mission:- (Read 1:16-17.)

It would be mainly evangelistic. Zechariah knew that many people had strayed from God. "He will turn (Gk. epistrepsei meaning bring back) many of the sons of Israel to the Lord their God." (1:16) This thrilled Zechariah. He would be compared with Elijah who was admired by all Jews who coveted his power; his son would have the spirit and power of Elijah (1:17). The prophet, Malachi, predicted four hundred years before that Elijah would herald the Messiah (Mal.3:1). He would be a second Elijah who would turn the hearts of the fathers to the children and he would hear about Elijah from his father. John's ministry will bring families together horizontally and spiritually. Elijah fired the imagination of Zechariah. His son would dress like Elijah; his humble task would be to make ready a people for God.

2) Zechariah's misgiving (Read 1:18.)

He was concerned about the age of his wife; doubt came to him in his greatest hour. How shall I know? This was a question of unbelief (1:18) unlike Mary (1:34). It was as if the angel's words were not enough.

3) The message of the angel (Read 1:19-20.)

The angel introduced himself as Gabriel meaning "man of God" or "God is my hero/warrior" (Fitzmyer) **(7)**, named in the Book of Daniel as a messenger of justice, (1:19) (Michael was a messenger of mercy in Jewish tradition). Here, the angel Gabriel was the bringer of good news and had a direct access with God; His message had great credibility (1:19). Because of his doubt, which showed his lack of faith, Zechariah would remain speechless for eight days after the birth (1:20). The cloud of judgement however, was lined with mercy and would portray God's disciplining grace. He could reflect upon the meaning of the herald of the Messiah, but he could not explain to people what had happened to him. He could not say the Benediction, but he could make signs with his hands. Luke saw it as a prelude to his story of the Messiah. These events will be fulfilled (Gk.plereo) meaning the completion of God's will and plan in their time (1:20; 24:44).

4) The wondering crowd and the silent priest (Read 1:21-23.)

The waiting of the people turned to wondering as Zechariah delayed in the Holy Place. The Greek verb "prosdokon" meaning "waited" suggests a long drawn out affair for Zechariah to complete the offering (1:21). Fitzmyer (8) says that "four other priests would have waited for Zechariah to complete the sacrifice." Other Jewish tradition about the Day of Atonement says that delay in the Holy Place was a matter of deep concern. (M.Yoma') (9) The people realised that Zechariah was dumb and that he had a vision (Gk.optasia), a supernatural appearance with God (1:22). Service in the Temple was that of "priestly service" (Gk.leitourgia) to God (1:23; Num.8:22). Priestly duty took place for one week in every six months. Zechariah had completed his week's service at the Temple as part of the division of Abijah (1:5) and he returned home to the hill country in Judea (1:23).

5) The birth of Elizabeth's child (Read 1:24-25.)

John was to be a contemporary of the Messiah. Elizabeth lived in seclusion and pondered the fact that God had removed her reproach in old age. She longed for the day of John's arrival when, at last, people would see that God had favoured her. She makes a spiritual response to her pregnancy. She had not realised that a close relation of hers would be the Messiah, although she knew her son would herald the Messiah's coming. She is filled with gratitude to God for His goodness to her and thanks Him for His kindness (1:25).[See Ch.5: Characteristics-Praise and Thanks.]

Pupil's Activity: Three

"A distinctive feature of Luke's Gospel are the similarities/parallelisms between the birth's of John and Jesus." (Evans) (10) Compare John's birth with that of Jesus by completing the list below. [See also Ch.7: Structure pp. 72-73.]

A comparison between John and Jesus' birth (Figure 2)

	John's Birth	Jesus' Birth
1	Elizabeth was old and barren (1:7).	Joseph and Mary were not married as yet. (1:26-27)
2	The angel appears to one parent, Zechariah (1:11-19).	(1:26-28)
3	Zechariah is troubled (1:12).	(1:29)
4	Zechariah is told not to fear (1:13).	(1:30)
5	Zechariah is promised a son (1:13).	(1:31)
6	Zechariah is given a name for his unborn son (1:13).	(1:31)
7	Zechariah's son will be great (1:15).	(1:32)
8	Zechariah doubts (1:18).	(1:34)
9	Zechariah is given a sign (1:20).	(1:36)
10	Joy at the birth of John – the neighbours and relations share in the parents' joy (1:58).	(2:15-18)
11	Neighbours react in fear, recognising God at work after the circumcision (1:65).	(2:31-38)
12	The Benedictus is sung (1:68-79).	(2:29-32)
13	The child grew and became strong (1:80).	(2:40)
	Conclusion	

Pupil's Activity: Four (Read 1:26-28.)

Brown **(11)** notes five features about the pattern of vision in the O.T. (Compare with Isaac's birth in Gen. 17: 13, 15-17) (1) The appearance of an angel (2) Fear in prostration (3) Annunciation message prefaced by, "Do not fear," followed by the visionary's name. (4) The objection as to how this would come about. (5) The giving of a sign for reassurance.

Pupil's Activity: Five

a) Design a questionnaire based upon Mary's vision and using Brown's **(12)** criteria. **(Figure 3)**

	Stages in the Narrative	Questionnaire	Yes	No
1.	The woman is about to be with child.			
2.	She will give birth to the child.			
3.	The name of the child.			
4.	The meaning of the name.			
5.	The future accomplishments of the child.			

b) Complete the questionnaire for Mary's vision. How many of these criteria featured in Mary's vision. Tick the boxes.

Pupil's Activity: Six
a) When the angel, Gabriel, appeared to Mary (1:30-33), what titles were used by the angel to describe her son?
b) What was the significance of those titles?

> The title, **Son of God** is to show that Jesus' human origins are based in God's creative activity; this title can allow for a pre-existent state.

[2] Announcement of the Messiah's birth to Mary in Nazareth (Read 1:26-38.)

A) Setting the scene and announcing the birth (Read 1:26-27.)

The angel Gabriel appears to Mary. Her name Mariam or Mary probably means "excellence." (Fitzmyer) **(13)** She recognised his identity. Probably he announced his name as with Zechariah or when swopping notes with Elizabeth. Luke possibly got the detail of the vision from Mary. The vision happened during the betrothal, when she was pledged to be married to Joseph. Although they were not married they were legally regarded as man and wife and she is called his wife. Women could be betrothed as young as twelve! Luke does not tell us Mary's age. The word 'virgin' refers here to one who has not had sex relations (1:27).

B) A fearful and calm greeting (Read 1:28-30.)

The angel says to her "Hail" (1:28). She is greeted in a way which emphasises grace (Gk. chaire), which (Marshall) **(14)** translates as, "hello or greetings", while (Fitzmyer) **(15)** regards as "O favoured one, the Lord is with you!" God is at your side Mary, in the sense that He has come to your aid. Klostermann **(16)** and Creed **(17)** see conception as later because of the future tenses in (1:31-33). God's favour (Gk.kecharitomene) rests upon her (1:28). She is specially chosen by God's grace and not through any merit of her own. "She is the recipient of God's grace." (Fitzmyer)**(18)**This is very perplexing (Gk.dietarachthe) for her (1:29) and indicates a deeper curiosity and concern than Zechariah, who was perplexed (Gk. etarachthe) at the angel's appearance. Her curiosity is dealt with when she is told to stop fearing (1:30).

C) The announcement proper to Mary of the birth of the Messiah (part 1) (1:31-33)

The birth of the child is predicted and his ministry is described (1:32-33). The signs of God's grace are a son (1:31a) and His name will be a sign of blessing (1:31b), "You will call His name Jesus." A God given name always related to the destiny of the person. Unlike Matthew, Luke does not give us the meaning of the name Jesus (Matt. 1:21).

D) The description of who Jesus is and what is His Ministry (Read 1:31-33.)

Firstly, His personal superiority shows "He will be great" in holiness, in His judgement of heaven and as a result, in power and influence (1:32a). Secondly the phrase "and will be called the **Son of the Most High**" means he will be recognised to be **the Son of God** and corresponds to His true nature. "He will be called" means "universally recognised" because He is such in fact. The title, "**Son of God**" is to show that Jesus' human origins are based in God's creative activity; this title can allow for a pre-existent state; Divine Sonship is mentioned first and is the foundation behind Davidic Sonship. (Marshall) **(19)** Brown however says this title is only a description of a Jewish hope of the Davidic Son of God unlike 1:35 which he says has Christian ideas read into the event. **(20)** Nevertheless, the emphasis is on Jesus' role rather than His nature: this is His Divine title and shows His future and eternal sovereignty (1:35). Thirdly, "The Lord God will give Him the throne of David for ever." (1:32) Fourthly, He is the Davidic Messiah (1:32-33). Fifthly, He is the King whose reign is eternal (1:33), "He will reign over the house of Jacob forever." The duration of Jesus' reign will be forever; neither Jewish rejection nor crucifixion will hinder God's plan for the Davidic king (1:33b). Later Luke will go on to disclose how the Davidic ruler will have complete authority over all human beings.

> The title, "**The Son of the Most High**" means he will be recognised to be the Son of God and corresponds to His true nature.

E) The manner of the reception of the message (Read 1:34-38.)

Mary asks her trustful question "How can this be?" She is puzzled as to how the birth can take place since she does not have a husband (1:34). "The power of the Most High" (1:35) is an explanation of Son of the Most High (1:32). It may not convey the idea of pre-existence. He shall be called holy, the Son of God (1:34b). He still had to keep the commandments. His birth gave Him liberty not to sin but did not take away from Him the liberty of sinning. (Godet) **(21)** Mary is not given a sign but the sign is clear in the promise to her. When she sees in Elizabeth the promised sign, her faith will be confirmed. The virgin birth makes Jesus totally unique. Mary is a model in obedience in accepting God's will for the birth of Jesus (1:38). The Holy Spirit will come upon Mary and the power of the Most high "overshadow her." (1:35)

F) The announcement proper to Mary (part 2) (Read 1:35.)

The Holy Spirit acts in history and is a linked with the power of God. The birth of Jesus happens because the Holy Spirit came upon Mary. She will have a child who fulfils the Davidic promise for the nation. He will be a royal Messiah superior to John the Baptist, "the child to be born will be called **holy, the Son of God**." **Jesus is the Holy One. He is the Messiah, Son of God from birth;** He was this before birth (1:41-45). Elizabeth, Mary's relation has conceived and is six months into her pregnancy (1:36). Her pregnancy shows that nothing at all is impossible with God; it is His total power at work.

[3] Mary's visit to Elizabeth in the unknown hill country in Judea (Read 1:39-56.)

The meeting of the two women (1:39-45): Zechariah and Elizabeth lived in an unspecified town in the hill country of Judea (1:39-40). [See p. 227.]

A) The arrival of Mary (Read 1:39-41.)

Mary starts her journey as soon as possible (1:39). Mary's first thought is to visit Elizabeth in haste which may reflect her obedience. From Nazareth to Judea was a distance of about eighty to one hundred miles away from Judea and the journey lasted three-four days. Until Mary came to Elizabeth, Mary did not know who the Messiah was to be or when he was to come. The movement of the foetus in the womb was to be a sign to Elizabeth that she was face to face with the Messiah's mother. She was given special intuition. The foetal John testifies to the presence of Jesus by leaping in the womb of Elizabeth (1:41a). Luke comments that (Elizabeth was filled with the Holy Spirit) and when Mary greeted Elizabeth, the baby leaped for joy in her womb. The idea of the Holy Spirit and power are combined here: this is a frequent combination in Luke/Acts and shows God's creative power (1:41,44).

B) Elizabeth greets Mary: (Read 1:42-45.)

> Mary is a vessel specially chosen by God's grace. She is "more" blessed (Gk.eulogemene) or "most" blessed among women and she is specially blessed because of the child she will bear (1:42).

1) Mary and her son (1:42)

2) Elizabeth and her son (1:43-44)

3) Mary and her happiness: Elizabeth gives a final blessing to Mary (Gk.makaria) (1:45) and shows ther confidence that God will bring everything to pass: God's promises are finally going to be executed (1:45). Elizabeth was able to confirm to Mary what the angel Gabriel had said to her, so reassuring her that this was not of her own imagination. Elizabeth shows a generous heart in being content with the lesser honour of being the mother of the herald. Elizabeth recognises Mary's unique blessedness (Gk.eulogemene) "You are most blessed of women." (1:42) This is a Semitic superlative (Judg. 5:24) in which the second line gives the cause of the blessedness. Mary is carrying the messianic child and that child is unique in his identity and role. (Nolland) **(22)** Brown **(23)** Mary is a vessel specially chosen by God's grace. She is "more" blessed (Gk. eulogemene) or "most" blessed among women and she is specially blessed because of the child she will bear (1:42). Our word eulogise comes from this word. The fruit of her womb is an O.T. expression for a fruitful womb seen as a blessing from God and is related to faithful obedience. "Blessed (Gk.eulogemenos) is the fruit of your womb." (1:42; Deut. 7:13; 28:1) She is twice blessed (Gk.eulogemene) (1:42a, 42b). All of these blessings bestowed upon Mary indicate that she is an exemplary servant touched by God's grace.

Pupil's Activity: Seven   Class discussion

The first movement of the foetus is an indication of life within the womb and is proof that the child to be born is an independent human being. Discuss this statement in the light of abortion today.

C) The Magnificat (Mary's Song) (Read 1:46-55.)

General points: The word "Magnificat" comes from Latin "magnificare" to magnfy and expresses Mary's praise of God for the way in which He has treated her. The style is that of Hebrew poetry and it is modelled upon the psalms. The spirit of the song fits well with the happy coming together of the two women. The phrase "my soul" praises (1:46) is another way of saying "I" praise and it is in synonymous parallelism with "my spirit." She calls God "Lord" (Gk. Kurion) and also God "my Saviour." She identifies God as "my Saviour" which anticipates the concern with salvation in the Infancy Narratives. (Green) **(24)** A key statement in the song is that God has regarded His handmaiden's low estate and all future generations would call her blessed. Mary was blessed here (Gk.makariousi) (1:48b). "For behold, henceforth all generations shall call me blessed;" not because of her faith as in (1:45), but rather because her blessedness depended on her son and His greatness. [See also (1:28).] This blessing is not a call to bless or praise Mary but affirms that Mary stood in a state of blessedness. (Stein) **(25)** Many blessings are bestowed upon Mary to show that she is a faithful servant touched by God's special grace.

She is also twice blessed (Gk. makaria) (1:45,48b). That which she cherished in her mind will spring to life at the opportune moment. The song really belongs to the O.T. in that it looks back to the past with thanks for what God has done. She expresses a very high view of God: God is her Saviour. He does not terrify although He will scatter the proud and overturn thrones. God is gracious and will exalt the humble. Mercy is used twice:- "It is for those who fear God.

God has remembered Israel His servant."

"The hungry are fed with good things." (1:53a) Even though she came from peasant stock, her child would introduce new values into society. "The humble will be exalted." (1:52) Her hymn of praise to God would be an inspiration to others.

Pupil's Activity: Eight

a) Produce a class powerpoint or acetate on the Magnificat using some of the ideas in Figure 4 and other related material.

b) Pick out the key themes in the Magnificat which are a foretaste of things to come in Luke's Gospel.

c) What thee characteristics of God does Mary praise in (1:49-50)?

d) Which features of Mary's character are seen in this song?

C) (Cont'd) The Magnificat as a declarative hymn of praise to God: a Psalm of thanksgiving [The Magnificat] (Read 1:46-55.)

1. Mary praises God for what He has done for her (1:46-49).

a) She thanks (present tense) God for the gracious way He has dealt with her, a woman of lowly birth (1:46-49). "My soul magnifies (Gk.megaluno) means makes great, praises or exalts the Lord." She lifts up the Lord (1:46a, 58).

b) She acknowledges Him as Sovereign Lord (Gk.Kurion), recognising her own humble state as God's servant (1:45-48).

c) She praised and identified God as Her Saviour (1:47). [past tense] She rejoiced (Gk.egalliasen) [past tense] in the Lord when the angel brought his message to her. My spirit has begun to delight in God my Saviour (1:47; Ps.35:9).

d) She gives three reasons for her praise: Firstly, God saw her humble position/low social position [past tense], "for He has regarded the low estate of his handmaiden." She is the handmaiden (Gk.doules) slave of the Lord (1:48a, 38; Ps.138:6). Secondly, although her position is a humble one, God has looked favourably upon her (1:48a). "From now things will be different; "all generations shall praise her and call her blessed."(1:48b) [future tense] She identifies herself as God's servant, the slave or handmaiden (Gk.doules) of the Lord (1:48). Thirdly, she praises God for all the mighty things which He has done for her: God is the Mighty One who creates the child and gives her a special role (1:49,35; Pss.24:8; 50:1; 71:19; 89:9).

e) This is a "declarative psalm of praise": it combines the word of praise with the reasons for praise (Pss. 8, 33). (Green) **(26)** Mary rejoices because God has regarded her lowly social status (1:47-48). The use of the three tenses shows Luke's interest in the events of the past, present and future and their meaning. She rejoiced beacuse had regarded her lowly status(1:47,48).

2. Mary praises God for His actions to the community (1:50-53).

a) God's mercy is on those who fear Him. She proclaims God's saving works (1:50). God's holiness is not separated from His mercy (1:49-50).

b) The faithful are blessed because God will bring His promise to completion and it will stretch "from generation to generation," which is a Hebrew expression for God's faithfulness (1:50). Mary speaks of God showing strength with His arm (1:51).

c) God acts to all who fear Him proud, hungry and rich. There are contrasting social consequences for the rich and the poor. The poor are more dependent upon God than the rich. The words Mary uses to describe God's character are taken from everyday activities, for example "scatters" the proud; "puts down" the mighty; "fills" the hungry (1:51-53; Ps.103:9,17). She anticipates God's vindication of those who fear Him (1:51). Later Jesus' opponents would grasp for social respect, positions of honour and exclude the less fortunate and socially unacceptable. She knows that God will stretch out a mighty hand to those who are humble. What God has done for her He does for others who are also humble; "God exalts those of low degree." (1:52b; Pss.107:41;113:7-8)

d) She knows that God is faithful to His word and will help those in need (1:53).

3. Mary praises God for all His actions to His people Israel (1:54-55).

a) For His gracious acts to His people Israel, God has remembered mercy (Ps.98:3); mercy is God's love in action (1:54).

b) He is faithful to His promises to His people Israel who are in covenant relationship with Him (1:54-55).

c) Mary sees herself as "Abraham's seed." "As He spoke to our fathers, to Abraham and his posterity forever."(1:55)

d) She is certain that God's promises are forever (1:50, 55).

e) God alone is worthy of praise and He is wonderful because His character is true.

f) Mary acts as an O.T. prophetess in this song. She represents Israel and willingly obeys God despite the personal cost. She interprets God's saving works (1:47,50). She rejoices in God as her Saviour. Only sinners need a Saviour.

4. Summary on Mary

• Mary is a model of trust (1:38). (Talbert) **(27)** "Let it be according to your word." (1:38) The same idea is in (8:9-21 the parable of the sower and (11:27-28), "Blessed (Gk.makaria) are those who hear the word and keep it." (11:28) She is believing. "Blessed is she who believed." (1:45) Mary's question, "How can this be?" (1:34) She does not express doubt, but asks for an explanation and therefore, implies faith. Unlike Zechariah (1:37-38), she takes God at His word and is a model believer. Her astonishment is that of a pure conscience. (Godet) **(28)**

• She sincerely worships God, "My soul magnifies the Lord." (1:46) She faithfully keeps the ceremonial law.

• Mary is of David's line and nothing is known of her home life up to this time. Luke aims to show the supernatural nature of the birth of the Messiah.

• "Luke wants us to identify with Mary's example, and not to unduly exalt her person." (Bock) **(29)**

• She refers to herself as "the bond slave of the Lord" (Gk. doule) showing her sense of submission and obedience. "Behold, I am the handmaid of the Lord;" (1:38) The word "doulos" means a galley slave. [See also the Magnificat 1:46-55.]

• She is a proclaimer of the birth of Jesus and she interprets God's saving work for His people. His mercy is on those who fear Him (1:50).

• She is twice blessed (Gk eulogemene)(1:42 a, b) and twice blessed (Gk.makaria)(1:45,48b).

• To share in the events which Jesus brings is an honour worthy of joy (1:47), because she along with Elizabeth has taken part in these blessings. Elizabeth blessed Mary because of her faith in God's promise that would be fulfilled in her (1:45).

D) The Magnificat as a poem (A2 level CCEA)

In the Greek text many lines begin with a strong action verb with a conjunction before. Tannehill **(30)** says that it has two strophes: (1:47-50) and (1:51-55). A mood of celebration is established as in Hebrew poetry.

1. Luke 1:47 has two statements of praise in **synonymous parallelism**: a device which enriches the thought.
"My soul magnifies the Lord,
and my spirit rejoices in God my Saviour," **Synonymous parallelism (Figure 4)**

My soul magnifies the Lord (1:46b)   **=**   and my spirit rejoices in God my Saviour (1:47),

2. Luke 1:48a and 49a are synonymous in that they describe the same event but also provide a contrast between the humble and the great. (Tannehill) **(31)**

• **In 1:52-53** Luke has **antithetical parallelism** : a device which heightens the sense of contrast and proclaims a dramatic reversal in society:-
"He has put down the mighty from their thrones
and exalted those of low degree;
He has filled the hungry with good things   **Antithetical parallelism (Figure 5)**
and the rich he has sent empty away."

2   and exalted those of low degree (1:52);   →   3   He has filled the hungry with good things (1:53a),

1   He has put down the mighty from their thrones (1:52),   4   and the rich he has sent empty away (1:53b).

• **In 1:51-53,** Mary is saying that God has overturned society in favour of the oppressed. "He has shown strength with his arm," (Ps. 44:3) "He has scattered the proud in the imagination of their hearts," (18:9-14; Num. 10:35)
"He has put down the mighty from their thrones, rulers will be removed from their thrones and exalted those of low degree;" social positions will be in reverse (1 Sam.2:7).
"He has filled the hungry with good things," The social consequences are seen in Ps.107:9; 146:7 and the rich he has sent empty away (Job 15:29; Jer.17:11).

3. In 1:51 Luke uses **synthetic parallelism**: two descriptions which describe one event. The second line goes beyond the thought of the first line. **(Figure 6)**

He has shown strength with His arm (1:51 a),   **Synthetic parallelism: (Figure 6)**

He has scattered the proud in the imagination of their hearts (1:51b): the arrogant will be dispersed.

"The arm of the Lord" in the O.T. is a symbol of strength (Deut. 4:34; Ps. 44:3; Is. 53:1). The power of God as seen in the O.T. is demonstrated in the birth of the Messiah (1:51a). God will also scatter his enemies by way of judgement (1:51b).

4. In 1:52-53 Luke uses **antithetical parallelism** which forms an **inverted synonymous parallelism** (chiasm) with each other:- [See later the Benedictus as a chiasmus.] This device heightens the contrast and shows up the dramatic reversal in society: the left side of the equation decreases and increases in reverse proportion to that of the right side.
(A) "He has put down the mighty from their thrones,
(B) And exalted those of low degree." Society will be overturned and we are to compare extremes.
(A) "He has filled the hungry with good things," means everything the rich have and the poor lack.
(B) "The rich He has sent empty away."

Inverted synonymous parallelism (Figure 7)

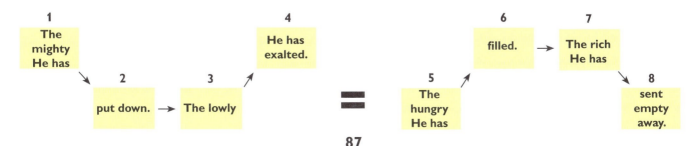

[4] John's birth in an unknown hill country in Judea (Read 1:57-80.)

A) John's birth (Read 1:57-58.)

Setting: Mary extends her stay and returns to Nazareth just before the birth of John (1:56). The relatives and neighbours provide the moral support for Elizabeth even though they are unaware of the child's uniqueness, and they rejoice at the special mercy of God to Elizabeth (1:58).

Zechariah was filled with the Spirit and prophesied in the words of the Benedictus (1:67).

B) The naming of John (Read 1:59-66.)

Zechariah inwardly rejoiced. Each time he went to speak he was reminded of his unbelief. Due to his lack of faith, Zechariah was unable to join, at first, in the praise for the birth of a son. His dumbness remained for the first eight days of John's life. This puzzled Zechariah as the angel had told him that his speech would return when the child was born. Did he fear the loss of speech forever? His speech returned on the day of circumcision. A prayer was offered, the child given a name and welcomed into the family of Israel. Elizabeth named the child John. This was confirmed by Zechariah who wrote the name on a tablet. All the relatives were amazed that the child was not called after his father (1:63). Zechariah's obedience was complete; physically he returned to normal. The bystanders saw it as a miracle and years later they would realise that John was no ordinary Israelite (1:66).

C) The Benedictus: the song of Zechariah (Read 1:68-79.)

1. The setting of the Benedictus: Zechariah was filled with the Spirit and prophesied. (1:67) The title Benedictus comes from the Latin meaning "speak well of" and expresses Zechariah's thoughts as he surveys God's plan through John the Baptist, to the heir of David. Zechariah's first words are of praise to God (Ps.41:13; 72:18; 106:49) for He has come and redeemed His people (Ps. 111:9). God's visitation of His people is a main theme in Luke's Gospel (1:78; 19:41-44; Zech. 10:3). Zechariah was under the **power of the Holy Spirit** and was influenced by Jewish prayers such as "Eighteen Benedictions of the Shemonah Ezreh from the O.T." All of these eighteen were used at the casting of lots in the Temple (1:9). The fifteenth one said, "Blessed be Thou, O God who causes the horn of salvation to sprout forth." Zechariah now believed that the Messiah would come. Luke's main theme is this salvation which Jesus brought. The term Saviour occurs in (1:47; 2:11) and the word "salvation" in (1:69, 71,77 and 19:9). It is not a political idea but deals with the response of the individual by faith (7:50; 8:12; 8:48, 50; 17:19; 18:42) to God, and forgiveness of sins (9:24).

2. Zechariah's song : Praise to God for the Messiah is the theme of the hymn/song, announced in (1:68-70) and the rest is the explanation of this theme. "Praise to the Lord the God of Israel for He has visited and redeemed His people (1:68). The promised time of salvation has come, God has already come to His people (1:69a). Zechariah's hymn reveals Jesus' role in salvation and does not mean that Simeon was "the first redeemed man" as argued by (Farris) **(32)** and Grundmann **(33)** The redemption for Israel will be through the house of David (1:69b). This shows the importance of the Davidic descent of Jesus (2 Sam.7:12-16). The Messiah is called a "horn of salvation;" horn is a symbol of strength in the O.T. (1:69b; Ps. 18:2; Ps. 132:17). The Messiah will fulfil O.T. prophecy. The reference to the holy prophets emphasises God's plan, "As He said through His holy prophets of long ago." (1:70) The Messiah will deliver the faithful from the clutches of the foreign enemies and will exercise authority over them. "Deliverance from those who hate us," (NIV) could refer to the local tyrants who hated the faithful (1:71). Deliverance refers to both political and spiritual enemies of God's chosen people. (Fitzmyer) **(34)** Believers are saved from their enemies at the second coming (1:71).

3. Why did God send the Messiah? (Read 1:71-75.)

The Messiah is seen as a powerful leader to deliver the nation from its enemies. God's mercy and His covenants are brought together (1:72). Marshall **(35)** sees this as explaining the purpose of salvation. Salvation produces and displays God's mercy and faithfulness. Messianic salvation leads to God remembering (Gk.mnesthenai) His holy covenant, which has the idea of God putting His promise into action and not just a matter of recall. This is the covenant with Abraham which is referred to here and it shows that God is faithful to His original commitments. "The oath He swore to our father Abraham." (1:73) The purpose and outcome of the Messiah's mission, Zechariah expressed in (1:74-75), "We might serve (Gk.latruein) Him fearlessly in holiness and righteousness before Him all the days of our life." (1:74) The goal of salvation is to serve God in holiness and righteousness (Mal. 3:33). This covenant appeals to the one treasured by all Jews but Zechariah does not refer to the New Covenant.

4. The mission of John the Baptist (Read 1:76-79.)

Prophecy about Jesus and John - the Benedictus also describes the role of John the Baptist. Zechariah addresses his baby son who would be prophet of the Most High (1:76a). His role was to inform and to prepare. God will provide a herald for the Messiah (1:76b; Is.40:3; Mal.3:1; 4:5): his theme will be one of salvation and forgiveness of sins as part of the **Messiah's mission.** "To give knowledge of salvation to His people." (1:77) The O.T. language called his mission the faint light over the horizon: a prelude to the coming day and a light to dispel the darkness and guide the traveller. "The Sun of Righteousness will rise with healing in His wings." (Mal. 4:2; Jn. 1:5) Zechariah has to trust that God will deliver on His promises and he now responds in obedience. Even the faith of very spiritual people like Zechariah, who earlier is praised for his faith (1:6), can pause and then grow in depth. Mary never hesitated in her obedience. The birth of John is an indication that God's salvation through the Messiah draws near (Num. 24:17; Mal.3:1).

5. A further picture of the Coming-Messiah (Read 1:78-79.)
Salvation is possible because of the tender mercy of our God (1:78). The word mercy characterises the entire plan. The coming of the Messiah is referred to as "the rising of a star or sun." "Gk.anatole" the word used means literally that which springs up. "The day shall dawn upon us from on high." (1:78b) "To shine on those living in darkness and in the shadow of death," continues the image of the rising sun or star. God will visit His people as the coming light. God sends His Messiah as the bright dawn of salvation shining upon the face of people (1:78) "The man whose name is the Branch shall build the Temple of the Lord." (Zech. 6:12) Jesus brings light to those sitting in darkness both spiritually and physically and He guides people into the way of peace. Salvation described in terms of peace is one of Luke's key themes (1:79). John will preach salvation but Jesus will take the people into it.

6. The Growth of John (Read 1:80.)
Does the description of John going to live in the desert or wilderness mean that John was an Essene, (a sect of Judaism) a member of the "desert party?" Fitzmyer sees it as plausible that John was a member of the Qumran Community. If this view is correct John would have rejected his parents to go and live in a community. John is more like a prophet than like the Qumran "holy ones" as he taught one baptism and not several washings. John's message was not one of separation (3:10-14). **(36)** John did not teach legalism or ritualism as in Qumran. Therefore John was not an Essene but he probably knew about the Qumran community as he lived in the desert. (Bock) **(37)**

7. The Benedictus as a chiasmus (1:68-79)
Alternatively, the Benedictus can be seen as a chiasmus; this is a style of Hebrew poetry which can be likened to the place settings at the Lord Mayor's banquet. All the cutlery has been laid out around each plate and the diner starts at the outside and works inwards with each course to reach the plate in the centre. In the same way the chiasmus follows a pattern with the "plate" or centre being (1:72-73).

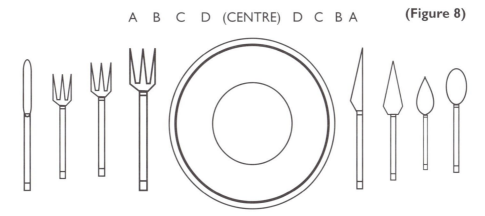

A   B   C   D   (CENTRE)   D   C   B   A   **(Figure 8)**

Part One - The Messiah (Praise to God for the Messiah's deliverance)
A Blessed be the Lord God of Israel, for He has **visited and redeemed His people** (1:68),
B and has raised up a **horn of salvation** for us in the house of his servant David (1:69),
C as He spoke by the mouth of **His holy prophets** from of old (1:70),
D that we should be **saved from our enemies,** and from the hand of those who hate us (1:71).

CENTRE to perform the **mercy promised to our forefathers and to remember His holy covenant (1:72), the oath which He swore** to our father Abraham (1:73).

D that we, **being delivered from our enemies,** might serve Him without fear (1:74), in holiness and righteousness all the days of our life (1:75).
Part Two - The child John: to celebrate the greatness and significance of the role of John the Baptist in his work of deliverance
C And you, child, will be called **the prophet of the Most High;**
for you will go before the Lord to prepare His ways (1:76),
B to give **knowledge of salvation** to His people and in the forgiveness of their sins (1:77),
A through the tender mercy of our God, when **the day shall dawn upon us** from on high whereby the dayspring will visit us (1:78), to give light to those who sit in darkness and in the shadow of death, to guide our feet into the way of peace (1:79).

Pupil's Activity: Nine
Look up the meanings of these names using a Bible Concordance and show how they are relevant to the text of the song. a) Zechariah   b) Elizabeth   c) John

[5] Jesus' Birth in Bethlehem (Read 2:1-20.)

A) The Messiah is born: the census (Read 2:1-3.)

The Jews expected a Messiah centred in Bethlehem, but not the way it happened (Mic.5:1-2 is not referred to by Luke). The Roman Emperor, Octavius Caesar in 31 B.C. had adopted the grand title "Augustus" and modestly declared himself on his coins to be "the saviour of the world!" His rule was called the reign of peace. God raises up a child of peace. The census or tax registration took place when Quirinius was Governor of Syria [that is: the imperial legate in Syria-Cilicia between A.D. 6-9 whereas the birth of Jesus must have been ten years earlier. [See Ch.6: Luke as a historian.] While there is no record of this world-wide census being held at this time under Augustus Caesar, there is evidence that Quirinius was legate twice over and held the position at the time of the birth. The census started with Herod and was not completed until the time of Quirinius ten years later. There is insufficient evidence to dispute the fact of a census at the birth of Jesus.

B) The journey to Bethlehem, the Davidic City (Read 2:4-5.)

God used a pagan census to bring about the birth in Bethlehem and Joseph shows his obedience to the Roman government in participating in the census. Joseph and Mary came to Bethlehem because of the census ordered by Augustus (Latin "exalted one") to complete his records for tax purposes. Each one went to the place of origin. Joseph and Mary went from Nazareth to Bethlehem: Joseph belonged to the Davidic family. Jesus' royal and Davidic connections are being expressed by Luke. Mary is referred to as Joseph's "betrothed" which suggests that the marriage has not been consummated and implies a virgin birth (2:5). (Marshall) **(38)** The animal trough where Jesus was born could have been a stable next to the place of lodging or a cave as caves were commonly used as stables. The Gk. word "kataluma" could refer to a reception room or a private house or a public shelter, since this public shelter (inn) was full up, Mary and Joseph had to take refuge elsewhere.

C) The humble birth of Jesus (Read 2:6-7.)

The lowliness of the Messiah's birth was important. Mary gave birth to the child in a stable, wrapped him up and placed him in an animal food trough (2:7).

> **God used a pagan census to bring about the birth of Jesus in Bethlehem and Joseph shows his obedience to the Roman government in participating in the census.**

D) Reactions to the birth: shepherds, others and Mary (Read 2:8-20.)

1) The setting (2:8-9): this is the third announcement in Luke and it is to shepherds watching over their flock. The field has been identified as the "Shepherd's field" two miles from the town. (Brown) **(39)** The shepherds represent all people. Heaven confesses who Jesus is and reveals his identity (2:10-11, 14): he is the Davidic child, who brings good news and peace to God's people and He is Saviour and Lord.

2) The angel's announcement to the shepherds (Read 2:10-12.)
The appearance of the angel (angelophany) to the shepherds announcing the birth calms their fear as happened with Zechariah (1:13), Mary (1:30) and Peter (5:10). Previously N.T. scholars did not rate the shepherds very highly in Israel and called them the "down trodden and the despised." (SB.) **(40)** As this evidence is a fifth-century rabbinic source, scholars today think the bible is much more positive about shepherds and refer to them as "the lowly and humble" who respond to the message of God (1:54). (Fitzmyer) **(41)** The shepherds represent all ordinary people who would offer homage to the same Messiah. Some shepherds tended sheep reared for sacrificial purposes; these were regarded as wealthier shepherds. With the messenger came the bright presence of the Lord's glory. In (2:9) glory (Gk.doxa) is the majestic presence of God, the bright Shekinah glory referred to in the O.T; this "glory" was God's special presence to His people. References to the revealing of God's presence among His people are Ex. 16:7, 10, 24:17, 40:34; Ps. 63:2; Luke 2:14; 9:30-31 the Transfiguration. His coming was marked by the glory of the Lord, the glory shining around the overawed shepherds, filling them with fear. The message of the angel is one of good news and the response will be one of great joy for all the people of Israel. The birth of Jesus is proclaimed (2:11). The national focus is still uppermost in Luke at this stage. It is good news and a joy because it is the messianic Saviour who is to be born and it is a fulfilment (2:4). Three titles are used for Jesus; (1) Saviour, (2) Christ, (3) the Lord. These do not appear together anywhere else in the N.T. **"Saviour"** (Gk.soter) is someone who delivers from physical and spiritual danger: God's deliverer for God's people. This title sums up Jesus' **humanity and compassion** and is Luke's most distinctive title for Jesus. Today in the city of David, a Saviour, is born to you, He is Christ the Lord (2:11). **Christ the Lord** can mean **Messiah**, which points to His office as God's promised, Anointed One: "Lord" denotes His sovereign authority. The specific directions for finding the Messiah in the city of David are given (2:12a). With the announcement comes a sign, the shepherds are to look for a newborn baby, (Gk.brephos) lying in an animal's feed trough (2:12b).

3) Heavenly Praise! (Read 2:13-14.)

This title "Saviour" sums up Jesus' humanity and compassion and is Luke's most distinctive title for Jesus.

The angel of the Lord is in the middle of the angelic attendants (2:13). What is unusual here is that there is a select group (Gk. stratias) meaning hosts of angels who come from the whole array of angels and normally serve God (1Kgs. 22: 19; 2 Chron.18:18; Dan. 7:10). Heaven is telling the earth about the significance of Jesus' birth. "Glory" can be the majesty of God or can be used for describing praise to God (2:14). While heaven offers praise, human beings will have peace which is a key idea in the Third Gospel (1:79; 10: 5-6; 19:38,42). It is for those who respond to the coming of Jesus. Jesus comes for all (2:10) but not all wish to receive the benefits of his coming (2:14). It is for those on whom His favour rests. The heavens praise God for salvation's outworking and the people will experience harmony and benefits. The concluding anthem ascribes glory to God and announces peace to men (2:14). The contrast between so heavenly a display of glory and the few humble shepherds was part of God's sovereign plan for the Incarnation. In the doxology (2:14) (Gk.doxa) is the glory ascribed to God in heaven and differs from the glory in (2:9). The glory of the angelic choir (2:13-14) is repeated by the shepherds (2:20), and the crowd of disciples when Jesus entered Jerusalem (19:37-38). [See Ch.5: pp.52-53.]

4) The shepherds confirm the message of the angels and pay homage. (Read 2:15-20.)

When the angels depart, **the shepherds** discuss what they have heard and resolve to go to Bethlehem to see this sign (2:12,15) and "word" which God has made known to them (2:17). They respond in faith, go to find Mary and the child in the feed trough as the angel had promised (2:16) and tell others what made them take up the search. They testify to the saying (Gk.rhema) meaning the word which had been told to them (2:17). Danker calls the shepherds the "first evangelists." **(42) The people** in turn react to the witness of the shepherds by marvelling (Gk.ethaumasan) at the events. This however does not mean that they entered into full faith but shows their surprise at what they heard (2:18). The report warmed their ears but it may have missed their hearts. This in turn leads to Mary's response of keeping this information in her heart; it is one of continual meditation. It is contemplation which tries to put thoughts into a comprehensive whole. As in (2:33) she "mulls these things over in her mind" and the reader is meant to identify with her response (2:19). Mary, Joseph and others hear that this child is going to be the Saviour for them, Christ the Lord (2:11). Now the angels and the shepherds are singing from the same hymn sheet. A fuller understanding by the people will come later. The **shepherds** tell everything which they have seen and heard. The shepherds believe which shows the different responses to the birth of Jesus. They return home with their faith confirmed and deepened. They see, hear, testify and experience a great sense of joy as they honour God with praise and glory. Glory (Gk.doxazontes) here means verbally giving honour to God for His wonderful deeds (2:20).

5) What was the significance of the sign to the shepherds (2:12)? "Sign" means a mark or token. The titles for Jesus are in direct contrast to the poverty of the sign, a baby in a manger wrapped in strips of cloth (2:11,12). What kind of a sign was it? The sign to the shepherds does not the take the same form of an exceptional display of God's power like the dumbness of Zechariah (1:22) and Elizabeth's conception (1:36, 57-58). Although these signs are similar, the sign to the shepherds functions in a different way. In the O.T. signs help to bring out the meaning of the message and are accompanied by a formula "this shall be the sign for you (Ex.3:12; 1 Sam.2:34; Is.37:30)." (Giblin) **(43)** [See pp.176, 197.]

Pupil's Activity: Ten
a) Examine the main features of the birth and infancy narratives presented in Luke's Gospel
(Edexcel A/S 2002/2004)   [14 Marks]
b) Consider how a study of these narratives contributes to an understanding of the mission of Jesus.
(Edexcel A/S 2002)   [6 Marks]
c) How far do these features reflect the author's understanding of the divinity of Jesus.
(Edexcel A/S 2004)   [6 Marks]

Pupil's Activity: Eleven
a) Outline and examine the main features of the birth and infancy narratives presented in Luke's Gospel.
(Edexcel A/S 2001)   [14 marks]
b) How far does the presentation of the birth and infancy narratives reflect the author's understanding of the humanity of Jesus? (Edexcel A/S 2001)   [6 marks]

Pupil's Activity: Twelve
a) Outline your knowledge and understanding of Luke's account of the events leading up to the birth of Jesus.
(CCEA A/S 2001)   [30 marks]
b) Explore the claim that Luke presents Mary as a model of trust and prayer in this account. Justify your answer.
(CCEA A/S 2001)   [15 marks]

The sign is accomplished by drawing out the significance of the scriptural echoes: the Saviour, Messiah and Lord, wrapped in strips of cloth lying in a feeding trough. With the coming of the Saviour God's people are returned to the One who sustains them (Is.1:3). Because of God's prevenient action in the birth of His Son, Israel may find a way back to God. Therefore sign has a Christological function adding interpretative detail to the names given to Jesus (2:11). There is also a theological role of the sign, showing God's gracious act to renew the embrace of His people through this child.

6) Summary features of Luke's account of the birth of Jesus

• The birth of the Davidic Saviour occurs in a place normally reserved for animals. His birth was humble (2:7).
• The extraordinary joy associated with the good news is one of Luke's themes. All are to share in this joy of the coming of Jesus (2:20).
• Events happen just as was spoken by the angels.
• Three titles are used for Jesus. Firstly "Saviour," which tells of His role as a deliverer. Secondly "Messiah," which points to His office as God's promised, Anointed One, and thirdly, "Lord" which denotes His sovereign authority (2:9, 11).
• Luke features the different responses to the birth: the shepherds by faith in going to see the child, the bystanders who marvel, and Mary's faithful response in naming the child as it had been revealed to her and yet she struggles to understand what it means (1:13). The Messiah would be a delight to His people. The shepherds may not have understood the universal note in the announcement. The Jews found it hard to see that the Messiah would be for the Gentiles as well. The good news is linked with peace which is a spiritual and not a political peace. The shepherds would only have had a glimpse of the Messianic peace. God had broken into history and therefore the Christian Church also worships.
• The pastoral scene was a witness to a historical event.

7) Summary: the Nature of the Messiah

He was Saviour and Lord, bringing deliverance and exercising sovereign authority.

• He was **Saviour and Lord**, bringing deliverance and exercising sovereign authority. As **Saviour,** His **role is one of deliverer.** See above where the title **Saviour** is used to sum up Jesus' humanity and compassion. For Luke, this child and not the Roman Emperor Augustus (Latin exalted one), who also called himself "the saviour of the world" is the key figure in history; Jesus is the Davidic Saviour (2:11).
• The title, **Messiah** points to His office as the promised Anointed One of God. His Lordship became an essential part of the early view of Him as part of an early Christian confession (cf. Rom. 10:9). The Emperor was also called "Lord" but it was a limited concept compared with the rich meaning of the Lordship of Jesus the Messiah. Bethlehem was David's town to stress Jesus' messianic claim to fulfil God's plan.
• Joseph and Mary had heard about the **Messiah's special saving mission** as it was focused on the name of Jesus. Mary is faithful because the name Jesus revealed by the angel is now given to the child (1:31).
• He is the Son of the Most High God (1:32).
• His coming was marked by the glory of the Lord. In the O.T. "shekinah" as "glory" was God's special presence to His people. References to the revealing of God's presence among His people occur in Ex. 16:7,10; 24:17; 40:34; Ps.63: 2. Events happened just as the angels had said and show that God is in control; His word comes to pass just as He says (2:20). "Just as they had been told" refers to the fulfilment of O.T. prophecy (2:20). God can be trusted and as the heavens rejoice so also should the earth. The Incarnation was glorious in its execution. The shepherds were filled with fear when they saw the glory of God. The only adequate explanation is that it was a supernatural manifestation.

Pupil's Activity: Thirteen (Read 2:8-20.)

What were the responses of:
a) the shepherds   b) others and   c) Mary to the birth of Jesus?

Pupil's Activity: Fourteen

a) Read the script of "The Shepherd and the Psychiatrist." b) Put the biblical evidence beside the "psychiatrist's" explanation.
c) With which of these explanations do you agree? d) Give reasons for your answer.

The Shepherd and the Psychiatrist

Cast: A Psychiatrist and a Shepherd
Doctor   Next please! Good morning (looking up). Name please?
Shepherd   Adam Sheepdip.
Doctor   Adam Sheepdip (writing). Occupation?
Shepherd   Nuclear physicist.
Doctor   (Looks up, then writes.) Shepherd. Now, what seems to be the trouble, Mr Sheepdip? Why do you need to see a psychiatrist?
Shepherd   The visions, doctor. I've been having visions.
Doctor   I see. And where were you when you had these .... visions?
Shepherd   Well, me and my mates were just, like, in the fields.
Doctor   Let me guess. Keeping watch over your flocks?
Shepherd   By night. That's it. Then I had the visions. In the sky. A bright, shining wondrous light.
Doctor   Really? Hmmm. (making notes) Seeing lights in the sky at night (looking up). It seems to me Mr Sheepdip that you may be suffering from what we in the profession call nocturnal-cosmic-photo-syndrome.
Shepherd   Oh. It looked more like the glory of God to me!
Doctor   So, how did you react to this light in the sky?
Shepherd   Well, we were afraid weren't we?

Doctor	(Writing) Afraid. Hmmm. Evidence of anxiety-neurosis, a touch of paranoia.
Shepherd	Then I looked up and found myself staring at an angel!
Doctor	An angel? I see. You mean a sort of heavenly being with a shining appearance floating around in space?
Shepherd	Something like that.
Doctor	(Humouring him) And, of course, he had wings? (sarcastically)
Shepherd	Ah, you've got me there, doc. It was too bright to see. But he did speak to us.
Doctor	He.....spoke to you? (Writing) Audio-visual hallucinatory tendency. And what did he say to you, this.....angel?
Shepherd	He told us not to be afraid - so you can cross out that bit about anxiety-neurosis. He said that he had good news of great joy for the whole world.
Doctor	And what was this good news?
Shepherd	That a Saviour had been born in Bethlehem - the one God had promised - and that we would find this baby wrapped in cloths lying in a manger - a long open trough that cattle eat out of. It's from the French word 'manger' which means to eat, you know.
Doctor	(Not really interested) Oh really. Seems a little unlikely. So, what happened next?
Shepherd	Well, suddenly the angel was surrounded by a heavenly host.
Doctor	Pardon?
Shepherd	Sorry - lots and lots of angels appeared, singing about the glory of God and peace on earth. It was amazing.
Doctor	Hmmm. (Writing) Pan-celestial-multi-faceted-audio-visual-hallucinatory-tendency. So, I suppose you trotted off to Bethlehem?
Shepherd	Ah, you've got me there, doc. It was too bright to see. But he did speak to us.
Doctor	He.....spoke to you? (Writing) Audio-visual hallucinatory tendency. And what did he say to you, this.....angel?
Shepherd	He told us not to be afraid - so you can cross out that bit about anxiety-neurosis. He said that he had good news of great joy for the whole world.
Doctor	And what was this good news?
Shepherd	That a Saviour had been born in Bethlehem - the one God had promised - and that we would find this baby wrapped in cloths lying in a manger - a long open trough that cattle eat out of. It's from the French word 'manger' which means to eat, you know.
Doctor	(Not really interested) Oh really. Seems a little unlikely. So, what happened next?
Shepherd	Well, suddenly the angel was surrounded by a heavenly host.
Doctor	Pardon?
Shepherd	Sorry - lots and lots of angels appeared, singing about the glory of God and peace on earth. It was amazing.
Doctor	Hmmm. (Writing) Pan-celestial-multi-faceted-audio-visual-hallucinatory-tendency. So, I suppose you trotted off to Bethlehem?
Shepherd	You bet. But we ran rather than trotted. We didn't go to any of the posh hotels in Bethlehem. We looked in the back streets and alleys. Eventually we bumped into this man who told us about a young couple from Nazareth who had begged him for a room because she was going into labour. He'd found them a place in the cow-shed round the back.
Doctor	So you went round to the cow-shed?
Shepherd	At once. And there they were - Mary and Joseph and the baby lying in a manger.
Doctor	A big manger, was it?
Shepherd	No (pointing to the doctor's notes). That's Mary and Joseph, comma, and the baby lying in a manger.
Doctor	And how did you find the mother and baby?
Shepherd	It was easy - we just went in and there they were.
Doctor	No, I mean were they doing well after the birth?
Shepherd	Oh yes - they were both in a stable condition.
Doctor	So, this baby - supposed to be the Saviour of the world - in a feeding trough - in a cow shed.
Shepherd	Well, it does seem unlikely. And the parents were from Nazareth! (Both laugh). And the baby didn't seem anything special - they all look the same to me. But, doctor, the presence of God was in that stable. It was like stepping into the 'holy of holies' in the Temple. It gave me the shivers. As though something really big was going on - right there in a stable in Bethlehem, and we were the first to know about it - a bunch of scruffy shepherds! Then this feeling of peace with God and deep down joy came over me.
Doctor	Hmmm. And what did they call this baby?
Shepherd	(Reverently) Jesus. It means 'saviour' you know. Just like the angel said.
Doctor	Right. I think I've got the background. Now, how can I help you Mr Sheepdip?
Shepherd	Well, doctor, the thing is....it can't really be true, can it? This baby in the trough, born to an ordinary girl from Nazareth, This can't really be God becoming a human, can it? This baby can't be the one to save the world?
Doctor	Well, as you say, it does seem rather unlikely.
Shepherd	But it happened - the lights, the angel, Bethlehem - it all actually happened. And what if it is true? The world can't ever be the same again, can it? If God comes to us like that then even an old shepherd like me has a chance.
Doctor	Or even a sceptical old psychiatrist like me (sceptically).
Shepherd	Every one of us. It's as if God is saying "I've stepped into your world to help you out." What do you think, doctor? Can it be true? Or am I just a stupid old shepherd suffering from that pan-celestial thing syndrome? What should I do about it all?
Doctor	Well, Mr Sheepdip, as a professional, my advice is to forget all about it.
Shepherd	Forget all about it?
Doctor	Yes. Just try to put it all out of your mind.
Shepherd	Sorry, doc. There's no way I can just forget it. What happened that night will live with me for the rest of my life! I can't just forget about it!
Doctor	Well alright then. I'll tell you what. Just think about it, say, once a year. Yes, that's the way to deal with it. Once a year allow yourself to remember the visions and the angels and the baby in the manger. And then forget about it for the rest of the year and get on with your life. (Leaning forward seriously) Mr Sheepdip, your sheep need you.
Shepherd	(Picking up his crook and starting to leave) Thank you, doctor. Yes, I suppose I'd better get back to my sheep and forget about it.
Doctor	Was there anyone else in the waiting room when you came in?
Shepherd	Just some wise guy going on about a star.

Author: Anon

Pupil's Activity: Fifteen

a) On the map based on the birth narratives find the following places:- [See map Ch. 9: John the Baptist.]

(1) Bethlehem (2:4,15)   (2) Jerusalem   (2:22, 25, 38)   (3) The hill country of Judea (1:39, 65)

b) Identify the main features of the birth and infancy narratives in Luke's Gospel.

(Edexcel A/S 2004) [14 Marks] (4) Qumran (1:80)   (5) Judea (2:4)   (6) Syria (2:2) (7) The desert/the Judean wilderness (John the Baptist) (1:80)

c) How far do these features reflect the author's understanding of the divinity of Jesus. (Edexcel A/S 2004)   [6 Marks]

[6] The presentation of Jesus in the Temple in Jerusalem (Read 2:21-40.) [See p. 227.]

A) The obedient naming of Jesus at circumcision (2:21)

The Jews had to conform to Jewish ritual so Jesus had to be incorporated into the covenant people through circumcision. Jesus opened the way into a New Covenant without circumcision. His parents "took" him up to Jerusalem (Bethlehem was five miles from south of Jerusalem) to be cicumcised (2:21; Gen. 17:9-14; Lev. 12:3).

B) The Jewish purification law (Read 2:22-24.)

1) Luke refers to "their purification" meaning that of Mary and Joseph or Mary and Jesus. It is likely that this refers to Mary's purification and "their" means Joseph, his inclusion showing family solidarity, Joseph wanting to be identified with Mary. This incident takes place forty days after the birth and thirty days after circumcision. This would have been **for purification of Mary** which required a sacrifice being offered at the Nicanor Gate in the Court of Women (2:22a; Lev. 12:2-4).

2) The presentation of the first-born to the Lord (Ex.13:2) required the payment of five shekels as a ransom "for the redemption of the first-born." (Num.3:47-48; 18:15-16) Luke does not mention this payment.

3) The dedication of the first-born son to the Lord's service (1 Sam.1:11, 22, 28) in 2:23 is the consecration of Jesus to His Messianic ministry.

4) Mary's purification required a sacrifice of purification based upon Lev.12:8; 2:24. Mary faithfully follows the O.T. law in presenting a lamb as a burnt offering and a turtle dove as a sin offering to be offered up by the priests (Lev. 12:2-4,6). Mary and Joseph used the offering for a poor person. The Messiah's coming was independent of favourable circumstances: the lowliness of birth showed the purpose of His coming to be a servant. The parents followed the law in bringing the child to the Lord.

==He is the Saviour-Messiah come to redeem the whole world.==

C) Simeon's prophecy (2:25-32)

The name Simeon means, "God has heard." (Fitzmyer) **(44)** Simeon's response is in the words of the Nunc Dimittis from the Latin meaning "Now let your servant (Gk.doulon meaning bond slave) depart." (2:29) Simeon is waiting (Gk. prosdechomenos) for "the consolation (Gk.parakleson) of Israel": he is waiting for God to come and comfort His people and he refers to the hope of the deliverance of Israel (2:25; Is.40:1; 49:13; 51:3; 61:2). Later rabbis would call Him comforter. (SB.) **(45)** Simeon was well known for his piety as he was just and devout. He was forward looking; his imagination was fired by the Messianic promises and he longed for the Messiah to come.

Simeon's received revelation from God: **God's Spirit came upon him** and, when that happens, a person speaks for all time (2:25). He was told that he would see the Messiah (2:26). Simeon receives the child. Luke uses the term "parents" perhaps to show that Joseph was the adopted and legal father of Jesus (2:27). The parents were taking their first-born to the Temple area (Gk.hieron) to dedicate their child according to the law. This would have been the Court of the Gentiles or the Court of Women. Later, Luke says (3:23), "Jesus being the son of Joseph (as was supposed)." Luke uses the expression, "his father and mother" (2:33) to show their natural relationship to Jesus. Mary and Joseph marvelled at what was said (2:33).

D) Nunc Dimittis (Read 2:28-32.)

1) Simeon praises God; Simeon could die in peace knowing that God had kept His word. "Lord, now let your servant depart in peace" is a Semitic expression for, "Let me die." (2:28-29; Num.20:29) Lord means Sovereign Lord (Gk. despota), who is in control. Simeon recognised the wider aspects of the **Messianic mission**. He gave as his reason for praise, that of having seen Jesus: he has seen God's salvation (2:30). **Jesus**, "a light to the nations and for glory to Israel:" (2:31-33) light (Gk.phos) is an image for the Son of David. His purpose in coming was to be the **Messiah: a light** for the **Gentiles** and also for the **glory** (Gk.doxa) **of Israel** (2:32). The Gentiles were in moral decline; Israel's glorious heritage had departed. Both needs were met in Jesus. This verse can also be translated "light, for revelation to the Gentiles, and for the glory of your people Israel." Light has the idea here of illumination coming into a dark place (1:79). (Marshall) **(46)** It is as a saving light, "I will also make you a light for the Gentiles, that you may bring my salvation to the ends of the earth." (Is.49:6) The Gentiles are attracted by the brightness of the glory and the light. Godet **(47)** notes that the Gentiles are placed first by Simeon. Did he realise that the salvation of the Jews can only happen after the nations have been enlightened? Had he realised that Israel was about to reject the Messiah? Simeon recognised that Jesus would be the Messiah for the whole world. This is the clearest indication of the worldwide aspect of Jesus' work of redemption. For Israel the coming of the Messiah spells glory which is always associated with brightness and so with light and revelation. "I will bring my deliverance, it is not far off, and my salvation will not tarry; I will put salvation in Zion, or Israel my glory." (Is. 46:13) "Arise, shine; for your light has come, and the glory of the Lord has risen upon you. For behold, darkness shall cover the earth, and thick darkness the peoples; but the Lord will arise upon you, and His glory shall be seen upon you. And nations shall come to your light, and kings to the brightness of your rising. Then you shall see and be radiant." (Is. 60:1-3,5) The Gentiles will take part as equals in the glory by receiving the revelation. Jesus, as the light, brings salvation to everyone and "illuminates them into God's way." Jesus for the first time is seen as the **"Servant"** hope of Is. 40-66, the note of victory rather than the Suffering Servant. (Bock) **(48)** He is the **Victorious Servant**. This hymn shows the whole universal scope of the work of Jesus. The royal, Davidic, messianic Saviour-Servant has come to redeem not just Israel but everyone, the **Saviour-Messiah** come to redeem the whole world.

2) Jesus' parents marvel. (Read 2:33.)

The response of the parents of Jesus is one of wonder and amazement (Gk. thaumazountes), because of the new note of universality about the ministry of Jesus; would be a natural response after a revelation.

> "Lord, now let your servant depart in peace" is a Semitic expression for, "Let me die." (Num.20:29) (LXX) "Lord" means Sovereign Lord (Gk. despota), who is in control (2:29).

3) Simeon blesses Jesus and addresses Mary. (Read 2:34-35.)

Mary's son is set for the fall and rise of many in Israel (2:34b). Jesus as a figure will be opposed by many people and He will not be their hope of promise. It will not be plain sailing for God's anointed. As well as bringing victory He will bring division. The Messiah would be an object of hatred and a sign to be resisted (2:34c). The sword is a broad two-edged sword (Gk. roumphaia) which will bring extreme, emotional pain to Mary. "A sword will pierce through your own soul." (2:35) This foreshadows the sufferings of Jesus (2:35; 5:35).

4) Anna's reaction (Read 2:36-38.)

Anna, whose Semitic name means "grace," is waiting for the "redemption of Israel (Jerusalem)": she is waiting (Gk. prosdechomenois) for God to come and rescue His people (2:38). Redemption (Gk.lutrosin) refers to God's decisive act of salvation for His people (Is. 40:9; 52: 9; 63:4), like Joseph of Arimathea, who also was waiting (Gk.prosedecheto) for the kingdom of God (23:51). She was probably widowed in her early twenties if married at the age of thirteen or fourteen. If so she was widowed for at least sixty-five years. She had chosen a life-time of service to God rather than remarriage. Anna was well known in the Temple as she worshipped (Gk.latreuousa): her total focus was upon serving God in prayer all day there constantly. She is called a prophetess and therefore she recognised the coming Redeemer. The Messiah became the topic of her conversation among the people who expected the Messiah. Here, a very spiritual woman of the city, testifies to Jesus. She turns to offer thanksgiving to God. She addresses her remarks to those who also waiting for the consummation of God's plan. Simeon and Anna praise God for the Messiah, while Jewish leaders later failed having rejected and crucified Him. In these birth narratives some men, women and shepherds all come to appreciate the child Jesus. [See p. 227.]

Pupil's Activity: Sixteen   Revision exercise

Identify the people and their expectations by completing the grid based upon Chs. 1-2. **(Figure 9)**

Refs.	People	Their expectations
1:21		
2:25		
2:38		

[7] Jesus in Jerusalem aged twelve –The Nazareth years (Read 2:41-52.)

A) Upbringing in Nazareth (Read 2:40.)

Luke records that Jesus grew physically and mentally and was noted for His strength and wisdom. He found favour with God: He grew in the wisdom and fear of God (2:40). Reference to Jesus being filled with wisdom and strong in spirit prepares us for this incident in the Temple where Jesus shows His wisdom. His life was viewed with favour by people and He obeyed His parents. The years of Mary's patient care over the developing life of Jesus were important for God's plan for the Messiah. Boys at school were taught to recite Scripture starting with Leviticus and later they were taught how to interpret Scripture. The very clever were instructed in oral law and graduated from a particular school of law. Jesus probably did not receive the highest education. Those who did not receive this higher education were despised as those who were seen as ignorant and unlearned. The Messiah had good rapport with the general public as he matured socially. **His mission** was prompted by humility and not academic achievement. Other children were born to Mary as Jesus' brothers and sisters are mentioned later; His brothers Joses, Simon, James and Jude are named in Matt. 13:55, but His sisters are not mentioned. James and Jude wrote N.T. letters but we do not know anything about the other two brothers. Nazareth was not noted for producing leaders (Jn.1:46).

B) The Temple visit to Jerusalem (Read 2:41-51.)

The infancy section begins and ends in the Temple as does the Gospel of Luke: Jesus never turned His back on Judaism. His parents kept the Passover which shows He was brought up in a religious environment and the tense of the verb "went" (Gk.iterative imperfect) indicates that they went to Jerusalem habitually to celebrate the Passover (2:41). This event happened when Jesus was twelve at the Jewish Passover festival in March/April and gives us a special insight into **the humanity of Jesus.** Jewish men were commanded by O.T. law to go to Jerusalem three times a year for the feasts of Passover, Pentecost and Tabernacles but in the first-century the very religious who lived far away, could travel once a year. Jesus' parents may have stayed the seven-day period. His parents assumed that Jesus was with the relations. As whole villages would have travelled together this might explain why His parents were not concerned about their missing boy. [See Ch.6: Luke the historian.] The parents returned and Jesus stayed behind (2:43). The Greek word "pais", child is used here for Jesus, showing the event happens early in the life of Jesus. This is the first time the title is used of Jesus. Before this event the Greek word "paidion", "little child" is used (2:17, 27, 40) and the usage of this indicated **Jesus' physical growth and humanity at this stage**. His parents assumed Jesus was in the caravan with the other children and that he was safe with family and friends.

> Reference to Jesus being filled with wisdom and strong in spirit prepares us for this incident in the Temple where Jesus shows His wisdom (2:40).

C) A day elapsed before the parents realised Jesus was missing (2:44). Immediately His parents headed back to Jerusalem searching for Him everywhere (2:45). After three days they found him (2:46). Jesus' role as a teacher can be seen here and also in 4:20-27; 5:3. It is thought that He was found in Solomon's portico the outer Temple court and not the inner Temple sanctuary (Acts 3:11). Here he is taking instruction (not giving it) which shows his thirst for knowledge and his ability to discuss spiritual questions. From an early age we can see his wisdom; he is on equal footing with the Jewish teachers. The central phrase of the incident, which consists of 170 words, is "among the teachers." The crowd are astonished (Gk.existanto means the wonder which comes from the insight shown by the answers he gave) at his wisdom. Jesus shows no awareness of His divinity as His parents do not understand his remarkable spiritual insight. He is seen here as someone remarkably gifted by God and endowed with wisdom. Those around show respect for the quality of his questions (2:46) and answers (2:47).

His parents are overwhelmed by the events and are full of amazement and relief, even though they were anxious about finding Jesus (2:48). Mary points out that they have searched for him with deep anxiety, mental pain and stress. They want to know why he has acted so insensitively and their language is one of complaint. By his reply, his parents have failed to understand his real mission and they seemed to be more concerned about getting home (2:48). Mary refers to Jesus as "child", and then asks "why have you treated us so?" She continues by saying "**your father and I** have been looking for you anxiously." Jesus replies with a question. Was this question, "Why did you not know where I would be in the Temple?" or was it, "Why are you searching for me all over?" The parents were amazed at the way in which his sonship showed itself.

> Jesus' Davidic descent is indicative of His humanity; He is the Davidic Messiah, "descended from David according to the flesh." (Rom.1:3) "The Lord God will give Him the throne of His father David." (1:32-33)

D) By the age of twelve Jesus recognised His Filial relationship to His Father and was obedient to Him. O.T. tradition suggests that Samuel started his prophetic ministry aged twelve. (Josephus) **(49)** "This incident is about **Jesus' sense of mission** and His preparation for it."(Evans) **(50)** Jesus said, "Did you not know that I **must** be in my Father's house?" (2:49) It is the first time Jesus uses the expression "I must." Jesus shows His allegiance to His Heavenly Father in aligning Himself with God's purpose even if it appears to contradict His relations with his parents: his parents fail to understand the comprehensive scope of his mission (2:50).

After this Jesus returns home with his parents to Nazareth. He submits himself to them for the next seventeen years during which time Joseph died. In obedience to them he shows his humanity (2:51). Mary took note of all that happened, accepted his retort and pondered all these things in her heart. This may be a clue into the source of the birth narratives and it is likely she contributed much of the material. Mary kept all those thoughts to herself. Unique to Luke is the word "increased" (Gk. proekopte)(2:52). Jesus increased in insight (wisdom), stature (physical stature), grace (moral growth) and favourable perception (2:52; Prov.3:3).

Luke presents the growth of Jesus very naturally. Firstly, in (2:16), he is a (Gk.brephos) meaning a baby, "the shepherds found Mary and Joseph, and the babe lying in a manger." Secondly, he is a "Gk.paidion" meaning a little child (2:40), "the child grew and became strong, filled with wisdom and the favour of God was on him." Thirdly, the Greek word "pais" meaning child, when the feast was ended the boy Jesus stayed behind in Jerusalem (2:43). Finally there is the name Jesus, "Jesus increased in wisdom and stature, and in favour of God and men." (2:52) This also shows how far Jesus' self-understanding of Himself went; Jesus is the Messiah-Servant who knows Himself to be the Son of God. (Bock) **(51)** Mary's presence shows her spiritual commitment to the upbringing of Jesus as only men were required to go on this journey to Jerusalem at the feast of the Passover (2:41). The trip would take three days as it was an eighty-mile journey from Nazareth to Jerusalem. The custom of Bar-Mitzvah, for a thirteen-year old boy, was not in place at this time. (Fitzmyer) **(52)**

> Jesus shows His allegiance to His Heavenly Father in aligning Himself with God's purpose even if it appears to contradict His relations with His parents, who fail to understand the comprehensive scope of His mission (2:50).

E) Summary of the humanity of Jesus in the birth narratives
• At the Annunciation of the Messiah's birth, Mary is told that she will conceive in her womb and bear a son (1:31). Jesus' Davidic descent is indicative of His humanity; He is the Davidic Messiah (Rom.1:3). "The Lord God will give Him the throne of His father David." (1:32-33)
• **"Saviour"** (Gk.Soter) is someone who delivers God's people from physical and spiritual danger: it sums up Jesus' **humanity and compassion** and is Luke's most distinctive title for Jesus. "Today in the city of David, a Saviour is born to you, He is Christ the Lord." (2:11) Mary calls Jesus, "My Saviour." (1:47)
• The incident of Jesus at the Temple with his parents:- (Read 2:41-52.) The term parents (Gk.goneis)[2:41,43b] and the reference to his "his father and mother" all point to the humanity of Jesus (2:33).
• When Jesus aged twelve said that he must be in "the house of his Father": he was not initially understood by his parents regarding the real meaning of his mission. Mary refers to herself and Joseph as, "Your father and I." (2:48) Jesus as a twelve-year old boy has a real sense of his personal mission (2:48). His parents could not comprehend his self-understanding. His struggle with his parents is not dissimilar to that with his disciples. This incident presents Jesus as very wise and knowing.

By the age of twelve Jesus recognised His Filial relationship to His Father and was obedient to Him. (2:49)

• The description of Jesus as the child "Jesus" (Gk.pais) (2:43) is in sharp contrast with him as a (Gk.brephos meaning baby) (2:16) and as a little child Jesus (Gk.paidion) (2:17, 27, 40). He is described as "among the teachers." Luke presents the development of Jesus quite naturally. (Morris and Bock) **(53)** [For contra see note **(41)**.] Each term changes from one event to another until finally there is the name Jesus. The teachers are astonished (Gk.existanto means the wonder which comes from the insight shown by the answers given by a twelve-year old boy) and at his wisdom.

• Jesus shows no awareness of His divinity as His parents do not understand his remarkable spiritual insight. This incident is not the only time in the Gospel that those close to Jesus will fail to understand him (9:54).

• He is seen here as someone remarkably gifted by God and endowed with wisdom. Those around show respect for the quality of his questions (2:46) and answers (2:47).

• Luke presents Jesus as a twelve-year old/young man who is able to think for himself. The teachers were amazed at his exceptional understanding and his answers (2:47).

• On the return journey from Jerusalem to Nazareth in Galilee (2:51), his parents discovered that he had not accompanied them. They found him in the Temple discussing with the teachers. Mary questioned Jesus as to why he had treated them with so much insensitivity and making them anxious regarding his personal safety, well-being after a three-day separation (2:48). We have searched for you with great anxiety (Gk.odunasthai). Why have you treated us so painfully? This is the language of complaint.

• The obedient Jesus returns with his parents to Nazareth as Mary mulls over these things in her heart (2:51).

• Luke concludes this section with a note on the growth of Jesus (2:52) compared with one similar note about John (2:52; 1:80). Wisdom (spiritual insight), stature (physical growth) and favour with God (moral growth) and people all (socially) show Luke's human portrait of Jesus. Everyone recognised these four ways in which Jesus had grown (2:52,40). Human maturing even in perfect form involves not only physical growth but development in wisdom and doing that which is pleasing to God and humankind. His humanity can be clearly seen in the fourfold ways in which he developed. Jesus between the ages of 5-13 would have been sent to the community school for elementary education for boys in the synagogue. (Blomberg) **(54)**

Pupil's Activity: Seventeen
a) Outline your knowledge and understanding of Luke's account of the presentation of Jesus in the Temple and Jesus' visit to the temple at the age of twelve. (CCEA A/S 2003)   [30 marks]
b) Explore the claim that Luke had a particular interest in the early life of Jesus. Justify your answer.
(CCEA A/S 2003)   [15 marks]

F) A summary of the key issues in the birth narratives: [Adopted from Green **(55)**]
• Deep spirituality – 1:5-6; 2:22-24, 25-27
• Presence and power of the Holy Spirit – 1:15,35,41,67; 2:25-27
• Hope for deliverance – 1:51-53,68-75 ; 2:25
• Joy, exultation and praise – 1:14,28,44,47,68; 2:10, 28-29
• Lord/Master and slave – 1:38,47-48; 2:29
• Peace – 1:79; 2:14,29
• Saviour, salvation, instrument of salvation – 1:47, 69,71,77; 2:11,30
• Advance preparation – 1:17,76; 2:31
• Universalism – 2:1-14,31-32
• Dawning light – 1:78-79; 2:9,32
• Sifting of Israel – 1:16,20; 2:34-35
• Social transposition – 1:51-53; 2:34

> **Wisdom (spiritual insight), stature (physical growth) and favour with God (moral growth) and people (socially) all show Luke's human portrait of Jesus. Everyone recognised these four ways in which Jesus had grown (2:52, 40).**

Luke has been building up a picture of Jesus' mission and His role in God's purpose. In many ways Simeon exemplifies these qualities. He is the agent of the Holy Spirit and he lives in the Temple where he uses O.T. ideas from Isaiah to show his praise to God (Is. 66:1).

1. Simeon looks forward to the consolation of Israel (2:25). Simeon is told that he will see the Lord's Messiah (2:26). Simeon sees God's instrument of salvation (2:30).

2. Simeon would not see death before he sees the Messiah (2:26). He is now ready to die (2:29).

3. It has been revealed to Simeon by the Holy Spirit (2:26). It has happened according to the word of God (2:29).

This outline goes from **promise to fulfilment** to **response of praise** and operates on these three levels.

G) Conclusion

Are the birth narratives to be regarded as symbolic? This is largely the view of Caird **(56)** who argued that the three ingredients of prophecy, history and symbolism are so woven together in the birth narratives that they are inseparable. Luke does not say that any prophecy is fulfilled but as the prophecies underlie the message of Gabriel to Zechariah and Mary (Mal. 3-4:6; Is.7:14) so Micah 5:2-5 is woven into the fabric of the narrative. "But you, O Bethlehem though you are small among the clans of Judah from you will come one who will be ruler over Israel."

In the town of Bethlehem a mother gives birth to a son, a prince of the ancient lineage, who will be a shepherd of the scattered sheep of Israel, standing in the glory of God (2:9) and extending His authority to the ends of the earth, with a proclamation from heaven (2:14). Caird says that for Luke the promise of God had become true because of a decree by the Imperial power an enactment of the Roman government (2:1). God's purposes were being worked out in the hesitancy of Zechariah (1:18), the joy of Elizabeth (1:59), the quiet faith of Mary (1:30); Caesar Augustus too like Cyrus (Is. 45:1) had an unwitting part to play in the salvation which would encompass the whole world, his entire empire. Regarding the census (2:1), Caird **(57)** says, "There is no question about the symbolic value to Luke even though it presents historical problems."

"The arm of the Lord" is a symbol of strength in the O.T. (1:51a; Deut. 4:34; Ps. 44:3).

Other symbolisms Caird says are:
• "No place for them at the inn." (2:7) which was the common guest room of the inn. Just like the Son of Man who had no place to lay His head, (9:58b) the king of the Jews would have no throne but a cross.
• The first worshippers, the shepherds were despised by the orthodox because their occupations made them neglectful of religious observance. (Caird) **(58)** They are the forerunners of multitudes of humble people who thronged Jesus in His public ministry (2:8-20).
• The chorus of angels who anticipate the joy which rings throughout the Gospel of Luke especially when a lost sheep is found (2:14; 15:7).
• The wonder with which the shepherds' story was greeted prepares us for a deeper and more abiding wonder to come (2:20).
• Examples of O.T. imagery used as symbolism and not recognised by Caird as symbolism:
1. "the horn of salvation". O.T. images are used in the birth narratives as symbols and act as a foreshadow of what is to come. Caird however, does not seem to recognise the symbolism used in that of O.T. imagery as in the expression, "He has raised up a horn of salvation." Horn in the O.T. and in this context is a symbol of strength (1:69; Deut. 33:17; Ezek. 9:21). "As an animal's strength is in its horn, so God is a horn in effecting His mighty act of salvation." Ellis **(59)** The use of horn in this context is similar to Pss. 89:17; 132:17 where a horn is raised and sprouts up from David. Morris **(60)** says as horn was a symbol of strength so "a horn of salvation" means a "mighty salvation" or a "strong saviour". The Song of Zechariah reiterates this promise and combines two O.T. images or motifs, Jubilee and David's dynasty.
2. "the day shall dawn upon us from on high." In (1:78), God sends His messenger as a bright dawn of salvation upon the face of people. Zechariah combines two O.T. images that of the Davidic Messiah, the Shoot from Jesse (Is.11:1) and the star from Jacob (Num. 24:17), who is to visit men from on high, God's dwelling place (2 Sam. 22:17). The sunrise from above is about to dawn (1:78) and it will mean redemption (1:68), salvation (1:69), deliverance and freedom to serve God (1:74-75), forgiveness of sins, freedom from the fear of death and peace (1:77-79). Gooding **(61)** "God has raised a horn of salvation for us (RSV), a mighty saviour for us (NRSV) from the house of David." (1:69) This horn is Jesus and not John.
3. The Song of Zechariah (1:67-69) is full of O.T. symbolism to show how profound is the salvation now unfolding.
4. "the arm of the Lord" is a symbol of strength in the O.T. "He has shown His strength with His arm." (1:51a; Deut.4:34; Ps.44:3)
5. The symbolic interest in the 70 weeks: "the six months" between the two annunciations (1:11) = 180 days; 9 months = 270 days for Mary's pregnancy; and 40 days from there to the presentation: total days = 490 days (7 weeks). The 70 weeks of Daniel 9:24 are the basis of this view. This view cannot be held with certainty. (Burrows) **(62)**
6. Some other scholars today argue that the shepherds were symbolical of the hatred towards Jesus. This view was based upon Rabbinic teachings. O.T. motifs about shepherds are very positive, for example Abraham, Moses and David. [See 2:8.]

Pupil's Activity: Eighteen
a) Examine the main features of the birth and infancy narratives in Luke's Gospel which reflect both the humanity and the theological importance of his birth. (Edexcel A/S 2003) [14 marks]
b) To what extent are the birth and infancy narratives symbolic rather than historically accurate?
(Edexcel A/S 2003/2005)   [6 marks]

Pupils' Activity: Nineteen
a) When the angel Gabriel appeared to Mary (1:30-33) what titles were used by the angel to describe her son?
b) What was the significance of those titles?

Pupils' Activity: Twenty
a) In Ch.2:8-14, when the angel of the Lord appeared to the shepherds, what titles did the angel use for "the babe wrapped in swaddling clothes"?
b) Why was Jesus' role as Saviour so important to Luke and how did it fulfil the O.T. predictions? (When doing this activity, background music from "Handel's Messiah" could be used, or C.D. starting from the recitative "There were shepherds abiding in the field......." "Glory to God in the Highest."

Pupil's Activity: Twenty-one

Which of the titles used for Jesus in the following carols appear in the first two chapters of Luke?

A. He came down to earth from heaven
Who is God and Lord of all,
And his shelter was a stable
And his cradle was a stall;
With the poor and mean and lowly
Lived on earth our Saviour holy.
("Once in Royal David's City" verse 2   Mrs. C.F. Alexander)

B. Christ by highest heaven adored,
Christ the everlasting Lord;
Late in time behold him come,
Offspring of a virgin's womb.
Veiled in flesh the Godhead see
Hail the Incarnate Deity.
Pleased as man with man to dwell
Jesus our Immanuel!
Hark the herald angels sing,
"Glory to the newborn king."

Hail the heaven born Prince of Peace!
Hail the Sun of Righteousness!
Light and life to all he brings,
Risen with healing in his wings.
Mild he lays his glory by,
Born that man no more may die.
Born to raise the sons of earth.
Born to give them second birth.
Hark the herald angels sing,
"Glory to the newborn king."
("Hark the Herald Angels Sing" verses 2
and 3 Charles Wesley)

C.As Joseph was a walking he heard an angel sing,
This night- shall be born—our heavenly King,
He neither shall be born in housen nor in hall,
Nor in a place of Paradise, but in an ox's stall.
Noel, Noel.
("Joseph and the angel" verse 1 and chorus.   Author anon.)

Pupil's Activity: Twenty-two

a) Identify the three hymns in Luke Chapters 1-2.
b) Explain the meaning of the titles of each of them.
c) Outline your knowledge and understanding of these three hymns.

Pupil's Activity: Twenty-three

a) Give an account of the different kinds of people who experienced joy at the coming of Jesus.
b) What does this tell us about the appeal of Jesus?

Pupil's Activity: Twenty-four

(1) For revision purposes which of these titles or expressions for Mary (see below) occur in the Birth Narratives of Luke's Gospel?
(a) Mother of God, (b) A virgin betrothed to a man, (c) Queen of Heaven, (d) Virgin Mary, (e) "Hail, O favoured one," (f) the handmaiden of the Lord, (g) "Blessed (Gk.eulogemene) are you among women and blessed (Gk.eulogemos) is the fruit of your womb." (h) "All generations will call me blessed." (Gk.makariousi) (i) "Blessed (Gk.makaraios) is she who believed there would be a fulfilment." (j) The Assumption of Mary, (k) the virgin's name was Mary/Mariam/Miriam, (l) The Immaculate Conception of Mary, (m) Co-Redemptrix (McCafferty) **(63)**

Pupil's Activity: Twenty-five

a) Outline your knowledge and understanding of Luke's account of the Annunciation and the visit of Mary to Elizabeth.
(CCEA A/S 2005)   [30 marks]
b) Comment on the claim that Mary plays a central role in the Infancy Narrative.
(CCEA A/S 2005)   [15 marks]
c) Outline and examine the main features of the birth and infancy narratives presented in Luke's Gospel.
(Edexcel A/S 2001)   [14 marks]
d) How far does the presentation of the birth and infancy narratives reflect the author's understanding of the humanity of Jesus? (Edexcel A/S 2001)   [6 marks]
e) Outline your knowledge and understanding of Luke's account of the events leading up to the birth of Jesus.
(CCEA (A/S) 2001)   [30 marks]
f) Explore the claim that Luke presents Mary as a model of trust and prayer in this account. Justify your answer.
(CCEA (A/S) 2001)   [15 marks]
g) Comment on the claim that Mary plays a central role in the Infancy Narrative. Justify your answer.
(CCEA (A/S) 2005)   [15 marks]

Pupil's Activity: Twenty-six

a) Examine the main features of the birth and infancy narratives presented in Luke's Gospel
(Edexcel A/S 2002/2005)   [14 Marks]
b) Consider how a study of these narratives contributes to an understanding of the mission of Jesus.
(Edexcel A/S 2002)   [6 Marks]
c) How far might the birth and infancy narratives be considered to be symbolic, rather than a historical account?
(Edexcel A/S 2002)   [6 Marks]

Outcomes

Students should be able to identify and have a knowledge and understanding of:
- the main events in the Infancy Narratives in Luke's Gospel.
- key characters, for example Mary as a model of trust and prayer. (CCEA)
- key concepts, for example the presence and power of the Holy Spirit, Saviour, salvation, angelophany, and universalistic message.

Students should be able to examine:
- the main features of these events in the Infancy Narratives. (Edexcel)
- the Infancy Narratives as symbolic. (Edexcel)
- the mission of Jesus and that of John the Baptist in the Infancy Narratives. (Edexcel)
- the humanity and divinity of Jesus in the Infancy Narratives. (Edexcel)
- Luke's special interest in the early years of Jesus.

Notes on Ch.8: Birth Narratives

1. Philip H. Wiebe's, Visions of Jesus: Direct encounters from the N.T. Today, Oxford Press, (1997)-criteria for assessing visions and miracles.
2. Joachim Jeremias, Jerusalem in the Time of Jesus; Economic and Social Conditions in the N.T. Period. Philadelphia: Fortress Press, London, SCM, (1969) p.199.
3. Joseph A. Fitzmyer, op. cit. p.322.
4. Joseph A. Fitzmyer, op. cit. p.323.
5. Josephus Antiquites, 13.282f.
6. Darrell Bock, op. cit. p. 88.
7. Joseph A. Fitzmyer, op. cit. p.328.
8. Joseph A. Fitzmyer, op. cit. p.328. (ibid.)
9. M. Yoma' 5.
10. Craig Evans, New Testament Studies, NIBC based on the NIV, Paternoster Press, (1998) p.22.
11. Raymond E. Brown, The Birth of the Messiah: A Commentary on the Infancy Narratives in Matthew and Luke, N.Y. Doubleday, (1977).*
12. Raymond E. Brown, (ibid.)
13. Joseph A. Fitzmyer, op. cit. p.344.
14. Howard Marshall, op. cit. p. 65.
15. Joseph A. Fitzmyer, op. cit. p.346.
16. Klostermann op. cit. p.13.
17. J.M. Creed op. cit. p.17.
18. Joseph A. Fitzmyer, Vol. 1, op. cit. p.345.
19. Howard Marshall, op. cit. pp.67-68.
20. Raymond E. Brown, op. cit. pp. 310-316.
21. F. Godet, A Commentary on the Gospel of Luke, T. and T. Clark, Edinburgh, (1875) p.94.
22. John Nolland, op. cit. pp. 66-67.
23. Raymond Brown, op. cit. p.342.
24. Joel Green, op. cit. p.103.
25. Robert Stein, op. cit. p.142.
26. Joel Green, op. cit. pp.98-105.
27. Charles H. Talbert, op. cit. p. 24.
28. F. Godet, op. cit. pp. 93-94.
29. Darrell L. Bock, op. cit. p.90.
30. Robert C. Tannehill, The Magnificat as Poem , JBL, 93:263-75, (1974) p. 264.
31. Robert C. Tannehill, (ibid.)
32. Stephen Farris, The hymns of Luke's Infancy Narratives :Their Origin, Meaning and Significance, (1985) p.147.
33. Walter Grundmann, THZNT, Berlin, (1963) p.90 cited in Bock p.245.
34. Joseph A. Fitzmyer, op.cit. p. 384.
35. I. Howard Marshall, op. cit. p. 92.
36. Joseph A. Fitzmyer, op. cit. p.389.
37. Darrell L. Bock, op. cit. p. 198.
38. I. Howard Marshall, op. cit. p.105.
39. Raymond E. Brown, op. cit. p.342.
40. Herman L. Strack and Paul Billerbeck, (1922-28) 2: 113–14; Sanh.25b; Midr. Ps.23.2.
41. Joseph A. Fitzmyer, op. cit. p. 408.
42. F.W. Danker, op. cit. p. 60.
43. Charles Giblin, Reflections on the Sign in the Manger, CBQ, (1967), 87-101, "Sign of the manger" pp. 90-95.
44. Joseph A. Fitzmyer, op. cit. p. 426.
45. S.B., (1.6683,195).
46. I. Howard Marshall, op. cit. p.121.
47. F. Godet, op. cit. p.139.
48. Darrell L. Bock, op. cit. p.245.
49. Josephus, Antiquities, 5:348.
50. Craig Evans, op. cit. p. 255.
51. Darrell L. Bock, op. cit. p. 255.
52. Joseph A. Fitzmyer, op. cit. p. 440.
53. Leon Morris, op. cit. p. 91. This record of Jesus' child development is recognised by Morris and Bock p.274 but rejected by Brown, op. cit. p. 483.
54. Craig Blomberg, op. cit. p.44.
55. Joel Green, op. cit. p. 144.
56. George Caird, op. cit. p. 61.
57. George Caird, cites Shek., 7.4; Baba, K, 7,80 a. For an up-to-date comment see **(41)**.
58. George Caird, (ibid.)
59. Earle Ellis, op. cit. p. 78.
60. Leon Morris, op. cit. p. 80.
61. David Gooding, op. cit. p. 49.
62. E. Burrows, The Gospel of the Infancy and other Biblical Essays, Ed. E.F. Sutcliffe, London: Burns, Oates and Washbourne, (1940), Infancy, pp.41-42.
63. Fr. Patrick McCafferty, Letter to the Belfast Telegragh, (16-04-04) "Mary was with her Son in His mission but not as His equal."

* This reference is highly recommended.

CCEA A/S and **Edexcel A/S**

Targets:
- Identify all the main Lucan narratives which relate to John the Baptist.
- Identify John's mission, "the greatness of John", titles for John in the Benedictus, the importance of John's ministry, his message, his character, "more than a prophet" and O.T. fulfilment.
- Identify the key concepts and expressions relating to John such as "forerunner", "fruits of repent ance," a "greater baptism," the Coming-One, "My Son, the Beloved," "bridge builder" and new Elijah.
- Recognise the differences between the role of Jesus and that of John the Baptist.
- Recognise the differences between John's ministry and that of Jesus.

The Work and Importance of John the Baptist
[1] The birth of John [See also Ch.8: the Infancy Narratives.] (Read 1:5-25.)

This event begins in the most sacred site of the nation, the Temple in Jerusalem, in the days of King Herod, when Zechariah a country priest is serving. Zechariah and Elizabeth were devout, God fearing people. God steps in to act as in the O.T. births of Isaac, Samson and Samuel, giving a special child to a childless mother. Children born in these circumstances are always significant. God is continuing to act as He did years ago. At the most sacred time of Zechariah's career as a priest, God steps in to deal with the nation's hope and his family disappointment. The angel Gabriel appears to Zechariah (1:8-11), telling him that his prayer has been answered. His prayer for national deliverance and for a child are fused into one petition (1:13). The child would be called John and the birth of the child would cause many to rejoice (1:14); he would be great before God, live a very upright and devout life and be filled with the Spirit right from conception (1:15). Like the O.T. prophets he would be an evangelist, turning many of the people of Israel back to God (1:16). He [John] will act like Elijah of old, "he [John] will go before him [Jesus] in the spirit and power of Elijah." (1:17a) This refers to his preaching and to his role in the last events when there was a hope that Elijah would reappear and be part of the restoration of Israel (Mal. 3:1; 4: 5-6).

Unlike Elijah, John did not perform miracles, however, he did warn the people to prepare for God or face judgement. Families would become reconciled, parents and children would be brought together (1:17b) and the disobedient turned into the just (1:17c). Luke's account raises many hopes in Israel. John will make ready "a people prepared." (Is. 43:7) John's role is to get ready for what God is about to do. He is going to work for His people Israel (1:17d).

John's mission: "he will turn many in Israel to their God and go before them in the spirit and power of Elijah." (1:17) "To turn to God" (Gk.epistrepsi) alludes to a change of orientation and direction in a person's relationship to others. Repentance is relational and is seen in the way we treat others: not in an overbearing manner or in misuse of authority Zechariah understands enough of human biology to raise the question of how Elizabeth could give birth given that she is past the age of childbearing (1:18). Gabriel assures him that God's hand is in all these events and Zechariah will be deaf and mute until all these things happen (1:20). Sure enough when Zechariah reappears from the Temple, he is unable to utter a blessing and returns home silent because he doubted the word of the angel (1:22-23).

Pupil's Activity: One   (Read 1:15-17.)
a) What was the nature of John's greatness (1:15)?
b) What was John the Baptist's mission?

[2] Mary's visit to Elizabeth [See Ch.8: The birth narratives.] (Read 1:39-56.)

When Mary and Elizabeth come together, John is still in the womb. The foetal John leaps within Elizabeth as a witness. This shows that the angel's prophecy was being fulfilled, "He will be filled with the Spirit, even from his mother's womb and God's word will come to pass (1:15). Elizabeth, being filled with the Spirit, extends a blessing to Mary and to Mary's child (1:42). Elizabeth acknowledges the superior position of Jesus by referring to Mary as "the mother of my Lord." (1:43) Mary had believed that the angel's word would be fulfilled. "Let it be according to your word." (1:38)

[3] The naming of John the Baptist and praise for his birth (Read 1:57-66.)

John was born just before the death of Herod the Great (5-4 BC). Zechariah goes against all the cultural norms in obeying the angel and naming the child John. The birth of the child is seen as an act of God's mercy, considering the age of the parents. As God-fearing Jews, the parents bring the child for circumcision (1:59). Elizabeth chooses the name John and the crowd ask the father to confirm this, as no relative is called by that name. Zechariah, still deaf and mute, writes on a wax tablet that the child is to be called John, much to everyone's surprise. Immediately (Gk. parakrema) his speech is restored and he starts to praise (Gk.eulogon) God for his goodness to him (1:63, 64): this means that "immediately" often accompanies a miraculous event (1:64; 4:39; 5:25; 8:44, 47).

Reactions at the birth of John: his father Zechariah learnt from his period of silence that God worked in amazing ways. Rather than call the child after his father, he was given the name which God had chosen for him, that of John (1:13).

The question is raised, who is this child? The answer is provided: John raises the curtain on God's salvation. He is the prophet who will prepare the people for God's visit in the Messiah. He [John] prepares the way rather than being the way; God's promises and His word will come to pass.

[4] Zechariah being filled with the Spirit, and to honour the birth of his son makes a prophecy in the words of the Benedictus. (Read 1:67 and 1:76-79.)

John will be a "prophet of the Most High to prepare the way." (1:76; 3:4-6; Is. 40:3-5) This title is a reference to the transcendence of God. John is subordinate to Jesus; Jesus is the Son and John is the prophet. John will give knowledge of the forgiveness of sins (1:77). How will John prepare the way? He prepares the way through all that God will do through the Messiah, "to give the knowledge of salvation to His people." (1:77) There is a close link between salvation and forgiveness, "to give a knowledge of salvation in the forgiveness of sins." (Marshall)**(1)** John brought an experience of forgiveness of sins because the person brought a repentant heart to the rite of baptism. (Bovon)**(2)** Forgiveness of sins is a precondition to peace with God. Peace, faith and salvation go together (8:48).

(Figure 1)   **Stages in the knowledge of salvation**

| faith (8:50) | → | repentance (24:47) | → | forgiveness (24:47) | → | peace with God (8:48) | → | knowledge of salvation (1:77) |

John's whole ministry is based upon God's merciful compassion which He will send upon the people, "when the day shall dawn upon us from on high." (1:78) The Messiah will be like a light to those who sit in darkness and death (1:79a), and His work will guide them into a path of peace (1:79b). John prepares for God's work which will be mediated through the coming of the promised one who is the light, guiding the people into peace. John is also **the prophet** who goes before the long awaited Son of David. In the birth of John, Zechariah is certain that God's plan of salvation will be completed (7:25). Jesus is the one who will take away the sins of the people.

Archaelogists have discovered ritual baths used in the Temple and in homes in Jerusalem and Sepphoris, going back to Roman times, showing the practice of ritual washing. The Levitical code required men and women to wash at different times for purification. "Lest the people die in their uncleanness and defile my tabernacle that is in their midst." (Lev.15:31)

Pupil's Activity: Two   **Class Discussion**

a) Do you agree with stages in forgiveness? Look at Figure 1 above, in which order do you think the stages should occur? Does the rite of baptism bring forgiveness or is it a sign of forgiveness?

b) Outline your knowledge and understanding of the prophecy of John's birth and its fulfilment as recorded by Luke. (CCEA A/S 2002 Resit)   [30 marks]

c) Explore the claim that in the infancy narrative, Luke portrays John as the forerunner of Jesus. Justify your answer. (CCEA A/S 2002 Resit)   [15 marks]

[5] The growth of John (Read 1:80.)

John grew physically and spiritually and spent his pre-ministry in the wilderness(es) plural. The plural is thought to refer to a general locality rather than to several places. His ministry would have been a national and exclusive focus to Israel. Josephus comments about different Jewish nationalists who promised deliverance urging the people to withdraw to the desert and wait for God to deliver Israel from Roman rule. (Josephus) **(3)** The wilderness became a symbol of hope for God's deliverance of His people.

[6] The ministry of John the Baptist (Read 3:1-6.)

A) General points: the events centred around John the Baptist in these verses means understanding events, rituals and

promises in the O.T. Luke locates John's ministry in the history of the Roman Empire to show his universal concern and provides the historical setting (3:1). His ministry began about A.D. 28-29 in the fifteenth year of Tiberias Caesar (3:1-2a). John would have been thirty years old. The O.T. priests started their ministry at thirty (Num. 4:3), the same age as Jesus when He started His public ministry (3:23a).

B) Luke highlights John's role as a prophet in saying, "the word of God came (Gk.egeneto) to John in the wilderness." John has been for some considerable time in the wilderness (1:80; 3:2). The words used here (Gk.rhema theou/word of God) means the coming of a clear and direct revelation from God. John preaches a baptism of repentance (3:2b-3). Isaiah promises a Coming One who would be a preparer for salvation. He adds to the quote from Is.40:3-5 to emphasise that, "all flesh shall see the salvation of God." (3:4-6) God's salvation will be seen in the Spirit's baptism. Luke alone explains how John prepared for Jesus. The coming of John was anticipated in O.T. Scripture. The ministry of John is a fulfilment of Is.40.3-5 and is introduced by the formula, "it is written." (3:4)

C) John as God's herald, calls for a moral preparation in the wilderness, "Make (Gk. poieo) His paths straight (Gk. euthus)," means clearing the way for God's coming. John is God's herald (3:4). The repentant heart must express itself in action and wait for God's deliverance. God's coming will be powerful to the extent that physical obstacles will be removed from God's people as He delivers them. "Every valley (Gk.pharagx/ravine) shut in by a precipice shall be filled up and every mountain and hill (Gk. bounos) shall be made low, smoothed down (Gk. leios)." (3:5; Is.40:3-5) A way shall be cleared for God's people who show humility and lowliness. God's coming will be without obstruction; the landscape will be levelled. Glory in this context can mean salvation (Is.40:5).

D) Other O.T. ideas in John's opening ministry, "Remove every obstacle from my people's way - I dwell with him who is of a humble and contrite heart." (Is.57:14-17) "Build up the highway, clear it of stones." (Is.62:10) The physical levelling clears a path for God's entrance and pictures the severity of God's coming. "The mountains brought low," (Is.40:4) is the same expression for the people who are brought low in Is.2:9,11,12,17. The proud will be destroyed and the morally crooked people (Gk. skolios) could represent in a metaphorical sense those who are perverse (Acts 2:40) and face the prospect of the judgement of God. If they repent they will be made straight (Gk. euthus).

Pupil's Activity: Three
a) What features of John's character are evident in Luke 3:1-20?
b) Play as background music the extract from Handel's Messiah, "Every valley shall be exalted." (3:5-6; Is. 40:4)

[7] John's message of repentance (Read 3:7-9.)(Matt.3:7-10.) (Q)
Luke includes John's warning to the crowds (Gk.ochlois) who have come to be baptised (3:7). Matthew says that John warns many of the Jewish leaders who have come for baptism (Matt.3:7). Marshall **(4)** comments that Luke had a wider audience fits Luke's emphasis: the message is for all. Matthew on the other hand tends to single out the Pharisees and Sadducees for criticism. Later, Luke says that the Pharisees and the lawyers rejected the purpose of God for themselves, not having been baptised by John (7:30). The Jewish leaders must produce fruit in keeping with repentance (Matt.3:8). Luke applies this to the crowds (3:8). Failure to do so will result in coming judgement; the axe is lying (Gk.keitai) at the root of the tree meaning ready for action. "Even now the axe is laid to the root of the trees." (3:9; Matt.3:10) Having come for baptism, these leaders refused to be baptised by John (7:30).

Firstly, John was saying (Gk.elegen means to present action in a vivid way to the readers as that action continues) to his audience that those who come for baptism should not take lightly the warning to flee wrath. John compares his audience to snakes fleeing the fire in the wilderness, forced out of protective cover by the heat (3:7). Those who come for baptism need God's forgiveness and are to pursue a life of right living, as a time of judgement and blessing approaches.

Secondly, the people are to bear fruit that befits repentance and not rely on their ancestors as a "way in" to God's blessing saying, "we have Abraham as our father." (3:8) God can create His children out of stones if need be (3:8). Those who know God are not limited to a certain race, because God's children are transformed from the heart (3:8).

Thirdly, God's judgement is at hand. Like an axe laid at the base of the tree, unfruitful branches will be cut off and cast into the fire of judgement. In his call for a response, John was preparing the way for God's work (3:9).

[8] The fruits of repentance (Read 3:10-14.) (L)
True repentance responds to God and treats people justly. Genuine repentance for the crowd meant changing how you relate to others. John does not appeal to Jewish ritual or to an ascetic life style but to serve others by meeting their need for food and clothing (3:11). John relates his ministry to three distinct groups: the crowd, the tax collectors and the soldiers who would have been either the army of Herod Antipas in Perea, which would have included non-Jews or the Judean police who helped with the task of tax collecting. It is these three groups who respond to John's ministry (7:29). The tax collector must only collect what he is due and the soldier is neither to rob nor make false accusations nor complain about his wages paid for by the state. John's response links with 1:16-17. The tax collectors responded favourably to John's ministry; the Gk. word "edikaiosan" means they accepted God's judgements as right because they realised that God's call for repentance was correct: they listened to John's preaching and accepted his baptism for the forgiveness of their sins (7:29). (Marshall)**(5)** However on the other hand the Pharisees rejected (Gk.ethetesan) the counsel or purpose of God (Gk.boule) while the people and the tax collectors responded and turned to God (7:30). They were the "many" referred to in the promise (1:16; 3:1-14, 21). The promise in Luke 1:17 was fulfilled in 3:10-14 "He will turn many in Israel to their God and go before them in the spirit and power of Elijah." "To turn to God" means how one relates to others. Repentance is relational and is evident in the way we treat others and not be overbearing in the use of authority.

John's reply re-echoes the O.T. prophets. "Wash yourselves make yourselves clean; remove the evil of your doings before my eyes; cease to do evil, learn to do good; seek justice, correct oppression; defend the fatherless, plead for the widow." (Is.1:16-17; 58:7-8) "Do justice and love kindness and walk humbly with your God." (3:10-14 (L); Mic.6:8) Luke adds that John gave ethical instructions and made radical demands. Luke includes a longer quotation from Is.40:4-6 to include the prophecy, "all flesh shall see the salvation of God." (3:6) [See Ch.6: Luke's characteristics.] In this section there are many references to the idea of the wilderness: stones, barren trees and snakes. John uses his desert surroundings to relate to spiritual truths.

[9] The preaching and promises of John the Baptist (Read 3:15-18.)

John's preaching about Jesus : John is subordinate to Jesus and the real promise and hope comes from Jesus who is mightier than John. This is an emphasis by Luke. Luke also presents the speculation by the people about whether John was the Christ, "the one to come."(3:15) John promises a **greater one to come** (3:15-17). He further promises a **greater baptism** (3:16-17). Despite the distinctive ministry of John, Jesus would be superior; He would be stronger, bring a better baptism than John and He is also the judge. John's baptism would be with water but that of Jesus "with fire and with the Spirit." (3:16) John's humility is noted. He is not worthy to untie a sandal from the feet of Jesus. Even a Hebrew slave would have considered this to be a very degrading action (3:16). John's ministry predicted a "Coming-One", a Messianic title based upon Ps.118:26, "Blessed is He who comes (enters) in the name of the Lord" and Is. 5:26-27, "He will raise a signal for the nation and lo speedily it comes." "He who is coming is mightier than I." (3:16)

Further judgement is seen in the imagery of the threshing floor as the farmer sifts the wheat from the chaff. (3:17; Is. 41:16) This purge is for Jews as well as Gentiles, "the chaff will be burnt with unquenchable fire." (Is.34:8-10; 66:24) This is the language of the final judgement. The coming of the Spirit is like a refining fire, purifying that which cannot withstand the heat and burning the rest, showing its worthlessness. John preached good news and he is part of the movement in Israel towards salvation, setting the mood for it (3:18). The words "now also" are a summary of what has gone before, "with many other exhortations" (Gk. parakaleo) means to comfort (Marshall) **(6)** and not to admonish (3:18). (Nolland) **(7)** John preached "good news to the people," as part of the kingdom age and not simply as the last prophet of the old age (3:18). Jesus breaks up the ground for God's message (3:18). John is the transition figure between the old and the new era. Jesus is the one who will bring the Spirit and takes away sin. There is continuity between Jesus and John: both break up the ground for the message of God (3:18). [See Ch.18: Forgiveness (John's preaching).]

Pupil's Activity: Four

What according to the preaching of John are the cause (3:7-9; 16,17), nature (3:8,10-14) and outcome (3:3, 15-17) of repentance?

John's teaching about repentance   (Figure 2)

Repentance	References	Comment
the cause	3:7-9, 16,17	
the nature	3:8, 10-14	
the outcome	3:3, 15-17	

[10] (A) The imprisonment of John and (B) the Baptism of Jesus (Read 3:19-22.)

A) Luke notes that Herod's unlawful marriage to Herodias was not the only reason for John's imprisonment. Luke speaks of all the evil things Herod had done. Josephus the Jewish historian says that Herod saw John as a political threat, as a moral attack would undermine Herod's credibility. [See below Figure 3.] (Josephus) **(8)** John was like Elijah in the way he challenged the political authorities (3:19; 1 Kgs. 21:17-26). John had also rebuked Herod in public over his unlawful marriage. The worst crime of all Luke says was the imprisonment of John designed to suppress the prophet's criticism of Herod (3:20). Sin tends to pay attention to the threat rather than the source of the sin itself. Luke omits the details about the death of John. His only statement is that Herod beheaded John (9:7-9). "For Herod had him put to death, though he was a good man and had exhorted the Jews to lead righteous lives, to practise justice towards their fellows and piety towards God and to join in baptism." There is no contradiction between Josephus and the Gospel writers. In the view of Josephus, this was an essential preliminary if baptism was to be acceptable to God. They must not employ it to gain pardon for whatever sins they committed, but as a consecration of the body indicating that the soul was already thoroughly cleansed by right behaviour. Forgiveness is a major emphasis in Luke's Gospel (4:18). [See also Ch.16: Forgiveness.]

> **Josephus, the Jewish historian's view of John**
> **"But to some of the Jews the destruction of Herod's army seemed to be divine vengeance, and certainly a just vengeance for his treatment of John, surnamed the Baptist. For Herod had put him to death, though he was a good man and had exhorted the Jews to lead righteous lives, to practice justice towards their fellows and piety towards God, and so doing to join in baptism. In his view this was a necessary preliminary if baptism were to be acceptable to God." (Josephus) (9)**

Pupil's Activity: Five

What aspects of John's ministry are highlighted by Josephus and how far does this concur with Luke's account of the baptism by John?

In Luke 4:18, there is a double use and meaning of forgiveness, "to proclaim **release** (Gk. aphasin) to the captives," (4:18b) and "to set at liberty those who are **oppressed** (Gk.en aphesei)." (4:18e) In the O.T. this meant release from exile; in Luke it means release from sin and spiritual captivity: come to God on His terms and accept His forgiveness as provided in Jesus, who frees the oppressed. Matthew points out that the Pharisees and Sadducees were coming to **where**, John was baptising (Matt 3:7) (NIV) and Luke points out that "the multitudes (Gk. ochlos) an assorted group of people came out to be baptised by him." (3:7 RSV)

B) The Baptism of Jesus (Read 3:21-22.) (Matt.3:13-17; Mk. 1:9-11; Jn.1:29-34)

All the Gospels record that Jesus' public ministry began with His baptism at the Jordan.

The setting: Luke provides the setting by highlighting the popularity of John when a huge throng (Gk. laon meaning not all of the people) responded to his call. "When all the people (Gk. laos) were baptised," and Jesus had been baptised and was praying, the Kingdom of God could now be preached (3:21 RSV).

The event: God sends His Spirit to come upon Jesus and in Luke John is not specifically named in the baptism (3:22). Luke focuses all the attention on Jesus' prayer and the divine voice (3:22b). Luke alone speaks of the descent of the Spirit in "bodily form", like a dove, indicating that it was a visible experience. The manner of the Spirit's descent was like a dove in that the Spirit came gracefully upon him in the same manner in which a dove glides through the air.

The nature of the event: Jesus had a private experience of the Spirit and John was able to testify to the event.

C) The identity of Jesus (3:22): He is identified as God's Son confirming 1:35.

"You are my Son, the beloved; with you I am well pleased." (NRSV)

"You are my Son, whom I love; with you I am well pleased." (NIV)

"You are my beloved Son; (my Son, my Beloved)(margin); with you I am well pleased" (RSV)

1) Jesus is called the "Son". "You are my Son." This is linked to "You are my Son, today I have begotten you," which is a Royal Psalm suggesting that Jesus is the royal figure giving the Psalm a Messianic concept (Ps.2:7). The title plus the setting provides the interpretation. Luke shows that Jesus was about thirty years of age when he started His ministry which was the age for men to enter the priesthood (Num.4:3).

2) The expression "the Beloved" (3:22b) could be linked to Is.41:8, "But you, Israel my servant, Jacob, whom I have chosen the offspring of Abraham, my friend;" This may also refer to the chosen and intimate relationship which Jesus had with His Father. "Thus said the Lord who formed you from the womb and will help you." (Is.44:2)

3) "With you I am well pleased." (3:22c) "God is well pleased with His Son." "Behold my servant, whom I uphold, my chosen, in whom my soul delights." (Is.42:1) This reference emphasises the Father's pleasure in the Son.

There is a royal and Messianic endorsement of Jesus (3:22). In accepting John's baptism, Jesus endorses John's ministry and message. Was John's baptism from heaven or from men (20:1-8)? Jesus links His cause with that of John. Jesus in His baptism shows His identification with sinners. He identifies with John's message of repentance and endorses the people's need to repent (1:76-77; 3:3). John's baptism showed that people needed to have their sins forgiven. Jesus emerges as the Coming-One to whom John pointed and who brings a greater baptism (3:15-18). Luke alone says that Jesus was praying when the voice came (3:21). The picture of the heavens opening shows God's dramatic action in using a vision from heaven. The baptism is a call to start a ministry and an inauguration of the kingdom. At His baptism there is the divine confirmation that Jesus is the Messiah-Servant; Heaven has testified that Jesus is the Beloved Son and God has shown who will reveal His plan. Jesus receives confirmation about His mission. He is anointed by God for divine service.

Pupil's Activity: Six

Complete the grid analysis of the titles for Jesus used at His baptism to show O.T. links and fulfilment (3:22).

Titles for Jesus used at His baptism   (Figure 3)

	Luke 3:22b	O.T.	Comment
1	My Son	Ps.2:7 "You are my Son, today I have begotten you."	What is the significance of the title 'Son'?
2	the Beloved	Is.41:8; 44:2	What does the title "Beloved" tell us about Jesus?
3	well pleased	Is.42:1	What Servant roles does Jesus fulfil at his baptism?

Pupil's Activity: Seven

Play the exerpt from Handel's Messiah, "But who may abide the day of His coming and who shall stand when He appeareth? For He is like a refiner's fire." (Mal. 3:2) and "And He shall purify the sons of Levi." (Mal. 3:3)

Pupil's Activity: Eight

a) What threefold testimony is given to Jesus at His baptism?

b) What was the significance of the baptism of Jesus?

[11] Questions about Jesus and John (Read 7:18-35.) (Matt. 11:2-19) "Q"

The key issues in this passage are based upon the relationship between Jesus and John and are centred around three basic questions.

A) What does Jesus think of Himself? John questions Jesus about His ministry (7:18-23).
1) The setting: John was imprisoned at Machaerus, a fortress east of the Dead Sea. This is omitted by Luke but recorded by Josephus. **(10)** John is in prison and his disciples tell him about the healings of Jesus, His preaching and His teaching. John's two disciples ask what kind of Messiah would this Coming-One be (7:18-19)? John sends two witnesses to Jesus (Deut.19:15) to guarantee the truthfulness of the report (Deut. 19:15). "On the strength of two or three witnesses shall a charge be sustained." (7:25) Jesus' style does not seem to fit most Jewish eschatological ideas. John wants to know if Jesus is the expected end-time Messiah. Is Jesus really more than the people think? "A great prophet (Mal.3:1; 4:5) has risen among us!" and "God has visited His people!" (7:16)
2) What kind of Messiah would Jesus be if He really were the Messiah? Is He a Messianic hope or an eschatological hope? Jesus' miracles would show that He is bringing in the last events, which would parallel Isaiah's prophecies (Is.29:18; 35:5; 42:6; 61:1).
3) Does John doubt who Jesus really is because there is no real political aspect to the ministry of Jesus?
This was not John's first step of faith as Creed **(11)** suggested but rather that John is seeking confirmation of Jesus' ministry. John's question put by the envoys (7:20-21) are unique to Luke (7:20). John is described as "the baptizer" The messengers ask the exact question which John had given to them. John was very interested in who Jesus really was; Jesus' reply reflects the type of miracle John was hearing. The envoys saw and heard these healings of plagues, evil spirits and many were graced with sight. This description links Jesus with the Servant of Isaiah 61 and the fulfilment of Lk.4:18-19. Grace and mercy are seen and these are key ideas linked to the Messiah, through the horn of David's house (1:68-69).
4) The messengers have to report what they have seen and heard (7:22; Matt. 11:4-5).
All are healing miracles except the last one which is preaching good news to the poor. It comes as a climax because it is distinctive. A special time of blessing has come. These events show the presence of the final events and reflect a picture of paradise. Jesus clearly is not just a prophet but the Coming One (Is.35: 5-6). Jesus makes a call to faith to those who hear His remarks and the general blessing (Gk. makarios) He gives, includes John. Jesus is the personal focus of the blessing. "Blessed is he who takes no offense at me." (7:23) Blessing comes to people who are not offended by Jesus. This is a general call for all by Jesus. John's perplexity about Jesus, shows how unprepared people were for the type of messianic activity that Jesus brought.

Pupil's Activity: Nine
Play the recitative from Handel's Messiah, "Then shall the eyes of the blind be opened and the ears of the deaf unstopped," CD, CD Rom or video.

B) What does Jesus think of John? (Read 7:24-30.)
1) The setting : the disciples of John depart and Jesus talks to the crowd asking some revealing questions about John (7:24). John is not like a tender reed (Gk. kalamos) which is easily blown about by the wind (1 Kgs.14:15; 2 Kgs.18:21). He is a man of great conviction. The people did not go out to see a pretty view of the Jordan river. It was not soft clothing which attracted the people but a prophet who drew their attention. Did you go to the desert to see a well-dressed man from the wealthy classes? If it was expensive clothes you wanted to see you would go to a palace and the court of a king. People were drawn to the wilderness by the message of John and not his clothing. Although Luke does not include the description of John's clothing, he seems to be aware of it. "What did you go out into the wilderness to see? A man clothed in soft raiment?" (7:25) [See p. 179.]

Pupil's Activity: Ten (Read 7:18-35.)
a) What was the doubt in the mind of John the Baptist and why was he perplexed (3:16-17)?
Why did Jesus take John back to the Scriptures (21-23; Is. 8:14-15; 35:4-5; 61:1)?
b) How does Luke compare John's ministry with that of Jesus (7:31-35)?
c) Outline your knowledge and understanding of the stories in Luke's Gospel concerning John the Baptist. (CCEA A/S 2004 Resit)   [30 marks]
d) Explore the claim that Luke seeks to compare and contrast the roles and of John the Baptist and Jesus. Justify your answer. (CCEA A/S 2004 Resit)   [15 marks]

[12] The description of John (Read 7:26-28.)

John as more than a prophet prepares the way (7:26). He is the greatest of the O.T. period as He belonged to a special time and should be seen as a transitional figure rather than tied to one period. He links the period of promise with that of fulfilment (7:26-28). (Fitzmyer) **(12)** He is the forerunner like Elijah, yet all who are in the Kingdom are greater than this the greatest among the prophets. He denies that he was Elijah but wants to be identified with the prophet who cried out from the wilderness, "Prepare the way of the Lord," (Is. 40:3; Jn. 1: 21-23) To reject John is to reject the plan of God. Jesus chooses to minister to sinners who are sensitive about their sin (7:36-50). "For John the Baptist has come eating no bread and no wine; and you say, 'He has a demon.' "(7:33) Luke uses Ex. 23:20 "Behold I send an angel before you to guard you." (7:27; Mal. 3:1) "This is he of whom it is written, "Behold, I send my messenger before your face, who shall prepare the way before you." Ex. 23:20 refers to the "Shekinah" glory going before Israel to prepare the way. Creation is to prepare morally for God's coming (3:4). The highway which clears the way for God's coming is a purified heart (Is.40:1-11). God's glory is shown to all because He brings salvation. At this time the community at Qumran called the people to study the law before the Lord returns. (Qumran) **(13)** Some Jews anticipated a new Exodus as when the nation was formed (Is.42:13; 48:12; 52:12).

John represents the greatest person ever born in the old era, yet he is the least person in the new era. The lowest person in the new era will be greater than John (7:28). Participation in the new era in forgiveness, total acceptance of God's children and the enabling of the indwelling Spirit gives the new era a greater position. The people responded to God's requirement of forgiveness and His call to repentance (7:29). The religious authorities refused to accept John's baptism rejecting John's ministry and God's way of salvation. Even the lawyers who were skilled in the interpretation of the laws missed out on God's purpose for their lives (7:30).

[13] Jesus' view of this generation: the parable of the complaining children (Read 7:31-35.)

These verses are a rebuke on those who reject Jesus and John. Judgement will come upon Israel for rejecting John and Jesus. The people's reaction to John led Jesus to make one final picture of the present generation. Jesus tells the proverb of the children, likening this generation to those children who do not want to play with their friends. "We piped to you, and you did not dance; we wailed, and you did not weep." Those who reject are like spoilt children who sit down and refuse to play any games. They complain that the other children will not play according to their rules and they change their tune constantly as they complain. Being like the complainers who think that John is too ascetic for their taste, they accuse him of having a demon. They accuse Jesus of mixing with the wrong people and joining in with their revelling (7:31-34). John in their eyes has been possessed by a demon and Jesus keeps company with the wrong people (7:33). Despite this rejection of God's servants, wisdom is shown to be right by her children (7:35). Wisdom's children by contrast with the children in Luke 7:32, are those who are identified with God's purpose as seen in the person and work of Jesus. Both John and Jesus are also "wisdom's children" and fulfil God's purpose. The Pharisees and lawyers had rejected John, were people of this generation and were not "wisdom's children", while the common people had been baptised by John. God's wisdom will show itself to be right even though it is different from what people anticipated (7:29).

[14] Evidence of the death of John (Read 9:7-9.)

Popular reports about Jesus come to Herod.   News about Jesus' ministry has spread to the palace of Herod Antipas after Jesus had raised the widow's son (7:16). Herod reflects upon Jesus as a prophetic figure. Eventually Herod's curiosity leads to the setting up of a meeting (23:6-12). Herod is perplexed about the different views about Jesus with some saying that Jesus was a resurrected John (9:7). What is certain is that John the Baptist is dead by this time. Herod says, "John is no longer with us, I beheaded him, but who is this about whom I hear so much?" (9:9) Only Luke says that Herod beheaded John the Baptist.

> John is the "bridge figure" spanning the old era of promise as the last of the great O.T. prophets (7:28) and the new era of inauguration, the new period of Jesus.

[15] For revision purposes: a general summary of John's public ministry
A) The greatness of John

• He will be great before God, live a very upright and devout life, be filled with the Spirit and be empowered by the Spirit right from conception (1:15). His greatness is anticipated in Jesus' statement "there is no one greater born of a woman than John the Baptist." (7:28) His greatness reflects his character and mission.

• "He is great in God's judgement because John lives to serve the Lord." (Brown) **(14)** "He will be great before the Lord." (1:15) He is an eschatological messenger of salvation.

• Like the O.T. prophets, John will be an evangelist, turning many of the people of Israel back to God (1:16).

• His greatness is seen in his prophetic role. The Spirit will come upon John and make him "a prophet of the Most High." (1:76)

• He will lead an ascetic life of strict discipline, which will be in contrast with the life of Jesus (7:33-35).

• A further aspect of his greatness is seen in the fact that John would be a special instrument chosen by God to play a unique role in His plan. "God's hand was with him." (1:66) This is a Semitic expression to show that God's power and guidance are with John.

• John's greatness is also seen in his role as a forerunner to Jesus (1:14-25; 57-80). John prepares a people who are ready for God's salvation. His ministry is influenced by the O.T. ideas: the Lord speaks of a prepared people, a special people whom God has drawn to Himself, often called a remnant (2 Sam.7:24; Is.43:7). He is the prophet who will prepare the people for God's visit in the Messiah: he prepares the way rather than being the way.

B) His mission is seen in terms of "going before", "turning" and "preparing." (1:17)

• John's mission in Israel would be to "many" and in the sight of the Lord." (1:14-15) He will turn many in Israel back to the Lord but not all will respond to God's call. His ministry will be exclusive to the Jews the sons of Israel (1:16).

• His mission is described as "going before": to represent the Lord before His people (1:17). This mission will take place in the manner of Elijah: John will go before Him [the Lord] in "the spirit and power of Elijah". (1:17)

• "John's mission will be to reconstitute a moral unity of the people by restoring the broken relation between the patriarchs and their descendents." Godet **(15)** This verse could also mean that families will be united through this reform or by "turning" (Gk.epistrepsei) and John will inform people about God's standard of righteousness. (Marshall) **(16)** The expression "turn" has O.T. roots (1:16-17; Deut 30:2; Hos.3:5; 7:10). The people turned to the Lord in their distress. (2 Chron.15:4) The fathers will look with favour upon Israel (Is.29:22). John will bring many in Israel back to the Lord in the same way as the Servant's role in Israel was to restore Jacob to himself (Is.49:5). He will be like Elijah (Mal.4:5). As a result of his ministry, the disobedient will accept the wisdom of the just: the resultant outcome will be a "prepared people" for the Lord (1:17).

• John's humility is noted. He is not worthy to untie a sandal from the feet of Jesus. Even a Hebrew slave would have considered this to be a very degrading action (3:16).

• John's mission was to prepare the way for Jesus. All the people came to be baptised by John as promised and fulfilled (1:16; 3:21). Later, the crowds and the tax collectors acknowledged that God's way was the correct one, when they were baptised by John (7:29).

C) His ministry predicted a "Coming-One", which is an O.T. Messianic title as in, "Blessed is the king who enters in the name of the Lord," (19:38; Ps. 118:26) "He will raise a signal for the nation afar off, ... and lo, swiftly speedily it comes!" "He who is mightier than I is coming." (3:16) John baptised merely in water, the Coming-One would baptise in the Spirit. John's ministry came to fulfilment in the Spirit's outpouring at Pentecost (3:15-20).

D) His message is clear: judgement is close at hand (3:7-9) and repentance means treating others well (3:10-14).

• While many aspects of his message reflect back to the great days of the prophets, John's life reflects a new era.

• He preaches a baptism of repentance, the forgiveness of sin and baptism (3:2b-3; 24:27); he fulfils Isaiah promise of a Coming-One who would prepare the way of salvation. The coming of John was anticipated in O.T. scripture: the ministry of John is a fulfilment of Is.40:3-5 and is introduced by the formula, "it is written". (3:4) Luke adds to the quote from Is.40:3-5 that "all flesh shall see the salvation of God." (3:4-6) God's salvation will be seen in the Spirit's baptism. John is God's herald.

• He further promises a greater baptism (3:16-17). Despite the distinctive ministry of John, Jesus would be superior; He would be stronger, bring a better baptism than John and He is also the judge. John's baptism would be with water but that of Jesus " with fire and with the Spirit." (3:16)

• His message involved preaching good news (Gk. euengelizeto) (3:18).

E) John is the "bridge figure": he is the **"bridge figure"** spanning the old era of promise as the last of the great O.T. prophets (7:28) and the new era of inauguration, the new period of Jesus (1:14-17,76-79 3:4-6).

• He is the bridge figure in whom the promise of fulfilment is made. (Marshall) **(17)**

• He is the key person sent by God into the history of Israel at the end of an era.

• Luke stresses that John's ministry is that of "good news." "I (Gabriel) bring you (Zechariah) this good news." (1:19) "He [John] preached good news to the people." (3:18) Jesus sees Himself as bringing in the Kingdom as His actions are paralleled in the O.T. (Is. 29:18; 35:5; 42:6; 61:1).

F) Who is the new Elijah? Is it Jesus or is John?

• In Luke's Gospel it is Jesus and not John the Baptist who is the new Elijah. (Danker) **(18)** The use of Mal. 3:1 in Luke 7:27 to describe John makes this a difficult interpretation. John refuses to identify himself with Elijah (1:17). John denies he is the ascended Elijah who has come to earth as the Jewish nation expected (2 Kgs. 2:11-12; Enoch 90.31;89.52; Sirach 48:10).

G) What is the difference between John and Elijah?

• Although John operates like Elijah (in the spirit of Elijah), he is not Elijah; He gives a fresh twist to Jewish expectations (Matt.17:12). Jesus is greater than John and therefore must be the Messiah, the new Elijah. For John, people are accountable to God whose salvation is approaching.

• John is the forerunner predicted by Malachi and is the greatest prophet of the O.T. period (7:27). The lowest member of the kingdom is higher than the greatest O.T. prophet (7:28).

H) Why does John baptise?

• His baptism is a preparation for the real ministry of Jesus which is still to come and it represents a washing or cleansing. This paves the way for "a spirit baptism". For John, Jesus is a powerful figure who brings victory and judgement. Jesus is the one who takes away sin and brings the Spirit (1:76-79, 3:15-17).

I) Similarities and differences between Jesus and John's ministry

• John and Jesus are alike in some ways: Jesus often aligns Himself with John.
• Both are agents of God's call to His people.
• Both call for repentance and are rejected by their contemporaries.
• However, it is in Jesus' preaching of the Kingdom of God and His role in bringing in God's promise of salvation to Israel that Jesus' role and purpose differ from that of John the Baptist. Although John is "a prophet of the most High" (1:76), his disciples will not share in the promised Holy Spirit, whereas Jesus' followers will be baptised in the Spirit (3:16; Acts 1:5; 2:1ff.). It is possible to say John predicted two baptisms by Jesus, one with the Holy Spirit and the other with fire. "I came to cast fire upon the earth." (3:16; 12:49) (Green) **(19)** John is the servant of God and in so doing magnifies the God he serves (Jn.3:25-30).
• John promises a greater baptism than his own (3:16-17). Despite the distinctive ministry of John, Jesus would be superior; He would be stronger, bring a better baptism than John and He is also the judge.
• John preached "good news to the people;" (3:18) Jesus breaks up the ground for God's message. "I must preach the good news of the kingdom of God to the other towns also, because that is why I was sent." (4:43)

Conclusion

There is a common denominator between the message of Jesus and that of John in that they both are used to break up the ground for God's message. Later, Luke compares and contrasts the two ministries (7:31-35). Jesus speaks of the law and the prophets existing until or through John the Baptist. ; since then the good news of the kingdom is preached." (16:16a; 7:24-30) This Greek words "apo tote" in Luke means "from now on" and denote a significant turning points in the events that follow (1:48; 5:10; 12:52; 22:18,69).

• John is the bridge between the old and the new eras. John appears to have a foot in both the old and the new eras. As a forerunner He points to the new era and his ministry marks the end of the old era in announcing the coming of Jesus and in preaching the good news of the kingdom. Sometimes Luke emphasises one side of the bridge while on other occasions he notes the other side (7:24-30; 16:16). (Bock) **(20)**
• The preaching of the kingdom is no longer a distant promise but is to be preached in nearness and arrival.
• Humanly speaking, John does not appear to have had a very successful ministry, having landed himself in jail for his public rebuke of Herod Antipas. However, he is a faithful and courageous prophet, whose lifestyle is exemplary and one who condemns a political figure, who does not repent of the evil he has committed, as the people before him had done (3:10-14).
• John is presented as the first of many servants of God, who will suffer at the hands of those who reject the message. The faithfulness of John's preaching stands out in this passage and he upholds God's moral standards (3:10-14).

Outcomes
Students should have a knowledge and understanding of:
• **all the main Lucan narratives which relate to John the Baptist.**
• **John's mission, his greatness, titles for John in the Benedictus, the importance of his ministry, his message, his character, "more than a prophet" and O.T. fulfilment.**
• **key concepts and expressions relating to John such as "forerunner", repentance, "fruits of repentance, a "greater baptism," the "Coming-One," "bridge builder" and "new Elijah."**
• **a comparison and contrast between the role of Jesus and that of John the Baptist.**

Pupil's Activity: Eleven
a) How does the role and purpose of John's ministry compare and differ from that of Jesus?
(Edexcel A/S 2004)   [14 marks]
b) Why were John the Baptist and the disciples so important to the ministry of Jesus?
(Edexcel A/S 2004)   [6 marks]
c) Why was John the Baptist so important to the ministry of Jesus?
(Edexcel A/S 2005)   [6 marks]

Pupil's Activity: Twelve
a) Outline your knowledge and understanding of the role of John the Baptist in Luke's Gospel.
(CCEA A/S Resit 2006)   [30 marks]
b) Explore the view that the baptism of Jesus by John is a turning point in Luke's Gospel. Justify your answer.
(CCEA A/S Resit 2006)   [15 marks]

Notes on Ch. 9: the importance and work of John the Baptist

1. Howard Marshall, op. cit. p. 93.

2. Francois Bovon, Luke 1:1-9 :50 EKKZNT Verlag (1989) p. 108.

3. Josephus, Antiquities, 20.8.10.185-188 on Luke 1:80.

4. Howard Marshall, op. cit. p. 139.

5. Howard Marshall, op. cit. p. 298.

6. Howard Marshall, op. cit. p.149 on Luke 3:18 says the Greek word "parakalein" means to comfort or encourage which is a characteristic of John's ministry to the people.

7. John Nolland, op. cit. p.154 on Luke 3:18 says (Gk. parakaleo) means admonish. Marshall's interpretation is preferable as Luke uses the (Gk parakaleo) consistently for comfort or encourage. (7:4; 8:31f, 41; 15:28; to comfort 16:25)

8. Josephus, Antiquities, 18. 5. 2. 116-119.

9. Josephus, Antiquities, 18.5.2 116-8.

10. Josephus, Antiquities, 18.5.2 Par 9.

11. J. M. Creed, op. cit. p. 105.

12. Joseph A. Fitzmyer, op. cit. p.671.

13. Qumran, The Dead Sea Scrolls, 1QS 9.19-20.

14. Raymond Brown, p.273 cited in Bock, p.84.

15. F. Godet, op. cit. p.81.

16. Howard Marshall, op. cit. p.58.

17. Howard Marshall, op. cit. p.149.

18. F.W. Danker, op. cit. p.163.

19. Joel Green, op.cit.p.182 says about Luke 3:16; 12:49, It is possible to say John predicted two baptisms by Jesus, one with the Holy Spirit and the other with fire. "I came to cast fire upon the earth."

20. Darren Bock, op. cit. p.326

Israel in the Time of Jesus

1. Jesus in Samaria (9:52)
2. Jesus in Bethany (9:57-62)
3. Jesus passes between Samaria and Jericho (17:1-11)
4. Jesus in Jericho (19:1-10)
5. Jesus approaches Jerusalem (19:34-44)

CCEA   A/S   **"37% of Luke's Gospel is contained in the Journey Narrative: 424 verses out of 1,151 verses." (Bock) (15)**

Targets:
- Identify the journey narrative in Luke's Gospel and know why it is so-called.
- Identify the main theme and sub-themes of the journey narrative in Luke's Gospel.
- Recognise the central importance of the journey narrative in Luke's Gospel.
- Recognise the place of Jerusalem in the journey narrative in Luke's Gospel.
- Identify the key concepts, for example discipleship, 'the way', suffering and rejection, chronological journey, generic view of journey, chiasmus and mission.

The Journey Narrative (9:51-19:48)

Introduction

As Jesus was praying alone, He asked the disciples. "Who do the people say I am?" (9:18) After Peter declares Jesus to be the Messiah (9:21), Jesus talks about His need to suffer. "The Son of Man must suffer many things and be rejected by the elders, chief priests and scribes and be killed and on the third day be raised." He then goes on to tell the disciples not to tell anyone about it (9:22). Jesus took Peter, John and James up to pray with Him and as He was praying, the appearance of His countenance was changed (9:28-29). At the Transfiguration, Moses and Elijah appeared in glory and spoke of His departure (Gk.exodon) which He was sent to accomplish in Jerusalem (9:31). Jesus predicted His sufferings again. "Let these words sink into your ears; for the Son of Man is to be delivered into the hands of men."(9:44)

Following on from two sessions of prayer, Luke then begins the travel section. "As the time drew near when Jesus would be taken up to heaven, He set his face to go Jerusalem." (9:51) Up to this point Luke has been using Mark's Gospel, now he goes on to use "Q" + "L" as his source (9:50). [See Ch.3: Sources p. 51.] and Ch.7: Structure p. 70.]

[1] Common issues, main themes and expressions in the Journey Narrative (9:51-19:48)

These chapters cover three main themes: Jesus' movements from Galilee to Jerusalem, Jewish rejection and the New Way. [See Ch.7: General Structure.] The arrangement of these chapters is not haphazard, but is governed by themes.

A) General Points

The journey narrative consists of miracles, parables, stories, events and teachings arranged as a continuous story, that of Jesus' journey to Jerusalem. They are contained in ten chapters which comprise over a third of the whole of the Gospel of Luke. Much of this material is unique to Luke's Gospel (L), approximately thirty-seven percent, four hundred and twenty-four verses out of one thousand, one hundred and fifty-one verses. [See p. 23.]

In this section Luke uses "Q" (material common to Matthew and himself) and (L). These are mainly the teachings of Jesus. (Goulder) (1) Approximately one third of the material overlaps with Matthew. There are fewer chronological or topographical notes in any other section of similar length in any Gospel. (Egelkraut) (2) The message is that Jesus provides a new way to follow God which is to, "listen to Him." Luke arranges his material in such a way that the focus of attention is Jerusalem as a preparation for the passion narratives (Chs.22-23). The references to Jerusalem could be references to the death of Jesus or Luke may be using John's Gospel where Jesus makes several visits to Jerusalem during His final year to participate in the Jewish festivals. [See Figure 4 "Chronological Journey" and p. 113 "Jewish Festivals."] The idea of journey is used nine times by Luke in this section (also a theme in Mark's Gospel) and Jerusalem is named eight times. The Jerusalem journey begins and ends in failure and rejection (9:51-56; 19:41-44). There are twelve narratives which focus on individuals.

B) Miracles in the Journey Narrative

There are only five miracles in this section compared with the Galilee Section (3:1–9:50) which has thirteen; they are all healing miracles, which are scarce in this section.

The five healing miracles in the Journey Narrative (Figure 1)

	Miracles in the journey narratives	Refs.
1	The dumb man	11: 14- 23
2	The crippled woman	13: 10-17
3	The man with the dropsy	14: 1-6
4	The ten lepers	17: 11-19
5	A blind beggar near Jericho	18: 35-43

Note: the idea of journey is used nine times by Luke in the "journey narrative" and it is also a theme in Mark's Gospel.

C) Parables unique to Luke in the Journey Narrative. [See Ch.7: Structure and Ch. 12: Parables.]

There are eighteen sayings and parables which are one of the main features of this section. Fourteen of these parables are unique to Luke. Teaching is of supreme importace in this section.

Jesus' use of the O.T. in the (L) parables in the Journey Narrative (Figure 2)

	Title	Reference	Theme	Comments
1	The good Samaritan	Lk.10:29-37; Deut.7:1-26	neighbourliness (mercy)	Addressed to the lawyer. This parable may have its roots in the O.T. (2 Chron. 28:8-15).
2	The friend at midnight	Lk.11:5-8; Deut.8: 4-20	persistence in prayer	At the other level it is the story of a man asking a reluctant friend for three loaves.
3	The rich fool	Lk.12: 13-21; Deut.12:17-32	"possessionitis" greed	A person in the crowd wants Jesus to give advice on dividing the family inheritance. Jesus' mission is too urgent for a request that a rabbi could settle.
4	The barren fig tree	Lk.13-6-9; Deut. 14:28	repentance of the nation of Israel	The events of 13:1-5 should awaken a realisation that judgement is near. People will not always have the opportunity to repent.
5	The tower builder	Lk.14: 28-30; Deut. 20:1-20	counting the cost of following Jesus	The cost of a project must be calculated carefully before you start.
6	The rash (warring) king	Lk.14: 31-33; Deut. 20:1-20	counting the cost of following Jesus	Fitzmyer (3) says this parable alludes to 2 Sam. 8:10. "King Tou sent his son to congratulate King David on his victory."
7	The lost coin	Lk.15: 8-10; Deut.15:15; 22:4	mercy	Addressed to the Scribes and Pharisees
8	The prodigal son	Lk.15:32; Lev.11:7; Deut.14:8 ; 21:17	mercy and forgiveness	Addressed to the Scribes and Pharisees (Deut. 21:17). The first-born son had to receive a double portion of his father's inheritance (Lev.11: 7).
9	The shrewd manager	Lk.16: 1-13; Deut 23:15-24:3	prudence with money	Addressed to the Pharisee and the publican. (The Qumran Community called themselves the "sons of light".)
10	The rich man and Lazarus	Lk.16: 19-31; Deut.24:6-25:3	attitude to wealth	It is the poor man who is received by father Abraham and the rich man enters hell. The "religious" thought that health and wealth would include God's blessing, while sickness and poverty show God's cursing. This is a dangerous conclusion to make.
11	The servant's duty	Lk.17: 7-10	humility	The servant does not deserve thanks for doing his job. In serving God, His people are only doing what is expected.
12 13	The importunate widow and the unjust judge	Lk.18: 1-8 (L); Exod. 22:21-24; Deut.24:17-18; Pss.65:8; 82:2-7; 146:9	prayer	Ps.25: 2-3 "Do not let my enemies triumph over me." Because of the widow's persistence she receives justice against her adversary. Even though the judge is uncaring and fearless he acquiesces to the pleas of the widow. The disciples are to learn that persistence in prayer pays off.
14	The Pharisee and the tax collector	Lk.18: 9-14; Exod.20: 12-16; Deut.5:16- 20; Deut.30:15-20	mercy	The error of the Pharisee is that he has a high regard for himself: he has performed his religious duties faithfully. He has no sense of his own unworthiness before God. The tax collector confesses his sin and cries out for God's mercy.

mercy	prayer	money	discipleship	Kingdom, Israel, repentance

Colour code

D) A common expression in the Journey Narrative

1) "When the days drew near (Gk.egeneto) it came to pass," is a common expression in Luke's Gospel for the start of a new unit (9:51). Main events in the life of Jesus "draw near." (1:5; 2:1; 3:21; 5:1,12,17; 6:1,12,17; 7:11; 8:1; 8:22; 9:18, 28, 37) "When the days drew near for him to be received up, He set His face to go to Jerusalem." It is the coming in time of a fulfilment of God's plan. "And when He drew near and saw the city, He wept over it." (19:41) "He drew near" (19:29) and "as He was drawing near" (19:37), "drawing near" continues the journey theme as in 18:35; 19:11,37, 41 and again suggests that key events in the life of Jesus are drawing near. This is key a issue and is one way of identifying the main events in the Journey Narrative.

2) Talbert (5) sees two clear motifs: Jesus going to His death and instructing His disciples.

E) The main theme of the Journey Narrative: Jesus' teaching and discussion with opponents
The main theme is the teaching of Jesus which is interspersed with instructing the disciples and discussion with His opponents. (Reicke and Ellis) **(4)** The teaching and instruction themes fit the wider concept of salvation in Luke and are not just restricted to discipleship as in Mark. In Luke, the grace of God and the response of the hearers are the main themes.

F) Where does the Journey Narrative end?
The end point is also debatable. There are approximately nine different views as to the conclusion of the Journey Narrative. However all the scholars agree that it starts at 9:51.

	Refs.	The views of scholars regarding the end of the Journey Narrative (Figure 3)
1	18:14	C.F. Evans, Goulder, Hendriksen, Klostermann, Luce.
2	18:30	Feine, Lagrange, Liefeld.
3	18:34	Blomberg, Nolland.
4	19:10	Marshall
5	19:27	Blomberg, Craig Evans, Fitzmyer, Godet, Guthrie, Miyoshi, Resseguie, Schurmann.
6	19:28	Plummer
7	19:40-41	Morganthaler, Robinson.
8	19:44	Bock, Carson, Moo and Morris, Ellis, Geldenhuys, Talbert, Trites, Wilcock.
9	19:48	Achtemeier, Bailey, Egelkraut, Green.

G) Four different interpretations of the idea of "Journey" in this section. (Figure 4)
How many journeys did Jesus make to Jerusalem? What was the nature of the journey Jesus made to Jerusalem?

1) A chronological journey

How many journeys to Jerusalem did Jesus make? The conservative view is that Jesus made several journeys to Jerusalem during the final year of His ministry and also in the earlier part of His ministry, to participate in the Jewish feasts referred to in John's Gospel. (Figure 5)

Ref.	Event	Date	Jer. visits
Jn. 2:13	1st Passover	Ap. AD 30	one
Jn.2:20?	2nd Passover	Ap. AD 31	?
Jn.5:1	Feast of Tabernacles	Oct. AD 31	two
Jn.6:4	3rd Passover	Ap. AD 32	three
Jn.7:2,10	Feast of Tabernacles	Oct. AD 32	four a secret visit
Jn.10:22-39; Lk 10:25-42	Feast of dedication / lights Hanukkah.	Dec. AD 32	five
Jn.11:47-57; Lk. 14:7-17:10; 19:29-34	Jesus returns to Jerusalem. 4th Passover of the Jews for pre-Passover purification.	Ap. AD 33	six
Lk 19:45-48	Jesus is back in Jerusalem in Passion Week for the Passover.	Ap. AD 33	seven

2) Journey in a general sense

The idea of journey is not one in a precise chronological order but only in a general sense that the events are set in the framework of a journey. The three journeys to Jerusalem are not in chronological order and do not exist in Luke. The three geographical references are:
1) In Luke 9: 51-56, Jesus is rejected in Samaria and He has to go on "to another village". This has been regarded by some as Jesus avoiding Samaria altogether and taking the popular Jewish route along the east bank of the Jordan via Perea. [See Ch. : 9.] However, it could also mean that Jesus went to a different village in Samaria.
2) In Luke 10: 38-42, Jesus visits Mary and Martha who live in Bethany outside Jerusalem (Jn. 11:1).
3) In Luke 17:11, Jesus is travelling along the border between Samaria and Galilee. In this section, there is no straight line journey from Galilee to Jerusalem. We need to see this section as Jesus "under the shadow of the cross," which He realised loomed large upon the horizon (9:51; Jn.11:47-57).

3) A theological journey (CCEA A/2, Edexcel A2)

Luke arranges his material for theological reasons so that a definite journey(s) is not intended. This is a very popular view of scholars who view the journey as symbolic. They see some vague references to time and space but these are only at the start of a section, for example (9:52; 14:1, 25).
• Bultmann regarded the Journey Narrative as Luke's personal composition.
• Conzelmann did see it as the report of a journey as Jesus did not make any progress on his way to Jerusalem.
• Chris Evans said the nine references to Jerusalem are too vague.
• Schurmann saw the journey as metaphorical.
• Craig Evans symbolises "the way of the Lord." It is the working out of the "Exodus" of Jesus.
• Fitzmyer says Jesus may not possibly have done any of these things on the way to Jerusalem. He rejects the historicity of the narrative.

4) A literary journey (CCEA A/2, Edexcel A2)

Some scholars see the Journey Narrative as a travel narrative based upon a precise literary outline. This section is regarded as part of a chiastic structure with the key motif of Jesus as the "Wise One."
Talbert, Goulder, Bailey and Liefeld follow this approach.

Scholars who accept a chronological journey	Scholars who accept journey in a general sense
1) Hendriksen **(6)** does not accept three journeys to Jerusalem in sequence and does not see a link between John's Gospel and that of Luke. He sees one general journey not in chronological order but does not give a clear reason why the travel motif is present . 2) Marshall **(7)** "the journey is the path to passion like Mark's Gospel and Luke points out that this journey is ordained of God. (13:33) It is a necessity (Gk.dei). 3) Bock sees the term journey as broadly descriptive and says it is in the movement of God's plan towards Jerusalem that Luke accurately presents a journey that is both theological and historical. It is a journey in time and not a direct geographical route. **(8)** 4) Guthrie) **(9)** says, it is preferable to call this section "from Galilee to Jerusalem" as the word "journey" suggests a detailed route. The idea of journey may not have been in Luke's mind. It looks as if Luke collected material he knew was from the closing period of Jesus' life and fitted it between the ministries in Galilee and Judea. The overall theme is "listen to Jesus." It deals with what Jesus taught and did as His ministry faced its end in Jerusalem.	1) Arndt **(10)** refers to this section as the "travel narrative" and identifies three journeys which Jesus made to Jerusalem saying that the final journey started in Luke 17:11 when Jesus healed the ten lepers. Arndt sees the journey in a broad descriptive sense. Some scholars say the final journey starts at 18:15; Mk.10:13-16. 2) Morris **(11)** sees the possibility of two journeys: (1) the feast of Tabernacles as in John 7, (2) Luke 17:11 where Jesus passes between Samaria and Galilee. (3) Other scholars say that Jesus went to Jerusalem for all the three main feasts during His ministry.

H) Conclusion about the travel motif.

Either Luke follows John's Gospel and Jesus makes several journeys to Jerusalem during the final year of His Ministry to attend the Jewish feasts or Luke keeps on referring to Jesus going to Jerusalem to remind his readers that Jesus is going to die there but that time has not come as yet. Therefore we are not meant to plot geographically or chronologically the route which Jesus might have taken. (Wilcock) **(12)**

Jewish festivals and calendar (Figure 6)

Jewish Feasts	Month	Month
New Year/ Trumpets	Elul	August
Day of Atonement, Tabernacles and Booths	Tishri	October-November
	Marchesvan	November-December
Dedication / Lights/ Hanukkah	Kislev	December-January
	Tebet	January-February
	Shebat	February-March
	Adar	March
Passover and Unleavened Bread	Nisan	April
	Lyyar	April-May
The Feast of Weeks	Sivan	May-June
	Tammuz	June-July
	Ab	July-August

I) Reasons for accepting the title Journey Narrative

Bock **(13)** gives four reasons for accepting the travel motif. It is in keeping with:

1) the nature of the ministry of Jesus which has been that of a journey and this is consistent with the emphasis in Luke/Acts which is also on travel.

2) the fact that Jesus did not go directly from Galilee to Jerusalem, shows that His mind was firmly set on the events which He faced in Jerusalem. Even though He travelled north again, His final destination was Jerusalem. It is in the movement of God's plan towarm that Luke accurately presents a "journey" that is both theological and historical and some sequencing may be in evidence.

3) The word "way" (Gk.hodos) does not appear in this section to describe the path of Jesus or the life of the disciples though it is used in (9:57) for road or way. "As they were going along the road," and in (10:4) "Salute no one on the road". It is only used in Luke 20:21 as the path of Jesus. "Teacher, we know that you speak and teach rightly and show no partiality

but truly teach the way of God."

4) Luke gives us very little evidence in the journey narrative where the events actually take place, for example there is no reference to Bethany as the village of Mary and Martha in Luke 10:38 as in John 11:1.

Other reasons:

5) The journey to Jerusalem and to His death are in respect of His sufferings and Jesus is described as "going ahead" of the disciples (19:28). (Talbert) **(14)**

6) The Journey Narrative starts with the rejection of Jesus by the village of the Samaritans (9:52) and ends in Luke 19:39-48 with Jesus in the city of Jerusalem. Talbert sees this as chiastic patterns. [See Ch.7: Structure.] The heavenly voice bears witness to Jesus, "This is my Son, my Chosen; listen to Him!" (9:35)

7) The end of the journey narrative should not be placed earlier than Luke 19:41, which refers to Jesus drawing near Jerusalem. (Bock)**(15)** Some recent scholars have tended to prefer the ending at Luke 19:48. [Figure 3]

[2] Themes in the Journey Narratives: Jerusalem, travel, suffering and the Kingdom of God
A) Jerusalem as the goal of Jesus' travels: the place of destiny (Read 9: 51, 53.) (L) [Figure 7]

Ref.	Text
9:51,53	When the days drew near for Him to be received up, He set His face to go to Jerusalem (9:51). But the people (of Samaria) would not receive Him because His face was set towards Jerusalem (9:53).

"When the days drew near (Gk.sumplerousthai)" means the days were fulfilled for Jesus "to be received up" (Gk.analempseos) "He [Jesus], set His face to go to Jerusalem." His going to Jerusalem did not happen by accident. This is a Hebrew idiom for determination to accomplish a task which literally means "to set one's face to go somewhere." God's plan is another step nearer to fulfilment (Is. 50:7; Jer. 44:12; Ezek. 21:2-3). The use of "draw near" followed by a finite verb "to be received" means the coming of a time in fulfilment of God's plan. (Marshall) **(16)** "Son of Man set your face to Jerusalem." The use of the verb "go" (Gk. poreuesthai) underlines the travel theme. It is used on seven occasions in this section (9:51, 56-57; 10:38; 13:31, 33; 17:11; 19:28). At the very start of His journey, Jesus announces that His goal is to go to Jerusalem. Jesus has been on the move since He went on a preaching tour of the synagogues of Judea (4:42). Main events in the life of Jesus "draw near." Jesus passes through Samaria. "The people (of Samaria) would not receive Him, because His face was set towards Jerusalem." (9:53) To set one's face is the O.T. word for resolve. Jesus is determined to do whatever God wanted him to do as in Ezek.21: 2-3; Luke 21:12. To be "received up" (Gk.analempsis) (9:51) can refer to Jesus' death, the resurrection-ascension (Acts 1:2; 11:22). (Marshall) **(17)** The approaching goal of Jesus is not only his death and resurrection but also His ascension.

B) The idea of travel as a concept of homelessness (Read 9:58.) (Matt. 8:20) Q [Figure 8]

9:58	"Foxes have holes, and birds of the air have nests; but the Son of Man has nowhere to lay His head."

This verse continues the travel idea with the concept of homelessness and this verse may also refer to the future passion "the Son of Man has nowhere to lay His head."

C) The continuing idea of Jerusalem as the place of destiny (Read 13:22-30.) L [Figure 9]

13:22	Jesus went on His way through towns and villages, teaching and journeying toward Jerusalem.

"He went (was passing) on His way through towns and villages, teaching and journeying toward Jerusalem." Jesus is on the move through the nation and heading towards Jerusalem. The verb "was passing" (imperfect tense Gk. dieporeuto) denotes a progressive movement and indicates that Jesus taught in all the inhabited areas of Israel. Entrance into the kingdom requires careful attention.

D) The Journey idea as seen in the context of the cross and resurrection: (Read 13:31-33.) L [Figure 10]

13:31-33	Some Pharisees warn Jesus that Herod wants to kill Him. Jesus says to them, "Go and tell that fox, (Herod) 'Behold, I cast out demons and perform cures today and tomorrow, and the third day I finish my course. Nevertheless I must go on my way today and tomorrow and the day following; for it cannot be that a prophet should perish away from Jerusalem.' "

This is a key saying which shows Jesus continuing His ministry undeterred by fear of Herod. "Nevertheless I must go on my way today and tomorrow and the day following; for it cannot be that a prophet must perish away from Jerusalem."

This verse shows that it is a path to the passion which is being referred to in this context which is part of God's plan. Jesus' ministry will come to an end in Jerusalem where Jesus anticipates His own death. "From the first prediction of His passion (9:22), Jesus is very conscious of the shadow of Jerusalem hanging over His ministry and He had His ultimate destiny in view." (Marshall) **(18)** The thought of suffering and rejection runs throughout this Gospel and in the journey section there is a heightened sense of suffering on the part of Jesus. Jesus sees his function as a prophet and his mission in terms of Jerusalem. His destiny is tied to Jerusalem by divine necessity. He is ready to become a sent one who suffers as a righteous messenger, rejected and wronged.

E) Nearing Jerusalem, His place of destiny, Jesus continues to show mercy and to call for faith. (Read 17:11.) (L) [Figure 11]

17:11	On the way to Jerusalem He was passing along between Samaria and Galilee.

"On the way to Jerusalem He was passing along between Samaria and Galilee," Jesus was met by ten lepers. As Jesus nears Jerusalem, He continues to act with mercy healing the ten lepers and calling for faith. This is the fourth of five miracles in this section. Significantly each of these miracles emphasises not the miracle but the teaching. The "thankful Samaritan leper" is commended for his faith compared with the "little faith" of the nine other lepers and shows the benefits of faith (17:5). This incident is an example of response to God's mercy and shows that God's grace works in the most surprising places Samaria. There is a growing expectation about what awaits Jesus in Jerusalem. Jesus is getting near to Jerusalem in a literary sense without being physically near.

F) Jerusalem as a symbol that Jesus must suffer (Read 18:31-32.) (Matt.20 17:19; Mk.10:32-34)
[Figure 12]   [Triple tradition]

18:31-32	"And taking the Twelve, He said to them, "Behold we are going up to Jerusalem and everything that is written of the Son of Man by the prophets will be accomplished. For He will be delivered to the Gentiles, and will be mocked and shamefully treated and spit upon: they will scourge Him and kill Him, and on the third day He will rise."

"Behold we are going up to Jerusalem." This is an expression from Mark's Gospel, placed before Jesus arrived in Jericho and is a detailed prediction of His suffering. All that is written about the Son of Man will be fulfilled and the Gentiles will share as participants in the slaying of Jesus. Luke 18:31-34 records the sixth announcement of the death of Jesus where He shows that what will happen in Jerusalem, will fulfil scripture and the disciples will fail to understand the remarks of Jesus. His sufferings are predicted in detail (18:32). In Luke 18:32, the verbs are all passive indicating what scripture says while Matthew and Mark show the human perpetrators "chief priests and scribes condemn Him and give Him over to the Gentiles;" He will be given over (Gk.paradidomi) to the Gentiles. This prophecy was fulfilled in Luke 23:22,25 but an abortive attempt was also made (20:20b). Jesus' arrest will be accompanied by mocking (Gk.empaizo). He will not receive any respect during His confinement. Jesus will be shamefully treated (Gk.hubrizo), an expression used only in Luke. It is the word which is used in the O.T. of the scoffers who work unrighteously and proudly against the righteous (Zeph.3:11-12). It is usually seen as another word for scoffing. Some will spit on Jesus (Gk.emputo) a custom which was often a part of the crucifixion process (18:33; Is. 50:6). This was fulfilled in John 19:1-6. Jesus will be killed (Gk. apokteino). Luke uses the active verb to show the intensity of the death of Jesus. They (the Gentiles) will kill Him. Jesus will be resurrected (Gk. anistemi) on the third day. All groups killed Jesus and this incident does not reflect an anti-Semitic approach by Luke as Sanders suggested. **(19)** Luke here is closer to Mark than to Matthew in the word he uses (Mk.10:32). Jesus is gradually and progressively giving more details about His suffering.

G) Jerusalem linked to teaching about the kingdom of God   (Read 19:11.) (L) [Figure 13]

19:11	He proceeded to tell them a parable, (the parable of the pounds) because He was near to Jerusalem, and because they supposed that the kingdom of God was to appear immediately.

Jesus tells the parable of the pounds because He was near to Jerusalem. His disciples have a false expectation about the consummation of the kingdom; they thought it would be an earthly kingdom which would come in Jerusalem. The location for this teaching of the parable of the pounds is Jericho and is connected to the Zacchaeus incident. The disciples had struggled to understand Jesus' departure (9:45; 18:34). Jesus wants them to see Jerusalem as a place of passion and not the place of the second coming. The disciples have to act responsibly during the interim period in faithful service until the return of the King as the parable teaches. Jesus was despised and rejected by men, a man of sorrows and acquainted with grief (Is.53). "We do not want this man to rule over us." (19:14)

H) The journey motif seen in respect of His suffering: (Read 19:28-29.) (L) [Figure 14]

19:28-29	And when He had said this (the parable of the pounds), He went on ahead, going up to Jerusalem. When He drew near to Bethphage and Bethany at the mount which is called Olivet, He sent two of the disciples saying,... .

This is a bridge verse and follows on from the parable of the pounds. "Going up to Jerusalem" – the city was on a higher elevation than the surrounding area. It is in respect of His sufferings that Jesus is described as "going on ahead" of the disciples. (Talbert) **(20)** Jesus enters Jerusalem as a King but is rejected by the leaders of the Jews (19:38-40). Luke identifies certain locations around Jerusalem to show Jesus' entry into the Holy City because here the Temple was the symbol of God's presence. Jesus has repeatedly run foul of the Jerusalem leaders and others who challenged His authority of scripture and the nature of salvation (5:17). As Jesus approaches Jerusalem, a crowd of disciples praises God in loud voices for all the miracles which they have seen (19:38). Jesus is given the greeting reserved for all pilgrims who have come to Jerusalem to celebrate the Passover. Luke includes the idea of King in the quote from Ps.118:26 rather than kingdom (Mk. 11:10) to emphasise that it is the King who has come when Jesus enters the city and not the kingdom. The use of the word "kingdom" would have led to great misunderstanding. His arrival in Jerusalem is the fulfilment of what awaited Him in the city of His destiny. Luke is unique in tying the setting to the journey's end (19:28).

I) Jesus weeps for Jerusalem because of the unexpected destruction that will come upon the unrepentant city. (Read 19:41 - 44.) (L) [Figure 15]

19:41-44	And when He drew near and saw the city He wept over it, saying, "Would that even today you knew the things that make for peace! But now they are hid from your eyes. For the days shall come upon you, when your enemies will cast up a bank about you and surround you, and hem you in on every side, and dash you to the ground, you and your children within you, and they will not leave one stone upon another in you; because you did not know the time of your visitation."

a) "And when He drew near (Gk.engizo) and saw the city He wept (Gk.klaio) over it, saying, "Would that even today you knew the things that make for peace! But they are hid from your eyes." Jesus is not indifferent to the nation; He laments for Jerusalem, weeping in a manner which means "full sobbing." Fitzmyer **(21)** Jesus laments in irony that the so called city of peace Jerusalem which literally means "I shall see peace" does not know what to do to secure peace. Peace was hidden from the eyes of Jerusalem (Ps.122:6; Jer.15:5). Instead of peace, blindness comes from a failure to respond. What potentially Jerusalem had will ultimately be taken away (8:10).
b) Judgement on Jerusalem will be evidenced in three ways (19:43). Firstly, fierce siege in "the days that are coming" – an O.T. expression for a coming event of great significance, secondly, barricades and earthen mounds will be placed around the city and thirdly, an enemy will come and attack the city. These events are all in the future showing that Jesus is speaking as a prophet. This description is like the collapse of Jerusalem in A.D. 70 when Titus built a barricade around the city. (Josephus) **(22)**
c) The fall of the nation is described in two ways. (Read 19:44.)
Firstly, the nation and secondly its children; both will be dashed (Ps. 136:9) and razed to the ground (Is.3:26). This is a picture of dead bodies. The description of one stone not being left on another is the idea of the city being levelled (cf. 13:35 and 21:6). Rome will leave the city for dead.
d) Jesus gives the reason for the terrible destruction. (Read 19:44.) The nation missed the opportunity to respond to His visitation. They did not recognise the time of the visitation of Jesus. "You did not know the time of your visitation." The nation will experience judgement while Jesus will be exalted. The sword does not just pass through the heart of Mary (2:34). Luke 19: 41-45 is unique to Luke and ends the Jerusalem Journey Narrative. Jesus knows that the people have already turned their backs on Him. Jesus cleanses the Temple; He acts physically and the leaders portray Him as a threat to peace (19:45-48). This drives the Jewish leaders to plot against Jesus. This is a prophetic act and Jesus' confession to be a king is still ringing in their ears. "Blessed be the king who comes in the name of the Lord." (19:38) The journey begins as it ends in a note of failure. The disciples respond improperly to rejection (9:54) and the people do not recognise the time of visitation (19:44).

J) Summary on the significance of Jerusalem
• Throughout the journey narrative, Jesus warns about the possibility of national failure (11:50-51; 13:31-35). Like Jer. 9:2; 2 Kgs. 8:11, the tears are of pain, anger and frustration that rejection causes in one who serves God. Peace was hidden from the eyes of the nation caused by blindness, failure to respond, resulting in darkness.

- It is interesting to note that references regarding His suffering and passion as predicted by Jesus, tend to cluster near the end of the journey, so that they are more than just travel notes.
- Jerusalem did not recognise the time of its visitation and this visitation was precisely the presence of Jesus in the Temple (19:44). Marshall **(23)** says, "The Temple is the focal point of the rejection of Jesus by the Jews."
- Jesus travels to Jerusalem to meet His destiny there. Even though the context is one of journey the overall theme is that of "the way": the way of following Jesus.
- Why did Jesus want to go Jerusalem? Jerusalem was the capital city of the Jews at that time both politically and religiously. The Jewish Temple was here and it was the centre of the Jewish faith and power. [See note 21.]

Pupil's Activity: One   **"The Temple is the focal point of the rejection of Jesus by the Jews." (Marshall) (23)**

a) Play as background music relevant extacts from Handel's Messiah. "The Lord gave the word; great was the company of the preachers." "Then shall the eyes of the blind be opened, and the ears of the deaf unstopped. Then the lame man shall leap as an hart, and the tongue of the dumb shall sing." (Is.35:6a) "Rejoice, greatly, rejoice O daughter of Zion! Shout, O daughter of Jerusalem! Behold, Thy king cometh unto Thee (Zech.9:9). He is the righteous Saviour, and He shall speak peace unto the heathen." "He was despised and rejected."(Is,53:3) "He trusted in God let Him deliver Him, if He delight in Him."

b) Discuss these passages from Handel's Messiah in the light of the "Journey Narrative."

Pupil's Activity: Two   **Revision**

Outline your knowledge and understanding of the place of Jerusalem in the Journey Narrative (CCEA A/S 2002). [30 marks]

K) The theme of Jesus' suffering and rejection in the Journey Narrative
Ideas for internal assessment on suffering (CCEA)

The suffering and rejection of Jesus in the Journey Narrative (Group: 1) [Read 9:21-22.] (Figure 16)
- Introduction: **Jesus tells the disciples He will suffer and be rejected by the elders, chief priests and scribes and be killed, and on the third day be raised.**
- This is the first time Jesus indicates that He will walk a difficult road.
- His power which is seen in Luke Chs. 7-9 will be withdrawn as He submits to rejection.
In what four ways is Jesus' career summarised here?

Jesus predicts His betrayal. (Group: 2) [Read 9:44-45.] (Figure 17)
"Let these words sink into your ears; for the Son of man is to be delivered into the hands of men." But they did not understand this saying, and it was hid from them, that they should not perceive it; and they were afraid to ask Him about this saying."
- Jesus speaks about being "given over," though the disciples do not understand what He is telling them.
- Jesus says "take completely to heart" or more commonly as in "He who has ears let him hear." (8:8)
- Jesus does not say who is to give Him over and why as in the earlier prediction (9:21-22).
- Jesus' popularity is not going to last. Often God's work is not appreciated by those whom He loves.
- "The exodus" will take place shortly at Jerusalem.
What did Jesus mean by this (9:31)?

Jesus' desire to complete His task.
(Group: 3) [Read 12: 49-50.] (Figure 18)
"I came to cast fire upon the earth; and would that it were already kindled! I have a baptism to be baptised (Gk. baptisma) with; and how I am constrained until it is accomplished!" **What did Jesus mean by this statement? "I came to cast fire upon the earth and I have a baptism to be baptised with."**
- Jesus had to undergo rejection and bear God's judgement before the Spirit came. Unless Jesus undergoes rejection and bears God's judgement, the Spirit of God cannot come.
- Jesus wants to suffer and save humankind and at the same time, He is going to be overwhelmed by the judgement of God for the sins of mankind, be rejected and suffer.

The theme of suffering and rejection in the Journey Narrative cont'd

---

Jesus defines His mission in terms of Jeruslem. (Group: 4) [Read 13: 31-33.] (Figure 19)

"Behold I cast out demons and perform cures today and tomorrow, and the third day I finish my course. Nevertheless I must go on my way today and tomorrow and the day following; for it cannot be that a prophet can perish away from Jerusalem."

• Why do the enemies of Jesus (the Pharisees) warn Jesus that Herod wants to kill Him?
• Look up 11: 38-54; 14:1-6. Were the Pharisees trying to scare Jesus out of Galilee into Jerusalem to meet His end or were they some of the sincere Pharisees who tried to warn Jesus? What do the references to "today, tomorrow and the day following" mean?

The timing and coming of the Kingdom - Jesus predicts His suffering and rejection. (Group: 5) [Read 17: 20b-25.] (Figure 20)

"The Kingdom of God is not coming with signs to be observed; nor will they say 'Lo, here it is,' or 'There it is,' for behold, the kingdom of God is in the midst of you."(20-21) And He said to the disciples, "The days are coming when you will desire to see one of the days of the Son of Man and you will not see it. And they will say to you, 'Lo there!' or 'Lo, here!' Do not go, do not follow them. For as lightning flashes and lights up the sky from one side to the other, so must the Son of Man be in His day. But first He must suffer many things and be rejected by this generation." (17:22-24)

• How do we know that the Kingdom of God is not a country or a building?
• How does Jesus indicate that the Kingdom is delayed?
• Why will Jesus not come as the Pharisees wish (17:21)?
• How does Jesus instruct them in the way He will not come (17: 22)?
To what does "one of the days of the Son of Man" refer (17: 22)?

Rejection of the authority of Jesus leads to judgement. (Group: 6) [Read 18:35-19:27.] (Figure 21)

"As they heard these things," He proceeded to tell the parable of the pounds, because they supposed that the kingdom of God was to appear immediately (19:11). "But as for these enemies of mine, who did not want me to reign over them, bring them here and slay them before me." (19:27)

• Who are the enemies of Jesus who are referred to here? Are they the Jews who have rejected Jesus or is this a specific reference to the Fall of Jerusalem by the Romans and the slaughter of its enemies? (Fitzmyer) (24) How does this parable follow the pattern of politics of old? [See also 18:31-32.]

Jesus warns about being ready for His return/ The entry into Jerusalem (Group: 7) [Read 19:27-28.] (Figure 22)

"And when He had said this, He went on ahead, going up to Jerusalem. When He drew near to Bethphage and Bethany at the mount which is called Olivet, He sent two of the disciples saying, 'Go into the village opposite where on entering you will find a colt tied, on which no one has even yet sat; untie it and bring it to here…. The Lord has need of it.' "

• This is a bridge verse and follows on from the parable of the pounds. "Going up to Jerusalem" the city was on a higher elevation than the surrounding area.
• It is in respect of His sufferings that Jesus is described as "going on ahead" of the disciples. (Talbert) (25) Comment: The exact location of Bethphage (Aramaic word meaning "house of unripe figs") is unknown but is generally thought to be south-east of Bethany and the Mt. of Olives, called today Abu Dis. Jesus had warned the nation about becoming an unproductive fig tree (13:6-9). [See map in Ch.9.] Bethany means "House of dates" and can be identified as El Azariyeh today. (Marshall) (26) The Mt. of Olives is seen in Zech. 14:4-5 as the place where the Messiah will show Himself. Luke does not comment on this but in Acts 1:11 one of the angels notes that Jesus will return to the Mt. of Olives. How did the crowd greet Jesus at His entry into Jerusalem? What was the significance of their cry (19:37-38)?

Pupil's Activity: Three　　　　　　　　　OHP presentation

Divide the class into nine groups, one group for each of the references to Jerusalem and bring all the groups together for a class presentation either by power point or OHP entitled "Jesus' suffering and death in the Journey Narrative".

Jesus weeps for Jerusalem (Group: 8) [Read 19:41-42.] (Figure 23)
"And when He drew near (Gk.engizo) and saw the city He wept (Gk.klaio) over it saying, 'Would that even today you knew the things that make for peace! But they are hid from your eyes. ' "
• Jesus is not indifferent to the nation.
• Jesus' lament for Jerusalem is unique to Luke and ends the Jerusalem Journey Narrative (19:41-44). Jesus knows that the people have already turned their backs on Him.
• Throughout the journey narrative Jesus warns about the possibility of national failure (11:50-51; 13: 31-35).
• Like Jer.9:2 and 2 Kgs. 8:11 the tears are of pain, anger and frustration that rejection causes in one who serves God.
• Peace was hidden from the eyes of the nation caused by blindness, failure to respond, resulting in darkness.
• It would have pleased me if you had known the things that make for peace! [See Fitzmyer **note 21**.] **Why did Jesus weep for Jerusalem (13:34)? What is the significance of the word peace in this verse?**

Judgement on Jerusalem (Group 9) [Read 19:44.] (Figure 24)
"And they will not leave one stone upon another in you: because you did not know the time of your visitation."
• The references regarding His suffering and passion predicted by Jesus are more numerous towards the end of the journey and are not just travel notes.
• Jerusalem did not recognise the time of its visitation and this visitation was precisely the presence of Jesus in the Temple (19:44). [Marshall **note 22**]
• Jesus travels to Jerusalem to meet His destiny there. Even though the context is one of journey the overall theme is that of "the way"; the way of following Jesus.
• **Why did Jesus want to go there? Jerusalem was the capital city of the Jews at that time both politically and religiously.** The Jewish Temple was here and it was the centre of the Jewish faith and power. This "journey" stretches ten chapters to Luke 19:44 or 48. Mary's heart is not the only one through which the sword passes (2:34).

[3] Three concluding themes in the Journey Narrative (Read 19:28-44.)

A) Jesus is a prophet who confronts people just like Moses.
In this passage Jesus becomes like an O.T. prophet calling the people to see their need for repentance. Despite the warnings, the people reject the message of God's judgement. The people fail to heed the call (19:41-44) and become like their unfaithful forefathers (11:14-54). Jesus continually warns about the need for repentance (9:51- 13-35). He also warns about destruction and rejection but again the people fail to listen (14:15-24). Jesus' journey to Jerusalem is portrayed as a "new exodus" like the first exodus by Moses from Egypt. At the Transfiguraton, Moses and Elijah were speaking with Jesus about His "exodus" which translated means departure (9:31). The command, "This is My Son, whom I have chosen; listen to Him," at the Transfiguration is linked to Deut.18:15. "The Lord your God will raise up a prophet like me from among you, him you shall heed." (9:35)

B) Jesus is greater than Moses (9:35) and He shows the ethic which God requires.
Jesus points out the way of discipleship in the face of opposition; He leads a new exodus into God's presence and promises a seat at God's table (14:15-24); faithfulness in humility is the basis of the spiritual life which is exemplified in the Good Samaritan, Zacchaeus the tax collector (19:1-10) and the blind man of Jericho (18:35-43). The parables on spiritual loss all show God's concern for different kinds of "lostness": the heedlessly lost, the sheep; the helplessly lost, the coin and the wilfully lost the son (Ch.15). Jesus' disciples are to walk in the way of love, generosity, rejection and suffering.

C) Jesus as the successor to Moses as in Deut. 18:15-18 could be implied in Luke 9:51 "The days drew near for Him to be received up." (Evans) (27)

[4] What is the way? (Read 9:51-10:16.)
This title could also be viewed as a summary of the in-service training for the disciples. Discipleship Training: selected passages on discipleship from 9:51-19:17. The idea of discipleship and journey are interwoven in the Journey Narratives. The basics of discipleship training are contained here in this section: **mission**, commitment, love for God, love for neighbour, devotion to Jesus, prayer and His teaching (9:51-11:13). There is a strong emphasis on the importance of welcoming Jesus, His message and messengers and showing hospitality and care as in the incident of Mary and Martha in listening and serving (9:57-62). Discipleship, trusting God, advice to disciples on possessions, preparedness and repentance are the key ideas of this section (12:1-13). Discipleship in the face of rejection is the main topic of this section (14:25-35). Seeking the lost, rejoicing in finding lost sinners, service to other people and being generous with resources are also part of discipleship (15:1-32). Discipleship training on generosity, handling money and possessions are key themes, as are money, its use and misuse (16:1-31). Discipleship teaching about service, false teaching, forgiveness and service (17:1-10) is uppermost here.

A brother or sister who sins is to be forgiven, even if they sin seven times (17:3). The disciple is to live in the hope of the return of Jesus (17:11-18:8). Jesus predicts His suffering and heals as David's Son (18:32-43). The mission of Jesus is epitomised in Zacchaeus as the transformed, wealthy outcast (19:1-10). The disciples and the nation must be faithful as they are accountable to God (19:11-17).

Summary on discipleship:

• Following Jesus is like joining Him on a journey (like Pilgrim's Progress) and in proclaiming the kingdom of God (9:51-10:42): Jesus and the Samaritans / the mission of the seventy (two). These incidents are highlights in the life of the disciples because they received an insight into the person and mission of Jesus and one in which they enjoyed great success.
• Chs.9-13: this section brings out the difference between Jesus' teaching and that of Judaism. (The seeds of discontent leading up to the death of Jesus are all in evidence here).
• Jesus enters Jerusalem as a King but is rejected by the leaders of the Jews (19:28-40).
• Israel faces God's judgement if they fail to respond (19:41-44).
• The concerns of Jesus are represented as a journey. It is a journey which Jesus takes with His disciples.
• Jerusalem is the place of divine destiny and the centre of hostility to Jesus.
• Key features of the journey are those of discipleship training. Sadly however the Twelve oppose the message and by the end of the journey appear to have vanished from sight having failed to identify with Jesus.

[5] The main sub-sections of the Journey Narrative adopted from Marshall, Bock and Blomberg
[See Ch.7: the Skeleton of Luke. (Bock note 13)]

1. Discipleship, the way of the cross (9:51-62)　2. The mission of the seventy (two) (10:1-24)
3. The double love command (10:25-42)　4. Teaching on prayer (11:1-13) [See Ch. 6: Characteristics.]
5. Controversy with the Pharisees (11:14-54)　6. Preparing for judgement (12:1- 13:9) [See [4]- What is the Way?]
7. Kingdom reversals (13: 10 –14:24) [Ch.13: Miracles.] 8. The cost of discipleship (14:25-35) [See Ch.14: Discipleship.]
9. God's love for sinners (15:1-32) [See Ch. 12: Parables.] 10. Generosity; handling money and possessions (16:1-31)
[See Ch. 17: Wealth.] 11. Faith, forgiveness and service (17:1-11) [See Ch. 18: Forgiveness.] 12. How the Kingdom will come? (17:20 -18:8) 13. How to enter the Kingdom? (18:9-30) 14. Conclusion (18:31-34) 15. Jesus in Judea (18:35-19:27) [See Ch. 13: Miracles.] 16. Jesus in Jerusalem (19:28-48)

Jesus enters Jerusalem (19:28-38), [See above concluding themes in the Journey Narrative.] Jesus predicts the Fall of Jerusalem, weeps for the city (19:41-44) and drives out the money changers from the Temple (19:45-46). The Jewish leaders plot against Jesus. (19:47-48)

These sub-sections reflect the key points. There is a conflict between the Jewish leaders and instruction on discipleship. Jesus points out to the Jewish leaders how not to walk with God. In 11:37-54, He condemns their leadership. The turning point is in (13:31-14:35), where the nation rejects the Messiah. This leads to Jesus' lament over Israel's desolate house. This in turn leads to Jesus' explosive teaching on discipleship involving commitment (14:25-35). Apart from brief critical comments about the Pharisees and scribes there is little reference to them.

They return again in Luke 15-18 where Jesus gives specific teaching on how to live in the light of rejection. Luke emphasises discipleship, rejection and suffering. Towards the end of this section in 18:35-43 the Davidic character of Jesus reasserts itself. This section ends on a sad note. Jesus enters Jerusalem and weeps for it, because He knows the short-term consequences of the nation's rejection of Him. Blessing will come for everyone but the nation will suffer greatly (19:38-48).

1. The first sub-section of the Journey Narrative: the way of the cross (Read 9:51-10:24.) [See p. 157-8.]
Luke combines some events about people who have an interest in Jesus' way. The common thread in all three is "follow" (9:57, 59, 61) [See below.] "In Ch.10 the disciples are "sent-on ahead of Him." To be involved in the way is to:
(1) come after Jesus (9:57-62), (2) to go before Him (10 :1-16) to be His followers, (3) to be His heralds. (Wilcock) **(28)**

The first event (Read 9: 51-56.) (L)
A) Discipleship in the middle of rejection by the Samaritans:- Background to the Samaritans: to the Jews they were the half-castes, the ethnic traitors. Samaria was the old name for the northern kingdom when the north was ruled by king Omri and was divided from the south (1 Kgs.16:21-24). They had intermarried with other peoples in the area and had their own Temple for worshipping God at Mount Gerizim. They only accepted the Pentateuch (the first five O.T. books) as inspired by God. Jesus' attempt to reach out culturally to them was unusual and was like a priest from the Falls Road ministering to Protestants on the Shankill Road or a Protestant minister from the Shankill conducting a mission on the Falls Road for the Roman Catholic people. This incident is the only one which presents the Samaritans in a negative way and shows that Jesus is rejected beyond the borders of Israel (10:25-37; 17:11-19). In the earlier story of the Gerasene demoniac, a similar Gentile rejection takes place (8:37). Tension between the Jews and the Samaritans intensified when the Samaritan Temple was destroyed around 128 B. C. Jews preferred to take the longer route around Samaria even though it took three days to pass through the region. Through this incident the disciples were still learning what their **mission** was all about, while the **mission of Jesus** was seen through His response. The disciples are submissive to Jesus and refuse

to act without his approval. "Lord, do you want us to bid fire come down from heaven and consume them?" (9:54) It was important at this stage to see that Jesus was shortly "to be received up" - to die, rise, and ascend and He is on His way to that outcome (9:51). The Jerusalem journey begins and ends in failure and rejection (9:51-56; 19: 41-44).

B) Rejection by the Samaritans

> **The Jerusalem journey begins and ends in failure and rejection (9:51-56; 19:41-44).**

Jesus sent some disciples on ahead to test the reactions of the people and to prepare the townspeople in Samaria for His arrival (9:52). The Samaritan villages did not welcome Jesus as a Jew travelling to Jerusalem (9:53). This shows the contrasting attitudes of Jesus and His followers to the refusal by some Samaritans. The report of the disciples was not favourable. The Samaritan villages refused to give the disciples a safe passage, not even for pilgrims. They had not grasped the fact that the Messiah was with the disciples (9:53). The disciples took this personally as an affront against Jesus. James and John boiled up within themselves in indignation and felt that drastic action was required, nothing short of divine judgement. They thought that the people deserved the judgement of fire from heaven. It may have been a desire to emulate Elijah and the prophets of Baal on Mount Carmel (1 Kgs.17). They thought that they had false power to command fire from heaven like Elijah, though they were sensible enough to ask Jesus' permission before trying it out. Jesus' **mission** was not to destroy this village. He had to rebuke their foolishness (9:54). The current period was not one of instant judgement but one of offering grace to all people. Hence Jesus and the disciples go on to another village (9:56b; 2 Pet.3:9). This story shows the loneliness of Jesus as He set his face to go to Jerusalem. Clearly the disciples needed more in-service training if they were to qualify as ambassadors of peace in a world of strife. The travel narrative opens with opposition to Jesus, just as the Galilean one started with rejection, so Jesus' ministry heads towards rejection and death. (Fitzmyer) **(29)**

> **The travel narrative opens with opposition to Jesus, just as the Galilean one started with rejection, so Jesus' ministry heads towards rejection and death. (Fitzmyer) (29)**

Pupil's Activity: Four (Read 9:51-56.)
Why was this experience of the Samaritan rejection a learning curve for the disciples and what did they learn from it?

C) The cost of discipleship: the way to be His follower (9:57-62.) (Matt.8:18-22) "Q"

The second event - the first would-be follower (Read 9: 57-58.)
On the way others were filled with desire to join the company of disciples. One man offered to follow (Gk.akoloutheso) literally wherever Jesus was going. The Greek word also has the meaning of wanting to belong to the close group of disciples who accompanied Jesus on His travels rather than the wider group (9:57). The man's offer was magnanimous and zealous but he had not recognised what was involved. The foxes and the birds had more settled accommodation. The man had not realised that Jesus was moving towards a cross : followers of Jesus cannot be content with a laid back lifestyle but have to learn to trust God despite rejection. The demands of discipleship are the same irrespective of how a person comes to Jesus. [See also Ch. 14: Discipleship.]

The third event - a second would-be follower (Read 9: 59-60.) "Q"
Another man was invited to follow (Gk. akolouthei) Pres. Imperative) "Be my follower"(9:60) but declined as he thought he had a good excuse, he must attend to his filial responsibilities. In Judaism burial took precedence over every other Jewish ritual. After the death of his father he would be willing to follow. Jesus does not tolerate his excuse. To wait for such a reason is to show spiritual deadness and be unaware of the urgency of the task. Immediate action was required in proclaiming the kingdom. The **mission** must come first and the burial be left to others.

The fourth event - a third would-be follower (Read 9: 60-62.) "Q"
Fitzmyer **(30)** says it may be unique to Luke and calls it, "an independent context in the ministry of Jesus". The third man seems to have a genuine excuse he says, "I will follow you (Gk.akoloutheso) but let me go home and say farewell." (9:61) Jesus sees the danger. The man was really turning away from his responsibilities, like a farmer ploughing a field and keeping his eye on the furrow ahead. In Palestine if the farmer looked back in ploughing he was more likely to make mistakes in preparing a field as the ground was rocky and to look back was to run the risk of going off course. This man would not be able to survive the heat of the kitchen and the demands of the kingdom. "Once they begin to plough the only way to drive a straight furrow- 'one that is fit for the kingdom'- is to keep looking ahead and not back." (Wilcock) **(31)** Jesus demands self-denial and complete devotion to the kingdom. "Those who look back are not fit for the kingdom of God."(9:61-62)

2. The second sub-section of the Journey Narrative: the mission of the seventy (two) (How to be a Herald!)-the fifth event (Read 10:1-16.) [Triple tradition] (Matt. 9:37-8; Mk. 6:8-11) [See p. 222.]
After setting His face to go to Jerusalem, Jesus appoints seventy (two) on a mission to preach the kingdom.
They are to prepare the way for Jesus and work as labourers in the harvest. **(32)** In 9:1-6, "the Twelve" were sent out to preach and to heal. Unlike "the Twelve," the seventy (two) are not given special authority, but they received extraordinary power. They were warned that they would receive the same reception as "the Twelve" by encountering hostility, "like lambs surrounded by wolves." They were to go in pairs as Jesus does not encourage individualism in the work of the kingdom. They were not allowed to have casual conversation on the way. Social conversation and good "craic" are fine in their own place but they are not an asset when urgent business is required for the kingdom. To shake the dust off one's feet is a symbolic action for leaving a city if the message is rejected; leaving the dust behind shows the city stands alone before God and has to answer for its own actions (10:11). Luke includes the denunciation of certain cities in Galilee: Chorazin, Bethsaida and Capernaum. [See map p. 110.] This gives a background to the mission of the seventy (two). Of the three cities, Capernaum had been the most favoured, since it was the headquarters of the Galilean mission and it became the home of Jesus. It had no grounds for pride as Jesus predicted its downfall to Hades and it is sombre to observe that all three cities have ceased to exist to this day (10:13-16)! The cities like Tyre and Sidon with reputations like Sodom will come out better in the judgement than those cities in Galilee, even though Sodom was the wickedest city in the O.T. and became dust at the judgement of God because of its sin.   **The disciples when they return from their mission are overjoyed at the outcome of their ministry.**

The sixth event - the return of the seventy (two) (Read 10:17-20.) (L)
They are overjoyed at the outcome of their ministry; they refer to Jesus as Lord (10:17). The main theme of their report was the subjection of demons to those who were sent out. This was more impressive to them than the response of the people to their announcements about the Kingdom. For them to subdue demons was more spectacular and the immanence of the Kingdom meant defeat for the Kingdom of darkness. They recognised that that they do not exercise their own authority as the demons were subject to them. "The demons were subject to us in your name." (10:17)
Jesus recognised the spiritual conflict for Himself and the disciples when He said "I saw (was seeing) Satan fall like lightning from heaven." (10:18) Was this a prophecy or a vision? It could be both. This statement surprised the disciples but not Jesus who knew that the hour was approaching when He would defeat the prince of this world. This ministry of the disciples was a present defeat for Satan (10:20). Another present defeat of Satan can be seen in Luke 11:20. "If by the finger of God I cast out demons, then the Kingdom of God has come to you." The future defeat of Satan will be seen on the cross (Jn. 12:31-32) and the ultimate overthrow of Satan seen in Rev.12:10-12; 20:1-3. The disciples had not realised the significance of these future events. They are to take comfort and to be encouraged for Satan's power cannot remove their secure position before God (10:20). Every exorcism was a proof of Satan's fall. Jesus issued a timely rebuke to His disciples, they should have been rejoicing far more that their names and those of the others were being written in heaven. This was a greater spiritual victory than exorcism. "Behold, I have given you authority to tread upon serpents and snakes." (10:18) Jesus makes them into messengers who can proclaim the message effectively. (Wilcock) **(33)** The seventy (two) were no more than "babes" (10:21), though they were given the thrill of victory. Was there symbolism in the number sent out? It has been suggested the seventy represents the number of Jacob's family when he went down to Egypt. This could be a symbol for the people of Israel which in turn could refer to the church today. They were more favoured than kings and prophets who wanted to see the coming of a better age, but had to make do with looking forward. They had to overcome all the power of the enemy. In conclusion the way is described from two viewpoints: [See p. 176.]

     Another defeat of Satan can be seen in Luke 11:20, "But if it is by the finger of God I cast out demons, then the Kingdom of God has come upon you."

(1) Jesus calls people to follow Him and to be His followers,
(2) disciples and learners; and as they learn of Him, so He sends them out ahead of Him to be His heralds, His messengers and His servants. In both aspects the way is to be one of complete devotion to Jesus.

3. The third sub-division: discipleship, the double love of God and neighbour (Read 10:25-42.)
A) The seventh event – Good neighbours – loving God and our neighbours (Read 10:21-37.) (Matt. 11:25-27; 13:16-17) "Q"
Luke links the joy of the seventy (two) with the rejoicing of Jesus in which he thanks His Father. In both Luke and Matthew these follow the rebuke of the Galilean cities for refusing to believe. Jesus has a deeper reason for rejoicing. He sees the victory in His mind as having been won already, so close was His fellowship with His Father and there was no doubt where the initiative lay. The Father was in control; "for such was your gracious will." (10:21) A lawyer, an expert in the law equivalent in rank to that of a scribe, tries to trap Jesus by asking Him about eternal life. Jesus gives a traditional Jewish answer, "You shall love the Lord your God with all your heart, and with all your soul and with all your strength, and with all your mind and your neighbour as your self." (Deut. 6:5; Lev. 19:18) Relationship to God gives life, "Do this and you shall live." Man's chief purpose is to love God wholly.

The lawyer thinking of his own ethnic group asks how far should the idea of "neighbour" extend? His concern was for his own people. What about my own sort? Do not forget my people? Who is my neighbour? The lawyer hopes that some people will not be his neighbour (10:29)!

Jesus tells the story of the Good Samaritan (10:25-37). The seventeen-mile journey from Jerusalem to Jericho was notorious for robbers and bandits, like many urban areas at night in Western Europe. Josephus **(34)** says that many travellers took weapons to protect themselves on this road. It is not the O.T. town of Jericho but the town built by Herod the Great south of the plain of Jordan, which is referred to here. (Fitzmyer) **(35)** A man is attacked by a band of robbers and left to die by the roadside. By a stroke of good "fortune" a priest happens to be going that way! He crosses to the other side and keeps on going (10:31). Along comes a Levite, (an assistant to a priest) who served in the Temple, possibly a singer in the choir. He also sees the man and likewise crosses over to the other side (10:32). The priest and the Levite were unable to help the man in case they became ceremonially unclean and defiled (Lev. 21:1-3; Num. 5:2; Ezek. 44:25-27). An alternative view to this is Jeremias. **(36)** The fact that the priest was travelling alone and not in a group indicates he was going back from the Temple and not to it. The point is no love was shown. Jesus puts the question. "Which of the men was the neighbour to the man who fell into the hands or the robbers?" (10:36) Note: the lawyer cannot bring himself to say "Samaritan". He replies, "The one who showed mercy to him." (10:37a) The man sees the point but it has not penetrated his prejudice. Jesus could be showing the disciples how they are to respond to the Samaritans by showing mercy (9:51-56).

Jesus replies to the lawyer, "Go and do likewise." (10:37) This is a continuous response, keep on doing (Gk.poiei). Jesus does not offer any excuses for them. It could have been they were afraid of being attacked themselves or by being considered unclean (handling blood before going to the Temple). From the example of the Samaritan, disciples today must show compassion to everyone in need; this is what it would mean in Jesus' time for a Jew to be eating pork with a Samaritan. Both were to be avoided at all costs. Doing one's religious duty is no excuse for not showing love. The punch line is that even the enemy is your neighbour. Do not try to limit the idea of neighbour so that you limit your responsibility. "To love the world for me is no chore; my biggest problem is the guy next door!" Compassion (Gk.esplanchnisthe) "to show compassion" (10:33) response and love make a neighbour not race, creed and gender. A neighbour is anyone in need and who is made in God's image. The positioning of the word "compassion" is placed in the centre of the unit in Greek; it is preceded by sixty-eight words and followed by sixty-seven words. Disciples are to love God completely and to show that love to others. Neighbourliness is not found by living in a certain locality. [See p. 169.]

> **A neighbour is anyone in need and who is made in God's image; disciples are to love God completely and to show that love to others. Neighbourliness is not found by living in a certain locality.**

Summary of the actions of the Samaritan (10:33-35) (Figure 16)

	The Samaritan's actions	Comments
1	He comes up to the man,	The man could have been a businessman. (Marshall) **(37)**
2	binds up his wounds,	This may have required cutting up some of his own clothes for bandages: his head cloth and linen underwear. (Jeremias) **(38)**
3	anoints him with oil to comfort him,	He anoints the wounds with oil and wine. The oil is for soothing and the wine in case infection sets in. In some Jewish eyes it was not permissible to receive oil and wine from a Samaritan (Is.1:6; Shabbath 19:2).
4	puts him on his mule,	The Samaritan would have had to walk on from there.
5	takes him to an inn,	These inns were not noted for their care. By offering money up front the man ensures the treatment will continue until he is healed.
6	cares for him by paying for his whole stay. He stays the whole night with him.	Two denarii would have been the equivalent of two days wages which would have been the cost of a month's stay at an inn. He does not leave him there and do a runner.

Pupil's Activity: Six

This parable has its roots in the O.T. (2 Chron. 28: 8-15). After Samaria had defeated Judah in battle, the Samaritans treated the people with mercy as the prophet Oded had advised. They clothed them, gave them food and drink, anointed them, carried the weak on donkeys and took them to Jericho.

Compare this parable of the Good Samaritan with the O.T. story in 2 Chron. 28: 8-15 by completing the grid. [See Figure 17.]

An O.T. connection (2 Chron. 28:8-15) with the parable of the Good Samaritan (Figure 17)

Refs.	1	2	3	4	5	6
The Samaritans 2 Chron. 28:8-15	showed mercy,	clothed the naked,	gave them food and drink,	anointed them,	carried the weak on donkeys,	and brought them to Jericho.
The Good Samaritan Luke 10:29-35						

B) A home in Bethany, discipleship and Jesus balancing work and meditation (Read 10:38-42.) (L) - the eighth event.

This incident is introduced by a Journey Narrative expression. "Now as they went on their way," Jesus seems to be on the outskirts of Jerusalem [Bethany]. (Talbert) (39) Jesus stresses hospitality, having commissioned the seventy(two) for their task, He had advised them to concentrate on the houses in which they had been received but not to waste time on the others. At Bethany, the home of Mary and Martha, He is especially welcomed. Providing hospitality requires household chores for while Martha was busy with the pots and pans preparing a meal, Mary sat and listened to Jesus. Martha seems justified in her complaint. She was annoyed at the indolence of Mary, who had left her to do all the work. Resentment soon spreads when it sets in! Jesus should have consideration for her even if Mary does not hear it. For her Jesus did not seem to care. The "way" means "to be with Jesus, to learn of Him and to know Him." (Wilcock) (40) The choice is between doing something which is good and doing that which is better. To the disciples, Jesus is saying, sit at my feet and take in my teaching. "To sit at the feet" of someone is a Semitic expression for being a disciple of that person. [cf. Paul was taught by Gamaliel (Acts 22:3).]

> **"To sit at the feet" of someone is a Semitic expression for being a disciple of that person.**

This is the most important meal. Jesus is not as much condemning Martha as commending Mary, who has her priorities in the right order; hearing and obeying are more important than being busy with other matters (10:40). Discipleship means suspending tasks while fellowship remains. "Lord, do you not care, that my sister has left me to serve alone?" A domestic squabble has taken place. "Tell her to help me." Jesus' method is significant. He says nothing about Martha's criticism of His own lack of action nor does He say that Martha was wrong in doing her work. When common duties cause anxiety, it is time for self-examination. For Martha, domestic routine was more important than enlightened conversation. Perhaps Mary would have helped after spending time listening to Jesus. Martha had not learned the importance of spending time listening to Jesus, whose teaching had astonished multitudes, who had hung on His words (10:42). She was good at organising the household chores but had no time for spiritual instruction. She needed to be reminded that people do not live by bread alone. Jesus found refreshment in this home as the early Church saw the importance of hospitality in spreading the gospel. Mary had found "the way" to be with Jesus and to learn from Him. For the rabbis, learning the Torah was the most important thing of all (Aboth 2.8; 3.2.).

4) The fourth sub-section of the Journey Narrative: the what and why of prayer - discipleship and prayer (Read 11:1-13.) (Matt. 6:9-13) "Q"

> **Luke records more on prayer than any other Gospel writer.**

A) The disciples' prayer (Read 11:1-4.)

Luke records more on prayer than any other Gospel writer. It is thought that Luke used the common written source "Q". Luke records this prayer in the "journey narrative" (and not in the Sermon on the Plain) to show the need for faith and "stickability" in prayer. Matthew however includes it in the Sermon on the Mount to show the right way to pray as distinct from the "showy" prayers of the hypocrites (Matt. 6:5) and meaningless repetitions of the Gentiles (Matt. 6:7). He frequently refers to the prayer habits of Jesus and notes that Jesus always prays before all the major crises. Prayer was crucial in the life of the Messiah. Jesus was teaching the disciples to be bold, persistent and full of faith in their praying. Jesus speaks of the importance of looking to God, approaching Him at all times because of His Fatherly care. It was the custom of the Jews to pray three times a day. [See Ch.5: p.49.]

The disciples wait for Jesus to finish praying and then Luke records the request of the disciples, "Lord, (Gk. Kurie) teach us to pray as John taught His disciples." (11:1) The disciples recognised their need to pray. They watched Jesus and were annoyed at the ease with which He communed with God His Father, but prayer did not come easily to them and John had instructed his disciples in prayer. A closing Jewish prayer, the Qaddish, at the end of the synagogue could have been based upon this prayer: "Exalted and hallowed be His great name in the world, which He created according to His will. May he let His kingdom rule in your lifetime, of the whole house of Israel speedily and soon." However it could be a short Jewish prayer. "Perform your will in heaven and bestow satisfaction on earth upon those who revere you." (Berakoth) (41)

The disciples made a similar request for help from their master. Jesus recognised the usefulness of a set form of prayer and did not resort to a Psalm or use a form of community prayer which John had taught his disciples. Judaism at this time had Eighteen Benedictions, two of which were requests for an annual supply of food (requests 9 and 18). The community in Qumran also had many hymns and prayers. (Qumran) **(42)**

Jesus taught them the Disciples' Prayer though it is usually known as the Lord's Prayer (11:2). "When you (plural) pray you (plural) say. It is a community prayer, designed by Jesus as a pattern for the disciples rather than for reciting. Jesus encouraged the disciples to approach God "Abba" as a Father which is an analogy for close and familiar relationship with God and not that of an unapproachable ruler. At the same time it is not the intimate term "Daddy." (Barr) **(43)** The disciples are called to be childlike in their trust and not in a shallow childish intimacy; the disciples are meant to feel close to God and to have access to Him. God is as close to you as a loving father. They have to show respect for His authoritative rule and they can approach Him as "a caring, kind Father." (Marshall) **(44)** "Father, hallowed be Your name." In Luke, the prayer concentrates on a person's right relationship with God.

Part a is concerned with God's name being kept sacred (11:2): it is asking God to establish and show His uniqueness, along with the inauguration of the kingdom. "Your kingdom come." (11:2b) This is asking God to show Himself and the use of the passive means looking to God to act.

Part b is the petition asking God to gives us each day our daily bread (11:3). This is a community prayer for God's provision for each succeeding day.

Part c is the prayer to ask God to forgive us our sins because we are to forgive everyone who sins against us. We cannot ask God to forgive us if we harbour grudges and unforgiving thoughts towards others (11:4). It is a community prayer for forgiveness. Judaism also recognised this connection. "Forgive your neighbour for what he has done, and then your sins will be pardoned when you pray." (Sirach 28:2)

Part d is a petition for spiritual protection that God lead us not into temptation (11:4b). Temptations or testings will come upon those who follow Jesus especially the days before the coming of the kingdom of God. These will include persecution, violence and being enticed away by false teachings and worldly living. If "trial" is the meaning of the words then this could refer to Gethsemane. It is a prayer for the protection of the community. Judaism had the same idea. "Bring me not into the power of sin, nor into the power of guilt, nor into the power of temptation." (Berakoth) **(45)** The way to avoid sin is to depend upon God. [See Ch.7: p.49.]

> **Jesus taught them the disciples' prayer though it is usually known as the Lord's Prayer (11:2).**

B) The parable of the persistent or importunate friend (Read 11:5-8.) (L)

There is no inconvenient time for God to answer the prayer of His people. In ancient times food was not as available as it is in Western Europe today. Food was prepared every day and they did not have a deep freezer. Hospitality was a cultural way of life. The man who receives a late night visitor has a problem; how is he to feed the guest? He has either to be rude and refuse the guest or ask a neighbour for some food even it is past bedtime. In Palestine at this time most homes only had one room and this would mean waking up the entire household. From a cultural aspect he would be expected to fetch the food. However, his neighbour initially refuses to get up, as his children are all in bed with him. It is likely that the whole family would have been sleeping on one mat. To go and fetch some bread would disturb the whole household and it would be quite a performance getting the children back to sleep again!! However because of his friend's persistence (Gk.anaideian) he will get up and give him the food. This word for "persistence" and "boldness" is only used once in the whole bible. [See p. 49.]

Pupil's Activity: Six   Class discussion

Is the idea of the power of prayer to move God to act or is it the power of God who allows His children to share in His revealed purposes?

C) Action required by the disciples - trusting God to meet your needs (Read 11: 9-13.) (Matt.7:7-11) "Q"

Jesus applies the parable by exhorting the disciples to make their requests to God. The disciples are to go on asking (Gk. aiteo). This is an invite to pray (11:10). "For everyone who asks receives." In seeking they are to go on pursuing God's will (Gk.zeteo) and the goals of His kingdom (13:24). They are to keep on knocking (Gk.krouo); that is continue to come into God's presence and blessing. Ask and it will be given. As God is the supplier, He will supply graciously in terms of the request. It is not that one gets exactly and always what one asks for. The disciple will find if he seeks the answer earnestly and brings the request to Round the door will open. An open door is for the disciple who is not too shy to ask. Jesus gives another example on prayer which shows God's compassion (11:11-13). If a child asks for a basic meal of fish or eggs will the father give him something dangerous like a snake or a scorpion. God is more gracious than human parents who know how to give good gifts to their children. God has the specific gift of the Holy Spirit in mind here which in turn is a request for God's presence, guidance, and close relationship. God cares for the needs of His children in the same way that we seek the help of a neighbour in a time of need or a child seeks help from a parent.

Pupils Activity: Seven
a) Why should this prayer be called the "disciples' prayer"?
b) What was Jesus trying to teach His disciples about prayer?
c) What important lessons on prayer was Jesus trying to teach His disciples in this parable?

5. Fifth sub-division: controversies with the Pharisees and calls to trust (11:14-54)
A) Controversy with the Pharisees / opposition to Jesus (Read 11:14-54.) - the tenth event.
Was Jesus wrong, crazy, lying or sent from God? The religious leaders question the source of Jesus' powers to heal and say that it is of Satan. Some of the people also take a hard line against Jesus.
Jesus shows that His miracles are audiovisual aids of God's plan and power at work. [See Ch.13: p. 185.] Jesus exorcises a demon that caused a man to be struck dumb and the crowd are amazed that the man can speak again (11:11). Different opinions are expressed by the doubters. Some regard Jesus as controlled by demons and see his power coming from Beelzebub "the prince of demons" (originally a name for a pagan god but here it is used as a derisive title for Satan meaning "Lord of the Flies." Others adopt a wait and see approach and by way of proof ask for a sign. They could not ignore His claims or His actions. Jesus demanded that people consider His identity. Despite their opposition, the people did not doubt that miracles do happen and that what they saw was a miracle. People today who deny the supernatural not only do they question Jesus but curiously enough His opponents. (Bock) **(46)** Jesus says if the people question His work they must also question that of His disciples ("your sons"). Jesus uses another argument, "But if it is by the finger of God that I cast out demons, then the kingdom of God has come upon you." The miracles provide evidence of God's power and rule. The kingdom has arrived or has come (Gk.ephthasen). Does it continue from the O.T. or has it just only just begun? The miracles are a clear call that God's ruling power has arrived, Satan's power is being challenged and has already been defeated. The establishing of God's kingdom will take a long time and the promise will not be completely fulfilled until He returns again. God is slowly breaking into creation through Jesus to reclaim us from the grip of Satan. This miracle provides evidence that the power of Jesus is greater than that of the demons and His power and authority can reverse the effects of sin.

B) The parable of the strong man (Read 11:21-23.) (Matt. 12:29-30; Mk. 3:22-27) [Triple tradition]
The strong man, Satan, is defeated by someone stronger-Jesus. Jesus frees the agents of Satan who are possessed of demons. Jesus can ransack the stronghold and carry away the armour and the spoils. Jesus has done this hence the frequent references to healing and exorcisms in Luke. Jesus' healings show that Satan the strong man has been overcome by Jesus who goes through Satan's house and removes Satan's works. Jesus casts out Satan's work. The charge of the Pharisees was incorrect. On the cross, Jesus destroyed the Evil One's hold on us. There is no in between; either one is with Him in the sense of believing in him or else one is against Jesus and rejects Him. In the battle a person either helps Jesus to gather in the things of the kingdom or a person scatters the harvest and in so doing hinders the kingdom (11:23).

C) What directs our lives? - warnings about response (Read 11:24-36.) (Matt. 12:43-45) "Q"
1. The parable about the return of the unclean spirit expresses the danger of experiencing God's work, only to leave a person's spiritual condition unfilled with anything from God (11:24-26). This is a double tradition parable. The man who has been exorcised is like a house which has been swept clean. Nothing has taken the place of the demon that once lived in the house. The spirit then brings in seven other spirits more wicked than itself. The situation of the man is now worse than it was before. The disciples have to ensure that their inner house is not empty and that they take in light, as a vacuum will lead to darkness. "There is a risk in not being occupied by God's protecting presence, which comes from faith." (Marshall) **(47)**
2. A beatitude for those who hear God's word and obey it (11:27-28): this was Jesus' reply to the beatitude of the woman "Blessed (Gk.makaria) is the womb that bore you and the breasts that gave you suck." Marshall **(48)** translates as "Happy is the mother of such a son or such a mother must have been specially blessed of God." A mother was valued through the achievements of her son. This would have been a very brave response from the woman in a mixed audience, which could have shown the woman's gratitude for the Ministry of Jesus. Jesus is more concerned about response rather than applause. She was quick to clap Jesus and He is quick to reply, "Blessed (Gk. makarioi) rather are those who hear the word of God and keep it." Marshall reads as "Nay rather, or on the contrary (Gk.menoun) blessed are those who keep (Gk.phalasso) God's word and law (11:28). "Her sentiments are in keeping with 1:42,48. "Blessed (Gk.eulogemene) are you among women and blessed (Gk.eulogemenos) is the child you will bear." [See also Green **(49)**.] "All genarations will call me blessed (Gk. makariousin)."

Pupil's Activity: Eight
a) What answer did Jesus give to His disciples when they said to Him, "Lord teach us to pray?"
b) Why was training in prayer so important for the disciples?
c) Give an outline of two parables, which Jesus taught on prayer, in the "journey narrative". What was He trying to teach His disciples?

(Figure 18) [See p. 86.]

	Refs.	Summary of comments on Mary in the birth and journey narratives
1	1:26-38	Mary as one who hears and reflected upon Gods' word. [See Ch.8 Birth Narratives.]
2	1:46-55	Mary as one who proclaims God's word in a prophetic way in the words of the Magnificat.
3	1: 42,45	Elizabeth, inspired by the Holy Spirit, declared Mary to be "blessed" (Gk. eulogemene) because of Mary's faith.
4	2:19, 51	Mary as one who responds to God's word.
5	11:27	Mary declared as "blessed" (Gk. makaria) because of the status of her son.
6	11:28	Does Jesus give special status to Mary or is it an invitation for everyone to hear and keep the word of God? "Blessed rather are those who hear the word of God and keep it."

D) Jesus warns and rebukes those still looking for a sign. (Read 11:29-32.) (Matt.12:38-42; Mk.8:11-12)
Jesus gives two calls to respond to the light (11:33-36). Light in a lamp is not intended to be hidden but displayed so that it can provide guidance. The disciples are called to be the light (11:34-36). If we take in light and are possessed by it, we will be bright. However to ignore the light is to live in darkness or alternatively we can respond to God and grow spiritually. Jesus is greater than Jonahbecause He brings a greater message and has greater authority.

E) Dinner at the house of a Pharisee (Read 11:37- 54.) (L) - the eleventh event [See p. 240.]
In the house of a Pharisee Jesus does not wash His hands before a meal. The Pharisee rebukes Jesus for his attitude and confronts Him for not keeping the rules regarding ceremonial washing before the meal (m.Yadayim 1-2). Jesus rebukes the Pharisees and the Scribes. He replies with six woes, three against the Pharisees and three against the Scribes. Jesus sees them as hypocrites, ignoring God's justice, burdening the people with demands they could not keep up with, following their murderous ancestors and blocking the entrance to heaven. Failure to lead others led to their own defilement. Although some scholars treat this as similar, this event appears to be unique to Luke and distinct from Matt. 23:25-26 and Mark 7:1-9. [See Ch.7: Structure - Journey Narrative.] (14:25-35) [See Ch. 14: p. 222.]

Pupil's Activity: Nine
a) Identify the journey narrative in Luke's Gospel? b) Why is it called by this name? c) Justify your answer.

Pupil's Activity: Eleven
a) Why is the journey narrative so important in Luke's Gospel?
b) How does Luke structure his material in the journey narrative in his Gospel?

Pupil's Activity: Twelve
a) What is the main theme of the journey narrative?
b) Select two incidents from these narratives and show how they tie in with the theme.
c) What was Jesus trying to teach the disciples in these incidents?

Pupil's Activity: Thirteen   Revision
a) Outline the main events in the journey narrative. (CCEA A/S 2002 and 2005 (Resit)) [30 marks]
b) Comment on the claim that the journey narrative is of central importance in Luke's Gospel. Justify your answer. (CCEA A/S 2005 (Resit)) [15 marks]
c) Use Liefeld's **(51)** chiasmus as an aid to memory for the journey narrative. Look out for sixteen identifiable themes.
[See Ch. 7: Structure p.71.]

Pupil's Activity: Fourteen
The Journey Narrative has been described as resembling a ride on the "Big Dipper" or Roller Coaster, the highs being the high water mark of Jesus' identity and the lows the disappointments with the disciples and the opposition to Jesus. Do a class audit of the events in the Journey Narrative as "highs" and lows" by completing the totals and draw a diagram to show the attitudes of the disciples, the crowd and the Jewish leaders to Jesus as He journeyed to Jerusalem. Identify each event as a high or low by completing the grid (Use PC Excel.) for example in Luke 9:18 Who do men say I am? (High) The first two events act as a way into the "Journey Narrative". Draw a graph on a scale 0-10 to indicate how people reacted to Jesus, for example from opposition – silence – indifference – listening – following Jesus. Add your own descriptors.
(Figure 19)

Events in the journey narrative (9:51-19:48)   (Figure 19)

	Refs.	Events	Context and Content	
1	9:18	Peter's confession	"But who do you say I am? "Peter answered, "The Christ of God." This became a key title at the trial of Jesus (22:67), and at the cross (23:35). Peter sees Jesus as more than a prophet.	High/ low
2	9:28-36	Jesus' Transfiguration at either Mt. Hermon, Mt. Tabor or Mt. Meron (NW Sea of Galilee)	After eight days Jesus takes Peter, James and John up a mountain to pray. (L) The cloud which overshadowed them could refer to His "shekinah" glory as at the Exodus. (Marshall) (50) A heavenly voice endorses Jesus as the Son-Prophet. "This is my Son, my Chosen; listen to Him."	High High
3	9:51-56	The Samaritans reject Jesus.	The people of the Samaritan village refused to receive Jesus because He set His face to go to Jerusalem and the disciples call for judgement upon them. It is not the time for judgement. God gave the people time to respond. The Samaritans did not recognise Jesus.	
4	10:1-42	Proclaiming the Kingdom	The disciples receive a new insight into the mission and person of Jesus. Sending out the 70 (2)	
5	10:11-12	Jesus predicts the fall of the unbelieving cities.	Rejection of Jesus is worse than that of that most wicked cities. Despite the rejection of their message, mission involves responsibility and privilege.	
6	11:14	Jesus heals the dumb and possessed man.	The crowds are amazed at the healing.	
7	11:15-23	The Beelzebul controversy	The crowd are sceptical and accuse Jesus of casting out demons by the prince of demons. Others tested Jesus by looking for a sign, "But if it is by the finger of God I cast out demons, then the kingdom of God has come upon you." Jesus' miracles attest to His power and authority (11:20).	
8	11:37-54	Jesus dines in the house of a Pharisee	Jesus rebukes the scribes and Pharisees about His failure to wash His hands before a meal to uphold ritual cleansing. The scribes have failed to enter into true knowledge and hinder others.	
9	11:53-54	A trap by the Pharisees	Their motive is a picture of a trap ready to spring. Jesus they already had identified as an enemy. In blocking the way to God the leaders had refused Jesus' teaching, rejecting the messenger.	
10	12:54-59	The weather signs	Jesus calls the crowd hypocrites because they can discern the weather but they do not the see what God was doing in their midst. They rejected His miracles; they were blind to God's plan.	
11	13:10-17	Healing the woman with the "crooked" spine	Jesus heals the woman on the Sabbath in the synagogue. Jesus' opponents are put to shame. Some of the people rejoice at God's salvation revealed in Jesus. The woman praises God (13:13).	
12	13:31-35	Herod Antipas has a plan to kill Jesus. The national officials show their opposition to Jesus.	Some Pharisees warn Jesus that Herod wants to kill Him. "Go and tell that fox, Behold, I cast out demons and perform cures today and tomorrow, and the third day I finish my course." O Jerusalem, Jerusalem, killing the prophets and stoning those who are sent to you! How often would I have gathered your children together as a hen gathers her brood under wing but you would not!" Israel fails to recognise Jesus as God's sent one. Your house is forsaken. The nation rejects Jesus and the fig tree is going to be uprooted (13:6-9).	
13	14:1-6	Jesus heals the man with the dropsy on the Sabbath.	Jesus goes to dine on the Sabbath at the house of a Pharisee. They were watching Him closely. This is a rule miracle where Jesus' authority is challenged. They reject His ability of Jesus to heal the man. The reaction of the Pharisees is one of silence after Jesus heals the man. They were unable to refute Jesus. The leaders have learnt nothing about Jesus from His teaching. Luke is anxious to show that Jesus dined with the Pharisees (7:36-50; 11:37-54).	
14	14:20-35	Cost of discipleship	The Jewish leaders fail to enter the Kingdom by refusing God's invitation which is for everyone.	
15	16:1-13	The shrewd manager	The disciple is not to be like the Pharisees in the way they handle money (16:14). The Pharisees are a negative example in the journey narrative (12:1; 14:7-14; 18:9-14). A disciple should use money not selfishly but with generosity.	
16	17:20-37	The coming of the kingdom	The Pharisees ask when the Kingdom of God will come. Jesus said, "For as the lightning flashes and lights up the sky from one side to the other, so will the Son of Man be in His day."	
17	18:15-17	Jesus blesses the children	The disciples rebuke Jesus for bringing young children to Jesus.	
18	18:31-34	Jesus predicts His rejection passion and resurrection.	"Behold everything written of the Son of Man by the prophets will be accomplished. He will be delivered to the Gentiles, and He will be mocked and shamefully treated and spit upon; they will scourge Him and kill Him, and on the third day He will rise." But they understood none of these things; this saying was hid from them and they did not grasp what was said.	
19	18:38	Jesus heals a blind man.	The crowds follow Jesus. The blind beggar recognises who Jesus is. "Jesus, Son of David have mercy on me." Jesus heals as David's Greater Son which is a Messianic title. The man becomes a follower of Jesus and glorifies God. All the people praised God.	
20	19:1-10	Zacchaeus	The crowd murmur at Jesus going to dine with a tax collector. Zacchaeus becomes a faithful "son of Abraham". He calls Jesus "Lord" (19:8) Behold, Lord, half of my goods I give to the poor."	
21	19:27	The parable of the pounds	A rebellious group did not want Jesus to reign (19:14). This group represent the Jewish leaders "But as for these enemies of mine, who did not want me to reign over them, bring them to me and slay them before me." The disciples have false expectations regarding the Consummation of the Kingdom. Some disciples saw themselves as followers of Jesus and carried out responsibilities in His name but Jesus says He does not know them.	
22	19:38-40	Palm Sunday: a crowd of disciples praise: God for Jesus.	The disciples who understand Jesus' purpose in coming rejoice. The miracles of Jesus are the "source" of the praise. (L) "Blessed be the King who comes in the name of the Lord! Peace in heaven and glory in the highest." Jesus triumphs by suffering. Jesus enters Jerusalem as a King but is rejected by the Jewish leaders. The disciples fail to see Jerusalem as the place of passion.	
23	19:41-44	Lament for Jerusalem	"Would that even today you knew the things that make for peace! But know they are hid from your eyes." (L)	
24	19:45-46	Cleansing the Temple	Jesus faces confrontation in Jerusalem. Israel fails to respond. Jesus rebukes the Jewish leaders about their unjust commercialism in the Temple.	
25	19:47-48	The Jewish leaders conspire against Jesus.	Everyday Jesus was teaching in the Temple. The Jewish leaders see Jesus as a threat to peace and plot against Him. They devised a plan because of Jesus' popularity with the crowd. The journey narrative ends with two questions who is Jesus and how should we worship God?	

Outcomes
 Students should know and understand:
• the main events in the journey narrative in Luke's Gospel and know why it is so-called.
• where the journey narrative ends.
• the main theme and sub-themes of the journey narrative in Luke's Gospel.
• the central importance of the journey narrative in Luke's Gospel.
• the place of Jerusalem in the journey narrative in Luke's Gospel.
• key concepts, for example discipleship, 'the way,' suffering and rejection, chronological journey, 'journey,' chiasmus and mission.

Notes on Ch. 10: The Journey Narrative

1. Michael D. Goulder, The Chiastic Structure of the Lucan Journey, Studia Evangelica, Vol. 2 Ed. by F. L. Cross, Christ Church, Oxford (1964) p.455.
2. H.L.Egelkraut, Jesus Mission to Jerusalem: A Redaction Critical Study of the Travel Narrative, Luke 9:51-19:48 (1976) Bern. Lang. pp.16-24. Over a third is unique to Luke and a third has parallels in Mark.
3. Joseph A. Fitzmyer, op. cit. p.1066.
4. Bo Reicke , op.cit. pp.206-216 and E.E. Ellis op. cit. p.146.
5. Charles H. Talbert, op.cit. p.112.
6. William Hendriksen, op. cit. pp. 542-543.
7. Howard Marshall, op. cit p.150.
8. Darrell L. Bock, op. cit. p. 961.
9. Donald Guthrie, op. cit. p. 92.
10. W.F. Arndt , The Gospel of Luke, Concordia (1956) p.271.
11. Leon Morris, op. cit. p.257.
12. Michael Wilcock, BST, The Message of Luke , IVP, (1979) p.117.*
13. Darrell L. Bock, op. cit. p.963.
14. Charles H. Talbert, op. cit. p.112.
15. Darrell Bock , op.cit. p. 957.
16. Howard Marshall, op. cit. p.405.
17. Howard Marshall, op. cit. p.403.
18. Howard Marshall, op. cit. p.152.
19. J.T. Sanders, The Jews in Luke-Acts, Philadelphia: Fortress, (1987)
20. Charles H. Talbert, op. cit. p.112.
21. Joseph A. Fitzmyer, op. cit. pp.1256-9.
22. Josephus , op.cit. Jewish Wars, 5.11.4§ 466; 5.12.2 § 508.
23. Howard Marshall, op. cit. p.155.
24. Joseph A. Fitzmyer, op. cit p.1238.
25. Charles H. Talbert, op. cit. p.112.
26. Howard Marshall, op.cit. p. 712.
27. Craig A. Evans, St. Luke, NIBC, Paternoster, (1990) p.167.
28. Michael Wilcock, op. cit. p.827.
29. Joseph A. Fitzmyer, op. cit. p.833.
30. Joseph A. Fitzmyer, (ibid).
31. Michael Wilcock, op.cit. p.118.30.
32. Jesus appoints seventy/two on a mission. Some biblical texts refer to seventy/two as distinct from seventy disciples going out on this mission.
33. Michael Wilcock, op.cit. p.121.
34. Josephus, Jewish Wars, 2.8.4 /125.
35. Joseph A. Fitzmyer, op. cit. p.886.
36. Joachim Jeremias, p. cit. pp.203-4.
37. Howard Marshall, op. cit. p.449.
38. Joachim Jeremias, op. op. cit. p.204.
39. Charles H. Talbert, op. cit. p.111.
40. Michael Wilcock, p. cit. p. 124.
41. The Talmud, Berakoth, 3,2.
42. Qumran, op. cit. 1 Q34;4Q507-9.
43. James Barr, "Abba Isn't Daddy," JTS, n.s. 39 (1988) pp.28-47.
44. Howard Marshall, op. cit. p.456.
45. The Talmud , Berakoth, 60b.
46. Darrell Bock , IVPNTCS, (1994) p. 209.
47. Howard Marshall, op.cit. p.480.
48. Howard Marshall, op.cit. p.481.
49. Joel Green, op. cit. p. 461 says Marshall sees it as a rebuke and as an adversative. This is also the view of the following scholars: Arndt p 302; Plummer p. 305; Fitzmyer, p.77; L.T. Scott Schneider p.289 and Danker p.235. They interpret as "yes, but" and suggest that Jesus did not contradict her but adds to the statement of Mary's blessedness. Her remark is correct but not exhaustive.
50. Howard Marshall, op.cit. p.387.
51. Walter L.Liefeld, Luke, The Expositor's Bible, Ed. F.E. Grabelin, Grand Rapids :Zondervan, (1984) p.932.
* This book is highly recommended especially for pupils.

CCEA A/S and Internal Assessment on "Suffering" (CCEA) and Edexcel A2

Targets:
• Identify the key themes and events in the passion narrative in Luke's Gospel, for example the betrayal of Jesus, the Last supper, the Passover and plot, the institution of the Lord's Supper, Peter's denial predicted, the Trials and the Death of Jesus, the sayings from the cross, the events which accompanied the Death of Jesus, His Burial, and Jesus' prediction about His death.
• Identify the main events of the Resurrection and the Ascension of Jesus in Luke's Gospel and the key concepts such as, betrayal, compassion, death as a necessity, innocence, Sanhedrin, Son of Man, Son of God and types of suffering. (CCEA)
Students should be able to examine and critically analyse:
• the symbolism contained in the cruxifixion and resurrection, the conflict with the Religious Authorities at the death of Jesus, why Pilate sentenced Jesus to death? The relevance of the resurrection to Jesus' teaching on salvation and eschatology. (Edexcel A2)

The Passion and Resurrection of Jesus Chs. 22-24

She ripped open a sleeve to reveal a tattooed number from a Nazi concentration camp.

2 In another group [an African-American boy] lowered his collar. "What about this? he demanded, showing an ugly rope burn! Lynched … for no crime but being black!"

A pregnant school girl with sullen eyes said, "Why should I suffer?" she murmured. "It was not my fault."

The Long Silence

Introduction

1 At the end of time, billions of people were scattered on a great plain before God's throne. Most shrank back from the brilliant light before them. But some groups near the front talked heatedly-not with cringing shame but with belligerence. "Can God judge us? How can He know about suffering?" snapped a pert young brunette. She ripped open a sleeve to reveal a tattooed number from a Nazi concentration camp.

"We endured terror…beatings…torture…death!"

An African/American boy-lynched … for no crime but being black!"

3 In another crowd, a pregnant schoolgirl with sullen eyes. "Why should I suffer?" she murmured. "It was not my fault."

4 Far out across the plain there were hundreds of such groups. Each had a complaint against God for the evil and suffering He permitted in this world. How lucky God was to live in heaven where all is sweetness and light, where there is no weeping or fear, no hunger or hatred. What did God know of all that man had been forced to endure in this world? For God leads a pretty sheltered life, they said. Continued on next page.

So each of these groups sent forth their leader, chosen because he had suffered the most. A Jew, a negro, a person from Hiroshima, a horribly deformed arthritic, a thalidomide child.

a Jew

a negro

The Long Silence
• **Nazi concentration camp**
• **lynched**
• **pregnant school girl**
• **a Jew**
• **a negro**
• **Hiroshima**

a person from Hiroshima

5 In the centre of the plain they consulted with each other. At last they were ready to present their case. It was rather clever. Before God could be qualified to be their judge, He must endure what they endured. Their decision was that God should be sentenced to live on earth – as a man!

6 Let Him be born as a Jew. Let the legitimacy of His birth be doubted. Give Him a work so difficult that even His family will think Him out of His mind when He tries to do it. Let Him be betrayed by His closest friends. Let Him face charges, be tried by a prejudiced jury and convicted by a cowardly judge. Let him be tortured.

"At the last, let Him see what it means to be terribly alone. Then let Him die. Let Him die so that there can be no doubt that He died. Let there be a great host of witnesses to verify it." As each leader announced his portion of the sentence, loud murmurs of approval went up from among the throng of people assembled. And when the last had finished pronouncing sentence, there was a long silence. No-one uttered another word. No-one moved. For suddenly everyone knew that God had already served His sentence.

Our suffering became more manageable in the light of His. He entered our world of flesh, and blood, tears and death. He suffered for us. There is still a question mark against human suffering , but over it we boldly stamp another mark, the cross which symbolizes divine suffering. (Stott) **(1)** 'The cross is God's only self-justification in such a world as ours.'(Stott) **(1)** "The impact that God's pain made on suffering humanity is immense."(Fernando) **(2)** The despised and displaced, the homeless and poor, the imprisoned snd tortured, realise that God far from being remote had suffered their pains. God did this to free them from pain and death forever.

Pupil's Activity: One
a) List all the examples of suffering in the above passage in "The long silence." b) How did Jesus suffer in the ways described in the passage? c) According to this story, why did God send Jesus into the world? d) What does this mean for Christians today?

(Figure 1) Differences between Luke and the other Synoptics regarding the Passion Narrative

No	Luke omits:	Mark	Matthew
1	Jesus predicts the disciples' failure and their being scattered.	14:26-28	26:30
1	Gethsemane by name and instead refers to the Mount called Olivet (21:37; 22:39).	14:32	26:36
2	Golgotha by name.	15:22	27:33
3	the offer of drugged wine.	15:23	27:34
4	the time the crucifixion began, though he says "when it became dark." "It was about the sixth hour and there was darkness over the whole land until the ninth hour (23:44b)." Mark says, "it was the third hour they crucified Him."	15:25, 33	
5	the first cry from the cross,"Father forgive them for they do not know what they do."	15:34	27:46
6	the crowd's mention of Elijah.	15:35-36	27:47-49
7	Jesus predicts the failure of the disciples and their being scattered.	14:26-28	26:30

(Figure 2) Incidents unique to Luke in the betrayal and farewell of Jesus   (22:1-38) (L)

	Refs.	Luke's account of Jesus' betrayal and farewell includes:
1	22:3	Satan enters Judas (Jn. 13:2).
2	22:15-23	a first cup followed by the bread and then a second cup (22:17,19-20).
3	22:18	Jesus desiring to have the Passover meal with His disciples. He eagerly anticipated it.
4	22:24-30	Who is the greatest? This conversation in this context is unique to Luke.
5	22:31-34	Jesus' speaks to Peter. Peter even denies he knows Jesus is also unique. "Simon, Simon, Satan has demanded to have you, that he might sift you as wheat, but I have prayed for you that your faith may not fail,"
6	22:33	only one remark which comes first. "Lord, I am ready to go with you to prison and to death."
7	22:35-38	dangerous times which lie ahead - need for a purse, bag and sword. Is. 53:12 will be fulfilled. "And He was reckoned with the transgressors."

(Figure 3) Incidents unique to Luke at Jesus' Crucifixion   (22:43-23:49) (L)

	Refs.	Luke account of Jesus' Crucifixion includes:
No 1	22:40-42	Jesus warns the disciples to pray before He departs (22:41), Jesus prays a stone's throw from the disciples and kneels in prayer. Use of only direct speech in the prayer of Jesus. "Father, if You are willing, remove this cup from me; nevertheless not my will, but Yours, be done."
2	22:43-46	The mention of the help of the angels and sweating great drops of blood (22:43-44). Jesus is comforted by an angel on His way to the Mount of Olives. He goes on to address all the disciples (22:45-46).
3	22:51	the healing of the ear of the high priest's servant.
4	23:4,14,22	the three times Pilate says that Jesus is innocent.
5	23:6-16	the trial before Herod.
6	23:27-32	the weeping of the women in Jerusalem.
7	23:34	the three sayings from the cross: **(1)** "Father, forgive them; for they know not what they do."
8	23:43-44	**(2)** "Truly, I say to you, today you will be with me in Paradise."
9	23:46	**(3)** "Father, into your hands I commit my spirit." Jesus' third cry on the cross was based upon Ps.31:5.
10	23:35	the Jewish rulers mock Jesus with reference to Him as "The Chosen One", rather than call Him King of the Jews.
11	23:36	the soldiers mock Jesus about being King of Israel (Mk. 15:26; Matt. 27:37).
12	23:39-43	Jesus' discussion with the two thieves.
13	23:45	the second reference to darkness, 'the sun's light failed.'
14	23:47	quotes the centurion as saying that Jesus was innocent instead of referring to His divine Sonship.
15	23:48	the crowd watching and mourning.
16	23:49	the disciples watching from a distance.
17	23:49	the women who were present and all came from Galilee, watching from a distance.

Incidents 2-9 all shed further light on the cross and contribute to another perspective on the events at Calvary.

[1] Betrayal and a farewell - preparation for the Passion (22:1-46)

A) Judas' plans to betray Jesus (Read 22:1-6.)

The Jewish leaders decide to enlist Judas (one of the Twelve) in their plot to have Jesus put to death. Their problem was how to arrest Jesus when the city was full of pilgrims, many of whom supported Jesus; these leaders were looking for an opportunity to put Jesus to death (22:2). Their only hope was to wait until after the Feast or to arrest Him at night. This betrayal would have been a personal disappointment for Jesus. The name Judas has four possible meanings:

(1) "man of Kerioth", the Hebrew word for a region in Judea. This would make Judas the only non-Galilean from among the Twelve. Kerioth is west of Masada near the Dead Sea. [See p. 110.]

(2) "Sicarios" Latin word for assassin or dagger man was also the word used for "Zealot".

(3) "False one" a wing of the Zealots (the name comes from the word "Seqar", Aramaic for falsehood). This is preferable as it reflects Judas' unfaithfulness and means his defection would be on moral grounds. The Zealots were fanatical Jewish nationalists determined to deliver Israel from the colonial power of Rome.

(4) His name can mean "Judas the Dyer": a reference to his job. Sometimes rejection and failure come from within one's own ranks as in the case of Judas. [See also Ch.14: Jesus and the Disciples.] This final act of betrayal takes place over the two feasts, the Feast of the Passover and the Feast of Unleavened Bread (Ex.12:1-20; Deut.16:1-8). (Josephus) (3) The two feasts came directly after each other. Passover was on Nisan 14. The Feast of Unleavened Bread was Nisan 15-21. Passover was to celebrate the Exodus from Egypt while the Feast of Unleavened Bread commemorated both the Exodus journey and the start of the harvest season. [See Lev. 23:5-8 and Jewish feasts in the Journey Narrative.] Together both feasts celebrated salvation. [See p. 114.]

Luke exposes the sin of rejecting Jesus, and the leaders fear a backlash from the people. The leaders were seeking to destroy Jesus (22:2); the Greek word anaireo meaning destroy and Luke uses it twenty-one times. Satan enters Judas, called Iscariot, and puts it into his heart to betray Jesus (22:3). Before this, Judas went to the chief priests and offered to betray Jesus. When Satan enters a life, it leads a person in sinister directions. Judas confers with the chief priests and the officers. The expression "Satan enters Judas" is unique to Luke among the Synoptic Gospels (22:3). (L) Judas acts but the impetus for the action is from Satan. Satan leads Judas to discuss betrayal with the Jewish leaders. John 13:2 indicates the time Satan put into the heart of Judas to betray Jesus and at that moment Satan entered to take entire possession of His will (Jn.13:27). Only Luke mentions the discussion between Judas and the authorities and refers to the Temple police Gk.strategoi), whose job it would be to arrest Jesus (22:4). An understood sum of money is exchanged. Luke does not disclose the amount. Matt. 26:15 says Judas is paid thirty pieces of silver which later are thrown down in the Temple. Judas' involvement suits the leaders because they can operate away from the crowds and take Jesus in private. The leaders agree to pay Judas, which shows he was greedy or coveteous. The leaders were pleased with their transaction (22:5). Judas tried to use his advantage as a disciple to regain favour with the rulers, having gone out of favour (22:5). (Godet) (4) Double-dealing has led to betrayal by Judas. He is at the bottom of the list of the apostles (6:16). As one of the Twelve, Judas would know where the group would meet, when they would be alone, so he looked for an opportunity to hand over Jesus when there was no-one present (22:6).

> **Jesus knew that this would be His last Passover and that all future Passovers would be irrelevant (22:16).**

Pupil's Activity: Two

a) Discuss the two statements in Luke 22:3 "Satan entered Judas to betray Him," and (22:22) "for the Son of Man goes as it has been determined; but woe to that man by whom He has been betrayed."

b) Explore the claim that Judas betrayed Jesus merely for money (22:5).

B) Preparation for the Last Supper (Read 22:7-13.)   **[Events before the Passover]**

The upper room events extend from 22:7-38. This is the seventh meal mentioned in Luke's Gospel to date. Here table friends can enjoy fellowship and reflect on events. A Passover meal is being celebrated. "On the day of Unleavened Bread, the Passover Lamb had to sacrificed." (22:7) Jesus and His disciples make plans to prepare for the Passover meal. Peter and John are sent into Jerusalem to meet a man carrying a jar of water. This was a task usually done by women. The house owner will give the disciples a large upper room fully furnished and the disciples are to make the preparations (22:12). It was exactly as Jesus said it would be (22:13). All traces of leaven, which represented an embodiment of evil, had to be removed, and every part of the house searched and the leaven destroyed. Only then was the Passover Feast and household prepared. Jesus knew that this would be His last Passover and that all future Passovers would be irrelevant (22:16). They asked for a guest-house (Gk.kataluma) (22:16; 2:7). A lodging could be a room in a private house. Did Luke see a link with the birth? They were given an upper guest room (Gk.anogeon) which is the "the extension room." Marshall (5) This room would be more secluded and Jesus would be able to give farewell truths in private. The house owner may have provided the lamb; no Passover feast was celebrated without the lamb. Would Jesus have used a lamb if He knew that He was to be the Lamb of God at this feast? Did Judas wonder how Jesus came to have such a splendid room without his knowledge of it? He may have wondered if Jesus suspected treachery!

> **Luke alone says that Jesus "earnestly desired", (Gk.epithumia) means literally "with desire, I have desired to eat this Passover with you." It is a double desire (22:15) and a joyous occasion.**

C) The Passover and the plot [22:14-23.] [Events during the Passover] (Read 22:15-20.)

Luke alone says that Jesus "earnestly desired", (Gk.epithumia) means literally "with desire I have desired to eat this Passover with you." It is a double desire (22:15) and a joyous occasion. He is with them and they are with Him as in a Holy Communion service today. Jesus vowed not to eat the Passover again until it finds fulfilment in the Kingdom of God (22:15). This is unique to Luke. In Acts 10:41, Jesus eats with the disciples because it inaugurated the Kingdom. Jesus showed Himself not to all the people but "to us chosen by God as witnesses, who eat and drank with Him after He rose from the dead." He is the source of the believer's spiritual nourishment at the feast (Acts 10:41).

The Messianic Banquet (22:16a): Jesus says, "I will not eat it again until it finds fulfilment in the Kingdom of God." The same idea is in verse 18 only this time He refers to the cup. "I will not drink of the fruit of the vine until the Kingdom of God comes," meaning that He will abstain from eating such a celebration until the plan is complete. "It" in verse 16 refers to the Passover or Messianic banquet. The incidents referred to in Luke 24:30, 41-43 and Acts 10:41 are not contradicted in Luke 22:16a.

D) The words of institution [Read 22:17-23.] (22:21)

Luke mentions the cup first (22:17). The cup could have been one of the four used at the Passover and perhaps the first one with which the meal starts. After the cup, Jesus took the unleavened bread, raised it, and prayed for a blessing on it (22:19). He broke the bread to symbolise the breaking of His body which people would eventually see. He shared the pieces with the disciples saying, "This is my body." (22:20a) These words were kept to a minimum perhaps for recall. After "this is my body," Luke adds, "which is given **for you,**" thus showing a very personal touch. "This cup which is poured out

for you is the new covenant in my blood." (Marshall) **(6)**(Green) **(7)** The disciples would reap the benefits personally as it was for sinners that Jesus would shed His blood to establish a new covenant, which would be written on the hearts of the people (22:20c; Is.53:12; Jer. 31:31).

> After "this is my body," Luke adds, "which is given for you," thus showing a very personal touch. "This cup which is poured out for you is the new covenant in my blood." (Marshall) **(6)**

The signs and what they signify: Jesus is speaking figuratively when He gives the **symbols of bread and wine** fresh meaning. The bread, He says, " This is My body which is given for you. Do this in remembrance of me." (1 Cor.11:24-25) He does not say that the bread becomes the actual body called "transubstantiation," nor does He say that He enters the bread with His presence as in "consubstantiation". The bread is a picture of His death and represents His self-sacrifice. The elements remind and proclaim; they are not transformed. Compare the story of the elderly cyclist from North Down who saw a signpost saying Belfast 12 miles and thought she had cycled to Belfast when she had only seen the sign pointing to Belfast. This idea of symbol continues in (22:20b) when Luke records Jesus taking the cup after supper and saying, "This is my body which is given for you." (22:21) As the meal continues, Jesus announces His betrayer. This is unique to Luke. The atmosphere becomes very tense and the disciples want to know who is going to betray Jesus since He says, "The hand of him who betrays me is at the table." (22:21) Luke points out the necessity of the death of Jesus (22:22a), "For the Son of Man goes as it has been determined; "Woe to that man by whom He is betrayed!" (22:22b) The betrayer was the one who shared the meal. The disciples were unable to apply the picture of the suffering Son of Man to Jesus Himself. They could not cope with the idea of a crucified Messiah and were caught unawares when the tragedy struck. All the disciples begin to question, "Is it I?" The disciples had not fully grasped that Judas was the one, as they thought that he had gone either to buy something for the feast or else give money to the poor (22:23).

> "Simon, Simon I have prayed for you that your faith will not fail;" (22:31)

Query : Why did Jesus choose Judas?
This will always be a mystery. The events are destined (22:22). The Greek word horizo means "as it has been determined, to decree or to destine" and our word horizon comes from it. God's plan is at work yet Judas is responsible for his own action and is subject to the wrath of God. Woe (Gk.ouai) can mean pain or displeasure. God knew by design that the Son of Man would be betrayed and Jesus knew that His betrayer would be Judas. Judas must stand before God for his own actions in betraying Jesus (22:22). Even though betrayal is part of God's plan, it does not excuse the action of Judas. The disciples speculate about the identity of the betrayer (22:23). Jesus would not have been mistaken about Judas' character; Jesus would know that Judas' heart would gradually harden during His ministry. Judas seemed impervious to all the gracious acts of Jesus. In later life, the disciples would reflect that they had been protected from a moral and spiritual decline like that of Judas. "Simon, Simon I have prayed for you that your faith will not fail;" (22:31) The disciples would have marvelled at the patience Jesus had shown towards the betrayer on the eve of His passion. Judas is an example of someone who associates with Jesus but is not really a friend of His: someone who makes a false profession of faith and whose defection shows them up in their true colours.

> For Jesus, the one who serves is greater than the person who sits at the table (22:27).

E) Discussion after the Supper - who is the Greatest? (Read 22:24-30.)
Who is at the top of God's list of the "Top Disciples"? The greatest disciple is the one who sees himself as the youngest or the least significant (22:24,26). In Jewish society, the humblest and hardest work was given to the youngest members of that society (Acts 5:6,10). In the ancient world the greater person sat at table while the lesser served the meal. The leading Christian should be the serving one. This teaching of Jesus on being a servant is unique to Luke. It would be the Father's task to allot places of honour and not the prerogative of Jesus. Jesus raised the issue of social convention. For Jesus, the one who serves is greater than the person who sits at the table. Those disciples who have served him faithfully will share his Messianic banquet and will sit on thrones judging the twelve tribes of Israel (22:30).

F) The prediction of Peter's denial (Read 22:31-34.) (L)
Luke 22:31-33 is unique to Luke. Jesus addresses His word to the disciples that Satan might sift them like wheat. "Satan demanded to have you (plural) that he might sift you (plural) but I have prayed for you (singular) that your faith may not fail." (22:31) This last part is addressed to Simon to show that Jesus was praying for him before his denial. Satan tried to destroy the faith of all the disciples. Jesus answers Peter that He has prayed for him that his faith may not fail. Peter will suffer a momentary lapse, but he will recover and return to Jesus, and will strengthen his brothers. He warns them about the moral danger which threatened them. Peter affirms his loyalty (22:33). He is ready to go to prison or even to death for Jesus. Jesus prophesies that, before the rooster crows that day, Peter will deny Him three times (22:34). Luke's wording is distinct from Matt.26:34; Mk.14:30; Jn.13:38; Luke adds Peter's denial that he knew Jesus which intensifies the denial. Luke is the only one to use the direct address "Peter". His version is shorter and looks to be in summary form. He agrees with the other Gospels in the following details: the denial will be today, and it will be a triple denial (22:34).

Peter affirms his loyalty (22:33). He is ready to go to prison or even to death for Jesus. Jesus prophesies that, before the rooster crows that day, Peter will deny Him three times (22:34).

Pupil's Activity: Three   Class Discussion
What is the difference between a temptation and a trial for Christians (22:31-32; James 1:12-15)?

G) The final conversation in the Upper Room with the disciples (Read 22:35-38.) (L) [See p. 150.]
This passage in which Jesus prepares Himself for His Passion by prayer near the Mount of Olivet is unique to Luke. **Note**: Luke does not mention Gethsemane. On the way to the Mount of Olives, Jesus surprised the disciples with the question, "When I sent you out without purse, bag or sandals did you lack anything?" (22:35) From now on they are on a different **mission**. It would be one of spiritual conflict and not one of proclamation. This time the disciples are to take purse bag and sword. They were to sell their cloak to buy a sword. Was Jesus advocating violence? This would be contrary to His character. Jesus warns the disciples about the end of time and reminds them of the security and protection they had enjoyed during His Ministry. Jesus quotes Is.53:12 as a reference to the suffering and rejected Messiah, "He was reckoned with the transgressors."(22:37 b) The use of Is.53 also reflects both suffering and exaltation. Later Jesus rebukes Peter for using a sword to cut off the ear of the high priest's servant (cf. Jn.18:10). "All who live by the sword die by the sword." They have to defend themselves and provide for themselves but not through the shedding of blood. (Bock) **(8)** The fight requires special weapons. Jesus is looking for faithfulness and humility; looking to Jesus they can face suffering and the world. Jesus cuts off the conversation about the two swords. "It is enough," said Jesus (22:38). The conversation would be continued later.

[2] The Trial and Death of Jesus (Read 22:39-23:56.)
Introduction
The key theme here is the innocent suffering of Jesus. Even at the end, Jesus is offering salvation to those who cry out to Him. [See the incident of the thief on the cross (23:32-43).] Jesus agrees to follow God's will to the death. He healed the severed ear of the one person who came to arrest Him. He exemplifies His own teaching (22:50-51; 6:27-36). Although Jesus suffers unjustly, it is God's will that He ministers to those He came to serve.

The cup of suffering was His appointed lot, even though the human flesh wanted to shrink from it. The cup is a metaphor for His impending suffering." (Jn.8:52; Is.51:22) (Stein) (10)

A) Jesus prepares Himself for His Passion through prayer near the Mount of Olives. (Read 22:39–46.)
Jesus arrived at the Mount of Olives where the spiritual battle would intensify. Luke does not refer to Gethsemane. Jesus withdraws a short distance. He urges the disciples to pray that they might not be led into temptation. The disciples never forgot the prayer of Jesus, "Father, if You are willing, remove this cup from me; nevertheless not my will, but Yours be done." (22:42) The disciples fell asleep due to excessive weariness (22:45). No one has ever plumbed the depths of this prayer and the disciples certainly could not do it. Jesus knew that the cup could not pass but He prayed that it might. This prayer shows His perfect humanity. All problems are resolved in the will of God. This was not fatalism but acceptance of the perfect plan of God. Jesus had no desire to save Himself as the Father had sent Him to save others. "Behold I have taken from your hand the cup of staggering ; the bowl of my wrath and you shall drink no more ; and I will put it into the hand of your tormentors." (Is.51:22-23) This refers to the infliction of punishment associated with the wrath of God; in this sense it is also a **cup of wrath.** (Marshall) **(9)** (Stein) **(10)** (Evans) **(11)** (Green) **(12)** (Ps.11:6; Is.51:17,19) His main concern is doing God's will; it is important that He obeys God despite His wish that things be different. Jesus is ministered unto by an angel (L) almost like an answer to His prayer which continues with great emotion. He prays earnestly and so hard that His sweat falls like drops of blood to the ground. As a medical man, Luke would know that the cause of this was intense strain and it shows the spiritual conflict in which Jesus was engaged. The disciples are told again to get up and pray that they will not fall into temptation (22:40, 46). The presence of the angel empowers Jesus to pray more fervently (22:43). Angels often appear in Luke's narratives to give a message and to help God's people (1:26; 2:9; 12:8,9,11; 15:10; Acts 5:19; 8:26; 10:3;
12:7; 27:23). Jesus arose from prayer (in a kneeling position) (22:45). He discusses God's will and resolves to fulfil His divine calling. Derogatory remarks are not made about the physical failure of the disciples in falling asleep, but they are excused on the basis that they are overwhelmed by grief (22:45). For a second-time Jesus says, "Rise and pray that you may not enter into temptation," [RSV] or "into the time of trial." [22:46 NRSV] Their failure was neither final nor fatal.

Pupil's Activity: Four
a) Why was Jesus in such a state as He faced death, yet many of His followers in the early Church face death quite calmly? b) Evaluate the claim that on the Mt. of Olives [in the Garden of Gethsemane], Jesus saw the full cost of obedience to the Father.

B) Betrayal and arrest (Read 22:47– 53.)[50-51(L)]
Judas hypocritically betrays Jesus. Luke names Judas as among the twelve apostles (6:16) and refers to him as the one who "became a traitor" meaning that he would reject the purpose of God and oppose His **mission**. Luke does not mention that Judas did actually kiss Jesus to identify him as in Mark 14:45, Matt. 26:49 in the Garden. Perhaps Luke saw the action of Judas as unworthy of inclusion. Luke's account is shorter here and he gives no explanation why the action was taken.

The kiss is to make sure there are no mistakes in identifying Jesus. The expression, "one of the Twelve", used by Luke to describe Judas is unique to Luke among the Synoptics (22:47). The account of the betrayal and arrest, initially focuses on Judas, who leads the group and Jesus who is doing the speaking.

Judas knew that Jesus had visited the Garden of Gethsemane when He wanted a time of quiet and he was sure, therefore, that Jesus would be there that night. Judas had arranged for a band of men to carry out the arrest and had a pre-arranged sign of a kiss to avoid mistaken identity. Judas is called "one of the Twelve" (22:47) as if the disciples never got over the shock of it. Jesus shows no panic and, although He knows the answer, He asked for whom, they were looking. Jesus asked, "Judas, would you betray the Son of Man with a kiss?" The Son of Man suffers because Judas betrays Him (22:48). One disciple (Peter) struck out with a sword, which cut off the ear of the high priest's servant (22:50-51) (L). Jesus healed the servant

[Judas drew near to kiss Jesus (22:47).] and commanded Peter to put his sword back. Peter had misunderstood the mission of Jesus that He would drink the "cup" which the Father had given to Him. Jesus challenged the Jewish leaders at this critical moment. "Have you come out as against a robber with swords and clubs? When I was with you day after day in the Temple, you did not lay hands on me. But this is your hour, and the power of darkness." (22:52-53) Jesus controlled the flow of events at His arrest. As the hour of the power of darkness comes, Jesus faces it in love.

As the hour of the power of darkness comes, Jesus faces it in love.

C) Summary of the different reactions to Jesus
• Judas represents someone in close proximity to Jesus who turns on Him in vengeance. Jesus asks, "Would you betray the Son of Man with a kiss?" (22:48)
• The disciples represent those in panic who try to take matters into their own hands. "Lord, shall we strike with our swords?" One of them answers on his own, by appealing to force. Jesus' way is not one of violence (22:49).
• The healed servant shows that the opportunity is there to experience God's grace (22:51).
• Those who arrested Jesus are those who remained defiant. They reacted with hostility and Jesus put the question to them, "Have you come out against a robber with swords and clubs?" They chose not to lay hands on Him in public; sin loves to work in secret (22:52). The power of darkness hid behind this human activity. Darkness must fall before a new day can come. It was a time when darkness reigned (22:53).

D) The trials and denials (Read 22: 54-71.)
The eleven had deserted Jesus, although Peter followed at a distance. The Messiah faced His judges alone. Peter watched from afar. He noticed a number of people warming themselves by the fire. These were members of the household staff of the high priest (22:54). This was the start of the evening trial (22:54a).

(1) Peter's denial of Jesus (22:54-62)
First challenge:- One of the female servants recognised Peter. She said, "This man was with Him." Peter denied it (22:56). She had noticed Peter's features in the light of the flames. She had no sympathy for the mission of Jesus and she implied guilt by association. Peter withdrew to the porch with confused thoughts. It was an indirect way to avoid the question. He replied. "Woman, I do not know Him." (22:57)
Second challenge:- This came from a man who made a similar charge with the emphasis on **"you"**. **"You** also are one of them." Peter tries to parry the blow with, "Man, I am not." (22:58)
Third challenge:- A second man made another challenge. "Certainly this man was with Him; for he is a Galilean." Again he denied it. The crowing of the rooster and the look Jesus gave him brought home the memory of Jesus' words to Peter. He knew he had let Jesus down. Peter's conscience was battered and he went out and wept the bitterest tears of his life (22:61-62). The injuries from His friend must have cut into the spirit of Jesus. The training of "the Twelve" seemed to be a failure and His most ardent fan denied all knowledge of Him. Jesus did not fear the outcome as He had prayed for Peter that his faith would not fail (22:31).

(2) Jesus before the high priest and the mocking of the soldiers (Read 22:63-65; John 18:13.)
Jesus was mocked and beaten before the high priest (Annas) (22:63-66). The guards blindfolded Jesus and asked Him to prophecy to determine who had hit Him. Jesus suffered violence but not a moral collapse. No judgements are made. This is possibly an initial trial. Luke says nothing about the false accusation of the two witnesses who said Jesus threatened to destroy the Temple (Acts 6:13-14). He was brought in the morning before the Sanhedrin. Luke has only one trial (22:66-71) which was before the Jewish council which consisted of: seventy-one members with the high priest as its leader, Sadducees, Pharisees and middle-class laymen called elders and had authority over all Jewish issues except the authority to put Jesus to death (22:63-66).

> **Jesus was asked the first question, by the Sanhedrin, if He were the Christ (22:67a). His first reply was to say that, as the Son of Man, He would be seated at the right hand of God (22:69).**

1. Then Jesus was asked the first question by the Sanhedrin, if He were the Christ (22:67a). Jesus is certain that they will not believe or answer a question if He asks one (22:68). His **first reply** was to say that, as the Son of Man, He would be seated at the right-hand of the power of God (22:69).

2. Then they asked Him a **second question** if He was the Son of God (22:70a), a self-designated leader? Jesus said, "You say that I am." (22:70b)

The **second reply**: Jesus did not deny His Messianic identity. He affirmed his Coming Triumph; He was to be seated next to God, at the right hand of the power of God. Not even the disciples would believe Him. These proceedings before the Sanhedrin showed the real cause of the hostility. There was no real legal charge against Jesus. Luke shows clearly that Jesus was falsely accused. He weaves together three titles for Jesus **(1)** Christ (22:67), **(2)** Son of Man (22:69) and **(3)** Son of God (22:70). [See p. 74.]

It is these claims, which Jesus makes about Himself, that finally send Him to the cross. To the Jews this is highly offensive. It is worse than claiming the right to walk into the Temple and live permanently in the "Holy of Holies". The Jews had fought the Maccabean War over the Greeks who thought they had the right to profane the Temple: the Temple represented the presence of God to the Jews. Jesus' saying that the Son of Man would sit at the Right hand of God (22:69) offended their understanding of the holiness of God. Jesus makes no effort to save His life by denying who He is; His confession leads to His conviction (22:71).

> **Luke shows clearly that Jesus was falsely accused. He weaves together three titles for Jesus (1) Christ (22:67), (2) Son of Man (22:69) and (3) Son of God (22:70). It is these claims, which Jesus makes about Himself, that finally send Him to the cross.**

Comment: Luke's trial scene remains focused on one main issue-who is Jesus? **This is the key question in Luke's Gospel (22:67).** It is an echo of His earlier discussion about Himself and John the Baptist (20:1-8).

The key title for Jesus in Luke's Gospel is Messiah or Christ, the Anointed One (Gk. Christos) found in 2:11; 3:15; 9:20. Luke in 23:2, 35, 39; 24:26,46 returns to this title. The issue of Jesus' promised regal status is important to Luke. To confess Jesus as Messiah is to confess His rule, as the title denotes Royalty. It is the authority of Jesus as the One sent by God, which is uppermost here in Luke. From now on Jesus is the Son of Man (Lord) who will be seated at the Father's right hand and He fulfils David's promise that one will sit on David's throne (22:69; 2 Sam.7:12-13). This title Son of Man emphasised God's sovereign power and might. It was not wrong in Judaism to claim to be Messiah as seen in the revolt by Bar Kochba in A.D.132. Jesus says He is more than the Messiah, He can go directly into the presence of God and rule at His right hand and therefore they cannot judge Him. This could also allude to His Resurrection-Ascension. The title Son of Man is the one which Jesus uses about Himself throughout the Gospel and goes back to Daniel 7:13-14. As Son of Man, Jesus makes the following claims about Himself (22:69):

- He claims to have authority from God which He will exercise from now on (22:69).
- He will eventually be seated at God's right hand in heaven (22:69).
- He has authority over the Sanhedrin and will be their judge.

> **The key title for Jesus in Luke's Gospel is Messiah or Christ, the Anointed One (Gk. Christos) found in 2:11; 3:15; 9:20.**

(3) The trial before Pilate, the governor (Read 23:1-5.)

This took place in Pilate's court. Here the charge was political; Pilate was hated by the Jews and, in turn, despised by them. Because of his misrule and violence he was removed from office. Now Jesus was accused of challenging the political power of Caesar by subverting the Jewish nation or it can mean "subverting our customs." (NIV) "This man perverts our nation." (23:2) They show contempt by calling Jesus, "this one" (23:2), seeing Him as a threat to their nation's tradition and misleading the people. They see Him as opposing payment to Caesar and failure to act against someone who opposes Caesar means not being a friend of Caesar (23:2). In claiming to be Christ a King, Jesus is presented as a dangerous revolutionary (23:3). The Sanhedrin wanted Pilate to believe that Jesus was a political threat to Caesar. Pilate could not find a basis for fault in Jesus (22:4), but the Sanhedrin pressed Pilate, accusing Jesus of stirring up the people all over Judea by His teaching. This subversive activity, Pilate was told, started in Galilee and spread all the way to Jerusalem (23:5). **"He stirs up the people."** The reference to Galilee gave Pilate the opportunity to send Jesus to Herod, the ruler of Galilee.

(4) The trial before Herod (Read 23:6-12.) (L)

Herod happened to be in Jerusalem at this time, which he was pleased about because:

- he wanted to see Jesus do a great miracle (23:8).
- for political reasons he wanted to develop his new found relationship with Pilate. Jesus gave Pilate no indication about His identity: He refused to perform a miracle before Herod to satisfy the king's curiosity.
- He had noted Jesus' popularity and once thought that Jesus was John the Baptist risen from the dead. Jesus had, on one occasion, called him "that fox." Herod draped Jesus in a gorgeous robe and sent him to Pilate. Herod pronounces that he

Both Herod and Pilate found Jesus innocent (23:12).

can find no guilt in Jesus. Thus both Herod and Pilate found Jesus innocent.

(5) Pilate summons the Sanhedrin and the people and Jesus is sentenced to death. (Read 23:13-15.)
Pilate tells the Sanhedrin and the people (Gk.laos) that he finds this man innocent. Pilate reports that Jesus is innocent having been examined by two supreme courts. He offers to punish Jesus by whipping, as a warning to avoid future trouble. All the Jewish groups want Jesus put to death. Pilate then offers to release to the people Barabbas or Jesus and the people shout for the release of Barabbas (23:8). It was Pilate's custom to release a prisoner and the Jews appealed to this. While there is no evidence of this in secular history, it could have been a deliberate policy of Pilate's to appease the people. They prefer a man of violence and a murderer who fits the bill as a cruder popular messiah rather than Jesus. Thus Luke put the blame for Jesus' death on the Jewish religious leaders. While Jesus was executed by the Roman authority, He had been pronounced innocent three times by this same authority. Jesus was executed because Pilate lost his nerve. Pilate's attempt at appeasement did not work.

Summary of events (23:1-25)
• Pilate speaks to the chief priests and says he finds Jesus innocent. "I find no crime in this man." (23:4)
• Pilate speaks to the chief priests, rulers and the people and says that Jesus was innocent. "I do not find Him guilty of any your charges." (23:14-16)
• Pilate speaks again to the above group. "I have found in Him no crime deserving death." (23:22)
• The crowd demands Jesus' death and Barabbas' release (23:18-23). He acts according to the crowd's wishes. The sentence finishes with the emphasis on their 'shouts' (NIV) and not the verb (23:23). "Their shouts prevailed."
• Jesus is condemned and Barabbas is released (23:24-25). Luke notes the human aspect. Jesus is delivered to the demands of the crowd (23:34): God's purpose is fulfilled (Acts 2:23). "Jesus was handed over to you by God's purpose..."

While Jesus was executed by the Roman authority, He had been pronounced innocent three times by this same authority. Jesus was executed because Pilate lost his nerve.

(6) The crowd's demand for Jesus' death and Barabbas' release. (Read 23:23-25.)
Pilate makes three attempts to release Jesus against the efforts of the crowd and their leaders to put Jesus to death.
(1) (23:13-19) **(2)** (23:20-21) **(3)** (23:22-23) Twice Pilate says he was unable to find a basis for the death sentence, so he offers to have Jesus flogged before He is released (23:14-16, 22). Pilate makes a third attempt (23:20). The Jews and their leaders **'shout out together'** (23:18) and **'keep on shouting'** (23:21) and **'urgently demanding with loud shouts'** (23:23) until their voices prevailed (23:23). This event has two opposing wills: Pilate's desire to release Jesus (23:20) and the desire of the Jewish crowd and their leaders to have Jesus put to death. In the end their will is granted (23:25). At this point the will of the crowd should be seen against the 'Big Picture' of God's over all plan (24:25-27; Acts 3:17-18). Luke emphasises the innocence of Jesus and the Jewish determination to have Jesus put to death. Pilate tries to placate the Jews by attempting to have Jesus flogged; finally Pilate decides to release Barabbas a murderer-insurrectionist, and hands Jesus over to be crucified.

Again there are two conflicting pictures in the use of the term 'release' (17,18, 20, 22, 25). There is the contrast between Pilate and the Jewish people and their leaders. The other is between Jesus repeatedly declared to be innocent and Barabbas imprisoned for murder and insurrection for which crucifixion was the fitting punishment. Pilate wants to release the one not guilty, the one they want to crucify. The crowd want Pilate to release one who is guilty, one who should be crucified.

A) Jesus' innocence is declared (23:13-16): Jesus was sent back to Pilate by Herod. Pilate convenes a town meeting to announce his judgement. **Both the people and the leaders all shout together, 'away with this fellow!'**
(23:18) The Jewish people and their leaders who reject Jesus are the same people who align themselves with Barabbas. Pilate summarises the charges against Jesus: **He perverts the people (23:4) and is a false prophet.** Pilate adds his own judgement to that of Herod. He introduces the idea of capital punishment. In branding Jesus as a false prophet the Sanhedrin had indirectly introduced the death penalty (Deut.13). "To flog" is to introduce a lesser form of punishment as an alternative to capital punishment, to gain favour with the Jews.
B) The crowd cries for Barabbas (23:18-19). The crowd is unanimous in their resistance to the release of Barabbas. The people join in their rejection shouting, **'away with this fellow'** (4:16-30;19:14) and demanding the release of Barabbas. Pilate shows a willingness to release Jesus because He is innocent and provides no legal basis for the release of Barabbas. The Jewish leaders and the people align themselves with Barabbas against Jesus.
C) All the crowd call for the crucifixion of Jesus (23:20-21). Crucifixion was designed to humiliate the victim, who was bound or nailed to a stake, tree or cross. It was a slow death over several days as the body gave in to shock and asphyxia. It was preceded by flogging and criminals were required to carry their own cross beams to the site of the crucifixion. They were nailed or bound to the cross with their arms outstretched, raised up or even put on a wooden peg. It was reserved for those who resisted the authority of Roman rule. The body was left to rot or as food for scavenging birds.
D) Pilate wonders whether Jesus has done any wrong (23:22-23). This scene is almost identical to 23:14-16. The intensity of Jesus' innocence is important for Luke's presentation of Jesus as the righteous one who suffers and will be vindicated, despite Jewish opposition to Pilate's plan to flog and release Jesus. The voices of the crowd and the leaders intensify to a crescendo (18:21,23) and become stronger than Pilate's resolve to release Jesus; Pilate preserves peace

rather than justice. Luke does not refer to Pilate washing his hands of responsibility for Jesus' death (Matt.27: 24) or the Jews accepting responsibility for His death (Matt.27:25) or to Pilate wishing to satisfy the crowd (Mk. 15:15). Luke draws attention away from Pilate to the crowd with 'their voices': the voices of the crowd prevail (23:24).

E) Pilate gives his verdict: Jesus is condemned and Barabbas released. (23:24-25) 'To give a verdict' means to pronounce an edict or issue a sentence (23:24). Here the implication is a miscarriage of justice (Gk.ekrino). Pilate accepted the crowd's demand; their action comes to a climax (23:24). Pilate acts according to the wishes of the crowd. The criminal goes free because the crowd asked for his freedom. Luke omits the mockery of the soldiers clothing Him in purple, putting a crown of thorns on His head, and calling him King of the Jews (Mk.15:17-20). The innocent one is placed among the criminals (22:37; Is.53:12), Jesus is delivered to the crowd's demand (23:24) yet, God's purpose is fulfilled in the crowd's decision (Acts 2:23).

Conclusion

• The Jews had rejected their long awaited Messiah.
• They demanded He be treated in the way all Romans dealt with their compatriots.
• The cross was the symbol of the deepest hatred of the Roman occupation.
• They had joined the conquerors against the greatest Israelite ever.
• Pilate was prepared to sacrifice an innocent man, rather than risk a Jewish uprising.

> **He [Jesus] tells the women not to weep for Him but for their own children. He did not despise their tears for He wept for Jerusalem, as He was aware of the coming destruction of the city (23:28).**

Pupil's Activity: Five   Class Discussion

As a revision exercise why did the Jews regard Jesus' words as blasphemy (22:69)? Discuss with the class the following answers: [See p. 74.]
1) the Holy One of God (4:31),
2) Jesus' claims to be Son of Man and be able to forgive sins (5:24; 7:48), the crowd who see Him as a great prophet (7:16),
3) the demoniac from the territory of the Gerasenes regarded Him as Jesus, Son of the Most High God (8:28).
4) Peter confesses Jesus as the Christ of God (9:20).
5) Jesus is called a false prophet and magician (11:19).
6) the voice from heaven which said, "You are My beloved Son; with You I am well pleased." This was a claim that Jesus was the Servant-Messiah at His baptism (3:22) and the Transfiguration (9:35).
7) the claim of Jesus to be the Son of Man who came to seek and to save the lost (19:10).
8) the crowd of disciples who say of Him, "Blessed is the King who comes in the name of the Lord!" (19:38)
9) the claim to be the Son of God (19:45-48; 22:70).
10) the charges against the Temple do not seem to have a role in Luke (19:45-48; Mk.14:55-59).
11) the claim to sit at God's right hand (22:69; Mk.16:19; Matt.26:64). While Jesus initially fulfils the Davidic Covenant (2 Sam.7), there is much more to follow. A human being seated beside God, in the eyes of the Jews, would lower God's stature. In early Rabbinic tradition only God sits in heaven; anything else is an insult to His person. One could stand in God's presence but not sit with Him. Only Moses and the Son of Man were regarded as exceptions (1 Enoch 51.3; 61.8). Thus when Jesus says He can sit at the side of God, this remark to the Jews, profanes the person of God. The very remarks that the Jews think lower the status of Jesus, in actual fact indicate how exalted Jesus is.

Pupil's Activity: Six

a) Outline and show your knowledge and understanding of Luke's account of the crucifixion and death of Jesus.
(CCEA A/S 2001/2005)   [30 marks]
b) Comment on the statement that Luke is concerned to show Jesus as innocent. Justify your answer.
(CCEA A/S 2001)   [15 marks]
c) Outline and show your knowledge and understanding of the trials of Jesus before Pilate.
(CCEA A/S Resit 2002)   [30 marks]

Pupil's Activity: Seven

a) Explore the claim that Luke portrays Herod as reluctant to condemn Jesus. Justify your answer.
(CCEA A/S Resit 2002)   [15 marks]
b) Outline and show your knowledge and understanding of Luke's account of the Last Supper.
(CCEA A/S 2002/2004)   [30 marks]
c) Explore the claim that betrayal is an important theme in the Passion Narrative. (CCEA A/S 2002) [30 marks]

Pupil's Activity: Eight

a) As a revision exercise complete the grid to show Luke's use of the title Messiah.
b) Identify the events and comment on the biblical texts to show your knowledge and understanding of them.

Luke's use of the title "Messiah" (Figure 4)

Refs.	Quotation	Name and comment on the event
2:11	"For to you is born this day in the city of David, a Saviour, who is Christ the Lord."	
2:26	It has been revealed to him [Simeon] by the Holy Spirit that he should not see death before he has seen the Lord's Christ.	
3:15	All men questioned in their hearts concerning John, whether perhaps he were the Christ.	
4:41	Demons also came out of many, crying, "You are the Son of God!"	
9:20	Peter answered, "The Christ of God."	
20:41	"How can they say that Christ is David's Son?"	
23:2	"He says He himself is the Christ."	
23:35	"He saved others let Him save Himself if He is the Christ of God, His Chosen One!"	
23:39	"Are you not the Christ? Save yourself and us!"	
24:26	"Was it not necessary that the Christ should suffer these things and enter into His glory?"	
24:46	"Thus it is written that Christ should suffer and on the third day rise from the dead, and that repentance and forgiveness of sins should be preached in His name to all nations."	

7) The crucifixion   (Read 23:26-49.) [27-42 (L)]
The journey to the place of crucifixion   (Read 23:26-31.)

Jesus is handed over for execution to satisfy the will of the people. Condemned people were expected to carry their own cross, but, as frequent scourging made them weak, bystanders could be forced to carry a cross. Simon of Cyrene was forced to do this having just come into Jerusalem from an outlying district. All the crowds followed behind Simon with Jesus going ahead (23:26).

A group of women took on the task of mourning for condemned prisoners on the way to executions. They were practised in wailing and showed their sympathy in this way (23:27-32) (L). Jesus spoke for the first time since leaving the Judgement Hall. He tells them not to weep for Him but for their own children. He did not despise their tears for He wept for Jerusalem, as He was aware of the coming destruction of that city (23:28). Since they would have no children to lament, He declared that barren women would be more blessed at this time compared with a whole generation heading for disaster (23:29). Jesus quotes a parable to the women. He foresees a time when people would prefer to be crushed by rocks than expose themselves to the horrors of existence. "For if they do this when the wood is green, what will happen when it is dry?" "Green time" was the present time. As fire spreads more quickly through a dry forest than a wet one, so Jesus' words warn of a situation in the future even worse than the present events of the crucifixion. The Romans were crucifying an innocent man - the Messiah. When the times become dry will they act any differently towards the Holy City? Jesus' thoughts right up to the end were for others (23:30-31).

If God is willing to allow such a disaster as the death of the innocent Jesus, how much more severe will guilty Jerusalem's disaster be! Jesus and the other two criminals are taken to the place of the skull called Golgotha. Jesus was offered drugged wine (gall or myrrh) at the start of the crucifixion. He refused this offer in order that He might bear the fullness of His suffering; Jesus wanted to be fully conscious to complete His mission (Matt. 27:34; Mk.15:23). Later, He was offered vinegar (cheap wine) just before His death (Jn.19:29).

Pupil's Activity: Nine
a) Explore the claim that the Last Supper is a central theme in Luke's Passion Narrative. Justify your answer.
  (CCEA A/S 2004)   [15 marks]
b) Outline and show your knowledge and understanding of Luke's account of the trial and questioning of Jesus by Pilate and Herod. (CCEA A/S 2005)   [30 marks]
c) Comment on the claim that it is difficult to decide who was responsible for the death of Jesus. Justify your answer.
  (CCEA A/S 2005)   [15 marks]

8) Words from the cross in Luke's Gospel: the first saying   (Read 23:34.) (L)
There is no bitterness of mind with Jesus: no resentment that people should treat Him this way. He feels deeply moved for them and prays to the Father to forgive them. The nailing of Him to the cross was symbolic of the attitude of men in general. It showed the need for an act of redemption that they were helping to effect. On hearing this prayer the people would wonder that any man could be so gracious under such suffering towards those who were inflicting it. This prayer could be linked to Is.53:12: the Servant suffers for the transgressors.

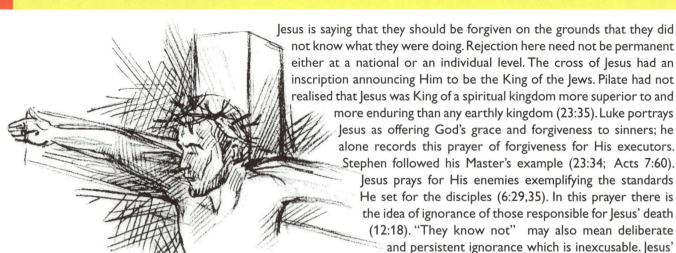

[“Father, forgive them for they know not what they do.” (23:34)]

Jesus is saying that they should be forgiven on the grounds that they did not know what they were doing. Rejection here need not be permanent either at a national or an individual level. The cross of Jesus had an inscription announcing Him to be the King of the Jews. Pilate had not realised that Jesus was King of a spiritual kingdom more superior to and more enduring than any earthly kingdom (23:35). Luke portrays Jesus as offering God's grace and forgiveness to sinners; he alone records this prayer of forgiveness for His executors. Stephen followed his Master's example (23:34; Acts 7:60). Jesus prays for His enemies exemplifying the standards He set for the disciples (6:29,35). In this prayer there is the idea of ignorance of those responsible for Jesus' death (12:18). "They know not" may also mean deliberate and persistent ignorance which is inexcusable. Jesus' humiliation and condition does not diminish in relationship with God when he continues to call him Father. "Them" refers to Jews and Gentiles who combine in their opposition to Jesus. Luke uses Ps. 22: 18, "they cast lots to divide His clothes," meaning a complete loss of dignity and personal identity (23:34).

> **Pilate had not realised that Jesus was King of a spiritual kingdom more superior to and more enduring than any earthly kingdom (23:35).**

9) The reactions of those who saw Him die: (Read 23:35-43.) (40-43 L)

A) The rulers/scoffers sneered at Jesus saying that He should save Himself and do something supernatural if He really were the Christ of God, the Chosen One. They did not realise that Jesus was unwilling to descend from the cross. The jibes of the Jewish leaders showed that they also thought that Jesus should escape from the cross (23:35). The people (Gk. laos) stood watching (23:35 NIV). Only Mark says the people hurled insults at Jesus, wagging their heads. Are you supposed to be the Messiah, God's promised Saviour, "Save yourself, and come down from the cross!" (Mk.15:29) They challenged Jesus' claim to be the Messiah.

> **Salvation is self-giving not self-saving.**

B) One of the thieves also hurled insults at Him saying, "Save yourself and us." (23:39) The other thief asked to be remembered by Jesus, when He came into his kingdom (23:42).

C) The indifference of the soldiers who cast lots for His garments (23:34).

D) The soldiers, who mocked by offering Jesus vinegar (23:36), failed to see the Divine purpose behind the cross. They missed the meaning of the passion and resorted to derision and scoffing (23:36). The first reference to the Roman militia in Luke's Gospel is (23:36). Surely He would save Himself if He was the King of the Jews (23:37)? Salvation is self-giving not self-saving. They should have said, "He saved others because He did not save Himself." Only Luke says the soldiers offered the wine to mock Him (23:36; cf. Ps.69:21). "They put gall in my food and gave me vinegar for my thirst."

E) Another group was the bystanders who watched were the people (Gk.laos) who saw Him die (23:35). Their actions are not as hostile to the sufferer and they appear to be just curious and neutral (23:35a; Ps.22:7). However, they may want to see the outcome of their demand for the death of Jesus (23:21, 23). Their actions may not be as bad as the Jewish leaders but by the same token they are not Jesus' supporters. Later, they beat their breasts and are compelled to have second thoughts (23:48). The people (Gk. laos) watch Jesus die (23:35).

F) The thief recognised that Jesus **was innocent** and began to fear God. He had only a vague notion of the Kingdom but it was enough. This is the sixth confession of Jesus' innocence from a third source, Pilate and Herod also called Him **innocent** (23:4,14,15,22, 41b). It is interesting to note that the criminal does not make a specific request to be forgiven although it is implied in his request. "Remember me when you come in your kingly power." (23:42) Jesus used the word "paradise" to describe the dwelling place of the just (23:43b). (Stein) **(13)** (Smail) **(14)** (Tidball) **(15)** The word "today" (Gk. semeron) means immediate presence and not an unspecified future (2:11; 4:21; 13:32-33; 22:34).

10) Words from the cross: the second saying (Read 23:43.) (L)

A) Jesus said to the thief on the cross, "Truly, I say to you, you will be with me in paradise." This was the response of Jesus to the criminal who said to Him. "Jesus, remember me when you come into your kingly power." Jesus had entered into dialogue with this man who had recognised that Jesus really was innocent and began to fear God. He had a vague idea about the kingdom but it was enough. Jesus uses the word "paradise" which describes the dwelling place of the just, the righteous dead. This word "paradise" comes from the LXX. translation of "garden" meaning "walled garden".

It came to mean a future bliss for God's people (Is. 51:3) and a symbol for heaven and its joys (2 Cor.12:4; Rev. 2:7). The paths of glory lead not to the grave but from the grave. This man confesses his guilt and throws himself upon the mercy of Jesus and His power to rescue. The expression, "Truly, I say to you," was always a word of assurance from Jesus.

B) Words from the cross: the third saying   (Read 23:46.) (L)

In His last breath Jesus committed His spirit to His Father. Those who stood by heard Him. The words show the triumph that issued from the seeming tragedy. "His noble spirit expressed to the end the priceless quality of serene trust." (Guthrie) **(16)** These were the last words of Jesus the Messiah fully in keeping with His own teaching. The peace He gave to others was a reality to Himself. Then Jesus, crying with a loud voice said, **"Father, into Your hands I commit my spirit!"** The righteous sufferer has won by obedience to His Father and has accomplished a great victory. All of these three sayings on the cross are unique to Luke. Jesus quotes from Ps.31:5 often used in Jewish evening prayer, commending oneself into God's care during the night's sleep. His last words are a comment on His death and life.

Pupil's Activity: Ten

The paths of glory lead not to the grave but from the grave.

a) Explore the claim that forgiveness is a central theme in Luke's Passion Narrative. Justify your answer.
   (CCEA A/S 2005)   [15 marks]
b) Outline and show your knowledge and understanding of events in the garden of Gethsemane as recorded in Luke's Gospel. (CCEA A/S Resit 2004)   [30 marks]
c) Explore the claim that this story is a key moment in Luke's Gospel. Justify your answer.
   (CCEA A/S Resit 2004)   [30 marks]

Pupil's Activity: Eleven

a) Outline and your knowledge and understanding of Luke's record of betrayal and denial in the Passion Narrative.
   (CCEA A/S 2003)   [30 marks]
b) Explore the claim that for Luke the death of Jesus was inevitable. Justify your answer.
   (CCEA A/S 2003)   [15 marks]

In His last breath, Jesus committed His spirit to His Father. Those who stood by heard Him say, "Father, into Your hands I commit my spirit!" (23:46)

11) The events accompanying the death of Jesus (Read 23:44-49.) [23:48 (L)]
A) At the sixth hour (midday) darkness descends upon the earth which lasts for three hours. A sense of judgement is evoked by the failure of the sun and emphasise that this is a sombre event. At this time of day the sun should have been at its brightest (23:44).
B) The curtain of the Temple was torn in two. This could be either the curtain at the entrance of the Holy of Holies or the curtain separating the outer court from the Temple. Jewish tradition said that the two curtains were used; one within the Holy Place and one parallel to it in the Most Holy place with a cubit (approx.18 inches) between. What did it mean? The separating partition which made God remote from the people of Israel had been removed. It could mean: (1) judgement on the Temple and the end of the Old Covenant (Heb. Chs.8-10), (2) judgement on the nation, (3) everyone has equal access to God, (4) Jesus opens the way to Paradise (23:34). Luke is quite positive in his attitude to the Temple. He sees it as:
• the centre of teaching and religious observation and a place of divine revelation.
• Jesus was God's agent, sent to reform the Temple and to restore God's purpose for it (19:45-48). For this, Jesus was opposed by the Temple leaders.
• The Temple represented the symbolic separation between Jew and Gentile, priest and people, men and women. For Luke the tearing of the Temple veil does not mean the end of the Temple, although Jesus had predicted the destruction of Jerusalem and the Temple (23:28-31). The Temple at that time was still standing and Jesus' followers still continued to relate to it. The centre of the early Church's mission to the nations would be from Jerusalem to the end of the earth (Acts 1:8).
C) Jesus commits His life in death to his Father (23:45). (See above 'Words from the cross.') In the midst of the physical darkness, God is present and Jesus' relationship with His Father is not in doubt. Jesus addresses God as His 'Father' using words from Ps.31:5, which speaks of the Suffering Righteous One, entrusting himself to God's care. Death and resurrection are combined in Jesus' passion predictions (9:22; 18:31-33). Jesus in this prayer, has faith in His Father, who raises from the dead (Acts 2:27-28).
D) After the events are complete, the pilgrims in the crowd returned to where they were staying for the Passover, having desired the death of Jesus, they now regret it (23:48).
E) The effects of the death of Jesus upon (1) the centurion (2) the gathered crowd (3) Jesus' followers: all three groups are related by the common motif of 'witness': 'saw', spectacle, and watching (23:47-49). The centurion 'sees' and recognises Jesus' identity and realises the presence of God even in Jesus 'final moments'. The crowd express remorse and prepare for their repentance early in Acts. They witness "these things even from afar." Included in this group are those whose opposition to Jesus led to His rejection, the cross and ridicule. He shows the effect of time keeping by slowing down the narrative

to emphasise the gravity of the events and to probe and interpret the events. He introduces the motif of darkness in the third hour of the sun's failure (23:44). In Classical literature, it was not uncommon for unusual signs to accompany the death of a famous person. The Roman historian Pliny tells of the portents and long eclipses of the sun, when Julius Caesar was murdered (Pliny Nat. Hist. 2.30 Par. 98.).

> **The crowd, who witnessed the sight, returned from the place of crucifixion, smote their breasts in lamentation, although it was not the end as they supposed. Some of them had been forced to think again (23:48).**

[**"All His acquaintances and the women who had followed him from Galilee stood at a distance and saw these things."(23:49)**]

(1) The centurion recognises Jesus as a righteous or "innocent man" (Gk.dikaios) (23:47). This use by Luke could be an allusion to Ps.31:5/or the Righteous One (Is.53:11). The centurion's verdict emphasises Jesus' innocence and the injustice of the execution. This is the seventh confession of innocence on these events in 23:4,14,15 (twice) 22,41. The centurion saw what had happened and he praised God saying, "Certainly this man was innocent!" (23:47) This Gentile recognised that Jesus could save him (23:42-43) and he saw the hand of God at work in Jesus (23:47).

(2) The crowd who witnessed the sight, returned from the place of crucifixion, smote their breasts in lamentation, although it was not the end as they supposed. Some of them had been forced to think again (23:48), when they saw what had happened. Again Jesus' prayer has results in people gaining insights into His status before God (3:21-22; 9:18-20, 28-36). **(3) The disciples**, who were on hand as witnesses to the events, are described as "acquaintances"; later they would resume the ministry of Jesus (23:49a). They are different from the crowd as they have travelled with Jesus and knew Him. This crowd (Gk.ochloi) are not the people (Gk.laos) referred to earlier but a mixed group of gathered people who were greatly affected by what they saw, as were Jesus' disciples. They may not be the crowd who pressed for the death of Jesus but they see the signs and could have heard the reaction of the centurion. They stayed faithful to Jesus and now saw what was happening (23:49a). Their presence is reminiscient of Ps.37:12; they regret what has happened to the Innocent One. Other disciples/His acquaintances could be a reference to the disciples and the apostles themselves (23:49a).

(4) The Galileans and the women from Galilee (L), stood at a distance watching from afar (23:49b). Luke uses a purposeful participle meaning "so that they could see" (Gk.horosai) the happenings. They are not "the daughters of Abraham" referred to in 23:28 and they are not named, perhaps because some of them would have been included in 8:1-3. Luke pays particular attention to these women disciples showing that they had followed Jesus from Galilee (8:1-3). Later they recall the events of the Resurrection (23:55; 24:6). They will go onto play a major role in Acts. As with Peter (22:54) they are distanced from Jesus. Comparison can be made with Ps.38:11 where the suffering Righteous - One complains "My friends stand aloof from my affliction and my neighbours stand far off. They have stayed with Jesus but are geographically remote, showing that they were not prepared to identify with Him in His death. They endured inexpressible grief at a distance.

Pupil's Activity: Twelve
a) Consider critically the importance of the resurrection for the original readers of the Gospel
(Edexcel A2 2005)   [8 marks]
b) Examine and analyse the meaning of three religious features contained in the crucifixion narrative in Luke's Gospel.
(Edexcel A2 2005)   [12 marks]

Pupil's Activity: Thirteen
a) Examine the reasons why Jesus came into conflict with the Religious Authorities. (Edexcel A2 2005) [12 marks]
b) Why did Pilate sentence Jesus to death? (Edexcel A2 2005)   [8 marks]

Pupil's Activity: Fourteen
As a revision exercise complete the grid in (Figure 5) to show the innocence of Jesus in His trials and death (23:1-49).

> Luke continues his interest in the Holy Spirit as the Spirit's role in empowering the disciples at Pentecost is predicted (24:48-49).

(Figure 5) People who said that Jesus was innocent.

	Refs.	Identify the context, discuss and comment.
1	23:4 (L)	At the trial of Jesus, Pilate said that he could find no fault in Him.
2	23:14 (L)	
3	23:15	
4	23:15	
5	23:22 (L)	
6	23:41	
7	23:47	

12) The Burial of Jesus (Read 23:50-56.)

The Romans were not concerned about the burial of their victims, but Jews had scruples about the burials. Joseph of Arimathea, Sanhedrin member, being a wealthy man, prepared his own tomb (Gk.mnema) and wrapt the body of Jesus in a linen cloth (Gk.sindon). This refence to a shroud does not give us enough evidence to make a comparison with the 'Turin Shroud'. He had heard Jesus preach about the kingdom of God and the future possibilities of this had fired his imagination (23:51). He received permission from the governor to remove the executed body. The burial had to be done quickly as the Sabbath was approaching; Jews did not believe in letting a body linger. Jesus was not buried among thieves as this would have been considered a dishonour.

The setting: Luke notes the timing of the event, the Day of Preparation is Friday when the Sabbath had to be made ready (23:54). The women all from Galilee watch Joseph to see how Jesus is buried (23:56), while Mk. 15:47 says they looked where He was buried and decide not to return until after the Sabbath, so that they can anoint His body with spices to take away the smell (23:55). The women were faithful in their preparation, keeping the Mosaic law and resting on the Sabbath: they did not anticipate a resurrection (23:56). Jewish tradition would have allowed the women to care for a corpse on the Sabbath (SB 2:52-53). In this way the women kept the Jewish law.

> The appearance of the two angels fills them with so much fear and terror (Gk.emphobos) that they bow their faces to the ground (24:48).

[3] The Resurrection and Ascension of Jesus (Read 24:1-53.)

Introduction: Luke's account of the Resurrection is longer than any of the other Gospels.

1) Jesus fulfils all the O.T. Scriptures (24:26-27,44-49). Luke's main emphasis is on the fulfilment of prophecy, in the offer of salvation and forgiveness to all who repent (24:47).

2) Jesus is made known in "table fellowship" sharing a meal together among His people (24:30-35).

3) The reality of Jesus' humanity and bodily resurrection is underlined as a defence against false teaching (24:36-43).

4) The Spirit's work continues as the Holy Spirit's role in empowering the disciples at Pentecost is foretold (24:48-9).

5) All of Luke's resurrection appearances take place in Jerusalem and the disciples return to the Temple, highlighting the central role of Jerusalem in God's plan for His people (24: 47, 52-53).

6) The narrative of the ascension is unique to Luke 24: 50-51 and if Luke/Acts is seen as chiasmus then the resurrection and the ascension become central in the chiasmus. [Ch.7: Structure p.75. ¶ 2 (Talbert) (17).]

A) The women discover the empty tomb (Read 24:1-12.) (Matt. 28:1-8; Mk.16;1-8; Jn. 20:1-13)

1) The setting : the women having prepared spices and ointments and rested on the Sabbath to obey the law (23:56; Ex.20: 8-11; Deut. 5:12-15), come to the tomb on the first day of the week (our Sunday). The time Luke says is "deep" or "early dawn," the first initial glimmer of light (24:1).

2) The discovery: the first hint of the resurrection of Jesus is the rolled-away stone (24:3).

Note: the contrast between what the ladies found on arrival (an empty tomb) and what they did not find (the body of Jesus). The tomb (Gk.mnema unique to Luke) is open and empty, the stone is rolled away and there is no sign of the body. The expression "hewn out of stone"(Gk.laxeutos) is unique to the NT. Luke explicitly says that the women did not find the body of Jesus. In first century Israel, a round stone disc was often placed in a channel carved in the rock so that it could be opened easily or to plug the entrance without a channel.

3) The report of the two men (angels): two men in bright clothes stood beside the women. (Read 24:4-7.)

The witness of two persons to the Resurrection is common in Luke. The reference to the two men seen as angels is unique to Luke. Luke later in 24:23 refers to them as angels. They announce to the women that Jesus has been raised from the dead and remind them of His predictions about His cross and resurrection. "He is not here but has been raised (Gk. egerthe) by God." "Christ has been awakened from the sleep of death (24:6a)." Fitzmyer [See p. 231-232.]

> **Peter is not so sure [about the report of the women] and he runs to the tomb, stoops and looks in seeing the linen clothes. He is amazed (Gk.thaumazon) at all the things which have taken place. (24:12)**

(4) The response of the women: (Read 24:8.) At first they are perplexed (Gk.aporeo) as they did not expect an empty tomb (24:4). The appearance of the two angels fills them with so much fear and terror (Gk.emphobos) that they bow their faces to the ground (24:5). This is a sign of the recognition of heavenly beings; they know that something is happening but have no idea what it is. The angels rebuke the women for not seeking "the living" among the dead. The women are wondering about this, despite the fact that Jesus made six distinct predictions regarding the resurrection in Luke: "The Son of Man must suffer many things and be rejected of men and be killed and on the third day rise again." (9:22) Moses and Elijah appeared in glory and spoke of His departure (Gk.exodus) which He was to accomplish at Jerusalem (9:31). The stress is on his death, resurrection and ascension which would happen in Jerusalem. They will scourge Him and kill Him and on the third day He will rise (18:32-33). Although this incident against the Sadducees is not a prediction, Jesus endorses the resurrection as it is the promise of God and a future hope for His people (20:27-40). But from now on the Son of Man shall be seated at the right hand of the power of God (22:69). The angels tell the women to recall Jesus' teaching near Bethsaida in Galilee (9:22) which alludes to His death and resurrection, "The Son of Man must suffer many things and be rejected by the elders, chief priests and scribes and be killed and on the third day be raised." Also in 18:32-33, "For He will be delivered to the Gentiles, and will be mocked and shamefully treated and spit upon; they will scourge Him and kill and on the third day He will rise."

Luke summarises Jesus' prediction. "The Son of Man must be delivered (given over/Gk.paradothenai) into the hands of sinful men and be crucified (Gk.staurothenai) and on the third day rise (Gk.anastenai)." (24:7)

• Though humans are responsible for the handing over and crucifying Jesus, God allows these actions to take place. He is not here but has risen (RSV marg. 24:6). His resurrection was his own doing (18:33; 24:46)! (Stein) **(18)**

• Reference to crucifixion is unique to Luke here in the passion sayings as is the focus on the third day.

• The women further respond in remembrance. They recall the teaching of Jesus and take the first small step to an Easter faith. They are not commissioned but they received Jesus' words and understood them which confirms their discipleship (24:8). While the witness of the women was not acceptable at that time, Luke still records their testimony (24:9).

(5) The report of the women (Read 24:9-11.) The women are called Mary Magdalene, Joanna, Mary the mother of James, and the other women (24:10). In Luke, there is no direct appearance by Jesus to the women as with the other Gospels (Mt. 28:9-10; Mk. 16:9; Jn. 20:14-17). They report all these things to the Eleven apostles where the women are met with unbelief, their story considered to be an idle tale (24:12).

(6) Peter's response (Read 24:12.) He is not so sure and he runs to the tomb, stoops and looks in seeing the linen clothes. He is amazed (Gk.thaumazon) at all the things which have taken place. Our word 'thaumaturge' comes from this Greek word.

Pupil's Activity: Fifteen

a) Compare these events with the vision of Mary in Luke 1:26-38 with 24:1-12.   b) What do they have in common?

c) Why did the disciples not believe?   d) What were the different reactions to their story?

> **He ate bread with them to show that He was the risen Messiah (24:31).**

B) The walk to Emmaus   **(Read 24:13-35.) (L)**
1) The meeting and the conversation   **(Read 24:13-16/17-27.)**

The Jewish historian, Josephus, refers to Emmaus in his writings as "thirty stadia from Jerusalem." A stadia is 607 feet /192 metres (7 miles). The disciples had heard rumours that Jesus had risen. They were not disposed to believe and only first-hand evidence would convince them; their sadness was seen in their faces. They seemed uninformed about the events that had taken place in Jerusalem. Jesus knew better than any one else what had taken place. The disciples spoke of Jesus of Nazareth, a prophet mighty in deed and acknowledged all that He said and did but did not know who He was (24:18). Cleopas is the shortened form of Cleopatros (24:18). This is the only time he is named in Scripture although there is a Cleopas named in Jn.19:25, Cleopas and his companion knew the grim facts about the death of Jesus and their own disillusioned hopes that He would redeem Israel. They had heard of an empty tomb but were not very impressed. The people (Gk.laos) witness Jesus' mighty works (24:19).

Jesus told them about all that the prophets had predicted regarding the Messiah. He then explained to them starting with Moses and the prophets, what had been said about Him. God opened their eyes to recognise Jesus and to identify Him. They recognised that the presence of Jesus and interpretation of Scripture had been like fire burning within their hearts. It was in the act of remembering the Lord's death that the full impact of Easter could be grasped. They had thought about these things many times but it had never dawned upon them that the Messiah would suffer. As He expounded these things, the cross became less of a tragedy. They saw the importance of the O.T. in interpreting the death of Jesus, who was not someone who was in the wrong place at the wrong time. What happened to Cleopas and friend must have happened to many others. The rest of this final chapter is unique to Luke.

> Jesus appears to the disciples, greets them and shows them His wounds to provide physical proof of His resurrection.

2) The amazing meal (Read 24:28-32.) (L)

The two travellers strongly urged Him to dine with them at their home (24:29) and intended to accommodate Him for the night (24:30). Jesus "took bread", "blessed it", "broke it" and gave it to them, enabling them to see Him (24:30). These people had been confused as the report of the women did not convince them. His followers were slow to believe all that the prophets had spoken (24:25) and to recall all His teaching about the necessity of **suffering** (24:26). He ate bread with them to show that He was the risen Messiah (24:31). After the recognition He was gone; His presence made a deep spiritual impact upon them. God opened their eyes to recognise Jesus and to identify Him. They recognised that the interpretation of Scripture had been like fire burning within their hearts (24:32). The "tale" of the women had become an amazing truth. Jesus opened the scriptures to them (24:32) and their minds (24:45). Jesus acting as the host led to the recognition. Through breaking the bread divine intervention, the two disciples recognise Jesus. The events recall the feeding of the five thousand (9:10-17) and the Lord's Supper in the breaking of the bread (22:19).

3) The return to Jerusalem to report the event (Read 24:33-35.) (L)

The two travellers reported all of this to the Eleven disciples (24:33) and an unspecified number of followers. who had stayed in Jerusalem. The Eleven is a collective term for the remaining apostles and would suggest that Thomas was not fully convinced until a week later (Jn.20; 24:29). They were so thrilled with the experience that they thought nothing of the return journey of seven miles, despite the late hour. They discovered that Jesus had already appeared to Simon so they shared their experience. Evidence for the resurrection was growing and also the expectancy of great things to come. The title 'Jesus is Lord' became linked with Jesus' resurrection. "The Lord has risen indeed, and has appeared to Simon!" (24:34) Peter's experience of seeing the risen Lord is reported though it is not related to show Peter as an eyewitness and his place of priority among the apostles as eyewitnesses of the resurrection. It was in the act of remembering the Lord's death that the full impact of Easter could be grasped (24:34). The word "Lord" shows the authority of the risen Jesus.

Pupil's Activity: Sixteen

a) Why did the two disciples not recognise Jesus at first? b) How did they come to recognise Jesus?
c) How do you account for the fact that Luke records all the resurrection appearances of Jesus in Jerusalem?
d) Why is Jerusalem so important to Luke in his Gospel?

> Jesus eats the piece of broiled fish as final proof, since angels and spirits do not eat. Luke says that He eats in their presence "before them" (24:43) in their doubt and incomprehension which give way to belief and understanding.

4) The appearance of Jesus at a meal (Read 24:36-43.)(L)

Jesus appears to the disciples, greets them and shows them His wounds to provide physical proof of His resurrection. He provides further proof when He eats with them. He also reminds them that all these things were promised in the O.T. Scriptures, especially His suffering, His resurrection and the preaching of repentance in His name for the forgiveness of sins to all nations. While the two are still talking about their experience, Jesus stands among them. It is likely that ten disciples would have been present and not Judas and Thomas. Suddenly He approached. They did not see Him come and the door had not opened, yet He was inside the room. Frightened, they thought they saw a ghost or spirit (24:37).

The first proof is one of touch (24:38-40). Jesus asks them why they are frightened, asking questions and doubting in their hearts (24:38). The Gk. word "kardia" means inner person. Why are you alarmed? Jesus identifies Himself by saying for emphasis 'myself,' "See my hands and my feet, that is I myself," (Gk.autos) means myself (24:39a). Jesus tries to tell them that they should recognise Him so He shows them His hands and feet. Thus Jesus is real and is recognised because of the nail prints. His physical reality is evident because they can feel Him. "Handle me and see; for a spirit does not have flesh and bones as you see that I have."(24:39b) The human body cannot develop into a resurrection body unless God brings about the change (1 Cor. 15:50). This shows the transformed nature of the resurrection body of Jesus. He can be touched, the scars of the nails can be seen. He has "flesh and bones" (24:39). He eats fish (24:42-43). [See pp. 219-20.]

The second proof is one of sharing a meal (Read 24:41-43.)

Jesus asks for food which He ate before them to show that He was not an apparition. They gave Him broiled fish and He eat it. This Jesus is real for the disciples and this incident is used to counter arguments that the disciples only saw a ghost (24:43-44). Jesus eats the piece of broiled fish as final proof, since angels and spirits do not eat. Luke says that He eats in their presence "before them" (24:43) in their doubt and incomprehension which give way to belief and understanding.

5) Commission, plan and promise of the Spirit (Read 24:44-53.) (L) [See pp. 219-20.]

The disciples are ready for their final instructions before the Lord departs from them for the last time (24:44). Jesus points out that the O.T. had to be fulfilled. Everything must be fulfilled. Again Luke notes that this is a **necessity.** Fulfilment is dependent upon and centred in Jesus who is the completion and fulfilment of the promises in Scripture and hope.

6) Luke's threefold summary of God's plan (Read 24:44-46.) (L)

• Christ should suffer.

God anticipated the sufferings of Jesus in Pss. 22:31, 69, 118, Is. 53. The book of Psalms plays a key role in the theme of the suffering of the innocent righteous. (Brown) **(20)** Suffering by the Messiah was not part of the first-century Jewish expectation but it became linked to the whole idea of forgiveness of sins in the early Church (Acts 20:28). [See Figures 4/5.]

• The promise of a quick resurrection: the Jewish hope to be resurrected at the last day (24:44) was based upon two points Pss.16:10 and 110:1. As Jesus has suffered and been raised from the dead, the message can go forward.

• The future of God's plan is to preach: a) in the name of Jesus. In the O.T. this meant in the authority of Yahweh - **an authority transferred to** Jesus and shows **the authority of the glorified Jesus.** b) repentance which is also rooted in the O.T., meaning turning, change in thinking about God and the way to Him, turning to God and embracing Him by faith. c) forgiveness of sins enabling a person to enter into a relationship with God because the sin barrier has been removed.

> **The book of Psalms plays a key role in the theme of the suffering of the innocent righteous. (Brown)**

7) The disciples are named as witnesses (24:48).

The disciples are to be witnesses of these things. They can testify to these events because they have seen them. These events include the passion, resurrection, and the work of Jesus. In the absence of Jesus, these disciples are to be witnesses to the things Jesus did and taught. **The command to wait for the Holy Spirit (24:49).** Jesus gives two further commands. Firstly, **He promises to send 'Him' the Holy Spirit**, and indicates that **He [Jesus] has authority over the distribution of the Holy Spirit.** As a result of the resurrection, Jesus mediates the benefits of salvation and promises. The coming of the Spirit represents the inauguration of the Kingdom's blessing, promised by the Father in the O.T. Secondly, the disciples are to go Jerusalem and wait to be clothed from on high. These are different gifts, which God gives to believers to 'wear' in their daily walk with Him. Jesus describes the Spirit's coming as 'power from on high'; the Spirit gives boldness to declare the message (Acts 1:8). The disciples have to wait for God's enabling.

> **By "stitching together" Luke and Acts in Luke 24 and Acts 1, Luke shows that the O.T. Scriptures are the essential foundation for both the Messiahship of Jesus and the mission of the Church.**

8) The Ascension (Read 24:50-53.) (L) Jesus' blessing and departure (24:50-51)

Luke describes concisely the departure of Jesus. Jesus greets the disciples with peace and departs after blessing (Gk.eulogeo) them (24:50). Other examples of blessing are 1:1:42, 64; 2:28,34; 6:28; 9:16, 13:35; 19:38; 24:30, 51, 53. The act of raising hands and bestowing benedictions adds to the solemnity of the event and are also given to close the proceedings (24:50). Jesus commends His disciples to God's care and protection. God is watching over them. (Fitzmyer) **(20)** He parted from them and was carried up to heaven. The response of the disciples is to await for the blessing. They go to Jerusalem to obey the commands; their attitude is one of obedience. They are filled with joy and stay continually at the Temple praising God. There is no need to see this as a "final" departure. Luke uses the word (Gk.dieste) for departure here (24:51). This is used rarely and only in Luke 22:59 when a third person insisted Peter was a Galilean. Only Luke presents Jesus' departure to heaven. Jesus at His trial predicted His departure to heaven. "From now on the Son of Man shall be seated at the right hand of the power of God." (22:69) The Ascension shows that His claims to sit at God's right hand are correct. It is not just a departure but an arrival and the start of His heavenly reign and the forerunner of the benefits given to believers seen in the fact, that Jesus now prays for the believers (Rom.8: 34; 1 Jn.2:1).

> **Jesus emphasises His close relationship with the God by calling Him "My Father". It shows Jesus as a mediator. Jesus also has authority over the distribution of the Holy Spirit, "I will send the promise of My Father upon you." (24:49) The Holy Spirit will come upon the disciples.**

9) Reaction: worship, joy and giving thanks (Read 24:52-53.) (L) [See pp. 51-52.]

The group return to the city worshipping (Gk.proskunesantes) Jesus and full of joy. Joy in Luke is always a present experienced through taking part in the event. The disciples go to the Temple and bless (Gk.eulogountes) God there. Luke ends the Gospel as he began it in the Temple (1:5); God is to be praised for the blessings that come in Jesus. The disciples were continually (Gk.diapantos) in the Temple. They await the coming of the Father's promise. God is to be praised for His work in Jesus Christ, the exalted Lord. Luke ends on an open note of the disciples waiting for the Spirit to come and shows Jesus reigning at God's side. Jesus is alive offering hope and blessing to all who come to Him.

> **The coming of the Spirit represents the inauguration of the Kingdom's blessing, promised by the Father in the O.T.**

10) The message of hope is to all nations. (Read 24:47.) (Is. 42:6; 49:6.) (L)

This is a universal message to all from any nation. It starts from Jerusalem Acts 24:49 but is designed to go to the ends of the earth. Luke shows that Jesus is Lord of all humanity, so the message of the Gospel can go to all. Jesus had gone up to Jerusalem to meet His fate but now the mission goes out from Jerusalem. Jesus is raised to the right hand of the Father to provide the benefits of salvation to those who repent and come to Him. Everything from suffering to world-wide presentation of the Gospel was foretold in Scripture. There is continuity in the plan of God. This is a very important aspect of Luke's whole work. By "stitching together" Luke and Acts in Luke 24 and Acts 1, Luke shows that the O.T. Scriptures are the essential foundation for both the Messiahship of Jesus and the mission of the Church. Consequently we need to know our O.T. to discover the early ideas and concepts of Messiah and mission.

[4] Themes from the Passion and Resurrection -Theme One: Suffering (CCEA Internal Assessment)
Christ had to suffer. (Read 24:46b.)
A) Jesus predicted His own suffering: "The Son of Man must suffer many things and be rejected by the elders, chief priests and scribes and be killed and on the third day be raised." (9:22) "For the Son of Man is to be delivered into the hands of men." (9:44) "But first He must suffer many things and be rejected by this generation." (17:25) "Everything that is written of the Son of Man by the prophets, **will be accomplished**." (18:31-33) "And He was reckoned with the transgressors for what is written about me **has its fulfilment**." (22:37)
B) His death was anticipated in Scripture (Read 24:46a.)
Suffering had been anticipated by God, even though the idea of a suffering Messiah was not part of Jewish teaching at this time. Luke quotes Ps.118:22 in describing the rejection of Jesus and includes part of Isaiah 53 in relation to His suffering. [See Figures 4 and 5.] Luke alludes to Pss. 22:6-8; 16:18; 31:5; 69:21. All these are included in the Passion Narrative. Luke sees it as a quick resurrection since the Jewish concept was one of a resurrection on the last day.
C) The Messiah was to be raised which includes Pss.16:10; 110:1; 118: 22-26. The disciples are experiencing this as Jesus speaks but there is more to come (24:46c).
D) What has still to be accomplished? – mission statement (Read 24:47a.)
Repentance and forgiveness should be preached to all. Repentance means a change in thinking, a reorientation of the mind regarding sin. It also means turning to God and embracing Him by faith (24:47a). All authority is in the name of Jesus. Yahweh's authority in the O.T. has been transferred to Jesus (24:47b). The message is one of hope for all the nations and will start in **Jerusalem** (24:47c; Acts 1:8). It is a universal message open to all nations both Gentiles and Jews because Jesus is Lord of all humanity (Is. 42:6; 49:6). Jesus had gone up to Jerusalem to meet His fate but now the direction is in reverse and His **mission** is to go out from Jerusalem.
All are to be His witnesses (Gk.martures) from which our word martyr is derived (24:48). The disciples are to be witnesses of these historic events. They can testify to them because they have seen the passion, resurrection, teaching and work of Jesus. Judas' replacement among the apostles, had to be a witness of these events (Acts 1:22).

> **The key point in Luke is that everything from suffering to preaching worldwide was predicted in Scripture and indicates the continuity of God's plan. Jesus has authority over salvation as a result of His resurrection.**

They would receive the Father's promise of the Holy Spirit (24:49). Jesus emphasises His close relationship with the God by calling Him "My Father". It is shows Jesus as a mediator. Jesus also has authority over the distribution of the Holy Spirit, "I will send the promise of My Father upon you." (24:49) The Holy Spirit will come upon the disciples. The Spirit in the believers is the gift Jesus promises from the Father and is also an O.T. promise (Joel 2:28-32). The key point in Luke is that everything from suffering to preaching worldwide was predicted in Scripture and indicates the continuity of God's plan. Jesus has authority over salvation as a result of His resurrection. They were to wait in Jerusalem until they would receive power from on high (24:49). They had to wait for the vital power The disciples are go to Jerusalem and wait to be clothed from on high (Gk.kathizo) "to sit" or "stay". They are to wait (stay) in Jerusalem for God's gift of enabling, His gift of power (Gk.dunamis). Our word dynamite comes from this Greek word.

Theme Two: relating Chs. 22-23 to suffering in Isaiah 53
References relating to Luke's use of Isaiah 53 regarding suffering in the Passion Narratives. **(Figure 6)**

	Refs. from Isaiah	Refs. in Luke	Comment	Characteristics of the Servant
1	Is. 53:12; 49:24-26 "I will apportion to him the many, and the strong he will allocate as spoil." "Can the prey be taken from the mighty, or the captives of a tyrant be rescued?" (Motyer) **(21)**	The parable of the strong man **(11:22)** Note: this reference is outside the Passion Narrative.	"He shall divide the spoil with the strong." The dividing of the spoil recalls the imagery of Is. 53:12; 49:25-26. Jesus' work means that Satan is no longer in control of the house.(Bock) **(22)** This verse may be an echo of Is.49:24; 53:12 following the (MT). (Marshall) **(23)** Unclean spirits in bonds to Satan are freed. The strong man is bound and his plunder is taken from him. (Jeremias) **(24)**	

	Refs. from Isaiah	Refs. in Luke	Comment	Characteristics of the Servant
2	Is. 53:12	**O.T. Scripture is fulfilled (22:37).** Jesus in His last discourse said, "I tell you that scripture must be fulfilled in Me, And He was reckoned with the transgressors;' for what is written about me has its fulfilment." Jesus grounds His own fate and that of His followers in Is. 53:12. (Green) **(25)** Jesus applies Is.53 to Himself and us.	"He was reckoned with the transgressors." This could have been fulfilled in the baptism of Jesus or with the thieves on the cross. Isaiah anticipates the fulfilment which Jesus brings. In Luke, the Servant is Jesus. Luke reflects Jesus' exaltation and suffering (24:44-47). Luke 22:37 shows Jesus' suffering as a rejected one. His suffering would be a shameful one between two criminals anticipated in Scripture. (Bock) **(26)** Luke in 22:37 follows the emphasis in Is.53 which moves from suffering to exaltation; Jesus refers to Is. 53:12 grounding His fate and that of His disciples on Is 53;12. "And he was reckoned with the transgressors." (Green) **(27)** Fulfilment in Jesus is a necessity (Gk.dei).	Jesus' Identification with sinners - the reference in 22:37 can mean numbered with the lawless but this would mean Jesus was responsible for disturbing the peace between the Jews and the Romans.
3	Is.53:7-9	**The trial before Herod (23:9)** Herod questioned Jesus at some length but He made no answer. Jesus was silent before His judges.	"He was oppressed and He was afflicted, yet He opened not His mouth." "And there was no deceit in His mouth." The silence of Jesus was the best response to this harsh injustice of Herod. Today, Christians see (23:9) as the fulfilment of Is.53:7-9. (Jeremias) **(28)** His silence was reminiscent of the Servant of Yahweh with whom He is identified	He is silent which is like Yahweh's Servant. It was criminal at this time for philosophers to parade their teaching before tyrants.
4	Is.51:22	**The cup (22:42)**	See text and notes p.136.	He is the obedient, prayerful servant.
5	Is.53:12	**On the cross Jesus said, "Father, forgive them; for they know not what they do." (23:34)**	"He poured out His soul to death."(Is.53:12) "He made intercession for the transgressors." The passage in Luke is linked with Is.53:12 where the Servant suffers for the transgressors.	The servant who suffers for sinners.
6	Is.53:9	**The burial of Jesus (23:50)** Now there was a man named Joseph from the Jewish town of Arimathea. He was a member of the council, a good and righteous man.	"And they made His grave with the wicked and with a rich man in His death." Matt. 27:57 (M) describes Joseph as "a rich man from Arimathea."	Matt.27:57 was fulfilled in Joseph, the rich man providing a tomb for Jesus.
7	Is.53	**The Emmaus road experience (24:26)** Luke comments, "Was it not necessary that the Christ should suffer these things and enter into His glory?"	What took place was all part of God's plan and Luke notes that all of these events were necessary. While first century Judaism did not anticipate a suffering Messiah, Jesus shows here that the O.T. prophets had such an expectation. Glory here means **the authority or majesty** of Jesus as at the Transfiguration. Resurrection means being received into **heavenly authority.**	This theme of suffering comes from Ps.118 and Is.53 presenting the righteous sufferer. (Danker) **(29)**

Pupil's Activity: Seventeen

a) From which O.T. book does Jesus quote most frequently during Holy Week? b) Produce a class power point to show references to Isaiah in Luke's Gospel. c) What characteristics of the Servant are in evidence in these passages? d) What do these references tell us about the sufferings of the Servant?

Pupil's Activity: Eighteen

Outline your knowledge and understanding of the importance of the following people in the story of the crucifixion: the women who mourned for Jesus, the two criminals on the cross, the Roman soldiers.

Theme Three: significant references to Psalms linked to the idea of Messiah in the Third Gospel

The Psalms play a key role for the theme of the innocent righteous who suffer. The idea of Messiah in Luke and in the book of Psalms are linked closely to the theme of suffering.

Suffering as a key theme in the Book of Psalms and in Luke's Gospel (Figure 7)

Events before and leading up to the Passion Narrative

	Psalms	Luke	Comment
1	**Ps. 118:22** "The stone which the builders rejected has become the head of the corner." The Psalmist uses the symbol of the foundation stone that is important to a building. Probably the Psalmist meant the nation of Israel which was small and insignificant among the big empires but central in God's plan for humanity.	**Luke 20:17** "The very stone which the builders rejected has become the head of the corner." (20:42-44) "From now on the Son of Man will be seated at the right hand of the power of God." (22:69) This verse is also referred to in Luke 13:35 and 19:38.	This verse shows that God will vindicate His rejected leader. Jesus is the foundation stone of God's plan. Even though some will reject Him, He is the centre piece of God's overall plan. This precious and chosen stone cannot be replaced. Humiliation and rejection are part of the Divine plan and as Messiah He represents the role and mission of Israel.

	Psalms	Luke	Comment
2	**Ps. 110:1/ Ps.109: 1 (LXX)** The Lord (Yahweh Jehovah) said to my Lord: (Adonai) (Messianic King) "Sit at my right hand, till I make your enemies your footstool." Comment: "Sit at my right hand," is a position of honour and expresses the rule of the right-hand regal figure and a close link with God. It also means to exercise protection, power and authority. The Psalmist says that through David's Son, all the king's enemies will be defeated (1:67-79).	**Luke 20:42-44** "How can they say that Christ is David's son? For David himself says in the Book of Psalms, David thus calls Him Lord; so how is He his son?" The Lord said to my Lord: "Sit at my right hand, till I make your enemies a stool for my feet." (Ps.109 : 1) (LXX) Jesus raises the question with the Jewish leaders, how can the leaders say that Christ be David's son and David's Lord? As David's descendent Christ will be His inferior; as His Lord, He is clearly his superior. Jesus does not give the answer here but later the early church came to see Jesus as the Son of David and the exalted Lord (Acts 2:32-36) and the risen Christ (24:46).	In what sense is the Messiah, David's son? In this text the Messiah is seen as a King with authority, though Judaism did not make this connection. The Messiah as David's Lord is greater than David, as David's descendent he is in a sense inferior. The answer lies: 1) in the double nature of Jesus: as man he is David's descendent, while as God He is David's Lord. (Wilcock) **(30)** 2) in the resurrection through which David's son Jesus was exalted to God's right hand as His Lord. The key title here is Lord and not David's son even though Luke uses the title "son of David" in other texts. "The Lord God will give Him the throne of His father David." (1:32ff)
3	**Ps. 11:16; 75:8**	**Luke 22:42**	See textual comment p. 136.
4	**Ps. 110:1** The Lord says to my lord, "Sit at my right hand, till I make your enemies your footstool."	**Luke 22:69** "But from now on the Son of Man shall be seated at the right hand of the power of God."	The Son of Man was about to end His earthly ministry, suffer and die but through His exodus (9:31), He would enter His glory. (24:26)
5	**Ps. 22:18** "They divide my garments among them and for my raiment they cast lots."	**Luke 23:34** They cast lots to divide His garments. Compare the regal robes put on Jesus (23:11).	Comment on (23:34): to be treated like a debtor was to have one's clothes divided up. It meant loss of dignity, status and identity.
6	**Ps. 22:7-8** "All who see me mock at me, they make mouths at me, they wag their heads; He committed His cause to the Lord; let Him deliver Him, for He delights in Him !" The psalmist speaks of someone whose status is less than human 'a worm' scorned, despised and mocked.	**Luke 23:35-37** And the people stood by watching; but the rulers scoffed at Him saying, "He saved others; let him save himself, if he is the Christ of God, his Chosen One!" (23:35) The soldiers also mocked Him, coming up and offering Him vinegar (23:36). One of the criminals, who were hanged (on a cross) railed at Him (23:39). Compare 18:32 with the actions of the Sanhedrin in 23:11. The actions of the Romans is like that of the Sanhedrin, Herod and his soldiers.	The activity of the rulers who "scoff" at Him. There are three phases of mockery here: (1)the religious leaders (23:35), (2) the Roman soldiers (23:36), and (3) the executed criminal (23:39), who scoff, mock and blaspheme Him. A huge rift develops between those who are offended by the cross and those who are not. The people look on. Today, Christians see His Royal Identity and salvation as closely linked with suffering in the Third Gospel (9:22; 17:25; 18:31-32). Jesus' opponents saw His suffering and death as a denial of His vocation. This aspect of Jesus as a Righteous sufferer in this situation is absent from Luke.
7	**Ps. 37: 32** "The wicked watches the righteous."	**Luke 23:35** The people stood by watching.	
8	**Ps. 22:16** " Yea, dogs are around me; a company of evil doers encircle me; they have pierced my hands and feet." Comment: the writer is surrounded by a pack of dogs and cannot escape.	**Luke 23:36** This could allude to all who put Jesus to death. The second part of this verse 16b alludes to John 20:25 "His hands were nailed" and Luke 24:40 "Handle me and see, for a spirit has not flesh and bones as you see that I have."	In 23:36, Jesus suffered pain at the hands of evil-doers and like the Psalmist was despised, taunted and surrounded by opposition like a pack of dogs. Luke like the other Synoptics does not specifically say that Jesus was nailed to a cross but says He was crucified (23:33).
9	**Ps. 69: 21** "And for my thirst they gave me vinegar to drink."	**Luke 23:36** "The soldiers also mocked Him, coming up and offering Him vinegar (Gk.oxos), which was a sour or dry wine thought to quench thirst and better than water. It was also used among the poor. The offer of "sour wine" is thought to be an insult. This form of mocking is reminiscent of Ps. 69:21 where the gift of vinegar is an insult. "The soldiers treated Jesus like a carnival king offering, Him sour wine, mocking Him, rather than superior wine fit for a King." (Brown) **(31)** [See also textual comment.]	Neither Jew nor Gentile knew what they were doing in nailing Jesus to a cross. Luke omits the bystander giving Jesus a sponge full of vinegar, (Mk. 15:36; Matt. 27:48) because Luke does not include Aramaic phrases like 'Eloi, Eloi, lama sabachthani.' (Mk. 15:36)
10	**Ps.31:5** "Into your hand I commit my spirit !" (MT 31:6) The Psalmist's prayer is that of a Righteous Sufferer, who wants to be delivered from his enemies and shows that he puts his future into God's hand. This was the typical response of the righteous in the O.T. It was not a response of personal vengeance. (Fitzmyer) **(32)**	**Luke 23:46** The final words of Jesus "Father (Gk. Pater), into Thy hands I commit my spirit!" Luke notes that Jesus cried out with a loud voice. A loud cry by someone near dead may seem unusual but not impossible. (Marshall) **(33)** Ps. 31:5 was often used in Jewish evening prayer, commending oneself into God's care during the night's sleep. (Numbers Rabbah) **(34)** The term Father (Gk.Pater) is often used in Luke and shows Jesus' special filial relationship with God (3:34; 10:21; 11:2; 22:42). Death follows the last saying of Jesus.	Jesus' prayer of trust shows His submission to God's will and indicates that God will deliver Him. The reference to the spirit of Jesus means His person. Jesus made many predictions about His resurrection (9: 22; 18:33; 22:69; 23:43). (Green) **(35)** Luke identifies Jesus with the suffering Righteous One of Psalm 22 and 31. Jesus calls God His 'Father' taking the words from Psalm 31:5. Jesus shows His own faith in God His Father, Who will save Jesus from the hand of His enemies (23:46).
11	**Ps. 31:18** "Let the lying lips be dumb, which speak insolently against the righteous in pride and contempt."	**Luke 23:47** "Certainly this man was innocent (RSV)!" For the Psalmist, the righteous suffer at the hands of those who speak with lying lips.	The centurion says that Jesus was a righteous, innocent man. Jesus as the innocent sufferer later becomes a key theme in Acts.

12	**Ps. 38:11; 119:136** The Suffering Righteous complains. "My friends and companions stand aloof from my plague."	**Luke 23:49** "All His acquaintances and the women --- stood at a distance and saw all these things."	In Luke's account the friends and companions (kinsmen) have remained 'with' Jesus even though they are distanced from Him.
13	**Ps. 16:10** "For thou dost not give me up to Sheol, or let thy godly one see the Pit." (RSV) The (NIV) translates as decay.	**Luke 24:44** "Thus it is written, that the Christ should suffer and on the third day rise from the dead." Luke points out how the whole of the O.T. fits together as a promise. Luke adds an element not contained in Judaism: a suffering Messiah. (Bock) **(36)** The three Divisions of the O.T. also occur here: the law of Moses, the Prophets, and the Psalms. Note: Luke shows that all of the O.T. fits together as promise and in a holistic way, the O.T. Scriptures refer to the Messiah. He adds the one aspect lacking in Judaism, that of a suffering Messiah.	King David anticipated a resurrection. This verse was the basis for the Jewish hope of the resurrection at the end. The law promised a prophet like Moses. Although the Messiah is not mentioned in the Pentateuch, promises about God's plan are included. The prophets are often referred to in Luke 1:70; 16:16, 29, 31; 18:31; 24:25, 27 and discuss an ideal rule and ruler, the "promised anointed one." Many prophetic texts from the Psalms appear in Luke, for example 13:35; 20:17, 41-44; 22:69.
14	**Ps. 22: 6-8.** He will suffer, "But I am a worm, and not a man; scorned by men and despised by the people."	**Luke 24:44** "Thus it is written, that the Christ should suffer."	
15	**Ps. 22: 6-8** (1) He will suffer, "But I am a worm, and not a man; scorned by men and despised by the people." **Ps.16:10** (2) He will be raised. [See above.] This verse and Ps.110:1 were the basis of Jewish hope in the resurrection.	**Luke 24:46-47** "Thus it is written, that the Christ should suffer and on the third day rise from the dead and that repentance and forgiveness should be preached in His name to all nations beginning at Jerusalem." The usual Jewish hope for resurrection was on the last day.	The Psalmist speaks as one whose status is less than human, a "worm" "scorned" "despised" and mocked. To be stripped of human clothing was a sign of gross indignity and loss of personal identity (23:35-37). [See also the earlier references to Is. 53.]

Pupil's Activity: Nineteen
As a revision exercise divide the class into six groups and using evidence from **(Figure 7)** and your own sources, produce a power point presentation for the whole class entitled "The idea of Messiah in the Psalms and in Luke's Gospel".

Pupil's Activity: Twenty
What kinds of suffering are portrayed here? How were these fulfilled by Jesus in the Third Gospel?

> **The most outstanding feature of the death of Jesus is the care and compassion He showed to people, as He wended His way to the cross, when He had every right to be preoccupied with His own suffering. (Tidball) (37)**

Theme 4: Compassion
Tidball **(37)** remarks that the most outstanding feature of the death of Jesus is the care and compassion He showed to people, as He wended His way to the cross, when He had every right to be preoccupied with His own suffering. Luke minimises the failure of the disciples in the garden in that they want to defend Jesus (22:49-50), he highlights the hostility of the crowds (mainly from the rulers 23:35), the sorrow of the women of Jerusalem at His death (23:27) and the remorse of the people as they return home from the spectacle (23:48 NRSV). It is the Saviour's compassion which stands out and which can be seen in four incidents.

Four incidents which show the compassion of Jesus
I. The healing of the high priest servant's ear (Read 22: 49-51.)
The disciples thought that the use of force would release their Master from His captors. They took their swords with them to the Garden and used them when Judas arrived with the posse. Jesus might have been able to escape while Peter and the others kept the guards busy. However in the melee the servant of the high priest lost his ear, Jesus commands the disciples to stop this skirmish at once, brings peace to the unruly situation, touches the man's ear and heals him. Jesus was the only one to get hurt in the coming hours. Luke does not provide us with the name of the servant (22:51). Only John refers to the servant as Malchus (Jn.18:10).

II The women of Jerusalem (Read 23: 27-28.)
Some of the crowd showed sensitivity to the tragedy, as Jesus made His way up the Via Dolorosa; the women of Jerusalem mourned and wept for Him. Later others shared this grief when they returned home from the cross, beating their breasts which was a sign of mourning or sorrow (23:48). Jesus was not concerned for Himself but rather for them as their future would be full of suffering. Jesus, who had wept for Jerusalem, continues to show His compassion and love towards people caught in wickedness, even on the way to the cross (19:41-44).

III. The prayer of forgiveness (Read 23:34.)

There are three sayings, which are only mentioned in Luke, by Jesus on the cross: the first is a prayer in which Jesus is asking for forgiveness, "Father forgive them, they know not what they do." The cry of Jesus was not limited to the Roman soldiers who carried out the execution; they were only doing their job. They may well have been the focus of His compassion and pardon while He was on the cross. Their lack of concern is seen in the way they were more concerned about dividing up His possessions. Jesus' cry went out to all His executioners: Jews, Romans, rulers and the people. The ox (calf) was an O.T. sacrificial animal. Jesus sacrificed Himself for the whole world. He breaks down all the barriers between Jew and Gentile. [See p. 267.]

> **Jesus' compassion embraces the most unlikely people; a dying thief, a hardened centurion (23:47), the women, and a Jewish leader (23:50-54). In this, the symbol of the ox is very appropriate for the Third Gospel. It was always the role of the ox to carry the weight of others and to be sacrificed for sin.**

IV. The dying criminal (Read 23:40-43.)

"Jesus, remember me when you come in your kingly power." (23:42) The compassion of Jesus extended to a convicted criminal (Greek kakourgos) "someone who commits gross misdeeds and is guilty of serious crimes." (Tidball) **(38)** Josephus uses the term for a political activist or "terrorist" who is prepared to kill and murder for political reasons. He was an anarchist who decommissioned his arms, gave up his anarchism, repented and asked to come into the kingdom of Jesus as an obedient servant. He received mercy from Jesus during the closing minutes of his life. "I tell you the truth , today you will be with me in Paradise." (23:43) He rebuked the other criminal for not believing in God (23:40). He believed that one day, Jesus would come again to reign. Jesus promised him the home of the righteous "Paradise". Jesus continues to show His love for the marginalized right up to His death. Jesus rescued him and did not just enter into His pain. Jesus' compassion embraces the most unlikely people ; a dying thief, a hardened centurion (23:47), the women, and a Jewish leader (23:50-54). In this, the **symbol of the ox (calf)** is very appropriate for the Third Gospel. It was always the role of the ox to carry the weight of others and to be sacrificed for sin. In each of the unique incidents that Luke records, "someone burdened with fear or weakness or evil is liberated from their burden by their proximity to the cross." (Senior) **(39)**

> **The compassion of Jesus extended to a convicted criminal (Gk. kakourgos) "someone who commits gross misdeeds and is guilty of serious crimes." (Tidball) (38)**

Pupil's Activity: Twenty-One

Play, show on video or CD Rom relevant passages from Handel's Messiah, the recitative " All they that see Him, laugh Him to scorn; they shoot out their lips, and shake their heads, saying : He trusted in God that He would deliver him, let Him deliver Him, if He delight in Him," (Ps. 22:7-8) the recitative " He was cut off out of the land of the living: for the transgression of my people was He stricken,"(Is. 53:8) and the aria, "But Thou didst not leave His soul in hell; nor didst Thou suffer Thy Holy One to see corruption." (Ps.16:10)

Pupil's Activity: Twenty-Two

a) What final instructions did Jesus give to His disciples?
b) Outline your knowledge and understanding of Luke's account of Jesus' meeting with the disciples on the road to Emmaus.
(CCEA A/S 2003)   [30 marks]
c) Explore the claim that this event helped Jesus' followers to believe in the Resurrection. Justify your answer.
(CCEA A/S 2003)   [15 marks]

Pupil's Activity: Twenty-Three

a) How far was the Christian Gospel and the Christian mission a fulfilment of the Scriptures and not an innovation?
b) Why is the symbol of the ox appropriate for the Third Gospel?

(Figure 8) The symbol of the ox (Book of Kells)

Pupil's Activity: Twenty-Four

For revision purposes draw a spidergram to show the scene at the cross, identifying eight different groups or people.

The religious features and symbolism in the accounts of the crucifixion and the resurrection (Figure 9)

	Religious features and symbolisms	N.T. fulfilment
1	**The Jewish Temple** in Jerusalem was the sacred symbol of socio-religious power to legitimise the separation of Jews and Gentiles. It is an example of an O.T. symbol presented as a 'type' or model depicting the presence of God in Israel.	**Jesus** is the **true Temple**, the final meeting place between God and sinful humanity who are made in His image. Jesus recognised the interminable presence of God, the Father to whom He commits His life in death.
2	**The Passover Lamb:** Jesus celebrates the Passover with His disciples to commemorate the exodus and the harvest season (22:1-46). Jesus saw this as the final Passover (22:16). Was this the First or the Last Supper? Here the Passover Feast was celebrated without a lamb. In the O.T. the Passover Lamb is the symbol of an ox or calf to depict suffering. As the true Passover Lamb who was sacrificed for our sins, Jesus carried the weight of others and was sacrificed for sin. The dying thief was freed from his sin (23:42).	Jesus is the **true Passover Lamb** who was sacrificed for our sins. He carried the weight of others just like the ox which was used in the O.T. sacrificial system. The ox, which depicts suffering has become the symbol for Luke's Gospel. Jesus knew that He was to be the Lamb of God at the feast. Jesus vowed not to eat the Passover again until it finds fulfilment in the Kingdom of God (22:15). He will not also drink the cup (22:18). • When He eats with the disciples Jesus inaugurates the Kingdom. • He broke the bread to symbolise the breaking of His body "This is my body which is given for you. Do this in remembrance of me." (22:20a) • The cup is also "the new covenant in His blood."(22:20c) • As Jesus poured out the wine so His blood would be poured out for our sins. • Jesus gave Himself as a sacrifice for the all the world. • All the divisions between Jews and Gentiles are removed.
3	**The cup** "Father, if you are willing remove this cup from me." What does the cup symbolise (22:42)?	**The cup** can mean: • the cup of wrath, • the cup of suffering, • the cup of blessing, • the cup of calamity and death, • the cup of remembrance.
4	**Darkness and the Jewish leaders** Jesus said to the Jewish leaders, "But this is your hour when darkness reigns." (22:53) (NIV)	**Darkness and the Jewish leaders:** Jesus said to the Jewish leaders, "But this is your hour when darkness reigns." (22:53) (NIV) Jesus sees the temple guards as instuments of Satan, Darkness here is a symbol for Satan (22:53; Acts 26:18).
5	**Darkness** a) After the crucifixion darkness also came over the whole land at the death of Jesus (23:44a). The sun's light also failed (23:45). Despite the darkness God is still present. Jesus' death fulfils God's purpose. b) The veil of the Temple separated the the Holy of Holies from the rest of the inner Temple. The veil of the Temple was torn in two (23:45b). This event did not mean the end of the Temple in Luke although Jesus has already foretold the Fall of Jerusalem; the Temple is still standing in Ch.24. God turns from the Temple to fulfil His plans by other means. The Temple would not be central to the worship of the new community. These events did not symbolise the final destruction of the Temple in Luke. Although Jesus had already foretold the Fall of Jerusalem (23:28-31), the Temple was still standing at the end of Luke 24. God turns from the Temple to fulfil His plans in a different way. The rending of the veil of the Temple is a symbol for the end of the Temple as a symbol for the presence of God. **The torn Temple curtain** Fitzmyer says symbolises the reign of evil during the time of the passion of Jesus, has come to an end. **(43)**	a) **Darkness** has an eschatological significance related to the last days of the Lord (Joel 2:30-31). For Luke "last days" are a mission to all people (Acts 2:17-21). Darkness anticipates and gives way to the universal spread of God's light. It can be a symbol of the darkness into which the soul of Jesus plunged. Jesus bore our sins in silence. (Acts 26:18). (Green) **(41)** (Stott) **(42)** b) In O.T. the Temple in Jerusalem was a sacred symbol of socio-religious power used as a legitimate separation between Jews and Gentiles, priest and lay people, male and female. It represented the presence of God. • Now Jesus is the true Temple, the ultimate meeting place between God and sinful people who are made in His image. • The veil of the Temple which was torn in two at the death of Jesus meant equal access to God for Jews and Gentiles. • Luke portrays the rent veil as a symbol for the Destruction of all the symbols associated with the Temple. • This rending of the veil is an apocalyptic sign based upon Joel 3:4 "wonders in heaven and signs on the earth." • Jerusalem will become the centre of the ministry of the church to the world (Acts 1:8). Rather than go up to Jerusalem, the church will go from it to the ends of the earth.
6	**The O.T. priest** "Are you the Son of God?" "You say that I am."	**Jesus is the ultimate priest** as the ultimate Son of God (22:70). (Green) **(40)**
7	**Paradise** On the cross Jesus said to the repentant thief, "Today you will be with me in paradise." (23:43)	**Paradise** is a symbol for heaven and its joys (23:43; 2 Cor.12:4; Rev.2:7).
8	**The Messiah** "Thus it is written, that the Messiah is to suffer and to rise from the dead on the third day and that repentance and faith is to be preached to all nations."	Jews in the first-century expected **two Messiahs** (1) a Davidic line (2) a priestly one. Jesus fulfilled both of these. All nations have to believe and obey Him (24:47).
9	**Bread** Jesus took **the bread** and blessed it when He had a meal with the two people He met on the Emmaus Road (24:30).	**This bread** recalled the many predictions he made that He had to die. "He bore the sins of many.' 'Surely He has borne our griefs and carried our sorrows." (Is.53) The broken bread was a symbol for His body broken for us.

Pupil's Activity: Twenty-Five

a) Examine and interpret the meaning of the religious features and symbolism contained in the accounts of the crucifixion and resurrection in Luke's Gospel. (Edexcel A2 2002)   [20 marks]

b) To what extent was the resurrection of Jesus relevant to Jesus' teaching [on salvation and eschatology]? (Edexcel A2 2004)   [8 marks]

Outcomes

Students should be able to identify, know and understand: (CCEA)

• **the key themes within the passion narrative in Luke's Gospel.**

• **the betrayal of Jesus, the Last Supper.**

• **the Passover and plot, the institution of the Lord's Supper, Peter's denial predicted, the Trials and the Death of Jesus, the words from the cross, the reactions to the Death of Jesus, the events which accompanied the Death of Jesus, the Burial of Jesus.**

• **the Resurrection and Ascension of Jesus.**

• **key concepts such as, betrayal, compassion, death as a necessity, innocence, Sanhedrin, Son of Man, Son of God, types of suffering.**

• **the key concepts such as, betrayal, compassion, death as a necessity, innocence, Sanhedrin, Son of Man, Son of God and types of suffering, (CCEA)**

Students should be able to examine and critically analyse: (Edexcel A2)

• **symbolism contained in the cruxifixion and resurrection, the conflict with the Religious Authorities at the death of Jesus, why Pilate sentenced Jesus to death?**

Notes on Chapter Eleven: The Passion Narratives and the Resurrection

1. John Stott, The Cross of Christ, IVP, (1999) p.312.

2. Ajith Fernando, I Believe in the Supremacy of Christ, Hodder and Stoughton Press, (1997) p.204.

3. Josephus, Ant .3.10, par.249.

4. F.Godet, on Luke 22:5 op. cit. p.280.

5. I. Howard Marshall, on Luke 22:13 and 2:7 op. cit. p.107.

6. I. Howard Marshall, op. cit. p.805 on Luke 22:17 "Jesus took a cup" sees as the cup the third cup of the Passover, following the meal, the cup of blessing. Luke mentions the cup first (22:17). The cup could have been one of the four used at the Passover. After the cup Jesus took the unleavened bread, raised it, and prayed for a blessing on it (22:19).

7. Joel B.Green, on Luke 22:20 op. cit. p.764. This cup which is poured out for you is the new covenant in my blood." The "you" are the disciples who have joined Him at the table. This verse has far reaching significance to the death of Jesus as it has the idea of "the cross' substitutionary role", for all who embrace the "good news for the poor."

8. Darrell L. Bock, Luke 3: NTCS, IVP, (1993) p.354.

9. I. Howard Marshall, on Luke 22:42 op.cit. p.831 sees cup in this context as a cup of wrath.

10. Robert H. Stein, Difficult Sayings in the Gospels, Grand Rapids, (1985) p.558 sees the cup as a metaphor for the sufferings of Jesus. 11. Craig Evans, op. cit. p. 329 says the idea of destiny Is.51: 17, 22; Ps.16:5 is also an important insight into the humanity of Jesus and sees the cup as one of destiny.

12. Joel Green, op. cit. p.780 interprets the cup as one of calamity and death.

13. Robert Stein, op.cit. p.593 says of the thief that he sought for "the Lord's mercy" and "amazingly found salvation."

14. Thomas Smail, Windows on the Cross, DLT, (1995) p.73. The thief is the model for all in that he asked for mercy. It is an example of salvation by faith alone.

15. Derek Tidball, BST, Bible Themes: The Message of the Cross, IVP, (2001) p.162. "The sight of Jesus with us in our pain is the promise of our healing; the sight of Jesus sharing our death is the promise of our life."*

16. Donald Guthrie, on Luke 23:46 (L) op. cit. p.352.

17. Charles H. Talbert, op. cit. p.37.

18 Robert Stein, op.cit. p.605.

19. Raymond E. Brown, op. cit. pp.1453-1455.

20. Joseph A. Fitzmyer, op. cit. p.1590 on Luke 24:51,53. Jesus is not acting as a priest here. Throughout the Gospel, Luke does not emphasis Jesus as a priest.

21. Alex Motyer, Isaiah, IVP, (1990) p.422.

22. Darrell L. Bock, op. cit. p.211.

23. I. Howard Marshall, op. cit.p.477 on(11: 22).

24. Joachim Jeremias, The Parables of Jesus, SCM Press, (1954) p.122 says that Luke 11:22 perhaps is directly associated with Is. 53:12. The strong man is bound and his plunder is taken from him. Those bound by Satan are set free. W. Grundmann, TDNT, (1964), p.402 cited in Jeremias p.122 says "the strong man is bound and his plunder is taken from him." The Coming One the conqueror will despoil the strong of their prey.

25. Joel B.Green, New Testament Theology: The Theology of the Gospel of Luke, Cambridge Press, (1995) p.25.

26. Darrell L. Bock, on Luke 22:37, op. cit. p.1748.

27. Joel Green, on Luke 22:37, op. cit. p. 25.

28. Joachim Jeremias, on Luke 23:9, TDNT, p. 713.

29. F.W. Danker, Jesus and the New Age Commentary on the Third Gospel, St. Louis Clayton, (1982) on Luke 24:26, p.393.

30. Michael Wilcock, op. cit. p.185.

31. Raymond E. Brown, The death of the Messiah from Gethsemane to the Grave, Anchor Bible, New York: Doubleday, (1994) Vol. 2. p.997.

32. Joseph A. Fitzmyer, op. cit. p.1519 on Ps.31:5 "Into thy hand I commit my spirit;! (MT 31:6) spirit means "any life": "the whole of the living person."

33. I. Howard Marshall, op. cit. p.875.

34. Numbers, Rabbah 20.20 , Midrash Psalm 25.2.

35. Joel B. Green, on Luke 23:46, the final words of Jesus, "Jesus identifies His death with the Righteous Sufferer of Ps. 31:5," op. cit. p.25.

36. Darrell L. Bock, on Luke 24:44, op.cit. p.1937.

37. Derek Tidball, op. cit. p.152.

38. Derek Tidball, op. cit. p.161. Walter Bauer, Greek English Lexicon, University of Chicago, (1957) on Luke 23:42, cited in Tidball.

39. Donald Senior, The Passion of Jesus in the Gospel of Luke, Michael Glazier Press, (1984) p.163.

40. Joel B. Green, op. cit. pp. 825-6

41. Joel B. Green, (ibid.)

42. John Stott, The Bible though the Year, Easter, Candle Books, (2006)

43. Joseph A. Fitzmyer, op. cit. p.1519, cited in Evans p.344.

*This book is highly recommended.

CCEA A/S + part of A2 + Edexcel A/S level

Targets:
- **Identify the parables of mercy in Luke's Gospel: Jesus as the compassionate teacher [See pp.206, 266.]**
- **Recognise the different types of parable in Luke's Gospel.**
- **Identify the key concepts, for example 'parable', similitude, example story, extended metaphor, extended synecdoche, 'Dyadic', classification of the parables, God's joy when sinners repent.**
- **Identify the main points in two-three parables on mercy in Luke's Gospel.**
- **Identify the main purposes and origins of the parables in Luke's Gospel.**
- **Identify the different responses to the parables in Luke's Gospel.**
- **Identify the nature of forgiveness in the teaching of Jesus in the parables in Luke's Gospel. (Edexcel)**

The Words and Deeds of Jesus with reference to the Parables of God's Mercy

The parables of Jesus have been compared to a child's magic painting book which at first looks ordinary until brushed with water, so that the colours "magically" appear. The parables of Jesus have hidden meanings.

Introduction
a) What is a parable?

Luke is interested in prayer, wealth, discipleship, kingdom and outcasts (invitations to a feast) and he arranges the parables around these themes.

(1) The Greek word for parable is "parabole" and comes from two words "para" and "bole" meaning "to throw alongside" : a comparison or an analogy in which Jesus was comparing familiar things on this earth with the kingdom of God. The kingdom is like a "mustard seed" (13:18-19) or the kingdom is like a woman who takes some "yeast". (13:20)

2) There is another classical meaning from Latin "parabola" meaning comparison, discourse or allegory. This is a much broader view of parables. Jesus describes the meaning of the parable of the sower or "the soils" (8:11) when His disciples asked Him what the parable meant. He replied, "Now the parable is this." He then goes on to interpret it as an allegory. There is therefore a limited amount of allegory in some of the parables of Jesus. "Those who are well have no need of a physician, but those who are sick." (5:31)

(3) The Hebrew word for parable is "mashal", which means sayings, proverbs, a common saying from everyday use, allegories, similies and prophetic discourses or a profound saying which makes you think. This is also a much broader interpretation of parable compared with the Greek view.

(4) A parable has also been described as a story with two levels of meaning; the story level which provides the reality through everyday things in Palestine and that which also mirrors aspects of the kingdom of God; the wise and foolish builders (6:47-49), the binding of the strong man (11:21-23) and the return of the unclean spirit (11:24-26).

(5) Parable as a literary form has been described as an imaginative story with a beginning, middle and an end, developed from everyday life and told for its teaching value. In the parable of the shrewd manager, Jesus asks, "You know how it is in the world out there, why have you not learned to apply what you know to life before God? " (16:8-9 The parables are not words of comfort but demand a response.

(6) Some scholars define parable on the basis of the laws of structure: a parable is a concise statement based around two elements; a person (people) and an object, told from the perspective of one figure with secondary figures not usually present, feelings rarely mentioned, but when mentioned are important. [See pp. 163-4 "Dyadic parable."] (Kissinger) **(1)**

(7) Parable has been called a literary, rhetorical form of argument, designed to instruct believers, hiding truth from those who reject the message, and shocking the listener through the imagery to think again about how one sees the world and God.

(8) Recent research based on literary analysis sees the parables as not just illustrations but " weapons of warfare." People are attracted by what appears as an innocent story only to be confronted with the demands of discipleship. What Jew would ever have considered a Samaritan as a hero in a story in which your enemy is your neighbour?

b) Some general facts about Luke's parables:

(1) Approx one third of Jesus' teaching is in parables and most of these parables are of the "L" material.

(2) There is little evidence to suggest that parables were used frequently before Jesus.

(3) The parables of Jesus were based on every day life in Palestine.

(4) Most of the parables in Luke appear in the "journey narrative". (9:51-19:48) which some say is chiastic in structure.[See Ch. 7: Structure.]

(5) Luke is interested in prayer, wealth, discipleship, kingdom and outcasts (invitations to a feast) and he arranges the parables around these themes.

(6) Jesus told some parables on more than one occasion; in the parable of the " lost sheep" He told the parable in the context of repentance in Luke 15:1-7 while in Matt. 18:12-14 it is in the context of disciples who go astray.

(7) Discipleship is another key theme in Luke's Gospel; being a disciple is no easy task and the cost has to be considered the tower builder (14:28-32) and the warring king (14:31-33). In the parable of the owner and his servant obedience is expected (17:1-10). In the parable of the two builders, the wise person is the one who hears and obeys the teachings of Jesus (6:47-49). In the parable of the Good Samaritan where obedience to God is required and His law, acts of mercy are also demanded (10:29-37).

The mercy parables all show that God wants to help people by seeking them, forgiving and accepting them.

(8) The main focus of the parables is the coming of the kingdom of God.[See Figure 2 below.]

(a) The kingdom is present in the way God spreads His word as in the parable of the sower; the kingdom goes on growing even though people reject it. In the parable of the mustard seed the band of disciples is small but they will ultimately bear fruit (13:18f). In the parable of the banquet (14:15-24) the feast is ready to begin and people should come now. Some parables reflect the refusal of many of the Jews to accept Jesus, for example the barren fig tree (13:6-9). In the parable of the banquet the invitation is an expression of God's grace (14:15-24). The mercy parables all show that God wants to help people by seeking them, forgiving and accepting them. [See no.2 Figure 10.]

(b) The kingdom is future -This idea is seen in the parables which speak of judgement; the crisis which faces the Jewish people (13:6-9) and in (16:19-31) the rich man and Lazarus, the judgement is more immediate.

(9) The parables are the preaching and teaching of Jesus and have to be interpreted; the large number of parables in Luke's Gospel shows that Jesus was a teacher who provided valuable insights into His teaching.

Colour Code	Kingdom present	Kingdom future	discipleship	mercy	Jewish leaders

Classifying Luke's parables in topics and themes [adopted from (Bock) (2)] (Figure 1)

No	Ref.	Parable	Topic	Meaning and response
1	5:33-39	Unshrunk cloth and wineskins	Kingdom present	A new approach to God 'But new wine must be put into fresh wineskins.' Jesus' presence means a choice between Him and the old ways of Judaism. To show the difference Jesus does not fast. Do not do things for the sake of tradition!
2	6:47-49	The two builders – one man dug down deep and laid the foundations on a rock. In a storm his house will stand. A house built without a strong foundation will not hold up when the floods come. "Immediately the house fell and great was the ruin of that house."	discipleship	Obedience to the words of Jesus is spiritual wisdom. Jesus said, 'Everyone who comes to me and hears my words and does them is like the man who dug down deep and laid the foundation on the rock (6:48). Everything the second man had was lost. Tragedy results when people do not respond to Jesus. Obeying Jesus means being able to stand up to life's pressures. Jesus preaches God's wisdom. People are required to listen to Jesus (9:35). A house built without a strong foundation will not hold up when the floods come.
3	7:31-35 (L)	Complaining children	Jewish leadership	rejection by the Jews of Jesus and John the Baptist
4	7:41-50(L)	Two debtors	discipleship	forgiveness, love, faith and mercy
5	8:5-8, 9-15	Sower/different soils	kingdom (present)	four responses to the word of God (Gerhardsson) (3) God spreads His wordwidely among all kinds of people.
6	8:16-18	Lamp on a lampstand	discipleship	You cannot experience God's grace without extending that grace to others. 'Pay attention to how you listen!' What God gives us will increase if we use it. If we do not use it we will lose even what we think we have.
7	10:25-37 (L)	Good Samaritan	discipleship	Mercy and love for your neighbour 'Go and do likewise.' (10:37) Grace comes in surprising ways and from sources people seldom suspect.
8	11:5-8(L)	Friend at midnight	discipleship	Prayer- Gk. 'anaideia' means 'shamelessness or persistence, boldly knocking on the door.
9	11:21-23 (L)	Binding the strong man	discipleship	Spiritual conflict-the power of God to defeat the enemy
10	11:24-26	Return of the unclean spirit	discipleship	Spiritual conflict in evangelism
11	12:13-21 (L)	Rich fool	discipleship	Wealth and money (12:20-21) 'Store up treasure in heaven.' The rich fool only thought of his own enjoyment in using his wealth but did not think about the source of that wealth or that life is more than possessions.
12	12:35-38	Preparing for the Master's return from a wedding feast	kingdom (future) discipleship	be awake and responsible – The Master serves the servants because they were faithful.
13	12:39-40	Thief in the night	kingdom (future) discipleship	be awake and responsible/ stewardship and faithfulness to God
14	12:41-46	Faithful and unfaithful steward	kingdom (present)	be faithful and compassionate

	Ref.	Title of Parable	Topic	Theme/Response
15	13:6-9	Barren fig tree (L)	judgement on Jewish leaders	repentance–time is brief
16	13:18-19	Mustard seed	kingdom (present)	growth
17	13:20-21	Yeast	kingdom (present)	growth
18	13:22-30	Two ways /doors	Kingdom (future)	Surprises in the membership of the Kingdom- entrance into the Kingdom does not depend upon human achievement. There is a time limit on the offer.
19	14:7-14	Seats of honour	discipleship	humility
20	14:15-24	Wedding banquet	kingdom (present) judgement on Jewish leaders	don't refuse invitation/open to all/ mercy (14:24)
21	14:28-30 (L)	The tower builder	discipleship	People are warned about counting the cost of discipleship. "Which one of you...?"
22	14:31 -33 (L)	Warring king	discipleship	Counting the cost of following Jesus- 'None of you can be my disciple if you do not give up your possessions.'(14:33) Josephus **(4)**
23	14:34-35	Salt	discipleship	being a useful disciple 'He who has ears to hear let him hear.' (14:34)
24	15:4-7	Lost sheep	discipleship evangelism/ mercy	seek the sinner, joy at repentance /mercy 'There is joy in heaven over one sinner who repents.' (15:7)
25	15:8-10 (L)	Lost coin	discipleship evangelism/ mercy	seek the sinner, joy at repentance/ mercy 'There is joy in heaven over one sinner who repents.' (15:10)
26	15:11-32 (L)	Lost son	discipleship evangelism/ mercy(15:32)	seek the sinner, joy at repentance, Do not be harsh on the forgiven, show mercy 'There is joy in heaven over one sinner who repents.' (15:32)
27	16:1-9(L)	Shrewd manager	Discipleship + wealth	Be generous with money -'You cannot serve God and money.' (16:13)People in the world understand the shrewd use of resources better than the disciples understand the economies of the Kingdom.
28	16:19-31 (L)	Rich man and Lazarus	Discipleship + wealth	Values and money "If they do not listen to Moses and the prophets, they will not be convinced if someone rises from the dead." This parable teaches the eternal consequences of failing to show mercy. To be a disciple of the Kingdom is to have one's priorities recognised with regard to finances.
29	17:7-10(L)	Humble servant	discipleship	serve dutifully and obediently.
30	18:1-8 (L)	Unjust judge/ persistent widow	discipleship	prayer/trust God's faithfulness 'Every one who exalts himself will be humbled and he who humbles himself will be exalted.'
31	18:9-14 (L)	Pharisee and tax collector (L)	judgement on the Jewish leaders	pride and humility/mercy- This parable is addressed to all who are self-righteous.
32	19:11-27	Pounds	discipleship	stewardship to God
33	20: 9-19	Vineyard	kingdom/ Jewish leadership	Do not presume about God's promises. The Kingdom is open to all especially the Gentiles.
34	21: 29-33	Fig tree	discipleship	Time is near so watch!

(11) Jesus sometimes teaches His parables in pairs to reinforce the same basic point. (Figure 2)

Titles of Paired Parables	Reference	Teaching point
The tower builderand the warring king	14:28-30/31-33	counting the cost of discipleship and commitment
The lost sheep and the lost coin	15:3-7, 8-10	mercy/seeking the sinner, joy at repentance

Pupil's Activity: One
Name and identify other pairs of parables in Luke's Gospel showing their common teaching point by completing the grid in Figure 2. (See also Figure 1.)

(12) The fact that there are a large number of parables in Luke's Gospel shows that Jesus was a teacher and valuable insights are provided into that teaching through the parables. (Figure 3)

(13) In the Synoptic Gospels parables make up the following percentages:

16 %	Mark
25 %	"Q"
40 %	(M)
52 %	Luke

Pupil's Activity: Two [For schools offering a computer skills based course at A/S level]
ICT task - Using PC Excel produce a pie chart to show the percentages of the Synoptic Gospels which are in parables and showing which percentage of Luke's parables are unique to him. [See Figures 2/3 and Ch.10.]
a) What does this tell us about the composition of Luke's Gospel?
b) How many of these parables are in the "journey narrative" section?
c) Draw a graph to show the percentage of: triple tradition parables in the journey narrative, [Fig.4] double tradition parables in the journey narrative [Fig. 4] (L) parables in Luke's Gospel, [Fig.1] (L) parables in the journey narrative, [Ch.10: p.112.] Luke's shared parables with Matthew plus "Q".[Fig.5]
d) How many parables outside the journey narrative are unique to Luke's Gospel? (Figure 4)

> In the parable of the sower (8:4-8,11-15), Jesus probably saw Himself and His rejected message as a parallel to Isaiah, the rejected prophet (Is.6:11-13b).

Pupil's Activity: Three
a) What are the key themes in the parables of Luke? b) For revision purposes draw a histogram to show how Luke has thematically arranged his parables.

(13) Triple and double tradition parables (Figure 5)

	Title		Matt.	Mark	Lk. and OT connections
1	The guests of the bridegroom		9:15	2:19-20	5:33-39
2	The unshrunk cloth		9:16	2:21	5:36
3	New wine		9:17	2:22	5:37-39
4	Binding the strong man		Matt. 12:29-30; Deut.9:10; Ps. of Sol. 12:28	3:22-27	11:21-23
5	Sower		13:1-9, 18-23; Deut. 6: 4-6	4:1-9/ 13-20	8:4-8,11-15
6	Lamp and measure	(D.T.)		4:1-9,13-20	8:16-18
7	Mustard seed		13:31-32	4:30-32	13:18-19
8	Salt		5:13	9:49-50	14:34-35
9	Wicked tenants		21:33-46	12:1-12	20:9-19; Is.5:1-7 (Song of the vineyard)
10	Budding fig tree		24:32-36	13:28-32	21:29-33; Is.40:18; 55:10-11 ; Ps.119:89
11	Watchman	(D.T.)		13:34-36	12:35-38

(14) Parables and sayings shared by Matthew and Luke ["Q" parables?] (Figure 6)

	Title of the parable or saying	Matt.	Luke
1	Wise and foolish builders- hearing and doing the word	7:24-27	6:47-49
2	Father and children's requests- on answers to prayer discipleship	7:9-11	11:11-13; Ps. 111:9; Is.5:16; Ez.20:41
3	Two ways/ doors – condemnation of Israel-the Pharisees and many other Jews have not responded. Time is short the door will close and it will be too late. The way to salvation is narrow. to enter the door means coming in God's terms. People from all nations will come to sit at the table in the Kingdom.	7:13-14	13:22-30
4	Leaven (yeast)	13:31-32	13:18-21
5	Lost sheep – God's mercy	18:12-14	15:1-7
6	Wedding banquet	22:1-14	14:15-24
7	Thief in the night- faithfulness	24:42-44	12:39-40
8	Faithful and unfaithful steward	24:45-51	12:42-46
9	Talents and pounds - stewardship	25:14-30	19:11-27
10	The return of the unclean spirit "He [the wicked one] never ceases to scatter".	12:43-45	11:24-26; Is. 53:12; Ps of Sol. 12:28

Pupil's Activity: Four
a) What do you observe about the "triple tradition" parables (Figure 5) compared with the parables and sayings in Matthew and Luke (Figure 5)? b) Draw a graph or pie chart to show the two sources and compare them with the (L) parables.

[1] The origin of the parables

A) O.T. connections and antecedents
Evans **(5)** links twelve of the parables in the Journey Narratives with Deuteronomy (Figure 4) saying Luke edited his

material to show that Jesus was the promised prophet like Moses. However, it could be that Luke follows Deuteronomy in the travel section because Luke interacts with the theology of election and he wants to show that the gospel extends to the supposedly non elect-Gentiles.

1) The parable of the Good Samaritan may have its roots in the O.T. (2 Chron.28:8-15). [See Ch.11.]

2) In the parable of the wicked tenants, there are some words which are similar to Is. 5:1-7 "the song of the vineyard." In Isaiah, it is the people who are guilty and the prophecy is fulfilled in 586 B.C. when Nebuchadnezzar conquered Jerusalem. Here it is the Jewish authorities who are the wicked tenants.

3) In the parable of the sower (8:4-8, 11-15), Evans **(6)** says that Jesus probably saw Himself and His rejected message as a parallel to Isaiah the rejected prophet (Is.6:11-13b). As Isaiah referred to the judgement of Assyrian invasion on Israel and later to the Babylonian destruction of and the coming of a "holy seed" (Is.6:13c), so Jesus' words of judgement could refer to the second destruction of Jerusalem by the Romans and the parable of the sower. The three soils represent the three requirements in the Great Commandment in Deut.6:4-5. (Gerhardsson) **(7)** (1) The fruitless soil does not "love the Lord with all his heart;" the rocky ground lacks endurance, "does not love the Lord with all his soul." (Evans) **(8)** The seed choked by the thorns, "Does not love the Lord with all his might," could reflect Is. 55:10-11; Jer.4:3. "Break up your unploughed ground, and do not sow among thorns."

B) Rabbinic sources: Not one single parable has come down to us from the period before Jesus. (Jeremias) **(9)** The first parable outside the N.T. does not occur until Jochannan ben Zakkai A.D.80.

C) Were there Greek and Semitic antecedents? Jesus was the first person to teach by parables and stories. There may have been Greek and also Semitic antecedents but there is no evidence of anyone using parables as an approach in teaching in the first-century before Jesus. Did Jesus draw His themes and structures from a Jewish source? Some say His approach was entirely new as there are no parables in Qumran and in the Apocryphal books.

D) Every day life and events in Palestine including domestic issues set in rural and urban situations
These would have included leaven, the lost coin, the lamp and the measure in a home situation, the mustard seed and the sower, the rich fool, the lost sheep from an agricultural situation and some parables combining the two environments–the lost son contrasting the far country and urban life style with the farming background.

E) Jewish inter-testamental apocryphal writings: parables are unique to the Similitudes of Enoch (after A.D. 30).

F) Jewish pseudopigraphic writings - Binding the strong man (11:21-23) may be based upon the Ps. of Solomon 12:28 dated (50 B.C.) or upon Is. 53:12.

G) Source theory and the parables: Streeter's Two-Four Source theory said that fourteen of the parables in Luke were from "Q" source": for example, the Good Samaritan, the Rich Fool, and the Unjust Judge. Matthew and "Q" could have overlapped with Matthew using "Q" and Luke using (L). (Bock) **(10)** These include many fresh sayings and parables of Jesus. Luke changes and improves the style of passages in Mark and in "Q." He abbreviates Mark and omits details which are non-essential to his purpose as in the parable of the Sower below.

The Sower

Luke 8: 4-15	**Mark 4:1-20** **(Figure 6)**
4. And when a great crowd came together and people from town after town came to Him, He said in a parable: 5. A sower went out to sow his seed; and as he sowed, some fell along the path, and was trodden under foot, and the birds of the air devoured it. 6. And some fell on the rock; and as it grew up it withered away, because it had no moisture. 7. And some fell among thorns; and the thorns grew with it and choked it. 8. And some fell into good soil and grew and yielded hundredfold. "As He said this, He called out, 'He who has ears to hear let him hear.'" 9. And when the disciples asked Him what this parable meant, 10. He said, "To **you** has been given to **know** (Gk.gnoai) **the secrets (Gk. musteria) of the kingdom of God;** but for others they are in parables, so that **(Gk.hina** in order that, purpose) **seeing they may not see and hearing they may not understand."**	1. And He began to teach beside the sea. And a very large crowd gathered about Him, so that He got into a boat and sat in it on the sea ; and the whole crowd was beside the sea on the land. 2. And He taught them many things in parables, and in His teaching He said to them: 3. "Listen! A sower went out to sow. 4. and as he sowed, some seed fell along the path, and the birds came and devoured it. 5. Other seed fell on rocky ground, where it had not much soil, and immediately it sprang up, since it had no depth of soil; 6. and when the sun rose it was scorched, and since it had no root it withered away. 7. Other seed fell among the thorns and the thorns grew up and choked it, and it yielded no grain. 8. And other seeds fell into good ground, growing up and increasing and yielding thirtyfold and sixtyfold and a hundredfold." 9. "And He said," He who has ears to hear, let him hear.' " 10. And when He was alone, those who were about Him with the twelve asked Him concerning the parables. 11. And He said to them, "To **you** has been given **the secret of the kingdom of God,** but for those outside everything is in parables ; 12. so that **(Gk.hina)** they may indeed see but not perceive and may indeed hear but not understand: lest they should turn again and be forgiven." 13. And He said to them, "Do you not understand this parable? How then will you understand all the parables?
11. Now the parable is this: The seed is the word of God. 12. The ones along the path are those who have heard; the devil comes and takes the word away from their hearts, **that (Gk.hina)** they may not believe and be saved. 13. And the ones on the rock those who, when they hear the word receive it with joy; but these have no root, they believe for a while and in time of temptation fall away. 14. And as for what fell among thorns, they are those who hear, but are choked by the cares and riches and pleasures of life, and their fruit does not mature. 15. And as for that in the good soil, they are those who on hearing the word, **hold it fast in an honest and good heart**, and bring forth fruit with patience.	14. The sower sows the word. 15. And these are the ones along the path, where the word is sown; when they hear, Satan immediately comes and takes away the word which is sown in them. 16. And these in like manner are those sown in rocky ground, who when they hear the word immediately receive it with joy; 17. And they have no root in themselves, but endure for a while; then when tribulation or persecution arises on account of the word immediately they fall away. 18. And others are the ones sown among thorns; they are those who hear the word, 19. but the cares of the world, and the delight in riches, and the desire for other things, enter in and choke the word, and it proves unfruitful. 20. But those that were sown upon good soil are the ones who hear the word and **accept** it and bear fruit, thirtyfold and sixtyfold and a hundredfold."

Pupil's Activity: Five

Four of Luke's parables overlap with Matthew but Matthew shows them in fresh light. [See Figure 7.]
a) Select similar abbreviations in both accounts for example Luke 8:10 has secrets or mysteries meaning parts of the plan while Mark 4:10 has "secret" meaning the whole plan. b) How does Luke improve the style of some of the passages in Mark? c) What details does Luke omit in this parable? d) Look up 8: 8:4-21 especially vs 11,18, 21 to see how all thee passages deal with hearing and obeying the word of God. In Palestine sowing always precedes ploughing and the farmer would have intentionally sown on the path. When he ploughs up the path, he will plough up the seed!

A comparison between the "Q" parables   (Figure 7)

	Ref.	Title	Comment
1	12:39-40	The thief in the night	Matt. 24:53 the images in Matt./L are similar but the vocabulary is very different. On the basis of this Marshall suggests two different versions of "Q" **(11)** Matt. 24: 44 is like 12: 40 apart from word order and a different introductory term "But know this." Matthew has "therefore." The stewards are referred to in 12: 41-46. This is a parable about stewardship and faithfulness to God.
2	14:15-24	The great supper	Deep contrast with Matt. 22 where many servants are sent.
3	15:1-7	The lost sheep	Luke has "lost sinners" where Matt. 18:12-14 has "wayward believers." Two traditions may have existed. (Marshall) **(12)** "It is God's will that none of these little ones should perish." The disciples are to exercise pastoral care over the weaker members of the community, harming no member.
4	19:11-27	The pounds	There are too many differences with Matt. 25:14-15 which suggests two traditions of "Q": Matthew and Luke used two different "Q"s.

H) A chiastic source especially for the parables is unique to the central section. [See Ch.10 [Figure 5] Journey Narrative Luke 9:51-19:44 based upon Liefeld's theory.] (Talbert) **(13) (Figure 8)** Gooding however says that this kind of symmetrical structure approach does not cast further light on or further emphasis on the detail of the chiasmus. Gooding queries the whole point of the symmetry, (Gooding) **(14)** but feels they might have been used as a teaching aid. He takes the example from 4:31-41- 6:17-49 compared this section with 8:26-39-8:4-8,16-21. Gooding's argument is upheld in Figure 8: the barren fig tree and the lost sheep do not correspond within the chiasmus.

(Figure 8)

A The Good Samaritan (10: 25-37) The Samaritan outcasts are seen as heroes.

  B The Friend at Midnight (11:5-8) Prayer

    C The Rich Fool (13:12-21). Riches

      D Watchful Servants (12:35-38)

        E Barren Fig Tree (13:6-9)

          F The Great Banquet (14:7-24) The climactic centre of the chiasmus has the theme of reversal, poor/rich, Christ's return.

        E The lost sheep, coin and son (15:1-13) [Three parallel texts on repentance: two short and one long]

      D The unjust steward (16:1-13) Servant parables: the right and wrong use of stewardship

    C The Rich Man and Lazarus (16:19-31): Eternal danger due to the misuse of riches

  B The unjust judge (18:1-8): God will vindicate His elect quickly. The Son of Man will be looking for those who are looking for Him (18:8). Prayer

A The Pharisee and the Publican (18:9-14) Jewish leaders are seen as bad role models. Outcasts

I) O.T. parables

The O.T. has seven parables which are antecedents to the parables of Jesus but only Nathan's parable of the poor man and his ewe lamb is a true parallel with the parables of Jesus (2 Sam. 12:1-10).

Pupil's Activity: Six

a) Outline your knowledge and understanding of any two parables of God's mercy as recorded in Luke's Gospel.
(CCEA 2001 and 2004 Resit)   [30 marks]
b) Explore the claim that Jesus used these parables because they are simple stories with a clear message. Justify your answer. (CCEA 2004 Resit)   [15 marks]
c) Expore the claim that these parables show Jesus as a compassionate teacher. Justify your answer.
(CCEA 2001)   [15 marks]   [See Ch.18 :Forgiveness pp. 267-68.]

[2] Five ways of classifying the parables in Luke: firstly, classification by type

A) Snodgrass **(15)** has identified four main types of parable. **(Figure 9)**

	Type	Ref.	Example from text-definition and comment
1	similitude	a) 5:36 b) 5:37-39 c) 5:18-19 d) 13:20-21	a) The patch on the new garment b) New wine in old wineskins c) The kingdom of heaven is like a mustard seed. d) The kingdom of heaven is like leaven (yeast). A similitude is an extended simile using "like" and "as" which relates to a typical or recurring event, for example (13:19, 22).
2	An "example" story called by Julicher an examplary story.	a) 10:37 b) 12:13-21 c) 16:31 d) 18:10-14	a) These are all (L) parables. They have a positive or a negative ending either as an example to be imitated or one to be avoided, e.g. the Good Samaritan "Go and do likewise." b) The rich fool "Fool! This night your soul is required of you." c) The rich man and Lazarus- "If they do not hear Moses and the prophets, neither will they be convinced if someone should rise from the dead." d) The Pharisee and tax collector, "For everyone who exalts himself will be humbled and he who humbles himself will be exalted."
3	extended metaphor	a) 15: 15-24	The Great Banquet – a parable which refers to fictional events in the past to express a moral or spiritual truth in that it shows Jesus' care for the outcast, downtrodden, unfortunate and the poor. • Julicher **(16)** calls these 'synecdoche' the name for the part of the whole or the one for the many. • Madeleine Boucher **(17)** calls them 'extended synecdoches' says they present one particular example to illustrate a general principle.
4	allegory	a) 8:4-8 b) 15:11-32 (The prodigal son) c) 11:5-10 (The importunate friend)	a) Some scholars in the past argued for only one meaning of all the parables but some e.g. the parable of the sower can be seen as allegories to show four different receptions of the word of God. Boucher says that allegory is not a literary device at all but a device of meaning. All parables are allegories either as a whole or in their parts: they are stories with two levels of meaning; (1) at story level as a mirror to perceive reality (2) at a spiritual level. Any parable which has a literal and a metaphorical meaning is an allegory. The rhetorical purpose of the parable distinguishes it from the allegory. b) Boucher **(18)** sees this parable as an allegory. On one level it is the story of a lost son's return to his father on the other it is a lesson about God's merciful love towards repentant sinners. (15:11-32) c) Boucher sees the parable as an allegory. At one level there is the story of a man asking a reluctant friend for three loaves of bread at an inconvenient time; on another level it is a precept on persistent prayer.

Second classification: by themes [See p. 163.]

B) Jeremias **(19)** identified ten themes in the parables. He also saw four parables dealing with God's mercy

Pupil's Activity: Seven

Identify other mercy parables. **(Figure 10)**

	Theme	Refs.	Title and comments
1	"Now is the day of salvation."	a) 5:36-38 ; b) 8:16-18 ; c) 11:33-36	a) Unshrunk cloth/new wine b) Lamp - " Take heed then how you hear; " - obedience c) Lamp on stand - "be careful lest the light in you be darkness."
2	God's love for sinners	a) 7:41-43; b) 14:16-24; c) 15:11-32; d) 18:9-14	a) The two debtors "The one to whom he forgave more will love more." b) The wedding banquet "None of those men who were invited shall taste my banquet." c) The prodigal son - forgiveness d) The Pharisee and the tax collector - humility
3	The great assurance	a) 11:5-8; b) 13:18-19; c) 13:20-21; d) 18:7-10	a) The friend at midnight - "For everyone who asks receives." b) Mustard seed c) Leaven (yeast) d) Humble servant
4	The immanence of catastrophe	a) 11:34-36; b) 12:16-21; c) 12:49-50,54-56; d) 13:60-69	a) Light and darkness b) The rich fool c) The coming crisis d) Reading the times like the weather
5	It may be too late!	a) 13:6-9; b) 14:15-24	a) The barren fig tree b) The wedding banquet

Pupil's Activity: Eight

a) What can be learned from the teaching of Jesus about the nature of forgiveness in the (1) Parable of the of the Lost Son (Edexcel 2003) (A/S)   [7 marks]

b) Why was Jesus' teaching on forgiveness so controversial at this time? (Edexcel 2003) (A/S)   [6 marks]

	Theme	Refs.	Title and comments
6	The challenge of the hour	a) 6:47-49; b) 11:24-26; c) 12:58-59; d) 16:1-8; e) 16:19-31; f) 17:7-10	a) The wise and foolish builders b) The returning spirits c) Call to settle with the accuser d) The crafty steward e) The rich man and Lazarus f) The humble servant
7	Realized discipleship	a) 10:25-37; b) 12:24-30	a) The good Samaritan b) Earthly possessions and heavenly treasure
8	The Via Dolorosa and exultation of the Son of Man	a) 9:58; b) 17:25	a) Warning about alienation from the world-the homelessness of the Son of Man who has no where to lay His head b) The Son of Man must suffer many things and be rejected by this generation.
9	The consummation	a) 6:20-26; b) 14:11; c) 17:26-30	a) Four beatitudes and four woes b) Taking the last seat c) The nature of the coming of the kingdom - Noah's day and Lot's day
10	Parabolic actions	a) 15:1-2; b) 19:5-6; c) 19:45-48	a) Approach to sinners and tax collectors/Grumbling of the Pharisees and scribes b) Jesus' initiative to stay with Zacchaeus c) Temple cleansing

C) Thirdly, classification by categorization: Dodd's five-fold category

	Theme	Explanation
1	Kingdom parables	describe the kingdom of God
2	Kyrios parables	compare God to an owner or someone in authority
3	Growth parables	focus on nature, food, or fish and make comparisons with the kingdom of God
4	Crisis parables	allude to the tension of awaiting Jesus' return or to the need for immediate decision.
5	Seed parables	compare the handling of God's message to the growth of seed.

D) Fourthly classification by movement of imagery: Crossan

Imagery	Example	Classification
1. advent parable	Kingdom parable	An advent parable describes the Kingdom that has come. The kingdom is like a mustard seed, the kingdom is like a sower.
2. reversal	Moral parables	The rich man and Lazarus, Prodigal son, Vineyard, Good Samaritan
3. action	Decision parables	Servant parables and Lord parables

E) Fifthly, classification: by literary structure: Blomberg (A2 level CCEA)

Blomberg **(22)** views the parables of Jesus like the rabbinic parables as allegories, which usually have two or three points to make depending on the number of main characters in the parable. This view is based upon literary criticism and follows the laws of structure. He argues that there are a limited number of allegories in the parables. A monarchic parable is told from the perspective of one figure.

(1) Triadic and monarchic

(1) Triadic parables have three main characters as in the prodigal son, if the parable is a record for the Samaritans then it is a model of compassion, if it seen from the injured man's perspective it means even an enemy can be your neighbour, if from the perspective priest and Levite then religious duty is no excuse for lovelessness. A monarchic parable has an authority figure usually a king, father or mother who acts as a judge between two subordinates.

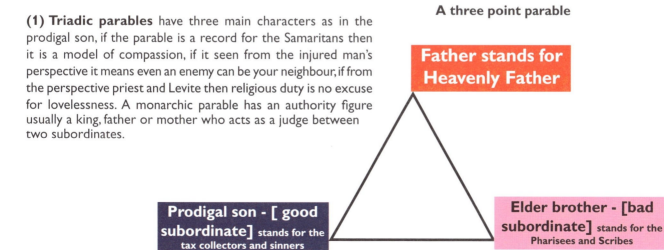

A three point parable

Father stands for Heavenly Father

Prodigal son - [good subordinate] stands for the tax collectors and sinners

Elder brother - [bad subordinate] stands for the Pharisees and Scribes

(2) A triadic and a non-monarchic parable

In **(2)** there is a master character, the Samaritan, two contrasting subordinates, the injured man, the priest and Levite. The central figure is not elevated, he/she can act as a judge between the other passers-by but is not in authority over them. Jesus answers the question who is my neighbour (10:29) and not how to inherit eternal life (10:25).

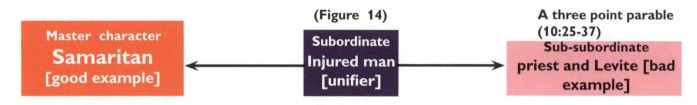

(Figure 14)

| Master character **Samaritan** [good example] | ← Subordinate **Injured man** [unifier] → | A three point parable (10:25-37) Sub-subordinate **priest and Levite** [bad example] |

(3) A dyadic and a monarchic parable

A two point parable (18:9-14)

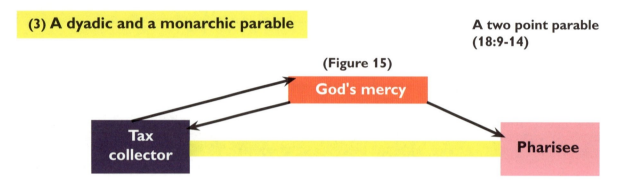

(Figure 15)

God's mercy

Tax collector   **Pharisee**

B) Dyadic parables – feature two people or a person and an object for example the tax collector and the Pharisee (18:9-14). This is a two point parable in **(3)**

The parable of the creditor and the two debtors, the creditor is the master and the subordinate is the servant forgiven the large debt and the sub-subordinate is the servant owing the small debt (7:35-50). This is a nonmonarchic parable. It is a dyadic parable. Justification only comes by throwing yourself on the mercy of God as in the parable of the tax collector and the Pharisee (18:9-14).

In the Children's Game in the market place the playmates stand for Jesus and John the Baptist. The children who do not want to play the game stand for Jesus' and John's contemporaries who rejected them (7:31-35; Matt. 11:16-19). The parable of the unjust judge teaches about God's character and the widow shows the proper response of God's people (18:1-8).

C) Monadic parables have one main character, for example Treasure hunter (Matt. 13:44), the pearl (Matt. 13:45-46), the mustard seed - the farmer (13:18-19) and the yeast - the housewife (13:20-21). The point of these parables is the inherent power in the seed as seen in Jesus healing the woman with the bent back, which precedes the parable of the mustard seed (13:14-16). The yeast shows the inherent power of the kingdom (13:21), the tower builder and the warring king (14:18-23) are one point parables.

[3] The purpose of the parables in Luke's Gospel

A) Some features regarding Luke's special (L) source are parables which are not often introduced as kingdom parables but as Jeremias says they are equally full of the kingdom. The purpose of the parables is to provide signs to be heard. "If you have ears to hear-" and the parables compel the hearers to come to a decision about the person and mission of Jesus (10:23). (Jeremias) **(23)** Jesus used parables for instruction, exhortation and defence. (Jeremias) **(24)** The purpose of the parables comes out in the parable of the sower to teach people about the kingdom of God and to communicate effectively about that kingdom. Jesus used parables as a form of good story telling. The use of parables demonstrate that whenever Jesus depicts the goodness of God, this is seen as Jesus "seeking the lost." (19:10; Ezek.34) Jesus went on to tell the parable of the pounds. Parables provide a pattern for the ministry of Jesus in which some people receive the meaning, while others do not. This was also the pattern of Jesus' ministry as a whole, some respond while others do not, others are blind and refuse.

B) The parables were designed to help people see (8:10b). Jesus concludes the parable of the Sower by saying "so that seeing they might not see and hearing they may not understand." The secrets and mysteries of the kingdom are known (8:10a), "to you (plural) have been given to know the secrets of the kingdom of God; but for others they are in parables." Jesus used parables to make people think: they require a response, "He who has ears to hear let him hear." Jesus teaches in parables as a gift to some and a judgement to others. This verse refers to two different types of people:

1) those to whom the mystery is given: those on the inside who understand the interpretation.

2) those who are on the outside, to whom everything is in parables. The parables are a form of judgement where the story is perceived but not understood. [See Figure 6 p. 160.]

The interpretation was addressed to the disciples in all three Synoptic Gospels. The context here is one of different responses to the word of God. In Scripture, election and freewill run on parallel tracks and appear to us as antinomies (seemingly contradictory); both are taught. The outsider's failure to understand is a sign of God's judgement on the people's hardness of heart as it was in the prophet Isaiah's situation in Is. 6:9-10. God in judgement removes the benefit of revelation. (Fitzmyer) **(25)**

C) In Luke's Gospel, the three parables-lost sheep, lost coin and lost son are all responses to the Pharisees and Scribes when they object to Jesus eating and drinking with tax collectors and sinners. In Luke, the lost sheep refers to the sinners with whom Jesus ate and not "the small child" as in Matthew.

D) Jesus used parables to answer those who confronted him, "This man receives sinners and eats with them." (15:2)

E) Some of the parables are warnings to the wealthy: the rich fool (12:16-21), the unjust manager (16:1-12), the rich man and Lazarus (16:19-35). Luke does not accept an order in society in which riches are esteemed and poverty despised. God has His way of upsetting our sociological distinctions and finding His saints in unexpected places. (C.M.M.) **(26)** [p.25]

[4] The parables of God's mercy for sinners in Luke's Gospel (Figure 16) [See pp. 152-3, 267-8.]

	Title	To whom was it addressed and situation	Refs.	Sources and comments
1	The healthy need the physician (a saying)	The teachers of the law who were Pharisees–in the house of Levi	5:31	Mark 2:16 ; Matt. 9:9-13 Only Luke uses Gk. hugiainontes for "healthy." This is a 3rd century A.D. proverb by Antisthenes. (Danker) **(27)** "Doctors associate with the sick but do not contract fevers."
2	The two debtors	Simon the Pharisee	7:41-50	(L)
3	The good Samaritan	The lawyer	10:25-37	(L)
4	The great banquet	An unknown person at table in the house of a Pharisee	14:16-24; 22:1-14	Luke + Matt.= "Q"
5	The lost sheep	The scribes and Pharisees	15:1-7; 18:12-14	Luke + Matt.= "Q" Is. 40:11; Ezek.34
6	The lost coin	The scribes and Pharisees	15:8-10	(L); Ezek.34
7	The prodigal son	The scribes and Pharisees	15:11-32	(L) Is. 40:11; 49: 22; Ezek.34
8	Pharisee/publican	The Pharisees	18:10-14	(L)
9	The wicked tenants	In reply to the chief priests, teachers of the law, and the elders.	20:9-19	Matt. 21:33-46; Mk. 12:1-12; Luke uses Is. 5:1-7 Song of the vineyard

The three parables in Luke 15 are based on Luke's theme of God's love for the outcasts and sinners (1) the lost sheep (15:4-7) (2) the lost coin (15:8-10) and (3) the lost son (15:11-32). Luke assures his readers of God's love and acceptance of them. These parables show that God accepts all the repentant sinners, no matter how outcast they may be. God's mercy is now described in these three parables and this ties in with Luke's emphasis on God's love and grace for the marginalized. (14:12-14, 21-23) God has shown His mercy (1:50,54, 58,72,78) by visiting the needy. (1:51-53) [See p. 262.]

Pupils Activity: Eight
Look for and identify a common audience in the contexts of these parables in Luke.

Pupils Activity: Nine
a) What does "prodigal" mean? Why do you think that this parable has also been called the "Merciful and Prodigal Father"? Complete the story predicting how you think it should end.
b) Outline your knowledge and understanding of either the parable of the Good Samaritan or the parable of the Prodigal Son. (CCEA 2002 Resit) (A/S)   [30 marks]
c) Explore the claim that the parables of Jesus were designed to provoke a response from the listener. Justify your answer. (CCEA 2002 Resit)   (A/S)   [15 marks]

(1) The first mercy parable in Luke - the parable of the two debtors (Read 7:41-50.)
The setting: in the house of Simon the Pharisee, when Jesus allowed a sinful woman to anoint His feet with an expensive perfume, costing a year's wage (7:38). Simon objected to the woman touching Jesus, especially if Jesus were a prophet. Jesus was able to read the thoughts of Simon (7:39). Jesus' failure to rebuke the woman shows He is not a prophet and for Simon, Jesus does not have the status of a prophet, otherwise He would not have allowed this woman to touch Him. The Pharisees had a theological objection: as devout and religious people they have nothing to do with sinners. Separationism or "we ourselves" was the name of their game. [See pp. 261-62.]

The contents of the parable

A) Two people are in debt. The first man's debt is for five hundred denarii which is ten times that of the second man who owed fifty denarii (approx. two months wage fifty denarii). Five hundred denarii was an unimaginable sum for a Palestinian peasant. The twist in the tail of the parable comes when the creditor wipes out both debts and forgives both men. **(Figure 20)**

Comparable Salaries in the first century	Amount	
Pilate, Roman procurator under Caesar Augustus	15,000-75,000 denarii (Nolland) **(28)**	Per year
State office holder under Pilate	2,500- 10,000 denarii	Per year
Labourer's/soldier's wage	1 denarium	Per day
Debt of first man	500 denarii	Labourer's wage 2 years
Debt of second man	50 denarii	Labourer's wage 50 days

B) Jesus compares the forgiveness of sins to economic forgiveness. The debtor has no bargaining position; only grace can remove the debt. Which debtor has the greater love? Simon the Pharisee replies. "The one to whom he forgave more." Greater forgiveness provides opportunity for great love. Jesus pursues sinners and welcomes them so that they may realise God's gracious forgiveness. Jesus explains why He openly associates with sinners (7:41-43). The woman has gone beyond the call of duty in showing humility and gratitude. She appreciates Jesus' offer of grace and seeks to honour it with devotion and love. Her actions reflect her experience of forgiveness from Jesus. Jesus commends her for her faith in action (7:50).

C) Jesus shows how to relate to people and combines ethics and theology. He shows His power and authority in saying that the woman's sins are forgiven. Here is Jesus forgiving sin, an act that only God can do, thus taking this authority unto Himself and making Himself equal with God.

D) Jesus challenges the Pharisee's idea of sin. The Pharisee saw himself as a little sinner (7:47b). "He who is forgiven little, loves little." The Pharisee judged the woman to gain a good feeling about himself." The heavenly Father will forgive debts when people turn to Him. **Forgiveness here is a synonym for salvation which comes through faith. (Stein)**

E) Simon's love was minimalist while that of the woman was maximalist. Simon had never seen himself as a debtor before God as the woman had. She was deeply aware of her need. Love is the fruit of faith and not prior to faith. Like the two debtors the woman had been liberated from the chains which bound her. Jesus' tender mercy towards her is a good example of His concern for broken lives. The Messiah had come to meet need at its deepest level. Simon on the inside track to forgiveness and salvation, is found outside of God's kingdom. The outcast woman found forgiveness, "Your faith has saved you ; go in peace." (7:50) Forgiveness here is a synonym for salvation which comes through faith. (Stein) **(29)** Jesus' Ministry spans gender diversity, social status and gives evidence of a growing division within Israel, "Who is this, who even forgives sins?" (7:49)

In 15:7, the parable concludes with the saying there will be joy in heaven over one sinner who repents than over ninety-nine righteous people who do not see the need for repentance.

(2) Luke's second mercy parable: the lost sheep shows the deep compassion of Jesus. (Read 15:4-7.)

A shepherd has one hundred sheep and one goes astray. The average flock was between 20-200 sheep in the Jewish tradition and 300 hundred was thought to be a large herd. In this parable Jesus shows the importance of the individual. The context of the parable is that of the scribes' and Pharisees' annoyance at Jesus eating with sinners, the Pharisees wanting to see the sinners destroyed not rescued. The shepherd was personally responsible for the sheep and would risk his neck for his sheep. As many of the flocks were communal, belonging to the villages, the whole village would rejoice when the shepherd would return home with his sheep across his shoulders.

Some differences between Luke and Matthew: the context in Luke is that of the repentant sinner (15:4-7) while in Matt. 18:10-14 it is that of the disciples going astray. In 15:7, the parable concludes with the saying "there will be joy in heaven over one sinner who repents than over ninety-nine righteous people who do not see the need for repentance." (15:6) Matthew concludes, "he rejoices over it more than over the ninety-nine that never went astray." The sheep was heedlessly lost or lost through "sheer folly." (Barclay) **(30)** The owner throws a party and invites the neighbours to celebrate. Heaven throws a party, when a sinner returns to God. The joy is a future joy (15:7).

Understanding the parable (Read 15:1-3.): the Pharisees were annoyed that Jesus was more in the company of the common people than He was with them. They did not expect common people to be in God's kingdom. (15:1-3) The Pharisees, for all their religious observance, never brought joy to God. Table fellowship in the Middle-East means to offer peace, trust, brotherhood and forgiveness. Jesus' meals with people indicate His Mission and Message. It is risky being a lost sheep as the sheep were attacked by predators. Jesus is pointing out what God is like. God rejoices when a lost person or sinner is found, as a shepherd is when a strayed sheep is found. The lost sheep receives special attention over those that are safe. Jesus' use of the shepherd image might have been inspired by Ezek. 34:11-16; Is. 40:11, "I will search for my sheep, and will seek them out .... I will seek the lost, and bring back the strayed." (Tiede) **(31)** [See p. 267.]

(3) Luke's third mercy parable : the lost coin (Read 15:8-10.) [See p. 167.]

It was a silver coin (Gk.drachma) which may have represented ten percent of the woman's savings or a day's wage for an average worker. The coin would have been one day's wage. (Josephus) (32) These coins were not circular and would not roll very far. The coin could be of more value than its monetary worth. It was one in ten while the sheep was one in one hundred. The woman had lost it but knew that it was somewhere in the house. She continues on a deliberate search, lights a lamp to help her see in a house without windows. She sweeps the house probably with a broom made of palm twigs to see if the coin fell into a corner. She goes to great lengths, searching diligently until she finds it. "Sweeping the house thoroughly until it is found" shows slightly more stress on the search in this parable than in the lost sheep. Recovering a sinner can take a lot of effort but it is worthwhile. The joy of finding it is emphasised and joy is a keynote in Luke's Gospel. The joy here is that of the present indicating that the sinners repentance brings present and future joy. It is the response of the angels and God. The priority of a disciple to find lost "sheep" and missing "coins," as Jesus practised during His Ministry and is required of His disciples today (12:8). The coin may have been part of the headdress and if so would be like losing a diamond from a wedding ring today! The search shows the Messiah's determination to pursue His Mission.

The parable contrasts with the approach of the Pharisees whose religious profession shows no compassion. Jesus is again rejecting the Pharisees' attitude to women in first-century society which was to treat them as inferior. The woman is a village peasant, living in a house with no windows. The Pharisees never plumbed the depths of Jesus' compassion nor did they understand the true nature of repentance because they never saw themselves as sinners. Jesus was always an enigma to them. The parable reflects God's search for people and is an example of "seeking mercy." (Barclay) (33)

Like the shepherd who gathers his male friends to celebrate, the woman gathers her lady friends (Gk.philas) and lady neighbours (Gk.geitonas) around her to celebrate the discovery of the lost coin. There is a gender difference with the parable of the lost sheep. So there is rejoicing in the presence of the angels over one repentant sinner. God's courts in heaven are full of praise when a sinner turns to Him. Barclay notes that the coin was lost through no fault of its own: people can be led astray and taught to sin by others. The coin was helplessly lost in that it could not speak for itself. (34) [See p. 236.]

God's courts in heaven are full of praise when a sinner turns to Him.

(4) Luke's fourth mercy parable: the lost son (Read 15:11-32.) [See pp. 267-68.]

This is a parable about the merciful father's response to his two sons. The younger son requests to have his share of the estate (the boy is single and in late teens). He asks for the portion of what his father's life (Gk.ton bion) will leave him (Deut. 21:17) which would be about one third of the elder brother's portion. Jews were not encouraged to divide their estate and distribution did not normally happen until death. In this parable the father grants the son his request. This is a picture of God letting the sinner go his own way.

Having divided the living or the property between the two sons, the father watches the son depart. The son soon loses everything in "loose living." The text says he scattered his resources and squandered his inheritance - it has the idea of tossing one's possessions in the wind. Natural disaster follows and "severe" famine strikes the land and he is in need. With no money, no family and suffering in a distant land, he hits rock bottom and has nowhere to turn. He resorts to feeding pigs, a great dishonour for any Jew (Lev. 11:7; Deut. 14:8; Is. 65:4; 66:17). "The swine is unclean to you." As a Jew working for a Gentile and caring for pigs, he can sink no further as he has taken the only job he can get. Even though he has a job he is still suffering and he longs (an idiom for hunger) "he intensely desired" (Gk.epithumeo) to eat the food of the pigs which was sweet beans from the carob or locust trees or "bitter thorny berries." (Bailey) (35) A rabbinic parallel said, "When Israelites resort to eating carob pods they repent." (Leviticus Rabbah 13.3) Even unclean animals are better off than he is. His condition is like that of the sinner. He reflects to himself even his father's servants are better off than he is. He is alone just like being outside of God's family with no one to help (15:16). The son was wilfully lost.

His plan of action is to confess his sin before his father and express his unworthiness

His plan of action is to confess his sin before his father and express his unworthiness This action showed his humility. All he could rely upon was the mercy of the Father. He returns home, his father's reaction is very telling (15:20). At a distance the father saw him, had compassion ran, embraced and kissed him. Jeremias (36) sees this as a break with middle Eastern protocol. The father is pleased to see the son return and expresses his joy by greeting his son with a kiss of affection.

Evans (37) says this parable corresponds to Deut. 21:15-22:4, the status of the first-born son who is to be honoured over the second-born son and receive a "double portion" of the inheritance. A disobedient son is to be taken out and stoned to death (Deut.21: (18-21).

However, in Luke 15, the emphasis falls on mercy and forgiveness. (Evans) (38) Jesus is only correcting a misinterpretation of Deut.21 which is laying down a civil law for Israel and does not exclude the possibility of repentance, forgiveness and restoration. This could be the thinking behind the attitudes of the Pharisees. How could Jesus, a man of God, have fellowship with people who should be excluded from Jewish society or even stoned? The son continues with his confession and is satisfied to be a slave but the father restores him to full sonship. The father orders the servants to bring the best robe, a ring for his son's hand and sandals for his feet. A fatted calf is prepared (15:21). The note of joy is crucial in the passage as it is the father's restoration of the privileges of the son; the son comes from destitution to complete restoration. This parable is an example of God's grace and mercy for the repentant sinner.

> **The elder brother is self-righteous, self-consumed with issues like justice and equity.**

The Elder Son

The Elder Son has missed all the action as he has been working in the fields. He hears the singing and dancing (Gk.sumphonia). In (15:25) the word is used for band music and our word symphony comes from it. This word is used only once in the bible. A servant explains to the elder brother what is going on here. The elder brother is enraged and refuses to join in the festivities. The younger brother on the outside is now on the inside. The father's compassion is incomplete as he tries to placate the elder brother who complains that his brother gets a five star meal while he ends up with the equivalent of a beef burger! The elder brother is self-righteous, self-consumed with issues like justice and equity. Like the complaint of the synagogue leader of someone healed on the Sabbath day, he refers to his younger brother as, "this son of yours." (15:30)

The Father's acceptance of the Elder Brother:

His aim is to reconcile the two brothers. He accepts his elder son and all the Father has is his. We need to celebrate and be glad. "This brother of yours was dead and is alive again, he was lost and is found." Justice demands that the younger son be accepted with joy and celebration-the sinner welcomed back with joy into God's family.

The theological significance of the story:

Schmidt **(39)** the "Sondergut" (key theme) highlighting Jesus' mercy for sinners is noticeably great here: it is Jesus' mission "to seek and to save the lost." (19:10) Luke forges stronger ties than anyone else between forgiveness and conversion especially in the return of the prodigal son

Summary: there are two main focal points of the thee parables.

1) Repentance means a reversal of status. The lost son is welcome back to the family: that is God's grace. God pursues sinners because He is merciful.

2) Others should rejoice when the penitent returns. Reconciliation involves not only God and the individual but the individual and the community.

• The younger son was deliberately and wilfully lost, callously turning his back on the father. The story is left hanging in the air. We do not know if the elder brother is ever reconciled with his brother or if he comes to the feast or not. It is an open ending. The listeners are to consider their own response. "The potential of God's grace drives Him to love others and pursue them." (Bock) **(40)**

• God is more merciful in His judgements than many an orthodox man and woman; the love of God is broader than the love of man and woman. He can forgive when men and women refuse to forgive. The father leaves the feast to plead with the elder son to show his love and mercy. The resentment of the elder is too bitter to soften the father's pleas. The Pharisees had a wrong view of God thinking God was unwilling to forgive sinners. They upheld the honour of God but not His mercy. The parable brings out the fact that the Pharisees obscured the most important part of God's character, His love. As God is merciful and gracious so also should His offspring be.

> **The parable brings out the fact that the Pharisees obscured the most important part of God's character, His love.**

Pupils Activity: Ten

a) What was the setting for the three parables on lostness?
b) How do these three parables reflect Jesus' attitude to the fallen and despised?
c) Why did the prodigal son leave home and what led him to return?
d) What does the expression "he came to his senses," mean?
e) During all of the sons's absence how did the father view his son?

Pupils Activity: Eleven

a) Outline your knowledge and understanding of the parables of the "lost" in Luke's Gospel.
   (CCEA 2003 resit)   [30 marks]
b) Explore the claim that the aim of these parables is to show God's joy when people repent.
   (CCEA 2003 resit)   [15 marks]

(5) The fifth mercy parable in Luke: the Pharisee and the publican (Read 18:9-14.)

The setting: this parable follows on from a previous parable on prayer. Jesus told the parable to those who were over confident of their own righteousness (18:9). This parable has been called "an example story" with the punch line, "He who humbles himself will be exalted." (18:14) It is a parable of two people praying. The Pharisee, a respected religious member and an honoured social group, and the tax collector who belonged to the most undesirable professions possible for a Jew. It is a parable about the two contrasting prayers of two people who went into the Temple to pray. People could enter the Temple to pray in the Court of Israel at any time though public prayer took place at 9am. and 3pm. "The Pharisee prays towards the front of the Temple's Court of Israel, in a prominent place." (Fitzmyer) **(41)** The tax collector would have stood at the back of the Court of Israel.

The Pharisee's Prayer (Figure 19)

This parable has been called "an example story" with the punch line, "He who humbles himself will be exalted." (18:14)

The Pharisee of high religious rank:	The tax collector of low social rank:
relied on himself because he was self-righteous and despised others. (18:10)	one of the "others" viewed with contempt by the Pharisee (18:9,11).
stood and prayed thus (18:11a)	standing afar - he would not lift his eyes to heaven, but beat his breast. (18:13a)
"God, I thank you that (RSV) (because) I am not like other men, extortioners, unjust, adulterers, or even like this tax collector. I fast twice a week, I give tithes of all that I get." Bailey **(42)** translates that (Gk.hoti) as "because." (18:11b-12)	"God be merciful to me a sinner!" (18:13b)
thanks God for his state of righteousness (18:11b-12)	addresses God in humility as a sinner and with a sense of unworthiness, asks to be reconciled to God (18:14a).
returned home without justification (18:14a)	returned home justified (18:14a).
"All who exalt themselves will be humbled." (18:14b)	"All who humble themselves will be exalted."(18:14b)

Jesus is targeting the attitudes and dispositions of the Pharisees in this parable. He points out the danger of trusting our own abilities and not trusting God. Do not regard other people with contempt and disrespect, rather see them as made in the image of God. Everyone is an object of God's grace and mercy. [See pp. 123-124.]

The Pharisee's - praying, fasting and tithing. He starts his prayer as if it were a psalm of thanks in which God is praised for something He has done. The prayer shows trust in one's self. His prayer really was "Thank you God that I am the greatest, I am so marvellous and I have been spared from a corrupt life." (5:33) His fasting was beyond the call of duty, twice a week. Jews were only required to fast once a year on the Day of Atonement (5:33). He tithes everything right down to the tiniest herb (11:42) and makes no request from God and God does not have to do anything for him. He has prayed with himself. His reference to others is derogatory." I am not like others." He puts himself in one camp and castigates all others in the category of thieves (Gk.harpax), rogues (Gk.adikos) and adulterers (Gk.moios) "robbers, rogues and roués". He caricatures all kinds of sin as thieving, reprobation and immorality. Everyone else is guilty of all of these sins.

Here it is a plea for mercy from a self-confessing sinner who asks God to show him mercy through atoning forgiveness.

The Tax Collector's Prayer   (Read 18:13b-14a.)
By contrast he is aware that he is approaching a holy God. He comes timidly from a distance, not lifting his eyes to heaven. The Pharisees stand at the front while the tax collector stands afar off and would not lift his eyes to heaven showing his humility and sense of shame and in "beating his breast," to show his own sense of repentance. His prayer differs from the blind man outside Jericho. "Have mercy on me" (Gk.eleeson). Here the tax collector says, "God have mercy (Gk. hilaskomai) on me a sinner." (18:14). This is a technical word used to cover sin "to propitiate" or to satisfy anger. Like the man who had a row with his wife and bought her a box of chocolates, which he called his "propitiation gift", to placate his angry wife when he said sorry and asked her to forgive him. Here it is a plea for mercy from a self-confessing sinner who asks God to show him mercy through atoning forgiveness. (Bailey) **(43)** says the word refers to an atonement sacrifice. Jeremias **(44)** agrees. "Paul's doctrine of justification has its roots in the teaching of Jesus." The Pharisee fasted twice a day which was more than was necessary. Jesus condemns those whose lives are built upon arrogance and contempt for other people. The tax collector relies completely on the mercy of God: he asks for mercy and wants to improve his spiritual health, not rest upon his laurels. "His only access to God is by divine mercy and God's grace." (Dan.9:18-19) Jesus points out that only one person who prayed went home justified, the tax collector. The tax collector has a humble heart. He is honoured by God and as this is an example story, we are all called to be like the tax- collector. (Bock) **(45)** "There was no vestige of self-righteousness nor a list of human achievements-only a confession of need and an implied trust in the mercy of God." (Guthrie) **(46)** In the prayer of the tax collector we see the essence of grace: he admits his sinfulness and pleads for God's mercy. (Ellis) **(47)**

6) A sixth example of a mercy parable: [See the Good Samaritan pp. 123-5.]
Pupil's Activity: Twelve
a) What is a parable?
b) Give a detailed summary of a parable in Luke's Gospel and explain its meaning, justifying your definition of a parable.

Pupil's Activity: Thirteen
a) Read the parable of the wicked tenants (20:9-19). b) To whom does it refer and what does it imply about the status of Jesus? c) Complete (Figure 20) below to show how this parable can be linked to the O.T.
d) How were these prophecies fulfilled in Jesus? (Figure 20)

Ref.	Parable of the wicked tenants	Comment	(Figure 20)
Is. 5:1-7	The song of the vineyard	Which people are guilty?	
Lk. 20:9-19	The parable of the tenants	Which group are guilty and to whom was Jesus referring?	

Pupil's Activity: Fourteen

a) Select a triple tradition parable and show how Luke's account differs from that of Mark and Matthew. b) How do you account for the similarities and differences? c) For revision draw a spidergram to show the origins of the parables.

Outcomes

Pupils should know and understand the:

• **parables of mercy.**

• **Jesus as the compassionate teacher in Luke's Gospel. [See Ch.18: Forgiveness.]**

• **the different types of parable in Luke's Gospel.**

• **the key concepts, for example 'parable', similitude, example story, extended synecdoche, 'Dyadic', classification of the parables, joy in heaven.**

• **main points in two-three parables of mercy.**

• **the main purposes and aims of the parables and origins in Luke's Gospel.**

• **the nature of forgiveness in the teaching of Jesus in the parables. (Edexcel A/S)**

Notes on Ch. 12: the Parables in Luke's Gospel

1. W.S. Kissinger, the Parables of Jesus A History of Interpretation and Bibliography Series, Scarecrow/ATLA, pp. 108-110.

2. Darrell L. Bock, op. cit. pp. 948-9.

3. B. Gerhardsson, The Testing of God - An Analysis of an early Christian Midrash CBNT 2/1 Lund: Gleerup (1966) pp. 165-193.

4. Josephus, Ant. 17. 206-223. Many Jews disliked Herod the Great's son Archelaus when it was time for him to ascend the throne in 4 B.C. Fifty Jews were sent to Rome to protest to Augustus, who compromised by allowing Archelaus to rule only as ethnarch, implying that he would have to earn the title as king which never happened. Around this prominent event Jesus built a picture of the consequences of rejection.

5. Christopher F. Evans, St. Luke, T.P. INT Commentaries, SCM Press/Trinity Press based upon the RSV (1990) pp.50-51.

6. C. Evans op. cit. p.129 cites F. Eakin, pp.87-107 writing about the parable of the sower based upon Luke 8:4-8, 11-15.

7. B. Gerhardsson, (ibid.)

8. Christopher F. Evans, op. cit. p.128.

9. Joachim Jeremias, The Parables of Jesus, (Revised Edition) SCM Press, (1972) p.12.

10. Darrell L. Bock, Article on The Gospel of Luke, DJG, p.497.

11. I. Howard Marshall, op. cit. p.538.

12. I Howard Marshall, op.cit. pp.600-601.

13. Charles H. Talbert and Ken Bailey both follow Liefeld, op. cit. p.932.

14. David Gooding, op. cit. p.362.

15. K.R. Snodgrass, Article on Parable, DJB , IVP, (1992) pp.593-601 .

16. Julicher, op. cit, cited in Boucher p.22.

17. Madeleine Boucher, The Mysterious Parable, Washington DC. CBAA, (1977) p.22.

18. Madeleine Boucher, op. cit. p.21.

19. Joachim Jeremias, op. cit. (1963) pp. 115-229.

20. Charles H. Dodd, The Parables of the Kingdom, London: Nisbet, (1961) pp. 122-56.

21. John D. Crossan, In Parables :The Challenge of the Historical Jesus, New York : Harper and Row, (1973).

22. Craig L. Blomberg, Interpreting the Parables, Downers Grove, IVP, (1990).*

23. Joachim Jeremias, op. cit. p. 230.

24. Joachim Jeremias, op. cit. pp. 42-48.

25. Joseph A. Fitzmyer, op. cit. p. 708.

26. Donald Carson, Douglas Moo and Leon Morris, op. cit. p. 130.

27. F.W. Danker, op. cit. p.126.

28. John Nolland, Vol. 1, Word Biblical Commentary on Luke, Dallas (1989) p. 355.

29. Robert Stein, op. cit. p.239.

30. William Barclay, op. cit. p. 206.

31. D. L. Tiede, Luke, Augsburg Commentary on the NT Minneapolis: Ausburg, (1988) p.274.

32. Josephus, (Antiquities 3.8.2/195).

33. William Barclay, op. cit. p.203.

34. William Barclay, op. cit. p.204.

35. Kenneth Bailey, op. cit. pp. 172-3.

36. Joachim Jeremias, op. cit. p.130 on Luke 15:20.

37. Christopher F. Evans, op. cit. p.48.

38. Craig F. Evans, op. cit. p.234.

39. Peter Schmidt, How to read the Gospels, St. Pauls Press, Maynooth (1993) p.160.

40. Darrell L. Bock, op. cit. IVPNTCS p.262.

41. Joseph A. Fitzmyer, op. cit. p. 1186.

42. Kenneth Bailey, op. cit. p.154.

43. Kenneth Bailey, op. cit. p.130-157.

44. Joachim Jeremias, op. cit. p.114.

45. Darrell L. Bock, op. cit. p. 297.

46. Donald Guthrie, op. cit. p.227.

47. Earle Ellis, op. cit. p.214.

CCEA + Edexcel A/S level

> **Targets**:
> • **Recognise the meaning of the words for 'miracle' as used in Luke's Gospel.**
> • **Identify different classifications of the miracles in Luke's Gospel.**
> • **Recognise the role of faith in the healing miracles.**
> • **Recognise the nature of Jesus' ministry from the account of the Transfiguration in Luke's Gospel.**
> • **Recognise the types of miracle in Luke's Gospel and the different words for the reaction to those miracles.**
> • **Understand the meaning of the function, purpose and the characteristics of the miracles in Luke's Gospel.**
> • **Identify the role of faith in the healing miracles and the key concepts.**

The Function, Purpose and Characteristics of Miracles in Luke's Gospel

Introduction

Two thousand years ago Jesus, a worker of miracles, healed people in public and in private as examples of His power and authority. Some people believed what they saw, others believed through what they saw but others were not quite so certain. Before we consider whether Jesus performed miracles or not we need to be certain what a miracle is.

Defining and identifying a miracle

Pupil's Activity: One   **Class discussion**
A) Are the following miracles?:
• a new scientific achievement - the cloning of Dolly the sheep - finding a cure for cancer.
• a great personal or corporate achievement - passing your examination with an A* grade-your school winning the Schools' Cup.
• an unusual event - being let off a homework.
• a seemingly impossible sporting achievement-a local football club beats Manchester United in the European Cup final.
• a Harry Potter magic spell.

Pupil's Activity: Two   **Class discussion**
B) What is a miracle?
• Is a miracle something which we do not fully understand for example how electricity works or making a tree, a plant or a seed to grow?
• Is it a scientific invention for example a hole in the heart operation?
• Is a miracle something that was impossible just a few years ago but is now part of every day life such as going to the moon?
• Is a miracle an unexpected event, like the ice skater in the last Winter Olympics who was at the rear for most of the race but won the gold medal because all the other skaters were involved in a pile up?
• Is it a miracle when you say, "everything that exists is a miracle"?
• Is a miracle a "freak of nature"?
• Is a person's personal charisma a miracle, for example David Beckham and Victoria Spice, Sir Alex.?
These are not real miracles even though they cause us to wonder.

Pupil's Activity: Three   **Class discussion**
C) What is a real miracle?
Discuss these definitions of miracle. Are these definitions real miracles?
• An act which is unique in itself. You have been able to train your pet cat to sing songs from the charts.
• An act which is unique and exclusive in itself of an other person or thing. You discover that you can fly like a bird without any assistance.
• An act which is beyond the power of man or woman to bring it about.
• A woman who gives birth to a child when all medical experts have said that it is impossible to conceive.
• An act which cannot be explained through science and which defies the laws of nature. Someone who has had a marvellous cure from cancer.
• An act of God performed for the good of His creatures. Someone who has been "brain dead" for two days and he/she is able to continue a normal life style.
• An act in which the person healed or rescued sees the experience as significant for the religious life.
• Someone who has been wonderfully healed or rescued at sea.

Pupil's Activity: Four   **Class discussion**
D) Do miracles happen today and do they only happen to believers?
Discuss some of these happenings above. Which of the examples cited above are miracles and which are not?
How would you define a miracle today? Is a miracle an act of God performed for the special good of His creatures no matter whether they are believers or not? Do you have to believe through a miracle before you believe in a miracle i.e. do you have to experience a miracle to believe in a miracle?

Pupil's Activity: Five   **Class discussion**

E) Discuss these definitions of miracle today.

• Miracles are the religious factor in determining an event.

• A miracle is a supernatural event. (H.H. Farmer)

• A miracle is being able to see things from a third dimensional aspect rather than just a flat surface two dimension. (C.S. Lewis)

• A miracle is an extraordinary and welcome event attributed to a divine agency. (The Oxford Compact English Dictionary 2000) To say that a miracle is contrary to the laws of nature implies that the universe somehow runs on its own steam and that God is absent from the regular ordering of the universe.

• A miracle is an event that is contrary to the established laws of nature and attributed to a supernatural cause. (Collins Dictionary 1986)

[1a] Miracles in the Synoptics (Fig. 1)

Miracles in all three Synoptics	Luke	Mark	Matthew
1. Possessed man in the synagogue on the Sabbath in Capernaum	4:31-37	1:23-26	
2. Peter's mother-in-law on the Sabbath in Capernaum on leaving the synagogue	4:38-39	1:30-31	8:14-15
First summary of miracles: Jesus withdraws from His public ministry of healing.	4:40-41	1:32-34	8:16
3. Man with leprosy - Jesus heals by touch on the Sabbath.	5:12-16	1:40-42	5:12-13
Second summary of miracles: the news of Jesus spread so that the crowds flock to Him.	5:15	1:45	8:17
4. Paralysed man	5:17-26	2:3-12	9:2-7
5. Man with the withered hand	6:6-11	3:1-5	12:10-13
Third summary of miracles: shows Jesus' power and healing by touch.	6:17-19	3:10	4:23
Fourth summary of miracles - many are healed.	7:21		4:24-25
6. Calming the storm	8:22-25	4:37-41	8:23-27
7. Gerasene demoniac	8:27-39	5:1-15	8:28-34
8. Raising Jairus' daughter	8:41-42,49-56	5:22-24, 38-42	9:18-19, 23-25
9. The woman with the issue of blood	8:43b-48	5:25-29	9:20-22
10. Feeding the five thousand	9:10b-17	6:35-44	14:15-21
11. The demon possessed boy	9:37-46	9:17-19	17:14-18
12. Two blind men (Matthew) one in Luke/Mk	18:35-43	10:46-52	20:29-34
Miracles only in Matthew and Luke	**Luke**		**Matthew**
13. The Roman centurion's servant	7:1-10 (Q)		8:10-15 (Q)
14. The blind mute and the possessed man	11:4-5 (Q)		12:22-23 (Q)
Miracles unique to Luke (L)			
15. The first catch of fish	5:1-11 (L)		
16. Raising the widow's son at Nain	7:11-17 (L)		
17. Demons cast out of Mary Magdalene	8:2 (L)		
18. The crippled woman	13:11-13 (L)		
19. Man with dropsy	14:1-4 (L)		
20. The ten leper	17:11-19 (L)		
21. The high priest's servant	22:50-51(L)		

B) General comments on the miracles in Luke's Gospel

• There are twelve triple tradition and two double tradition miracles in Luke.

• There are four summaries of the miracles in Luke: [See Figure 1.]

firstly, " Now when the sun was setting, all those who had any who were sick with various diseases brought them to Him; and He laid His hands on every one of them and healed them. And demons also came out of many, crying, 'You are the Son of God!' But He rebuked them and would not allow them to speak, because they knew that He was the Christ."

(4: 40-41), secondly, (5:15) thirdly, (6:17-19) and fourthly (7:21).

• Jesus' first miracle recorded in Luke's Gospel is an exorcism (4:31-44), showing Jesus as the Anointed One, having great authority and power. [See Figure 1.]

• The first three miracles in Luke follow on from each other on the Sabbath day, the possesed man in the Synagogue.

Jesus began to teach in the synagogue and everyone praised God (4:15). Jesus was anointed to preach the Gospel in the synagogue in Nazareth (4:18). Jesus came to Capernaum and taught on the Sabbath days (4:31). Jesus said, "I must preach." (4:43) The people pressed upon Him to hear (5:1). Jesus entered the synagogue and taught (6:6). A great crowd came to hear Him (6:17). When he ended all these sayings... (7:1) He went through every city and village preaching (8:1).

He called His Twelve disciples and sent them to preach (9:2).

• The first six miracles in Luke are in a context of teaching and healing. [See Figure 1.]

• Jesus is the one with the **authority** to defeat the evil forces that affect life and control people.

• There are combined miracles between (8:22-56) which all attest the power of Jesus over a variety of forces: forces from without (nature or demons), forces from within (disease or death).

[2] Classification of the miracles in the Third Gospel

A) Fitzmyer's classification of the miracles in the Third Gospel into four categories: (Figure 2)

Miracle	Ref.	Type	Purpose
1. Calming the storm	8:22-25	nature	Call to strenghen faith (8:25)
2. Gadarene demoniac	8:27-35	demons	A strong witness due to a changed life (8:39)
3. Raising Jairus'daughter	8:41-42, 49-56	death	Call to faith (8:50)
4. The woman with the issue of blood	8:43-48	disease	Call to faith (8:48)

One way to classify the miracles in Luke's Gospel based upon these four miracles is that of Fitzmyer **(1)**, who classifies the miracles in different forms: exorcisms, healing, resuscitation and nature. Another view is that of Theissen **(2)** who divides the miracles into six categories: exorcism, healing, epiphany, rescue, gift and rule. He divided up the nature miracles into those which express purpose in that they rescue or give provision. "Rule" miracles are those which involve healings where the goal is not just to heal but to show **authority,** as in the healing of the paralysed man (5:24). He distinguishes between exorcisms and healings; in exorcisms the case of the express mention of evil forces is determined by possession (4:33). This is an exorcism since a being possesses the man in the synagogue. The next miracle, that of Peter's mother-in-law, is a healing miracle (4:38-39). For Luke, there is a spiritual presence behind the scenes which is the real cause of the problem. People who reject the spirit world tend to give a natural or literary explanation for exorcisms.

B) Theissen's classification of the miracles in the Third Gospel into six categories (Figure 3)

Miracle	Ref.	Type	To express purpose
1. Calming the storm	8:22-25	nature	Rescue people in danger
2. Gadarene demoniac	8:27-35	exorcism	To show there is a "spiritual" presence, which is the real cause of the demoniac's problem.
3. Raising Jairus'daughter	8:41-42,49-56	rescue	To show that Jesus can restore whatever the condition
4. Feeding the 5:000	9:12-17	gift	To give provision of food
5. Peter's mother- in- law	4:38-39	healing	Restorative-Jesus wants her to be well again and to continue her work in the home.
6. The paralysed man	5:24	rule	A healing miracle with the purpose of showing authority - who is in contol in Jesus' challenge of the Pharisees.

[3] An imaginative writing about the miracles in the Third Gospel with special reference to the healing of the paralysed man (5:17-26).

Dear Theophilus,

In my Gospel, I have put much emphasis upon the miracles of Jesus, including at least twenty-one incidents of miracles and four summaries of miracles. Throughout the Gospel, I have used four different types of miracles: healings, exorcism, nature (gift, rescue, provision) and resurrection. The context of the healing of the paralysed man was that of healing and teaching (5:17). As Jesus was teaching, there were Pharisees and teachers of the law sitting by, from every city in Galilee and Judea and from Jerusalem and the power of the Lord was with Him to heal (5:18).

The **function** of this miracle was to acknowledge that God was at work through the healing and to show the link with prayer. In (5:16), I have written how Jesus had withdrawn to the wilderness and prayed; I have included this practice of prayer by Jesus on other occasions (e.g. 3:21; 9:29). Many others are linked to miracles. Generally speaking, all of the miracles provide concrete evidence of the fact that God is in control; He rules and His power is at work. By this I mean something very dynamic. Your word "dynamite" comes from the word I use which is (Gk.dunamis). I have used this word to describe how the power of the Lord was seen to be with Jesus, to heal the paralysed man when he was brought to Jesus by his four friends (5:17). The Pharisees were quite right when they said that only God had the power to forgive them their sins; what they did not realise was that Jesus really was the Son of God. That's why this miracle has also an Christological function, that is to tell us who Jesus really is. He is the Son of Man who has the power to liberate and restore people (5:24).

This miracle provides evidence of Jesus as God because He can forgive sins. "The Son of Man has power on earth to forgive sins." (5:20) This was Jesus' favourite title for Himself. It is the only time the title is directly linked to a miracle. I have used it twenty-five times but this is my first time to use it in my Gospel. Jesus used this title here to show the extent of His authority. He has the authority to forgive sins (5:24). However, this was not a purely physical healing miracle; it went much deeper than that when Jesus said to the man, "Friend, your sins are forgiven you." (5:20) When Jesus forgave the man his sins, the paralysed man entered into God's kingdom. God took control of the paralysed man's life. The miracle goes much further than the human eye can see; it raises the issue whether Jesus' claim to forgive sins is real or true. This miracle is evidence of the Kingdom of God at work and demonstrates God's sovereign will in action. The function of this miracle was to tell the people who Jesus really was: that He was God and had the power and authority to forgive sins. Despite this the people failed to recognise His unique character.

A key **purpose** of this miracle is evangelistic. Readers are faced with a response. Is Jesus really the promised One or was He deluded? When people are faced with the divine Jesus they have either to accept Him or reject Him. Faith in this miracle is also more explicitly stated and is evident when the friends bring the paralysed man to Jesus. This shows that the miracle was based upon the dependent faith of the friends. It is the first time in which I have used the word "faith." This miracle reinforced the existing faith of the friends which led to the miracle: Jesus on seeing the faith, both of the four men shuffling their friend to the house for healing and the man himself, responded by healing (5:20).

He is a liberator and restorer of people as seen in His authority to forgive sins (4:18). This points to an eschatological ("now and not yet") purpose in the miracle. Messianic times are here as Jesus gives the "knowledge of salvation to His people in the forgiveness of their sins."(1:77) He also shows empathy to those who have a sense of their need; in this case it is the paralysed man. There is also evidence of the power and authority of Jesus to heal and to forgive sins. With the help of my trusty concordance I have made these references to faith seen in miracles in the Third Gospel. Look them up to see how these miracles produced faith. Five of them are incidents after a healing miracle when Jesus commended people for their faith, for example (7:9) "I tell you, not even in Israel have I found such faith." Here are some further references to study :- (7:50; 8:48; 17:19; 18:42).

"Immediately," I have deliberately used the words (Gk.euthus and parachrema) as impact words to show that these miracles were instantaneous and supernatural. As you can see from the incident of the paralysed man, "Immediately he rose up before them, took what he had been lying on and went home, glorifying God." (5:25) There are seven other occasions when I use these words in the Third Gospel (1:64; 4:39; 5:13; 6:49; 8:44; 8:47; 13:13; 18:43). Those who were healed didn't need to go to their G.P. for further treatment; the Kingdom of God was at work. The miracles go hand in glove with the message. I am, however, conscious that your modern, or even post-modern minds might have difficulty in accepting the miracles. I have made allowance for this in 11:29 and 31. It was possible for the Pharisees to perceive nothing. Jesus insisted that those with eyes to "see" would be blessed for the hopes of the prophets of old were being fulfilled (10:23b-24). The miracles show that God's kingly rule is in action, but they do not always bring faith.

Some of the characteristics can be seen in the sub-headings in which I have set them out. Firstly, there is **the setting -** Jesus was teaching and the Pharisees and teachers of the law were sitting by, having come from every village in Galilee, Judea and Jerusalem. Secondly, **the condition of the man**: he was paralysed and was lying on a bed. Thirdly, **the approach or request to heal:** the friends of the man went up on the roof and let down the man with his bed through the tiles because there was no way through the crowd. Fourthly, **the act or the words of healing:** on seeing their faith, Jesus said, "Man your sins are forgiven you." "The Son of Man has power on earth to forgive sins." "Rise take up your bed and go home." Fifthly, **the healing is demonstrated:** " Immediately he rose up before them took up his bed and went home." Sixthly, **the reaction to the healing:** the man went home to his own house glorifying God (5:25). The people reacted by saying, "We have seen strange things today." The reaction of the crowd was one of total amazement. No wonder they were filled with awe and glorified God. The people were absolutely "gobsmacked," ecstatic (Gk.ekstasis), having witnessed this amazing event which was beyond their belief and explanation and yet they failed to recognise who Jesus really was (5:26). The Pharisees had reacted by asking two questions: "Who is this who speaks blasphemy?" and "Who can forgive sins but God only?" (5:21) They were offended at Jesus making Himself equal with God. Jesus you will note gave three commands to the man. "Rise, take up your bed and go home." The fact that the man was able to walk home was proof of his healing and should cause an observer to reflect on whether Jesus was an imposter or a liar or God? The three commands are all fulfilled, "He got up, took up his mat and went home." (5:25)

Jesus healed by the spoken word, when He said to the paralysed man, "I say to you, rise; take up your bed and go home." (5:24) Refusal to accept the authority of Jesus as a teacher and the source of His authority, as in the case of the Pharisees in (20:1-8), does not change the nature or the extent of the healing or the teaching. Despite the opposition of the Jewish leaders, the people continued to listen to Jesus everyday in the Temple (21:37-39).

The Scribes and Pharisees start to question by asking, "Who is this that speaks blasphemy? Who can forgive sins but God only?" Jesus, you will note, puts up with the unbelief of the Scribes and Pharisees, but it does not change who He is or what He can do. He still continues to minister with grace. You will observe that I have written of "the power to heal." (5:17) That spiritual power is with Jesus. God is working through the Teacher who is also the Healer. Like learning and teaching in the classroom in the twenty-first century, both are inter-related. The key issue in this miracle is the nature of authority as it is also in (4:22,36) and it is the nature of His authority to which the incident draws attention: I mean the forgiveness of sins. It didn't just prove that Jesus could forgive sins, but it upheld and collaborated the claim to be the Son of God. The Scribes and Pharisees were shocked at the power and authority of Jesus to forgive sins. This miracle aimed to show God's love in action as He healed the man with paralysis. This event becomes the turning point in the ministry of Jesus, as it can be seen in terms of forgiveness and not just healing from physical illness.

I should like you to note one further observation. You will be pleased to know that Jesus made it very clear that there is no direct link between paralysis and sin. Jesus was very opposed to the notion that illness came from sin as many Jews believed at that time. So next time someone is ill don't blame them for wrong doing! I hope you will discover more of the truth about Jesus and His miracles for that was one of my original intentions in writing to you Theophilus.

Your loving friend,

Luke

Pupil's Activity: Six
Write an imaginative letter to Theophilus indicating the function, purpose and characteristics of the miraculous catch of fish (5:1-11).

[4] What does Luke say about miracles?
They are signs of the power of God. In the O.T., the Israelites believed that God had delivered them out of Egypt and had parted the Red Sea, enabling them to cross (Ex. 14). Many O.T. prophets such as Elijah and Elisha, performed miracles. In 4:25-29, Elijah restored the life of the child of the woman in Zarephath (1 Kgs.17:22) and Elisha restored the Shunammite woman's son to life (2 Kgs.4:18-37). Jesus was standing in the great tradition of the Hebrew prophets. He implicitly compares Himself with these two prophets and the work they did among the non-Jews (4:23-24). At times Jesus is an anti-type to Elijah when He refused to bring down fire from heaven on the Samaritan villages (9:54-55; 2 Kgs. 1:10-12; Luke 9:62; 1 Kgs. 18:36-38).

In general Luke stresses the compassion of Jesus which was present in the miracle accounts. When the Lord saw her (the widow of Nain), He had compassion on her. "Do not weep." And He came and touched the bier (7:14). This would have been considered an act of defilement according to O.T. law (Num. 19:11), "He who touches the dead body of any person shall be unclean seven days." In the raising of Jairus' daughter, all were weeping and wailing but Jesus said, "Do not weep; for she is not dead but sleeping." (8:52) At the time of Jesus there were other miracle workers, especially in Galilee, but the effect and the meaning of the miracles of Jesus was different.

Luke uses this word "mighty deeds" for miracles fifteen times.

[5] What words does Luke use for miracles?
In the Third Gospel, four different words are used for miracle:
Firstly, the Gk word "dunameis" is plural means powers or acts of power with the emphasis on the source of all power, God is the main word to be used. Luke uses this word "mighty deeds" for miracles fifteen times. The power (Gk.dunamis) of the Most High will overshadow Mary in the birth of her Son (1:35). Power in this context is a synonym for God. The people of Nazareth were amazed when Jesus healed the man with the unclean spirit. "For with **authority and power** (Gk. dunamis), He commands the unclean spirits and they come out." (4:36) Luke often uses (Gk. dunamis) for miraculous power to heal (5:17; 6:19; 8:46; 9:1). The healing of the man with the unclean spirit in the synagogue at Capernaum is the first miracle, against the forces of evil, by Jesus, reported in Luke to show Jesus' command over the world of evil. The people are curious about His power and authority (Gk.exousia).

As Jesus was teaching, the power (Gk.dunamis) of the Lord was with Him to heal (5:17). When the woman with the issue of blood touched Him, Jesus perceived that power had gone out of Him (8:46). Luke tends to put more stress upon the conquest of Satan's power and domain. Jesus entrusted His power to His disciples to heal. "He gave them power and authority over demons and to cure diseases." Luke is unique among the Gospel writers in using the word Gk.dunamis here (9:1). "Woe to you Chorazin! Woe to you Bethsaida! For if the mighty works (Gk.dunameis) done in you had been done in Tyre and Sidon they would have repented long ago." (10:13) [See p. 123.] The seventy (two) who were sent out were given power (Gk.dunamis) over the enemy (10:19). When Jesus entered Jerusalem, the crowd of disciples began to praise God for all the mighty works (Gk.dunameis) they had seen (19:37). Jesus of Nazareth a prophet, mighty (Gk. dunatos) in deed (Gk. ergo) and in word (24:19). These "dunameis" show God's nature.

Secondly, Luke uses the Greek word (Gk. semeia) signs for miracles. [See p. 91.]

The angel said to the shepherds, "And this will be a sign (a mark or a token) for you." This is a miraculous sign (2:12) Here the sign helps to bring out the meaning of the message; it arouses astonishment and provides an understanding faith in the beholder. It is also an O.T. expression for miracle. (Ex. 3:12; Is. 37:30; 38:7)

Simeon describes Jesus as "a sign that is spoken against." Simeon knows that Jesus is God's hope though not everyone will respond. This is Luke's first indication that it will not be all plain sailing or a "bed of roses" for God's Anointed (2:34). In the healing of the paralysed man the crowd said, "We have seen strange [wonderful (Gk.paradoxa things)] today." The Greek word (semeron) "today" means that the present ministry of Jesus is unique and the crowds have the privilege of seeing an unusual event. Sins were forgiven combined with healing. This marked a turning point in the ministry of Jesus (5:26). Jesus did not want to be known as a worker of miracles and sometimes commands the healed people to be silent (8:56). On other occasions, they are to tell others, as in the case of the Gerasene demoniac (8:39). "While others, to test Him, sought from Him a sign from heaven." Even His enemies believed He worked miracles (11:16).

Jesus rebukes this generation for looking for signs. Even though Jesus is getting a growing audience it will not last. Jesus refuses to give a sceptical Pharisee a sign/miracle, "This generation is an evil generation; it seeks a sign but no sign shall be given to it except the sign of Jonah." (11:29) O.T. figures will up rise up in judgement against the leaders for their lack of faith. Jesus' audience and the Ninevites shared in hearing God's message (11:30). "Performing cures today and tomorrow." (13:32-33) "Today" (Gk.semeron) in Luke often means the immediacy of an event or the need to respond (19:5,9). These signs indicate purpose in that they signify the Messiah's claims.

What will be the sign when this is about to take place? (21:7) "There shall be signs from heaven." (21:11) "There shall be signs in the sun and moon."(21:25)

Herod was hoping to see some sign/miracle (Gk. semeia) done by Jesus and wants to be entertained by His power as a wonder worker (23:8). Luke has already warned his readers about people seeking miraculous signs (4:9-12, 23-24; 11:16,29).

==**Authority is His right to do something, while power is His ability to do it. (Arndt) (3)**==

Thirdly, authority (Gk.exousia) and power (Gk.dunamis) are used by Luke to describe the miracles of Jesus.

The miracle of the paralysed man raises the issue of who the Son of Man is and how does He possess such unique authority as to forgive sins? (5:24) Jesus bestows authority upon the Twelve to overcome demonic forces and be able to reverse disease. What is the difference between authority and power of Jesus? Authority is His right to do something, while power is His ability to do it. (Arndt) **(3)**

Summary of the authority of Jesus in Luke's Gospel [See pp. 185-202 Function and Purpose.]

• Jesus' authority is seen in action in the fulfilment of O.T. promises. "The Spirit of the Lord is upon me, because He has anointed me to preach good news to the poor." (4:18; Is.61:1-2) [See p. 181.]

• Jesus has the authority to defeat evil forces (4:36,41). [See p. 182.]

• The use of the term "Master" (Gk. Epistata) by the disciples is a sign of respect and acceptance of His authority; "Master" is a word used instead of "Rabbi" (5:5; 17:13). [See pp. 185, 208.] Jesus' authority is from God. The leper recognised this. "Lord, (Gk.Kurios) if You will, you can make me clean." (5:12)

• The miracle of the paralysed man raises the issue of who the Son of Man is and how does He possess such unique authority as to forgive sins (5:24)? Jesus is quite unique in having the divine authority to forgive sins. He forgave the sins of the paralysed man (5:21) and later the sinful woman (7:48). [See p. 187.]

• Jesus shows His authority regarding God's intended action on the Sabbath. The new way, which Jesus brings does not depend upon the authority of the Jewish religious leaders but on the authority of God. He is Lord of the Sabbath and not the Pharisees (6:5). [See pp. 188, 272.]

• When "the Lord" saw the widow of Nain He had compassion on her (7:13). The title for Jesus as "Lord" includes His authority. To her son He says, "Young man I say to you arise.!" (7:14) Jesus' authority extends to distance, disease and death, as in the case of the centurion's servant when healed from a distance (7:17). [See p. 191.]

• Jesus has the power and authority over nature, wind and water as in the stilling of the storm (8:25). His authority is growing in increasing spheres. [See p. 195.]

• The Gentiles witness this power and authority in the healing of the Gerasene demoniac (8:29). [See p. 196.]

• The disciples recognise that the authority and the power of Jesus to drive out demons and to preach was due to the Spirit's empowerment; their authority was delegated or a shared authority given to them by Jesus. Jesus bestows authority upon the Twelve to overcome demonic forces and be able to reverse disease (9:1-2). [See p. 199.]

• The power and authority of Jesus is seen in the sending out of the seventy (two) (10:1-13). [See p. 203.]

Fourthly, (Gk.ergon) means work. It has the same meaning as (Gk.dunameis) to show supernatural power. [See p. 74.]

"Jesus of Nazareth, a prophet mighty (Gk.dunamis) in deed (Gk.ergo) and word before God and all the people."(24:19) The title, Jesus of Nazareth, is usually used of Jesus' capacity as a miracle worker. The demons, which possessed the man with the unclean spirit in the synagogue of Nazareth, used the same title for Jesus. "What have you to do with us Jesus of Nazareth? Have you come to destroy us?" (4:34) "I know you are, the Holy One of God." Outside Jericho, the people said to the blind man, "Jesus of Nazareth is passing by." (18:37)

Fifthly, (Gk.terata is another N.T. word used for a miracle but does not occur in Luke. It is only used in the N.T. with (Gk.semeia) wonders as in Mark 13:22 and Matt. 24:24 signs and wonders.

> In stilling the storm, Jesus is affirming His sovereignty over storm and sea, as God did in the Exodus (8:22-25). (Liefeld) (4)

Pupil's Activity: Seven

What different words did Luke use for miracle?
What do they mean?

> Theissen (2) divides miracles into six categories: exorcism, healing, epiphany, rescue, gift and rule.

Pupil's Activity: Eight

As an exercise in revision complete the squares by classifying the miracles and giving examples of each type of miracle. The first box has been completed for you.

Four types of miracle	(Figure 3)
1. Nature or gift miracle a. The catch of fish b. Feeding the five thousand c. Stilling the storm	**2.** a. b. c. d.
3. Resurrection a. b.	**4.** a. b. c. d

[6] Luke use of three different words to show the reaction of the people to the miracles.

Firstly, Luke uses the word (Gk.thaumazo) to marvel and to describe the reaction to miraculous events or to teaching. Our word "thaumaturge" comes from this: someone who performs a wonderful happening (24:41). Here the reaction of joy and amazement could be to the teaching. All who heard wondered at what the shepherds told them (2:18). They were filled with wonder at the new note of universality about the Ministry of Jesus. Amazement after a revelation like that of the shepherds was a common response (2:19). Mary and Joseph marvelled (Gk.thaumazontes) at what Simeon said about Jesus (2:33). The Greek.word thaumos is unique to Luke. The people in Capernaum were amazed when Jesus exorcised the man with the unclean spirit (4:35). Peter was astonished (Gk.thaumos) at the catch and all those with him (5:9). [See pp. 51-52, 91.]

Secondly, he uses the Greek word ethaumazon "amazed".

The people of Nazareth gave a two-fold reaction; they were amazed at His gracious words and skill in rhetoric, but they also remembered His background. "Is this not Joseph's son?" (4:22) After the stilling of the storm, the people were afraid and marvelled (Gk. ethaumasa) at His power over wind and water (8:25). Only in this context are fear and wonder put side by side and that is at the response to Jesus' mighty work. Who then is this the people ask? Who but divinity can handle things like this? The calm sea testifies to the real identity of Jesus. [See p. 195.]

Jesus is affirming sovereignty over storm and sea as God did in the Exodus. (Liefeld) **(4)** Jesus shows His power and authority by healing a boy possessed of a destructive spirit (9:43). God's mercy is also in evidence. God is seen as wonderfully present in Jesus. The reaction of the crowd is one of amazement (Gk.thaumazonton) at the majesty or greatness of God. Luke concentrates on the power of Jesus rather than the failure of the disciples to heal the boy as in the other Synoptics (Mk. 9:19; Matt. 17:17). [See p. 202.]

The mute man who also had a demon (11:14). Luke records three simple steps in describing the event. [See p. 204.]

The **work** - Jesus exorcises a demon from a man who cannot speak,

The **result** - the man speaks, and

The **reaction**: the crowd marvel (Gk.thaumazo). They are "amazed" at the unusual work and not that it represents something good. People can be amazed and still not like what they see. Despite the amazement the crowd are divided over the work of Jesus. Compare (4:22, 29); they put Him out of the city and took Him to a brow of a hill to throw Him over a nearby cliff. The Scribes and Pharisees were not able to catch Him out over the tribute to Caesar but they marvelled (Gk. thaumazantes) at His answer (20:26).

Luke uses this word "mighty deeds" for miracles fifteen times.

Thirdly, Luke uses the word "awe" (Gk.paradoxa) meaning a wonderful event and expresses the response of the crowd: it means "strange things" and is an event which is beyond belief or explanation. (Kittel) **(5)** This is the only time this word is used in the N.T. but it is often used in the LXX. The crowd's reaction to the healing of the paralysed man was one of praise and awe. The unusual character of Jesus' ministry was noted although they failed to recognise His unusual character or uniqueness (5:26). This word was also used by the Jewish historian Josephus **(6)**, in which he described Jesus as doing "surprising works." Josephus **(7)** also speaks of a Jewish exorcist called Eleasar who used Solomon's incantations to draw a demon out by the nostrils, using a Baaras root. [See p. 187.]

Conclusion

• While some witnesses **marvel** at the miracle working activity of Jesus (8:56), others accuse Him of collusion with Satan (11:14-22) and others praise God (13:17). Those who witnessed the miracles of Jesus interpreted them in different ways and put them into different categories.

• Some of the Rabbinic writers compared Jesus with Honi the circle – drawer who in a time of drought prayed to God for rain and the prayers were answered. (Josephus) **(8)** Hanina ben Dosa who was reported as surviving a poisonous snake-bite. He is also said to have healed a person at a distance (Mishnah). **(9)** Jesus was aware of other exorcists at this time, "By whom do your sons cast them out?" (11:19) and (Tacitus) **(10)**

• Even though there are examples from the first century of extraordinary events and miraculous healings, there are no records of anyone who performed miracles and exorcisms in exactly the same way as Jesus did. Miracles were not the common occurrence of everyday life.

[7] Why did Jesus perform miracles?

The purposes of the miracles have been described as:

• evidential,
• evangelistic,
• empathetic and
• eschatological. (Moo) **(11)**

I. Evidential

They provide evidence to people to show them who Jesus is.

Jesus, when He preaches in the synagogue at Nazareth, sees Himself as the fulfilment of O.T. prophecy. "The Spirit of the Lord is upon me, because the Lord has anointed me to bring good tidings to the afflicted;" (4:18-19; Is.61:1)

A) Restorer of people

He can deal with evil and restore people as in the exorcism of the man with the unclean spirit in the synagogue (4:31-37). He can deal with evil forces as in the case of the possessed man (4:36). The bible distinguishes between healings and demon possession. Where healings occur hostile forces are not mentioned in Scripture. Not all disease is possession and not all possession is disease. (Van der Loos) **(12)** "Saviours" in Roman antiquity were often seen as healers. The centurion regards Jesus as a Saviour (7:6-7). [See p. 190.]

B) Anointed One

In this incident of the man with the unclean spirit, Jesus is also the "anointed one" who has power and authority over the forces of evil (4:31-37). [See p. 182.]

> Sometimes miracles can produce faith as in the case of the leper "Your faith has made you well." (17:19) and in the case of the woman with the flow of blood (8:48). "Daughter, your faith has made you well."

C) Divine - Messiah

Jesus is the divine Messiah "anointed one" and the kingdom of God is breaking into human history through His ministry. His idea of Messiah was not to bring political freedom from the Romans but to liberate and restore people from evil. The kingdom of God is in evidence when Jesus exorcises demons. "But if it is by the finger of God I cast out demons, then the kingdom of God has come upon you." (11:20) [See p. 205.]

D) Forgiver of sins

He can show His authority as in the healing miracles where He does not just heal but forgives sin as in the healing of the paralysed man. "Man, your sins are forgiven you." (5:20b) "The Son of Man has authority on earth to forgive sins." (5:24) [See p. 187.]

E) Son of Man

He is the Son of Man who has the power to liberate and restore people from evil (4:31-37). Luke uses this title, "Son of Man" twenty-five times but (5:24) is the only time it is linked to a miracle. [See p. 74.]

F) Provider

He can provide food for people as in the nature or gift miracle of feeding the five thousand (9:10-17). [See p. 200.]

G) Prophet

Jesus, when He preaches in the synagogue at Nazareth, sees Himself as the fulfilment of O.T. prophecy. "The Spirit of the Lord is upon me, because the Lord has anointed me to bring good tidings to the afflicted;" (4:18-19; Is. 61:1) Jesus explains His identity to John the Baptist's disciples by referring to Isaiah, "In that day the deaf shall hear the words of a book, and out of their gloom and darkness the eyes of the blind shall see."(Is. 29:18-19) "Then the eyes of the blind shall be opened, and the ears of the deaf unstopped; then shall the lame man leap like a hart, and the tongue of the dumb sing for joy." (Is.35: 5-6) Miracles provide attestation as to who Jesus is. [See p. 106.]

> In crossing these boundaries of purity, Jesus shows His compassion and empathy with people and manifested the kingdom as God's power (Lev. 13-14; Num. 5:2-3; 12: 10-12; Deut. 24:8).

II. Evangelistic

A) Sometimes miracles can produce faith as in the case of the healing of the leper, "Your faith has made you well;" (17:19) and in the case of the woman with the flow of blood. "Daughter, your faith has made you well." (8:48) It was a touch of faith and not a magic power by which Jesus healed her. However, it should be noted that not all miracles produce faith. There is no predictable relationship between miracles and faith. Nevertheless, sometimes faith does produce a miracle. To the blind beggar outside Jericho Jesus said, "Receive your sight; your faith has made you whole." (18:42) The emphasis on miracle as a catalyst for faith is a characteristic of Luke's Gospel. (Achtemeier) **(13)** Some scholars have argued that the miracles pre-suppose faith: they do not create faith and being healed is not the same as being saved. However, Jesus said to the Samaritan leper. "Your faith has made you well." The leper's faith had delivered him in the same way that faith had saved the sinful woman (7:50). The miracles show God's Kingdom in action but they do not always bring faith. (Stanton) **(14)** Sometimes miracles show the importance of believing that Jesus is capable of doing such great acts of healing, the woman with the flow of blood (8:48) and raising from the dead (8:50). In raising Jairus' daughter, Jesus worked a miracle in response to the faith of Jairus. (8:41-2, 49-56). "Do not fear, only believe and she will be well."

B) Sometimes miracles can produce a new sense of dependence upon God. In the miracle of the catch of fish, Jesus ministers to Peter (5:1-11). Peter stands as a sinner before God realising that such a catch is only possible because Jesus has access to the power of God. Grace was experienced by Peter. In this experience Peter is transformed from "sinner" to "fisherman". He recognised the greatness of God and it led him to a simple trust and reliance upon God. "But at your word I will let down the nets." (5:5b) Sometimes a miracle is meant to instil faith where it is lacking as in the stilling of the storm. "He said to them "Where is your faith?" (8:25) In this event the miracle strengthens faith.

C) Sometimes miracles produce faith outside Israel. Jesus said to the Roman centurion, "I tell you, not even in Israel have I found such faith." (7:9) Jesus praises the Roman centurion for showing faith and marvels at the quality of the man's faith. "Rise go your way, your faith has saved you." (17:19)

D) Sometimes miracles can provide missionary opportunities for the gospel especially in Gentile territory. The Gerasene demoniac was told by Jesus to go back home and tell people how much God had done for him. (Fitzmyer) **(15)** The miracles show God's Kingly rule in action but they do not always bring faith. (Stanton) [See above.] The emphasis on miracle as a catalyst for faith is a characteristic of Luke's Gospel. (Achtemeir) [See p. 208-9.]

Pupil's Activity: Seven

The following are references to faith in the miracles of the Third Gospel. Look them up to see how these miracles produced faith. Five of them are incidents after a healing miracle when Jesus commended people for their faith for example, "I tell you, not even in Israel have I found such faith." (7:9) Here are some further references to study:- (7:50; 8:48; 17:19; 18:42). Look them up! [See pp. 197, 208-9.]

III. Empathetic: to understand and share feelings with someone [See pp. 47, 237-248.]

Miracles provide evidence of the compassion of Jesus as in laying on hands on the sick and healing them (4:40) and touching the leper (5:13). They also indicated His willingness to heal even though such an act made Him ritually unclean(Lev. 14:46). Jesus takes the initiative in some of the healings to show His compassion. Jesus had compassion on the widow of Nain, who had lost her only son. "Do not worry," He said (7:13). The woman with the flow of blood touched the fringe of His garment (8:44). Jesus took Jairus' daughter by the hand to raise her from the dead (8:54). In the feeding of the five thousand, Jesus shows His capacity to meet the physical needs of the people (9:10-17). Jesus crosses boundaries of purity to show that the kingdom is the power of God and people will be made whole. In showing compassion to the marginalized He wants to restore people to wholeness and to fellowship among and with the people of God. Miracles can break down social barriers with Gentiles, lepers, women and people possessed of evil spirits; these people would all have been barred from entrance to the temple as they were regarded as ritually unclean. Jesus would have been regarded as unclean for touching a Gentile, a leper, a woman or a demoniac. All of these groups were those referred to as "release of the captives." (4:18) In crossing these boundaries of purity, Jesus shows His compassion and empathy with people and manifested the kingdom as God's power (Lev. 13-14; Num. 5:2-3; 12: 10-12; Deut. 24:8). Jesus did not begin by focusing on the purity of God's people as the Pharisees and the Essenes were doing, His concern was to restore the people of God.

> **Jesus would have been regarded as unclean for touching a Gentile, a leper, a woman or a demoniac. All of these groups were those referred to as "release of the captives." (4:18) In crossing these boundaries of purity, Jesus shows His compassion and empathy with people and manifested the kingdom as God's power (Lev. 13-14; Num. 5:2-3; 12: 10-12; Deut. 24:8).**

IV. Eschatological: ("now and not yet") the life of Jesus seen as the coming of the Kingdom of God

A) The eschatological background for the nature miracles

The gift miracle of the feeding of the five thousand foreshadows the Messianic feast (Is.25: 6-9) with the abundance of bread (as in the miracle of the manna in the O.T.) and the wine. The rescue miracle of calming the sea is meaningful against the horizon of Yahweh in the O.T. asserting His sovereignty over the sea in creation (Job 26; 12-13; Ps. 74:16-20): the last event (Is. 27:11). The Baptism and Transfiguration are examples of apocalyptic eschatology as (a) where visions with a revelatory medium are used and (b) where there is also an eschatological content. Jesus is identified as the eschatological agent, the Messiah. There is evidence in Luke/Acts that Jesus was regarded as the **Mosaic prophet** of Deut. 18:15,18 and so His miracles appear as signs and wonders. (Blackburn) **(16)** Jesus shows compassion and mercy which are qualities expected of the shepherd-Messiah.

> **Miracles can break down social barriers with Gentiles, lepers, women and people possessed of evil spirits; these people would all have been barred from entrance to the temple as they were regarded as ritually unclean.**

B) The Kingdom of God is breaking into human history.

The expression "Kingdom of God" is used thirty-one times in Luke. The present or future meaning depends upon the context. (Marshall) **(17)** Jesus saw His deeds as the manifestation of the Kingdom of God (8:18-23) compared with those who were waiting for the salvation of Israel. The total demonstration of the authority of Jesus on earth is the fulfilment of the promises made to Israel. The Kingdom of God is near or has drawn near and it is linked to the defeat of Satan (9:1; 10:18-19) and to Jesus' ministry of exorcism, "I saw Satan fall like lightning from the sky." (8:35, 39) A new era has begun: God is asserting His power over the world. The disciples are given a greater and more permanent empowerment than Israel in the O.T. Despite this, God's final purposes await future fulfilment. Jesus spoke of the future climax of the Kingdom moving backward toward the present. God's Kingly rule is in action. The Kingdom is present "already" (11:20), when Jesus exorcised the demons, showing evidence that the kingdom has come. It is also future, "not yet": His reign at God's right hand. There is an eschatological joy which people have when they enter the Kingdom of God. This is a feature of Luke's Gospel. [See p. 52, 205.]

Pupil's Activity: Eight

From the incident of Jesus preaching in the synagogue in Nazareth, what purposes did Jesus have in doing miracles and how were these accomplished in His ministry (4:16-30)?

(Figure 4)   **[8] Outline of Luke's miracles**

BIBLE TEXT / TITLE / GENERAL COMMENTS	FUNCTION: WHAT IS ACHIEVED?	PURPOSE : INTENDED RESULT [WHY?]	CHARACTERISTICS : HOW IS IT UNIQUE?
1.A] Read 4:14-16 the summary of the Galilean Ministry. a. Jesus comes to Galilee in the Spirit and His ministry is received with great popularity. His fame spread throughout Galilee. b. Luke 4:14-15 is triple tradition: Mark 1:14-15; and Matthew 4:12-17. **1.B] Read Ch.4:16-30** Jesus preaching in the synagogue in Nazareth this is triple tradition: (Mk. 6:1-6; Matt. 13:53-58) c. People are drawn at first by the teaching of Jesus d. Jewish eschatology saw history moving towards a future goal even though the prophets had expected God to bring in salvation and judgement. The Jews saw this goal as one of permanent salvation, peace and righteousness. Jesus took over these thought forms when He preached about the poor having the gospel preached to them (7:22). 'The poor' are those who have the special need of dependence upon God. e. In Luke's Gospel, Jesus does not discourage the idea of Himself as a prophet speaking in these terms in the synagogue message about Himself and seeing Himself as a prophet without honour (4:16-30). f. This is the first rejection of Jesus in His ministry in Luke (4:23,30). g. The nature of Jesus' task is described in three ways: (1) a prophet declaring good news, (2) the Messiah and ministering in the power of the Spirit to social outcasts, the needy, including Gentiles. The year of Jubilee (Heb. Yobel) is the year of release or forgiveness when slaves were freed one year in every fifty. This could be implied (4:18-19; Lev.25:10-13). A Jubilee in Palestine was held in A.D. 26-27.	**Jesus' preaching in Nazareth's synagogue provides evidence of:** - who Jesus is, the Son of God. - Jesus' missionary function/role as God's Anointed One/ The Messiah. - Jesus as the fulfilment of O.T. prophecy (Is.61:1-2; 58:6). - the power of the Spirit in His ministry. The references to the Spirit show a special anointing: "the Holy Spirit descended upon Him in bodily form, as a dove" after His baptism for a special task (3:22). **Jesus is the bearer of the Spirit.** He is the person begotten or has been born of the Spirit (1:35). - "Jesus, full of the Spirit, returned to the Jordan and was led by the Spirit for forty days in the wilderness." (4:1) - Having being elected to do God's business on behalf of people, Jesus returned to Galilee filled with the power of the Spirit (4:14a). Jesus says that He has been anointed by the Spirit of God at the start of His ministry 4:18. - popular support at the start of His public ministry (4:14b). He had come to preach (4:18,19) and to heal (4:18). - His Messianic function and task is seen in His coming as the One who brings release to the oppressed (4:18b). - Jesus' mission statement; the good news is a joyful announcement (4:18-19). - the kingdom of God at work. "Today, this scripture is fulfilled in your hearing." (4:22) - "today" is the promised time. Jesus announces a new era and brings to pass this salvation as the anointed Messiah (4:21). - His role as a suffering Servant is not specified here in 4:18-19 but association may be assumed in the use of Is.61:1.	**1. Evidential and Christological** a) This example of the teaching of Jesus, provides evidence as to who Jesus really is, i.e. the **Son of God, God's Anointed One, the Messiah** who brings release to fulfil His Messianic role. b) The emphasis in the incident is on power. (Talbert) **(18)** c) This sermon of Jesus is a thematic explanation of His ministry. (Stein) **(19)** **2. Eschatological:** a) This event shows that the Kingdom of God was at work (4:22). "Today" is the promised time, Jesus announces a new era and brings to pass this salvation as the anointed Messiah. b) It was the day for the poor, the prisoners, the blind and the oppressed. His own people demand signs but do not accept the claims as to who Jesus really is. The rejection of Jesus would indicate and confirm His identity as a prophet and the Messiah. Israel's captivity was not one merely imposed by the Romans but had been self-inflicted. The miracles would be a mission to Israel like the prophetic hope in the O.T. and would indicate a special time of God's activity. c) The incident foreshadows the future mission to the Gentiles. The Gentiles had received God's grace through the prophets Elijah and Elisha (4:25-27). God would reach out to those hated by Israel, the Gentiles. d) Jesus is the **eschatological prophet who declares good news at Nazareth** (4:18ff). (Fitzmyer) **(20)** Jesus is comparing His ministry to that of Elijah and Elisha. It is likely that this is the way in which the people in the synagogue saw Jesus. e) Luke however seems to link the incident to more than one event, the infancy and the baptism and these show Him as the anointed One, who proclaims the kingdom. **3. Evangelistic:** Jesus starts His ministry by preaching the good news of the Kingdom.	**1. The setting:** Luke's Gospel begins the ministry of Jesus with this incident in Nazareth. He enters the synagogue on the Sabbath. News about Jesus spread in Galilee and everyone praised Him (4:14-15). **2. General points:** Jesus stands up and reads from the prophet Isaiah, citing the passage (4:18-21). He closes the book and says that fulfilment has come. Everyone had a fixed gaze on Him; they have intense anticipation of how Jesus will interpret Is. 61:1;4:22. The crowds at first speak well of the gracious words of Jesus but hesitate when they see Him as Joseph's son. The relationship of Jesus to Joseph is questioned. The proverb "a physician should do good works and heal himself" could mean "Show your stuff, if you want credibility or a prophet's lack of honour" (4:23b), or 'do the signs you did in Galilee,' (4:14-15) the parallel with Elijah and Elisha (4:24). The crowd's anger is seen in desiring to throw Jesus over a cliff, Jesus passes through the crowd. **3. The reactions:** a) At first there was a universal response of praise in the synagogue for Jesus. (4:15) b) Jesus showed His power as He passed through the middle of the people in Nazareth, when they tried to kill Him, by throwing Him over a cliff top. Familiarity breeds contempt (4:30). The people who knew Jesus best had least regard for Him. They challenged Him to do miraculous signs (4:23). c) The later rejection of Jesus is foreseen (4:23-30). Jesus stands in line with the rejected prophets, "To let the oppressed go free" (4:24) **4. Conclusion:** Jesus combines Is.61:1-2, the hope of proclaiming deliverance, with Is.58:6-8 "the nation fast but do not honour God with their lives, even though they continue to worship God." Jesus calls for a genuine response to God. The Jewish Messiah would announce a year of Jubilee.

BIBLE TEXT / TITLE / GENERAL COMMENTS	FUNCTION: WHAT IS ACHIEVED?	PURPOSE : INTENDED RESULT [WHY?]	CHARACTERISTICS : HOW IS IT UNIQUE?
2 a. Read 4:31-37 the man with the unclean spirit in the synagogue in Capernaum on the Sabbath. b. This is a double tradition Mark 1: 21-38. c. It is both a healing and an exorcism. Capernaum was N.W. Galilee by the seaside. It was noted for its lush environment and had a Roman garrison. The population was between 1-2,000. The main trades were agriculture and fishing. It became the centre of Jesus' ministry and not Nazareth (4:31; 7:1; 10:15). d. Jesus went regularly to the synagogue here. Sabbath is in the plural which may indicate many visits. "He was teaching them on the Sabbaths." (4:31) e. This is the first miracle by Jesus in Luke's Gospel and it shows that Jesus can overcome hostile foes. The word "amazement" (Gk. thambos) is unique to Luke (4:36). [See Ch. 6 Outcasts.] f. An evil spirit is unclean compared to God's holiness and could cause physical filth in a possessed person. g. Jesus calls the evil into subjection by exercising His authority. Jesus is not the divine man-worker as the Greeks believed.	The exorcising of the man with the unclean spirit in the synagogue provides evidence of: - reaction of the people to the miracle as one of amazement (4:36). - the teaching of Jesus with authority which is recognised by demons and the powers of darkness (4:36). - the main stress which in Luke is in the **authority and power** of Jesus' teaching (4:36). - "What is this word? For with power and authority He commands the unclean spirits, and they come out." (4:36) His word was with authority (4:32). - the fact that Jesus also acts with authority. "Be silent and come out of him!" (4:35) - Jesus silencing the unclean spirit. Why! Is it that He does not want to appear to be leading a revolution against the Romans? At Qumran, some scholars taught that demonic control would end on the Day of the Lord (1Qm 1:10-14). Probably the Jews taught that the Messiah should only engage in certain kinds of self-proclamation and would be seen as a title with a very political force. - the emphasis on the authority of the 'word' (Gk. logos) of Jesus (4:36). - the function of the miracle is restorative, as the Messiah, Jesus would restore the possessed from evil and bring them into mainstream society (4:36). - Jesus initiating a ministry of "release" against all forces of evil.	**1. Evidential and Christological** a) This incident provides evidence as to who Jesus is, the Holy One of God, Messiah. b) The demons recognised Jesus as "the Holy One of God", who has power over the forces of evil. This title means Anointed One or Messiah. c) It shows that Jesus is the Anointed One whose **power and authority** rules the hidden world and the world forces. d) The healings fulfil the Scriptures and O.T. promises (7:16,2; Is.29:18). (Theissen) **(21)** **2. Empathetic** a) Jesus shows His compassion in exorcising the man. **3. Eschatological** a) The Kingdom of God breaks into human history by setting at liberty those who are oppressed and, in this situation, a man with an unclean spirit (4:18). b) Jesus is recognised as the **eschatological agent, the Messiah, the Mosaic prophet,** "I make them know the statutes of God and His decisions." (Deut. 18:15,18) c) A new age has begun. The coming of the messianic age depicts the demise of Satan's rule (Is, 24:21-22; Jn.12:31). **4. Evangelistic** a) The oppressed man is released from the unclean spirit when the Kingdom of God has come. b) Jesus was attacking the forces of evil as He proclaimed the gospel (4:43). c) The gospel spreads as the result of this miracle and this is a key theme in Luke.	**1. The setting:** Jesus is going down to Capernaum in Galilee to teach on the Sabbath(s) in the synagogue (4:31). **2. The condition of the man:** it is the public healing of a demon possessed man. **3. The approach to the healing:** the cry of the man, "Ah! (RSV) Let us alone (NRSV)! What have you to do with us Jesus of Nazareth? Have you come to destroy us? I know who you are, the Holy One of God." (4:34) **4. The exorcism:** Jesus gave a simple word of command on His authority and did not use incantation. Jesus said sternly, "Be silent and come out of him!" The demon threw the man to the ground and came out of him, without harming him (4:36). **5. The reaction:** all were amazed at the power and authority of Jesus over the demons. News of Jesus spread throughout the region (4:37). The power of God can free a person from evil forces. **Conclusion:** 1. In this miracle, **teaching is combined with authority,** healing and making disciples. 2. It also challenges Jewish tradition about healing on the Sabbath. 3. Luke builds his Christology from the earth upwards for the benefit of his readers. (Bock) **(22)** 4. The exorcism is done in full public gaze in the Synagogue (4:41). 5. Jesus would not allow the demon to speak (4:41).

BIBLE TEXT / TITLE / GENERAL COMMENTS	FUNCTION: WHAT IS ACHIEVED?	PURPOSE : INTENDED RESULT [WHY?]	CHARACTERISTICS : HOW IS IT UNIQUE!
3a. Read 4:38-39 Peter's-mother-in-law. b. This is an example of a healing miracle though some scholars call it an exorcism as Luke refers to Jesus "rebuking the fever." (4:39) c. This is a triple tradition miracle as it is in all three Synoptic Gospels: Matthew 8:14-15; Mark 1:29-31 and Luke 4:38-39. d. The emphasis in Luke is that it takes place on the Sabbath. e. At this point, Peter's call has not taken place (5:1-11). f. Peter is married (1 Cor. 9:5).	The healing of Peter's mother-in-law provides evidence that: - Jesus healed Peter's mother-in-law 'immediately'. The word (Gk. parachrema) 'immediately' is unique to Luke and has a sense of urgency and without delay. - she is grateful to Jesus for her healing ; she serves them (4:39). - **Jesus shows His authority** and power over the fever in the woman when He stands over the woman (4:39). This is common in exorcisms. - **Jesus' authority** has ever widening scope in healing Peter's wife's mother but He has to go to all His people through Israel with the message of God's coming kingdom (4:43). - the healed woman is anxious to serve	**1. Evidential** a) Jesus provides evidence of His power to heal and His authority over illness. **2. Empathetic** a) Jesus is willing to heal a woman even though it would make Him ritually unclean. b) This miracle shows Jesus' concern for a woman. c) Jesus' purpose is restorative. He wants Peter's mother- in- law to be well again and to continue her work in the home. **3. Eschatological** a) Jesus is seen as the restorer of people and a special time has come for God to deliver. "Tell John what you have seen and heard." (7:22-23) b) He cured many of diseases (7:21). This is a sign of Messianic times. c) The Kingdom of God has come in His preaching.	1. The **account** takes a common form: a) **The setting** : Peter's mother-in-law's house in Capernaum on the Sabbath. The setting is more private (4:31-33). b) **Her condition:** she suffered from a high fever. Her disease could be a high-grade fever which included dysentery. Only Luke describes it as a "high fever" (4:38). c) **A request to heal** is made, "an unspecified group begged Jesus to heal her." (4:38) (NLB) d) **The words or act of healing** are given: "He stood over her and rebuked the fever." (4:39a) e) **Evidence of the healing** : the fever left her and at once she rose and served them (4:39b). f) **Reaction to the miracle :** her service to others showed her grateful response for the healing. Her **response** is one of hospitality and gratitude and not one of amazement. She rose and served them (4:39). 2. **Conclusion:** The language is like that of a nature miracle in the description of the demon's departure. Some scholars see it as an exorcism, as it is the language of an exorcism which is used. He rebuked the fever and it left her (4:39). This word is unique to Luke in this incident. (L) 3. Unspecified people ask Jesus to help her (4:38). 4. They realised that He could help (4:38). 5. This is a semi-private healing (4:38).

BIBLE TEXT / TITLE / GENERAL COMMENTS	FUNCTION: WHAT IS ACHIEVED?	PURPOSE: INTENDED RESULT [WHY?]	CHARACTERISTICS: HOW IS IT UNIQUE?
4 a. Read 4:40-41 the sick are healed in the evening. b. This is a summary of the healings and the exorcisms of Jesus. c. This is a triple tradition Mark 1:35-38; Matthew 8:16-17. d. Luke distinguishes between the sick (4:40) and those possessed (4:41) which helps to justify the above distinction between healings and exorcisms.	**Provides evidence that:** - Jesus is the Christ. - the demons confess Jesus as the Son of God and know Him to be the Christ. - Jesus demonstrates His **authority** in rebuking the spirits. - Jesus had further opportunities to heal, which led to Him healing multitudes of people and exorcising those possessed with demons (4:40-41).	**1. Evidential** a) Evidence that Luke equates the title Son of God with the title Christ (4:41). b) The demons confess His divinity "Son of God" and also recognise His regal office as Christ. **2. Empathetic** a) Jesus attends to the sick individually and "lays hands on them" to show His personal concern and compassion (4:40). However, He does not always touch people to heal them (7:1-10). **3. Eschatological** a) The demons may have been expecting a popular political Messiah. b) The exorcisms show that a special time has come; people in captivity to demons are being released (4:18c). c) The good news to the poor is the good news of the kingdom (4:19; 4:43). This is the **mission statement of Jesus** showing His need to preach the good news of the Kingdom.	**1. The setting:** the crowds wait until the Sabbath is over, when the sun is setting, and then bring the sick to Jesus. This continues until the sun goes down (4:40). **2. The conditions** of the people: Jesus moves to public healings of people with a variety of diseases. The people struggle about who Jesus really is. **3. This summary** of the miracles gives the reader a sample of the work of Jesus. 4. Luke presents different aspects of the person of Jesus one-step at a time; first of all as Son of God and then as Christ. **5. The approach to the healings:** Luke refers to the laying on of hands as in Lk. 13:13, Mk. 5:23. **6. The reaction:** The demons recognise who Jesus is, "You are the Son of God!" and they further recognised Him as the Christ. (4:41).
4b]. a. Read 4:42-43 Jesus leaves Capernaum, and preaches the good news of the Kingdom in other cities. This is a double tradition (Mk. 1:35-38). **4c]. a.** Read Luke 4:44, a summary of Jesus' tour of Galilee and Judea. **b.** This is a triple tradition. **c.** Where Jesus says, "I have come," (Mark 1:38) Luke has "I was sent." This shows the relationship between God's sovereign purpose and the mission of Jesus.	**Provides evidence that:** a) the initial response at the start of Jesus' ministry was one of popularity (4:42). b) Jesus' mission to preach the good news of the kingdom to the other cities. c) Jesus' ministry is that of authoritative teaching (word) and healing (works). a) Jesus goes on teaching in Judea in the synagogues (4:44). The Kingdom is at the centre of the message (8:1; 9:2, 26; 10:9;16:16).	**1. Eschatological:** a) Jesus sees His calling in terms of proclaiming the arrival of God's promised rule (4:43). **2. Evangelistic:** a. The demons recognised Jesus as Son of God and the Christ. b) There is a strong sense of urgency in Jesus' evangelism; Jesus says, "I must preach the good news of the Kingdom." (4:43) Jesus preaches the gospel of the Kingdom to all Israel (4:43). c) Jesus' mission is seen in the words, "I was sent" (Gk. apostello). d) The Kingdom is the core of Jesus' message (4:43).	1. Jesus' mission is not limited to one locality and He does not desire that the focus be purely on the miracles (4:42-43). 2. The key features of the ministry of Jesus are the preached word and the supporting events (4:44). 3. Jesus preaches throughout the synagogues in Judea, which here has the broader sense of the entire land of the Jews (4:44). Compare with Lk.15, 6:17; 7:17 and 23:5 for a broader view.

BIBLE TEXT /TITLE / GENERAL COMMENTS

5a. Read 5:1-11 the miraculous catch of fish.

b. This is a nature miracle. It has also been called a 'pronouncement story', a 'gift' or 'provision' miracle because of the fish provided. (Theissen) (21) c. This is Luke's first nature miracle.

d. Does Luke develop Mk. 1:16-20? The call to become fishers is in both. In Mk 1:19, the fishermen are mending their nets not washing as in Lk.5:2. The same people are named in both accounts except for Andrew (Mk.1:16). e. This is unique to Luke and is a different event from the calling of the disciples (Matt.4:18-22; Mk.1:6-20). e. This miracle takes place in the context of the people coming to hear the word of God. Jesus used the boat as a pulpit.

f. It is an example of teaching and also a miraculous gift.

g. A recent discovery of a boat in the sea of Galilee 26 feet long and 7 feet wide shows that it would have been physically possible for Peter to fall at the feet of Jesus (5:8). (BAR) (22)

h. Fitzmyer (23) calls this a 'pronouncement story,' "henceforth you will be catching men." (5:1) 'Commission narrative' (Talbert) (24)

i. Is it the same as Jn.21:1-14? There are distinctive differences with Jn.21:1-14. In Lk.5:6, the nets are breaking. In Lk.5:8, Peter bows before Jesus and in John's Gospel, he flees (Jn. 21:7).

j. Other occasions when Peter calls Jesus "Master": "Master, Master we are perishing!" (8:24) Peter said, "Master, it is well that we are here let us make three booths." (9:33) "Master, we saw a man casting out demons in your name and we forbade him, because he does not follow us." (9:49)

FUNCTION: WHAT IS ACHIEVED?

The miraculous catch of fish provides evidence that/of:

- enabled Peter to see that Jesus has access to the power of God.
- only those who saw the miracle were summoned to follow Jesus, namely the three: Peter, James and John.
- who Jesus is in comparison with other people and highlights **His knowledge, authority and holiness.**
- It also lays the foundation for Peter's commission.
- It is a **"gift miracle."** Jesus initiates the event and in the end, provides for those around Him.
- In a sense the miracles are parables. This miracle is an **"audio-visual aid"** for a deeper spiritual reality. It points to Jesus' spiritual work and asks the reader to respond. Other examples are 5:17-36; 8:26-39; 11:14-23.
- Peter knew he was in the presence of the divine. He calls Jesus **"Master"** as a sign of respect and authority (5:5) and later he calls Him **"Lord"** (Gk.Kurie) (5:8).
- Discipleship means leaving the family and the family's business.
- Peter recognises the authority of Jesus in referring to Him as **"Master"** (Gk. epistata) a word used instead of Rabbi (17:13). Luke prefers the term **"Master"** (Gk. epistata) a term used by the disciples for Jesus. In Luke, the disciples never call Jesus "teacher" only those who observe Him, Simon the Pharisee (7:40); a lawyer (11:45); one of the multitude (12:13); some of the Pharisees in the multitude (19:39). Luke may do this out of respect for his non-Jewish audience, rather than use the term "rabbi".
- showing what happens when human sinfulness meets Jesus and that to receive the saving grace of Christ, a person must repent (5:8).
- This miracle also has a further discipleship function in that it inspires trust in and dependence upon Jesus.

PURPOSE: INTENDED RESULT [WHY?]

1. Evidential

a) It provided Peter with evidence which gave him an insight into Jesus' mission and His power in the healing of his mother-in-law, before he is asked to share in Jesus' work (4:38-39).

b) The call of Peter, James and John shows how Jesus received assistance in an overly successful ministry such as the healing of Peter's mother-in-law just before the incident.

c) Evidence of miracles, teaching and discipleship help to explain to Peter what is involved in his call to be a disciple.

d) It showed that Peter's discipleship was based upon his perception of himself as a sinner.

e) Evidence that Peter had entered the presence of Someone so powerful and holy that he pleads with Jesus to leave him. "Depart from me, I am a sinful man, O Lord." (5:8)

f) Peter calls Jesus "Master" and "Lord" and recognises **His authority** and sees him as divine.

2. Evangelistic: a) "Jesus uses Peter's boat as a pulpit to throw the net of the gospel over His hearers." (5:3) (Plummer) **(25)**

b) Peter is changed from "sinner" to "fisherman" and experiences a new sense of dependence upon God. "But at your word, I will let down the nets."(5:5)

c) Jesus still requires sinful people to join Him in fishing for people. Peter's faith is exemplary here.

d) A "provision or gift' miracle: the catch of fish was to represent the people who would be caught by the disciples.

e) From now on Peter will be catching people alive, engaging in continuous evangelism. It is a call to mission for the disciples (5:10b).

3. Eschatological:

a) The kingdom has come, when Peter realises that God is at work through Jesus.

b) After the great catch of fish, Jesus is going to send out the disciples to fish for people. The Kingdom of God has come.

CHARACTERISTICS : HOW IS IT UNIQUE?

1. **The setting:** Jesus is standing by Lake Gennesaret. The people are listening to Him preaching the word of God. Jesus uses Simon's boat as a pulpit. Crowds were becoming attracted to Jesus in Chs.4-5. People pressed upon Him to hear the word of God (5:1).

2. **The situation:** the four fishermen had "toiled all night and caught nothing" even when the conditions were favourable (5:5a).

3. **The words or act of the miracle:** "Put out into the deep and let down your nets for a catch." (5:4) When Peter responded to Jesus' words to let down the nets for a catch, it was on the basis of what he saw done for others (4:38-41). Peter has simple trust and dependence upon Jesus. "But at your word, I will let down the nets." (5:5b)

4. **The evidence of the miracle:** they enclosed a great shoal of fish; their nets were breaking and they had to get help from their partners. Both boats were so filled with fish that they began to sink (5:6-7).

5. **The response:** after the catch of a great shoal of fish, Peter realises that God is at work through Jesus and he confesses his unworthiness; "Depart from me, I am a sinful man, **O Lord.**" (Gk.Kurie) (5:8)

a. He is also astonished (Gk.thambos) at the great catch and all his colleagues with him. This is a common word in Luke for an amazing reaction to a miracle (5:9) Jesus promises Peter that he will share in the ministry of catching people.

b. The miracle of the catch of fish had a direct bearing on the call of the first disciple; they left all and followed Jesus (5:11).

c. Peter realised that Jesus could see into people's minds and hearts as He could detect fish in the Sea of Galilee.

6. **The Messiah had come to make people aware of their need.** These fishermen all responded at once.

7. **This miracle highlights** the knowledge of Jesus and His holiness. Jesus asked a sinful man like Peter to join Him in fishing for people.

8. Peter and the three fishermen with him leave their nets and start on a life's work of following Jesus, in the task of catching people. They had worked all night and caught nothing and followed Jesus when they saw the miraculous catch of fish.

9. Peter's call is a foreshadow of Jesus calling and choosing the Twelve and it showed Peter's future role in the Church (6:12-16).

10. Jesus and Peter are in the foreground. Andrew is not mentioned by Luke.

BIBLE TEXT / TITLE / GENERAL COMMENTS	FUNCTION: WHAT IS ACHIEVED?	PURPOSE: INTENDED RESULT [WHY?]	CHARACTERISTICS: HOW IS IT UNIQUE?
6. a. Read 5:12-16 the man with leprosy. [See p. 245.] b. It is a healing miracle. c. This is a triple tradition. Mark 1:40-45; Matthew 8:1-4. d. Leprosy was regarded by the Jews as the presence of sin: Lev.13:14; Num. 5:2-3; 12:10-12; Deut. 24:8. e. If the skin is declared leprous by the priest, the leper shall be pronounced as unclean (Lev.13:14). Put the leper outside the camp (Num. 5:2-3). f. Jesus accepts the Jewish norm, which required the leper to be declared healthy by the priest (Lev.14:1-32). g. This is the second summary of the miracles in Luke's gospel. The news of Jesus spread so that the crowds flocked to see Him (5:15). h. The Messianic act of healing was to be a "testimony to them"; Jesus' words echo Is.55:5-6 which says in the Messianic age those who do not see, hear, walk or speak will be healed. i. God's special agent had come; this is God's special time.	**The healing of the Jewish leper provides evidence that:** - Jesus acts and shows His **authority** to people who see their need. - He faces people with a choice: either He is a blasphemer or He has authority from God. - the function of this miracle is to show that the news of Jesus spread first to Galilee (5:15), Capernaum and then to Judea and Jerusalem (5:15,17). [See the map Ch.9.] - Jesus shows that His **authority** is from God (5:12). - multitudes gathered to hear the word of God and be healed of their diseases. - Messianic times are here. - the pattern to silence follows the approach in 4:41. Jesus would not allow the demons to speak. At first He wanted to do the works of the Messiah and to fulfil His basic mission of sacrificial suffering before being publically declared as the Messiah (5:14). - in calling Jesus "Lord" (Gk. Kurie), the leper recognised that Jesus could deal with his disease (5:12).	**1. Evidential** a) Evidence of the authority of Jesus and also that the power of leprosy is cancelled by the power of His word. **2. Evangelistic** a) This miracle provides people with a choice as to who He is: either He is a blasphemer or from God. b) Jesus' explicit purpose in coming was, "to preach the good news of the kingdom to the other cities." (4:43) c) The good news was first spread to Galilee (5:15). d) Crowds came to hear and be healed. **3. Empathetic** a) Jesus shows compassion to those who sense their need. b) Jesus healed by touch to show empathy towards the leper. c) In touching the leper, Jesus made Himself ceremonially unclean (Lev.13:42 in Nega'im), which would affect His participation in corporate worship. d) Luke shows His tenderness and sympathy "the people were troubled" with evil spirits. **4. Eschatological** a) Evidence of the sign of the "Messianic times." Jesus was "sent to preach release to the captives." (4:18b) Later it would also be an indication to John the Baptist that the Messiah had come, when "lepers are cleansed." (7:22) b) Jesus ministers unto the marginalized and the rejects of society. Lepers were socially and physically isolated to prevent others getting this contagious disease.	**1. Setting:** while Jesus was in one of the cities in Galilee (5:12). **2. The condition** of the man: full of leprosy (5:12). **3. The request for healing:** "Lord (Gk. Kure), if you will, you can make me clean." (5:12) **4. The act of healing:** a. Jesus stretched out His hand and touched the man who said, "I will be clean." (5:13) b. Jesus showed both His willingness to heal and His compassion by touching the man (5:13). **5. The healing demonstrated:** a. "Immediately the leprosy left him." (5:13). b. The man is also told to tell no one but go and show himself to the priest (5:14). c. The leper receives three instructions from Jesus: Jesus wants him to be silent until he is officially clean. The leper has to show himself to the priest, cf. (17:14) which reflects Lev.14:1-32. It took a week to get clearance from the priest. He had to offer a sacrifice before the priest as a proof (RSV) or testimony to the people (5:14). d. It was a testimony of God's power to heal and is a testimony that Messianic times are here (7:22). **6. The reaction to the healing:** a. the gathering of greater crowds. News of Jesus spread wider (5:15, 17). b. This is a fulfilment of (4:43-44), "Jesus must preach the good news of the Kingdom in other cities." c. Crowds came to hear and be healed.

BIBLE TEXT / TITLE / GENERAL COMMENTS	FUNCTION: WHAT IS ACHIEVED?	PURPOSE : INTENDED RESULT [WHY?]	CHARACTERISTICS : HOW IS IT UNIQUE?
7 a. Read 5:17-26 the paralysed man. b. This is a healing miracle sometimes called a "rule" miracle to show the authority of Jesus. (Theissen) (28) c. It is also an example of instant healing and is a triple tradition. [Mark 2:1-12; Matthew 9:1-8] d. The first miracles in Chs.4-5 show the extent of Jesus' power to deal with many different conditions and indicate how He revealed Himself. e. The comments of Jesus and the reactions to the miracles all explain why some people rejected Him. f. This is the start of formal opposition to Jesus. Jesus knew what was going on in the minds of the Scribes and Pharisees who accused Him of blasphemy and rejected His claim to be God and to forgive sins (5:22). g. God's kingdom had entered a human life. h. This is the first reference to the Pharisees in Luke's Gospel (5:17). i. People are faced with a response to Jesus. Is He the One that God has promised will come? j. This is the first miracle in Luke's Gospel against the forces of evil. k. "Today" is unique to Luke. "We have seen remarkable things (Gk. paradoxa) today." (5:26)	The healing of the paralysed man provides evidence of: - the uniqueness of Jesus, who has the divine authority to forgive sins (5:21). - Jesus met the man's two-fold need, his sin and his paralysis. Jesus was opposed to the idea that illness comes from sin as the Jews believed (Jn. 9:2). Jesus said that there is no direct link between paralysis and sin. - it provides evidence of the authority of Jesus in taking control of the man's life. - God's kingly rule is in action. - this miracle also raises the issue as to whether the claim of Jesus to forgive sins is real or empty? It cannot be proved wrong! - this is a "rule" miracle to show who is in control, in Jesus' challenge of the Pharisees. - Jesus shows that His miracles also carry a message of spiritual realities. - Jesus is reaffirmed as God's anointed agent "the power of the Lord was on Him to heal." (5:17 ; 4:18) - the power [Gk.dunamis] of God was seen in the power of Jesus to heal (works) and also in His teaching (words) in Galilee (5:17). - Jesus has the power to forgive sins: God does the healing and the forgiving. - faith. When Jesus saw their faith, He said, "Man your sins are forgiven you." (5:20)	1. Evidential/Christological a) Evidence of the power of Jesus to heal (5:17). "The power of the Lord was with Him to heal." b) All the crowd sought to touch him for the power came forth from Him and He healed them (6:19). c) Evidence of the authority of Jesus as, "The Son of Man has authority on earth to forgive sins." (5:24) d) Jesus sees Himself as more than a prophet. e) This is the first time the title "Son of Man" is used in Luke's Gospel and it is used twenty-five times; it is the only time it is used in relation to a miracle (5:24). f) Evidence that Jesus was exposing the opposition of the Pharisees. 2. Evangelistic a) Miracles put the rejection of Jesus into the "without excuse" category as they show that Jesus is divine. Readers are faced with a response. How will they respond? Is Jesus really the One who was promised? If Jesus is the source of the healing, what does this tell us about Jesus? b) The purpose of this miracle is to make a pronouncement to the paralysed man, "Man, your sins are forgiven you." c) God's saving work is evident to the crowd and they praise God. 3. Empathetic a) Jesus shows compassion to those who sense their need. 4. Eschatological a) Messianic times are coming, "release to the captives." (4:18) The hope of (1:77-79) is now taking place, "to give knowledge of salvation to His people in the forgiveness of their sins." Cleansing from sin could be a testimony to Messianic times. cf. 7:22: God's Kingdom has come. b) The event is the awaited eschatological "today." (4:21; 5:26)	1. The setting: Jesus was teaching and the Pharisees and teachers of the law were sitting there having come from all the regions. God's power was on Jesus to heal (5:17). 2. The man's condition: some friends brought a paralysed man on a bed to Jesus. Their way into the house was blocked by the crowds, who had come even as far as Jerusalem to hear Jesus (5:17). 3. The approach of the friends to the healing: they removed the mud layer above the beams and lowered their friend to Jesus (5:19). 4. The act and words of healing : Jesus addressed the man, when He saw the faith of his friends. This is the first time faith is used in Luke (5:20). Faith is explicitly expressed through the four friends bringing the paralysed man to Jesus. Their faith was powerful and active. "Man, your sins are forgiven you." (5:20) "The Son of Man has power on earth to forgive sins." (5:24) Three commands were given to the paralysed man: "Rise, take up your bed and go home." (5:24) 5. The healing is demonstrated: "Immediately" is used to show the impact of the healing. It was instantaneous and supernatural (5:25). 6. The reaction to the healing: a. the paralysed man goes home praising God (5:25). b. This miracle is followed by the public praise of God. "Then the people glorified God and were filled with awe." (5:26) The crowd says they have seen great things, wonderful things (Gk.paradoxa) happen today but failed to see the uniqueness of Jesus (5:26). d. The outcome is one of praise by the man and the crowd for God's saving work (5:25-26). God is glorified (Gk. doxazo).

BIBLE TEXT / TITLE / GENERAL COMMENTS	FUNCTION: WHAT IS ACHIEVED?	PURPOSE: INTENDED RESULT [WHY?]	CHARACTERISTICS: HOW IS IT UNIQUE?
8 a. Read 6:6-11 the man with the withered hand in the synagogue on the Sabbath. b. This is a healing miracle, sometimes called a "rule" miracle in which Jesus teaches and shows His authority. c. It is a triple tradition [Mark 3:1-6: Matthew 12:9-14]. d. Jesus does not abuse His power unlike Honi, the contemporary Jewish miracle worker (6:11). e. This miracle comes after three controversies that started in 5:33; all three provide a rationale for Jesus' style of ministry. Luke points out "like teacher, like disciple." [See Ch.7 Structure p.76.] f. For the Pharisees, the healing of the man with the withered hand, did not qualify for a Sabbath healing; the Sabbath could only be broken if life was threatened (Yoma 8:6; Shabbath 1:32a). g. From the Pharisees point of view, Jesus should have waited until after the Sabbath to heal the man as in the case of the crowds in 4:42-46. h. The man with the withered hand has the right to be healed on the Sabbath day, as the healing does not violate the idea of a Sabbath rest. i. This event is both a controversy about the Sabbath and a miracle. It is the first direct challenge to Jesus without referring to His disciples.	**Healing the man with the withered hand provides evidence of/that:** - the power of Jesus to heal and His **authority** about God's intention regarding the Sabbath. "The Son of Man is Lord of the Sabbath." (6:5) - Jesus confirms a claim He makes at the end of Lk. 5; He is bringing a new way. "New wine must be put into fresh wine skins." (5:37) - Jesus was an interpreter of the law regarding the Sabbath. - it is not an issue of doing good as distinct from doing nothing but doing good as distinct from doing evil. - those who like the old ways do not accept the reforms of Jesus. - Zeal can lead to unrighteousness. Jesus seeks to do good on the Sabbath, but the Pharisees want to destroy Him. Officials within Judaism had turned against Him; they were filled with fury and discussed as to what they might do to Him. Mark 3:6 and Matthew 12:14 say that they tried to destroy Him. The challenge to their faith and the religion of their fathers, was too great for the Pharisees. - Jesus brings new ways but people who like the old ways do not want His reforms. - the miracles differ from magic by the good character of those who do them. Jesus is not power hungry and therefore He is not like the wandering soothsayers in Galilee (11:19). - God's law does not inhibit the good.	**1. Evidential/Christological** a) Jesus is Lord of the Sabbath. He is a threat to traditional Judaism in the way He handled the Jewish Sabbath laws. b) Jesus shows His **authority** by just speaking a sentence. c) "Jesus as Son of Man is Master (Gk. Kurios) of the Sabbath." Jesus rules the Sabbath and not the Pharisees. d) The new way Jesus brings does not depend upon the authority of the religious leaders but on the **authority of God.** **2. Evangelistic** a) The Pharisees have chosen to reject Jesus and feel that something should be done about Him. b) The controversy has created a choice to resist or accept Jesus. **3. Empathetic** a) The ethic of compassion should be the basis for helping people in need. The "law of love" should be the basis for doing good on the Sabbath. The compassion of God and His power are evident in the healing. b. The purpose is to deal with the Jewish issue of doing good on the Sabbath and not that of a Sabbath rest for the disciples or Christians. c) Jesus takes the initiative in the healing, "Come and stand here" in front of everyone. (6:8) "Stretch out your hand." (6:10) **4. Eschatological** [See p. 76.] He has brought release to the captives in fulfilling the O.T. prophecy (Is.61:1) and the joy of the new age has come (4:18).	1. **The setting:** The sabbath in (6:1) could be the first after the feast of Passover and the second Sabbath after the Passover (6:6). Jesus entered the synagogue and was teaching there on another Sabbath (6:6). 2. **The man's condition:** he has a withered hand, possibly caused by paralysis. 3. **The approach to the healing:** Jesus knew the thoughts of the Pharisees and says to the man, "Come and stand here." (6:8) "I ask you. Is it lawful on the Sabbath to do good or to harm?" (6:9) 4. **The healing:** Jesus takes the initiative and commands the man to stretch out his hand and the outstretched hand is restored. "Stretch out your hand." (6:10) 5. **The healing demonstrated:** the man obeyed and his hand was restored (6:10). 6. **The reaction:** The event concludes with a plot to deal with Jesus. The Pharisees were furious [Gk. anoias] meaning mindless with illogical rage at Jesus (6:11). For the Pharisees, to heal or do any kind of medical work on the Sabbath was wrong unless that life was in danger. A midwife could work on the Sabbath. For the Jewish leaders, this event is in public and does not have any urgency; a sick or crippled person could wait until after the Sabbath, in the same way as a child born at twilight on Friday would have to wait to be circumcised after the Sabbath. Unless a person was near to death they could wait (Jn. 7:22-24; Yoma 8.6). 7. Jesus puts a question to the Pharisees. "Why delay a healing, when you can do good now?" 8. Jews could not initiate a battle on the Sabbath but if attacked would fight. [See p. 272.]

BIBLE TEXT / TITLE / GENERAL COMMENTS	FUNCTION: WHAT IS ACHIEVED?	PURPOSE: INTENDED RESULT [WHY?]	CHARACTERISTICS : HOW IS IT UNIQUE?
9. a. Read **6:17-19** people came from Judea, Jerusalem, Tyre and Sidon to hear and be healed by Jesus. b. This is a triple tradition [Mark 3:7-12; Matthew 4:24-25]. c. This is the third summary of the ministry of Jesus in Luke's Gospel and it is close to Mark 3:7-12. d. Other summaries are: [4:40-41; 5:15 and 7:21-22]. e. Luke emphasises Jesus as a teacher. He also shows the variety in the ministry of Jesus. f. This summary sets the scene for the Sermon on the Plain. g. Great crowds (6:17) indicate Luke's stress on the popularity of Jesus. There are two contrasting groups of people in (6:20): 1) the Pharisees with their emphasis on legalism and righteousness. 2) the many 'people of the land' who know little about rabbinic teaching and do not have regular religious traditions. h. Jesus had challenged this world view of the Pharisees (5:17; 6:11). They discriminated in their choice of 'table friends': those who do not fast and those who keep the Sabbath. Jesus challenges these views in 5:33-38; 6:36. "Be merciful, even as your Father is merciful."	**A third summary of the miracles provides evidence that/of:** - the power went out of Jesus to heal. - the priority of Mark as Mark omits the Sermon on the Plain and the Sermon on the Mount (Matt. 5-7). [See pp. 33-4.] - three groups of people who are present at the miracles: the apostles, a crowd of disciples and the people. - Jesus' power was drawn on by touch, cf. (8:43-46). - the authority of Jesus is in His works (healings) and word (teaching) (6:18). - "the people" are the prospective followers (6:17) and "the many disciples" are His larger circle of friends.	**1. Evidential** a) Provides evidence that people came to listen to Jesus as well as to be healed. b) That Jesus continues to be popular as His healings continue to attract the people. c) Evidence that the people are also interested in his teaching (6:17). d) Evidence that people are attacted by the power of Jesus. **2. Empathetic** a) Jesus heals crowds of people by touch (6:18). **3. Eschatological** a) Jesus is likened to Moses when He came down from the mountain (c.f. 6:17). "This is my Son, my Chosen; listen to Him!" (9:35) b) This has been likened to Deut.18:15, "The Lord your God will raise up a prophet like me from among you, from your brethren - him you shall heed." **4. Evangelistic** a) The people came fron Judea, Jerusalem (Jews) and from Tyre and Sidon (Gentiles) to hear and be healed. b) Here are Jews and Gentiles who came from afar and are open to the gospel.	**1. Setting:** Great crowds from Judea, Jerusalem (the religious centre of the faith), and the sea coast of Tyre and Sidon (the Gentile interest in Jesus), are coming to hear Jesus and to be healed (6:17). Jesus "came down" possibly meaning He came down from a mountain. **2. The medical condition of the people:** many people with diseases and those troubled with unclean spirits (6:18). **3. The request for help:** the crowd, both Jews and Gentiles, came to touch Him because they recognised His power to heal and to exorcise. **4. The healing demonstrated:** spiritual power came from Jesus and He healed them all (6:19). The healings distinguish between those who are possessed by demons and those who have physical illnesses. **5. The reaction:** Jesus' popularity spread and people's curiosity was whetted (6:17).

BIBLE TEXT / TITLE / GENERAL COMMENTS	FUNCTION: WHAT IS ACHIEVED	PURPOSE: INTENDED RESULT [WHY?]	CHARACTERISTICS: HOW IS IT UNIQUE?
10. a. Read 7:1-10 the centurion's servant. [p. 245.] b. This is a healing miracle. It is sometimes called a "quest" story. (Tannehill) (29) c. Fitzmyer (30) calls it a "pronouncement" on "commendable faith". d. It is the only occasion Jesus marvelled or is amazed (Gk. ethaumasen). [See also the parallel account in Matt. 8:10-15]. e. Jesus comes in response to an initial request by the Jewish elders (7:6a). f. It also showed the Jewish elders' respect for the Gentiles. g. It showed Jesus' concern for outsiders. h. It is a "telepathic healing" (healing from a distance), which shows that the power of Jesus could not be limited by distance or touch. i. This event marks the pivotal point in the progress of God's word from a Jewish context to the Gentile world. j. If Jesus had entered the centurion's house, He would have been criticised by the Jewish leaders. k. The centurion could have been a soldier in Herod's provincial army. Herod was known to have employed Roman soldiers.	The healing of the centurion's servant provides evidence of/that: - a Christological function: it shows who Jesus really is. The centurion recognises the great authority of Jesus. He recognised Jesus as Lord as a sign of the expansion of Jesus' ministry to the nations (7:6). - racial differences are not a hindrance to Jesus; the centurion is commended to Jesus. - Jesus' empathy extends to socially significant people and not just to the poor. - **the authority of Jesus extends to distance, disease and space.** - the Jews' appreciation of a religious, Roman Gentile. - Jesus' comparison of the Gentile faith with that of the Jews. - stress being placed upon the word (Gk. logos) of God, believed to have power (7:7; 4:32, 36). - the fact that race makes no difference to Jesus. - a third example of faith in Luke so far: Mary in (1:45) and the four men with the paralysed man (5:20). - Jesus referred to as "Lord" as a sign of respect by the centurion (7:6). - Jesus speaking to a large multitude 'who followed Him'. A large group of disciples is suggested in the word 'followed' (7:9). The centurion recognised the authority of Jesus which the Jewish council in Capernaum failed to do.	**1. Evidential** a) Evidence of Jewish respect for the Gentiles. "He is worthy to have you do this." (7:4) b) Jesus praised the centurion for his faith. "I tell you, not even in Israel have I found such faith." (7:9) Jesus is amazed at the quality of the man's response to Him, "He marvelled at him." (7:9) c) Evidence of the proof of the healing is, "they found the slave well." (7:10) **2. Empathetic** a) Jesus shows empathy to other races and to people of significant social standing. Racial and religious distinctions are not part of the gospel. This miracle shows the extent and depth of God's love. Gentiles could react more positively to a powerful demonstration of authority. b) Jesus ran the risk of Jewish defilement in His praise of the Gentile centurion (7:9). c) Jesus shows compassion to the servant of the army of occupation and has no racial limits. d) It is a "quest story" in which someone approaches Jesus looking for something important for the human well-being of another person. **3. Eschatological:** a. Some scholars see parallels with Elijah providing food for the widow and her son in 1Kgs.17:7-16. (Brodie) **(31)**(Green) **(32)** **4. Evangelistic:** a. Luke points out the importance of faith. The centurion has faith in the same way as Mary (1:45). The centurion believed Jesus had the power to heal, "But say the word..." (7:7).	**1. Setting: after the Sermon on the Plain,** Jesus journeys to nearby Capernaum (7:1). Jesus taught in the hearing of the people (7:1). **2. The slave servant's condition:** a Roman centurion has a sick servant, who was sick at the point of death. **3. The request for the healing:** The centurion sends Jewish envoys to Jesus to ask for healing. Gentiles were less enchained by tradition than the Jews. A Gentile centurion recognised that Jesus has the power to heal and help those with faith (7:9). This is the first meeting with a Gentile and it shows the centurion's willingness to respond to Jesus. Jesus acknowledged the Gentile centurion's generosity in building the synagogue in Capernaum (7:5) and also his sense of unworthiness. **4. The act of healing:** Jesus responds to the man's faith and humility. "Not even in Israel have I found such faith." (7:9) **5.** Luke places the two miracles of the centurion's servant and the widow's son before the query by John's disciples as to who Jesus is or whether they should look for someone else. **6. Reaction:** Jesus recognises this Gentile's humility and deep faith. The faith of a Gentile can be just as great or greater than that of a Jew. Faith here is a plea to ask Jesus for help even though the person is unworthy to receive it. "Lord do not trouble yourself, for I am unworthy to have you come under my roof." (7:6) He calls Jesus "Lord."

BIBLE TEXT / TITLE / GENERAL COMMENTS	FUNCTION: WHAT IS ACHIEVED?	PURPOSE: INTENDED RESULT [WHY?]	CHARACTERISTICS: HOW IS IT UNIQUE?
11.a. Read 7:11-17 raising the widow's Son at Nain in O.T. Shunem. (L) **b.** This is a resurrection miracle. Bock (33) calls it resuscitation. Against this view, Jesus alludes to the dead boy being raised (7:22). [See p.197.] **c.** It is an example of instantaneous healing. **d.** Burial customs for the Jews said that the person could not be buried until death was certain, clothes were torn as a sign of mourning and the eyes were closed, the body was anointed to prevent decay and a quick burial followed (SB 23,5). (34) **e.** This miracle has been called a **"parabolic miracle"** like Elisha–an enacted object lesson about the coming Kingdom. (Blomberg) (35) **f.** The title "prophet" was a **common way for unresponsive people to view** Jesus (7:16; 9:19; 24 19). **g.** Jesus is the prophet and the **compassionate teacher, the Benefactor of the poor.** **h.** Following death, the corpse was washed and anointed, the deceased was buried in their own clothes or a burial cloth carried on a bier or coffin and entombed in salt or sand. **i.** At a funeral even the poorest would hire at least two flutes and a professional mourner (Ketuboth 4:4). **j.** The widow epitomises 'the poor' having lost her husband and now her only son: Jesus came to preach good news to the poor. She is devoid of social status in her community. **k.** The miracle took place in public. Compare this miracle of Jairus' daughter, which was in private (8:49-56).	**Raising of the widow's son provides evidence of/that:** - a crowd showing Jesus' popularity - Jesus' compassion (7:12) and concern for the widow when He restores her son like Elijah (7:15; 1 Kgs. 17:22). - Jesus' power to raise the dead and inspire faith and His power and authority over death (7:13). - **reference to Jesus as Lord shows the great authority of Jesus (7:13).** - Jesus taking the initiative in the raising of the boy, comes at the beginning of the account (7:14). - the public response to declare Jesus a prophet like Elijah (1 Kgs. 17:17-24) and Elisha (2 Kgs. 8:37) and to praise God for visiting His people. - the personal authority of Jesus. "Young man, I say to you arise." (7:14) - the words and position of Jesus being made valid. The crowd see Him as a great prophet: it recognised God's hand in the miracle (7:16-17). - the fact that, for Luke and his readers, John was asking if Jesus was the Christ, Lord, Son of God, Son of Man and not the future second coming of the Son of Man. It is His first coming. - this event as a resurrection miracle and Luke reports that the boy had died. Therefore his death is not symbolic. "The young man got up." (7:15) - Luke's first use of the term "Lord" (Gk.Kurios) in his narrative shows His authoritative position after the resurrection. - Jesus risking defilement in touching the bier (7:14; Num.19:11.16).	**1. Empathetic:** a. Jesus knew the needs of the widow and shows compassion to her in her helplessness by comforting her. When the Lord saw her His heart went out to her (Gk, esplanchnisthe), and He said, "Do not weep." (7:13) He offers more than words in his comfort and more than others can give, b) Jesus goes on to do further healing miracles and exorcisms (7:21). This is a summary of His ministry linking the miracles and messages. c) The contemporaries of Jesus were privileged; they heard the word and saw the actions which are a fulfilment of ancient hopes. Jesus' compassion is focussed on the widow. Compassion is a key feature in Ch.7. **2. Eschatological:** a. The purpose of Luke in Ch.7 is to show Theophilus that Jesus is "the one who was to come."(7:19) After the raising of the widow's son the crowd recognised:- b) Jesus as a great prophet who had come, but they did not recognise Him as the Messiah. He was indeed the "One who was to come." c) The extent of God's love and the power of Jesus over death. d) A key issue here is, "What kind of Messiah would Jesus be, if He is the Messiah?" **The mission of Jesus** does not seem to match Jewish expectations about the "last days." They expected a Messiah but were confused about what the Messiah would be like. O.T. images of the Messiah include: Deut.18:15-18 (the Coming Prophet), Is.40:10 (a Shepherd to feed His flock), Hab.2:3 (a vision which awaits God's time), Mal.3:1 (God's messenger to prepare the way), Mal. 4:5 (the return of Elijah). In later Judaism, "the Coming One" was a Messianic title. (S.B.) **(36)** e) A major time of eschatological fulfilment has come, 'the dead are raised'. (7:22) **3. Evangelistic:** a. Jesus issues a beatitude which is a call to faith. "Blessed is he who takes no offence at me." (7:23) Jesus is more concerned about reaching out to people.	**1. The setting:** a funeral procession in the Galilean city of Nain, SE of Nazareth, when Jesus is accompanied by His disciples, a great crowd is in attendance. It shows Jesus' great popularity. The disciples and His companions are witnesses of the event (7:11). **2. The boy's condition:** an only son of a widow had died. **3.** There is **no request** for a miracle. Jesus takes the initiative. **4. Jesus shows compassion** to the widow who had lost her only son. When Jesus saw her, He had compassion and said, "Do not weep." This shows that Jesus expressed the great love which He has for people (7:13). **5. Jesus restores her son:** He came, touched the bier and said, "Young man, I say to you, arise." (7:14) Jesus also uses this word of the Good Samaritan (10:33) and of the father in the parable of the Prodigal Son (15:20). He comforts the widow (7:13). Jesus touched the bier, which ran contrary to the Jewish tradition (Num.19:11). The bearers stood still when He touched the bier; something unusual had happened (7:14). This would have been seen as unclean and He would not have been allowed to enter the Temple. **6. Evidence of the miracle:** the dead man sits up and begins to speak (7:15). **7. The reaction:** all the people were filled with fear (Gk.phobos) for the work of God and the public perception of Jesus as a prophet. The crowd acknowledged the healer and God who had sent Him. "A great prophet has risen among us and God has visited His people." (7:16) News about Jesus spread. **8.** Raising the boy offers answers as to who Jesus is in terms of power and praise. The crowd see Him as a great prophet: they do not know if He is the One who is to come. John and the Twelve had difficulty in recognising who Jesus was due to preconceptions about the Messiah. (Stein) **(37)**

BIBLE TEXT / TITLE / GENERAL COMMENTS	FUNCTION: WHAT IS ACHIEVED?	PURPOSE: INTENDED RESULT [WHY?]	CHARACTERISTICS: HOW IS IT UNIQUE?
12.A. a. **Read Ch.7:18-23** John the Baptist sends two messengers to Jesus to question Jesus about His Ministry. b. The messengers put two questions to Jesus. **"Are you the coming one, or are we to wait for another?"** (7:20) c. Jesus' reply to the envoys: the setting for this reply is in the fourth summary of miracles in Luke's Gospel (7:21-22). These include many miraculous acts: curing many of diseases, plagues and evil spirits, and on many who were blind, **He bestowed sight** (7:21). The expression 'bestowed sight' is unique to Luke (7:21). d. This is the fourth summary of the miracles and includes four different types: healings, exorcisms, resurrections and grace miracles. e. This is an example of double tradition (Matthew 11:2-6). f. Luke omits John's imprisonment. Matthew says that John was in prison at this time (Matt.11:2). Josephus says he was imprisoned at Machaerus, a restored fortress east of the Dead Sea. g. In later Judaism, "the Coming One" was a Messianic title (S.B.). (38) Some groups saw a connection between the event of the Coming One and healing based upon 1QH 18.14-15; Pesikta Rabbati 15.22; Aggadat Berishit 69.1 based upon Is. 35:5-6.	**Provides evidence of/that:** - grace/mercy as key ideas in Jesus' ministry. - a variety of healings and exorcisms which is further **indication of the authority of Jesus** and shows the kinds of things John was hearing. - Jesus' acknowledgement that John the Baptist was His forerunner and was much more than a prophet. There is no one born of a woman greater than John.' (7:28a) - Jesus' review of His Ministry in terms of Is.61: 2; 29:18-19; 35:5-6. - Jesus as the answer to John's question "Are you the one who is to come or are we to look for another"? (7:19-20) The answer is in Jesus' miracles: the blind receive their sight, the lame walk, lepers are cured, the dead are raised, and good news is preached to the poor (7:22). - Jesus as the true Messiah. - Jesus reveals Himself to John the Baptist (7:18-23). - Jesus' activity is the fulfilment of the prophecies of the coming age of divine blessing (7:22; Is. 35:5-6). - Jesus' role is made clear. He is **an end time prophet like Moses** who is a messianic type of figure. What kind of Messiah would Jesus be, if He is the Messiah?" **The mission of Jesus** does not seem to match Jewish expectations about the "last days." They expected a Messiah but were confused about what the Messiah would be like. O.T. images of the Messiah include: **The Coming Prophet** (Deut.18:15-18; Is.40:10), **'A Great prophet'** (7:16;1Q 9:11), **The Messiah (a Shepherd)** to feed His flock (Jn. 6:14;11:27), a vision which awaits God's time. (Hab.2:3), **God's messenger** to prepare the way (Mal.3:1), **the return of Elijah** (Mal.4:5). Luke's answer is in 3:15-16. Luke keeps this question in the forefront. [See p. 104.]	**1. Empathetic** a. God visits the outcasts and the needy with compassion when the Gospel is proclaimed to the blind, lame, lepers, deaf, dead and the poor. **2. Eschatological** a) Jesus fulfilled the Servant role of (Is.61:1-2: 29:8-19) in the gracious way, He restored sight to the blind (7:21; 4:18-19). b) He is the **true Messiah** who does not proclaim himself as such but does Messianic works; He heals the blind, the deaf, the lame, the dumb and fulfils Is. 42:7; 35:5-6. The Messianic age has come. Jesus is the Coming one spoken of in the O.T. c) Jesus' reply to John the Baptist, shows the belief that the people would experience healing in the Messianic age (Midrash,Tanhuma B. trad. Mezora 7. "All who suffer will be cured in the world to come." d) The final eschatological verdict depends upon people's attitude to Jesus. Final judgement will depend upon whether people are His followers, for example the person who hears and obeys God's word (6:47-49); takes up the cross daily and follows (9:23-26,48); and acknowledges Jesus (12:8-9; 14:26). e) "Go and tell John what you have seen and heard: the blind receive their sight, the lame walk, lepers are cleansed, the deaf hear, and the dead are raised up and the poor have the good news preached to them." (7:22) f) Jesus goes on to do further healing miracles and exorcisms. g) A major eschatological time has come the dead are raised (7:11-17). **3. Evangelistic** a. Jesus preaches good news to the poor. **4. Evidential:** Jesus is the coming One.	**The setting of John's question:** 1. John the Baptist was in prison, expecting Jesus to do something spectacular, nothing happened (7:18), so he sent envoys to Jesus to find out why and to provoke action (7:19). John sends two of his disciples to Jesus asking, 'Are you he who is to come, or shall we look for another?' (7:20) "In that hour" (Gk. hora) refers to a specific time in the ministry of Jesus, when Jesus cured many (7:21). Luke uses this word seventeen times. The fact that two witnesses were sent may reflect that truthfulness in the witness is guaranteed (Deut. 19:15). John's disciples report back to him about Jesus' healings, preaching and teachings. 2. In the summary of the miracles, general terms for illness are used (Gk. nosos) and (Gk. mastix), which refer to a very painful affliction; these are different from demon possession (7:21). 3. **Jesus graced many with sight.** This was free gracious exercise of His power (Gk. eucharistato) (7:21). This links Jesus' healing ministry with the Servant of Is. 61:1-2 "to proclaim the year of the Lord's favour." 4. **Why did John question Jesus** (7:19)? a. Is John's doubt caused by his imprisonment which seems the reverse of Jesus saying 'freeing captives from prison' (4:18-19)? b. Is John being impatient with Jesus' progress in His ministry? c. Was this pure doubt? Was it doubt produced by pressure as the background to the question? Even disciples like Peter did not fully understand the full nature of Jesus' ministry (Matt.16:22-23). All these questions give rise to the real question who is the Coming One? Luke's answer goes back to the Baptism of Jesus. [See p. 135.]

BIBLE TEXT / TITLE / GENERAL COMMENTS	FUNCTION: WHAT IS ACHIEVED?	PURPOSE: INTENDED RESULT [WHY?]	CHARACTERISTICS: HOW IS IT UNIQUE?
12.B **a. Read Ch.7:22-23 important questions about the ministries of Jesus and John the Baptist.** **b. Jesus' reply to John's messengers: Trust the O.T. pictures. Is.35: 5-6; 29:18-19; 61:1. "A cry of Jubilee"; "song of salvation" These O.T. texts look for God's deliverance.** **c. This is a double tradition with Matthew 11:4-5. (Q)** **d. The envoys have to report back to John all that they have seen and heard.** **1. Is Jesus saying, I have come not as 'a fiery reformer' and therefore not Messianic?** **2. Judaism expected the Messiah to do great miracles. Did they see the Messiah as the expected Son of David (18:38-39)? [See p. 209.]**	**Questions about the ministries of Jesus and John provides evidence of/that:** - who Jesus is to the envoys sent by John and also to John himself. - Jesus' ministry closely linked to the Servant in Is. 61:1-2. - all the miracles which Jesus did. These are proof of His authority and show the arrival of a new era (7:22). - Jesus having a central role in salvation; blessing or woe depends upon what people do with Jesus (7:23). - Jesus' miracles showing the scope and extent of His **power and authority** in healing the sick, exorcising evil spirits, curing fever, leprosy, paralysis, a withered hand, a flow of blood, and deafness. The "Messianic age" has come. - Blessing is not just for individuals but points to a special period of time. - Jesus alludes to a Messianic function when He declares and brings good news. He is not just a prophet (4:18-19). The events testify to a Messianic figure as in 4:18-19. - who possesses unique authority (7:22-23). Luke answers the question, "Who is Jesus?" The answer is clear; "Jesus of Nazareth is the Christ, the Son of God, the Lord."	**1. Eschatological** a) Jewish eschatology expected the Messiah to do miraculous works in the "eschaton (final event)." So the reply of Jesus is a Messianic one (7:22-23). b) These miracles show the presence of the "eschaton". Is.35:5-6 is a picture of paradise when God's rule is manifest in its fullness. c) Jesus is up front in saying, "I am **the Coming–One, the Messiah and not just a prophet.**" John prepares the people for the coming of the Messiah (Ex. 23:20). d) Jesus is not just a prophet but the **Coming–One, the Messiah**. "His miracles and preaching were not simply acts of mercy; they were part of an agenda whose goal was the restoration of Israel. (Scott) **(39)** Blessings and miracles point to a special time of blessing (7:23). **2. Evangelistic:** a. Jesus' role is central to salvation. "Blessed is anyone who takes no offence at me." (7:23) He blesses and accepts the person who accepts Him for what He is (7:23). Jesus' remark is open to 'anyone' or all who respond. b) This beatitude is a challenge as is "Blessed rather are those who hear the word of God and keep it!" (11:28) Blessing or woe will depend upon what people do with Jesus. Those who do not have preconceived ideas about the Messiah but judge by what they see happening, will know that Jesus is the Promised One and will be blessed. **4. Evidential:** Jesus has unique authority.	**The setting for Jesus' reply to John the Baptist** who has sent two messengers to Jesus (7:21). 1. Jesus tells the envoys to tell John all the things which they have seen and heard: the blind receive their sight the lame walk and lepers are healed, the deaf hear, the dead are raised up, the poor have good news preached to them (7:22). 2. According to Luke, John's envoys saw and heard these activities and they were eyewitnesses to the answers Jesus sent (7:22). 3. Jesus then puts a question about John to the crowds. "What did you go out to see?" (7:24) 4. John is "the already Elijah," while the "not yet" Elijah has still to come. Jesus calls John "great" as John is the bridge from one era to another (7:28). [See p. 108.]

BIBLE TEXT / TITLE / GENERAL COMMENTS	FUNCTION:WHAT IS ACHIEVED?	PURPOSE : INTENDED RESULT [WHY?]	CHARACTERISTICS : HOW IS IT UNIQUE?
13 A]. a. Read 8:2 demons cast out of Mary Magdalene. (L) b. Luke tells of those who supported Jesus: **the Twelve disciples, Mary Magdalene from whom He cast out the demons and the women.** c. **This is a summary statement of Jesus' touring ministry like 4:14-15; 4:43-44.** d. Luke indicates three categories of illness: evil spirits (8:2), diseases (8:2) and demon possession (8:3). They all experienced different measures of social ostracism. After their healing they may not have returned to their own families and communities but to a new community formed around Jesus. e. **Mary remained faithful as she watched the crucifixion** (23:55; Matt. 27:61; Mk.15:47). f. **This is the first time the disciples are called 'the Twelve' since they were called in 6:13; 8:1.** g. **At least eleven of the women named in Luke's Gospel are all in unique accounts.**	**The exorcism of Mary Magdalene provides evidence of/that:** - **the power and authority of Jesus to cast out demons from Mary Magdalene (8:2).** - Mary being freed from the presence of seven demons. This could denote very severe possession. - the effect of the ministry of Jesus in entering Herod's house, Joanna the wife of Chuza Herod's steward, Suzanna and many others (8:3). - Jesus emphasising that the fulfilment of God's promise was at hand and that God's agent through the blessing would come, was at hand (4:16-30; 8:1a; 11:20; 16:16). - another significant point in the progress of God's word in a Jewish context: that of entering Herod's court palace. - a Christological allusion to Jesus'power to heal and cast out demons (8:2). - God's grace coming to the outcast Mary. [See pp. 46, 243.]	**1. Evidential** a) Evidence of other women giving their support to Jesus. [See p. 219.] b) Evidence of the unusual practice of women to travel with a rabbi. The ministry of Jesus was gender inclusive and was not limited to the poor. **2. Eschatological** a) Evidence that "messianic times" have come in that Jesus cast out demons from Mary Magdalene (7:22; 8:2). b) Jesus fulfilled the O.T. messianic promises. God had indeed visited His people (1:68; 78; 7:16). c) The fact that the miracles occur (7:22) is proof that Jesus is the Messiah. (Stein) **(40)** **3. Evangelistic** a) The gospel has entered Herod's household (8:3). b) Jesus tours the region with the message of the Kingdom; He continues His preaching (8:1a). **4. Empathetic** a) These women supported Jesus and His disciples (8:3). This was a reflection of their faith and generosity by way of practical help on the mission. b) Because Jesus had been compassionate to Mary, she decided to serve Him who had healed her.	1. Women play a major role in responding and contributing to the ministry of Jesus. [See pp. 229, 233.] 2. "From city to village is an indication of His travelling (8:1b). 3. "Soon afterward" denotes an event after Ch.7. 4. Demon possession was not considered a sinful condition by some writers in the early church!! (Tertullian) 'On Modesty' 11 5. Those who have been touched by Jesus, minister onto Him and the Twelve. 6. 7. These women serve/provide "out of their resources." (8:3) It is likely that these women are single; it would have been easier to dispose of their resources "as they saw fit." 8. These women reflect the graciousness of Jesus and His self-giving. They serve others (22:24-37). 9. They exemplify Jesus' message on faith and wealth (Acts 4:32). Everything they owned was held in common. They hear and live out the word of God (6:46-49; 8:21). 10. Mary was from Magdala (today Migdal) N.E. of Tiberias. (See map at the end chapter 9.) She is not the sinful woman in 7:37-50. The reference to seven demons shows the magnitude of her former condition (11:24-26).

BIBLE TEXT / TITLE / GENERAL COMMENTS	FUNCTION:WHAT IS ACHIEVED?	PURPOSE : INTENDED RESULT [WHY?]	CHARACTERISTICS : HOW IS IT UNIQUE?
13B]. a. **Read 8:22-25 the stilling of the storm.** b. This is a nature miracle sometimes called a rescue miracle. c. It is also a triple tradition miracle. [Matthew 8: 22-25 and Mark 4:35-41]. d. It is another example of an instantaneous miracle. e. This is the first of four miracles which start with nature and moves to disease, to exorcism and finally to death. f. One of a trilogy of "Great Miracles." (German Grosswunder) g. The double use of the word "Master" expresses respect and terror (8:24). h. This miracle is deliverance or rescue through trial rather than from trial. i. The major theme is Christological to describe who Jesus is (8:25). He is "The Son of the Most High" (1:32); the Lord Christ (2:26) and the Lord (2:11).	**The stilling of the storm provides evidence of/that:** - the disciples were helped to realise that whatever the danger, Jesus is aware and is able to deliver. - the disciples were convinced of the unique power **authority** and character of Jesus over nature. In the O.T. Yahweh is Lord of the sea in creation and has the power to calm the raging storm (Pss. 29:3-47; 4:12-15; 104:7; 107:23-32; Job 26:12-13). He can divide the waters as at the Exodus (Ps.77:16-20). - the issue: "Who then is this, that He commands even wind and rain?" The disciples can trust Jesus because of who He is. What God used to do in the past, Jesus now does (8:25). - Jesus is more than a prophet or teacher. - the greatness of the **authority** which the disciples will receive. - the range of the **power and authority of Jesus** is seen in increasing spheres. - the disciples realise that because of the Lord's power there is no need to fear and to reassure the reader that God has acted through Jesus because of the power which is revealed. - very soon, Jesus will give the same **authority to His disciples (9:1-6).** - the disciples are slow to realise the identity of Jesus the Master. - Jesus has different ways for believers to serve Him.	**1. Evidential/Christological** a) Evidence of discipleship training: Jesus says to the disciples, "Where is your faith?" (8:24) The disciples are to apply faith in dangerous situations by deliverance through trial, rather from it. There was a momentary lapse in their faith. b) The sudden stopping of the wind shows the unique power and character of God and showed the disciples who Jesus really was. c) Jesus' power shows that He can be trusted. d) Even when He does not seem to be consciously with them, He can still meet their need. e) This miracle shows that Jesus is more than a teacher or prophet but is someone who is unique. f) The identity of Jesus is kept in centre stage from (8:22-9:17). g) The disciples should have been certain that they would get to the other side having been assured by Jesus (8:22). **2. Evangelistic** a) It confronts people with who Jesus really is. b) It is an "object lesson" about the nature and arrival of the Kingdom of God. c) At the end of the event the reader is left to ponder who Jesus really is (8:25). **3. Eschatological** a) Luke leaves the query unanswered as to who Jesus is. He is at least a prophet but is He more than that: He has the power to restore order and in Him there is real hope for the future.	1. **The setting:** this is the second nature miracle in Luke and is the first in a series of miracles centred around the Sea of Galilee, before Jesus sent out the Twelve. Jesus said to the disciples, "Let us go to the other side of the lake." (8:22) 2. **The condition of the disciples:** the account describes the physical need of the disciples. 3. **The request for help:** "Master, Master we are perishing!" The disciples panic, waken Jesus up and ask Him to save them, because they are at risk (8:24). 4. **Evidence of the miracle:** Jesus rebukes the wind and the raging sea. The waves cease and there was a calm (8:24). When things calm down, Jesus rebukes them for having such little faith. "Where is your faith?" (8:25) 5. **The reaction:** the disciples realise that a miracle of nature has taken place and they are afraid (Gk.phobethentes). Our word "phobia" comes from this. They further react by marvelling at (Gk.ethaumasan) and recognising the authority of Jesus (8:25). "Who is this, that He commands even wind and water, and they obey Him?" 6. Fear thrives where faith is missing. 7. **Conclusion:** a. The waves can only be calmed by the One who has the power to restore order. b. Only Someone fully Divine can handle wind and waves like this. c. However great the peril, Jesus can deliver. d. Very soon He will give the same authority to His disciples (9:1-6).

BIBLE TEXT / TITLE / GENERAL COMMENTS	FUNCTION: WHAT IS ACHIEVED?	PURPOSE: INTENDED RESULT [WHY?]	CHARACTERISTICS: HOW IS IT UNIQUE?
14. a. Read 8:27-38 the demoniac from the region of the Gergasenes. b. This is an example of an exorcism/healing. Gerasene is thought to be the neighbourhood and Gadara the name of the town. c. The Gerasenes are the inhabitants of Gadara, the people who inhabit the region of the Gerasenes (8:46). d. This is another visual-aid miracle. e. Was the storm at sea an attempt to prevent Jesus' arrival at Gerasene (8:22-5)? f. This miracle raises the question why does God in His Wisdom, Power and Love permit evil in the world? Satan though defeated, is still active (1 Pet. 5:8). g. The narrative does not say Jesus willed the destruction of the pigs. Jesus allowed the demons to enter the pigs; the man's healing would be verified when the pigs were destroyed. The man's cure is more important than the herd of pigs! They begged Jesus not to send them to the Abyss which is the place the demons wanted to avoid (8:28,31): this is the final destiny for the devil and his angels. h. Luke highlights the destruction of the evil forces and emphasises the isolation of the demoniac (8:27). Unbelief often runs away from meeting God (8:37).	The exorcising of the demoniac provides evidence of and testifies to the disciples of: - the power, authority and love of **God in Jesus Christ over the forces of evil.** - Jesus' **power and authority** among the Gentiles. - Jesus' concern for the mental well-being of the man. - the disciples' realisation that whatever the mental condition of the person, Jesus is able to deliver. - the power of the kingdom (cf.11:20), the power of the Messiah and the destructful effects of demon possession. - the Christian mission to the Gentiles. - demonic control of speech, shouting (8:28) and extraordinary strength (8:29). He was controlled by powers alien to God. The man's words and actions are not his own. He is in a state of mental and physical torture (Gk. basonizo). - demons' recognition of Jesus' deity (8:28). - the demons' intention to continue their alien work on the pigs. The swine's destruction is evidence of the success of the exorcism. - a Gentile wanting to join the travelling band of disciples. - a Christological function. Jesus' greatness is seen in His mastery of the demoniac. The story prefigures the future Gentile missions. [See p. 246.]	**1. Evidential/Christological** a) Evidence that Jesus controls vast numbers of spiritual forces allied against Him. b) Evidence of the good news of Jesus spreading into the Gentile areas. **2. Evangelistic** The transformed life of the man would be a powerful witness. The man's task was to stay and witness to his own people. This is really a missionary story as there is opportunity for witnessing in a Gentile area. (Fitzmyer) **(41)** **3. Empathetic** a) This incident shows Jesus' full acceptance and compassion for those who were socially, religiously and ethnically marginalized, living in tombs in the pagan, Gentile area of Decapolis. All mankind benefits from God's message. (Talbert) **(42)** b) The demoniac recognised the authority of Jesus. c) Jesus was concerned for the peace of mind of the man. **4. Eschatological** a) God's Kingdom was present when Jesus cast out demons (11:20). b) His miracles were part of His ministry to restore God's people. c) Jesus showed the power of God's spirit to overcome demonic forces which marginalised people from the rest of society. d) The eventual judgement of Satan and his followers in the 'Abyss' (Rev.20:1-3,10; 1 Enoch 15-16; Jub. 10:8-9; T. Levi 18:12).	**1. The setting:** the east side of the Sea of Galilee in the Decapolis region which was mainly Gentile but had a considerable Jewish population. Tombs were used as shelter by the very poor (8:26). **2. The condition of the man:** he lived naked (8:27)(L) showing disregard for personal dignity to indicate the theme of shame. His life was in social isolation among the tombs. He was possessed by multiple demons, had unusual strength: he broke his chains and fled to the desert. **3. The approach to the exorcism** by the man: "What have you to do with me, Jesus, Son of the Most High God?" (8:28) **4. The decisive act of Jesus:** He commanded the unclean spirits to leave the man and the multiple demons were cast out (8:29). Jesus extracted the name of the demons; "Legion" which shows multiple possession of demons (8:30). **5. Evidence of the miracle:** the man was sitting at the feet of Jesus, clothed and in his right mind (8:35). **6. The reaction** a. He proclaimed throughout the whole city how much God had done for him (8:39). When Jesus departed the man asked to accompany Him, but Jesus refused. He has to testify to God's work. Some like the exorcised man are called to stay at home and witness for Jesus, others are called to go with Jesus. "Return to your home, and tell how much God has done for you." (8:39) b. The crowd register their fear at seeing the man in a sane condition and cannot accept the presence of God (8:35). They are further filled with great fear and ask Jesus to depart (8:37).

BIBLE TEXT / TITLE / GENERAL COMMENTS	FUNCTION:WHAT IS ACHIEVED!	PURPOSE : INTENDED RESULT [WHY?]	CHARACTERISTICS : HOW IS IT UNIQUE!
15. a. Read 8:41-42a and 49-56 raising Jairus' Daughter. **b.** This is another triple tradition miracle [Mark 5:21-43; Matthew 9:18-26]. [See p. 235.] **c.** It is an example of instantaneous healing. He takes the child by the hand: touching the dead. **d.** This miracle is intertwined with that of the woman with the haemorrhage. **e.** Jesus was faced with tension; this was created for Jesus and the disciples by pressing the need for compassion for a woman who had been isolated from society because of her illness and prevented the impending death of Jairus' daughter. **f.** It shows how popular Jesus was and the great expectation they had in Jesus (8:40). **g.** The raising of Jairus' daughter was done in private, cf. the widow of Nain's son which was in public (7:16-17). **h.** Jesus tells the parents to say nothing (8:56b), in contrast to the woman with the haemorrhage. Jesus did this because He did not regard this miracle as central to His ministry. **i.** This miracle is an audio-visual aid relating to God's sovereignty.	**Provides evidence of/that :** - who Jesus is to the disciples and shows the power of Jesus over death. - the importance of believing that Jesus is capable of delivering people (8:50). - whatever the condition of the person Jesus is able to restore them. - the fact that Jesus does not wish to focus on the miracle He can do. To the parents He says, "Tell no one what had happened." (8:56) Misunderstandings by the crowd can be a distraction and Jesus could have been concerned about a wrong emphasis on Himself and His ministry (11:27-29). - to prevent misconception about the Messiah, this miracle took place in private. - the healing of Jairus' daughter is accomplished by summoning the spirit back to the body other than by resuscitating the body (Acts 9:41). (Marshall) **(43)** - the continuing authority of Jesus over disease and the importance of faith. - both a Gentile and a Jewish leader can recognise the power and authority of Jesus to perform great and powerful acts in raising from the dead. - faith is seen as the recognition of the power of Jesus and His goodness. - the healing brought a response of amazement (Gk. exestemi) as resurrections do not happen every day (8:56a). - risking defilement by taking the dead child by the hand (Num.19:11,16). - evidence that the girl's spirit returned to her (8:55).	**1. Evidential a)** The disciples recognise that Jesus is the Christ of God. **b)** There is sociological purpose in this miracle involving a synagogue leader and a child. Whether one is male or female, adult or child, clean or unclean makes no difference to Jesus. (Tannehill) **(44)** **c)** Jairus is confident about God's power and capacity to deliver the child from death and God's compassion (8:50). He is assured that she shall be well (she shall be saved) if he only believes. **2. Evangelistic a)** This miracle is a call to have faith. Jesus says to Jairus, "Put your trust in me!" to show the importance of faith at this moment (8:50). **b)** Jesus still called on Jairus to trust Him despite the interruption and the delay (8:50). Jairus is called to be patient when called to trust in God. God works in His time. This miracle shows that Jesus is worthy of Jairus' trust. God's power is absolute and death is not the end for human beings: facing God and knowing Him is more important. **c)** Jairus is told that if he really believed, healing, being made well and salvation would come to his daughter (8:50). The word "saved" is used to describe the woman's (with the flow of blood) healing (8:47) and the girl's resurrection (8:50). Her healing is called salvation and this came by faith. **3. Empathetic a)** Both incidents show the power and compassion of Jesus. The fact that the child was an only child adds to the compassion of Jesus and the emotion of the situation. **b)** Jesus shows His further compassion by requesting food for the child (8:56a). **4. Eschatological a)** It shows who Jesus is. He is the First and the Last Person to whom are given the keys of death and Hades. (Rev. 1:17-18) **b)** He has the **power and authority** to save from all situations, those who call on His name.	**1. The setting:** Jesus returned from the country of Gerasenes (to western Galilee side of the lake (8:40; Mk. 5:21). Some religious leaders accepted Jesus and recognised that He really was being used by God. Luke again shows the popularity of Jesus, 'the crowd welcomed Him and waited for Him.' (8:40) **2.a Jairus was the main elder** in the local synagogue and could have arranged the services. It is thought that he was not a member of the Sanhedrin but was a man of great social status, a leader in the city. His name means "he will give light" or "He (God) will awaken." (8:52) At twelve, in Jewish society his daughter was soon to be of marriageable age. **3. The condition of the girl:** Jairus' only daughter aged twelve was dying and he looked for the one who had healed so many (8:42). **4. The request for help:** He falls to his knees before Jesus to show his respect. Despite his high position, he requests Jesus to make a visit to his house to heal her. There is a balance in the detail of the two miracles: the girl is twelve years old and is dying (8:42) while the woman has had the haemorrhage for twelve years. In 8:49, the messenger announces the death of the girl and all hope seems to be lost. Some would be thinking that in stopping to heal a lesser condition, Jesus had allowed the girl to die. "Her spirit returned" (8:55) would suggest that she had in fact died. This would show that it was a resuscitation and not a resurrection of the girl's body, a calling back of her spirit. (Marshall) **(45)**

BIBLE TEXT / TITLE / GENERAL COMMENTS	FUNCTION: WHAT IS ACHIEVED?	PURPOSE: INTENDED RESULT [WHY?]	CHARACTERISTICS: HOW IS IT UNIQUE?
16. a. **Read Ch. 8:42b-48** the woman with the haemorrhage. This is a double miracle combined and intertwined with that of the raising of Jairus' daughter. Faith and Christology are key elements in this miracle. b. It is a triple tradition miracle: Mark 5:25-29; Matthew 9:20-22. c. The idea of peace is also a key to this miracle as it is closely linked to the ministry of Jesus in Luke's Gospel. The healed woman is now in a state of peace that exists between herself and God because of her faith. d. Church tradition links this woman with Caesarea Philippi. The word "edge" (Gk. kraspedou) could be the four tassels hanging from the edge of Jesus' garment or the edge of the garment. e. 'Power had gone out of Him' does not mean that Jesus' power was diminished. f. In the miracle of Jairus' daughter Jesus ordered the parents not to tell anyone while, in the case of the woman, the miracle takes place in public. The woman realised she was not hidden (8:47,51). g. After the raising of Jairus' daughter, Jesus tried to avoid publicity to prevent premature or misguided ideas about His Messiahship. He ordered the parents not to tell anyone (8:53).	**Provides evidence of/that:** - Jesus' concern for the peace of mind of the people. - the supernatural power of the Messiah. Inside two days: a storm was stilled (8:24). a demoniac delivered (8:33). an incurable disease is cured (8:43), and a girl restored to life (8:55). - the power of Jesus over disease. - Luke, having a more gentle description of the doctors who could not heal, describes her condition as "could not be healed by any one." (8:43) - the fact that even the timid faith of the woman can mobilise God. - the importance of believing that Jesus is capable of doing great things (8:48). - she departs in peace knowing that her relationship with Jesus have been restored (8:48). - a woman can recognise the power and authority of Jesus to heal her. - after the raising of Jairus' daughter Jesus tried to avoid publicity to prevent premature or misguided ideas about His Messiahship. - the woman departing in peace knowing that her relationship with Jesus has been restored. [See p. 230.]	**1. Evidential/Christological** a) God's power is seen in action as Jesus recognised that power had gone out of Him when the women touched Him. **2. Evangelistic** a) What was the nature of the woman's faith? If she was driven by superstition, imagining that the power of Jesus was almost magical and even if her faith was deficient, He heals and affirms her. Perhaps the "smouldering wick of her faith" was fanned into flame by the actions of Jesus (Matt. 12:20). (Liefeld) **(47)** b) "Daughter, your faith has made you well; go in peace." Literally this means your faith has saved (Gk. sesoken perfect tense) you (8:48). c) For Luke, faith is the basis for forgiveness of sins and salvation (7:50; 17:19; 18:42). After this, Jesus hears that Jairus' daughter has died which requires patience and a faith that endures. d) The woman spoke openly of what Jesus had done for her, and gives a public testimony to her faith and healing (8:47). **3. Empathetic** a) Jesus responds with gracious compassion and **authority.** Jesus' compassion and care extends to all who stretch out a hand to Him. b) This incident shows Jesus' full acceptance of those who were socially and religiously marginalized. c) This miracle shows that Jesus healed people who were considered by the Jews to be ritually impure (8:43-48; Lev.13:19-30).	1. **The woman's condition**: she had been suffering from bleeding for twelve years (8:43). 2. **The approach to heal**: she comes to Jesus furtively, 'up from behind Him.' She touched the edge (Gk. kraspedou) of His cloak. She would have been considered unclean and everything she touched (Lev. 15:25-31; Ezek. 36:17). Jewish custom was codified in M.Zabim. She could not live normally with others as she suffered from uterine haemorrhage. She recognised the power of Jesus when she touched Him. 3. **The act of healing**: The woman's desire was to go unnoticed (8:47) because of the embarrassment of her illness and having the boldness to break the ritual isolation to touch His garment. Immediately she is healed (8:47). To bring the woman forward Jesus said, "Who touched me?" 4. **The response**: Peter reminds Jesus that there are many present and is amazed at Jesus' question given the size of the crowd (8:45b). Jesus knew that there was something special about the touch of this woman since He remarks that power had left Him (8:46). Her touch was different from that of the crowd. 5. She explains why she touched Him, shows her respect by falling down before Him and begging for mercy (8:47). 6. It was not a magic touch but a touch of faith by which Jesus' power went to heal her. "Daughter, your faith has made you well; go in peace." (8:48) Jesus later refers to other exorcists who could cast out demons. "By whom do your sons cast out demon?" (11:19) The Pharisees' disciples practiced exorcisms. Reports of Jewish miracle workers in the first century show that they did not include cures of the deaf, dumb and the lame. (Guthrie) **(48)** 7. Jesus calls her "daughter" a term of affection to show she is part of Israel and no longer an outcast, her uncleanness having been removed. In the same way, Zacchaeus is called a "son of Abraham." (19:9)

17.

a. Read Ch.9:1-6 in which Luke recounts the mission of the Twelve.

b. These are exorcisms and healings.

c. This is a triple tradition: Mark 6:6b-13; Matthew 10:1,5-7.

d. The disciples are not to take an extra staff: they are to travel light (9:6) and trust in God.

e. Teaching and healing go together on this mission: those who are healed experience the power and the reality of the Kingdom of God in their bodies.

f. The Jewish Essenes and visitors to the Temple were all given similar instructions by the Jews (Josephus, Jewish Wars 2.8.4/125). Greek Cynics and philosophers usually asked for money in their itinerant role.

g. Luke uses two different words for healing Gk.therapeuo (9:6) and iaomai, each meaning the same thing. (Liefeld) **(49)**

The mission of the Twelve provides evidence of/that:

- the **power** (Gk.dunamis) of and **authority** (Gk.exousia) (9:1) of Jesus, seen in action to drive out all demons and to heal.

- the "**delegated authority**" or shared authority given by Jesus to His disciples as they were sent out to preach and to heal, including exorcism of all demons. No demon is too powerful for Him (9:1).

- the coming of the Kingdom of God by preaching (9:2) and in healing (Gk. therapeuo) the sick and exorcism. No demon is too powerful for Him (9:1).

- the time given to the disciples to reflect and discover who Jesus is (8:25), "Who then is this, who teaches and does such things?"

- the Kingdom which will not be based upon Jewish identity nor tied to the law but will call repentant people into a new community.

- Jesus empowered the disciples by the Spirit, which is a foreshadow of the future empowering, promised by the Father (24:49) and the Son (Acts 1:8), which would come at Pentecost.

- the disciples trusted God to supply their food, protection, and shelter.

- the disciples are to receive hospitality graciously.

- the person who supports the disciples will be privileged and a 'son of peace' (10:16).

1. Evidential

a) This **mission** shows that Jesus gave His disciples opportunities to spread the gospel. The Galilean towns heard the message of the Kingdom from the disciples, as Jesus could not visit them all by Himself.

b) This mission shows that the disciples have become "catchers of people." (5:10) (Tannehill) **(50) [See p.185.]**

c) Jesus was prepared to share His **power and authority** with His disciples.

d) This **mission** shows that Luke understood the "**authority**" of Jesus to drive out demons and to heal as due to the Spirit's empowerment. (Stein) **(51)**

e) Disciples must adopt a simple life style.

2. Evangelistic

a) They went through the villages preaching the gospel and healing (Gk.iaomai) everywhere. Jesus takes the gospel to them (9:6). To see and hear the Twelve is to see and hear Jesus.

b) As a symbol of judgement, the disciples are to shake off the dust from their feet if the town is not responding to the gospel. Repentance is a requirement for entrance into the Kingdom.

c) A greater judgement will fall upon the Galilean cities than upon Sodom and Gomorrah.

3.Eschatological

a) The message of the disciples is the kingdom of God (9:2). Their message would have been: the nearness of the Kingdom, the evidence of the power of the Kingdom, a special time had come and people were called to repent and enter the Kingdom.

b) Miracles were only evidence of the nearness of the Kingdom and displayed the power of God (11:18-21).

1. The "first missionary journey" of the disciples was a rehearsal for their future mission as witnesses to Jesus throughout the world, which would involve preaching, healings and exorcisms. (Stein) **(52)**

2. The ministry of the disciples is a mirror of Jesus' own ministry in Ch.8.

3. The Galilean cities, rejecting the Messiah, would incur more serious judgement than the cities of Sodom and Gomorrah in Abraham's time because of their wickedness. (Guthrie) **(53)**

4. This was a solemn reminder of the consequences of rejecting the message.

5. Jesus takes the gospel to the people.

6. This is the start of active ministry for the disciples and fulfils (5:10; 6:12-16). (Tannehill) **(54)**

7. The formation of the Twelve shows that Jesus intended to build a community around people, whom He expects will lead it. He named them apostles (6:13-16). He sends out the Twelve to call Israel (Matt. 10:5) to enter the Kingdom and to repent. The disciples display the coming of the Kingdom in their preaching and healing ministry (9:6). Jesus tells their leader Peter that He will build His Church after Peter's confession of Jesus as the Messiah (Matt. 16:18).

8. Jesus promises the Kingdom to the Twelve and their right to sit and judge the twelve tribes of Israel (22:29-30). Jesus is above the Twelve in authority and does not include Himself in the Twelve. The kingdom will not be based upon Jewish identity nor tied to the law but will call repentant people into a new community.
[See p.218.]

BIBLE TEXT / TITLE / GENERAL COMMENTS	FUNCTION: WHAT IS ACHIEVED?	PURPOSE : INTENDED RESULT [WHY?]	CHARACTERISTICS : HOW IS IT UNIQUE?
18. a. **Read 9:10b-17 feeding the five thousand.** b. **This is an example of a nature miracle. It is also referred to as a "gift or provision" miracle.** (Bovon) (55) c. **This event is included in all four Gospels** [Mark 6:32-44; Matthew 14:13-21; John 6:1-5]. d. **This is the only miracle recorded in all four Gospels to show that it is important.** e. **Even though He desired privacy, Jesus does not show any sign of irritation (9:10b).** f. **Bethsaida was outside the jurisdiction of Herod and some people may have thought that Jesus might not reappear in Galilee.** g. **John's death by Herod would have taken place recently; this showed Herod's opposition to the preaching of the Kingdom.** h. **In conclusion everyone was satisfied and twelve baskets of scraps were gathered. Luke records no reaction by the people.**	**The feeding of the five thousand provides evidence of:** - the mighty acts of the O.T. being fulfilled through Jesus: as God used Moses to feed Israel in the desert (Ex.16:1-36) and as Elisha fed one hundred men with the barley bread (2 Kgs. 4:42-44), so Jesus in a greater way is able to feed five thousand. - the **authority of Jesus** to provide a meal for five thousand. - Jesus the Messiah fulfilling Deut. 18:18. - the fact that many Jews came to expect the Messiah to re-enact this and other miracles (1 Kgs. 17:9-16; 2 Kgs. 4:42-44; Ps. 132:15). - parallels with the Lord's Supper. - the meeting of the needs of the people and recalls O.T. promises (Pss.37:1;81:16; 145:15-16). - the provision of the fish as when Jesus called the fishermen (5:1-11). - Jesus ministering to the total needs of the people as He taught, healed and fed the five thousand. It is uncertain whether Jesus had a prophetic role or a Messianic function in performing this miracle. - Jesus ministering to the total needs of the people as He taught, healed and fed the five thousand (9:11). - the image of Jesus as the Saviour who welcomed (Gk.apodexamenos) all who came and told them about the Kingdom (9:11). - the provision for the disciples in what they cannot provide for themselves.	**2. Evidential/Christological** a) Jesus is in part the answer to Herod's question. Who is this about whom I hear so much? It was thought that He was the resurrected John or the long-awaited Elijah. (Evans) **(56)** b) Jesus' abundant supply, when twelve baskets of scraps were picked up (9:17). c) A Christological purpose is seen in answer to the question Jesus was soon to put to Peter, "Who do you say I am"? Peter replied, "The Christ of God." (9:20) d) Jesus wants the disciples to develop a dependent spirit upon Him and they are to think on what He has done for them. He is the source of that provision. e) To train the disciples in trust and obedience **(Berger) (57)** and the work he wanted to do through them. **2. Empathetic** Jesus shows compassion to the crowd in meeting their need for food and welcoming them (9:11). **3. Eschatological** a) If this miracle is a partial fulfilment of the Messianic banquet (Is.25:6), then the Messianic age has begun. It would also point to Jesus as the Messiah, even though the Jews do not recognise Him as such. b) Lk. 9:16 foreshadows the words of the last supper in (22:19). c) It also prefigures the Messianic feast which features an abundance of bread and wine (Is. 25:6-9) and which has its parallel in the miracle of the manna in the O.T. However it differs from the Passover meal in that fish is the second element and not the wine. d) It is uncertain whether Jesus had a prophetic role or a Messianic function in doing this miracle. The event evokes images of the beginning and restoration of Israel. Luke alone links the event with the teaching about the Kingdom (9:11) (L). **4. Evangelistic** a. Jesus told all that came to Him, all about the Kingdom (9:11).	**1. The setting:** The disciples had been given authority to drive out unclean spirits and to preach the kingdom (9:1). News of the activities of the apostles had spread throughout Galilee, so that Herod began to wonder who Jesus was (9:10a). Jesus withdrew with the disciples to be privately alone with them in Bethsaida for a rest. **2. The approach to the miracle:** Jesus welcomes the crowd, tells them about the kingdom of God and does some healing miracles (9:11). By evening the disciples protest at Jesus' desire to feed the people and remark at the need to buy provisions (9:12). Jesus challenges the disciples to give the crowd something to eat (9:13). Two denarii would not be sufficient to feed a crowd (9:13; Jn. 6:7). Jesus asks the disciples to arrange the people in groups of fifty, making one hundred groups. **3. The miracle:** a. Jesus took the five loaves and the two fishes and, looking up to heaven, He gave thanks and broke them (9:16). Jesus is able to feed a multitude with five loaves and two fishes. b. The disciples minister to the people through His power and provision. They are not just "fishing for people" but are also providers of the basic food for life. The people are fed and filled. c. Jesus saw this miracle linked to: (1) the Elisha stories in the multiplication of the barley loaves for 100 men; (2 Kgs. 4:42-44) (Evans) **(58)** (2) the manna for Israel wandering in the desert (Ex.16). d. The disciples are to model Jesus' style of ministry, as they depend upon and what He can give them (22:24-27). e. This miracle precedes Peter's confession that Jesus is the Christ, which is the climax of the Galilean ministry with the focus on the disciples and not on the public.

BIBLE TEXT / TITLE / GENERAL COMMENTS	FUNCTION: WHAT IS ACHIEVED?	PURPOSE: INTENDED RESULT [WHY?]	CHARACTERISTICS: HOW IS IT UNIQUE!
19. a. Read 9:28-36 the Transfiguration. b. This is a triple tradition: [Mk. 9:2-8; Matt. 17:1-18] c. When prayer happens in Luke's Gospel, something significant takes place, compare His baptism (3:21). d. Classification is difficult. The following have been suggested: an enthronement, a prophetic vision, an apocalyptic vision, a transformation and a voice from heaven, regal imagery, a divine epiphany (heavenly glory manifested on earth), the exodus background, a Christian midrash based upon Ex.24:15-16 and 34:35, "The people saw that the skin of the face of Moses shone." Schweizer (59) a cult narrative, a story about Jesus, a legend [Taylor (60) and Bultmann]. (61) e. The voice from heaven repeats what had been said in private at His baptism, "This is my beloved Son; listen to Him!" (9:35) Lk.21:27 uses the singular for cloud rather than the plural in Mk.13:26 and Matt.24:30, which may link the second coming with the Transfiguration. f. This event follows on from Peter's confession about Jesus' identity, 'the Christ of God' (9:20,22), the prediction about His coming as the Son of Man, His death and the promise about His glory (9:26,32). All three themes are in the Transfiguration in reverse order: identity, prediction about suffering and glory. g. Moses and Elijah appear in glory (9:28) and Jesus is seen in glory (9:31).	**To confirm that:** - Jesus is unique and He is part of a plan which is being worked out by God; the plan to heed what His Son is saying. The fulfilment of the O.T. language of Ps.2:7, "You are my Son, today I have begotten you," and Deut.18:15 "The Lord your God will raise up a prophet like me among you, him you shall heed." He is the Son of God obedient to His Father and has **divine authority for His mission.** - the disciples of Jesus have access to the presence of Jesus and they are to heed what He says (Deut.18:15 LXX). (L) - the revelation of the heavenly glory of Jesus has been seen by some of the disciples. - Jesus is greater than Moses and Elijah in refusing to build the three booths and in His transformation (9:33-34). - a divine word is given (9:35-36). - though He speaks with Moses and Elijah only Jesus is transformed (9:29-31). - the timing of the event is significant following on from His word about suffering and His prediction about His own suffering and death (9:31). Despite this, He brings heavenly glory (9:31-32). - the event could have a clear purpose to answer the disciples' question, "Who is this, that He commands the winds and water and they obey Him?" (8:25) and Herod's question, "John I beheaded; but who is this about whom I hear such things?" (9:9) - the disciples had seen the Kingdom fulfilled in the Transfiguration (9:27). - Jesus speaks of His own impending departure (Gk. exodus), another prediction about His passion (9:31). - Jesus alone is the True Prophet, the Chosen Servant (L), and the Son of God (9:35; 23:35; Is.42:1).	**1. Evidential/Christological** a) The revelation of the glory in Jesus' transformation. b) A greater prophet than Moses or Elijah is here in that He refused to build booths (9:33-34). c) The divine testimony to Jesus as Son. He is the Messiah-the Servant, the Chosen One of Is.42:1. d) The call to listen to Him as the "prophet like Moses." (Deut.18:15) Evidence that the prophets of the O.T. affirmed God's plan (9:31). e) They saw this in the two references to glory; the glory of the returning Son of Man (9:26) [Gk.astrapto] (17:24) and at the Transfiguration (9:32). f) "His raiment became dazzling (Gk exastrapto) white." **2. Eschatological** a) This event is a word of testimony that Jesus is the messianic eschatological Son and this experience would encourage the disciples. b) Peter saw the event as having eschatological overtones and wanted the experience to continue (9:33). c) The Feast of Tabernacles looked forward to God's total provision at a later date. This incident marks a new era with Jesus and the glory that His presence represents. d) The predicted suffering will take place as part of God's plan, is seen in His departure (Gk. exodus) in Jerusalem. e) The O.T. saints are in a glorified condition.(L) "Moses and Elijah who appeared in glory." (9:31) f) The glory which the disciples see shows who Jesus really is and how He will finally manifest himself. Moses is the founding figure of the nation and Elijah is the prophetic figure of the coming event/the eschaton. g) Both testify to Jesus and are subordinate to Him. h) A hope is expressed for the return of God's glory in the eschaton or parousia, the second coming. [2 Macc.2:8] (Danker). (62) i) The voice from heaven fulfils Deut.18:15 which foretells of the Coming Prophet God would raise up. Jesus is the true prophet, the Chosen Servant and the Son of God. This points to Is.42:1. i) The identity of Jesus is the theme of the Heavenly proclamation (9:35).	**1. The setting:** this event occurs eight days after Peter's confession at Caesarea Philippi and after Jesus completed these sayings (9:26). This locale is not in Luke and it is either Mt.Hermon (9200ft.) Mt. Meron (4,000ft.) or Mt.Tabor (1,900ft.) which had a fortress at this time and is very unlikely. [See map Ch. 9] Luke uses the expression (Gk. egeneto) "it came to pass" to introduce a new unit and to show that a key event in the life of Jesus is about to take place. The (RSV) translates as "it happened that" to give the setting. **2. The event and those who witnessed it.** The context is one of prayer in which three of the disciples Peter, James and John accompany Jesus up a **mountain.** Jesus is physically transformed into a radiant figure whose brilliance extended to his clothing (9:29). Luke says His clothes were "a dazzling white." This description **portrays the glory of Jesus** (9:29; Dan.7:9; Rev.3:5). The three disciples are given a unique glimpse into the **glory of Jesus.** With Jesus are **Moses and Elijah** who represent the law and the prophets. It was anticipated that Elijah would be the prophet at the end of time (Mal.4:5). The three disciples are discussing the topic of the "exodus" or departure (RSV) is a reference to the death and ascension of Jesus which would take place in Jerusalem. (L) **3. Peter's request** to celebrate the Feast of Tabernacles (9:32-33): Luke notes that Peter and the others slept and then woke up to what was happening, missing out most of the conversation (9:32). With the impending departure of the O.T. saints, Peter tries to prolong the occasion by suggesting that they celebrate the Feast of Tabernacles which looked back to God's provision for Israel in the wilderness and Israel's deliverance. Peter wanted three booths to be built one for Jesus, one for Moses and one for Elijah (9:33). Luke alone says that Peter did not know what he said as he had not recognised the full force of Jesus' future suffering (9:33b). It could be that, in wanting to build the booths, Peter was making himself equal with the three figures. **4. The voice from heaven:** endorses Jesus as the Son-Prophet (9:34-35). A cloud, a sign of the God's "Shekinah" presence descends upon them as in Ex.13:21-22; Num.9:15; Lev.16:2; Is.6:4-5.

BIBLE TEXT / TITLE / GENERAL COMMENTS	FUNCTION: WHAT IS ACHIEVED?	PURPOSE : INTENDED RESULT [WHY?]	CHARACTERISTICS : HOW IS IT UNIQUE?
20. a. Read 9:37-43a the healing of the demon-possessed boy. b. This is an example of a healing and an exorcism. c. It is a triple tradition [Matthew 17:14-21; Mark 9:14-29]. d. This is the last of the thirteen miracles in the Galilean section. e. From Luke 9:62 onwards every pericope / unit / paragraph has instruction and correction for the disciples. f. In this culture, boys were highly prized. Luke says he was an 'only son.' Sons were considered to be very precious. g. Children were the lowest status at the bottom of the ladder. h. Epilepsy was viewed with much apprehension. It brought terror because of the association with darkness. i. This incident is followed by repetition of Jesus' prediction of His passion; it shows that Jesus' ultimate purpose goes beyond such a miracle as this (9:45b). j. There is repetition of the prediction of Jesus' passion (9:43b-45). [See p. 244.]	**The healing of the demon possessed boy provides evidence of /that:** - a direct link with Jesus' proclaiming of the Kingdom. - the power and mercy of God at work. - the **power and authority** of Jesus over demonic forces compared with the failure of the disciples. - Jesus' greatness and uniqueness. - God being present in Jesus. - the contrast between the power of Jesus and the impotence of the disciples. - the disciples' failure to understand Jesus' prediction about His passion (9:43-45). - patience on the part of the One who came to turn people to the right path of true life. - this generation portrayed as perverse has O.T. roots (Deut.32:5,20; Num.14:27). - the crowd marvelling at Jesus' greatness and majesty, when they saw all the miracles He did (9:43a). - the greatness of God. Luke concludes (9:43a) with the reaction of those that saw the healing (9:43). - Jesus' authority can be trusted but not that of the disciples when they act on their own. - the crowd recognised the authority of Jesus when they are amazed at His greatness (9:43). - Luke wants the readers to know that Jesus is unique. (Stein) (63)	**1. Evidential** a) The acclamation by the people, affirms that God is working through Jesus who, by performing miracles, is carrying out **His mission.** b) The miracles in Luke's Gospel are the "mighty works" seen by the people (19:37b). c) Trust in the miracle worker and in the power[s] responsible for the miracle is the expected response to the marvellous deed. d) Evidence of the authority of Jesus that the demons had to obey Him. e) Evidence of instruction to the disciples that they might learn. **2. Evangelistic** a) This miracle is a call to faith (9:41). b) God's saving work is evident in the healing. **3. Empathetic** a) God's compassion is seen through Jesus. b) Even though Jesus faces death, He still shows compassion. "Let these words sink into your ears for the Son of Man is to be delivered into the hands of men." (9:44) Jesus would have been "naive or ignorant," (Tiede) (64) not to have been aware of the peril He faced, as He approached Jerusalem. **4. Eschatological** a) The Kingdom of God has come near when the posessed boy has been healed.	1. **The setting:** the day after the Transfiguration when a great crowd met Jesus (9:38). 2. **The boy's condition:** a 'spirit seized' an **only** son. (L) He cried out, suffered convulsions and was foaming at the mouth. The boy is shattered and the spirit will not leave him alone (9:39a). 3. **The request:** "Teacher (Gk.Didaskalos), I beg you to look upon my son." (9:38b) The disciples were unable to heal the boy but the father still had high hopes in Jesus. Perhaps they thought that healing would be automatic after their successful mission (9:6). The disciples are filled with fear as the cloud surrounded them (9:34). 4. **The request to heal:** the concerned father seeks physical relief for his boy. 5. **The act of healing:** Jesus ordered the son to be brought to Him (9:41). Even as the boy came to Jesus he suffered another attack with physical cuts and convulsions. Jesus rebuked the unclean spirit and gave the son back to his father (9:42). 6. **The reaction:** a. The public were astonished (Gk. thaumazonton) at the majesty and greatness (Gk.megaleioteti) of God (9:43a) (NIV and RSV have "at everything He did" (9:43b) AV has "at the power of God." When Jesus rebuked the evil spirit, the boy was healed and God was praised (9:43-44). b. Jesus' response was to rebuke the disciples for their lack of faith in being unable to cast out the evil spirit in the boy. "Oh faithless and perverse generation, how long am I to be with you?" (9:41) Unbelief was unable to heal. c. God's saving work is the occasion for praise in the Third Gospel. (Green) (65) God was praised through the work which Jesus did. d. The unbelief and perversity of this generation is such that the Son of Man would soon be delivered into their hands (9:44).

BIBLE TEXT / TITLE / GENERAL COMMENTS

21A

a. Read 10:1-13 sending out of the seventy (two).

b. These are examples of healings and exorcisms.

c. This is a triple tradition miracle: [Mark 6:8-11; Matthew 9:37-38, 10:7-16].

d. The miracles were signs of the Kingdom.

e. Signs in Luke are supernatural events designed to bring out the meaning of the message, the kingdom of God has come near.

f. The disciples are like defenceless lambs and dependent only upon God.

g. If your host has the right attitude to God, he will receive the blessing of the kingdom (10:9).

h. "Son of peace" is an idiom for expressing someone's character as a destiny of which He is worthy.

i. The hearers were assured of the Kingdom in time and space, through the arrival of the ministry of Jesus' representatives (10:9). (Marshall) (66)

j. The title "Lord" (Gk.Kurios) is used for the commissioning of the disciples, the Lord appointed."

k. The title "Lord (Gk.Kurios) of the harvest" is God the Father, who hears and answers prayer (10:2). [See p. 218.]

FUNCTION: WHAT IS ACHIEVED?

Provides evidence of:

- Jesus having a vision of the fall of Satan (10:12).*

- the working of miracles as part of the proclaiming of the kingdom (10:13). When the sick are healed there is evidence that the Kingdom of God had come (10:9,11). The healings signify the start of a new divine age. However it does not mean that everything had finally come for example Acts 2, the coming of the Holy Spirit has not taken place. Luke lays out his view of the kingdom in clear related stages.

(Figure 2)

The kingdom seen in related stages.

	Kingdom	Ref.	Comment
1	The kingdom as the hope of God's rule.	Lk. 4:16-30, 43	Nothing can prevent the coming of the Kingdom.
2	The kingdom comes with Jesus and becomes a reality in the events of His power	10:9 (L)	The kingdom has come near (RSV, NIV) to you. or upon you.
3	The fall of Satan	4:16-18; 10:17; 11:14-23	The exorcisms by the disciples- "Lord, even the demons are subject to us in your name!" Jesus said, "I saw Satan fall like lightning from heaven."*
4	The lasting benefits of the Kingdom	Acts 2 4:16-30; 4:43	The coming of the Holy Spirit

PURPOSE: INTENDED RESULT [WHY?]

1. Evangelistic

a) to show that there are boundless opportunities but few take them.

b) "The harvest is plenty but the labourers are few." (10:2) The title 'Lord of the Harvest' refers to the urgent missionary task of the present age (Matt. 9:37-38).

c) Whoever hears the disciples hears Jesus and whoever rejects them rejects Jesus (10:16).

2. Eschatological

a) The question of the kingdom is an apocalyptic end time theme which describes "secret" events about the kingdom of God and the end of the world.

b) 'The kingdom has come near you (Gk. engiken) when the sick are healed.' (10:9)

c) For Jesus, God's kingdom and rule are the hope of Israel. The kingdom is the presence of God's rule. Did Jesus foresee the end coming in His life time?

d) Healing and preaching the kingdom are tied together as in the mission of "the Twelve" (10:9; 9:1-2,11).

e) To ignore God's warning means destruction like that of Sodom and Gomorrah. The cities of Galilee are as culpable as those O.T.cities. Capernaum's privilege of hearing Jesus preach often, does not guarantee fame or survival.

f) The title "Lord" (Ho Kurios) is used to show that all the instructions came from Jesus Himself.

CHARACTERISTICS: HOW IS IT UNIQUE!

1. The setting: 'After this 'refers to Jesus' teaching on the cost of discipleship (9:57-62). As Jesus draws near to His time of suffering and rejection, the disciples are sent to preach the coming of the Kingdom (10:9).

2. The ministry of those sent out: the seventy (two) were also given power to heal and exercise in the name of Jesus, to bless or remove blessing.

3. The miracles were signs that the Kingdom had come near (10:9).

4. The disciples preach the kingdom's approach and the authority of the kingdom.

5. Jesus notes that He saw "Satan fall like lightning from heaven."

6. When the disciples talked about their success, this could refer to Is. 14:12, a picture of a king who fell because of arrogance. Here it refers to the demise of Satan.*

7. The disciples are to be single-minded and not to get involved in time consuming greetings. 'Do not greet anyone on the road!' (2 Kgs. 4:29)

8. Christians are to support God's messengers (10:7).

9. God's Kingdom was effective as the ministry of Jesus against demons. When the disciples exorcise demons the forces of evil are shaken, symbolising the defeat of Satan (10:17; 11:20).

BIBLE TEXT / TITLE / GENERAL COMMENTS	FUNCTION: WHAT IS ACHIEVED!	PURPOSE : INTENDED RESULT [WHY?]	CHARACTERISTICS : HOW IS IT UNIQUE!
21B. a. **Read 10:17-20 the return of the seventy (two).** b. **This incident is unique to Luke.** c. **The authority of Jesus is from God, the scribes' authority is based upon tradition, from rabbi to rabbi.** d. **Jesus rejoices at God's mighty saving work (10:21-22).** e. **Exorcism must be done in the name of Christ and signifies His authority. "Lord even the demons submit to us in your name." (10:17)** f. **This mission points to Jesus' victory. In Judaism this would have meant the defeat of evil (1 Enoch 55:4).**	**Provides evidence of/that:** - Jesus giving authority to the seventy (two) to:- exorcize demons, tread upon serpents (10:19; Gen.3:5; Deut. 8:15) have power over the enemy [Satan], and be physically protected (10:19). - the miracles as such are only of secondary importance to having experienced conversion (10:20). - **the authority residing in Jesus to defeat destructive forces, which are opposed to people.** - healings are subordinate to conversion and salvation (10:21). (Blomberg) **(67)** - God's sovereignty in imparting His revelation (10:21). - the relationship between the Father and Jesus (10:21). This is His personal relationship with the Father rather than His functional role. - the privilege of the disciples in witnessing the messianic revelation and salvation.	**1. Evidental** a) When the seventy (two) returned after a successful ministry in which the demons are subject to the disciples, Jesus said, that having their names written in heaven is more important than the power to do miracles (10:20). This is God's special register of V.I.P.s. "The secure position of the disciples before God is more important than power." (Bock) **(68)** **2. Empathetic** a) The disciples showed their compassion to exorcise the demons like their Master. "Even the demons are subject to us in your name." (10:17) **3. Eschatological** a) Jesus is in an eschatological battle with Satan, whose power is vanquished as Jesus ushers in the age of the New Covenant. (Blomberg) **(69)** b) The conquest of Satan's power and domain is evidenced (10:18-20).	**1. The report of the seventy-two:** a. The disciples are excited and rejoice at their **authority over the demons (10:17).** b. They address Jesus as Lord (Gk.Kurios), indicating that they recognise who Jesus is (10:17). c. They recognise that their authority comes from God. Jesus tells the disciples about their wide-ranging power (10:19). d. They can overcome hostile creation and the power of Satan. **They have a greater joy than their authority: their names are in heaven (10:20).** **2. The response** a. Rejection is worse than that for the most wicked O.T. cities (10:16). b. The seventy (two) return excited about the work of God, "Lord even the demons are subject to us in your name!" (10:17)
22A. a. **Read 11:14-15 the healing of the (blind) and dumb demoniac.** b. **Matthew alone calls him blind (12:22-23).** c. **This is the first miracle of the journey section.**	**Provides evidence of:** - the source of Jesus' ministry and what His work really means. Is it from God or Satan? - the amazing power of Jesus over demons. - the awareness of the crowd of Jesus' power.	**1. Evidental** a) The Kingdom of God is breaking into human history. b) Evidence of the signs of Jesus' power over the forces of nature and demons. The ministry of the disciples is an extension of messianic power. **2. Eschatological** a) Messianic times are here as the blind receive their sight (4:18d; 7:22). b) Jesus reminded John the Baptist that a sign of Messianic times was the healing of the blind and deaf (7:22).	**1. The condition of the man:** a dumb man possessed by a demon. Matt.12:22 says he is also blind. **2. The exorcism:** Jesus exorcises a demon from a dumb man and now he is able to speak. **3. The reaction:** The reaction is as important as the narration of the miracle. a. The crowd marvel (Gk. thaumazo) at this unusual happening. b. Despite being amazed, the people do not like what they see and some are sceptic. "He casts out demons by the prince of demons." (11:15)

BIBLE TEXT / TITLE / GENERAL COMMENTS	FUNCTION:WHAT IS ACHIEVED?	PURPOSE : INTENDED RESULT [WHY?]	CHARACTERISTICS : HOW IS IT UNIQUE?
22B. a. **Read 11:16-28 the Beelzebul controversy.** b. **This is a triple tradition.** [Mark 3:22-27 (no miracle included) Matthew 12:22-30]	**The Beelzebul controversy provides evidence of/that:** - this miracle as a testimony to this authority of Jesus. - God as the source of the **power and authority** of Jesus as in reference to the "finger of God" (11:20): the source of His power is the finger of God (11:20). (Liefeld) **(70)** - this O.T. image for the Spirit of God (Exod. 8:19; Deut. 9:10; Ps.8:3). It could also mean the Power of God. - the connection between miracles and the Kingdom of God (11:20). - Jesus' saying identified as the word of God. "Blessed are those who hear the word of God and obey it." (11:28) - the Kingdom of God, when Jesus exorcises demons. "But if by the finger of God I cast out demons, then the Kingdom of God has come upon you." (11:20) - important Christological principles are established regarding Jesus' greatness. He is more important than John (3:16). He is truly the Lord, the One Israel longed for. (Liefeld) **(71)**	**1. Evidential/Christological** a) To show that Jesus is the divine Messiah and that the Kingdom of God has come in human history (11:20). b. "As Jonah was a sign to the men of Nineveh, so will be the Son of Man to this generation." (11:30) **2. Evangelistic** a) This healing compels people to decide who Jesus really is. Does He act by Satan's power or God's power? Luke's readers are left with a similar choice. **3. Eschatological** a) For Luke the healing of the mute is the sign that Jesus is the Coming One. b) The Kingdom has come with Jesus but not in its totality and completeness. The kingdom has been inaugurated and Satan's house is plundered and the spoils are divided (11:21-23). c) Does Jesus mean the Kingdom draws close in the present activity or that it arrives (11:20)? The Kingdom here is something present among humans. The king has come (1:32-33). Did Jesus' first coming inaugurate the Kingdom or did the Kingdom operate like an eschatological term, which refers to the consummation of God's rule on earth through Israel? The Kingdom of God is a present reality. "But if it is by the finger of God I cast out demons, the Kingdom of God has come (11:20). God's Kingdom is in evidence when Jesus exorcises demons. "But if it is by the finger of God I cast out demons, the Kingdom of God has come. " (11:20) Jesus teaches a realised eschatology in part (11:22) it will be further developed.	1. There was a **twofold reaction:-** a. amazement "Is this the Son of God?" b. disbelief…the Pharisees were convinced He was not the Son of God. 2. Jesus was called a false prophet and magician (11:19). 3. Luke attributes the impediment to the work of demons (11:14). "For, if by the finger of God I cast out demons, then the Kingdom of God has come/has come near (Gk.ephthasen)." (11:20) 4. The Kingdom of God is also future. "Your Kingdom come." (11:2) Among the Jews there were two kinds of hope: **(1) apocalyptic-eschatological hope** as in the use of the expression the Son of Man (Dan.7:13). **(2) a prophetic hope** as in the use of the term Messiah. In the idea of the Kingdom are both strands of hope but eschatological hope is more dominant. 5. The demons seek a human body and in order to repossess its previous abode, enlists the help of seven demons worse than itself (11:26; Is.13:21; 31; 34:4).

BIBLE TEXT / TITLE / GENERAL COMMENTS	FUNCTION: WHAT IS ACHIEVED?	PURPOSE: INTENDED RESULT [WHY]	CHARACTERISTICS: HOW IS IT UNIQUE?
23. a. **Read 13:11-13 the crippled woman on the Sabbath.** [See p. 272.] b. **This is a healing miracle and a "rule" miracle.** c. **It is unique to Luke's Gospel and is the second one in the journey section.** d. **It is also called a "mirror miracle"** in that it replays the Sabbath healings of 4:31–41, the healing of the man with the unclean demon, Simon's mother-in-law and the man with the withered hand (6:6-11). e. In Ch.12, Jesus has been telling the crowd to watch the weather as a warning that the healings are miracles. f. **This miracle is followed by two parables of the mustard seed and the leaven to show the inherent power in the seed and leaven as seen in the miracle. The two parables give added support to the miracle (13:18-19).** g. **The yeast (leaven) shows the inherent power of the Kingdom and Jesus as a compassionate teacher (13:20-21).** O.T.references to the bounty of God's favour are:Ps.104:12; Ezek.17:22-24,31; Dan.4:10-12,20-27. [p. 267.] h. In Luke 13:32-35 "Jesus' healings and miracles are a prelude to suffering which had been ordained by O.T. Scriptures."(Jer.12:7) (Blomberg) [note 69]	**The healing of the crippled woman on the Sabbath provides evidence that:** - the earlier Sabbath miracles are replays to Jesus' warnings (13:17). - the crowds and the leaders have responded to Jesus' warnings (13:17). - Jesus' action brings a division. - a healing by Jesus shows Satan is loosing his grip on the people. - Jesus is the one through whom God is at work. - Jesus takes the initiative when He sees the condition of the woman. - the **authority** of Jesus is seen over evil forces, "Woman you are freed from your infirmary." (13:13) She is freed (Gk.apoluo) from the power of Satan (13:16). - Luke's stresses the conquest of Satan's power and domain by Jesus (13:11-12). - **Jesus has the power and authority to reverse the condition of the woman.** - the woman remains in bondage no longer (13:12). - the miracle shows the extent to which the crowds and the leaders have responded to Jesus' warnings. - Jesus acts with God's **authority** when the woman straightened up and praised God (13:13). - the people side with the narrator (Luke) in recognising Jesus the authoritative teacher seen in the wonderful things He was doing,the gracious hand of God (13:17). (Green) **(72)** - the crowds were delighted with the ministry of Jesus as in 9:43.	**1. Evidential** a) People can come to Jesus at any time for healing and restoration. b) Evidence that the ministry of Jesus causes division. c) Evidence of the hostility shown by officials and Jesus breaking the oral traditions (5:33-39; 11 :37-44). d) Evidence of an instantaneous healing is a feature of Luke's Gospel. e) This is called a "rule" miracle: the woman remains in bondage no longer. **2. Evangelistic** a) The need to respond to Jesus while it is still time. b) Different reactions to message of repentance are evident Some remain stubborn and blind, while others rejoice. c) Miracles indicate the time and need for decision. d) God was visiting His people with the salvation promised long ago. **3. Empathetic** a) Jesus shows His compassion in exercising His power on behalf of the crippled woman and meeting her need. God's compassion is always available: it showed Jesus' compassion for the outcast woman. b) He takes the initiative in the healing. c) Jesus laid His hands upon her to heal and to identify with her (13:13). This miracle raises the issue as to whether tradition should have priority over compassion. **4. Eschatological** a) A special time in God's plan had come: the experience of "messianic salvation" (13:17) and joy at the coming of God's Kingdom (1:14). It is an eschatological joy which comes with the Messianic age (10:17; 24:41,52). b) Messianic times are here: the lame walk. c) This incident shows Jesus' struggle with Satan (7:22). **(Tannehill) (73)** [See pp. 272-3.]	**1. The setting:** this event follows on from Jesus telling the parable of the spared fig tree, in which the nation of Israel is given one more chance to respond. As Jesus was teaching on the Sabbath in one of the synagogues (13:10). He became aware of the woman **2. Her condition:** the woman had been crippled by a spirit for eighteen years indicating the severity of her condition. She was bent over and could not straighten up (13:11). Her condition could be due to demonic influence rather than possession. The woman's illness which was with her for eighteen years, shows also God's struggle with Satan. **3. The approach to the healing:** Jesus calls her forward. **4. The healing:** "Woman, you are freed from your infirmary." He put His hand upon her and at once (Gk. parachrema) she straightened up." This is an instant healing. **5. The response:** a. Jesus' healing on the Sabbath meets with the usual hostility from the leader of the synagogue (13:14). He is most indignant that this healing should not take place on the Sabbath (Ex. 20:9-10). b. The woman responds by praising(Gk.eudoxa) God, (13:13) showing Luke's interest in God's glory. c. However there is a reaction the other way. The Jewish leaders are put to shame and some of the people rejoiced at the variety of wonderful things which they saw (13:17). **8. It is significant in that Jesus healed a woman in a culture where men shunned women.** **9.** The woman is "freed" (Gk.aplouo) from the effects of the disease. She has entered a state of healing. This is a term usually used for the freeing of prisoners or releasing from a debt. (Josephus) **(74)**

BIBLE TEXT / TITLE / GENERAL COMMENTS	FUNCTION: WHAT IS ACHIEVED?	PURPOSE : INTENDED RESULT [WHY]	CHARACTERISTICS : HOW IS IT UNIQUE?
24. a. **Read 14:1-6 the man with the dropsy on the Sabbath. [p. 273.]** b. It is a healing miracle also called a "rule" miracle. (Theissen) (75) c. **It is unique to Luke's Gospel. This is the third miracle of the journey section.** d. **This is a Sabbath miracle.** e. **This miracle leads to confrontation with the Pharisees.** f. **It is another example of an audio visual-aid miracle.** g. This is the fourth controversy on the Sabbath in Luke' Gospel (6:1-5; 6:11; 13:10-17). h. **This miracle includes a healing, a conversation and a parable.** i. **Dropsy was often associated with uncleaness and immorality** (Midrash. Rabbah Leviticus 15:2. S B 1926:2:203). j. **Some rabbis said dropsy was due to sexual offences (Sab.33a) or failing to have bowel movements (b Ber.25a). [See pp. 223-4.]**	**The healing of the man with the dropsy provides evidence that:** - Jesus has power and ability to restore with God's power and approval. - **the Pharisees do not accept the authority of Jesus despite the fact that He rules.** - no response is possible and silence speaks louder than words. Luke wants the readers to compare the response of Jesus with that of the Pharisees. - the Pharisees are so fixed in their tradition that they have no sense of guilt about their belief. At Qumran a distinction was made between a person and an animal. A person could be rescued on the Sabbath but not an animal (Qumran). (76) - Jesus' greatness can be seen in the healing of the man.	**1. Evidential** a) Evidence that Jesus exposes the inconsistent teaching of the Pharisees. The practice of pulling up the ox which falls into a well on the Sabbath reflects Deut. 22:4; Sab. 18:3. b) The miracle becomes a rebuke and a call to repentance (14:5). c) Jesus points to the actions of the scribes and Pharisee themselves on the Sabbath. What would they do if a son or an ox was in danger on the Sabbath? **2. Empathetic** a) Despite opposition, Jesus continues to show compassion to those in need in touching the man and healing him (14:4). b) The appeal of Jesus is to do a basic act of compassion and rescue on the Sabbath. c) Jesus criticised the Pharisees for putting the treatment of animals before people. **3. Evangelistic** a) Jesus, in ministering to the Pharisees, continues to warn Israel. Previously He had warned about their rejection and declared judgement on Israel (Ch.13). b) Even on the Sabbath, Jesus continues to show mercy and compassion. **3. Eschatological** a) The poor are made rich through reversals, the oppressed are set at liberty. b) Messianic times are here.	**1. The setting** a. Jesus is invited to the home of a Pharisee or synagogue leader (14:1). b. This shows that Jesus had "table fellowship" with the Pharisees (7:36-50; 11:37-54). **2. The condition of the man** a. He suffered from dropsy (swollen limbs) due to access body fluids sometimes called "hydrops". (14:2) b. It is thought to be more of a medical problem than a disease. c. Dropsy is referred to in the O.T. (Lev. 15:1-12). It may also have been regarded as a curse for sin: "the water of bitterness which brings a curse." (Num 5:19) **3. The approach to the healing:** a. Jesus asks the lawyers and the Pharisees "Is it lawful to heal on the Sabbath or not?" (14:3) b. Jesus took the man and healed him (14:4). c. This is another Sabbath miracle after Jesus' prophetic warning to the nation. **4. The reaction** a. This miracle involves another confrontation with the Pharisees. The Pharisees are asking, "What will He do this time?" b. There is no reply by the Pharisees after Jesus acts and heals (14:4,6). c. The significance of the miracle is the reaction that it produces, which is that of silence, even though it may be a trap and they let Him go (14:6).

BIBLE TEXT / TITLE / GENERAL COMMENTS	FUNCTION: WHAT IS ACHIEVED?	PURPOSE: INTENDED RESULT [WHY?]	CHARACTERISTICS: HOW IS IT UNIQUE?
25. **a. Read 17:11-19 the ten lepers.** **b. This is a healing miracle.** **c. It is also called the thankful Samaritan leper.** **d. This is the fourth miracle of the journey section and is unique to Luke. "A pronouncement story" (Fitzmyer) (77) "A quest story" (Tannehill) (78)** **e. This miracle recalls the healing of Naaman the Syrian (2 Kgs.5:10-15).** **f. Jesus is referring to total salvation and not just to healing. "Your faith has saved you." (17:19)** **g. Each miracle in the journey section emphasises the teaching that following Jesus is more important than the miracle. [See p. 245.]**	**The miracle provides evidence of/that:** - the universal appeal of the Gospel and shows who Jesus is. - Jesus' current power as distinct from His power at His coming. - "foreigners" and "outcasts" appreciating Jesus, yet they could not go beyond the inner barrier of the Temple. (Josephus) **(79)** - an outsider praising God and showing respect for Jesus (7:15). - Luke emphasising the thankful Samaritan, yet being critical of Israel for lack of faith. (It is not an anti-Semitic miracle.) - this miracle could be called the "Thankful Samaritan Leper." Samaritans were considered as half-breeds and not part of Israel. - a Samaritan who praises God because a Jewish Messiah would not conform to Jewish expectations. - the leper being moved beyond the reception of kindness to the exercise of faith (17:19). - a Christological emphasis seen in Jesus' power and **authority** to heal lepers and in the praise of a believing Samaritan (17:15) who threw himself at Jesus' feet and thanked Him. (Stein) **(80)** - a soteriological truth. A person can experience God's work of grace as in healing and yet not experience or receive salvation. All ten lepers experienced the start of faith and went out in faith to show themselves to the priest but only the thankful leper persevered. (Stein) **(81)**	**1. Evidential/Christological** a) To show that the miracle of healing is of secondary importance to that of conversion, Jesus says, "Your faith has saved you." [17:19] **b) To show that the challenge of Jesus transcends nationalism.** **2. Evangelistic** [See p. 179.] a) He is commended for his faith which is unto salvation. He received what the others do not receive. The leper is "healed by faith." His miracle is pro-faith and challenges all to be like this foreigner. He receives the greater gift of salvation which is received by faith. Luke's reader is meant to identify with this Samaritan leper's example of faith. b) Luke sees the importance between faith and salvation. "Your faith has saved (Gk.sesoke) you." (17:19) Marshall **(82)** says that it is not clear if the other nine lacked faith. They may have been rebuked for their ingratitude and incomplete faith. The Samaritan was unique among the ten lepers. **3. Empathetic** a) Jesus acts with mercy to those who ask for it and commends faith. "Jesus, Master, have mercy upon us." (17:13) The lepers knew His name and called Him "Master." This is the only time non-disciples use this title Master. b) Ten lepers as a group show Jesus' continued general compassion. c) **A foreigner with sensitivity responds to the compassion of Jesus. He was the only leper who turned back to praise God because he was socially and physically restored (17:15).** **4. Eschatological** a) This miracle shows the presence of messianic times "lepers are cleansed". (7:22) (Arndt) **(83)**	**1. The setting:** this event happens as Jesus nears Jerusalem, passing between Samaria and Galilee. **2. The condition of the men:** all ten are suffering from leprosy and at least one of them is a Samaritan leper. **3. The request for healing:** a. They call Jesus from a distance because their disease is despised (Lev. 13:45-46; Num.5:2-30). b. They call to Jesus to show compassion. "Jesus, Master, have mercy upon us." (17:13) **4. Jesus upholds the Jewish law:** telling the lepers to go and show themselves to the priest to certify they had been healed and to re-enter society (17:14; Lev.13:19). **5. The healing:** the lepers depart as a group and were healed on the way, showing that Jesus healed from a distance (17:14) as in (7:1-10). All ten lepers are healed. Jesus did not heal the lepers at once (17:14). **6. The reaction:** a. Only one leper expressed his faith in coming back to give thanks to God. He was a Samaritan leper and, therefore, a religious and social outcast. He fell on his face at the feet of Jesus and gave thanks (17:15). b. The Samaritan leper alone benefited from Jesus' act of mercy and gained a relationship with God. (Arndt) **(84)** c. The response of the nine never went beyond receiving kindness to the exercise of faith. (Bock) **(85)** **7. This miracle** shows the value of faith as Jesus commends the Samaritan for his faith. Jesus said to the thankful leper; "Rise; and go your way: your faith has saved you." (17:19)

BIBLE TEXT / TITLE / GENERAL COMMENTS	FUNCTION: WHAT IS ACHIEVED?	PURPOSE: INTENDED RESULT [WHY?]	CHARACTERISTICS: HOW IS IT UNIQUE?
26. a. **Read 18:35-43 the healing of the blind beggar of Jericho.** b. This is the fifth and final miracle of the journey narrative. c. Other occasions in Luke when Jesus commends faith are: 7:50, 8:48, 17:19. [See p. 179.] d. This is the only healing of a blind person in Luke's Gospel. e. This is a triple tradition: [Mark 10:46-55; Matthew 20:29-34] f. "And it came to pass" includes a new unit. g. Sometimes this healing miracle is called an "epideixis" (to receive someone kindly). Bultmann, Fitzmyer, Berger. [pp. 52, 54.] f. This miracle emphasises the importance of faith (18:42): the man's faith was based upon the Messiahship of Jesus, "the Son of David". g. A unique feature of Luke's Gospel is the conjoint praise of the healed person and that of the crowd (L) (5:26; Acts 2:47; 3:9). Both the praise of the blind man and that of the people are unique to Luke's Gospel (18:43). h. A soteriological significance :the man has passed from darkness to light. By faith salvation is appropriated. A Christological emphasis: Jesus as the Son of Man (18:31), Son of David (18:38) shares the Messianic character. He is Lord (8:41). Stein (86)	**Provides evidence of/that:** - a cry for mercy which is an important aspect of the appeal for salvation. - a lesson about faith. However it is both the man's confession of Jesus, The Son of David, and his persistence that Jesus praises. - Jesus nearing His death in Jerusalem, experiences a flood of praise by the people in Jericho on seeing this miracle. (18:43). A positive response of praise to Jesus by the ordinary people is a regular theme in Luke's Gospel (4:15; 5:26; 6:17; 7:16; 9:43; 18:43; 19:37,48: 20:6; 19:26; 21:38, 22:2; 24:19). Check out this point by looking up the references! [p. 52.] - the first public confession of Jesus as "the Son of David" (a messianic title) as Jesus nears His death in Jerusalem (18:38). - Jesus continuing His ministry near Jerusalem, Luke continues to say "See, who Jesus really is as the blind man recognised Jesus". Sight is a matter not just of the eyes but also of the heart. Note: The Greek word "sesoken" in Luke is always linked to faith and means both physical and spiritual healing; that is a deeper experience beyond that of restored sight (7:50). - the blind man makes a Messianic confession "Son of David." - Jesus is the final eschaton (the coming-One, the coming event), which brings the work of the promised Son of David, the messiah, to those who respond to Him in asking for mercy and following Him by faith.	**1. Evidential/Christological** a) the 'poor' show evidence of sensitivity to spiritual things. **2. Empathetic** a. despite the pressure against him, Jesus continues to show compassion. b) Jesus always has time for compassion (18:40). c) Jesus shows compassion in reaching out to meet the needs of the poor and the rejected. This compassion continues even though He is aware of the pressures against Him and is becoming more intense. **Jesus' compassion and spiritual sensitivity of the poor remains two key themes in Luke's Gospel.** **3. Evangelistic** a) His faith had saved him. "Your faith has made you well." (18:42) Light now exists were darkness had previously lived. b) This miracle shows the qualities required for access to God's power and salvation. It is for those who ask for God's mercy and follow Him by faith. **3. Eschatological** a) The restoring of sight to the blind shows that the end time has come (4:18; 7:22). (Fitzmyer) **(87)** b) The needs of the poor and rejected are met. c) The blind man uses the Messianic title for Jesus "Son of David." This was a time of restoration and healing (4:17-18; Is.61:1). d) The blind man's cry for help is an appeal to God's mercy. [See p. 52.]	**1. The setting:** Jesus is approaching Jericho, the first city named in the journey narrative (18:35). **2. The condition of the man:** a poor beggar sitting by the road (18:35). **3. The approach to the healing:** the blind man heard the crowd and asked what was happening. (18:36) (L). The crowd respond by telling him, "Jesus of Nazareth is passing by." (18:37) It could mean Jesus from Nazareth or Jesus the Nazarene (Gk.Nazir) someone consecrated by a vow. He cries out for help. "Jesus, Son of David have mercy on me!" This is the only time Luke uses this as a confession. It is a plea for compassion and mercy which is key theme in Luke (18:38). Many in the crowd told him to keep quiet as Jesus would not be interested or it could be his use of the words "Son of David". (18:39) Jesus orders the man to be brought to Him and than asks him what he would like Jesus to do for him. **4. The man's request:** "Let me receive my sight." (18:41a) **5. The healing:** Jesus says, "Receive your sight; your faith has made you well (healed/saved Gk. sesoken)." (18:42) Jesus commends the man for his faith. **6. The reaction:** a) The man becomes a disciple who follows Jesus and glorifies God. The healing is immediately (Gk. parachrema) to show how instantaneous was the miracle. b) The people also respond by praising (Gk. ainon) God. This word (Gk.ainon) is used only here (2:14,20) and in Matt. 21:16 The praise is instant.

BIBLE TEXT / TITLE / GENERAL COMMENTS	FUNCTION: WHAT IS ACHIEVED?	PURPOSE: INTENDED RESULT [WHY?]	CHARACTERISTICS: HOW IS IT UNIQUE?
27. a. Read 19:37 Jesus enters into Jerusalem and a crowd of disciples praise God for the mighty work which they have seen. b. This comment is unique to Luke. c. Luke omits the quote from Zech. 9:9 as in Matt. 21:5, "Hosanna," the actual triumphal entry into Jerusalem. He shows us Jesus approaching the city, and after the crowd's welcome, Jesus is still approaching it (19:11).	**A crowd of disciples who praise God for the miracles Jesus did provides evidence that:** - Jesus' ministry has been one continuous demonstration of power (7:22). People understood the purpose of Jesus' coming and rejoice. - Jesus is the humble king riding on the colt (19:35). - Jesus is moving to the place of His rejection and therefore Luke omits the triumphal entry (13:33).	**1. Eschatological** a) The Mount of Olives has much eschatological importance (19:29). The cry of the disciples, when the king enters, makes this a portrait of the Messiah. b) So also is the use of the eschatological Ps. 118:26. "Blessed be He who enters in the name of the Lord!" c) Luke stresses the Messianic theme in the use of the word "King." (Ps. 118:26).	**1. The setting:** the event takes place on the Mount of Olives (19:37). 2. God's miraculous works are the source of the praise. 3. The reference to praise is unique to Luke. Luke distinguishes between the "people" (Gk.laos) who were responsive to Jesus, and the leaders and the crowds (Gk.ochloi) (19:48). His teaching drew all the people (Gk. laos). Later this group will turn against Jesus (23:13). 4. Luke omits the actual entrance into Jerusalem, he shows us Jesus approaching Jerusalem (19:41).
28. a. Read 22:48-49 (L) the betrayal of Jesus with a kiss. Only Luke speaks of Jesus teaching daily in the Temple (22:53). (L) b. Read 22:50-51. The right ear of the high priest's servant is severed and then restored by Jesus. c. This is the last miracle in the ministry of Jesus and yet it is an aside. d. Parts of Luke 22:50 are triple tradition with Matthew 26:51; Mark 14:47. e. None of the Synoptics identify the disciple who cut off the right ear of the high priest's slave.	**The restoring of the high priest servant's ear provides evidence that:** - God's plan is in motion; He controls those who are scheming against Jesus. - Jesus accomplishes God's will. - Jesus reminds His opponents that they could have arrested Him peaceably in public rather than under the cover of darkness at night (22:53a). Only Luke speaks of Jesus' teaching daily in the Temple (L). - only Luke records, "No more of this," (L) to emphasise love of one's enemy. "Let them (the police) have their way." (NEB) [See p. 52.]	**1. Evidential** a) God is in control of the events even when Jesus is being arrested and submits to the Jewish authorities (22:51). b) Jesus submits to God's will. c) God allows the forces of evil to do their own evil deeds. d) Only Luke records that this is their hour and the hour of the power of darkness (22:53). The battle has entered a very critical and sombre stage. Those who reject Jesus appear to have their way. **2. Empathetic** a) Jesus shows compassion in healing the ear of a wounded enemy, that of the high priest's servant. b) He sets an example of love to His disciples, "love you enemy." (6:27-36)	**1. The setting:** the approach of Judas and the crowd causes a reaction among the disciples. 2. Jesus says to Judas, "Would you betray the Son of Man with a kiss?" The disciples came to the defence of Jesus, when they saw what might happen to Him. "Lord shall we strike with the sword?" Either they feared the crowd would seize Jesus or thought they could use force. **2. The incident:** the right ear of the high priest's servant is severed (22:50). Only Luke and John says it was the right ear. Jesus rebukes the disciple who did this. Mark says Peter did this. **3. The miracle:** Jesus touched his ear and healed him (22:51). **4. The response:** for the disciples it is a time to stand up and fight. Jesus has to stop them. The disciples want to take matters into their own hands rather than let God work out His own will.

Pupil's Activity: Nine

a) Using the outline which is common with Luke describe the characteristics of the miracle of the healing of Peter's mother–in–law (4:38-39) and prepare can outline of the characteristics of miracle in Luke's Gospel involving an outcast. **(Figure 3)**

	Headings	Detail based upon the event	Ref.
1.	the setting		
2.	the medical condition of the person		
3.	the approach or request to heal		
4.	the words or act of healing is given,		
5.	evidence of the healing		
6.	the reaction to the miracle.		

Pupil's Activity: Ten

a) Outline your knowledge and understanding of **two** miracles recorded in Luke's Gospel.
(CCEA A/S 2002)   [30 marks]
b) Explore the claim that miracles have an important function in the Gospel of Luke. Justify your answer.
(CCEA A/S 2002)   [15 marks]

Pupil's Activity: Eleven

a) Outline your knowledge and understanding of Luke's account of either the healing of the centurion's servant or the raising of the widow's son at Nain or the story of the Ten Lepers.
(CCEA A/S 2003)   [30 marks]
b) Explore the claim that faith plays an important role in the healing miracles as recorded by Luke.
Justify your answer.
(CCEA A/S 2003)   [15 marks]

Pupil's Activity: Twelve

a) Outline your knowledge and understanding of the purpose and characteristics of the miracles in Luke's Gospel.
(CCEA A/S 2004)   [30 marks]
b) Explore the claim that the Jesus of Luke's Gospel is a man of compassion and prayer. Justify your answer.
(CCEA A/S Resit 2004)   [15 marks]   [See Ch.7: Characteristics (Prayer).]
c) Explore the claim that the miracles of Jesus show the power and authority of Jesus. Justify your answer.
(CCEA A/S 2004)   [15 marks]

Pupil's Activity: Thirteen

a) Outline your knowledge and understanding of any two nature miracles recorded in Luke's Gospel.
(CCEA A/S Resit 2006)   [30 marks]
b) Comment on the claim that miracles demonstrate the authority of Jesus.
(CCEA A/S Resit 2006)   [15 marks]

[9] A summary of the subordinate themes associated with miracles

• The main purpose of the miracles in Luke's Gospel is Christological: to show that Jesus is the Divine Messiah and that the Kingdom of God is breaking into human history (11:20).
• Miracles are by definition exceptional, supernatural events.
• There is evidence that miracles are more prevalent when God's reign is forcefully advancing into an area enslaved by the powers of darkness (8:27-35).
• Jesus claimed to cast out demons by the Spirit of God (11:20) and explained His identity to John by referring to the prophecies of Isaiah (7:18-23). This shows that He regarded His mighty deeds as a manifestation of the Kingdom of God in contrast to the expectations of others who hoped for the "salvation of Israel." His miracles were part of His Ministry to restore God's people.
• The Kingdom was present when He exorcised demons (11:20). "But, if it is by the finger of God that I cast out demons, then the Kingdom of God has come upon you." This is a key verse to the understanding of miracles as it is one of the few passages to make the explicit connection between miracle and the Kingdom of God. Among the people

healed were lepers, lame, deaf, physically deformed and those with a bodily discharge. All of these people were barred from the admittance to the Temple as they were regarded as ritually unclean. Jesus would have been seen as unclean for touching a dead person or even touching a Gentile. He crossed the boundaries of purity to show the Kingdom as the power of God and God will make His people whole.

• He showed the power of God's Spirit to overcome demonic forces which marginalized people from the rest of society. For this He was accused of being in collusion with Satan for the sake of releasing the captives (4:18; Is. 35:5 ; 61:1).

• His idea of Messiah was to restore God's people along different lines from the common standards of that time. Jesus never works a miracle for His own benefit: He operates on the basis of compassion. His concern is not to do the spectacular and He refuses to give a sign to the doubters. He prays to God before the miracle of the Transfiguration (9:29) but never utters some kind of mantra or incantation. The way in which the miracle takes place is rarely stated. All of the nature miracles are closely linked to the Kingdom of God. Luke in his miracles stresses the conquest of Satan's power and domain (10:18-20; 13:11-12). The miracles challenge Jewish tradition especially those of the Pharisees. He breaks down social barriers and shows compassion for the sufferers. These are all the main key sub-themes associated with miracles in the Third Gospel.

Pupil's Activity: Fourteen
Classify the miracles in Luke's Gospel. Identify each miracle according to your classification. Find out how many are:-
a) healing miracles b) nature miracles c) exorcism miracles d) resurrection miracles

Pupil's Activity: Fifteen   I.C.T. Activity
a) There are eighteen miracle stories in Mark plus four summaries of miraculous events, twenty-one miracle stories in Luke plus four summaries and nineteen miracle stories in Matthew plus four summaries. (Achtemeier) **(88)** For schools doing the "Skills Option" at A/S, identify each of these miracles. Draw a pie chart to show their differences indicating which Gospel has the largest proportion of its total in miracles. Use your computer software "Excel."

Pupil's Activity: Sixteen
a) Outline your knowledge and understanding of Luke's account of "the raising of Jairus' daughter", "the Widow of Nain's Son" and "the Man with the Withered Hand."
b) What were the main purposes Jesus had in mind in doing these miracles?
c) Identify and consider what can be learned about the nature of Jesus' ministry from:
1) The healing of the Paralysed Man;
2) The feeding of the Five Thousand.   (Edexcel A/S 2002)   [30 marks]
c) What can be learned from the nature of Jesus' ministry from:
1) the healing miracles;
2) the casting out of evil spirits?   (Edexcel A/S 2004)   [14 marks]

Pupil's Activity: Seventeen
a) What lessons did the Twelve learn and what impact did they have upon the villages they entered? How does Luke link the kingdom and the Gospel (9:1-6)?
b) What can be learned about the nature of Jesus' ministry from the Transfiguration?
(Edexcel A/S 2005)   [5 marks]

Pupil's Activity: Eighteen   Map Question
Mark on the map the following places named in the miracle stories in Luke's Gospel. In which towns did Jesus not perform a miracle in Luke's Gospel. Mark on the city of Nain on the map. (Figure 4)

Places	Miracles in Luke
1. Alexandrium	
2. Chorazin	
3. Bethsaida	
4. The country of the Gerasenes	
5. Jericho	
6. Capernaum	
7. Nazareth	
8. Tyre	
9. Sidon	

Pupil's Activity: Nineteen   Map Question
a) Identify the places marked on the map b) Which miracles in Luke's Gospel do you associate with these places?

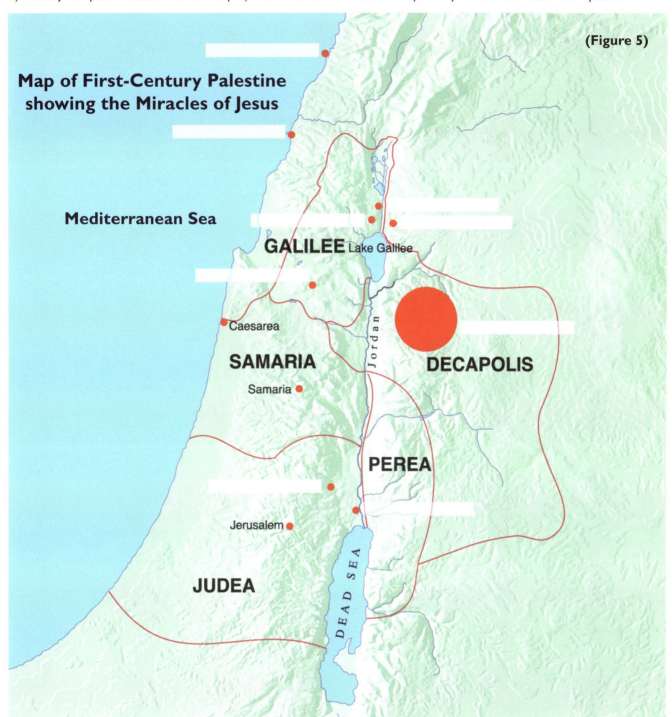

Map of First-Century Palestine showing the Miracles of Jesus

(Figure 5)

Mediterranean Sea

GALILEE   Lake Galilee

Caesarea

SAMARIA

Samaria

DECAPOLIS

Jordan

PEREA

Jerusalem

JUDEA

DEAD SEA

Outcomes
Students should have a knowledge and understanding of the:
• different classifications of the miracles in Luke's Gospel e.g. the views of Fitzmyer and Theissen.
• nature of Jesus' ministry as evidenced in the miracles in Luke's Gospel.
• different words for miracles in Luke's Gospel e.g. 'mighty deeds', 'signs', work, authority and power.
• role of faith in the healing miracles in Luke's Gospel.
• types of miracle in Luke's Gospel nature, gift, healing, rescue, exorcism, rule, resurrection and the different words for the reaction to those miracles, for example thaumaturge, amazed.
• function, purpose and the characteristics of the miracles in Luke's Gospel.
• key concepts linked to miracles, for example angelophany, eschatological, Christological, Son of Man.

Notes on Ch.13: The characteristics of the miracles in Luke's Gospel

1. Joseph A. Fitzmyer, op. cit. pp. 542-43.

2. Gerd Theissen, The Miracles Stories of the Early Church Tradition, Trans. F. McDonagh: Edinburgh T. and T. Clark, (1983) pp. 542-43.

3. W.F. Arndt, The Gospel According to Luke, (1956) p.250.

4. Walter Liefeld, Luke in the Expositors' Bible, Vol. 8 Matthew-Luke , Zondervan, (1984) p.911.*

5. G. Kittel, TDNT, 2:255.

6. Josephus, Ant. 18.3.3¶¶ 63-64.

7. Josephus, J.W.7.6.3 ¶¶ 180-85.

8. Josephus, Ant. 14.2.1 ¶ 32.

9. Mishnah, Ta'anit 3:8.

10. Tacitus, Hist. 4.81.

11. Douglas Moo, Synoptic Gospels, cited in Craig L. Blomberg, Jesus and the Gospels : An Introduction and Survey, Apollos, IVP, (1997) p.275 .

12. H. Van der Loos, The Miracles of Jesus, HTS, Supplement 9, Leiden: Brill, (1965) pp.78-79. 15.

13. Paul Achtemeier, J.B.L. Lucan Perspectives and Miracles, Edinburgh: Clarke, (1975) p.161.

14. Graham Stanton, The Gospels and Jesus, Oxford Press, (1989) p.219.*

15. Joseph A. Fitzmyer, p.734 comments that because of the ending, the account is really a missionary story and a miracle. (8:39) The demoniac has to stay at home to witness to his friends rather than be called to be with Jesus. Some are called to stay at home and some are called to be with Jesus.

16. B.L. Blackburn, Article on "Miracles and Miracle Stories," Luke's Gospel, IVP, DJG, (1992) p.559.

17. I. Howard Marshall, op. cit. pp. 128-136.

18. Charles H. Talbert, op. cit. pp. 52-53.

19. Robert H. Stein, op. cit. p.153.

20. Joseph A. Fitzmyer, op. cit. p.529.

21. Gerd Theissen, op. cit. pp. 223-224.

22. Darrell Bock, op. cit. pp. 109-121.

23. Gerd Theissen, op. cit p.321.

24. Biblical Archaelogical Review, Article on Galilee Bible Works, Vol. 14. 5:18-33, (1998):18-33.

25. Joseph A. Fitzmyer, op. cit. p.562.

26. Charles H. Talbert, op. cit pp.60-61.

27. Alfred Plummer, op. cit. p.143.

28. Gerd Theissen, (ibid.).

29. Robert C. Tannehill, op. cit. pp.111-116.

30. Joseph A. Fitzmyer, op. cit p.650.

31. Thomas Louis Brodie, Studies in Biblical Theology (1984) Greco-Roman Initiation as a partial Guide to Luke's use of Society, New Prospectives from SBT and Charles H Talbert: New York pp. 134-147.

32. Joel Green, op. cit p. 284 notes three parallels in (2 Kgs. 5 1-14), the story of Naaman the Syrian who is also a well-respected Gentile, a Jewish girl intercedes like the Jewish elders in LK. 7:3-5 and the healing also takes place at a distance.

33. Darrell L. Bock, op. cit. p.646. This view is also upheld by Blomberg who calls it 'revivification', op. cit. p.271 Jesus and the Gospels (1997), Murray J. Harris, The Dead are Restored to Life, Gospel Perspectives, Vol.6 pp.295-326.

34. S. B. op. cit. 23: 5.

35. Craig L. Blomberg, Jesus and the Gospels, Apollos, (1997) pp.269-71.

36. S. B. op. cit. 4:858-860.

37. Robert Stein, op. cit. p.225.

38. James M. Scott, Ch. 9: Jesus' vision for the restoration of Israel: Biblical Theology Retrospect and Prospect, editor Scott J. Hafemann, Apollos, (2002) p.135.

39. Robert Stein, op. cit. p.228.

40. Joseph A. Fitzmyer, op. cit. p.740.

41. Charles H. Talbert, op. cit. p.97.

42. Robert C. Tannehill, op. cit. p.135.

43. Howard Marshall, op. cit. p. 342.

44. Howard Marshall, (ibid.)

45. Gerd Theissen, op. cit. p. 342.

46. Walter L. Liefeld, op. cit. p. 916.

47. Donald Guthrie, Jesus the Messiah, Pickering and Inglis, Zondervan, (1972) p.133.

48. Walter L. Liefeld, op. cit. p.919.

49. Robert C. Tannehill, op. cit. pp.215-6.

50. Robert H. Stein, op. cit. p.269.

51. Robert H. Stein, (ibid.)

52. Donald Guthrie, op. cit. p.119.

53. Robert C. Tannehill, op. cit. pp.215-6.

54. Francois Bovon, op. cit. p.469.

55. Craig Evans, op. cit. p.141.

56. Peter Berger and Luckmann, The Social Construction of Reality: A Treatise in the Sociology of Knowledge, New York : Doubleday (1966) p.317.

57. Craig Evans, op. cit. p.146.

58. Eduard Schweizer, TDNT, (1982) 8:369.

59. Vincent Taylor, The Gospel According to Mark: Macmillan, (1966) pp.386-88.

60. Rudolph Bultmann, op. cit. pp.259-61.

61. Robert H. Stein, op. cit. p.287.

62. Frederick W. Danker, op. cit. p.201.

63. Robert H. Stein, (ibid.).

64. David L. Tiede, op. cit. pp. 182-3.

65. Joel Green, op. cit. p.390.

66. Howard Marshall, op. cit. pp.421-22.

67. Craig Blomberg, op. cit. DJG, p.303.

68. Darrell L. Bock, op. cit. Vol. 2, p.1014.

69. Craig Blomberg, op. cit. DJG, p. 303.

70. Walter L. Liefeld, op. cit. p. 950.

71. Walter L. Liefeld, (ibid.)

72. Joel Green, op. cit. p.526.

73. Robert C. Tannehill, op. cit. p.65.
74. Josephus, Ant. 3.11.3 ¶ 264.
75. Gerd Theissen, op. cit. p.113.
76. Qumran, CD, 11.11-17.
77. Joseph A. Fitzmyer, op. cit. p.1150.
78. Robert C. Tannehill, op. cit pp.118-120.
79. Josephus Ant. 15.11.5 par. 417.
80. Robert H. Stein, op. cit. p.434.
81. Robert H. Stein, (ibid.).
82. Howard Marshall, op. cit. p.652.
83. W.F. Arndt, op. cit. p.371.
84. W.F. Arndt, op. cit. p.372.
85. Darrell L. Bock, op. cit. Vol. 2 , p. 1406.
86. Robert H. Stein, (ibid.).
87. Joseph A. Fitzmyer, op. cit. p.1214.
88. Paul J. Achtemeier, J.B.L. Lucan Perspectives and Miracles, Edinburgh: Clarke, (1975) p.547.
* These books are highly recommended.

(Edexcel A/S + parts of CCEA A2)

> The word "disciple" (Gk.mathetes) means learner, pupil, follower of a great master and in the early Church, it came to mean a true believer.

Targets:
- **Identify the main events relating to discipleship in Luke's Gospel.**
- **Recognise the nature and demands of discipleship.**
- **Identify key themes and concepts relating to discipleship in Luke's Gospel, for example discipleship viewed as a journey, the women disciples, the Twelve, 'apostles', the call of the disciples, the call to mission, defection, coping with failure, the cost of discipleship. (CCEA A/2)**
- **Identify parables relating to discipleship and the challenge of discipleship. (CCEA A/2) [See pp. 157-8.]**

Jesus' Relationship with His Disciples and the Nature and Demands of Discipleship
Introduction

A) What is a disciple? The word "disciple" (Gk. mathetes) means learner, pupil, follower of a great master and later in the early Church (Acts 4:32), it came to mean a true believer; someone who had put their trust in Jesus. Jesus called His disciples and chose from them twelve (6:13). A disciple must be prepared to sacrifice everything for Jesus (14:25-33). The word "disciple" is used thirty-seven times in Luke's Gospel.

B) O.T. background Christian discipleship coheres with the faith of Israel and the concept of disciple goes back to the time of the Prophets when men like Isaiah gathered around them a group called "my disciples" (Hebrew limmud) (Is.8:16). These men were disciples of both Yahweh and Isaiah (Is. 15:13). By the time of Jeremiah, the idea of a "master disciple" started to provide conjoint support in the work of bringing God's word to Israel (Prov. 25:1) and this was continued with the wise counsellor idea (Jer. 18:18).

C) N.T. background By the time of Jesus it was common for different groups of leaders to have disciples. John the Baptist had his own disciples (5:33) as did the Pharisees (Matt. 22:15). In Jesus' time those seeking to become a scribe or a rabbi were called disciples. The other Gospel writers call Jesus "Rabbi" but Luke prefers to call Him "teacher"(Gk.didaskalos), a Greek title, which would appeal to the Gentiles (7:40; 8:49; 9:38). In the first-century the teacher-pupil relationship was a personal one as the learning was by oral instruction and not by book. The disciple becomes like the teacher because of the nature of the pupil-teacher relationship; the servant-master picture has the idea that the product is like the producer. The disciples of Jesus are to be like Him, "But I am among you as one who serves." (22:27b)

> The other Gospel writers call Jesus "Rabbi" but Luke prefers to call Him "teacher" (Gk.didaskalos), a Greek title which would appeal to the Gentiles.

[1] Jesus' relationship with His disciples
A) The call of the first disciples (Read 5:1-11.) [See p. 185.]

The life of discipleship began for four of the disciples-Peter, his brother Andrew (not named in this event in Luke), James and John (his companions) when Jesus called them by the lakeside in Galilee. The focus of the account is mainly on Peter. Jesus takes the initiative in calling these fishermen. He commissions Peter to catch people which has the idea of rescuing them from danger (Gk.anthropous ese zogron). This was a call to ministry; Peter would be called to engage in continuous evangelism (5:10). The account focuses on Peter as the leader and representative of the group. The disciples would become great evangelists in the Acts. Rarely do they exercise this gift during the earthly ministry of Jesus.

As followers the "called" disciples abandoned everything: their family ties, property and livelihood to follow Jesus (5:11). In Jewish idiom, pupils or protégés often followed their teachers. (Kittel) **(1)** The extent of the disciples, commitment can be seen in the expression "leaving all" (Gk.aphentes panta). Leaving home for the disciples was a radical change as the cultural responsibility was to submit to parents and fulfil all family obligations. Jesus did not draw up a short list for the job but took the initiative to command people to follow Him. The idea of following will become a standard image for discipleship: denying self (9:23), acceptance of the outsider who was an exorcist (9:49), the cost of discipleship (9:59-61) and a call to give all to the poor and follow Jesus (18:22). Peter notes that the disciples have given up all to follow Jesus (18:28); the blind man outside Jericho received his sight at once and followed Jesus. The Greek word "akoloutheo" "follow" has now become a technical word for discipleship (9:57-61). The disciples were called by Jesus and their call was a voluntary one (5:10-11, 27-28). This call was given to a specific group of disciples. Peter's discipleship was based upon his perception of himself as a sinner (5:8b). Jesus now has **companionship** in His relationship with His four disciples as He starts His Mission (5:11). Luke does not include the command, "Follow me;" instead he says that they left everything and **followed** (Gk.ekolouthesan) Jesus (5:11). This indicates the nature of their commitment. Jesus is the centre of their lives. [See Ch. 13: Miracles.]

B) The call of Levi.   (Read 5:27-32.) [See p. 240.]

Jesus called a social outcast to follow (Gk.akolouthei) Him (5:28) and this leads to a negative response by the Pharisees and the scribes, who reject fellowship with the unrighteous. Jesus singles out Levi. He saw this lower level tax collector (Gk. telones). Levi, unlike Zacchaeus who was a chief tax collector, would have reported to a line manager like Zacchaeus. The disciples are not to isolate themselves from sinners. There is spiritual and emotional healing for Levi who is accepted now as a person and who also accepts God's healing grace as a follower of Jesus. Luke emphasises discipleship and repentance. Levi leaves everything behind (5:10) and follows Jesus (Gk.ekolouthei imperfect tense): this is to show that what comes next exemplifies his discipleship (5:28). He shows his complete break with the past in having a great feast for Jesus and opens up his home to his friends especially his fellow tax collectors, introducing them to Jesus (5:29). Later the Pharisees raise their objections, grumbling (Gk.egongyzona denotes complaints about Jesus to outsiders) against the disciples of Jesus, asking why the disciples and Jesus were eating with such a rabble. The complaint was against Jesus and anyone who had an association with Him. "Why do you (plural) eat (Gk.esthiete) and drink (Gk.pinete) with tax collectors and sinners?" (5:30) This is a common charge against Jesus (5:33; 7:33-34). The Pharisees think that Jesus should decline all such fellowship. Jesus said that the disciples are to seek the lost and are to associate with sinners (5:30); Jesus formed relationships that would help lay the basis of an acceptance from which a person's lifestyle could be challenged. This is the first use of the word "disciples" in Luke's Gospel. The Pharisees' objection was on the basis of a call to holiness (Lev.10:10; 19:2) and separation (Neh.10:28). Jesus replied that He had come to call sinners to repentance and not the righteous (5:32). Jesus said His disciples must also seek the lost even if it means risking ridicule and associating with sinners. 'Tax collectors' were grouped with 'sinners' not so much because they were dishonest and practised distortion, but because they were regarded as traitors collecting taxes for the Romans (5:32). (Stein) **(2)** Jesus shows His concern for the marginalized, who now become the object of God's grace and who are regarded with suspicion by the religious authorities.

> **The word "disciple" is used thirty-seven times in Luke's Gospel.**

C) The disciples follow the example of Jesus (Read 6:1-3.) [See p. 271.]

The disciples plucked and ate the ears of corn on the Sabbath. For the Pharisees, this was tantamount to reaping, threshing, winnowing, and preparing food on the Sabbath. In this incident, Jesus and His disciples are again regarded as a group. **A special feature of Luke's Gospel is the idea of a group of disciples (6:3).** As they are His disciples, they are seen as following His example. Both Jesus and His disciples are challenging the custom of the Pharisees. Jesus defends the actions of the group of disciples against the criticism of the Pharisees. At this point the disciples add little to the narrative and Green **(3)** sees them as "stage props." Up to Ch.9:39 they are merely with Jesus, receiving instruction from Him alongside the crowds (6:17, 20; 7:1). [See 9:51.] In Luke, the list of "the Twelve" consists of three groups of four, in which the lead position is always occupied by Peter, Philip and James, the son of Alphaeus.

> **In Luke, the list of "the Twelve" consists of three groups of four, in which the lead position is always occupied by Peter, Philip and James, the son of Alphaeus.**

D) "The Twelve" (Read 6:12-16.)

1) The choice of Twelve: Luke alone says that Jesus chose twelve from a large pool of disciples. "He called to His disciples and chose from them twelve, whom He named apostles." Luke says that Jesus "elected" (Gk.eklexamenos) meaning He made a conscious and calculated choice of "the Twelve", calling them out of a group of disciples. There is much evidence to show that Jesus had an inner group of disciples called "the Twelve" and had a special relationship with them. As "the Twelve" were marked out from the beginning, they were always called apostles and regarded as the greatest of a broader group. Their authority was always seen as unique, going back to Jesus' choice of them. In Luke's usage of the term an apostle needs to be with Jesus from the start (Acts 1:21-22). (Schurmann) **(4)** It is quite likely that the disciples had three calls in Luke's Gospel. The first call cited above 5:1-11 and the second when Jesus called Levi to follow Him and he left everything, and rose and followed Jesus (5:27-32). Nolland sees choosing and naming "the Twelve" as a third call (6:12-16). **(5)** Although they are called by Jesus, they are not given any responsibility in the early ministry of Jesus. In Luke, the list of "the Twelve" consists of three groups of four, in which the lead position is always occupied by Peter, Philip and James the son of Alphaeus. (Plummer) **(6)**

(Figure 1) The list of "the Twelve"

1	Simon Peter	5	Philip	9	James the son of Alphaeus
2	Andrew	6	Bartholomew	10	Simon the Zealot
3	James	7	Matthew	11	Judas son of James
4	John	8	Thomas	12	Judas Iscariot

Peter always leads the first list and Luke always calls him Peter except for 5:8; 22:31; 24:34 when he is called Simon Peter. Peter is noted for his leadership qualities among "the Twelve." Jesus does not see Himself as one of "the Twelve" as He stands above them in authority. Green **(7)** notes that the line between the disciples and others is not always clearly drawn in Luke's Gospel.

The number twelve is significant as it could refer to the twelve tribes of Israel.

E) The significance of the number Twelve and the idea of a group (Read 6:12-17.)
Jesus chooses the Twelve and teaches them in the Sermon on the Plain (6:12-49). After a night of prayer, He chose twelve ordinary men to form a commissioned group around him. Jesus chose the numerical twelve and not eleven as an indication that He was above and outside the group. The disciple is not above his teacher (6:40). The number twelve is significant as it could refer to the twelve tribes of Israel. "I have appointed you to eat and drink at my table in my Kingdom and sit on the thrones judging the twelve tribes of Israel." (22:28-30; Matt. 19:28) In calling "the Twelve", Jesus is indicating that God is now establishing anew His people and will bring the O.T. promise to fulfilment. (Stanton) **(8)** In this view the Church parallels Israel. The choice of Judas is part of God's divine plan. (Plummer) **(9)** Jesus names the Twelve as His commissioned representatives (6:13) and as His apostles, giving them great authority (9:1-6).

Jesus names "the Twelve" as His commissioned representatives (6:13) and as His apostles, giving them great authority (9:1-6).

1) The Church as the New Israel
This is the view of Hendriksen **(10)** who sees the Church as the New Israel with roots going back into the O.T. through the twelve tribes of Israel. In this view the Church replaces Israel. Before the Sermon on the Plain, Jesus stood on a level place with a great crowd of His disciples showing that His teaching had been well received at first (6:17). Those who are selective about the people they sit beside at table, who do not fast on the right days (5:33-39), who forbid healing on the Sabbath (6:6-11) and spurn the offer of forgiveness (5:29-32), will not be able to identify with those referred to in the Sermon on the Plain (6:17-29). The disciples must show mercy. Jesus defines the new conditions of faith and life for the disciples. "Be merciful, even as your Father is merciful." (6:36)

2) The apostles: sometimes the disciples, "the Twelve" are called apostles (Gk. apostoloi), (6:13) (Hebrew salah "the sent ones") to increase their faith. "Salah" had the Jewish idea of acting with authority equal to the sender. (Fitzmyer) **(11)** Jesus names "the Twelve" as His commissioned representatives (6:13) and as His apostles giving them great authority (9:1-6). Later, the title "apostle" would become an exclusive office for the select twelve. After teaching His disciples about forgiveness, the apostles ask Jesus to increase their faith. Jesus relates the parable of the grain of mustard seed, and that of the sycamine tree, "You could say to this sycamine tree [black mulberry tree], 'Be rooted up and be planted in the sea,' and it would obey you." (17:5) Jesus went on to tell the parable of the unworthy servant (meaning slave Gk. doulos). Serving Jesus as a disciple is a duty and not a matter of negotiation. In the parable Jesus depicts a servant coming in from a hard day's work of farming or shepherding only to be asked to prepare his own dinner. The servant will not get a meal until the master is served. Further the servant will not be thanked as if he has done something special. He will prepare the meal out of a sense of duty (17:7-10). Committed service is a disciple's privilege. This was in complete contrast to the Pharisee in the parable who fasted twice a day and gave tithes of all he received (18:12). [See p. 168.]

F) "The Twelve" are sent out on a mission. (Read 9:1-6.) [See p. 201.]
a) The word "apostle" (Gk. apostolos) occurs six times in Luke's Gospel. Jesus is willing to entrust His disciples with power and authority to heal and to exorcise even though they are very insecure in their faith. After sending out the Twelve on a mission, on their return the apostles told Jesus what they had done (9:10). The twelve chosen were called to function as His representatives and mouth pieces for the good news of the Kingdom (9:1-6). The disciples were very involved in the ministry of Jesus by going on missions (9:1-6; 10:1-17). They were debriefed by Jesus (9:10; 10:18-24) and helped with the distribution of the bread and fish at the feeding of the five thousand (9:12-17). In their relationship with Jesus, the apostles report/recount (Gk. diegesanto) to Jesus all that had happened on the mission. This would have been an oral report (9:10a).
Other occasions when the title "apostle" is used: after giving the disciples teaching on forgiveness, the apostles said to the Lord, "increase our faith!" (17:5) At the last supper, Jesus sat at table and the apostles with Him (22:14). The three women and the other women told the apostles about their experiences at the empty tomb (24:10). Later, the title "apostle" became an exclusive office of the select Twelve.
G) The seventy (two) are sent out on a mission. (Read 10:1-24.) [See pp. 203-4.]
In the mission of the seventy-(two) disciples, Jesus gave them authority to preach and to heal; they were also the formal representatives of Jesus, "Whoever hears you hears me, and he who rejects you rejects me, and he who rejects me rejects Him who sent me." (10:16; Matt. 10:40; "Q") This shows Jesus' self-understanding as a prophet and His close relationship with His disciples (10:1-12). Despite having this power over Satan, the disciples are to rejoice that their names are written in heaven (10:20).

> **In the mission of the seventy (two) disciples, Jesus gave them authority to preach and to heal; they were also the formal representatives of Jesus.**

H) Questions the disciples put to Jesus: the disciples are curious about the meaning of the parable of the Sower and ask Jesus to explain its meaning. They realise that this is not a lesson on agriculture but teaching something about God (8:9). Jesus explains that God's word divides people, and parables reveal to disciples the mysteries of God's kingdom. The disciples have access to the mysteries of God (8:10). They also asked Jesus if they should bring fire down from heaven and destroy the Samaritan village which refused the message. Jesus rebukes them for wanting to judge immediately this unbelieving village of outcasts. The current time is not one for instant judgement but one for the disciples to offer God's grace (9:52,54,56). [See pp. 121-2.]

I) The others/the women who followed and who were part of a wider group of disciples: (Read 8:1-3,38.)
[See Ch. 15 : Women.] Apart from "the Twelve", a group of women, many of whom had been healed by Jesus, travelled with Him and supported His ministry. It was unusual for women to travel with a rabbi. The women provided for the whole group. At the turning point in the narrative, when Jesus moves from Galilee to Jerusalem (9:51), Green **(12)** notes that the disciples appear more often and have more active roles. However, they fail to recognise Jesus' identity and react with fear and amazement when He calms the wind and water (8:22-25). Despite this lapse, He entrusts them with power and authority to heal (9:1).

> **Due to the shortcomings of the disciples when on occasions they show their self-centredness, feelings of self-importance and failings, the disciples have a broken relationship with Jesus.**

J) The disciples' broken relationship with Jesus (Read 22:24-30.) [See pp. 135-6.]
1) Due to the shortcomings of the disciples when on occasions they show their self-centredness, feelings of self-importance and failings, the disciples have a broken relationship with Jesus. They raise the contentious issue which of them is the greatest. Who will have what role in the kingdom of God? This was an old thorny question among the disciples (22:24 ; Matt. 20:20-28; Mk.10:35-45). Jesus replies that the apostles are not to lead as the world leads by exercising power. Equality in Jesus has a great effect on a person's style of leadership. The apostles are not to exploit their age and position. "The Twelve" are not to be an elite group. Greatness is defined by service and not by authority. The disciples are to lead by serving. This verse is unique to Luke and points to a relationship of serving. "For which is the greater, the one who sits at the table or the one who serves?" Great people are served by those under them, but Jesus came to serve. Leadership will be seen not in great acts of power but in service (22:27). Even though Jesus is greater, He presents Himself as one who serves (22:28-29). Even those who will sit in judgement, have in God's kingdom, no greater status than any other.
2) A disciple who defects. (Read 22:48.) [See pp. 136-7.]
Jesus asks Judas is this the way - a kiss, in which a defecting disciple betrays the Son of Man? (22:48) Those [disciples] who fall away are like the seed sown on the rock, they receive the word joyfully at first but have no root. They believe for a while but like Judas in the time of testing, they fall away (8:13).
3) The disciples want to use force to defend Jesus. (Read 22:49.) [See p. 137.]
Sometimes the failings of the disciples are physical when they fall asleep with sorrow on the Mt. of Olives (22:45) and when He has to rebuke them for drawing their swords in His defence (22:51). He shows love for His enemies, which He had instructed His disciples to do (6:27-35). Jesus in restoring the ear of the high priest's servant, shows mercy and compassion towards His enemies (22:50-51). The disciples' weaknesses are forgiven by Jesus and their broken relationship with Him is restored. The disciples wanted to take measures into their own hands rather than let God work out His will. "Shall we strike with a sword?" (22:49)
4) The disciples will face trials: being a disciple will be a hard road to travel. (Read 12:4-12; 22:36, 56-61.)
The disciples must trust God and confess Jesus before people, so that Jesus will confess them before the angels (12:4-12). They must seek God's priorities and keep to His agenda as God is concerned about the fate of those who trust Him. God will help the disciples withstand the heat of the kitchen. Peter affirms his loyalty to Jesus (22:33) being ready to go to prison and death for Jesus. Jesus predicts that before the cock crows that day Peter will have denied Jesus three times (22:34). Jesus prays for Peter that his faith may not fail in the time of trial (22:36).
Peter, despite showing considerable interest and nerve in following Jesus to the courtyard of the high priest (22:54), fails on three occasions to stand up for Jesus. When the pressure comes upon Peter, he repeatedly fails to align himself with Jesus and denies Him three times (22:56-57; 22:58 and 22:59-60a). This is a very painful experience for Peter, as Jesus is fully aware of the events, turns and looks at Peter. "The Lord saw Peter." (22:61a) Peter then recalls the earlier prediction of Jesus had happened (22:61b). Jesus has to face His trial alone as He predicted would happen. He lost His companions in the hour of need. [See pp. 136-7.]
5) All the disciples are called to mission. (Read 24:36-53.) [See pp. 147-8.]
The disciples are still coming to terms with the Resurrection as seen in their fear (24:37). The suffering death and resurrection

of Jesus are all part of God's plan right back from the O.T. The disciples are to take this plan and the message of repentance (turning to God and embracing Him by faith) and forgiveness to all the nations in the name of Jesus (24:47). The disciples are witnesses of these things (24:48). They are to wait for the promised Holy Spirit who will be sent to them in Jerusalem. As Jesus departs, He blesses them and they return with great joy to Jerusalem worshipping Jesus and continue to bless God in the Temple for all His grace. He wants the disciples to know that God's plan continues as they wait for the Spirit. From these verses onwards the disciples are called to continue the work of Jesus. Prior to (22:28) they have been receiving training from Jesus. "You are those who have continued with me in my trials."

Pupil's Activity: One
Jesus defines discipleship as following Himself, a concept Luke develops above all by noting the presence of the disciples continually "with Jesus." (Green) **(13)** a) How do these references corroborate this definition of discipleship and what did companionship with Jesus mean? b) What do these references indicate about the meaning of discipleship?

(Figure 2) Incidents regarding the nature of discipleship in Luke's Gospel

	Refs.	Incidents regarding the disciples	Comment
1	6:17	He stood on a level place with His disciples.	
2	7:11	His disciples and a great crowd went with Him to Nain.	
3	8:1	He went through cities and villages preaching and bringing the good news of the kingdom of God.	
4	8:22	He got into a boat with His disciples. Compare (8:37-38).	Why does Jesus not allow the healed demoniac to be with Him?
5	9:10	Jesus took the disciples and withdrew apart to a city called Bethsaida.	
6	22:11	Tell the house holder, "the Teacher says to you, Where is the guest room where I am to eat the passover with my disciples?"	
7	22:14	He sat at table and the apostles with Him.	
8	22:28	"You are those who have continued with me in my trials;" Compare (22:23).	They began to question one another, which of them it was who would betray Him.
9	22:39	The disciples followed Him to the Mount of Olives.	22:61-62

[2] The nature of discipleship: discipleship viewed as a journey

A) Luke emphasises entrance into the way of salvation and discipleship, the way which is found by faith alone. To the sinful woman in the house of Simon the Pharisee, Jesus said, "Your faith has saved you; go in peace." (7:50) To the woman with the haemorrhage, He said, "Daughter, your faith has made you well; go in peace." (8:48) To the Samaritan leper, He said, "Rise and go your way; your faith has made you well." (17:19)
B) Discipleship as a costly way (Read 14:25-33.): discipleship also means counting the cost in being attached to Jesus. The "costly way" is a distinctive feature of Luke's Gospel. (Wilkins) **(14)** Jesus provides discipleship training relating to conditions for entering the Kingdom: family, wealth, nothing must detract from following Jesus. Discipleship also involves counting the cost: Jesus must be the first love. The disciple who loses saltiness becomes useless and is tossed out. The uncommitted disciple is like a builder who cannot complete a planned project, a silly king who enters a war he cannot win. These three issues putting God above one's family, bearing one's cross and leaving all, are issues which threaten discipleship. They are not entrance requirements into the kingdom but are the commitments for real discipleship (9:57-62; 14:26-33). (Tiede)**(15)** As time passed the disciples grew into some of these commitments. Above all the disciples are not to be useless disciples like tasteless salt (14:34-35). [See p. 158.]
C) The way as a narrow gate "to salvation": Jesus answers the question: will few or many be saved? People from all corners of the earth will sit at God's table in His Kingdom (13:22-30).
D) Discipleship as a testimony of the way (9:1-6): "the Twelve" are sent out. This is the start of an active ministry for the followers of Jesus. He sends out the disciples to speak about the coming of the Kingdom and shares His power and authority with them. They travel light and stay where people receive them. They have just witnessed an impressive series of miracles: a nature miracle, an exorcism, a healing and a raising from the dead (Ch.8). They are committed to following the way and have to go and pray that others will join them. They are called to a simple life of trusting God. The Galilean

ministry comes to a climax with Peter's confession and the call to discipleship before Jesus sets His face to go to Jerusalem (9:51). Even after the success of this mission, the disciples fail to ask Jesus to provide food for the crowd at the feeding of the five thousand (9:13). The instant reactions of the disciples are wrong. They have to realise that Jesus is the source of their life and ministry. Life on the Way, Jesus said, consists of daily self-denial, bearing one's cross and daily following in the footsteps of the Master, if the disciple is to survive the forces of the world. [See p. 199.]

> **Life on the Way, Jesus said, consists of daily self-denial, bearing one's cross and daily following in the footsteps of the Master, if the disciple is to survive the forces of the world (9:23-25).**

E) Confessing Jesus (Read 9:18-22.): Jesus asks the disciples, "Who do you say I am?" Even when Peter answers that Jesus is the Christ (9:20), the disciples have not understood that Jesus is the Messiah. The people had regarded Him as a prophet. They only see Him as more than a prophet. Jesus is the promised one who brings deliverance. From now on Jesus teaches the disciples that they will suffer and be rejected because of their love for Him. It is still early days in their discipleship as they have to learn hard lessons on prayer, humility and self-sacrifice.

F) A new way of suffering for the disciples (Read 9:23-27.): this discourse follows on from Peter's confession. Jesus prepares His disciples for future ministry. Life on the Way, Jesus said, consists of daily self-denial, bearing one's cross and daily following in the footsteps of the Master, if the disciple is to survive the forces of the world. Daily self-denial is unique to Luke (9:23). Judgement will be for those who are ashamed of Jesus. Salvation is for those who place their identity in the hands of God (9:24). Jesus predicts that He will suffer, be handed over, killed and raised. Suffering will be included in identifying with Jesus. Following Jesus is worth the cost since the story to follow lasts forever. Jesus requires a sacrificial allegiance to Himself by His disciples. He defines discipleship as coming after Him, denying self, taking up the cross daily and following Him. At the Transfiguration the disciples learn that they must listen to Jesus (9:35). Three disciples are privileged to hear the heavenly voice testify to the uniqueness of Jesus, who is pictured as the Messiah-Servant and the Prophet like Moses from whom they have much to learn.

[3] The demands of discipleship

> **The demands of discipleship are the same no matter how one comes to Jesus (9:57-62; Matt.8:21-22). (Stanton) (16)**

A) Coping with failure in their ministry: each incident involves constant correction by Jesus. (Read 9:38-40-9:62.) The disciples were faced with five examples of failure in their ministry as in the incident of their inability to heal the boy with the evil spirit. Even though they are given the power to be exorcists (9:1), they do not succeed (9:40). The radical nature of discipleship is seen in the "Q" saying as it cuts across respect for parents and proper burial for the dead, both of which were deep seated in the O.T. and Judaism (9:43b-50). Being a disciple does not mean power but sharing in Jesus' suffering and rejection. The disciples cannot look back once they identify with Jesus. [See p. 202.]

i) The disciples have much to learn as they listen to Jesus (9:35). They are to change in the way they see themselves and in the way they see others. They are struggling to understand what following Jesus really means (9:43). Jesus shares His betrayal but the disciples cannot see it in God's plan and are too uncertain to ask.

ii) They raise the issue who is the greatest (46-48)? Jesus uses a child to show such comparisons should not be made. Genuine ministry means receiving lowly people. As they look at themselves, they need to see that all are great.

iii) What about those outside the inner circle? Are they to be excluded from ministry? Interpersonal rivalry is not to be the trait of a disciple but co-operation is. Jesus teaches the disciples to receive all and the disciples relate that they have excluded someone from ministering. John tells about a man casting out demons in Jesus' name. The disciples stopped him because he did not follow Jesus. Jesus rebukes the disciples saying that people are not to be stopped, for anyone not opposed to the disciples is for them. Luke has the Greek word "epistata" for Master which is unique to him (9:49-50).

iv) "The demands of discipleship are the same no matter how one comes to Jesus." (Stanton) **(16) (Read 9:57-62; Matt.8:21-22.)** The disciples are to be united as Jesus turns to face Jerusalem (9:51). James and John want Jesus to bring fire down from heaven on the Samaritan village which failed to receive the message. Jesus teaches them that they are to be dependent upon God, love, accept others, associate with sinners and walk in the new way to God. In the journey narrative many of these issues resurface. The disciples James and John call for God's judgement on the Samaritan village. It is a misguided zeal for God's honour. They thought that the time was ripe for judgement to fall on people for lack of faith. The disciples took the Samaritans' rejection seriously. The implication is that the disciples have a prophetic like authority given by Jesus when ministry is given in His name. The disciples are not to act without the approval of Jesus. Is it your will that we do this (9:54)? An example of discipleship is that of the farmer who has to concentrate upon the furrow before him, guiding the plough with his left hand while goading the oxen with his right-hand. To look away would be to produce a crooked furrow (9:62). [See p. 122.]

v) Later in the ministry of Jesus, another example of failure was the way in which the disciples discouraged the women from bringing their children to Jesus to be blessed. Jesus is quite indignant with them. To the disciples, the presence of children was an encroachment on their time, "Let the children come to me." The trust of a child compares with someone who receives the kingdom. "To such as (Gk.toiouton) these [children] belongs the kingdom." (18:15-17) The disciples belittle the children who are brought to Jesus to be touched by way of blessing, and see children as unworthy of Jesus' attention, not really grasping that children are the kingdom and those who are like them (18:15-18). [See p. 244.]

vi) Later Jesus sends out the seventy (two) who experience the blessing of mission (Read 10:1-12; 17-20.). God's help will be present for the disciples when persecution comes (12:8-12). Jesus, in the parable of the rich fool, taught the disciples that they are not to depend excessively on material things (12:13-21). Trust God and do not be anxious. The disciple is to pursue the kingdom, be assured that God is with him/her and live in a way which acknowledges God's return (12:22-34). The disciple should show concern for others. In the parable of the great supper, it is the unexpected who follow Jesus. Many people exclude themselves from discipleship while others take the opportunity to sit at God's table (14:15-24). [See pp. 123, 204.]

> **Jesus shows that He is prepared to associate with all kinds of people including a self-confessed sinner like Peter.**

B) Discipleship as obedience and counting the cost of allegiance to Jesus: the incident of the young lawyer. The disciple must love God fully and show that love to others. Mercy and love must be extended to all: the disciple should act as the exemplary Samaritan has acted towards one's neighbour. There is an ethic for the disciples (10:25-37). The disciple must be a doer of the word. This requires obedience (11:27-28). [See p. 127.]

C) Discipleship as total commitment to Jesus: the incident of the ruler who asked Jesus what he must do to inherit eternal life (18:18-30). In the setting for this, Jesus discusses with a rich ruler and His disciples what total commitment means. The ruler thought he was devoted to God and was accepted by Him on the basis of his own good works. Jesus challenged him to sell all his possessions and give them to the poor. The condition of his own heart showed that God was not really Number One in his life. Despite the offer of a reward in heaven the ruler prefers earthly riches. Jesus pronounces that the rich will have difficulty entering the kingdom because they have difficulty leaving the false security of their wealth. The disciples are shocked at this remark as they see wealth as a sign of God's blessing. Peter notes that all the disciples have left "all their own things" (Gk. ta idia) to follow as disciples (18:28). They had already accepted the challenge of Jesus (5:11, 27-28). While Peter talks about leaving things, Jesus talks about leaving people, which is a greater sacrifice (18:29). God will vindicate those who cast their cares on him. (Marshall) **(17)** In making this sacrifice, the disciples receive "treasure from heaven." Jesus reassures Peter and the other disciples that God knows about their sacrifice and He will reward them for it. Only Luke includes leaving a wife for the sake of Kingdom of God means renouncing the possibility of marriage (18:29; Matt.19:10-12). To leave a house meant to abandon the security of a vocation for the sake of the kingdom (18:29). What God gives back to the disciple is much more than what is given up. The reward will be in both "this period", the kingdom now and the age to come. A fundamental lesson in the nature of discipleship is putting God first.

D) Discipleship in relationship to others: bearing fruit as a natural outcome of discipleship (6:43-49/19:11-27). It required loving and doing good to others (6:17-36), being a good steward of material possessions (6:35; 8:3) and being a servant (22:24-30). [See p. 135.]

E) Discipleship involving prayer for others: praying for more labourers in the harvest (10:2). The Disciples' Prayer shows the dependence that the disciples should have upon God as their Father (11:1). The disciples are further encouraged to pray (18:1-8). [See p. 49.]

F) The call to discipleship (14:25-35): losing one's old life and following Jesus alone (9:23-25; 14:27). Discipleship means giving total loyalty to Jesus. The disciples are to love God more than earthly loves, even the nearest and dearest (14:27). Devotion to Jesus must not be less than whole-hearted. It means cross bearing. In the parable of the tower builder Jesus says, sit down and count the cost whether you can afford to follow (14:28). Sit down and count the cost whether you can afford to refuse the demands of Jesus (14:31-32). Do not rush into discipleship without thinking what is involved! Three times Jesus says, "he cannot be my disciple." (14:,26,27,33) The disciple must renounce everything. In the parable of the tower builder Jesus says, sit down and count the cost whether you can afford to follow (14:28). [See p. 158.]

G) The disciples imitating their Teacher and Master's lifestyle (6:40): suffering like Him, showing compassion like Him, taking the same message to the people and practising the same religious traditions (5:33-39). To the disciples Jesus says that His mission statement is to bring fire upon the earth. "I came to cast fire upon the earth." (12:49) This is the image of judgement in which humanity will be divided (3:9,17; 9:54; 17:29), it can also refer to the coming of the Holy Spirit (3:16) or God's message through the prophets (Jer.5:14; 23:29). Jesus says that He is under great emotional duress (Gk.sunechomai) until His task is completed (12:50). All Jesus' emotional energy is directed towards completing that task which God requires Him to do (12:49-53). The Pharisees and their scribes ask Jesus why His disciples do not fast and pray like the disciples of John. Jesus tells them this is the time for celebration and not for fasting (5:33-39). The Pharisees fasted twice a week Mondays and Thursdays (18:12) while in Judaism there were five different occasions for fasting and prayer. (Bock) **(18)** [See p. 104.]

The disciples were commissioned by Jesus to proclaim the gospel among the nations, to those who have not received forgiveness of sins. The disciples have to continue the work which Jesus began in preaching repentance and forgiveness (24:46-47).

H) The disciples receiving in-set training in the Sermon on the Plain including sacrificial love and love for all humanity: this meant surrendering everything to follow Jesus (6:12-49). To experience God's grace means that God's children must be gracious. The disciple must be rich in mercy, just as God is (6:17-49). (Fitzmyer) **(19)** One day God will deal justly with everyone.

I) The disciples being blessed: they are eyewitnesses of the events. "Blessed are the eyes which see what you see." This remark is addressed to the disciples alone, people who do not respond to the events do not share in the blessing. It also applies to those outside the seventy(two). Power is not the most important aspect of God's plan but rather the disciples' secure position before God (10:23; 11:1; 14:26; 19:37-39). [See p. 123.]

J) Jesus breaks through the religious barriers in His choice of ordinary men to form a commissioned group of disciples around Him. He called "the clean and the unclean," fishermen like Simon Peter, Andrew, James and John, tax collectors like Matthew and Zacchaeus, a political revolutionary Simon the Zealot (6:15), a sceptic like Thomas who wanted proof of the resurrection (24:40; Jn. 20:24) and a future traitor Judas. Jesus had good and bad disciples. [See Ch. 12 Passion and Resurrection, Section on "the betrayer."] Jesus shows that He is prepared to associate with all kinds of people including a self-confessed sinner like Peter (5:8b). These men were all hand picked and did not appear by accident. [pp. 133-4, 147.]

K) Jesus warns the disciples about the scribes (Read 20:45-47.)
The scribes always appear in public places, synagogues, market places and banquet rooms to invite respect and preferment (11:42; 14:7-11). This is a warning about pride. Jesus knows what the scribes are like in seeking public esteem and recognition. The true disciple must give himself, to the poor, the outcast and the outsider. He warns the disciples about the Pharisees who tithe possessions which should have been shared with the needy. [See p. 148.]

L) The disciples were commissioned by Jesus to proclaim the gospel among the nations, to those who have not received forgiveness of sins. The disciples have to continue the work which Jesus began in preaching repentance and forgiveness (24:46-47).

Discipleship starts with repentance and leads to belief in the good news which Jesus preaches.

Conclusion
• Discipleship in Luke means following Jesus all the way to eternal life. The life of discipleship is a life of faith as in the parable of the dutiful servant which explains a theology of grace. The servant serves dutifully and the Master's gifts come unmerited and unearned and so it will be with God (17:10). God notices and commends the servant (17:7-10; 24: 44-49; 1 Cor.4:5). The dutiful servant does his duty and earns no merit. The Master's gifts come unmerited and unearned and so it is with God (17:10). (Baillie) **(20)**
 • The Pharisees overheard Jesus' teaching about wealth and money, even though the parable of the shrewd manager was addressed to the disciples (16:14). The Pharisees sneer at Jesus' teaching because they loved money. Jesus knows their hearts (Prov.21:2) : they are people who look on the outside.
• Discipleship starts with repentance and leads to belief in the good news which Jesus preaches. It has to be confessed in public (12:3) and the kingdom received as a gift (12:32). Often Jesus uses the phrase, "Your faith has made you whole," meaning physical and spiritual healing (7:50; 17:19). Despite the disciples' active service for Jesus (9:1-6) in the healing of demons and disease, the authority of Jesus per se is seen in the exorcisms and the healings. (L)
• Despite this early success, the disciples failed to recognise who Jesus really is and what He would do and accomplish in Jerusalem. All the detail about the final prediction of His passion by Jesus is quite baffling to the Twelve who cannot understand how this can fulfil scripture and how the Messiah could suffer (18:31-34). Before the feeding of the five thousand, the disciples question Jesus' ability to provide for the crowds (9:12) and fail to grasp the status of Jesus (9:21-27, 35, 37-50). Jesus takes "the Twelve" on one side and announces that He is going to Jerusalem. Luke speaks generally of Jesus being "treated shamefully".
• The disciples could not comprehend how the death of Jesus could mean hope and victory. How could a victorious Messiah be put into the hands of Gentiles and be slain (18:31)? Although, Jesus had first predicted His suffering and death after the Transfiguration, the actual meaning of His destiny was hidden from the disciples (9:43-45).
• The disciples are commissioned by Jesus to proclaim to the ends of the earth, the Gospel message to people who have not received forgiveness of sins (24:43b-45). Discipleship in Luke is a bridge between Luke Vol. 1/Acts Vol.2. (Green) **(21)**
• Jesus was a prophet-teacher who gathered a group of disciples around Him. The choice of twelve disciples was an indication of the nucleus of a renewed Israel and a new era.

Pupil's Activity: Two
a) Outline your knowledge and understanding of Jesus' relationship with His disciples.
b) Outline your knowledge and understanding of Jesus' teaching on the nature of discipleship.

Pupil's Activity: Three   **(Revision exercise on discipleship and parables)**
What aspects of discipleship was Jesus teaching in the following parables? (CCEA A/2)   [See Ch. 12.]   (Figure 3)

(Figure 3)   A summary of Jesus' teaching on discipleship in the parables of Luke's Gospel

	Parable	Refs.	Comment upon Jesus' teaching on discipleship in the parables
1	The house built on the sand	6:47-49	**e.g. hearing God's word and obeying it**
2	The good Samaritan	10:29-37	
3	The friend at midnight	11:5-8	
4	Binding the strong man	11:21-23	
5	The return of the unclean spirit	11:24-26	
6	The rich fool	12:13-21	
7	The fig tree	13:6-9	
8	Seats of honour	14:7-14	
9	Warring king	14:28-33	
10	Salt	14:34-35	
11	The shrewd manager	16:1-9	
12	Rich man and Lazarus	16:19-31	
13	The dutiful servant	17:7-10	
14	The unjust judge/persistent widow	18:1-8	
15	The pounds	19:11-27	
16	Fig tree	21:29-33	

Pupil's Activity: Four (Read 5:1-11.) [See p. 216.]
Outline your knowledge and understanding of the call of the first disciples in Luke's Gospel.

Pupil's Activity: Five   (Read 8:22-39.) [See p. 195.]
In the incident of the storm at sea, Jesus asked the disciples, "Where is your faith?" (8:25)
a) In what way was the faith of the disciples defective?
b) What lessons did they learn about discipleship and about Jesus?

Pupil's Activity: Six   (Read 9:1-17.) [See p. 199.]
a) What new method does Jesus use with His disciples (9:1-6)?
b) What lessons would they have learnt as a training for their future work and what effect would it have had on the places they visited?

Pupil's Activity: Seven   (Read 9:23.) [See p. 202.]
a) How does Jesus define discipleship in this verse?
b) In what five ways did some of "the Twelve" disciples fail? (Read 9:37-56.)

Pupil's Activity: Eight (Read 12:1-12.)
a) Why did the disciples need their faith strengthened and steadied? [See also 11:53-54; 12:1.]
b) What attitude should the disciples adopt in facing threatening danger?

Pupil's Activity: Nine (Read 14:25-35.) [See p. 222.]
a) Why did Jesus emphasise the cost of discipleship at this time?
b) What does discipleship involve (14:26-27)?
c) What four issues does Jesus raise regarding discipleship? What characteristics does Jesus require in true discipleship?
(Read 17:1-10.)

Pupil's Activity: Ten (Read 18:15-34.)
How did Jesus strengthen "the Twelve" at this time?

Pupil's Activity: Eleven   (Read 21:8-19.)
a) What two questions asked by the disciples outline what will happen before the Temple is destroyed?
b) How does Jesus answer these questions (21:20-24)?

Pupil's Activity: Twelve   (Read 22:24-38.) [See p. 136.]
In what different ways does Jesus' love and concern for His disciples show itself?

Pupil's Activity: Thirteen   (Read 22:33-60.) [See p. 136.]
a) Trace the stages in Peter's downfall.   b) What brought him to repentance?
c) Why did Jesus appear to Peter at the resurrection before any of the other apostles (24:13-35)?

Pupil's Activity: Fourteen
a) Examine the significant features of Jesus' teaching in Luke's Gospel concerning the nature of discipleship.
(Edexcel A/S 2003/2005)   [14 marks]
b) Why were John the Baptist and Peter so important to the ministry of Jesus?
(Edexcel A/S 2003)   [6 marks]

Pupil's Activity: Fifteen
a) Examine the main features of Jesus' teaching in Luke's Gospel concerning the nature and demands of discipleship.
(Edexcel A/S 2004)   [14 marks]
b) Why were John the Baptist and the disciples so important to the ministry of Jesus?
(Edexcel A/S 2004/2005)   [6 marks] [See also Ch. 9: John the Baptist.]

Pupil's Activity: Sixteen
a) Discuss any two parables concerning discipleship as recorded in the Gospel of Luke.
(CCEA A/2 2004)   [30 marks]
b) Critically assess the view that the challenge of discipleship in Luke's Gospel is very demanding.
(CCEA A/2 2004)   [15 marks]

Outcomes
Pupils should be able to examine: (Edexcel A/S)
• **the cost of discipleship in Luke's Gospel.**
• **the main events relating to discipleship in Luke's Gospel.**
• **the nature and demands of discipleship in Luke's Gospel.**
• **key themes and concepts relating to discipleship in Luke's Gospel, e.g. discipleship viewed as a journey, the women disciples, the Twelve, 'apostles', the call of the disciples, the call to mission, defection, coping with failure, the cost of discipleship.**
Pupils should be able to critically assess and discuss: (CCEA A/2)
• **the parables relating to discipleship and the challenge of discipleship in Luke's Gospel. [See Ch. 12: Parables.]**

Notes on Ch. 14: Discipleship in Luke's Gospel

1. G. Kittel, TDNT, op. cit. 1: 2130.
2. Robert H. Stein, op. cit. p. 182.
3. Joel Green, op. cit. p. 103.
4. H. Schurmann, op. cit. p.314.
5. John Nolland, op. cit. p.264.
6. A. Plummer, op. cit. p.172.
7. Joel Green, op. cit. p. 105.
8. Graham Stanton, op. cit. p.200.
9. A. Plummer, op. cit. p.172.
10. William Hendriksen, Exposition on Luke, NTC, Grand Rapids: Baker (1978) p.327, cited in Bock p.542.
11. Joseph A. Fitzmyer, op. cit. p.617.
12. Joel Green, op. cit. p.103.
13. Joel Green, op. cit. p.108.
14. M. J. Wilkins, Article on Discipleship, DJG , IVP, (1992) p. 184.
15. D.L.Tiede, op. cit. pp. 269-270.
16. Graham Stanton, op. cit. p.200.
17. I. Howard Marshall, op. cit. p.688.
18. Darrell L. Bock, op. cit. p.110.
19. Joseph A. Fitzmyer, op. cit. p.630.
20. Kenneth Baillie, op. cit. p.126.
21. Joel Green, op. cit. p. 102.

A key aspect of Luke's Gospel is his sensitivity to women. Evidence of this can be seen in the number of times women are mentioned, the kinds of interaction which Jesus allows women and the special importance and role of Mary.

(Edexcel A/S) + (CCEA A/2)

Targets:
• Identify Jesus' respect for women as persons of dignity and value, and be able to compare this with the religious and social practices of that time. (CCEA A/S) (Edexcel A/S)
• Recognise the contribution women make to Luke's Gospel. (CCEA A/S)
• Select and study at least two events in which women play a significant role. (CCEA A/2)
• Identify examples of women who showed courage and faithfulness. (CCEA A/S)
• Recognise motherhood linked to obedience.
• Identify the significant role played by women in the infancy narratives. (CCEA A/S)
• Show how Luke's Gospel challenges all kinds of discrimination. (CCEA A/2)
• Recognise key concepts, for example "pairing references".
• Recognise the social and cultural background of first-century Palestine's attitude to women. (Edexcel A/S)

Teaching on Women in Luke's Gospel

Bedouin woman and child, in the desert.

Introduction

[1] The social and cultural standing of women in the first-century A.D.
Background

In the first-century Greco-Roman patriarchal world, women had low status and esteem in society and were culturally and socially marginalized as expressed in the daily prayer of the Jewish man. "Thank you, I was not born a woman." (Mishnah) **(1)** "The law holds women to be inferior in all matters and therefore women should be submissive."(Josephus) **(2)** This marginalisation led to women being treated as outcasts in society and outside the boundary of God's grace. In Israel the status of a woman was inferior to that of a man and this also would have been true of most Gentile areas. [See Ch.16: Outcasts.] The Roman philosopher, Plato, described women in a crude chauvinistic way as, "A bad man's fate would be, in reincarnation, as a woman." (Timaeus) **(3)** The Greek philosopher, Aristotle **(4)**, saw women as "mutilated males. They are imperfect males accidentally produced by the father's inadequacy or by the malign influence of the moist south wind." The world of Jesus' time had little concept of the freedom or the importance of women. The role of women was limited to household chores.

The role of women was limited to household chores.

A woman had no legal rights. She was in her husband's absolute possession. There were however notable exceptions to this as some women had positive roles and some were known to be presidents of Jewish synagogues. One such exception was thought to be in Macedonia where women had a much higher standing in society. Some women were known as strong leaders as in the story of Judith (76-77 B.C.), others acted as priests in the Roman religions and some women had their own businesses (Lydia a seller of purple from Thyatira) (Acts 16:14). Job's daughters spoke the language of angels (The Testament of Job Beruriah). A key aspect of Luke's Gospel is his sensitivity to women: it is Luke more than any other writer who focuses on Jesus' approach to the subject of women. As a Gentile, Luke appreciated the different emphasis taken by Jesus in contrast to that of most of His contemporaries.

[1] Luke's sensitivity to women can be seen in the number of times women are mentioned.
A) Jesus' interaction with women in Luke's Gospel

The kinds of interaction which Jesus allows women and the special importance and role of Mary are evidences of Jesus' concern for women. All of these factors help to provide evidence that one cannot deal adequately with the ministry of Jesus without including and examining the role and value of women in making the Christian message come alive in a significant and dynamic way in the first-century. In all of Luke's writings women played a key role. There are far more women named and unnamed in Luke's Gospel than any other. There is also a greater interest in women in the life and ministry of Jesus in Luke's Gospel than any other Gospel.

Luke shows the importance of womanhood in the parts played by Elizabeth and Mary in the Birth Narratives. Elizabeth, Mary and Anna were proclaimers of Jesus at His birth and of His place in salvation as were their male counterparts Zechariah and Simeon. Zechariah and Elizabeth were both filled with the Spirit (1:42,67).

B) "Pairing references" [See p. 228.]
This is an aspect of Luke's writing style which provides insights into Jesus' understanding and valuing of women. Luke likes to use "pairing" references to men and women or "sets of complementary male-female examples." (Kopas) **(5)** When an action or saying is attributed to a man, a complementary model of a woman is used. This shows a degree of equality in Luke's Gospel. This pairing also indicates that a "substantial number of women constituted the Gospel audience." (Parvey) **(6)**

C) Other examples of "pairing references" to men and women in Luke's Gospel
In the birth narratives the announcements are to both Zechariah and Mary. Zechariah hears that his wife Elizabeth, who is still barren in old age, will give birth to a son (1:5-20) and the child will be the last of the great prophets. In the case of Mary and Joseph, Mary and not Joseph is the recipient of the angel's message. Mary is told that even though she is a virgin, she will conceive a son (1:26-38).
Elizabeth was from priestly stock, being a daughter of Aaron (1:5). It was common for Jewish priests to marry women from a similar background. She had a very spiritual background and ancestry as had Mary her kinswoman (1:36). Elizabeth and her husband were righteous before the Lord and kept the standards which God had laid down for Israel (1:6). They were blameless before God in that they faithfully obeyed Him (1:6). Luke shows the importance of womanhood in the parts played by Elizabeth and Mary in the birth narratives. Elizabeth, Mary and Anna were proclaimers of Jesus at His birth and of His place in salvation as were their male counterparts Zechariah and Simeon. Zechariah and Elizabeth were both filled with the Spirit (1:42, 67). [See Figure 1.] [See pp. 81, 85.]

D) Simeon and Anna as an example of pairing references   (Read 2:25-38.)
Simeon and Anna are in the Temple when Jesus is presented after his birth. Both utter their prayer of praise for what God has done for them and allowed them to see. They witness to the fulfilment of the promise and are faithful listeners and waiters. Anna is a prophetess and a woman of religious stature who speaks God's word for Israel. Elizabeth is filled with the Spirit on hearing of Mary's greetings (1:42-43) and Zechariah is filled with the Spirit when his speech is restored to him and he prophesies (1:67). Elizabeth (1:41) and Simeon (2:27) are all empowered by the Holy Spirit. [See also Birth Ch. 8: Birth Narratives.] [See pp. 47, 94.]

E) Comments on other examples of pairing in Luke
Luke pairs parables and stories so that one story about a man is always followed by that of a woman. Jesus heals the centurion's slave (7:2-10) and this miracle is followed by raising the widow of Nain's son (7:11-12). [See Figure 1 no. 5.] The parable of the Good Samaritan (10:29-37) is followed by the story of Martha and Mary (10:38-42). [See Figure 1 no.9.] The parable of the shepherd who lost one of his sheep (15:4-7) is paired with that of the woman who lost her coin (15:8-10). [See Figure 1 no. 14.] The return of Jesus will catch both men and women unawares. Two men will be in one bed; one will be taken and the other one left. Two women will be grinding corn together; one will be taken and the other one left (17:34-36). [See Figure 1 no.15.] [See pp. 82, 85]

F) The differences between the male and the female responses of Zechariah and Mary to the visit of the angel
Mary provides a better example of discipleship than her male counterpart particularly in the way in which she questions the angel, "How can this be (Gk.Pos estai touto), since I have no husband?" She is puzzled since she has had no sexual relationship with a man (1:34). In her questioning she shows how her faith is nourished by the search for understanding. Zechariah's question was a doubting one for biological reasons. "How shall I know this? (Gk. Kata ti gnosomai touto) For I am an old man and my wife is advanced in years."(1:18) How can I be sure that a child will be born if my wife is in old age? Mary receives a different response to her question than Zechariah who is struck dumb; she is blessed (1:34,42). She asks out of a sense of wonder. How can the promise of the angel come to pass, since she is a virgin? Her faith was willing to be moved to a deeper level of spiritual understanding. Mary identifies with the lowly and the oppressed in her song of praise, the Magnificat, by the way in which she shows her solidarity with those who have cried for deliverance and her confidence in a compassionate God (1:46-56). Both Mary and Elizabeth are seen as spokespersons for God and interpret the coming of Jesus and John into the world (1:42-45). [See pp. 82, 84.]

Cont'd on page 229 ⟶

Pupil's Activity: One

Complete the grid in Figure 1 commenting upon the male and female "pairings".

G) Sets of complementary male-female/pairing references   (Figure 1)

Male	Ref	Female	References	Comment and answer
1. Zechariah	1:5-22 (L)	Mary	1:26-38 (L)	Why does Mary appear as a better example of a disciple than her male counterpart Zechariah?
2. Simeon	2:25-35 (L)	Anna	2:36-38 (L)	Anna appears beside her male counterpart Simeon. What were their expectations?
3. Naaman the Syrian	4:27 (L) 2 Kgs. 5:1-14	The widow of Zarephath	4:25-26 (L) 1 Kgs.17:8-16	In the O.T. only a Gentile woman from an area between Tyre and Sidon and a Gentile Syrian commander are blessed by God by the prophets Elijah and Elisha.
4. The demoniac at Capernaum	4:31-37; Mk.1: 23-38	Peter's mother-in-law	4:38-39; Mk. 1:29-31; Matt. 8:14-17	Luke points out the role of women in serving Jesus. In Matthew, she serves the entire group. Jesus shows compassion to both sexes.
5. The centurion's servant	7:1-10; Matt.8: 5-13	The widow of Nain's son	7:11-17 (L)	Jesus shows His loving concern for the widow because of the death of her only son. "His heart went out to her." Both the servant and the widow epitomise 'the poor' and have little social status.
6. Simon the Pharisee	7:36/39-50 (L)?	The sinful woman	7:36-50 (L)?	The sinful woman is affirmed. "Your faith has saved you; go in peace."
7. The Twelve	6:12-16;Mk.3: 13-19a; Matt. 10:1-4;	Four women followers are named	8:1-3 (L)	Compare this event with the choice and mission of "the Twelve" (6:12-16, 9:1-6). Three of the names are (L).
8. Gerasene demoniac	8:26-39; Mk. 5:1-20; Matt. 8:28-34;	Woman with the issue of blood for twelve years	8:43-48; Mk. 5:21-34; Matt.9: 18-26	"Daughter, your faith has made you well; go in peace." She would have been older than Jesus. She is healed because she has faith.
9. Good Samaritan	10:29-37(L)	Mary and Martha	10:38-42 (L)	Jesus praises Mary for her devotion to Him.
10. The men of Nineveh were Gentiles who belie-ved the word in Jonah's time.	11:32 (L)	The Queen of the South was a Gentile, who believed the word of God in Solomon's time.	11:31 (L)	As the Queen of the South responded to Solomon, so the people should respond to Jesus, who is the bearer of a greater wisdom from God than that of the Queen of Sheba. Jesus' generation are without excuse if they do not listen to Him. The Queen of the south will rise at the general resurrection at the final judgement. (Stein) (7)
11. Man with dropsy healed on the Sabbath	13:10-17 (L)	Crippled woman healed on the Sabbath	14:1-6 (L)	Both the man and the woman are cripples and are healed on the Sabbath day. Jesus calls the woman "daughter of Abraham."
12. The ruler in the synagogue	13:14-16 (L)	The woman with the infirmity	13:10-16	These two people can be seen as a complementary pair. What do they have in common?
13. The man with the mustard seed	13:18-19; Mk.4: 30-32; Matt.13:31-32	The woman with the yeast	13:20-21; Matt.13: 13	Note the different roles of the man and the woman; the man plants and the woman cooks.
14. The man with one hundred sheep	15:4-7 (L) Jesus uses masculine imagery of a shepherd likening God to a shepherd who has lost a sheep.	The woman with ten coins rejoices with her female neighbours.	15:8-10 (L)	The shepherd rejoices with his fellow shepherds when he finds the lost sheep. The woman with ten coins rejoices with her female friends and female neighbours, when she finds the missing coin. Jesus uses feminine imagery likening God to the woman who lost the coin. It is the great effort of the woman which is highlighted; she searches diligently until she finds it. This shows God's gracious love for the sinner (15:8).
15. Two men sleeping	17:34; Matt.24: 40	Two women grinding corn	17: 35; Matt.24: 41	Luke alone says that the women were grinding together. Jesus will return when women and men are doing everyday household chores. One is rescued and the other is judged at the end.
16. Pharisee and publican	18:9-14 (L)	The importunate widow	18:1-8(L)	If a dishonest judge responds to a persistent widow, how much more will God respond to His children?
17. Scribes	20:45-47, Mk. 12:38-40	Widow's mite	21:1-4; Mk. 12:41-44	Do not judge the poor prematurely because some of them are very faithful to God in their stewardship. God looks at the way a disciple gives rather than the amount given. Jesus condemns the scribes for taking over the widows' homes and laments that they take a widow's livelihood from her.
18. Joseph of Arimathea	23:50-53; Mk. 15:42-46; Matt.27: 57-61	Women from Galilee	23:49,55-56; Mk.15:40-41; Matt.27:55-56	The women stood at a distance watching from afar. The Galilean women prepared spices for Jesus' body .
19. The disciples on the Emmaus road	24:13-35 (L)	Women at the tomb	24: 1-11; Mk.16 :1-8; Matt. 28:1-8	The women at the empty tomb are perplexed at what has happened. They find the tomb open, angels present but there is no body. They are the first witnesses but their report is not believed by the male apostles. Did Mary make two trips to the tomb? The women's report required courage, since they were not allowed to testify in this culture.

(Cont'd from p. 227)

Mary and Elizabeth have their (prayers Gk.deesis: a collective word for prayer) answered for a child, as do the people in praying for deliverance from the Romans (1:10,13). God's answer came at a surprising time, in a surprising place and in a surprising way. (Bock) **(8)** Mary's status comes from God and it is based upon her relationship with Him. Her family, which is her immediate source of social status is not mentioned by Luke and she does not appear to deserve any honour. Mary is called a relative (Gk.sungenis) or kinswoman of Elizabeth (1:36). (Green) **(9)** Only in this scene (1:36) do we learn that she belongs to the family of Elizabeth and shared the same ancestors. Up to this point Mary is seen as a Galilean far removed from Jerusalem, being betrothed to Joseph. She is thought to be as young as (10-13 years) (Green) **(10)** and Joseph is not her husband as yet. She is not introduced in any way as someone deserving honour. Mary would have had a very low rating on any status scale as regards age, family background and gender but she is the one who is favoured by God, finds her identity in obeying Him and in playing a key role in His redemptive purpose. [See pp. 82, 84.]

> **Mary provides a better example of discipleship than her male counterpart particularly in the way in which she questions the angel, "How can this be, since I have no husband?" (1:34)**

Pupil's Activity: Two
From Figure 1, find out the number of named and unnamed women who are unique to Luke's Gospel.

> **In Zechariah's prayer (1:13) God's answers came:**
> - **at a surprising time,**
> - **in a surprising place, and**
> - **in a surprising way. (Bock) (8)**

[2] Women make a unique contribution to Luke's Gospel

This is evidenced in the number of women who exemplify the following characteristics: barrenness (Gk. poreuomenoi); childlessness (Gk. steira) (1:7) which was thought in the O.T. to be the result of sin, a sign of divine punishment and a source of great shame; disobedience to the law could lead to a cursing of the womb (Deut. 28:15-18). However, in the case of Elizabeth and Zechariah, this is not likely as they were said to be righteous before God (1:5-6). Elizabeth recognises God's grace in removing the disgrace of childlessness (1:7, 25). Mary recognises her lowliness in God's sight (1:48). Luke recognises Anna's widowhood (2:37). [See p. 95.] Jesus recognises the spiritual and compassionate need of the widow of Nain (7:11-12). Service to the poor and others is recognised and God's grace comes to the outcast Mary Magdalene. Joanna is faithful being present at the crucifixion and the gospel has reached Herod's household and the Royal palace (8:3). Poverty has also been identified in the case of the widow who offers her two copper coins (21:1-4). Women are the first witnesses to the empty tomb (24:10). [See p. 81.]

A) Jesus' respect for women as persons of dignity and value and as recipients of healing in Luke's Gospel can be seen in the following incidents:
- the healing of Peter's mother-in-law of a fever (4:38-39).
- Jairus' daughter and the woman with the issue of blood for twelve years (8:40-56). [See Ch. 13 Miracles]
- Mary Magdalene from whom seven spirits had been exorcised (8:2)(L).
- the raising of Jairus' twelve year old daughter (8:40-56).
- the woman with the spirit of infirmity for eighteen years and bent back was a "daughter of Abraham" meaning the old Israel. She was of Abraham's seed, racially descended from Abraham (13:16) (13:10-17) (L). The combination of an evil spirit and malady was not unusual at this time in Judaism. (Qumran) **(11)** It was more important that a "daughter of Abraham" be freed from the binding power of Satan (13:16). Jesus initiates the healing. He heals a woman in a culture where men shunned women. [See p. 206.]

> **To the sinful woman, Jesus says, "Your faith has saved you; go in peace." This can also be expressed as, "Go into peace." (7:50) The woman went away with inward peace, the critics went away with a quibble. Jesus never answered them: forgiveness and peace were benefits too priceless to be dissipated by fruitless discussion.**

B) Other women who displayed faith and faithfulness
The well known sinful woman entered Simon's house and "gate crashed" the dinner (7:36-50). This was common in the ancient world to allow access to a meal in honour of a great teacher. Hence no one is shocked at the presence of the woman. The scandal is that she has drawn close to Jesus and He has allowed her to approach. It would have been all right if she had remained as a spectator. Jesus is anointed by the sinful woman in the house of Simon the Pharisee (7:38). For Simon if Jesus was a genuine holy man he would not get near to sinners. Simon had ignored all the courtesies for foot washing and oil for anointing (7:39). The perfume was precious, expensive and was used at civic feasts for the purification of priests in the Temple. (Josephus) **(12)** Anyone failing to do this had little respect for the guest. Simon clearly had no respect for Jesus and Jesus was not surprised at this breach of courtesy. Jesus did not mention it until Simon inwardly criticised Him for accepting the action of a disreputable woman (7:39). Here Jesus met deeply ingrained class distinction for which he had no sympathy. He did not inaugurate a social revolution to fight it but He did combat it by His gracious attitude towards those whom others treated with contempt. The presence of the woman upset the dignity of the meal and Simon was taken aback because she was noted for her immoral life. He may not have seen her until she had already washed the feet of Jesus with her tears. The odour of the ointment may have attracted Simon's attention.

Jesus could read the critical thoughts of Simon. This is another example of Jesus being able to read the minds of people in thoughts which had not been uttered. Simon was convinced that Jesus was no prophet as no prophet would allow himself to be defiled by the touch of a sinner or be unaware who she really is: Jesus' willingness to allow her action showed a lack of a prophetic gift on his part. Jesus tells the parable of the two debtors (7:41-43).
The woman was aware of her need. Simon never saw himself as a debtor before God. Jesus says to Simon, "Her sins, which are many, are forgiven for she loved much." (7:47) God's forgiveness of sin is not based upon a person's prior love for Him: love is not prior to faith but is a fruit of it. Jesus confirmed what she already knew by experience: her sins were forgiven. Her act of love showed her liberation from the chains which bound her. Jesus' tenderness towards the woman is the most striking example of His concern for broken and bruised lives. The group at table were more concerned about the theory of forgiveness of sin than the experience of forgiveness. "Who is this who even forgives sins?" (8:49) The woman went away with inward peace, the critics went away with a quibble. Jesus never answered them: forgiveness and peace were benefits too priceless to be dissipated by fruitless discussion. [See pp. 243, 261.]

C) To the woman who touched the fringe of His garment He said, "Daughter, your faith has made you well; go in peace." (8:48) In calling her "daughter," Jesus is using an affectionate term to reassure her that she is now recognised as part of Israel." (Fitzmyer) **(13)** Jesus regarded women as fully inclusive in the covenant community. Her "uncleanness had been removed; she is no longer an outcast." Through faith she received spiritual healing (8:48). [See p. 198.]
D) In the parable, the importunate widow will be vindicated. The persistence of the widow's faith in the parable is commended (18:1-8). [See pp. 49, 158.]

E) Jesus also commends another widow with her mite (Gk.leptra two small copper coins) as an example of a right attitude to material possessions (21:1-4). The Temple had fallen into the hands of those who used it for injustice. Jesus had indicted the scribes for taking possession of widows' homes (20:47) and then He goes on to warn them for taking away a widow's living. Widows were at the bottom of the pecking order in the first-century culture and were being ripped off by the scribes, having their homes taken over, with the loss of their livelihood. The Talmud complained about those who managed a widow's estate and gave themselves a healthy fee (b. Git.52a-b). [See p. 253.]

F) The faithful group of women from Galilee who followed Jesus were also faithful to Him at the cross. (23:49) The Greek word "sunakolouthousan" translated as "those who are following" is used for following in the sense of being a disciple. Marshall **(14)** says that the stress is on their accompanying Jesus from Galilee. They are distinct from His acquaintances (Gk.gnostoi) (23:49a) are part of a broader group of disciples than the eleven and watched the events at a distance (23:49). Some of the Galilean women followed (Gk.katakoloutheo) and saw the tomb (23:55). They returned to their home and made preparations to anoint the body of Jesus with a variety of perfumes and spices after the Sabbath (23:56). Unique to Luke is the incident of the women resting on the Sabbath; they honoured the Mosaic law of God by resting (23:57). The perfumes and spices were bought on the first day of the week (Mk. 16:1). [See pp. 144-5.]
The women were not anticipating a resurrection on the Sunday morning. Mary Magdalene, Mary the mother of James and the other women who saw the empty tomb, heard the message of the angels and proclaimed the resurrection narrative. Luke mentions that the women did not find the body of Jesus; he emphasises the faithfulness of their witness and their report falls on deaf ears. The male disciples call the report "useless chatter" (Gk.leros) because they failed to grasp the meaning of Jesus' suffering and resurrection and cannot comprehend the news shared with them (24:11). Compared to the male disciples, the women showed more faith and faithfulness (24:1-11). Culturally this would have been a world biased against women as witnesses (24:9-12). Although women could be called to be witnesses in a court, the testimony of a woman was avoided if at all possible. (Witherington) **(15)** Even Peter does not have the spiritual insight to recognise what has happened. Unlike the women he goes home with nothing to share. He is amazed (Gk.thaumazon) but he is not certain (24:12). Faith seems to be present with the women who were way ahead of their male counterparts. It required great courage to report what they saw since they were not allowed to testify in this culture. (Josephus) **(16)**

> Some of the Galilean women followed (Gk.katakoloutheo) and saw the tomb (23:55). They returned to their home and made preparations to anoint the body of Jesus with a variety of perfumes and spices after the Sabbath (23:56).

It was not until other men confirmed the events for them that the male disciples came to believe (24:34-35). Some of the women named in the Passion Narratives are present in the Upper Room in Jerusalem along with Mary, the mother of Jesus. It follows that some of them were in the crowd waiting for the Holy Spirit (Acts 1:15). The status of women was being redefined by Jesus; salvation did not depend upon sex and gender.
Jesus likens His concern for Jerusalem to that of a mother hen for her chickens (13:34; Matt.23:37), yet the Bible never speaks of God as "Mother." Jesus speaks of Himself as like a mother hen gathering her chickens. God is described as like a Mother but always known as Father.

Pupil's Activity: Three   **Class Discussion**
Should a Christian address God in prayer as "God our Mother"! Give reasons for/against your answer.

The status of women was being redefined by Jesus; salvation did not depend upon sex and gender.

[3] Summary of the event in which the group of women were first to hear the good news of Jesus' Resurrection (24:1-12)

After Joseph had given Jesus an honourable burial, the group of women from Galilee watched to find out where He was buried. Luke identifies these women as Mary Magdalene, Joanna, Mary the mother of James (Mk.16:1; Matt.28:1) and the other women, for example Salome (Mk.16:1; 24:10). Some of these women had accompanied and supported Jesus during His ministry. Later they were to be found at prayer with the apostles (Acts 1:14). Chronologically this event occurred on the Day of Preparation, which was the Friday, the day people prepared for the Sabbath (23:54). This would have been late Friday afternoon. Both the Jewish feast and the Sabbath come together on the same day.

A) The Galilean women who followed, saw the tomb (23:55). In the minds of the women the body may not have been prepared properly. These women noted how the body had been laid in the tomb (23:55b): they identified the site of the tomb, having followed the movements of Joseph of Arimathea (Acts 16:17).
• Then the women returned to their homes and made preparations to anoint the body of Jesus with a variety of perfumes and spices, after the Sabbath (23:56). The myrrh which was used would have been purchased on the Sabbath. Jews did not embalm so spices and perfumes helped to remove the stench and the smell of decomposition. Preparing a body for burial was permitted on the Sabbath (Sabbat 23:5).
• The women had stick-ability in seeing things through to the end and showing great care for the body of Jesus.
• As work was not permitted, they rested on the Sabbath day, honouring the Mosaic law of God (23:57) (L).

B) The setting: the women return to the tomb to anoint the body (24:1). The perfumes and spices were brought on the first day of the week (Sunday) (24:1; Mk.16:1). These women were not anticipating a resurrection on the Sunday morning.

C) The empty tomb (24:2-3)
• They saw "the stone rolled away", the tomb open and empty and the body of Jesus was missing. This event came as a great surprise to the women; they were at a loss to know why this had happened (24:3).

D) The report of the two angels (24:4-8)
• The women were perplexed at what has happened (24:4a). Suddenly two men, whose bright clothes appeared like lightning, stood beside them (24:4b).
• They were terrified at the appearance of the angels, bowing their heads in recognition of the presence of the heavenly messengers (24:5). The angels rebuke them for not looking for the living among the dead (24:5-7).
• They heard the message of the angels, which reminded them of Jesus' prediction (9:22) about His death and Resurrection. They proclaimed the resurrection narrative (24:9). "Two" is a common thread running through the resurrection appearances to denote two witnesses of the resurrection. The angels point out that these events were necessary. Luke stresses God's plan and movement in divine history, more than any other Synoptic Gospel, an emphasis which goes hand in hand with Luke's strong fulfilment motif (24:7). What is happening is no surprise; it is a part of a divinely wrought event sequence. (Bock) **(17)** God's plan involved Jesus' being given over to sinful men, crucified and raised (24:7). God is allowing this to happen even though human beings are responsible for the first two actions; sinful people are allowed to hand over Jesus and arrest Him. Despite Jesus' teaching about the resurrection it was too incredible an event for the disciples to believe until after it took place (24:6).

E) The response of the women
• The women are to understand that the resurrection is an expected part of God's plan.
• They recall the teaching of Jesus and take the first small step to an Easter faith (24:8). They are not commissioned but they received Jesus' words and understand them, which confirms their discipleship (24:8).

F) The report of the women (24:9-11)
• The women return from the tomb and report all these things to the apostles and the rest of the disciples; the women respond in faith. While the witness of the women was not acceptable at this time, Luke still records their testimony (24:9).

God's plan involved Jesus being:
• **given over to sinful men,**
• **crucified and**
• **raised (24:7).**

• Luke mentions that the women did not find the body of Jesus; he emphasises the faithfulness of their witness but their report falls on deaf ears (24:11).
• This group of women would have been part of the travelling entourage of Jesus' followers.
• The male disciples call the report "useless chatter" because they failed to grasp the meaning of Jesus' suffering and resurrection and cannot comprehend the news shared with them (24:11).

Pupil's Activity: Four (Read Chs. 1-2.)
What significant roles did the women play in the birth narratives?

Conclusion
Why was it not surprising that the women were the first to hear the good news of the Resurrection?
• Compared to the male disciples, the women showed more faith, courage and faithfulness (24:1-11). The women are met with unbelief because the men thought that the resurrection of the dead would come at the end of time.
• Culturally this would have been a world biased against women as witnesses (24:9-12).
• Although women could be called to be witnesses in a court, the testimony of a woman was avoided if at all possible. Even Peter does not have the spiritual insight to recognise what has happened. Unlike the women, he goes home with nothing to share. He is amazed but he is not certain. Does this indicate that Peter is incredulous? (24:12) It would seem that his visit to the empty tomb did not produce faith despite the evidence. He wondered at what he saw (24:12 RSV margin; Jn.20:8). He was amazed at what he saw (24:12 NRSV). In Luke "wonder" means things that are hard to understand. It does not imply belief of unbelief. Therefore, Peter is still unbelieving because his visit to the empty tomb fails inspite of the evidence (Jn. 20:8). (Liefeld) **(18)**
• Faith seems to be present with the women, who were way ahead of their male counterparts. It required great courage to report what they saw, since they were not allowed to testify in this culture. It is amazing that eventually they were believed especially in this first-century culture. "But let not the testimony of women be admitted, on account of their levity and boldness of their sex." (Josephus) **(19)**
• The apostles in their unbelief were not able to comprehend the reality the women were trying to convey (24:11).

Pupil's Activity: Five (Read 8:40-56.)
a) Contrast the raising of Jairus' daughter with the healing of the woman with the haemorrhage.
b) What do these miracles tell us about Jesus' regard for men and women?
c) How do these incidents show the importance of faith and continuing faith?

Pupil's Activity: Six
How does Jesus challenge the culture of the times regarding women?

> **Touching a bier or wooden plank on which the body was carried would make Jesus ritually unclean (Num. 19:11; Sirach 34:30).**

Pupil's Activity: Seven   **Revision**
Prepare a spidergram or powerpoint entitled "Women in Luke's Gospel."

> **Jesus shows equal treatment to the widow of Nain's son when He touched the bier making Himself unclean in the eyes of the Jewish authorities (7:7-8).**

Pupil's Activity: Eight
a) With reference to **THREE** different incidents in Luke's Gospel, discuss the attitude of Jesus towards women.
(Edexcel A/S (2001)   [15 marks]
b) How far does a knowledge of the social and cultural background of first-century Palestine contribute to an understanding of these incidents? (Edexcel A/S (2001)   [9 marks]

> **Jesus ended the curse of the Fall, reinvesting the woman with her partially lost nobility and reclaimed for His new kingdom community, the original blessing of sexual equality. (Stott) (26)**

Pupil's Activity: Nine
a) Discuss two incidents in Luke's Gospel in which women play a prominent part.
(CCEA   (2002) A/2)   [30 marks]
b) Critically evulate the claim that this Gospel challenges all forms of discrimination. [See Ch.16: Outcasts.]
(CCEA   (2002) A/2)   [15 marks]

[4] A) Why did Jesus exclude women from "the Twelve"?

Luke draws attention to Jesus' high regard for women and highlights this theme for the Christian community to adopt. As Jesus selected "the Twelve" who were all men, why was this? "The Twelve" were "to be with Him" as constant companions. If women had been included in this group it would have raised all kinds of problems, accusations and difficulties. It was "the Twelve" who were sent out in (9:1-6) and not the women travelling companions (8:1-3).

B) The ministering women (Read 8:1-3.)

Some "well heeled" women became disciples of Jesus through healing miracles and Luke notes that they travelled with Jesus (8:2). "The Twelve" were with him and also some women who had been healed of evil spirits and diseases." It was unusual for women to travel with a rabbi. It would not have been culturally possible to have included women in that most intimate group of Jesus' followers. (Scorer) **(20)**

These women clearly contributed to the kingdom by their resources (8:1-3). Their service was not just waiting upon tables and household chores; the women were "with Jesus" like "the Twelve." Jesus is doing the preaching in this context. Later, authority would be given to "the Twelve" and the seventy (two). These women reflect the graciousness of Jesus as a provider: they serve others (22:24-27) and exemplify Jesus' teaching on faith and wealth. It is these women who are portrayed in 8:1-3 as followers who hear and live out the word of God and not "the Twelve." (6:46-49 ; 8:21) **In His choice of twelve men, Jesus accepted the social and cultural patterns of His day and yet challenges these social patterns in His choice of women as travelling companions.** On the basis of this analysis, it has been concluded that Jesus regarded women as of equal worth with men. (Giles) **(21)** While their status was equal, the roles they performed were different. In Jewish law only a man could bear witness. "Let not a single witness be credited; but three or two at least, and those such whose testimony is confirmed by their good lives. But let not the testimony of women be admitted on account of their levity and boldness of their sex." (Josephus) **(22)** Jesus challenges this male-centred culture and misogynist attitude to women.

> **In the incident of Mary of Bethany, Jesus taught women as well as men, which ran counter to the culture of the time, where rabbis regarded it as a sin to teach a woman.**

While it is not unique for wealthy women to support religious leaders, (Josephus) **(21)** Luke draws attention to the women who provided financial support for Jesus' work (8:1-3). One was Mary Magdalene, who was released from seven spirits or rescued through an exorcism. This is something similar to the sinful woman who responded to Jesus' work of grace (7:36-50). Secondly, Joanna the wife of Herod's steward, shows that the good news had penetrated into the upper strata of society, even the palace. This shows the upper class status of the women and the comparative wealth of these ladies. The third woman to be named is Susanna about whom there is no information. **The ministry of Jesus was gender and socially inclusive; it was not limited to 'the poor'.** Jesus taught women as well as men, which ran counter to the culture of the time, where rabbis regarded it a sin to teach a woman. [See pp. 46, 219, 229, 233.]

[5] Jesus healed many women some of whom were named and others were unnamed.

Some examples of unnamed women in Luke's Gospel (Figure 2)

	Event	Ref.	Other Synoptic refs.
1	Peter's mother-in-law healed of a fever	4:38-39	Matt. 8:14-15; Mk. 1:29-31
2	Jairus' daughter	8:40-56	Matt. 9:18-26; Mk. 5:21-43
3	The woman with the issue of blood	8:40-56	As above
4	The eighteen-year old crippled woman, whom Jesus addressed as a "daughter of Abraham"	13:11-17	(L)
5	The widow of Nain	7:11-17	(L)
6	The widow's mite (two copper coins)	21:1-4	Mk. 12:41-44

Pupil's Activity: Ten   **Class Discussion**

a) Give reasons why you agree or do not agree that Luke leaves women in their expected roles in the patriarchal world of the first-century.

b) Give reasons why you think Luke does or does not encourage a "discipleship of equals" (Fiorenza) **(23)**.

A list of incidents which are unique to Luke's Gospel and which involve women (L) (Figure 3)

	Women in Luke's Gospel (L)	Refs. in Luke	Identify the events in Luke's Gospel involving women.
1	Elizabeth	1:24-36	
2	Anna the prophetess	2:36-38	
3	The widow of Zarephath	4:25-26	
4	The widow of Nain	7:11-17	
5	The sinful woman who anoints Jesus in Simon the Pharisee's house	7:36-50	
6	The ministering women Joanna, Susanna	8:1-3	
7	Martha and Mary	10:38-42	
8	The woman in the crowd	11:27-28	
9	The woman Satan had bound for eighteen years	13:10-17	
10	The daughters of Jerusalem who wept	23:27-31	

Pupil's Activity: Eleven
a) What do we learn about Jesus' attitude to women from Luke's special material (L)? **(Figure 3)**
b) What does it tell us about Luke?

Pupil's Activity: Twelve
a) There are at least eleven women referred to in Luke's Gospel who are not mentioned in other Gospels. [See above **Figure 3**.]
b) From the list above identify the events associated with these women.

[6] Mary of Bethany sat at the feet of Jesus listening to all His words. (Read 10:38-42.)
A) Jesus commends Mary of Bethany [See pp. 125, 243.]
Jesus affirms her choice in that she has chosen the good portion which shall not be taken away from her (10:42). Mary focuses on one specific thing while Martha is concerned with many household activities. Mary (and with her those of low status used to living on the margins of society) need no longer be "defined by socially determined roles." "Everyone must act on the priority of the guest before them extending to Jesus and His messengers the sort of welcome in which the authentic hearing of discipleship is integral." A key aspect of Luke is the sensitivity of Jesus to women. (Green)**(24)** Jesus refuses to reduce Mary to the role of domestic servant in favour of her identification as a disciple. She reflects the image of women as disciples as equal with men. Here is evidence that Jesus taught women as well as men which ran counter to the culture of the times, where rabbis regarded it as a sin to teach a woman. Jesus is spending time exclusively with women which is culturally unusual as is the image of Mary sitting at the feet of Jesus like a disciple. Jesus is concerned about Martha's attitude to Mary's choice. Mary made a good choice for her needs. "She sat at His feet" is a Semitic expression for being taught by Jesus as a student (10:38-42). **[See 7a.]**

B) Anna [See also Ch. 8: Birth Narratives.] (Read 2:36-38.)
She is a God fearing prophetess who had been married for years and could have been widowed for eighty-four years (NIV margin) and therefore one hundred years old. In her widowhood, she spent her time worshipping in the Temple, fasting, praying and waiting for God to come and rescue His people. She is endowed with the Spirit of God. She thanks God for what is happening, recognising the significance of the child coming as a Redeemer. He is the answer to all her prayers. Luke emphasises the reliability of Anna's witness to Jesus even more than her reaction. In the case of Simeon and Anna both a man and a woman praise God. [See p. 95.]

Pupil's Activity: Thirteen (Read 7:11-17; 8:40-56.)
a) Compare the raising of the widow of Nain's son with that of the Jairus' daughter.
b) What do these incidents tell us about Jesus' regard for women?

[7] Motherhood linked to obedience (Read 11:27-28.) (L) [See p. 125.]
A) Blessedness comes from obedience to the word of God and not just praise: Jesus wants application rather than applause. Jesus responds to the beatitude for the womb that bore Jesus and the breasts that fed Him. This positive response to the ministry came from an unnamed woman in the crowd and this incident is unique to Luke (11:27-28).

A key aspect of Luke is the sensitivity of Jesus to women.

In a mixed audience women were expected to be silent. (Arndt) **(25)** A mother would have been valued in the achievements of her son. "Happy is the mother of such a son." (11:27) Blessing is for those who hear and keep God's word (11:27-28). Jesus is not concerned about status based upon one's ancestry but on obedience to God.

Jesus is not concerned about status based upon one's ancestry but on obedience to God (11:28).

B) Jairus' daughter and the woman with the haemorrhage (Read 8:40-56.)

Timid faith shown by the woman can mobilise God. The woman did not draw attention to herself but realised that Jesus could heal her. When confronted she spoke openly of what Jesus had done for her. Jesus went to great lengths to get the woman with the haemorrhage to relate her healing (8:45-47). He tells the woman that her faith has brought her salvation (Gk.sesoken/meaning saved). The woman confesses to all and tells why she had touched Jesus (8:47). The woman's mention that she touched Jesus is unique to Luke. Her bowing is a sign of respect for Jesus and a begging for mercy; it is not a sign of worship. Her condition would have forced her to live detached from normal life. Anyone in contact with her would become ritually unclean until evening and anyone who touched her would have to inquire if she were unclean (Lev.15 :19-33). To touch a dead person made one ritually unclean for a week (Num. 19:11-12).

A Jewish male was not allowed to talk to a woman on the street: even if she was his wife, sister or daughter. Jesus in breaking this law restored the original blessing of creation of sexual equality (Gen.3:16). Peace (Heb. shalom/Gk. eireinen) has the sense of wholeness, the lady having been healed both physically and spiritually (8:48).

In the case of Jairus' daughter, Luke has, "child (Gk.pais) arise." Jesus restores the little girl, reaches out, taking her by the hands as He addresses her. By O.T. Jewish standards, this would make Jesus unclean but restoring her is more important than ritual cleanness. Jesus did not have to touch her in order to heal her but that He did so was to show compassion to her (Is. 41:13; 42:6). (Fitzmyer) **(26)** Jesus shows equal treatment to the widow of Nain's son when He touched the bier making Himself unclean in the eyes of the Jewish authorities (7:7-8; Num. 19:11; Sirach 34:30). As meeting human need was the main issue, Jesus did not worry about ceremonial issues. Josephus **(27)** says that it was the practice at this time to use an open bier. [See pp. 197-8.]

Anna is endowed with the Spirit of God and thanks Him for what is happening, recognising the significance of the child coming as a Redeemer. He is the answer to all her prayers. Luke emphasises the reliability of Anna's witness to Jesus even more than her reaction.

Jesus calls the little girl loudly out of her sleep, "Child arise," as if she were having a siesta (8:55). He makes a similar loud call to the widow's son, "Young man, I say to you arise."(7:14) Jairus and his wife are absolutely amazed and grateful as resurrections from the dead are not a daily happening. Jesus commands the parents not to tell anyone which contrasts with the Gerasene demoniac who was told to make his healing an opportunity for evangelism (8:39). Why did Jesus request the parents to be silent about the resurrection of their daughter? Jesus did not regard these events as central to His ministry (10:21). Jesus was requiring a discipleship which meant suffering and not a cosy existence (9:22, 36, 57-62). Jairus was required to have faith when all seemed lost through a delay. He still has to trust Jesus even though the timing was not what he thought it should be. Jairus exercises a patient faith while the woman with the haemorrhage exercises a timid faith. God responds to both the patient faith of Jairus and the timid faith of the woman with the issue of blood. Luke takes it for granted that women will be part of God's plan as much as men. [See pp. 199, 201.]

Conclusion [See Ch. 18: Forgiveness.] (Read 7:36-50.) [See pp. 243, 261, 268.]

• Jesus' attitude to women in His ministry restored to women the measure of dignity that had been lost by the Fall. Jesus was probably the first person to treat the sinful woman with dignity; previously men had only misused her. "It was not just His birth of a woman, however which restored to woman that measure of dignity lost by the Fall, but His attitude to them". He accepted the love of a prostitute to wet his feet with her tears (7:36).

• Jesus ended the curse of the Fall, reinvesting the woman with her partially lost nobility and reclaimed for His new kingdom community the original blessing of sexual equality. (Stott) **(28)**

• Both men and women were among Jesus' followers as disciples and proclaimers. [See also Ch.16: Outcasts.]

Pupil's Activity: Fourteen

a) Explore the view that it was not surprising that women were the first to hear the good news of Jesus' resurrection.
b) Justify your answer. (CCEA   A/S   2006   Resit)   [30 marks]

Pupil's Activity: Fifteen   Revision

Complete the OHP on Women in Luke's Gospel using the following headings and answering the questions.

[8] Summary of women in Luke's Gospel   (OHP)

• Jesus has respect for women valuing them as persons with dignity. Give examples and comment upon them.

• In Luke's Gospel, the status of women was redefined by Jesus with salvation no longer depending upon sex and gender. How did Jesus achieve this? To demonstrate this point summarise an appropriate incident from Luke's Gospel?

• Jesus challenged the social patterns of His time in His choice of women as travelling companions. Comment on this.

• Jesus saw women as of equal worth with men even though they may perform different roles. Give evidence from Luke's Gospel to show this.

• Jesus challenged the male centred misogynism of His time. Give examples to show if this statement is correct.

• Contrary to the culture of the time, Jesus taught women as well as men. How did He achieve this? Summarise an example.

• Jesus called women to be His disciples (8:1-3). Who were they and what insights do these verse give us regarding female discipleship?

• Women are presented as reliable proclaimers of the good news about Jesus in Luke's Gospel. Who were they and what significant contribution did they make?

• Luke uses a style of writing called "pairing references" to show some examples of equality between women and men. Give concrete examples of this style of writing from Luke's Gospel. How effective was it?

• A key aspect of Luke's Gospel is his sensitivity to women and Jesus' gender inclusivity. How many women are mentioned in Luke's Gospel and how many of these are unnamed?

• Women are exemplars of faith and faithfulness in Luke's Gospel (24:1-11).

• Luke in his Gospel underlines the equality of women in the teaching of Jesus and names thirteen women who do not appear in the other Gospels.

Outcomes

Students for (CCEA A/S) should be able to know and understand the following issues in Luke's Gospel:

• the significant role played by women in the infancy narratives and resurrection appearances.

• motherhood linked to obedience.

Students for Edexcel (A/S) should be able to examine and consider:

• Jesus' respect for women as persons of dignity and value, and be able to compare this with the religious and social practices of that time.

• key concepts, for example "pairing references".

• the social and cultural background of first-century Palestine's attitude to women.

Students for (CCEA A/2) should be able to critically evaluate and discuss the following issues in Luke:

• show how Luke's Gospel challenges all kinds of discrimination. (CCEA A/2)

• the contribution women make and at least two events in which women play a significant role.

• examples of women who showed courage and faithfulness.

Notes on Ch. 15: Women in Luke's Gospel

1. Mishnah, Berakot 7.18 (Heb. for repetition) a book slightly bigger than the bible by Rabbi Judah Ha-Nasi about A.D. 200).
2. Josephus, Against Apion, 2.25 para 202.
3. Plato, Timaeus, Loeb Classical Library, Heinemann, (1929) p.249.
4. Aristotle, The Generation of Animals, Loeb Classical Library, Heinemann, (1943) p.175.
5. Jane Kopas, Jesus and Women: Luke's Gospel, Theology Today, 43 (1986) p.193.
6. Contance Parvey, The Theology and Leadership of Women in N.T. Religion and Sexism ed. R. R. Ruether, New York : Simon and Shuster, (1974)pp.117-49.
7. Robert Stein, NAC, 3 Luke, Broadman Press, (1992) p.374.
8. Darrell Bock, Vol. 1, BECNT, Luke, Baker Press, (1994) p.83.
9. Joel Green, The Gospel of Luke, NICNT, Eerdmans, (1997) p.142.
10. Joel Green, (ibid.)
11. Qumran, (1 Qap Gen) 20. 16-29.
12. Josephus, Antiquities, 3.8.6 par.205.
13. Joseph A. Fitzmyer, Anchor Bible, Luke, Doubleday Press, (1981) p.747.
14. I. Howard Marshall, NIGTC, Luke, Paternoster Press, (1978) p.877.
15. Ben Witherington, (3), Women in the Ministry of Jesus: A Study in Jesus' attitude to women and their roles as reflected in His Earthly Life. SNTSMS, 51 Cambridge University Press, (1984) pp.135-6.
16. Josephus, Antiquities, W. Winston trans. the Works of Flavius Josephus 4.8.15 par 219.
17. Walter Liefeld, op. cit. p.1049.
18. Darrell Bock, op. cit. p. 1893.
19. Josephus, Antiquities, W. Winston trans. the Works of Flavius Josephus 4.8.15 par 219.
20. D.M. Scorer, Article on Women, DJB, IVP, (1992) p.886.
21. K. Giles, Interchange, 19 (1976) p.136.
22. Josephus, (ibid.)
23. E.S. Fiorenza, cited in Green op. cit. p. 144.
24. Joel Green, op. cit. p.437.
25. W.F.Arndt, The Gospel According to Luke, St. Louis: Concordia (1956) p.302.
26. Joseph A. Fitzmyer, op. cit. p.749.
27. Josephus, Antiquities, 17:197; Vita 323.
28. John Stott, Issues Facing Christians To-day, Marshalls Press, (1984) p.240.*

*This book is highly recommended.

(Edexcel A/S + A/S CCEA A/S + ("discrimination" CCEA A/2)　　　A main feature of Luke's Gospel is his great interest in and concern for those in society who were marginalized.

> **Targets:**
> • Identify the different groups who were marginalized in Luke's Gospel in Jesus' time, for example Samaritans and Gentiles, tax collectors and sinners, women, the poor, shepherds, children, lepers.
> • Classify these different groups, for example culturally, ethnically, economically, morally, socially, physically and according to religion.
> • Identify the events in which Jesus helped these outcasts and the main titles for Jesus which reflect this concern.
> • Recognise Jesus' concern for the outcasts, downtrodden and the oppressed (CCEA A/S) and why this issue was so controversial. (Edexcel A/S)
> • Identify the key words and concepts, for example "the poor", the "upside down kingdom", "ascribed status", "performance status and diminished status".
> • Identify Jesus' attitude to women and the religious and social practices of the time. (Edexcel A/S)
> • Identify the different forms of discrimination which Luke challenged. (CCEA A/2)
> • Identify ways in which Jesus' teaching at that time differed from that of the Jews. (Edexcel A/S)

Outcasts in Luke's Gospel (Other aspects of Human experience: human suffering)

Introduction

A main feature of Luke's Gospel is his great interest in and concern for those in society who were marginalized. Here are eight groups who for different reasons are regarded as downtrodden:

A) religion-the Samaritans. Jesus transcends Jewish nationalism in visiting Samaria on his way to Jerusalem and healing a Samaritan leper (17:18). [See p. 208.]

B) political and religious-tax collectors [See p. 252-3.] and [Ch.11: p. 116.]

C) gender-women were considered to have negative roles in society. [See Ch. 15: Women pp. 226-236.]

D) economical-"the poor", the needy, helpless and disadvantaged, the widow of Nain, and the widow's mite.

E) moral and social-the prostitutes, a sinful woman anoints Jesus' feet in a Pharisee's house (7:36-50).

F) cultural and social-little children were considered to be the nobodies, certain types of slaves and shepherds who also fell into this category. [See Ch. 15: Women + pp. 90, 96.]

G) physical-the lepers, their disease was often linked to uncleanness and immorality. The blind, the dumb and people possessed of evil spirits were also seen as outcasts. [See pp. 182, 186, 204, 209.]

H) ethnical-the Gentiles, e.g. the Gentile centurion (7:1-10) and the Gerasene demoniac (8: 26-36). [See p. 190-6.]

[1] Jesus' humanity and compassion for the outcasts of society

Eight types of outcasts in first-century Palestine

(Figure1)

	Forms of discrimination and examples in the first century	First century social and cultural background in Palestine	Jesus' attitude to discrimination
A	**Religious, ethnical and sectarian reasons** a) the Samaritans (9:51-56) b) the thankful Samaritan leper. Jesus refers to the Samaritan leper as "this foreigner." (17:18) "Was no one found to return and give praise to God except this foreigner?" c) the Samaritan hero in the parable (10:25-37) d) There is a notable contrast between Jesus' rebuke of the disciples in wanting to bring down fire from heaven on the hostile Samaritans (9:52-56) shortly before the narrative of the Good Samaritan (10:25-37).	a) The Samaritans were stricter in their keeping of the law than the Jews. (b. Qidd) (1) b) Samaritans were not averse to murdering pilgrims going up to Jerusalem. (Josephus) (2) c) The Samaritans have a history of racial and religious hostility that makes it difficult for them to accept a Jew. d) Jesus was not welcome in the Samarian village (9:52) because He was a Jew going up to Jerusalem (9:53). e) The Jews took the longer way around Samaria even though it took three days to pass through. f) The Samaritans were seen as Jewish half-casts and ethnic traitors with their own centre of worship at Mt. Gerizim. [See p.107.]	a) Jesus provides an opportunity for the Samaritans to hear the gospel but they refuse. Jesus transcends Jewish nationalism in visiting Samaria on His way to Jerusalem (9:51-56). Jesus has no racial prejudice. b) The foreignness of the grateful Samaritan leper is stressed (17:11-19). Jewish and Samaritan lepers lived together outside the village. They called to Jesus from a distance because lepers were despised (17:12). c) All ten lepers were healed both the honourable and the dishonourable (de Silva) (8) but only one is commended by Jesus: the one who showed gratitude. d) Racial-religious distinctions are not part of the gospel. "Jesus' disciples are to care for the non-elite: Jesus conferred on them the honour of being His brokers." (de Silva) (9)
B	**Political, religious, social and economical reasons** e.g. the tax collectors a) Levi (5:27) b) Parable of the Pharisee and the publican (18:9-14) c) Zacchaeus (19:1-11) d) Jesus dines at the house of Simon the Pharisee. e) On a second occasion, He dines with a religious leader (11:37-41). f) On a third occasion, He dines with a very prominent Pharisee (14:1-24). Jesus turns the tables on His critics.	a) The tax collectors gathered revenue for the Roman army of occupation. The Pharisees murmured and chided Jesus because He allowed tax collectors and sinners to come to hear Him preach and He ate with them (15:2). b) They are often put alongside other sinners (5:30; 7:34; 19:1-11). c) They broke the cultural and religious norms of Judaism. "Table fellowship" for the Pharisees did not mean mutual acceptance. d) Luke refers to Jesus as "Lord" (11:39), who is thought to be a deviant by His behaviour.	a) Despite the opposition, Jesus dines with a Pharisee on at least three occasions (7:35; 11:37-41; 14:1-24). However, the Pharisees accuse Jesus of receiving and eating with such degrading people as tax collectors and "sinners." (15:2) b) Jesus taught mutual acceptance of all people. He came to call sinners to repentance and not the righteous (5:31-32). c) Jesus uses the imagery of the shepherd to show His love for tax collectors. He came to seek and to save the lost (19:11; Ezek.34:16). d) Jesus acts as the host who has the right to say what is or is not impure (11:39).

C	**Gender and social reasons:** generally women were socially ostracised and had a very low social status. e.g. a) Anna, b) Elizabeth and Mary, c) Mary of Bethany, d) the sinful woman [See E below.], e) the crippled woman, f) the woman with the haemorrhage (8:42-48), g) Some notable exceptions (8:1-3).	a) Many women were thought to have negative roles in society. b) The woman with the issue of blood was a social and religious outcast because of her physical condition 8:42-48). c) They broke the cultural and religious norms of Judaism. 'Table fellowship', for the Pharisees did not mean mutual acceptance. d) In 11:31-41, the Pharisee who ask Jesus to dine with him accuses Jesus of being ritually unclean in not washing His hands before the meal. Jesus replied, "But give what is inside the dish to the poor, and everything will be clean for you" (11:41 NIV).	a) Jesus gave dignity and worth to women by healing. b) He healed the crippled woman (13:11-13). c) He healed the woman with the issue of blood (8:42-48). To the Jews, this woman was continuously and ceremonially unclean (Lev.13:19-30; 15:25-31; Ezek.36:17; m Zabim 2:3; 4:1; 5:7). Being socially ostracised was worse than her actual physical condition. Her healing was a greater relief socially and culturally than physical.
D	**Economical reasons:** a) "The poor", widows, the needy and helpless-"poor" (Gk. ptochos) in Luke b) the widow of Nain (7:11-17) c) the crippled woman (13:10-17) This group could also include the physical outcasts who are invited to the banquet. [See G below.] d) the widow's mite.	a) In the O.T. the 'nawim' are the economically poor and weak who lived in complete dependence upon God. The rest are those who are spiritually complacent and lay up treasures on earth for themselves. b) In the N.T. culture of that time "poor" meant low status: the lack of education, gender, family heritage, religious purity, vocation and economics; the word "poor" had a wider meaning than "economically poor." Luke uses ten times as a collective term for the disadvantaged. c) The loss of a son to a widow would have meant the loss of protection. Her clothing or the absence of a husband in the procession would have indicated that she was a widow (7:12). d) 'The poor' are those who experience oppression, helplessness, real suffering and insecurity.	a) Widows e.g. (the widow of Nain) (7:11-17) b) (4:18) He preaches good news to the poor. (4:18) He is concerned about the greater spiritual need of these people. c) His strategic plan and tactics were to "proclaim release to the captives, recovery of sight to the blind [a metaphor for sight and experiencing salvation and inclusion into God's family] liberty to the oppressed, and proclaiming the year of Jubilee." (4:18; Lev.25) This is Jesus' great mission statement. d) Jesus said to the Pharisees, "But give for alms those things which are inside the dish to the poor, and everything will be clean for you." (11:41) The Pharisees were concerned about ritual purity.
E	**Moral and social reasons:** a) prostitutes and b) adulteresses were treated as outcasts.	a) The Pharisees and the people could have objected to an unclean woman who showed no regard for the Pharisaic rules and entered Simon the Pharisee's house (7:36-50). b) For her to have been in the house was not impossible (SB). (3)	a) In the case of the sinful woman who anointed Jesus in Simon the Pharisee's house, in the eyes of the people in general, her presence would have been objectionable but not for Jesus (7:36-50).
F	**Cultural and social reasons:** a) shepherds b) children c) slaves	a) Children are the nobodies, the insignificant of society, those whom the world holds cheap. (de Silva) (4) Jesus has conferred on these non-elite, weak ones the honour of being His broker. b) In later Judaism, shepherds were seen as thieves. (SB) (5) c) Slaves	a) In Luke's Gospel, children exemplify God's mercy to 'the poor', the weak and the marginalized. A son is born to a childless woman (1:7,25), and a lowly "handmaiden" (1:48). An "only" son, demon-possessed boy is healed, (9:37-43) and Jairus' daughter is raised (8:41-42a-49-56). b) It is very young children (infants) who are brought to Jesus and whom He calls (18:15-17). c) Jesus says, "Whoever welcomes this little child in my name welcomes the One who sent me." d) Shepherds (2:8-20): a shepherd's work made him ceremonially unclean. The gospel came to these social outcasts of that time, peasant shepherds and not to Caesar and Herod.
G	**Physical reasons:** a) The lepers (5:12-16: 7:11-19); b) blind (18:35-43); c) dumb (11:14-15); d) dropsy (14:1-4) e) lame (5:17-26) f) the man with the withered hand (6:6-11) g) people, who are possessed of evil spirits (5:12). h) the man with the unclean spirit (7:22-23) Jesus is deeply concerned about the physical and spiritual needs of people (Acts 10:38). Release from captivity is a spiritual activity involving release from sin.	a) The sign of 'an honourable client' was to return honour and thanks for benefits (1:46,49; 2:20). In the case of the lepers, all ten were healed the honourable and the dishonourable (17:11-19). b) Only one leper was commended by Jesus, the one who showed gratitude (17:19). c) Dropsy (14:1-4): was often linked with uncleanness and immorality (Lev.15:1-12; Num.5:11-27). d) Some rabbis linked dropsy with sexual offences (Sab.33a) and bowel failure (b Ber. 25A). (6)	a) Paralysis: Judaism saw paralysis as the result of sin; they said there was a link between personal sin and paralysis. (1 Macc.9:55; 2 Macc.55). Jesus was opposed to this attitude (Jn.9:2-3). b) For Jews, exile could be imposed on lepers (Lev.13:13; Num.5:2-3;12:10-12; 2 Kgs.5:27). c) It is the poor, maimed and blind who are invited to Jesus' Messianic banquet, while the wealthy are excluded (14:21).
H	**Ethnical and racial reasons:** the Gentiles a) the Roman centurion and his servant (7:1-10); "The Gentile centurion could have served in Herod's provincial army stationed over Jewish and not over Roman soldiers (7:1-10). However, he could have been in the service of Herod, who employed non-Jewish soldiers. b) the Gerasene demoniac (8:27-35)	a) To praise a Gentile could run the risk of defilement (7:9). Roman soldiers were not stationed in Galilee until 44 A.D. and therefore not in Capernaum but could have been employed by Herod. Therefore it is highly likely the centurion was a Roman (7:1-10). b) The centurion is a man of means and generosity who gave support for synagogues as it prompted order and morality in the community. (Josephus) (7) c) Salvation extends to the Gentiles (4:26-27; 24:44-49).	a) Luke speaks favourably about those the Jews found unacceptable. "The centurion loves our nation and built us our synagogue." (7:4-5) b) Racial differences are not a problem for Jesus. His mission is primarily to Israel, but from the beginning it foreshadows the wider mission to the Gentiles. (Marshall) (10)

Pupil's Activity: One Revision

a) Based upon Figure 1 draw a spidergram to get a bird's eye picture of the downtrodden and the oppressed in Luke's Gospel.

b) Give reasons for their marginalisation.

Adopted from Herzog's (11) Social groupings in Palestine and how they functioned. (Figure 2)

	%	Class distinctions in Israel	Examples
1	1-2%	The aristocrats who had 50% of the total wealth.	The emperor and his court, key political and military leaders, the landed gentry and influential religious leaders would have been in this category.
2	4%	The bureaucrats who served the upper class. e.g. one of the rulers (Gk.archonton) of the Pharisees (14:1).	This group would have been considered as "rich" and would have included the "well to do" women who financially supported Jesus (8:2).
3	14%	The middle class who had modest savings from small earnings	Zebedee, who had more than one servant, would have been in this category (5:10; 6:12 [James and John] Mk.1:20). This group consisted of priests, Pharisees, merchants, traders, artisans, craftsmen, bankers and tax collectors.
4	70%	The lower class who were in the majority. Even they were relatively poor, this group would have had at least one servant. Jesus compares the disciple with a servant who works all day in the field and then returns to prepare his master's meal. The servant will not eat until the master has been served. Disciples, when they obey God are to say they are only "unworthy servants"(Gk. achreioi). Their worth is seen in a faithful relationship with God (17:7-10).	This group consisted of struggling farmers, shepherds, fishermen and labourers who worked for others on the land or in "factories." They lived in poverty by modern standards. Any surplus money had to be saved. The disciples would have come from this social class (17:7). "Will anyone of you, who has a servant ploughing or keeping sheep say to him when he has come in from the field, 'Come at once and sit down at table?' Will he not rather say to him, 'Prepare your supper for me and gird yourself and serve me, till I eat and drink; and afterwards you shall eat and drink?"
5	10%	Outcasts and the expendables	This group lived below the subsistence level and starvation was a real threat.

Whatever wealth the disciples may have had from their business and the sons of Zebedee having more than one servant could have been a bit more prosperous (Mk.1:20), the disciples gave this up to follow Jesus. Jesus and the disciples were supported by a group of wealthy ladies (8:1-3). Another class who cut across these divisions were the slaves.

Pupil's Activity: Two Class discussion

a) Look at Figure 2 to find out from which rung of the social ladder did Jesus come (2:24; Lev 12:8)?

b) Which two groups are omitted by Hertzog?

c) In which category would you place the Levite and the priest in the parable the Good Samaritan, the father in the parable of the prodigal son and Joseph of Arimathea?

A) Religious, ethnical and sectarian outcasts: the Samaritans as outcasts on religious grounds (Read 4:51-6; 17: 11-19.)

Despite the fact that Luke alone records the rejection of Jesus by the Samaritan village (9:51-56) (L), he also records the parable of the Good Samaritan (10:25-37), the story of the ten lepers who were healed and the Samaritan leper who returned to give thanks (17:11-19) (L). The compassion of Jesus does not stop at the boundary of Israel. There was a place for the Samaritans in the ministry of Jesus. Despite the rejection by the Samaritan village, Jesus refuses to take vengeance upon them (9:51-56). The hero in the parable is the Samaritan and not the religious, priestly Jewish aristocrats. In the healing of the thankful Samaritan leper who was a religious and social outcast, Jesus transcends Jewish nationalism. Yet He upholds the Jewish law by telling the lepers to go and show themselves to the priest to certify that they have been healed. The Samaritans were regarded as semi-pagan, being a fringe group of the Jewish world. They are mentioned favourably in 10:30-37. Even though Jesus' disciples were rejected by the Samaritans because they were going to Jerusalem (9:53), Jesus does not by-pass Samaria (9:51-56). A Samaritan plays a major role in the parable, "who is my neighbour?" (10:25-37) In this healing Jesus shows no racial bias; racial differences are not a problem to Jesus. [See pp. 121-24.]

> The compassion of Jesus does not stop at the boundary of Israel; there was a place for the Samaritans in the ministry of Jesus.

B) The tax collectors as socio-economic outcasts yet recipients of God's grace (Read 5:27; 7:34,37; 11:37-41;14:1-24; 15:1-2; 16:20; 18:9-14; 19:7.)

This is an unusual combination for us today. "Sinners" were those who blatantly broke the cultural and religious norms of Judaism as in the parable of the Prodigal Son (15:11-31). The tax collectors were those who acted as "tollhouse keepers" for the occupying army of the Romans, collecting customs and duties for them. People who gathered to hear Jesus preach were referred to as "tax collectors and sinners." This passage is also unique to Luke's Gospel and is an example of reversal of expectation as to who is right with God (18:9-14).

> The tax collectors were those who acted as "tollhouse keepers" for the occupying army of the Romans, collecting customs and duties for them.

1) Levi (Read 5:27-32.)

The Pharisees make a similar complaint against Jesus. "Sinners" refers to anyone who needs healing and not just the worst of sinners (5:31-2). Unique to Luke are the words "eating and drinking" and additional details about the disciples (5:33; 7:33-34). In the eyes of the Pharisees, Jesus should decline fellowship and not recline with sinners especially as Jesus took the initiative with Levi (5:27). **The issue is the scope of Jesus' mission and the focus of the disciples' concern.** They are to seek the lost (5:32). While the gospel of grace and forgiveness is for all (2:10), repentance is a prerequisite to its reception. Jesus says that He must associate with sinners because they appreciate being forgiven (5:32). Tax collectors and sinners came to a banquet for Jesus, given by Levi, after Jesus called Levi to be a disciple (5:30). Levi was a local tax collector. The murmuring and grumbling Pharisees and scribes accused Jesus of eating and drinking with tax collectors and sinners (5:30). They took exception to Jesus' seeking out and welcoming these people: later in His ministry the crowd of people in Jericho did not like His association with Zacchaeus especially when Jesus was a guest at Zacchaeus' table (19:7). The expression "with sinners" (5:30) indicates the crowd's evaluation of tax collectors and the social offence they felt towards them, because of the advantage they took from the people, when they collected their taxes. Jesus shows His concern for tax collectors like Zacchaeus in terms of the activity of a shepherd of God's flock (Ezek.34:16). This imagery is similar to (15:3-7) and the task of Jesus is to "seek and to save the lost." Jesus eats with these people and sinners to show God's love to them. [See p. 217.]

2) Jesus dines in the house of Simon the Pharisee: the sinful woman who was marginalised for moral and social reasons. (Read 7:36-50.) The use of the Gk. word "kataklino" recline (7:36) does not prove that this was a "symposium." No self-respecting Pharisee would have arranged this type of Greco-Roman type of entertainment. Luke has the greatest number of comparatively positive references to Pharisees, regarding their relationship with Jesus. Luke does not use the standard terms for prostitute (Gk.porne and koine) but rather the general word sinner (Gk. hamartolos). The woman is either quite wealthy which would be unusual for a first-century prostitute or she is making a great sacrifice. Her actions at best are culturally inappropriate; Bovon **(12)** and at worst so sexually suggestive as to be shameful. Those who assembled disapproved of her action. The fact that she touches Jesus magnifies the offence. (Blomberg) **(13)** She was weeping and continued to wet His feet with her tears, wiped them with her hair, kissed His feet and anointed them with an expensive ointment. This ointment could have been intended for His head as was the Jewish custom but she has no access to His head, only His feet. Jesus becomes the teacher with the Pharisee who was the host; the roles are in reverse (7:40). Far from being corrupted by the woman in her scandalous behaviour, Jesus has imparted some of His holiness to her. Whether this happened on a previous occasion or at this time, purity is being passed on which involves the entire person not in degrees or gradations as elsewhere in Judaism. (Moritz) **(14)** [See pp. 165, 261, 268.]

3) Jesus dines in the house of a Pharisee: a meal turned sour. (Read 11:37-54.)

For a second time Jesus dines with a Pharisee. This was either an early morning breakfast or a midday meal (Gk.aristese). Well-to-do Pharisees would have eaten twice on weekdays: a light meal in mid-morning (Gk.ariston) and a main meal in late afternoon (Gk.deipnon); a snack meal might be taken before starting work. Three meals were eaten on the Sabbath, the main meal being at midday after the synagogue service. The Gk. word "ariston" suggests the earlier meal but the main Sabbath meal may well be intended. (Marshall **(15)** If this had been a Sabbath meal Jesus would have been reclining (Gk. anapipto). His host is amazed at Jesus' failure to wash His hands reflecting oral Torah. This was not a written requirement in the O.T scriptures. Washing was for ceremonial reasons and not for hygienic reasons (Stein). **(16)** Jesus may have passed on the bowl to the next person without using it or neglected to use the bowl standing nearby. Luke focuses little attention on the actual meal or the wine drinking. Jesus challenges the Pharisaic ritual purity and their hospitality practices. Luke refers to Jesus as "Lord" (Gk.Ho Kurios) (11:39) who was considered to be a deviant in His behaviour by those around Him. Jesus raises the issue of external and internal purity. Only what comes from inside a person makes him unclean. "Give alms for what is within and behold everything is clean for you."(Blomberg) **(17)** Jesus plays the host who has the right to say whose behaviour does or does not produce impurity. Jesus turned the tables on His critics in accepting all foods as clean: He did not adopt the ritual washing of the host, who could have concluded that Jesus' contact with the crowds left

'Outside the Private Sector!' **OUTCASTS IN LUKE'S GOSPEL**

Him consistently impure. (Nolland) **(18)** Jesus goes on to accuse the Jewish leaders of hypocrisy in ignoring God's justice, adding extra burdens on to the people which the Pharisees themselves do not keep and blocking the way into heaven for the people. They are like their ancestors who murdered the prophets.

Jesus condemns the insensitive legalism and hypocrisy of the Pharisees. He challenges the Pharisee's ritual purity and hospitality practices. It is those with social status who are humbled, while the poor and the outcasts are exalted. Jesus turns the table on His critics by playing the host who has the right to say which is correct.

4) Jesus dines in the house of a very prominent Pharisee: a cagey host and a rude guest! (Read 14:1-24.)

This man was one of the rulers of the Pharisees (Gk.archonton). On this occasion Jesus was being watched very carefully (14:1). He proceeds to heal a man with dropsy and as this takes place on the Sabbath he faces conflict with the Pharisees over legal tradition regarding the Sabbath (14:2-6). Meals were often used to show social hierarchy. (Green) **(19)** Jesus is recognised as a teacher and it would have been the custom to invite Him for a meal to "eat bread"(14:1). Jesus would have attended already and preached in the synagogue. Dropsy was thought to be a disease in which people, who drank too much and became bloated, ironically still felt parched with thirst. (Blomberg) **(20)** At the meal people had chosen seats for themselves with possibly a formal setting (14:1-6). Jesus recognised that the invited guests had chosen the best seats (14:7). In the parable (14:8ff) Jesus teaches that guests should humble themselves, take the place of the least honour and allow the host to exalt them as he pleases(14:9). "Standard patterns of reciprocity and concern for those of our social standing are overturned here."(Nolland) **(21)** [See p. 273-74.]

A second mini parable (Read 14:12-14.)

Jesus tells about giving a small lunch or breakfast or all kinds of meals are intended as He is laying down a general principle. Jesus does not actually forbid people inviting their friends or others who cannot repay them but an invitation to a meal should not be motivated by the hope of favours extended in return.

In the parable of the great banquet (14:15-24), the final guests are the riff-raff from outside the city and included undertakers, tanners, drovers, squatters, those involved in butchery, refugees, runaway slaves, prostitutes, roving beggars. (Braun) **(22)** Jesus is toppling the familiar world of the ancient Mediterranean, overturning its socially structured reality and replacing it with what must have been regarded as a scandalous alternative. (Blomberg) **(23)** It is those with social status who are humbled, while the poor and the outcasts are exalted. (Blomberg) **(24)**

5) The parable of Pharisee and the tax collector (Read 18:9-14.) [See pp. 49, 168.]

The Pharisee assumed that he was more right with God: Jesus recognised that the tax collector was more justified than the religious leader. It was the tax collector who realised that the only way he could be justified was to throw himself at the mercy of God. Jesus welcomed the tax collectors. The Pharisee's prayer was Pharisaic in terms of separation from others. Separation itself was not reprehensible as a distinctive group was required to maintain a religious stance against the increase of pagan Hellenism. Unfortunately their attitude became one of self-righteousness by many Pharisees but not all of them. The Pharisees were dedicated to upholding the purity of the Jewish faith and life. They obeyed strictly the law and tradition including religious rites of purification and separation from all whose moral or ritual purity might be questionable (5:29-30). Table fellowship to them implied mutual acceptance. The Pharisees thought they were the only righteous ones (5:31-32). They tithed (18:5) even the herbs (11:42). They fasted twice a week, which was more than was required. God is only mentioned once at the start of his prayer. At the time of Jesus, it was the religious Pharisee who deserved acceptance by God and not the despised tax collector, when business depended upon the despised Roman Imperial power.

6) Zacchaeus (Read 19:1-10.) [See pp. 129, 253, 265.]

His name comes from Heb. Zakka meaning clean or innocent. Luke told another story in which the chief tax collector or district manager was the hero: the conversion of Zacchaeus (19:1-10). His shortage of stature could have led to public ridicule and climbing a tree could have exposed his shame in the eyes of the on-lookers. Here is an undignified action for a well-to-do male claiming status in the community. (Green) **(25)**The crowd is there as an obstacle to Zacchaeus. Jesus takes the initiative in the conversation, shocking the tax collectors and the crowd with His command and predictions, "Zacchaeus, come down at once, I must stay at your house today." Zacchaeus welcomes Jesus at once (19:6). The crowd object. For them to stay in such a person's home was tantamount to living in sin. (Marshall) **(26)** All the people and some Pharisees call Zacchaeus a "sinner" and chief tax collector. Zacchaeus sought salvation more than anything else. Jesus shows His great willingness to associate with such a well-known sinner even in the intimate contact of table fellowship. (Blomberg) **(27)** Zacchaeus says if he has swindled or defrauded anyone, he is now willing to repay and to repay with interest. If he has pressurised someone for personal gain or secured something through intimidation he will repay four-fold. This is not a legal requirement. In Jewish law a thief was required to return only an additional one-fifth (Lev.6:2-5). Roman law required four-fold restoration in certain circumstances especially wrongful accusation in the courts. As a son of Abraham, Zacchaeus is still Jewish. Not all of Jesus' meals include Gentiles. Here he refers to inclusiveness within Israel. As God cares for the "down and out" He also has compassion for "up and out" among the people. Jesus cares for those who are rightly or wrongly stigmatised by society: He ignores the conventional restrictions in intimately associating with them. He is willing to go to their homes. He insists upon going to Zacchaeus' home: shares his food and lodging but never for the sake of inclusiveness. A call to repentance is always implied, unless as here, Zacchaeus takes the initiative to declare His change of heart and behaviour. (Blomberg) **(28)**

The crowds see Jesus as accepting hospitality from a man whose wealth has acquired by ill-gotten gains and see Jesus becoming a partner with him in his crimes. "Son of Abraham" means a true Jew. This could refer to the Messianic Banquet in which all the spiritual descendents of Abraham and all the Patriarchs will participate (Matt.8:11). This passage can be explained in non-Hellenised Jewish terms, "Today, salvation has come to this house since this man is a son of Abraham." (19:9)

Summary: five characteristics of type-scenes with outcasts in Luke's Gospel [See pp. 129, 165.]
• Jesus or His representatives eat with those who in some sense are thought to be second-class citizens in Israel.
• These outcasts regularly respond to Jesus' message with joy.
• Pharisees and scribes by way of contrast, equally commonly grumble about Jesus' behaviour.
• The episodes are consistently introduced by calls to discipleship.
• Finally, the scenes regularly conclude with a statement of Jesus' mission and redemptive purpose in order to refute the objections praised against His behaviour. (McMahan) **(29)**
• Tax collectors and sinners came to a banquet for Jesus, given by Levi, after Jesus called him to be a disciple (5:30). Levi was a local tax collector. The murmuring and grumbling Pharisees and scribes accused Jesus of eating and drinking with tax collectors and sinners (5:30). They took exception to Jesus' seeking out and welcoming these people; later in His ministry the crowd of people in Jericho did not like this also (19:7).
• His association with Zacchaeus especially when Jesus was a guest at Zacchaeus' table (19:7). The expression "with sinners" (5:30) indicates the crowd's evaluation of tax collectors and the social offence they felt towards them, because of the advantage they took from the people when they collected their taxes. Jesus shows His concern for tax collectors like Zacchaeus in terms of the activity of a shepherd of God's flock (Ezek.34:16). This imagery is similar to (15:3-7) and the task of Jesus is to seek and to save the lost.
• Jesus eats with these people and sinners to show God's love to them. [See pp 267-68.]

[C] Women as social and cultural outcasts because of gender [See pp. 167, 242.]
The women were culturally outcasts. Luke says more about women in his Gospel than any other.
1) Elizabeth and Mary are key players in the birth narratives; these stories are presented from their perspectives (Chs.1-2). It is Elizabeth and Mary, who first hear of Jesus' coming and not Zechariah and Joseph. This is an example of role reversal. It is these two women who praised and blessed and who were the first to sing and prophecy about the child to be born.

2) Anna, the prophetess, (2:36-38) appears beside her male counterpoint Simeon (2:25-35). [See Ch. 15: Women.] Anna had departed from all cultural norms in that she fasted and prayed day and night; a form of hope that in praying to God, He would put things right for Israel (2:37). Most Jews had only a certain number of fast days in the year (Bock) **(30)**; daily fasting was not a requirement in Judaism (2:36). [See Ch. 10: birth narratives.] [See pp. 95, 227.]

Pupil's Activity: Three
a) Outline your knowledge and understanding of Jesus' interest in the downtrodden and oppressed.
(CCEA A/S 2002)   [30 marks]

Pupil's Activity: Four
a) Critically evaluate the claim that the Gospel challenges all forms of discrimination.
(CCEA A/2 2002)   [15 marks]

Pupil's Activity: Five
a) Identify the different groups of marginalized people in Luke's Gospel.
b) Outline your knowledge and understanding of one of these groups through an encounter which Jesus had with him or her.

Pupil's Activity: Six (Read 4:16-30.)
a) Who are "the poor" in Luke's Gospel and what did Jesus do for them? [See Figure 3.] [See p. 247.]
b) What do we learn about the kingdom of God from Jesus' treatment of the outcasts in Luke's Gospel?

> **Anna, the prophetess, had departed from all cultural norms in that she fasted and prayed day and night; daily fasting was not a requirement in Judaism (2:36).**

3) Mary of Bethany is praised by Jesus for her devotion to His teaching against the cultural pattern of the times (10:42b). Mary and those of low status used to living on the margins of society need no longer be defined by socially determined roles; "Mary has chosen the better part, which shall not be taken away from her." (10:42b) [See pp. 228, 234.]

4) Only Luke describes Jesus public ministry as being funded by the gifts of some "well-heeled" ladies who accompanied Jesus on His travels (8:1-3).

5) Jesus' concern for a marginalized woman: the sinful woman (Read 7:36-50.) (L) [See also E: Moral and social outcasts.] [See pp. 228, +230.]

> **Only Luke describes Jesus public ministry as being funded by the gifts of some "well heeled" ladies who accompanied Jesus on His travels (8:1-3).**

D) "The poor" (Gk. ptochoi) **as social, economical outcasts are helpless and downtrodden.** In the O.T. "the poor" are called the 'nawim', the marginalized who were materially poor but spiritually pious. In Is.61, they are the impoverished Israelites trying to rebuild their country. Jesus addresses the poor in the Sermon on the Plain, "Blessed are you poor, for yours is the kingdom of God." (6:20) In His first sermon in the synagogue in Nazareth, He indicated that He fulfilled the mission of the servant of Isaiah when He came "to preach good news to the poor." (4:18) The offering made by Joseph and Mary was that prescribed for the poor people (2:24; Lev.12:8). At the start of His ministry in Nazareth, Jesus shows that He came to "preach good news to the poor" in fulfilment of Isaiah's prophecy (4:18). Jesus' message to John the Baptist as a summary of His ministry includes "good news being preached to the poor." Jesus does not teach that poverty is a virtue but He is concerned for the greater need and helplessness of the poor. His concern for the sick and dispossessed who are unable to help themselves is seen in the parable of the great banquet (14:7-24). This group of outcasts also includes the maimed, the blind and the lame, who are invited to the feast when the rich and the respectable failed to come. When these outcasts are invited and attend, this is a sign of the fulfilment of God's promised salvation (7:22). [See Ch.17: the widow's mite.] [See pp. 249-50, 253.]

> **Jesus does not teach that poverty is a virtue but He is concerned for the greater need and helplessness of the poor.**

E) Prostitutes (adulteresses) as social and moral outcasts (Read 7:36-50.) [See Ch. 15: Women.] [pp. 229-30] A sinful woman anoints the feet of Jesus at the house of a Pharisee. This incident is unique to Luke even though similar incidents occur in Matt. 26:6-13; Mk. 14:3-9; Jn. 12:1-8. It indicates the willingness of Jesus to associate with a sinful woman and His right to forgive sins. Even though Jesus had tensions with the Pharisees, He accepts the invitation to dine at the house of Simon the Pharisee. Interested observers were allowed to sit on the fringes and listen to the conversation. This was a social custom which allowed needy people to visit such a banquet to receive some of the leftovers. The scandal was that she had drawn close to Jesus and He has allowed her to approach Him. As a spectator, she should not be a major player. The sinful woman came up to where Jesus was eating and began to anoint His feet with expensive ointment costing a year's wages, two-three hundred denarii per pound. The woman showed great courage and nerve in performing this act of homage. Throughout the event, she is weeping and lets down her hair to wipe the feet of Jesus. This act would have been culturally shocking and unacceptable. Her kissing of Jesus' feet was also offensive. People were saying what a nerve she has. So great is her love that it has caused her to be so bold in expressing appreciation to Jesus (7:39).
Simon the Pharisee objected, blaming Jesus, saying religious people do not get close to sinners. She continually touches (Gk.haptetai) Him; the woman's conduct is outrageous and intolerable. Pious prophets should have nothing to do with sinners and Jesus cannot therefore be a prophet, seeing He lets her anoint His feet (7:39). Simon objects to Jesus allowing the woman to do this. Jesus should have known the type of person she was. The act of kissing the feet and anointing them with ointment was a sign of great reverence and devotion (7:38). (Nolland) **(31)** Simon calls Jesus "teacher" (Gk.didaskale) (7:42) and not Rabbi. This could be Luke's way of showing deference to the Gentiles. Her love goes beyond the call of duty. She shows humility and gratitude. Jesus has made her feel welcome. No washing of feet, kiss or greeting had met Jesus at the Pharisee's door but this woman supplies them. Jesus comments on the faith that led to her actions (7:50).
Jesus reaffirms the faith of the sinful woman, seen in her actions and also shows that He is much more than a prophet. "Your faith has saved you; go in peace." (7:50)

Jesus tells the parable of the two debtors (7:41-48) to show that He knew exactly what the Pharisee was thinking. One had a debt of 50 denarii (two and half month's wage) and the other a debt of 500 denarii (two years' wage). Neither of them could pay but had their debt forgiven. Jesus asks which of the two would love the creditor more. Simon provides the correct answer; "The one, to whom I suppose, he forgave more." (7:43) People who think they have been forgiven little have only a little devotion but those who experience great forgiveness show great love (7:47). Jesus points out the lack of gracious acts towards himself by Simon in not providing water for His feet, no kissing of His feet and no anointing of His head with oil. Jesus tells the woman she has been forgiven and this upsets the people at the table (7:49). [See p. 165.]

> **People who think they have been forgiven little have only a little devotion but those who experience great forgiveness show great love (7:47).**

They ask, "Who is this, who even forgives sins?" In Luke, Jesus is the One who has special care for women. Women are thankful to Jesus, even though they cannot go beyond the Women's Court in the Temple. Unique to Luke is the reference to the women who wept for Jesus on His way to the cross (23:27-31). [See also pp. 141, 149.]

> **Jesus reaffirms the faith of the sinful woman, seen in her actions and also shows that He is much more than a prophet. "Your faith has saved you; go in peace." (7:50)**

F) Shepherds, children, and slaves as social and cultural outcasts (Read 2:8-20.)

1) Shepherds: Luke is interested in the disreputable. The shepherds in the fields outside Bethlehem received the angels' message at the birth of Jesus. They were greatly despised in the time of Jesus (2:8-20). [See Figure 1 Group F.] Working with animals, especially dead ones would have prevented them from meeting the requirements of ceremonial cleanness and they were famous for sheep stealing. A man was not encouraged to train his son to be a shepherd as "their craft is the craft of robbers." (m. Qidd) **(32)** They were not allowed to give testimony in courts as they were seen as untrustworthy. (Talmud) **(33)** The good news comes to peasant shepherds and not to rulers like the Jewish ruler Herod or the Gentile ruler, Augustus Caesar. [See pp. 90-91.]

2) Children [See p. 207.]

Children also feature in the birth narratives and in references to the "only" son and the "only" daughter in some of the miracles (7:12; 8:42; 9:38). To teach the disciples about humility, Jesus set a young child in the centre. It is interesting that He did not have to send for one (9:47). Jesus taught His disciples that there would only be two types of people in heaven, children and those like them. Jesus speaks about children a number of times (10:21; 17:2; 18:16). He watched the children of Jerusalem at play (7:31-35). It is not age which is in view in 18:15-17 but childlike qualities of trust, openness and the absence of a holier-than-thou attitude. Jesus has compassion on children (Gk.brephe) too young to understand the difference between right and wrong. The older children are also invited. Jesus' words about little children is another example of receiving God's grace. The person who welcomes the infant child 'the little one', will in fact welcome Jesus (9:46-48 NRSV). (de Silva) **(34)** In the first-century people were always seeking a favour of a greater or more powerful people in Palestine. As a means of gaining access to even greater or more powerful patrons the weaker in society were never asked to be mediator's of God's favour. Jesus says that whoever welcomes the weak, insignificant child, welcomes Him.

> **Jesus taught His disciples that there would only be two types of people in heaven, children and those like them. "For to such [children] belongs the kingdom of God." (18:16b)**

3) Slaves (Read the healing centurion servant 7:1-10): This social class cut across most of the economic distinctions in Figure 2.

The slaves were the victims of conquest by the Romans as prisoners-of-war, for example the centurion who had the servant who was dear to him (7:2). Others were born slaves or sold themselves into slavery to pay their debts. They were allowed to own property, earn money and could buy their own freedom. Other slaves were forced to work down the mines. Josephus at the end of the first-century said, "Israel depended relatively little on exporting and importing, being a relatively self-supporting farming society." **(35)** [See p. 190.]

Pupil's Activity: Seven
a) Why were the teachings of Jesus concerning wealth and outcasts so controversial at that time?
(Edexcel A/S 2005)   [6 marks]

Pupil's Activity: Eight
a) Outline Jesus' teaching in Luke's Gospel concerning: (1) wealth (2) outcasts
(Edexcel A/S 2004)   [14 marks]
b) To what extent did these teachings differ from Jewish teaching at that time?

Pupil's Activity: Nine   **Revision**
a) Draw a spidergram to show how Jesus challenged the different forms of discrimination in the first-century.

> The good news comes to peasant shepherds and not to rulers like Herod or Augustus Caesar.

G) Physical
This group of outcasts also includes the maimed, the blind and the lame who are invited to the feast when the rich and the respectable failed to come. When these outcasts are invited and attend, this is a sign of the fulfilment of God's promised salvation (7:22). The O.T. poor were called the 'nawim' the marginalised who were materially poor but spiritually pious. In Is. 61 they are the impoverished Israelites trying to rebuild their country. [See pp. 249-50.]

> Luke's entire Gospel can be summed up in one verse "For the Son of Man came to seek and to save the lost." (19:10)

1) Lepers are also physically and ceremonially unclean outcasts, e.g. the ten lepers. (Read 17:11-19.)
Leprosy was a dreaded and terrible disease in the ancient world. It has been described as "a living death." (Godet) **(36)** It was disfiguring and fatal; quarantine was the only answer. A leper was considered to be ceremonially unclean (Lev. 13:45); contact with leprosy would make Jesus ceremonially unclean (Lev.13:42-46), which would effect his involvement in corporate worship. (M. Nega'im) In the incident of the ten lepers, Jesus sends the healed sufferers to the priests to have their cure confirmed (17:11-19). The priests acted like heath inspectors to prove that the cure had taken place (Lev.14:2ff.). Luke notes that the one leper, who returned to give thanks to God was the Samaritan leper, a foreigner (17:16,18). This event shows that Samaritan and Jewish lepers lived together. Normally they would not share the same bowl. All ten suffering lepers stand outside the village and are distanced from Jesus, in keeping with O.T. law, "The lepers stood at a distance because their disease was despised." (Lev.13:46) Foreigners and outcasts are thankful to Jesus, but they can only enter the Gentile court of the Temple.

> Jesus promoted an "upside down kingdom" in seeking to save the lost and outcast of His society and in making the same demands of His disciples.

2) Jesus also heals a leper. (Read 5:12-16.) In touching this man, Jesus would have made Himself, by tradition, unclean. In doing this Jesus shows His compassion. Jesus sent him to the priest in accordance with the law. In the O.T. to have leprosy was often seen as picturing the presence of sin and priests were not expected to provide healing for a leper (Lev.13-14; Num. 5:2-3). (Bovon) **(37)** A leper was ostracised and isolated from society as commanded in the O.T. (17:12; Lev.13:45-46). Jesus' act of healing freed this man to return to a normal life. The man shows himself to the priest to fulfil the O.T. law (Lev.13:49).
Jesus has mercy on social outcasts; He accepted the Jewish norms which required that lepers go for the required priestly declaration of health (Lev.14:1-32). God's grace extends beyond the Judaism to the ceremonially unclean lepers who receive special attention (5:12-16). The leper asked for pity and calls Jesus "Master"; He did not make a specific request. To the Jews, leprosy was viewed as the presence of sin (Lev.13:1-4; Num.5:2-3; 12:10-12; Deut. 24:8). The leper was declared as unclean and put outside the camp of Israel. Jesus ministered to the marginalized lepers who were socially and physically isolated to prevent the contagious disease spreading (5:12-16). Other miracles took place by mere speaking of the word, this one was by touch (5:13). [See p. 186.]

3) Jesus in healing a man with a withered hand on the Sabbath in the synagogue, shows that compassion should be the basis for helping people. God's "law of love" should be the basis for doing good on the Sabbath; God's law of love was never intended to inhibit the good (4:31-44).

4) Jesus also heals a man with an unclean spirit. Judaism taught that demonic power would be crushed in the Messianic age (TZ) **(38)** Jesus assumes this role (7:22-23). This is Jesus' second encounter with the forces of evil (4:1-11). In Qumran some thought that demonic control would end on the Day of the Lord. (Fitzmyer) **(39)** Why does Jesus silence the unclean spirit? Stein **(40)** says the Jesus does not wish to appear as revolutionary against the Romans. It is probable that Judaism taught that the Messiah should only engage in certain types of self-proclaiming and the title Messiah would be regarded as signifying a very political force. [See pp. 182, 186.]

H) Gentiles as ethnic outcasts, for example the centurion's servant (Read 7:1-10.) and the Gerasene demoniac (Read 8:27-35.) [See p. 196.] Racial differences are not a hindrance to Jesus.

1) The centurion's servant (Read 7:1-10.)(Matt.8:5-13) [See p. 190.]
In the case of the centurion's servant, Jesus shows compassion to an eminent socially significant Roman soldier, the hated army of occupation, and not just to "the poor" servant slave (7:1-10). The Roman centurion never actually meets Jesus (7:2-10). Two separate groups are sent to Jesus asking for His help. In doing this, the centurion is seeking a benefit from Jesus. Only God (a deity) can meet his need in healing the sick servant. The centurion has heard of Jesus' healings and recognises that Jesus can provide a favour. The centurion at first sends a group of Jewish envoys. How can an officer of an unwelcome Gentile army of occupation force Jesus a miracle worker for Gentiles to secure him a favour from Jesus? The Gentile centurion has received the favour of Jesus' fellow Jews by building them a synagogue in Capernaum. Roman

The term "poor" often in Luke appears to be a collective term for people who are disadvantaged.

support for building Jewish synagogues was not uncommon (7:5). (Josephus) **(41)** These Jews must pay the centurion a favour with a favour. The Jewish messengers act as brokers saying that the centurion is worthy of a favour from Jesus (7:3-5). Jesus grants the desired request: racial differences are not a hindrance to Jesus and racial-religious distinctions are not part of the gospel when a person follows Jesus (7:6a; Eph.2:11-22). This incident also shows the huge social and religious gap between Jews and Gentiles in first-century Palestine. The centurion then shows further respect for Jesus by sending his "friends" (members of the closest circle of his clients) saying there is no need for Jesus to come to the house.

The second group of messengers meet up with Jesus a short distance from the centurion's house. The messengers say that Jesus need not come as far as the house to heal the servant: the centurion's humility and faith stands out (7:6b). The indication is that Jesus can heal from where He is. "Say the word and let my servant be healed." (7:7) "I am not worthy to have you under my roof." (7:7) Before Jesus great people pale into insignificance irrespective of whether they are Jews or Gentiles. Jesus shows compassion to the socially significant centurion even those who may not be accepted ethnically. The word of Jesus is given to heal the precious servant from a distance and is unseen (7:7b). Even though Jesus is physically absent his presence is effective.

The Jews in the incident appreciate the altruism of the centurion (7:5). The centurion shows respect for Jesus in calling Him "Lord." (7:6) Gentiles are now responding positively to the powerful demonstration of Jesus' authority. The centurion was concerned for the well-being of his slave servant. Gentile faith is just as significant as Jewish faith. He shows great spiritual insight in recognising more clearly than his fellow Jewish countrymen that here in Jesus is the One in whom all authority has been entrusted by God. He was probably a God-fearer like Cornelius (Acts 10:2). (Nolland) **(42)** If the centurion as a member of the Roman army is obeyed, so the spiritual forces that are subject to Jesus will obey His word (7:8). Jesus is amazed at the quality of the Gentile's response to Him. This is only the second time Jesus is said to be amazed in the Gospels: He is amazed at the unbelief of His fellow countrymen (Mk.6:6). Jesus commends this centurion for his faith as something not found in Israel (7:9). The healing of the servant is noted: the has produced a newly found health (7:10).

Jesus could not be accused of visiting someone from another nation seeing Gentile houses are unclean (Acts 10:28; (m). Ohol. 18:7). The centurion sees himself as unworthy to have Jesus enter his house or for Jesus to associate with a Gentile. It was mainly due to their carelessness in food matters that Gentiles were ritually unclean people for a religious Jew to meet socially. Contact with Gentiles was not categorically forbidden; but it did make a Jew ceremonially unclean, as did entering a Gentile building or handling articles belonging to Gentiles. Strict Jews would not share bread, milk or olive oil coming from Gentiles, nor flesh from an unclean animal or sacrificed to a pagan god and which contained blood. To sit at a table with Gentiles was forbidden. Only in Luke is the Gk. pais "servant" used for a slave. Normally it is one of the words used for a child (7:6). It should also be noted that in the healing of the Syro-Phoenicean woman's daughter, Jesus does not have contact with the healed girl: this healing also involved a Gentile (Mk. 7:24-30).

2) Gerasene demoniac (Read 8:27-35.) [See p. 196.]

Jesus accepted those people who socially, ethnically and on the grounds of religion were marginalised, living in tombs in Decapolis, a Gentile area. The demoniac is the first Gentile who wants to become a travelling disciple. Jesus tells him his task is to stay and witness to his fellow Gentile community. This incident prefigures future Gentile missions.

[2] Titles used for Jesus which show His concern for the outcasts

a) Saviour (Gk.soter) – this word sums up Jesus' humanity and compassion, "for to you is born this day in the city of David, a Saviour, who is Christ the Lord." (2:11) This word is used eight times in Luke's Gospel. The entire Gospel can be summed up in one verse "For the Son of Man came to seek and to save the lost." (19:10) [See p. 74.]

b) Prophet -After the raising of the widow's son in Nain, the crowd respond by saying "a great prophet has risen among us." (7:16) This incident is unique to Luke as it is like the raising of the Shunammite woman's son (2 Kgs. 4:8-37). Jesus refers to Himself as a prophet, "It cannot be a prophet should perish away from Jerusalem." (13:33) Jesus is the messenger sent from God to warn a stiff-necked people of its coming destruction as in the great banquet and of its rejection, "none of those men who were invited shall taste my banquet." (14:24) [See p. 74.]

c) Teacher of parables - the parables of Jesus in Luke are mainly about down to earth, simple examples for Jewish peasants. Some are called example stories because they are less symbolic in nature than most: the good Samaritan (10:25-37), the rich fool (12:13-21), the rich man and Lazarus (16:19-31) and the Pharisee and the Publican (18:9-14). [See Ch. 12.]

[3] Summary

a) Jesus promoted an "upside down kingdom" in seeking to save the lost and outcast of His society and in making the same demands of His disciples. His main concerns were those of mercy and justice. The quality of mercy was predicted by Mary in the Magnificat:

• "His mercy is on those who fear Him from generation to generation." (1:50) God's holiness expresses itself in mercy and His favour is on those who fear Him. Mary is one of the many God fearers who are blessed.

• "To perform the mercy promised to our fathers and to remember His covenant." (1:72) This covenant with Abraham is the basis of God's acts of love and mercy and was promised to the fathers of the nation. "He has helped His servant Israel, in remembrance of his mercy." (1:54)

b) John the Baptist in his teaching on mercy and justice says to the crowd, the tax collectors and soldiers, that taxes are to be gathered without extortion, surcharges or pay-offs or bribes (3:10-14). The business man is to conduct his affairs in fairness unlike the corrupt tax collectors (3:13). The soldier is not to abuse his position nor is he to take an unfair advantage over those who are under him. He is not to receive additional money by force to improve his wages. A soldier received as a wage his basic food and a minimal subsistence. By being content with their wages John is telling the soldiers not to take advantage of people by supplementing their military income (3:14). [See p. 103.]

• To three groups of people John says, "Be compassionate, loving and fair to your fellow humans and do not leave them destitute for your own selfish gain." This is the nature of true repentance. Concern for God is expressed through concern for others. John's teaching on social injustice in the end cost him his life.

c) Jesus presented His manifesto in His first address: "to preach good news to the poor." "Poor" (Gk. ptochos) in Luke is a collective term for the disadvantaged and it is used ten times. In Matthew and Mark the term is used only five times. Jesus' strategic plan and tactics were to "proclaim release to the captives, recovery of sight to the blind [a metaphor for sight and experiencing salvation and inclusion into God's family] liberty to the oppressed, and proclaiming the year of Jubilee." (4:18; Lev. 25) In the culture of that time "poor" meant low status: the lack of education, gender, family heritage, religious purity , vocation and economics. "Poor" had a wider meaning than "economically poor." Jesus' ministry was universal, bringing healing of spirit and body to the social outcasts, the poor, Samaritans, Gentiles, women, children and the sick particularly the lepers who were the "untouchables." His parables showed His grace and mercy (15:1-32) and His desire for social justice (18:1-8) which transcends all cultural distinctions - even your enemy (Samaritan) is your neighbour (10:25-37). The disciples are to implement the social concerns of Jesus and yet they are not to assume that these are ends in themselves lest people think that in gaining earthly freedoms they have prepared for eternity. It is a both/and exercise of following Jesus and having a social concern. [See p. 250.]

d) Was Jesus "the consummate party animal"? (Crossan) (43)
Blomberg **(44)** rejects this saying if the expression is used in the sense that we normally mean: a lover of food and other forms of entertainment with friends just for the pleasure of it. Jesus always had a purpose in attending banquets and other special meals. Yet, Jesus was always willing to socialise and have close table fellowship with anyone and everyone to fulfil His mission.

e) The Samaritans oppose the disciples who are challenged boldly to cross those humanly drawn boundaries in outreach and to look on each person not through the lens of any human prejudice, nor to respond to them in kind when they speak to us out of their prejudice (9:51-56), but to seek their redemption in God's love (de Silva) **(45).**

f) An anthropological view by H. Eilberg-Schwartz (46): this view examines the different ways in which status and purity were measured in priestly, early Christian and Dead Sea communities.
Firstly, "ascribed status" is imputed on the basis of family heritage, one's sex, other inherited genetic attributes. Genetic defects could result in exclusion from priestly status.
Secondly, "performance status" based upon education, or conformity to prescribed behaviours. People were born into priestly families and did not chose to be priests. Sons could be prevented from taking up office due to genetic and physical defects: hunchback, blind, lame, broken foot, dwarf, itching disease, mutilated face (Lev. 21:16-2). Similar restrictions were placed upon the Qumran community. A person's status could be determined by genetic disability factors. Jesus always includes the poor (Gk. ptochos) at the beginning of a list to show people who should be included except for (7:22) where the poor are at the end of the list of those who suffer. **(Figure 3)**

4:18	6:20	7:22	14:13	14:21	16:20,22
Poor	**Poor**	Blind	**Poor**	**Poor**	**Poor**
Captive	Hungry	Lame	Maimed	Maimed	Ulcerated
Blind	Mournful	Leper	Lame	Lame	Hungry
Oppressed	Persecuted	Deaf	Blind	Blind	
		Dead			
		Poor			

Outcomes
CCEA A/S Students should be able to know and understand in Luke's Gospel:
• the different groups who were marginalized in Jesus' time, for example Samaritans, tax collectors and sinners, women, the poor, shepherds, children, lepers, Gentiles and classify these different groups.
• the events in Jesus' ministry to show how He helped these outcasts.
• Jesus' concern for the outcasts, downtrodden and the oppressed (CCEA A/S) and why the issue was so controversial. (Edexcel A/S)
• titles for Jesus which reflect this concern. (CCEA A/S) (Edexcel A/S)
• the key words and concepts related to the outcasts, for example "the poor", the "upside down kingdom", "ascribed status" and "performance status and diminished status".
Edexcel A/S students should be able to:
• discuss the extent the teachings of Jesus differed from Jewish teaching at that time.
CCEA A/2 Students should be able to:
• critically evaluate all the forms of discrimination which Jesus challenges in Luke's Gospel.

Notes on Chapter 16: Jesus' teaching on outcasts in Luke's Gospel

1. b. Qidd. 76a.
2. Josephus Ant. 20. 118.
3. SB 1V: 2,615.
4. David A. de Silva, An Introduction to the N.T. , Contexts, Methods and Ministry Formation, Apollos, (2004) p.337.
5. SB .2,11 3 f.
6. b Ber.25a.
7. Josephus Ant. 16.6.2 §§ 162 –65; 19.6.3 §§.299-311.
8. David A. de Silva, (ibid.)
9. David A. de Silva, (ibid.)
10. Howard Marshall, N.T. Theology, Apollos, (2005) p.152.
11. William R. Herzog, Parables as subversive speech: Jesus as Pedagogue of the oppressed, Louisville; Westminster/John Knox (1994) pp. 53-73. This classification however excludes women and children, Gentiles and Samaritans and as regards outcasts it is not fully comprehensive.
12. F. Bovon, Luke 1, Minneapolis: Fortress, (2002) p.295.
13. Craig L. Blomberg, Contagious Holiness Jesus' meals with Sinners, NSBT, Apollos, (2005) p.134.*
14. T. Moritz, Dinner Talk and Ideology in Luke: The role of sinners, EJT (European Journal of Theology) 5:47-69 (1996) op. cit. p.57.
15. Howard Marshall, op. cit. Luke pp.493-4.
16. Robert Stein, op. cit. p.340.
17. Craig Blomberg, op. cit. p.143.
18. John Nolland, op. cit. p.663.
19. Joel Green, op. cit. p.545.
20. Craig Blomberg, op. cit. p.145.
21. John Nolland, op. cit. p.751.
22. W. Braun, Feasting and Social Rhetoric in Luke 14:1-24, Cambridge: Cambridge University Press. (1995) op. cit. p.148.
23. Craig Blomberg, op. cit. p.148.
24. Craig Blomberg, op. cit. p.161.
25. Joel Green, op. cit. p. 669.
26. Howard Marshall, op. cit. Luke p.697.
27. Craig Blomberg, op. cit. p.15.
28. Craig Blomberg, op. cit. p.156.
29. S.T. McMahan, Meals and Type scenes in the Gospel of Luke, (1987) Ph. D. dissertation, Southern Baptist Theological Seminary Louisville. (pp.118-119)
30. Darrell Bock, IVPTNC, (1994) p.110.
31. John Nolland, op. cit. p.135.
32. M. Qidd 4:14.
33. Talmud, b. Sanhedrin 25b.
34. David A. de Silva, (ibid.)
35. Josephus, Ag. Apion 1:12. 60-61.
36. Francois Godet, op. cit. Vol. 1. p.259.
37. F. Bovon, op. cit. p. 239.
38. Testament of Zebulon 9:9; Assumption of Moses 10:1.
39. Joseph Fitzmyer, op. cit. pp.545-6. cites 1QM 1:10-14 ; 14:10.
40. Robert Stein, op. cit. p.16.
41. Josephus, Ant. 16.6.2 Par.162-65.
42. John Nolland, op. cit. p.135.
43. John D. Crossan, The Historical Jesus: The Life of a Mediterranean Jewish Peasant, San Francisco, Harper: San Francisco (1991) cited in Blomberg (44) material not distinctive to Luke.
44. Blomberg, op.cit. pp.99-129.
45. David de Silva, op. cit. p.344.
46. H. Schwartz, The Savage in Judaism: An anthropology of Israelite religion and Ancient Judaism (Bloomington Indiana University Press, (1990) pp. 195-216.
47. David J. Bosch, Transforming Missions, Orbis, (1991) p.99.
* This book is highly recommended.

Poverty and Wealth in Luke's Gospel (CCEA A/S + Edexcel A/S) + [Poverty and Wealth in the Sermon on the Plain CCEA A2]

No other N.T. book shows as much concern about the Christian's attitude to material possessions as the Third Gospel.

Targets:
- Identify Jesus' teaching on wealth and stewardship in Luke's Gospel. (Edexcel A/S)
- Identify stories and sayings unique to Luke: parables which have wealth and possessions as their theme. [See Ch.12.]
- Identify key concepts, foe example "eye of a needle Christians", "the poor", alms giving, tithing, "the nawim", the widow's mite, a lepta, the "fool", the difference between wealth and money.
- Recognise the Pharisees' attitude to wealth. [See Ch.7.]
- Identify Jesus' teaching on wealth and poverty as a characteristic of Luke's Gospel. (CCEA A/S)
- Identify aspects of the Sermon on the Plain which exemplify Jesus' teaching on wealth in Luke's Gospel. (CCEA A/2)

Jesus's Teaching on Wealth in Luke's Gospel

Introduction:

"Wealth is the state of being rich, an abundance of valuable possessions or money." Oxford Dictionary **(1)** No other book in the N.T. shows as much concern about the Christian's attitude to material possessions as the Third Gospel. There is no attempt by Luke to show that Jesus was an ascetic who rejected outright the use of wealth, as He took part in dinner parties, leaving Himself open to the charge of being a "glutton and a drunkard." (7:34, 36; 14:1-24; 19:1-27) Jesus interacts with the peasants and the wealthy as both need God's good news.

[1] 'The Poor' (Gk. ptochos) A) The Old Testament

Stott **(2)** classifies the condition of 'the poor' in three ways in the O.T.:

1) **The indigent poor** who were economically poor deprived of food, clothing, shelter and the basic necessities of life. For some, their poverty may be self-inflicted through laziness, gluttony or extravagance (Prov.6:6-11). 'Lazy hands make a poor man.' However, generally in the O.T., poverty was seen as involuntary as in the case of orphans, widows and aliens who were more 'sinned against' than sinned and who are people to be helped. 'He who mocks the poor shows contempt for his neighbour.' (Prov.17:5) Jesus identified with this type of needy person for example the widow of Nain.

2) **The oppressed poor** who were powerless: they were socially and politically oppressed. Their condition may be due to social injustice (Ps.109:31; 140:12). 'The Lord maintains the cause of the needy and executes justice for the poor.' The prophets were fierce in their condemnation of injustice. God will judge the rulers in Israel because they trampled on the heads of the poor, crushed the needy and denied justice to the oppressed (Amos 2:6). These people were all victims of social injustice: their cause was fought for by the prophets.

3) **The humble poor** who were spiritually meek and dependent upon God and looked to Him for mercy. They were oppressed by mankind and could not liberate themselves. They were the meek and humble who trusted in their God and trembled at His word (Is.66:2; Zeph.2:3; 3:12). Compare in the N.T. the woman with the issue of blood (6:20). God helps the indigent poor:
- He fights the cause of the powerless poor and exalts the humble poor.
- In each case 'He raises the poor from the dust' whether it is the dust of penury or oppression or helplessness (Ps. 113:7), the poor are not regarded as "sinners" but as sinned against.

B) Who are 'the poor' in Luke's Gospel?

A significant feature of Luke's Gospel is his interest in the poor; Luke points out that God has a special interest in the poor. He uses this word ten times in his Gospel compared with five times each in Matthew and Mark. **Who are 'the poor'?**

a) After the birth of Jesus, Joseph and Mary went to the Temple, to make a sacrifice of a pair of turtle doves or two pigeons, the prescribed offering for poor people (2:24; Lev. 12:8).

b) Mary and Zechariah in their hymns of praise to God, speak of "a great reversal"- the powerful are rendered powerless and the lowly in Israel are exalted (1:46-55, 67-79).

c) At the start of His ministry in Nazareth, 'The Nazareth Manifesto', Jesus quotes from Is.61:1-2 to show that He was sent "to preach good news to the poor." (4:18) On this occasion, there is no overcoming of the wicked by force and the deliverance brought by Jesus is spiritual with wider effects. The offer of salvation is for the poor. (Marshall) **(3)** Jesus had a great concern for the poor because of their greater need and not because there is any real virtue in being poor. Jesus' mission is for all. Whatever the social, cultural or religious reasons people are marginalized, to a place outside the boundaries of Israel, Jesus came to remove these barriers (4:18). Words like "poor", "weep", "rich", "full" and "laugh" are to be viewed religiously and sociologically because the gospel canonises no sociological state." (Talbert) **(4)** Luke has a deep compassion for the poor and shows a profound interest in them.

d) In the Sermon on the Plain the poor are addressed: (CCEA A/2)

(1)"Blessed (Gk.makarioi) are you poor (Gk.ptochos), for yours is the Kingdom of God." (6:20) This can mean, "Blessed are those who are **materially poor**; their poverty brings them to dependence upon God." (Stein) **(5)** Another view is that of Green **(6)** who sees **"the poor" in Luke as a collective term for the disadvantaged**. These are the **socio-economic poor** in Judaism who are in desperate need and whose helplessness drives them to a deep dependence upon God (6:20). It can be translated as, "Blessed are you materially poor, who nonetheless look to God and His promise, for the kingdom of God is yours." Despite their poverty, the poor can now take part in the blessing of the Kingdom. [See Ch. 16: Outcasts see p. 254.]

(2) " Woe to you who are rich, for you have received your consolation." (6:24)(L) Woe comes to the rich not because they are wealthy but because they have chosen present pleasures over future blessing. Luke sees the rich as disregarding spiritual realities and often become wealthy at the expense of others (12:15-21).

(3) "Give to everyone who begs from you and of him who takes away your goods, do not ask them again." (6:30) This refers not just to beggars on the street, but to a genuine readiness to meet needs without prejudice. Luke stresses that all who ask you should be treated in this way. In the time of Jesus, poor people were often despised.

---

c) Issues for discussion   (CCEA A/2)

1) a) If we say that "blessed are the poor in spirit, for theirs is the kingdom of heaven," then (Matt 5:10) could mean "blessed are the rich too, if they act humbly." Therefore we have spiritualised the text. [Luke has, "Blessed are you poor, for yours is the kingdom of God." (6:20)]

b) If on the other hand we say "blessed are the poor" means "poor people are happy" we have secularised the text. Jesus combines Matthew's spirituality with Luke's sociality with the best of each." (Bruner) **(7)** Luke has a spiritual as well as a material component in 6:22-23 to those whom Jesus blesses in His beatitudes. (Blomberg) **(8)**

2) "Seeing Jesus in the face of the poor irrespective of their religious commitment," is an expression made famous by the late Mother Theresa of Calcutta. Blomberg **(9)** says at best this statement encapsulates only partial truth and at worst proves highly misleading. Some contemporary Christians have argued that God has a divine bias for the poor and disadvantaged and the Church needs to be more faithful in reflecting it. God takes flesh in the person of Jesus, living out His life in a special relation to the poor. (Sheppard) **(10)**

Words like "poor", "weep", rich", "full" and "laugh" are to be viewed religiously and sociologically because the gospel canonises no sociological state." (Talbert) **(4)**

d) Summary of the "poor" in Luke: [See p. 243.]

• a **generic term** for the disadvantaged in Luke's Gospel (Bosch) **(11)** Green **(6)** [See p. 243.]

• the "poor" can refer to the **materially poor** but more often the word applies to those who have been marginalised in the larger world for economic, social, cultural or religious reasons. By contrast, the wealthy are those with ample resources, who fail to recognise the needs of others.

• "the poor" are accustomed to living in the **margins of society** but the rich find themselves surrounded by friends, as they use their resources to strengthen their positions in society.

• "The poor" are those who are **most open to the message of Jesus**. The strong and wealthy do not accept the message but little children and those who are of little standing who make no claims about themselves are the poor (10:21). Not all the wealthy reject the message (Zacchaeus) (19:9) and not all the poor receive it (the unrepentant criminal) (23:39-41). (Marshall) **(12)**

• They are the "humble poor" who are spiritually meek and dependent upon God. (Stott)

• A cultural understanding of the poor seen in the light of Mediterranean culture and the social world of Luke/Acts. Here "poor" serves as a "cipher" for **people of low status** who are excluded according to normal canons of status and honour in the Mediterranean world. While the term is not devoid of economic significance, for Luke it has a wider meaning of **diminished status honour** and this is paramount. (Green) **(13)** For an anthropological view of status in society poverty seen as a diminished status (16:19-31). (Eilberg-Schwartz) [See p. 247.]

People can enjoy one luxury car or apartment but not five of each at once. "Take heed and beware of all covetousness; for a man's life (Gk.zoe/eternal life) does not consist in the abundance of his possessions." (12:15)

---

[2] Parables with warnings for the wealthy: the rich fool (Read 12:12b-15.) (L)

a) Setting of the parable: someone in the crowd wanted Jesus to tell his brother to divide his inheritance. Jesus refuses to arbitrate in this family dispute (12:13-14). He did not come to act an arbiter of family disputes (12:15). These issues were settled in the synagogue as Jesus did not have the legal right to arbitrate (12:14; Deut.21: 15-17). In fact the man really wanted an advocate rather than an arbitrator. Jesus gives a warning about all kinds of greed. "Watch out, take heed;

for a man's life (Gk. zoe means eternal life) does not consist in the abundance of his possessions." (NIV) "Life" here means "man's chief purpose, his true interest or the real end of his being (12:15)." "Take heed" means "be on one's guard," be vigilant about all kinds of greed." Concern for a fair and proper distribution of inheritance leads to Jesus telling the parable about the folly of storing up treasures on earth.

A) The parable of the rich fool (Read 12:16-21): Spiritual wealth means being rich in God's eyes or treasure in heaven (12:21). This parable is unique to Luke (L). It is linked to Jesus' teaching about the needless accumulation of wealth or covetousness, possessions and inheritance rights and is the first parable with a warning for the wealthy. Because of the abundant harvest, the rich man has to replace his barns with bigger ones. By implication the man is selfish and does not see this as an opportunity to help people in need (12:19-25). All the fool will have to show for his life will be bigger barns full of food. He has selfishly and greedily hoarded his worldly goods with the result that he does not finally benefit from them. The rich man failed to grow rich in spiritual wealth; instead he gathered wealth to himself. "I will pull down **my** barns and build larger ones; and there **I** will store all **my** grain and **my** goods. **I** will say to **my** soul, soul you have ample goods laid up for many years." The use of **I** and **my** shows his self-interest. He had measure [full barns] (12:16), treasure [a rich man with ample goods] (12:16), leisure [eat and drink] and pleasure [be merry] (12:19). The rich fool made three mistakes. He hoarded his possessions, he assumed that life can be secured and measured by possessions and he regarded property as his own. (Pilgrim) **(14)** Fool (Gk. aphron means mindless) in this parable means someone who acts without God; the O.T. idea (Pss. 14:1; 53:1), "The fool says in his heart there is no God." In Luke this means acting in a self-destructive way, using resources in a way which is displeasing to God. When God takes the man's life, his temporary possessions are left behind. [See p. 157 Figure 1 No. 11.]

B) The disciple is not to be worried about food and clothes which distract and show a lack of faith (12:28). If God cares for the relatively insignificant things such as birds and flowers will he not feed and clothe His own children?

C) The parable of the great banquet (14:12-24) A wealthy man has prepared a banquet and invited honoured guests and invitations in a socially appropriate way by using his servants. The

> **The rich fool made three mistakes:**
> • **he hoarded his possessions.**
> • **he assumed that life can be secured and measured by possessions.**
> • **he regarded property as his own.(Pilgrim)(14)**

poor, the maimed, blind and lame are to be invited (14:21; Matt.22:1-14; "Q"). This is an example of a characteristic of Luke's Gospel: his fondness for fours. The maimed were banned from full participation in Jewish worship (Lev.21:17-23). Jesus' association with the classless of society leads to reaction from His opponents. A third invitation goes out urging people to attend as they do not know the host and have to be encouraged to attend (14:23). [See Ch.15: Outcasts.] Give hospitality to those who cannot return the favour. "When you give a dinner do not invite your friends or brothers lest they invite you in return but rather invite the poor the maimed the lame, the blind, and you will be blessed. You will be repaid at the resurrection of the just." (14:12-14) Jesus exhorts the Pharisees to invite not their friends but the poor, crippled, lame and blind: those who have need and cannot return the invitation. Such people were excluded from the Temple and the Qumran community. Reciprocity should not be a factor in deciding whom to invite. (Marshall) **(15)** Hospitality should be provided without an alternative motive: God honours with exaltation those who are humble. At the resurrection of the righteous, which was also taught in Judaism when each one's stewardship is weighed, such kindness will be paid back by the Father, who is the source of the reward (2 Macc.7:9). The ethics of Jesus are based upon humility and openness. The disciple is to ask, "What can I do to meet the needs of others?" rather than "What can I do to receive the equivalent back in return?" [See p. 158.]

> **"Do not let greed, which is temporary, keep you from God's eternal treasure!"**

D) The unjust manager/the shrewd manager (Read 16: 1-13.) (L)
It is the second parable which is a warning for the wealthy. This parable is one of the hardest to grasp in meaning. It is based upon the steward who is fired but has the temerity to forgive some of the debts owed to his master. Jesus is teaching the disciples to use material wealth for eternal purposes. The unjust manager is commended for using his wealth shrewdly; believers must do the same for the sake of the kingdom. Jesus exhorts His disciples to use the resources of this world wisely (16:9). One cannot serve God and money (Heb. "Mammon" means firm or certain "that in which one puts trust." (Marshall) **(16)**; (Fitzmyer) **(17)** (16:13) "Do not let greed, which is temporary, keep you from God's eternal treasure!" This parable is a warning about greed and the pursuit of possessions. Sin is gathering riches for oneself. The dishonest manager cancels the profit that was due to him (the commission) and so reduces the debts. The disciples will recognise that by giving up a little now, in the future they will receive much more. [See p. 158.]

E) The rich man and Lazarus (Read 16:19-35.) (L) [See p. 158.]
This is the third parable which has warnings for the wealthy. It deals with the use and misuse of money and handling possessions and is a warning to the disciples to beware of praying in luxury while the poor in the world go begging.

F) The parable of the pounds (Read 19: 11-27.) (L) [See p. 158.]

The setting: this parable could be topical in that many Jews did not like Archelaus, the son of Herod the Great. When the time came for him to ascend to the throne after his father's death in 4 B.C., the Jews sent a delegation of fifty men to protest to the Emperor Augustus, who compromised by allowing Archelaus to rule but only with the title "ethnarch". This was to indicate that he would have to earn the title king, which he never did (19:11). (Josephus) **(18)**

The parable: a man of noble birth leaves home and his estate in anticipation of being appointed king. Before he leaves he entrusts ten of his servants with ten pounds (RSV). In his absence, some of his subjects sent a delegation to prevent the nobleman reigning as king. On his return as king he called together his servants to find out what they had gained. The first one had earned ten more pounds. This servant is commended and is put in charge of ten cities. The second had earned five pounds and was put in charge of five more cities. A third person hid his pound in a piece of cloth for fear of what his master would do if he lost it. The new king takes his pound away from him and gives it to the man who has ten pounds. The enemies of the king who oppose his kingship are then to be slain.

Summary

• This really is a parable about stewardship and judgement: the faithful will be rewarded generously.

• Jesus is teaching that His final return would be "after a long time". The punch line is "why did you not put my money into the bank, [the table of money changers] and at my coming I should have collected it with interest?" (19:23) The crowd think that this bonus is unfair as this man would in total receive twelve pounds. What justice is that if the poor servant is left destitute (19:25)?

• The parable commends the faithful servants who invest their wealth and make more money, but all the money reverses to the master for his service and use.

[3] Examples and warnings about attitudes to wealth: people who exemplify the right attitude to wealth:-

(1) Mary in her song, The Magnificat, points out the social consequences of God's work, "The rich will be sent empty away." The rich man's focus on himself produces a lack of concern for one's neighbour and this action is condemned by God. "Keep material things in perspective and use them generously to serve one's neighbour." (1:53)

(2) the Roman centurion who built a synagogue for the Jewish people in Capernaum is commended (7:5).

(3) in the parable of the Good Samaritan, Jesus said, "Take care of him (the injured man) and whatever more you spend, I will repay you when I come back (10:34-35). Jesus said to the lawyer who recognised the mercy of the Samaritan in the parable, "Go and do likewise." (10:37)

(4) wealth must never be allowed to come in the way of the disciples' love for Jesus (18:18-30).

Jesus said to the rich ruler, "Sell everything you have and give to the poor, and you will have treasure in heaven." (18:22)

(5) the women who followed Jesus and many others who provided for Him out of their means (8:3).

> **Jesus said to the rich ruler, "Sell everything you have and give to the poor, and you will have treasure in heaven." (18:22) Wealth must never be allowed to come in the way of the disciples' love for Jesus.**

[4] Warnings about wealth: the rich ruler (Read 18:18-30; Matt.19:20,22.) "Q"

Luke refers to the man as "rich ruler" and not "young" as in Matt. 19:20,22. Jesus is confronted by a leading member of society who is thought to be a lay person rather than a ruler in the synagogue. He tells the rich ruler, "You still lack one thing. Sell everything you have and give to the poor, and you will have treasure in heaven and come and follow me." (18:22) The ruler thought he was devoted to God and could earn acceptance on the basis of his good works. Jesus demanded of the rich ruler that he go and sell all that he had and give it to the poor and follow Him. Even with the promise of a reward in heaven, he prefers this earth's riches, which is in contrast to the blind man who receives mercy (18:35-43). Jesus looked at the rich ruler and surprised His audience by saying, "How hard it is for those who have riches to enter the kingdom of God!" (18:24) "For it is easier for a camel to go through the eye of a needle than for a rich man to enter the kingdom of God." (18:25) By the grace of God whatever is humanly speaking impossible becomes possible (18:27). This is the use of a Palestinian image in which the largest animal tries to pass through the smallest common opening. "Wealth can shrink the door of the kingdom down to an impassable peep-hole." (Bock) **(19)** The disciples wonder how anyone could be saved; they regarded riches and wealth as a blessing from God for faithfulness (Deut.8:1-10, 26:1-9; Prov.6:6-11). However, the O.T. and Judaism warned that wealth was not an automatic sign of blessing (Prov.28:6; 30:7-9; Jer. 5:28; Amos 8:4-8; Mic.2:1-5). (Talbert)**(20)** They asked, "Who then can be saved?" Is there any hope for anyone? What about those people who have left everything "our own homes" behind to follow Jesus? This is Peter's concern, leaving things behind. Jesus speaks about leaving people behind which is a more significant sacrifice (18:29). We have already made the choice which this man has refused (18:28). Jesus promises them their manifold reward in this life and in the next life to come (18:29-30).

There are two phases about their reward. Firstly, there are the temporal elements; disciples who leave all will receive "many times as much" in this life. He gives back more in terms of relationships; a new community is gathered. The second phase of reward is in the age to come, which is eternal life: being accepted forever into the presence of God. What God

gives back to the disciples is many times greater than what is given up. The disciples have done what the rich ruler failed to do. Talbert **(21)** calls this a "recognition story" since the young man learns something about himself.
Tannehill **(22)** sees it as a "quest" story as the ruler is in search of eternal life (18:18,23). People are asked to think whether they are relying on their possessions and themselves or whether they trust God. If wealth stands between ourselves and whole-hearted allegiance to Christ, then we must divest ourselves of it. Not all Christians are called upon to give up everything as the rich ruler was required to do. In the next incident Zacchaeus voluntarily agrees to give up everything up to half of his goods (19:1-10) and the faithful servants invest everything they have for their master's work (19:11-27).

> **Zacchaeus is an example of a rich man who went through the eye of a needle (18:24) and of someone who handled money generously. (16:9-13)**

[5] Zacchaeus, a ruler/leader of the tax collectors: wealthier than the rest (Read 19:1-10.)
In the story of Zacchaeus restitution is made; if he has extorted money from anyone he will repay fourfold (19:1-10). In his new life style, the chief tax collector who worked directly for the Romans, of his own accord, gives up half of his goods to the poor and restores fourfold to those he has cheated in his tax business. Rabbinic law only encouraged the giving of twenty percent (Lev. 6:5; Num. 5:6-7). Zacchaeus goes beyond the call of duty, but he still retains a fair proportion of his wealth. (S B) **(23)** Zacchaeus assumes the harsher double penalty the Mosaic law imposed upon rustlers (Ex. 22:1). Zacchaeus' encounter with Jesus has led him to change the way in which he handles money and rather than take advantage of people, he now serves them. Zacchaeus is an example of a rich man who went through the eye of a needle (18:24) and of someone who handled money generously (16:9-13). In his transformed life style, Zacchaeus is an example of how to handle money generously (16:9-13) and of Jesus eating with someone who had ill-gotten gains which made a person a "partner in the crime." Social ostracism was used as a deterrent at this time. [See pp. 129, 241-2, 265.]

[6] The example of the poor widow (Read 21:1-4.)
As a fitting contrast to the scribes who 'devour widows' houses' (20:47), Luke continues with Jesus in the Temple and commends the widow for her praiseworthy example in giving a very generous offering to the Temple treasury. The quantity was only two copper coins but the percentage of her giving was enormous compared with the generosity of the wealthy. Jesus is more impressed with how much we sacrifice than how much we give. The scribes (20:47) were cheating widows of their houses and estates while acting as executors of these properties. Poor defenceless widows were being ripped off by the religious-appearing scribes; the widow was being victimised for the sake of an oppressive religious system. Therefore the widow's wealth was being devoured (20:47). Thirteen trumpet shaped receptacles were placed in the forecourt of the Court of Women, used for the collecting of freewill offerings for underwriting Temple worship. Jesus would have heard an announcement as to how much was being donated. (Marshall)**(24)**

The widow walks up to the treasury and throws in two lepta (copper coins) equal to one eighth of a penny or one hundredth of a denarius. This would have been the equivalent of one hundredth of the daily wage of an average worker. It would have been

> **The point of the story is:**
> • **the meaasure of a person's giving does not involve how much one gives, but how much one keeps;**
> • **a gift is measured by the spirit in which it is given;**
> • **one's giving should be commensurate with one's means;**
> • **true giving means giving all one has. (Stein) (25)**

about six minutes work. One lepton would have been forbidden. The action of the widow is one of sacrificial giving; for the widow it was a huge personal hardship for her to make a contribution. In real terms, she gave the most, in that she gave all the living which she had (21:4). It cost her in terms of life's basics. She could have kept one lepton as a cushion but she did not. The "common person" can be more in touch with God than the "religious person." God does not look on the number of contributions we make but the way in which we make them. She gave knowing that God would care for her. Jesus laments what is happening in society; He does not praise it (21:3). This event precedes Jesus' prediction of the Temple's destruction (21:5-6). [See p. 230.]

Fitzmyer **(26)** suggests six ways in which the scribes 'devoured widows' houses' (20:47):
1. scribes accepted fees for legal aid, as though it was permitted;
2. acting as legal trustees, scribes cheated widows out of their estates;
3. using their religious and social prestige, scribes freeloaded upon widows;
4. the scribes may have mismanaged the property of widows who had dedicated themselves to Temple services.
5. scribes accepted payment for prayers.
6. scribes took possession of a property if it was impossible to pay the mortgage.

[7] Generosity and the giving of alms (Read 3:11.)
A) The proper fruit of repentance: John in his reply about the product of repentance points out to the crowd the need to help others. The fruit of repentance can be seen when,
"He who has two coats, shares with him who has none. He who has food is to do likewise." (3:11) Giving an undergarment to the person in need fits the O.T. prophet's concern for those in need especially the poor (Job 31:16-22; Is.58:7-9; Ezek.18:7-8; Mic.6:8). A spare possession is to be given to the person in need, in this case an undergarment (Gk.chiton) which was worn underneath the longer outer garment. What applies to clothing should also apply to food. [See p. 103.]

B) Sermon on the Plain: lend and expect nothing in return. "And if you lend to those from whom you hope to receive, what credit is that to you? Even sinners lend to sinners to receive as much again." (6:34-35) This verse is different from Matt. 5:42 in that Luke has "lend" while Matthew has "give" to the person who begs from you. Luke is saying that if you lend to those from whom you expect to get back, what favour does that bring you before God? Sinners make safe loans to each other. The verse refers to a lender who loans so that if a future need arises the lender can get a loan too. (Marshall)**(27)** Give without strings attached and do not say, "I'll scratch your back if you will scratch mine." If you only meet the needs of people who can meet your future needs, how are the future needs of the needy to be met, seeing they cannot pay (Deut. 15:7-11)? [See p. 250.]

C) Sermon on the Plain : God will honour generosity: "Give and it shall be given to you; good measure, pressed down, shaken together, running over, will be put into your lap. For the measure you give will be the measure you get." (6:38) God will honour generosity, while those who treat people harshly can expect their prayers to be hindered (1 Pet. 3:7-12). Jesus is using imagery from the market place for measuring corn. God is extravagant in His generosity in being neither stingy nor fair to Himself, but fills the measuring vessel to excess (6:38).

> **Give without strings attached and do not say, "I'll scratch your back if you will scratch mine." (6:33) (Marshall) (27)**

Filling up a corn vessel

First of all the seller crouches on the ground with the measure between his legs, then he fills the measure three-quarters full and gives it a good shake with a rotation movement to make the grain settle down. The measure is then filled to the top and he gives it another shake. The corn is then pressed together with both hands. Finally it is heaped into a cone, tapping it carefully to press the grains together; from time to time he bores a hole in the cone and pours a few more grains into it, until there is literally no more room for a single grain. In this way the buyer is assured of a full measure, when the container cannot hold any more. God promises to reward the disciples for their gracious acts to others. The standard one uses in relation to others, is the standard God will apply to the disciples (6:38).

D) Giving alms is a way of showing mercy. "But give for alms those things which are within; and behold, everything is clean for you." (11:41) Embrace people in need as if they were members of your own family. If God made the outside and the inside of a person, then both are important. It is the inside which is the most important (the attitude of the heart). Give sacrificial attention to inside things; those things tied to character, caring and spirituality – then cleanliness will be present and complete. In Judaism almsgiving was a sensitive religious concern and a way of showing mercy (Is. 1:10-31); it involved giving money to the poor to alleviate destitution. They should tithe but they should also be kind to their neighbour. Later in His ministry, Jesus relied upon the financial support of wealthy women (8:3).

e) Jesus warns the Pharisees not to major on minor issues. Even though the Pharisees gave a tenth of everything even of the smallest produce, they neglected justice and the love of God (11:42).

> **Later in His ministry, Jesus relied upon the financial support of wealthy women. (8:3)**

[8] General teaching on wealth in Luke's Gospel

A) Sermon on the Plain: a blessing is bestowed upon the followers of Jesus, while a woe is recorded for the rich. "Woe to you who are rich, for you have received your consolation." (6:24) A "woe" or an "alas" (Gk. ouai) is a warning of danger and the nearness of judgement. (Danker) **(28)** It should be borne in mind that the rich, like Zacchaeus and Joseph of Arimathea, are not excluded as a class because they belong to a socio-economic group but are included on the basis of their attitude. The danger of giving in to things temporal is very real and deceptive. The rich have all the consolation now that their wealth will ever bring.

B) Later in His ministry, Jesus relied upon the financial support of wealthy women (8:3). "Go sell all that you have and give to the poor." (14:33) Jesus meant that all the disciples must put Him above our family and our goods and possessions.

C) The correct attitude toward use of possessions (11:41; 16:9) [See Para (2e).]

The Pharisees had objected to Jesus not washing His hands before a meal. "But give for alms those things which are within; and behold everything is clean for you." Alms were the giving of money or food to feed the poor in the O.T. (Is. 1:10-31). Give sacrificially to inside things i.e. those things which are linked to character, caring and spirituality. The attitude of the heart (the inside) is most important. God made both the inside and the outside of the cup.

Why does Jesus regard the wealthy (those who have possessions) [Gk. hoi ta chremata echontes] as dangerous even if wealth is not evil of itself? (18:24) Jesus warns that no one can serve both God and mammon (Heb. mamonas) meaning that in which one puts trust (16:13). The rule of wealth is seen in theft, exploitation, hoarding, consumption and disregard for the outsiders and people of low status and need. Luke's presentation intersects with Josephus' view of the Essenes who despised riches, and practised sharing their goods in the community so that no one suffered from poverty. (Josephus) **(29)** Their view of wealth led to a social solidarity. The disciple should use money not selfishly but generously and faithfully so that a person may possess all the future riches God has for the disciple.

> **"Go sell all that you have and give to the poor." (14:33) Jesus meant that all the disciples must put Him above our family and our goods and possessions.**

Why do would-be disciples have to give up everything? (14:33) "So therefore, whoever of you does not renounce all that he has (Gk.pasi everything) cannot be my disciple." Luke adds "everything" while Mark 10:21 says, "Go sell what you have and give to the poor." Is it a universal must for all disciples? Jesus meant that all the disciples must put Him above their family, goods and possessions.

D) Is there a contradiction in Luke between having possessions and being a disciple? Having possessions and being a disciple are not contradictions; Joseph of Arimathea was a "rich man and a disciple of Jesus." (Matt.27:57) Zacchaeus gave half of his possessions to the poor (19:8). The husband of Joanna, one of the women who followed Jesus and provided for Him and for the disciples, was a steward in the Herod's household (8:3). It is not how little one can give that is the issue but how much God deserves. Putting God above family, bearing one's cross and leaving all are issues that threaten discipleship but are not requirement issues for entrance into the kingdom. Wealth is a temptation to prestige and security and is therefore suspect. In the parable of the rich fool, Jesus says, "Do not be anxious about your life, what you shall eat, nor your body what you shall put on (12:22)." Jesus taught the disciples to renounce all personal possessions (12:33; 14:33). The followers of Jesus are not to accumulate or hoard riches for themselves (12:21).

> **When giving one is not to expect anything in return. The disciples have to give freely. Give not expecting anything in return (6:27, 36).**

[9] The culture of the times

Economic sharing was closely related to social relations. To share and to expect a return was to treat a person as a member of your family: to refuse to share was to treat them as outside the community. When the rich ruler refused to sell all, he was making an economic plus a social decision (18:18-23). In deciding to hold onto his wealth, he distanced himself from the needy. Jesus came to "lift up the lowly" and to "fill the hungry with good things." (1:52-53) The Pharisees and Scribes are reprimanded for not sharing and for acts of greed and wickedness (11:39-41). The rich man, in the parable of the rich man and Lazarus, finds himself in Hades (16:19-32).

A) Sermon on the Plain

When giving one is not to expect anything in return (6:27-36). A patron has a commodity which a client requires, in exchange the client provides expressions of honour and loyalty to the patron. The client is under obligation of debt to the patron. This situation has all the potential for exploitation and exercise of control and powers of coercion. The disciples have to give freely, "Give not expecting anything in return." (6:27, 36)

To forgive debts is to treat one another as kin, giving freely and not holding over each other obligations for praise and esteem. Luke's teaching on wealth is interwoven into a broader picture than talk of money and treasure which it might seem at first glance but it goes deeper. It is geared to issues like status, power and social privileges. The way of discipleship raises the issue of possessions. Luke is calling for forms of distribution where the needy are cared for and the wealthy give without expectation of return. Riches can keep one from God's kingdom. Luke emphasises that the possessions of wealth tend to lead to arrogance and self-sufficiency and hence the warning, "Woe to you that are rich, for you have received your consolation (RSV) already received your comfort (NIV)." (6:24) The rich have all the consolation that their wealth can bring. At best it may last all their lifetime but for some it may be shorter than expected as the rich fool discovered. Riches are one of the primary reasons for the choking of God's word as in the parable of the seed sown among the thorns. They are choked by the cares and pleasures of life (8:14).

Pupil's Activity: One

a) Identify and examine the teaching of Jesus concerning wealth in Luke's Gospel.
(Edexcel A/S) (2002/2004)   [7 marks]
b) Why was Jesus' teaching on wealth so controversial at that time?
(Edexcel A/S) (2005)   [6 marks]

Pupil's Activity: Two

a) Identify and examine three people/groups of people who exemplify good practice regarding their attitude to the poor and needy.
b) Why are Zacchaeus and Joseph of Arimathea examples of rich people who went through the eye of needle?

(Figure 1) B) Summary of Jesus' teaching on wealth and possessions in Luke's Gospel

	Incidents relating to wealth	First-century Jewish attitude to wealth	Jesus' attitude to wealth
1	Inheritance (12:14)	a) One of the crowd wanted Jesus to act as an advocate not arbitrate in a family dispute over inheritance. "Teacher, bid (tell) my brother (to) divide the inheritance with me." (Num. 27:1-11; 36:5-9; Deut.21:15-17) b) We do not know if the man wanted to take his share of the family business.	a) Jesus refused to act as judge as these issues were settled in the synagogue. "Man, who made me a judge or a divider over you?" (12:15) Why did Jesus refuse to at as aj udgein this situaation? b) Jesus warns about all kinds of greed (12:16). Greed always looks for possessions and they become a substitute idolatry.
2	Parable of the shrewd manager (16:1-13)	a) Jesus commends the shrewd manager for his wise use of money. He rebukes the Pharisees for their love of money (16:13-14).	a) "You cannot serve God and mammon (trusting in wealth)."(16:13) What does this expression mean?
3	Parable of the rich man and Lazarus (16:19-35)	a) The rabbis viewed Lazarus' life as no life, depending on food from another, being ruled by one's wife and having a body covered by sores (g. Besa [Yom Tob] 32b). b) Lazarus is doubly deprived.	a) In the O.T. God's people are to care for the stranger, the fatherless and the widow, even harvest for them. b) To love God is to show compassion to humanity. c)What does treasure iinvested for God produce? d) What does treasure invested for self produce?
4	The rich ruler (18:18-30)	a) The Jews regarded wealth as an automatic sign of blessing from God for faithfulness (Dt. 8:1-10; Prov. 26:1-19). b) The O.T. did teach that wealth was not automatic. 'Better to be poor and to walk in integrity.' (Prov. 28:6; 30:7-9)	a) What does Jesus promise the disciples in this life and in the next (18:29-30)?
5	Zacchaeus (19:1-11)	a) Rabbinic law encouraged the giving of 20% by way of restitution (Lev.6:5; Num.5:6-7). Zacchaeus gave away half of his goods to the poor and fourfold if he had cheated anyone. b) He gave away more than O.T. law demanded: what was required for theft with killing or selling an animal (Ex.22:1; 2 Sam.12:6).	a) Why is Zacchaeus an example of a an 'eye of a needle' Christian.? b) Why is he not required to give up all his wealth? c) Zacchaeus sees the error of his way and repents of materialism, dishonesty and greed.
6	Parable of the pounds (19:11-27)	a) The people think that the idea of a bonus is unfair as the most faithful received eleven pounds. There is no justice if the poor become destitute (19:25).	a) The faithful are to invest their wealth and make more money but all the money is to be given back to the master for His use. b) There is a time of stewardship between the present time and the end.
7	The poor widow who gave two copper coins into the Temple treasury for Temple worship (21:1-4).	a) The Scribes 'devoured widows' houses (20:47a). b) They cheated widows out of their estates and houses while they acted as executors of these properties. c) The amount people paid into the treasury would have been announced in public!	a) Jesus commends her for her generous giving. "She has given out of her poverty."(21:3) Jesus is more concerned about sacrificial giving. b) He laments over what is happening in society. The scribes will receive the greater condemnation (20:47).
8	Almsgiving (3:11): generosity (6:34-5); showing mercy (6:38)	a) The Essenes despised wealth unlike the Pharisees who were lovers of money (16:14). b) In Judaism, almsgiving was a way of showing mercy: giving money to the poor (Is.1:10-31).	a) God honours generosity. b) Lend and expect nothing back in return. Give without strings attached (Deut.15:7-11).
9	Hospitality : the parable of the great banquet (14:12-24)	a) The poor, crippled, lame and blind were not allowed into the Temple and the Qumran community: they were banned from full participation in Jewish worship (Lev 12:17-23). b) The Jews believed there would be repayment at the resurrection of the just (2 Macc.7:9).	a) When you give a dinner do not invite your friends, lest they invite you in return but rather invite the poor, crippled, lame, and blind. b) Invite the needy who cannot reciprocate the invitation. c) In the parable, Jesus invites the poor to the Banquet. He taught eschatological reversal which is an O.T. concept (1:52-3; 6:21; 10:15; 18:14; Ezek.3:19-23; Sirach 3:19-23).

Pupil's Activity: Three
a) Identify and examine the teaching of Jesus concerning wealth in Luke's Gospel.

Pupil's Activity: Four
a) What does Luke's Gospel teach about Jesus' attitude to the rich?
b) Identify and consider two stories (unique to Luke's Gospel) which tell us about foolish rich men.

Pupil's Activity: Five   Revision
Complete the comment and answer section in **Figure 2.**

(Figure 2) C) Summary of Jesus' teaching on wealth and possessions in Luke's Gospel

	Ref.	Event or parable	Comment and answer
1	6:24	"Woe to you that are rich, for you have received your consolation (Gk. paraklesin)." In Luke consolation is usually a positive word but not in this context.	What does Jesus say about riches now? (James 1:9-11) In what way is their consolation the trophy of a loser-an empty bag? The world's values are in reverse here.
2	11:39-43	Jesus dines in the house of a Pharisee.	Of what does Jesus accuse the Pharisees?
3	12:13-21	Parable of the rich fool	What mistakes did the rich fool make about wealth?
4	12:32-34	"Sell your possessions, and give alms; provide yourselves with purses that do not grow old, with a treasure in the heavens which does not fail, where no thief approaches and no moth destroys."	How do possessions hinder the disciples' walk with God? What should believers concentrate upon (12:31)?
5	14:15-24	"Whoever of you does not renounce all that he has cannot be my disciple."	What does it mean to renounce all possessions?
6	16:1-9	The unjust manager / the shrewd manager	What was Jesus teaching about wealth in this parable?
7	16:19-35	The Rich man and Lazarus	What does Jesus teach about the use and misuse of money and possessions?
8	18:18-30	The Rich Ruler	Why is wealth a hindrance to entering the kingdom of God?
9	19:1-10	Zacchaeus	How did Zacchaeus' restitution show that he had entered God's kingdom?

Pupil's Activity: Six
a) Outline Jesus' teaching on wealth in Luke's Gospel. (Edexcel A/S 2004)   [14 marks]
b) To what extent do the teachings differ from Jewish teaching? (Edexcel A/S 2004)   [6 marks]
c) Why were the teachings of Jesus concerning wealth and outcasts so controversial at that time?
(Edexcel A/S 2005)   [6 marks]

Pupil's Activity: Seven
a) Discuss Jesus' teaching in the Sermon on the Plain. **(**CCEA A/2 2004)   [30 marks]
b) Discuss the main teaching of Jesus in the Sermon on the Plain. [See Ch.18: Forgivness.]
(CCEA A/2 2005)   [30 marks]
c) Critically evaluate the claim that this sermon challenges the followers of Jesus.
(CCEA A/2 2005)   [15 marks]

(Figure 3) A comparison between Jesus' teaching on wealth and stewardship in Luke's Gospel

18:18-30	19:1-10	19:11-27
The rich ruler	Zacchaeus	Parable of the Pounds
A quest or recognition story	Jesus' quest for the lost (Bock)**(30)** – the rich man who gets through the eye of a needle (Tiede) **(31)**	This is a parable with a saying tied to it (19:26). (Fitzmyer) **(32)** "To everyone who has more will be given; but from him who has not, even what he has will be taken from him. A reward for faithfulness will be given for those who really know and love the king."
"Sell all that you have and distribute to the poor and you will have treasure in heaven." (18:22)	"The half of my goods I give to the poor, but if I have defrauded any one of anything, I will restore it fourfold." (19:8)	"Why then did you not put my money into the bank, and at my coming I should have collected it with interest?" (19:23)

Pupil's Activity: Eight
What do these statements in Luke's Gospel teach about wealth and stewardship?

Outcomes

Students should be able to identify, examine (Edexcel A/S) know and understand (CCEA A/S):
• **Jesus' teaching on wealth and stewardship in Luke's Gospel. (Edexcel A/S)**
• **stories and sayings unique to Luke which tell us about foolish rich people.**
• **key concepts, for example 'eye of a needle Christians', 'the poor', alms giving, tithing, 'the nawim', the widow's mite, a lepta, the 'fool', the difference between wealth and money.**
• **the parables which are unique to Luke and have wealth and possessions as their theme. [See Ch.12.]**
• **how Jesus' teaching on wealth differed from that of the Jews. (Edexcel A/S)**
• **Jesus' teaching on wealth and poverty as a characteristic of Luke's Gospel. (CCEA A/S)**
• **why Jesus' attitude to wealth was so controversial at that time? (Edexcel A/S)**
Students should be able to discuss and critically examine:
• **why Jesus was opposed to the Pharisees' attitude to wealth. (Edexcel A/2)**
Students should be able to discuss and critically assess aspects of the Sermon on the Plain which exemplify Jesus' teaching on wealth. (CCEA A/2)

Notes on Ch.17: Wealth

1. Oxford Compact English Dictionary (2000).
2. John Stott, Issues facing Christians today, Marshalls, (1984) pp. 216-220.
3. Howard Marshall, (c) N.T. Theology, Apollos, (2004) p.144.
4. Charles H. Talbert, Reading Luke, New York: (1982) p. 70.
5. Robet H. Stein, op. cit. p. 52.
6. Joel Green, op. cit. p.103.
7. Frederick D. Bruner, The Christbook: Matthew 1-12, Waco: Word, (1987) p.135.
8. Craig L. Blomberg, Neither Poverty nor Riches-a biblical theology of possessions, Apollos, (2003) p.129.
9. Craig L. Blomberg, op. cit. p.126.
10. David Sheppard, Bias to the Poor, Hodder and Stoughton, (1983) p.16.
11. David J. Bosch, Transforming Missions, Orbis, (1991) p.99.
12. I. Howard Marshall, (c) N.T. Theology, Apollos, IVP, (2005) p.144.
13. Joel Green, op. cit. p.211.
14. W.E. Pilgrim, Good News to the Poor: Wealth and Poverty in Luke–Acts , Augsburg: Minneapolis (1981) p.112.
15. I Howard Marshall, (a) op. cit. p. 621.
16. I Howard Marshall, (a) op. cit. p. 584.
17. Joseph A. Fitzmyer, op. cit. p. 1109.
18. Josephus, Antiquities, op. cit. 17.8. 1 §188 background.
19. Darrell L. Bock, op. cit. p. 1486.
20. Charles H. Talbert, op. cit. p.173.
21. Charles H. Talbert, op. cit. p.172.
22. Robert C. Tannehill, the Narrative Critic, op. cit. pp. 111-27.
23. H. Strack and P. Billerbeck, KZNT on the Talmud and Midrash (1922-61) 4:546-47.
24. I. Howard Marshall, (a) op. cit. p.751 follows SBK 23-45.
25. Robert H. Stein, op. cit. p. 508.
26. Joseph A. Fitzmyer, op. cit. p.1318.
27. I. Howard Marshall, (a) op. cit. p. 263.
28. F.W. Danker, op. cit. p. 142.
29. Josephus, Jewish Wars, op. cit 2.8.3 §§ 122-23.
30. Darrell L. Bock, op. cit. p. 1513.
31. D.L. Tiede, op. cit. p. 319.
32. Joseph A. Fitzmyer, op. cit. p.1232.

CCEA A/S + Sermon on the Plain Edexcel A/S + Forgiveness in the Sermon on the Plain CCEA A/2

> "Luke puts greater stress on repentance than any other Gospel writer." Lunde (4)

Targets:
- **Recognise the importance of forgiveness in Jesus' teaching in Luke's Gospel.**
- **Identify incidents in Luke's Gospel which generally relate to forgiveness. (CCEA A/S)**
- **Recognise Jesus' specific teaching on the nature of forgiveness specifically in at least two parables in Luke's Gospel and in the Passion Narrative. (CCEA A/S + Edexcel A/S)**
- **Recognise the nature of repentance in the teaching of John the Baptist. (Edexcel A/S)**
- **Identify key concepts relating to forgiveness in Luke's Gospel e.g. repentance and faith, sinners, 'release', cancelling or forgiving a debt, pardon, cleanse, sin, iniquity and transgression.**
- **Recognise the controversial nature of Jesus' teaching on forgiveness at that time.**
- **Identify the main teachings on forgiveness in the Sermon on the Plain. (CCEA A/2)**
- **Identify parables in Luke's Gospel in which Jesus is seen as a compassionate teacher. (CCEA A/S)**

Forgiveness in Luke's Gospel

Introduction

The Oxford Dictionary defines forgiveness as, "stop feeling angry or resentful towards someone for an offence or mistake." This definition sees forgiveness purely on a human level and does not include divine forgiveness. Forgiveness in Luke's Gospel deals with God's forgiveness of people and people's forgiveness of each other as set out in Jesus' teaching and that of John the Baptist. Outstanding among the blessings brought by Jesus is the forgiveness of sins hinted at in Jesus' first sermon in Nazareth, "preaching good news to the poor and proclaiming release (Gk. aphesin) to the captives and recovering of sight to the blind, to set at liberty those who are oppressed (Gk. en aphesei)." (4:18) (Marshall) **(1)**

[1] Forgiveness in the O.T.

A) The O.T. has three words for wrong doing:
1) Transgressions, David said "blot out my transgressions". The Heb. word "pesha" means wilful rebellion against their king (19:4; 1Kgs. 12:9) and "blot out" means wipe away like writing a book (Ps.51:1).
2) Sin, David said "cleanse me from my sin!". The Heb. word "chattath" means missing the mark (Ps.51:2b).
3) Iniquities, David said "wash me thoroughly from my iniquity!" The word "wash" means laundering clothes; the Hebrew word "avon" means "perversity," "crooked." (Ps.51:2b).

B) The O.T. has three corresponding words for forgiveness:
1) The Hebrew word "nasa" means "to lift up a burden" or "remove a burden." "You [God] forgave the guilt of my sin." (Ps. 32:5)
2) The Hebrew word "salach" means "to cancel a debt," "send away," "let go" as in "Bless the Lord, O my soul, and forget not all His benefits who forgives all your iniquity." (Ps.103:3) This word corresponds to the N.T. word "aphesin" meaning "release from sin."
3) The Hebrew word "kaphar" means "to cover an ugly sight." "Yet He [God] being compassionate, forgave their iniquity (Ps.78:38)." These words were all used for the removal of sin and forgiveness.

C) Another key word linked to forgiveness is repentance. In the O.T. the Hebrew word "shuv" meant people "turning" from their sins, a very dramatic change of action, a "U" turn (1 Kgs. 8:35) or God turning from His anger against His people (Ex.32:12; Josh.7:6). The corresponding Greek words for this in the LXX are "epistrepho" and "metanoeo". The most common N.T. word for repentance is metanoia which meant a change of mind and thought. "Metanoia" corresponded to the Hebrew word "niham" to relent from ones' actions and be sorry. (Butterworth) **(2)** "The Lord repented concerning this." (Amos 7:3,6) "Have pity on your servant." (Ps.90:13) The Gk. word "Metanoia" refers to an **inward change** which takes place in the mind and heart of the sinner (3:18; Rom 2:4; 2 Pet. 3:9) whereas Gk. "epistrepho" means the **outward change** in the sinner's action as in Zacchaeus making restitution for his sins (19:8; 1:16; 1 Thess. 1:9). (Ryken) **(3)**

> "Metanoia" refers to an inward change which takes place in the mind and heart of the sinner (Rom 2:4; 2 Pet. 3:9) whereas "epistrepho" means the outward change in the sinner's action as in Zacchaeus making restitution for his sins (19:8; 1:16; 1 Thess. 1:9) (Ryken). (3)

[2] Forgiveness in the N.T.

A) A key word for forgiveness in the N.T. is the Greek word "aphesis" which in Luke always refers to forgiveness of sins. It can mean "to let go, loose, set free, acquit, dismiss and remit." By forgiving a person we set the other person free in removing the burden of our enmity. John the Baptist preached a baptism of repentance for the forgiveness (Gk.aphesin) of sins. "Aphesin" compares with the O.T. word "kaphar"; it is the most common word in Luke's Gospel for forgiveness and is used twelve times. Jesus' healings restore people into the community and gives them a status (4:18-19). Peter's mother-in-law serves people (4:39). The leper proves to the community that he has been healed (5:14). [p. 266.]

B) "Luke puts greater stress on repentance than any other Gospel writer." (Lunde) **(4)** "Repentance" is used for anything which hinders a wholehearted trust in God (18:18-30). It means acknowledging one's sinfulness as well as adopting a new life style and a new behaviour to others (3:8,10-14). John the Baptist uses words like "smooth" and "straight" to describe people who have undergone repentance. "The crooked shall be made straight, and the rough places shall be made smooth" means that if the people repent they will be made straight (3:5).

> **Forgiveness through Jesus is a characteristic blessing of salvation which Jesus offered during His earthly ministry.**

C) Another word closely linked to forgiveness is "sinners". Luke has the most extensive references to "sinners". (Wilkins) **(5)** He uses the expression "sinners" ten times, eight of which are unique to his Gospel. Faith is also closely correlated with forgiveness. To the woman He said, "Your faith has saved you; go in peace."

References to the word "sinners" in Luke's Gospel (L) (Figure 1)

	Biblical Text where the word "sinners" or sinful is used	Refs.
1	In the miracle of the miraculous catch of fish, Peter's recognises his sin and is overwhelmed by his unworthiness. He confesses Jesus as Lord and says, "Depart from me, for I am a sinful (Gk. hamartolos) man, O Lord."	5:8
2	In the Sermon on the Plain Jesus said, "If you love those who love you, what credit is that to you? For even sinners love those who love them. And if you do good to those who do good to you, what credit is that to you? For even sinners do the same. And if you lend to those from whom you hope to receive, what credit is that to you? Even sinners lend to sinners, to receive as much again. But love your enemies, and do good, and lend, expecting nothing in return; and your reward will be great and you will be sons of the Most High. For even sinners love those who love them."	6:32, 33, 34
3	Luke starts his account of the anointing of Jesus by the sinful woman in the house of Simon, the Pharisee, by saying, "Behold a woman of the city who was a sinner."	7:37
4	After the incident of the Galilean martyrs Jesus said, "Do you think that these Galileans were worse sinners than all the other Galileans because they suffered thus?"	13:2
5	In the parables on "lostness" Jesus says, "There will be joy in heaven over one sinner who repents."	15:1-31
6	In the parable of the Pharisee and the tax collector, the tax collector says, "God be merciful to me a sinner."	18:13
7	At the call of Zacchaeus, they [the crowd] all murmured, "He has gone to be the guest of a man who is a sinner."	19:7
8	The angels' testimony to the women at the empty tomb was, "The Son of Man must be delivered into the hands of sinful men."	24:7

Incidents in all three Synoptics, relating to "sinners" and "sins" (Figure 2)

	Common texts in the Synoptics	Luke	Mark	Matthew
1	In all three Synoptics, the Scribes and Pharisees murmured, "Why do you eat with tax collectors and sinners?"	5:30,32	2:15,16	9:10,11,13
2	"Behold a glutton and drunkard, a friend of tax collectors and sinners."	7:34		11:19
3	"Forgive us our sins as we forgive everyone who are indebted to us."	11:4		6:12

[3] Divine Forgiveness

At the heart of the gospel is Divine forgiveness which Jesus imparted to sinful men and women. Forgiveness through Jesus is a characteristic blessing of salvation which He offered during His earthly ministry.

Examples of Divine forgiveness in Luke's Gospel

A) Jesus has the Divine authority to forgive sins. In the healing of the paralysed man, He said, "Your sins have been forgiven." (5:23) This was Jesus' first controversy with the Pharisees and it concerned His power and authority to forgive sins (5:17-26). The fact that the paralysed man continued in this state of forgiveness is seen in the fact that Jesus uses the third person plural perfect indicative passive (Gk. apheontai) to forgive or pardon which shows that the paralysed man entered into a state of forgiveness there and then (5:20). "Man, your sins are forgiven (Gk. apheontai) you;" (RSV) (meaning have been forgiven) or "God forgives you." (Nolland) **(6)** [See p. 187.]

It can mean the continuing state of forgiveness. (Stein) **(7)** Later the present active infinitive "aphienai" is used to denote continuous forgiveness, "The Son of Man has authority on earth to forgive sins" (to continuously forgive sins) (5:24).

B) Another example of God's forgiveness and Jesus' concern for the social outcast is seen in the call of Levi the tax collector to be a disciple and Jesus' subsequent dining in Levi's house with his friends (5:27-32). This is the second conflict story over Jesus' association with tax collectors and sinners and is a call to repentance for sinners. Rejoicing and celebration are evidence of repentance here (5:27-29). Only Luke uses this expression "sinners to repentance" here (5:32). This is a common expression in Luke. Jesus says that His mission is for sinners rather than the righteous, for it is the sinners who can repent. The Pharisees are not open to their need of repentance. [See p. 217.]

C) The parable of the two debtors is the first parable Jesus taught about forgiveness (7:41-50). [See p. 157.] **The context of the parable:** the incident of the sinful woman who was forgiven by Jesus in the house of Simon the Pharisee. Greater forgiveness provides opportunity for great love. Jesus pursues sinners and welcomes them and forgives the sinful woman's many sins, He makes Himself equal with God. He challenges the Pharisees' idea of a minimalist view of sin. Simon the Pharisee saw himself as a little sinner (7:47b). "He who is forgiven little loves little." Jesus showed both His concern for the outcast and the offer of salvation to everyone (7:36-50). "Her sins which are many, are forgiven (Gk.apheontai), for she loved much; but he who is forgiven (Gk.aphietai) little, loves little. He said to her, "Your sins are forgiven" (RSV) (Gk.apheontai), perfect tense (NRSV and NIV) is preferable, "Her many sins, have been forgiven." (7:47) Jesus ministers to people who are sensitive about their sin (7:48). [See pp. 165-6.]

> **Forgive here can also means release from the power of sin (7:47-49).**

"**Forgive**" here can also mean release from the power of sin (7:47-49). This event shows Jesus' love for sinners, His association with them and His power and right to forgive sin. Sinners know that Jesus can be approached. Great forgiveness leads to great love. Her actions show the evidence of the great forgiveness which she had received. Faith is the basis for forgiveness and salvation. In anointing His feet with the ointment, her actions provide evidence of her faith, which brought about her forgiveness. The tears of the sinful woman who wept and wet Jesus' feet could have been tears of repentance for sin or joy over the forgiveness of her sin (7:38). (Stein)**(8)** Sinners know God will respond when they turn to Him in humility (7:38). The moneylender forgives and cancels the debt rather than force the debtors to pay up. It is completely out of the blue and totally unexpected. In the parable both debtors were forgiven (Gk.echarisato). Jesus does not look on the woman's past sins but what she could be through the love of God (7:42). [See p. 235.]

"**Forgive**" can also mean the cancellation of a debt. The Greek word charizomai is used here for forgiving a debt as in a business transaction of cancelling a mortgage or paying a debt on a car. It has the idea of a free offer of God's grace and is completely unmerited. Luke also uses this word in his summary of Jesus' miracles which John the Baptist would have heard about. Luke says that "Jesus bestowed sight (Gk.echarisato) on many who were blind," the free exercise of God's power. It means literally that Jesus graced many with sight (7:21). Her many sins shows that Jesus knew about her sins all along (7:47). Simon the Pharisee is the person who has loved so little and has little need of forgiveness. There are three elements of forgiveness here:

1) God's offer of forgiveness (as in the parable) (7:42);

2) the receiving of forgiveness by the woman, and (7:47);

> **The starting point of God's forgiveness was not the actions of the woman but her faith (7:47).**

3) God confirms that forgiveness has been received (as in the parable) (7:48). The point of the story is clear; God offers forgiveness to deal with sin. Those who receive forgiveness realise how much God has done for them and respond with deeds of love. The Pharisee who is "forgiven little" needs to see God's work as more significant and then make a proper response. His little sin still needed to be dealt with (5:31-32). The reaction of the Pharisees expresses Jesus' action for forgiveness [Gk. present tense "aphiesen"] to show that Jesus continued to show forgiveness. "Who is this, who even forgives sins [continues to forgive sins]?" (7:49) The starting point of God's forgiveness was not the actions of the woman but her faith. Faith is the key to forgiveness of sins and is closely tied to it. She departs with a sense of God's presence. "For she loved much." (7:47) Her act of love shows her the realization of forgiveness and her faith is the basis of her forgiveness and not her love. Another possible way of seeing this is to say, "the great love she has shown proves that her many sins have been forgiven." (7:47) (TEV) Jesus affirms the woman as a person recognising her true potential.

Pupil's Activity: One

a) From your understanding of Luke 7:36-50 why does Jesus associate with sinners?

b) What does this passage teach about forgiveness?

> **Three elements of forgiveness in 7:36-50:**
> • **God's offer of forgiveness as in the parable (7:41-43),**
> • **the sinful woman receives forgiveness (7:47, 49),**
> • **God confirms that forgiveness has been received as in the parable (7:41-43, 48).**

D) The way of escape into God's gracious arms comes in John the Baptist's call to realise one's need for God's forgiveness and in the need for baptism by John (7:18-35; 7:49). The Pharisees and lawyers did not see their need of John's baptism for the forgiveness of sins and they rejected God's purpose for themselves (8:30).

E) The three parables in Luke 15, the lost sheep, the lost coin and the lost son all emphasise God's mercy and forgiveness; it is Jesus' mission to seek and to save the lost (19:10). Jesus is despised by the Pharisees as the "friend of sinners". (15:2)

F) In the parable of the lost sheep, the shepherd rejoices when he finds the sheep which was heedlessly lost or lost by folly. Jesus says that heaven throws a party when a sinner returns; God rejoices when the lost sheep returns (15:7).

G) In the parable of the helplessly lost coin, Jesus shows that it requires a lot of effort to recover a sinner but it is well worthwhile. When the coin is found, the woman gathers together her lady friends and neighbours to celebrate. In the same way there is rejoicing in heaven over one repentant sinner. Heaven is full of praise when a sinner turns to God. In these three parables repentance is characterised by rejoicing and celebration while mourning and regret are aspects of rejection. The repentant tax collector says, "God, be merciful to me a sinner." (18:13-14)

H) The parable of the prodigal son/the forgiving father (15:11-32), shows God's search for people who are wilfully lost. While this parable does not use the word forgiveness, the theme is that of God's pardon for sinners. The Pharisees had a wrong view of God thinking that God would not forgive sinners. They objected that Jesus was more in the company of the common people than in their company. Jesus is correcting their wrong interpretation of Deut. 21:15-22:4 which was intended as a principle for a legal court. (The elders in Israel had the right to stone a stubborn, drunken and rebellious son.) Those who see themselves as more upright should not resent those who are "unworthy" of God's grace.

The father shows the extent of his love by running in an undignified way and throwing a party rather than requiring forgiveness. In the case of the prodigal son, it is God's grace for the repentant sinner which is uppermost. "Father, I have sinned against heaven and before you; I am no longer worthy to be called your son; treat me as one of your hired servants." (15:18) Here the prodigal son represents the tax collectors and sinners and the older son, the Pharisees and Scribes, who were critical of Jesus.

> In the parable of the lost sheep, the shepherd rejoices when he finds the sheep which was heedlessly lost or lost by folly. Jesus says that heaven throws a party when a sinner returns. God rejoices when the lost sheep returns (15:7).

I) Summary of the parables of the lost in Luke's Gospel (Read 15:1-32) [See pp. 166-7.]

First-century background: Jesus shows His concern for the social outcasts of His day. The tax collectors were marginalised because their work for the Roman army of occupation was thought to be dishonest, immoral and practised distortion. The Pharisees regarded the tax collectors as "sinners". The NIV uses special speech marks to show the way the Pharisees viewed them. In the O.T. God's people do not associate with sinners. "Sinners will not stand in the assembly of the rightous." (Ps.1:5) The Pharisees went beyond this by saying, "Do not welcome them and do not eat with them." The Pharisees had forgotten (Deut. 10:19), "You are to love the alien because you yourselves were alien in Egypt." [See p. 270.]

1] The lost sheep (15:1-7)

• The return of sinners to God should be a cause for joy to the religious leaders.

• Jesus says He is acting as God's representative.

• God takes the initiative in searching for the lost sheep. Some rabbis were unwilling to seek Gentile converts, while others were aggressive proselytisers (Matt. 23:15): they did not have a compassion for the lost.

• The emphasis is on the rejoicing in the rescue of the sheep (15:6).

• Jesus' seeking and receiving sinners is pleasing to God.

• Heaven rejoices (God rejoices) when a sinner returns. Jesus welcomes sinners (15:2).

2] The lost coin (15:8-10)

• The woman searches and sweeps until she finds the lost coin on the hard earthen floor (15:8).

• The extent of her joy is important in that it extends to her female kinsfolk and female neighbours (15:9).

• There is rejoicing in heaven in the presence of the angels of God, when a sinner returns (15:7).

• Sinners are welcome (15:10).

3] The lost son (15:11-32)

• God welcomes back repentant sinners.

• The Father (God) remains constant in His love (15:2).

• To come to one's senses in (17:12) is a Semitic expression for repentance.

• The Father represents God. The son says 'I have sinned against heaven' means I have sinned against God. The Father portrays the characteristics of God; the Father's compassion is uppermost (15:17-20).

• The son knew that he had no right to return as a son since he had squandered his money and he planned to earn his keep (15:19).

• "Dead", "alive", "lost" and "found" are words which would apply to one's state before conversion to Christ (Eph.2:1-5).

• It is a time to celebrate. We had (Gk. edei) to celebrate means "it was necessary" and urgent to celebrate (15:32).

• The elder brother like the Pharisees cannot understand the meaning of forgiveness.

• God is willing to receive "sinners" and rejoices when they return (15:24,32).

All three parables presuppose joyous feasting with returned prodigals. The celebration of the fatted calf (15:22-25) in the parable of the prodigal son, is a very Jewish, first-century, Galilean practice. (Young) **(9)**

J) Is there a sin which God does not forgive: blasphemy against the Holy Spirit? (Read 12:10.)
Jesus indicated that there was a limit to the forgiveness of God; blasphemy of the Spirit would not be forgiven but blasphemy of the Son of Man would be forgiven. This is a persistent and decisive rejection of the Spirit's work concerning Jesus. It is the totality of the person's response to the Spirit and not a momentary one. Blasphemy of the Son is an instant rejection (22:65; 23:39) and blasphemy against the Spirit is a permanent decision of rejection (Acts 7:51; 13:40-49; 28: 23-28). (Bock)**(10)** It involves a continual and wilful rejection of the truth.

> In Jesus' first sermon in the synagogue in Nazareth (4:18) there is a double use of the term forgiveness, "to proclaim release (Gk. aphasin) to the captives", (4:18b) and "to set at liberty those who are oppressed." (Gk. en aphensei) (4:18e)

[4] "Forgiveness" meaning release from sins

In Jesus' first sermon in the synagogue in Nazareth (4:18) there is a double use of the term forgiveness, "to proclaim release (Gk.aphasin) to the captives," (4:18b) and "to set at liberty those who are oppressed (Gk. en aphesei)." (4:18e) Jesus is the Saviour who forgives sin or who releases people. By forgiving we set the other person free. Jesus' release ministry is the opposite of the binding power of the demonic forces.

A) Peter as a sinner is overwhelmed by grace; he is a self-confessed sinner. When called and commissioned by Jesus Peter said, "Depart from me, for I am a sinful man, O Lord." Peter was released from his sins. He was filled with a sense of unworthiness as he faced the might and power of Jesus (5:8).

B) To the healed leper Jesus said, "Go to the priest and offer for your cleansing, as Moses commanded." (5:13-14) This ritual lasted a week and portrayed the cleansing and removal of sin and could have been a testimony to Messianic times. "Tell John what you have seen and heard, the lepers are cleansed." (7:22)

C) When Jesus went to feast in the house of Levi the tax collector, where He was accused of eating and drinking with publicans and sinners, He replied, "I have not come to call the righteous but sinners to repentance." (5:30-32)

D) To the paralysed man Jesus said, "Man, your sins are forgiven (Gk. apheontai) you." (5:20) "Who can forgive (Gk. aphienai) sins but God only?" (5:21) "Your sins are forgiven (Gk.apheontai) you." (5:23) "The Son of Man has authority on earth to forgive (Gk.aphienai) sins." (5:24) Did some in the audience see paralysis as the product of sin? (1 Macc. 9: 55; 2 Macc. 3:22-28) Healing here is seen as the restoration of a relationship with God and His people: this is forgiveness. Jesus opens up the boundaries which leads to spiritual and social retoration of these outcasts.

E) To Simon the Pharisee He said, "he who is forgiven little loves little." (7:47) To the woman taken in sin He said, "Your sins are forgiven you." (7:48) "Who is this that forgives sins?" (7:49) [See 3 above: Divine forgiveness.]

F) In the disciples' prayer Jesus said, "When you pray, say: Father, hallowed be Your name." (11:2) "And forgive us our sins." (11:4)

> Tax collectors can be forgiven; sinful Jews are not beyond the reach of God's mercy, which is like the shepherd seeking out the lost and bringing them back (15:3-7; Ezek.34 :16).

G) "He who blasphemes against the Holy Spirit will not be forgiven." (12:10) [See pp. 51, 54.]

H) Jesus tells Zacchaeus that He had come to forgive sin and he (Zacchaeus) is like the prodigal, the lost sheep, coin and son (19:10). Zacchaeus as a Jew was every bit as entitled to salvation as the most respectable of Jewish society. Tax collectors can be forgiven; sinful Jews are not beyond the reach of God's mercy, which is like the shepherd seeking out the lost and bringing them back (15:3-7; Ezek.34:16). Zacchaeus' works reflect the true repentance to which John the Baptist referred (3:8). "Bear fruit that befits repentance." And also like the tax man whose prayer was acceptable to God because he came to God humbly and responded to His call (18:9-14). [See pp. 129, 241-2, 253, 265.]

I) The Last Supper   (Read 22:20.)
At the last supper Jesus said to the disciples, "This cup which is poured out for you is the new covenant in my blood." Even though Luke does not explicitly refer to forgiveness of sins for the many, (Matt. 26:28) he personalises the remark: it is the blood shed "for you".

> Only Luke uses this expression "sinners to repentance" here (5:32). This is a common expression in Luke. Jesus says that His mission is for sinners rather than the righteous, for it is the sinners who can repent.

J) Fulfilment of Isaiah rejected   (Read 22:37.)
Jesus predicts Peter's denial and asks the disciples if they lacked anything when they ministered without a purse bag or sandals. Then He quotes from Is. 53:12 referring to the suffering and the rejection of the Messiah, "He was numbered with the transgressors." (22:37) This could have been fulfilled through Jesus' identification with sinners in His baptism and being numbered with the two criminals on either side of Him on the cross. There is evidence that Herod had no intention of repenting and becoming a follower or changing his life style and Jesus gave him no answers even though he wanted to see Jesus do a miracle (23:8-9).

K) Peter denies Jesus (Read 22:61.) (L)
Jesus looked at Peter and he remembered the words of Jesus. Peter wept bitterly, when he heard the rooster crow. These were tears of repentance. Blomberg **(11)**; Bock **(12)** sees these as tears of remorse for his denials (22:62). Peter acknowledges his own sinfulness. (Green) **(13)** This is like the sinful woman who wept and wet Jesus' feet with her tears. Her tears could have been repentance for sin or joy over the forgiveness of her sin (7:38). (Stein) **(14)**

L) On the Cross (Read 23:34.): Jesus prayed for both Gentiles and Jews, who put Him to death, "Father, forgive (Gk. aphe) them; for they do not know what they do." Those who put Him to death are to be forgiven on the grounds that they did not know what they were doing (23:34). This saying may have a conceptual link with (Is. 53:12e) where the Servant suffers for the transgressions of His people. "Yet He bore the sins of many."

> **Forgive and you will be forgiven (6:37b-38). "Forgive us our sins as we forgive everyone who is indebted to us." (11:4)**

Pupil's Activity: Three   Class Discussion
"Is there any time night or day that roosters do not crow?" (Brown) **(15)** What is the significance of this comment?

[5] "Forgiveness" meaning the cancelling of a debt

A) Forgiveness in the disciples' prayer (Read 11:4 a-b.)
The petitioner is to ask for forgiveness because he himself is forgiving to others. The Disciples' Prayer stresses that people may ask for forgiveness only if they have forgiven those who sinned against them. "Forgive (Gk. aphes) us our sins, for we ourselves forgive (Gk. aphemin) everyone who is indebted (Gk. opheilonti) to us. "Opheilonti" are wrongs (debts) which are willingly forgiven. Whatever you ask of God, you should be prepared to do to another. A forgiven person must be forgiving. Luke interchanges the words for sin (Gk. hamartia) and debt (Gk. opheilo). Thus cancelling a debt is closely linked to forgiveness and forgiveness has come to mean cancelling a debt. [See p. 49.]
This is similar to the Sermon on the Plain where Jesus said, "Be merciful, even as your Father is merciful." (6:36) Luke has mercy where Matt. 5:46 has "perfect". The disciples are to imitate their heavenly Father. God's character is the guide for the Christian's character. Again a similar concept was in Judaism: "As our Father is merciful in heaven, so be merciful on earth." (Tg.Ps.-J, on Lev. 22:28) God has a rule of mercy.

B) [See above: Divine forgiveness, the incident of the sinful woman.] (7:41-50)
To the woman forgiveness meant the release from the cycle of debt by the rich who controlled the lives of those without privilege and power.

C) In the Sermon on the Plain, the disciple who has experienced God's forgiveness is to love his/her enemies (6:27).
"Forgive and you will be forgiven." (6:37c) This verse does not mean ruling out any ethical evaluation at all.

D) Forgiveness meaning release from a diabolic power so that the person is healed (13:10-17). Jesus heals and frees
(Gk.lythenai) a woman who had a spirit of infirmity for eighteen years. Jesus says to the crippled outcast woman, "Woman, you are freed or loosed from your infirmity." (13:16)

[6] Forgiveness in the community of believers: Jesus' teaching on forgiveness (Read 17:3-4; Matt.18:5.)(Q)

A) Confronting the sinner and forgiving one's brother when he repents. Firstly, rebuke the person who sins: the disciples are to rebuke each other about sin and to forgive one another upon repentance (17:3). This is appropriate if the sin is "against you". This does not mean to meddle in the affairs of other disciples but Jesus wants the community of believers to desire righteousness and to be accountable to each other for the way they walk. The main issues in (17:3c) are showing mercy, being able to forgive, and refusing to judge harshly. The community of believers should be concerned about the best interests of each one. The call to rebuke was laid down in the O.T. and is a familial responsibility (Lev. 19:17). The disciples have to be quick to forgive when repentance is shown; people must be able to move on from their failures (17:3b).
It is the same principle which Jesus laid down in the Sermon on the Plain (6:37), "Judge (Gk. krinete) not and you will not be judged; condemn not and you will not be condemned; forgive (Gk. apoluete) and you will be forgiven (Gk. apoluthesesthe)." Do not be judgemental and censorious towards others in a way that holds them down in guilt and never seeks to encourage them towards God. (Bock) **(16)** The disciples are not to be indifferent to evil and at the same time they are not to bear a grudge. A key aspect of the teaching is the restoration of the believer and the ability to forgive. Luke emphasises individual responsibility while Mathew sees it as the corporate responsibility of the church (Matt.18:17). Be slow to condemn and quick to forgive. Do not hold an action permanently against the person who harmed you. Jesus has the idea of amnesty here and not acquittal. He is opposed to the attitude of the Pharisee (18:11-14). God's judgement falls on those who judge. Christians are not meant to take a hard-nosed, contemptuous, and supercilious attitude towards those whom they regard as sinners (2 Cor.11: 24).

B) How many times must the disciple forgive (17:4)?
Forgive again and again. Jesus says, "Seven times a day," meaning that the disciple is to forgive and forgive again and again without limits. "If he sins against you seven times, and turns to you seven times and says, 'I repent,' "you must forgive him." Seven has the idea of frequency of the sin and the forgiveness rather than the literal number. "Seven times a day I praise You for Your righteous ordinances." (Ps. 119:164) Forgiveness is unlimited. It is assumed here that the sin is directed personally against the disciple. Even if one were to question the genuineness of repentance every two hours, forgiveness should be granted.

C) Repentance means turning and repenting.

In the Disciples' Prayer (11:4), the sinner has to take the initiative and admit that he is wrong and ask for pardon. The command to forgive (Gk. apheseis) is in the future tense and has the idea that you must forgive. "You must continually forgive." (17:4 RSV) It is also used in the future tense for emphasis. (Fitzmyer) **(17)** "Forgive us our sins as we forgive everyone who is indebted to us." These words in the disciples' prayer are similar in thought to the words in the **Sermon on the Plain**. "Forgive and you will be forgiven." (6:37c) This prayer shows the regular need for confession of sins for cleansing of sins from all wrong doing. The word Luke uses is "sins" as Gentiles would know this term rather than debts which is a Hebrew term used in Matthew (6:12).

Pupil's Activity: Four

To what extent is forgiveness an important aspect of Jesus' teaching?

(Edexcel A/S 2002) [6 marks]

Pupil's Activity: Five **Class discussion**

a) Is Jesus laying down a principle for the individual or the state? (17:37c) b) Has the state a responsibility to provide a safe environment for its citizens? c) What is the responsibility of the courts?

[7] Forgiveness in relation to repentance and faith in Luke's Gospel

Faith and repentance are seen as requirements for forgiveness.

A) True faith requires genuine repentance which is a requirement for forgiveness. John had preached a baptism of repentance for the forgiveness of sins (3:3). John's message was a call to repentance and forgiveness of sins extended to Jews and Gentiles at the start of the messianic era. For John, repentance is a response to the kingdom linked to the coming judgement. Not all of Israel would respond to John's message of repentance.

> Jesus tells His disciples that repentance (Gk. metanoian) and forgiveness (Gk. aphesin) of sins should be preached in His name to all the nations (24:47). Repentance (Gk. metanoian) means a complete "turning" a turning away from one's sinful way of life and a change of mind.

Those who respond positively will be gathered like wheat into a granary and will take their part in the restoration and renewal of God's people. To the sinful woman Jesus said, "Your faith has saved you; go in peace." (7:50) This is the human response to God by faith. In the parable of the sower the devil snatches the word from the hearts of the people so that they may not believe and be rescued (8:12).

B) The second response is that of repentance which can be expressed in specific ways such as selling one's possessions and giving to the poor (18:22). Zacchaeus gave half of his goods to the poor. [See p. 241.] In the house of Levi, Jesus said, "I have not come to call the righteous but sinners to repentance." For Luke, faith and repentance were essentially two sides of the one coin. The thief on the cross who repented is an example of someone who did not have time to show evidence of faith by doing good works (23:43). [See also **Sermon on the Plain** as it is a community sermon and an individualistic one.]

C) Repentance and forgiveness: (Read 24:46.) the message which the disciples are to take out in Jesus' name. Finally, when Jesus is rejected and then exalted, He tells His disciples that repentance (Gk. metanoian) and forgiveness (Gk. aphesin) of sins should be preached in His name to all the nations (24:47). Repentance (Gk. metanoian) means a complete "turning" a turning away from one's sinful way of life and a change of mind. This is the "Great Commission" proclaiming repentance and forgiveness to all nations. In the "Great Commission" repentance is a key term for the response to the gospel message. People must change their mind as to who they are and how they can approach God. People who repent cast themselves on the mercy of God, His grace, His direction and plan. Forgiveness of sins comes to those who stretch out a needy hand to Jesus, clinging only to Him. It enables the sinner to come out of the darkness and into God's light, "to give light to those who sit in darkness." (1:79) It brings other blessings of righteousness, salvation, life and the Spirit. Lewis **(18)** says, "Christianity tells people to repent and promises them forgiveness. It has nothing (as far as I know) to say to people who do not know they have done anything to repent of and who do not feel that they need any forgiveness." Forgiveness and salvation come to those who repent and enter the kingdom for example the sinful woman (7:36-50); and Zacchaeus (19:9). True faith requires genuine repentance. For Luke, faith and repentance were essentially two sides of the one coin. The thief on the cross who repented is an example of some one who did not have time to do good works (23:43).

> Forgiveness and salvation come to those who repent and enter the kingdom, e.g. the sinful woman (7:36-50) and Zacchaeus (19:9).

[8] The call for national repentance: A Suffering God [CCEA Internal Assessment A/S]

(Read 13:1-5.) (L) Jesus is asked to access the theological reasons for two tragedies.

A) Some Galileans were put to death as they offered or prepared to offer a sacrifice. Pilate, the Roman administrator, used force and people were killed. The fact that the massacre occurred in the Temple area and could have been at Passover time when Galileans would have been in Jerusalem, aroused the passions of the Jews. Jesus uses the opportunity to warn the people of the need to repent. This type of violent event was common for example some Samaritans were massacred at Mt. Gerizim A.D. 36. (Josephus) **(19)**

This was a tragedy by human hands. Did the Galileans get their just reward because they were worse sinners than other Galileans? This would have been a common Jewish response to the massacre. (SB) **(20)** Jesus rejects this response and gives an additional warning about the threat of a tragic end for all. Only repentance will prevent a death which lasts (13:3).

B) The next incident is unknown and involved the tower at Siloam: a reservoir near the inter section of the south and east wall of Jerusalem. Eighteen residents of Jerusalem lost their lives when the tower or scaffolding fell upon them. This was a tragedy caused by natural causes (13:4). Tragedy is not necessarily related to a lower level of sin but it shows how life is fragile and the importance of knowing God. Another Greek word for sinner 'opheiletai' is the word used here and has the idea of debt. Those who do not repent will perish (13:5). The real threat is not being able to stand before God. This appropriately follows on from a warning to settle one's account with God (12:57-59). Talbert suggests that some people in the audience saw the absence of tragedy in their lives as a sign of God's approval and blessing. **(21)**

There may also be a subtle attempt to force Jesus to make a political statement against Pilate and then Rome would have to deal with Him. Jesus is emphasising that repentance is a universal need (13:1-5).

This is followed by the parable of the fig tree planted in a vineyard (13:6-9). The fig tree is a symbol for Israel (Matt. 21:18-19). What shall I do with an unproductive tree (13:6)? The fig tree is given one more brief chance to bear fruit or face destruction. The nation must repent if they are to avoid perishing. The other vines and fruit trees suffer because of the space taken up by the fig tree which deprives the ground of nutrients (13:7). The vine was another symbol for the nation (13:7). The vinedresser is to give the fig tree another chance within a year. He will care for it and fertilise it to provide nutrients to make it fruitful (13:8). Does the threat of removing the fig tree suggest making way for a replacement? (Marshall) **(22)** Others will come into the vineyard (20:9-18). Jesus is saying that there is a real need to prepare for repentance. (Fitzmyer)**(23)** This is like the rich fool, "Fool, this night your soul is required of you." (12:20) Jesus' audience will likewise perish if they do not repent. There is a final opportunity for the nation of Israel to repent before God's judgement. The destruction of the Temple in A.D.70 would be a temporal and spiritual judgement upon Israel.

Conclusion

Forgiveness in Luke's Gospel is concerned with God's forgiveness of people and people's forgiveness of each other as evidenced in Jesus' teaching and that of John the Baptist. For Luke, forgiveness meant God's forgiveness as evidenced in:

> For Luke, forgiveness meant God's forgiveness as evidenced in release from:
> • sins meaning forgiveness (7:47-49).
> • the binding power of Satan (13:10-17).
> • and a cycle of debt (6:27-36). (AGT) **(24)**

release from sins meaning forgiveness (7:47-49), release from the binding power of Satan (13:10-17), and release from a cycle of debt (6:27-36). (A G T) **(24)** The woman who had been bound for eighteen years was freed from this bondage. Receiving of sight is both a physical experience and a metaphor for the experiencing salvation and inclusion into God's family (1:78-79; 2:9, 29-32; 3:6; 6:39-42; 8:35-43).

Repentance goes hand in hand with faith.

[9] A summary of the meaning of repentance in Luke's Gospel

• Luke more than any other Gospel writer points out the need for repentance. The fruits of repentance are spelt out (3:8,10-14). Luke also adds the words "to repentance" to the saying of Jesus, "I have not come to call the righteous but sinners to repentance." (5:32) The word for repentance clearly has a high profile in Luke's vocabulary (13:3,5; 15:5,10; 16:30; 17:3).

• Firstly, a sick person in need of medical attention as in the healing of the paralysed man in urgent need of the doctor's skill. The person who repents comes to God for spiritual healing and blessing (5:31-32).

• Secondly, there is the Prodigal Son's action in returning to his father, showing that repentance is entirely based upon the mercy of the one to whom the request is made (15:7-21). Repentance and forgiveness of sins mean seeking God's mercy through Jesus as one approaches God on His terms (24:47).

• Thirdly, the tax collector expresses this attitude although there is no direct reference to repentance (18:9-14).

• Fourthly, Zacchaeus also expresses the same attitude; in his treatment of other people he shows his repentance. He discovered that Jesus cancelled personal debt. He is the rich man who gets through the eye of the needle (19:1-10).

• If repentance is genuine there must be evidence of a new life style as in the case of Zacchaeus who gave half of his goods to feed the poor. This shows that he had turned away from evil and indicates a new moral outlook (19:10). [See Ch.17: Wealth.] Conzelmann **(25)** said that Luke moralised the nature of repentance. Marshall **(26)** replies, "What else is repentance if it is not concerned with a man's moral life in the sight of God? This is evident in the ministry of John the Baptist when he speaks of the 'fruit of repentance'." (3:8) Conzelmann **(27)** argued that Luke changed the idea of repentance from that which describes the whole act of conversion to a precondition for salvation. Luke, he argued, narrowed the concept down to penitence (Mk. 1:4), an inward attitude to be followed by a changed life. To repent for Conzelmann is a "once and for all " act of penitence. Conzelmann also argued **(28)** to repent (Gk. metanoein) (11:32; 24:27,43-47) and to turn (Gk. epistrephein) (1:17; 17:4 ; 22:32;) have the same meaning. However, Mk. 1:15 goes on to refer "to repent and believe the Gospel." (Marshall) **(29)** Hence there is no difference between Luke and Mark on the meaning of repentance and repentance and faith are not synonymous in Mk. 1:4 as argued by Lohmeyer. **(30)** [See p. 259.]

• The Oxford Dictionary defines repentance as feeling "deep sorrow about one's actions and resolving not to continue a wrongdoing." This definition does not include the biblical idea of a complete turn around or a change in the "mindset" involving admission of guilt and sorrow for sin and a return to God. The dictionary definition may be applicable to the thief on the cross but not to Zacchaeus. Repentance goes hand in hand with faith. However, the thief made one final amazing request of Jesus. "Jesus, remember me when you come into your kingdom." (23:42) He realised that Jesus still had a future after His death." (Meynell) **(31)** If a person repents without believing by implication they rescue themselves. If a person believes without repenting or without a change in life style, this would mean continuing to live in God's world without a real dependence upon Him.

> **Jesus shows forgiveness towards His enemies when He touched and healed the ear of the high priest's servant (22:49-51).**

[10] Summary of forgiveness in the Passion Narrative (Chs.22-23) [See Ch. 11.] [See pp. 152-53.]
• Jesus shows forgiveness towards His enemies when He touched and healed the ear of the high priest's servant (22:49-51). Jesus practised what He preached (6:27-31). He rebuked the disciples for their use of force. John's Gospel says it was Peter who did this (Jn.18:10). There is no sense of bitterness of mind with Jesus and no resentment that He should be treated indifferently by the soldiers who cast lots for His garments (23:34).
• He was scoffed at by the Jewish rulers, "He saved" others let Him save Himself, if He really is the Christ of God, His chosen one!" (23:35).
• He was insulted by the criminal on the cross (23:39) and mocked by the soldiers who offered him vinegar (23:36).
• The soldiers mocked Him saying, "if you are the King of the Jews, save yourself and us!"
• When a large crowd followed Jesus and the women of Jerusalem mourned and wept for Him, He was considerate towards them as their future would mean suffering. They should not mourn for Him but for themselves (23:27-28). Jesus had predicted this (19:42-44).
• The prayer for forgiveness on the cross: "Father, forgive them; for they know not what they do." Jesus' prayer is for the Jews, the Romans, Jewish leaders rulers and the people who have acted in ignorance. On the basis of this prayer, there are no grounds for anti-Semitism (23:34).
• The dying thief who believed that one day Jesus would return. "Today you will be with me in paradise." His spiritual state and recognition of Jesus implies forgiveness (23:40-43).
• After the Resurrection appearances, Jesus in His final instructions to His disciples says, "Repentance and forgiveness should be preached to all nations." (24:47) Repentance, forgiveness of sins and faith bring a person into a right relationship with God and enables that person to enter His glorious light. The believer is forgiven through God's grace in Jesus Christ (1:79; Acts 26:18).
• The message of repentance for the forgiveness of sins is a key theme in Luke/Acts and is a key part of the gospel (24:47).

Conclusion
• The repentant thief rebukes the unrepentant criminal for not believing in God (23:40).
• Jesus shows forgiveness to the outsider right up to His death. "Jesus, remember me when you come in your kingly power." While this is not a specific request for forgiveness it is implicit. "I tell you the truth you will be with me in paradise. The thief on the cross accepted God's mercy, found salvation and by implication God's forgiveness (23:43).
• The hardened Roman centurion received forgiveness when He recognised Jesus as a righteous man. "Certainly this man was innocent (righteous)." Forgiveness in this incident is implied (23:47). As result of this the people returned home beating their breasts, which was a sign of remorse and assumed guilt and contrition (23:48).
• In the case of Joseph of Arimathea forgiveness is also implied (23:50-54).

Summary of Jesus as the compassionate teacher [See pp. 165-68, 206, 262.]
Jesus shows His concern for the social outcasts of His day. The tax collectors were marginalised because they regarded their work for the Romans as dishonest and immoral. The Pharisees, who saw the tax collectors as "sinners." interpreted Ps. 1:5 as saying, "Do not welcome sinners and do not eat with them." (15:1-2) They were annoyed at Jesus g with sinners. To meet this challenge Jesus taught three parables on lostness to express God's compassion for the helpless, the outsider and sinners. In these three parables Jesus taught that there is joy in heaven over one sinner who repents (15:7,10,32). God in His mercy searches and seeks out the lost, bringing back the straying.
A) The lost sheep (15:1-7) [See p. 228 Figure 1 No. 14.]
• In the parable of the lost sheep, the shepherd has one hundred sheep and one goes astray. The individual is important for Jesus. God takes the initiative in searching for lost sheep.
• Jesus' disciples have to search for lost sheep.
• God rejoices when one lost sheep is found like a shepherd when a straying sheep is found.
• The return of sinners to God should be a cause of rejoicing by the Jewish leaders. Some rabbis were unwilling to seek Gentile converts, while others were aggressive in their proselytising (Matt.23:15).
B) The lost coin (15:8-10)
• The woman goes to great lengths searching diligently until she finds her lost coin. This search shows the Messiah's

determination to pursue His mission. The Pharisees had no compassion; Jesus rejected their attitude to women in society because the Pharisees saw women as inferior. This is an example of "seeking mercy": "a love that will not let us go."
• God welcomes sinners.

C) The lost son (15:11-32) [See p. 168 elder brother.]
•This is a parable of the "Merciful Father." The younger son is granted his request for his share of his father's estate: God lets the sinner go his/her way.
• In the far country the son realised he had to rely upon the mercy of the father. As he nears home his father sees him in the distance, has compassion, runs, embraces and kisses him.
• God in His mercy welcomes back repentant sinners. Jesus used a Semitic expression for repentance in His teaching: "to come to one's senses" (15:17). In His mercy, God is willing to receive sinners and He rejoices when they turn to Him. When this happens there is time of celebration (15:32). Celebration was a very Jewish practice in first-century Galilee. (Bailey) (32)
• Repentance and forgiveness of sins means seeking God's mercy through Jesus as a person approaches God. "I have sinned against heaven and earth." (15:18-19)
• "Dead" and "lost" and are expressions which apply to the spiritual state of someone before Jesus looks for them while "alive" and "found" relate to their standing in Christ, thanks to His compassion (15:32; Eph. 2:1-5). Jesus seeking and receiving sinners is pleasing to God.

D) The parable of the two debtors (Read 7:35-50.)
• When Jesus was a guest teacher at the house of Simon the Pharisee his host said, "Tell me teacher." This is a common title in Luke for a Rabbi (7:47 NIV). After this parable Jesus said, "But he who is forgives little, loves little (7:47). The woman's sins which are many are forgiven for she loved much.
• Jesus shows His concern for a sinful woman. The woman's act of love showed that she had been forgiven: her faith is the basis for her forgiveness.
• In the parable the creditor cancels both debts and forgives both men. Jesus pursues sinners and welcomes them so that they can appreciate God's gracious forgiveness. Jesus openly associates with sinners (7:41-43). Jesus forgives sin and makes himself equal with God. His heavenly Father will forgive debts when people turn to Him. Jesus shows His concern for broken lives.

E) The good Samaritan (Read 10:25-37.)
• In this parable, mercy should be shown in helping the needy and helpless (10:37).
• God does not give the life of the Kingdom to those who reject the command to love (10:37). Three people show that they have not recognised how much they need God's love themselves: they are like Simon the Pharisee rather than the woman who was forgiven.
• The Samaritan "took pity" (Gk.esplanchnisthe) which means a deep feeling of sympathy. Here it involved sacrificial action in the use of his own wine (10:33), bandages (10:34) and oil as a soothing lotion. (Jeremais) (33) He put the man on his donkey and paid the innkeeper from his own money promising to pay more (10:35).

F) The great Banquet (14:16-24)(p. 157.) **G)** The Pharisee and the Publican (18:10-14) **H)** The wicked tenants (20:9-19)

Pupil's Activity: Six   Revision
a) What according to the preaching of John, are the cause (3:7-9,16,17), nature (3:8, 10-14) and outcome (3:3,15-17) of repentance?
b) Complete the grid on the preaching of John the Baptist to show different aspects of his teaching on forgiveness. [See Activity: Six and Ch. 9: John the Baptist.]

The preaching of John the Baptist   (Figure 4)

Repentance	The preaching of John the Baptist	Refs.
The cause of repentance		3:7-9, 16-17
The nature of repentance		3:8, 10-14
The outcome of repentance		3:3, 15-17

Pupil's Activity: Seven
a) With reference to TWO parables, examine the teaching of Jesus on the nature of forgiveness.
(Edexcel A/S   2001)   [8 marks]
b) What can be learned from the nature caf repentance from the teaching of John the Baptist?
(Edexcel A/S   2001)   [6 marks]
c) Draw a spidergram on forgiveness in Luke's Gospel.
d) Play appropriate selections from The Messiah on forgiveness or use a video of The Messiah by G.F.Handel. "Comfort ye my people." "Every valley shall be exalted." "He shall purify." "Let us break their bands asunder."
e) Play Max Bruck's cello concerto "Qol Nidra" on forgiveness played at the commencement of the Yom Kippur feast.

Pupil's Activity: Eight

a) What can be learned from the teaching of Jesus about the nature of forgiveness in: (1) the Parable of the Lost Son;
(Edexcel A/S 2003)   [14 marks]   (2) the Sermon on the Plain?
b) Why was Jesus' teaching on forgiveness so controversial at that time?
(Edexcel A/S 2003/2006)   [6 marks]
c) Why is forgiveness such an important part of Jesus' teaching in Luke's Gospel? (Edexcel A/S 2006) [6 marks]

Pupil's Activity: Nine

a) Outline your knowledge and understanding of the parables of "the lost" in Luke's Gospel.
(CCEA A/S Resit 2003)   [30 marks]
b) Explore the claim that the aim of these miracles is to show God's joy when people repent. Justify your answer.
(CCEA A/S Resit 2003)   [14 marks]

Pupil's Activity: Ten

a) Explore the claim that forgiveness is a central theme in Luke's Passion narrative.
b) Justify your answer. (CCEA A/S 2005)   [15 marks]

Pupil's Activity: Eleven

a) Discuss Jesus' teaching in the Sermon on the Plain.   (CCEA A2 2002/2005) [30 marks]
b) Critically evaluate the claim that it is difficult to live up to this teaching. (CCEA A2 2002/2005) [15 marks]
[See Vol. 2 to be published later for other aspects of The Sermon on the Plain.]

Outcomes
Students should have a knowledge and understanding of:
• **Jesus' specific teaching on forgiveness, for example at least two parables in Luke's Gospel and the Passion Narrative.**
• **forgiveness in the teaching of John the Baptist.**
• **key concepts relating to forgiveness, for example repentance and faith, sinners, "release", cancelling or forgiving a debt, pardon.**
• **key teaching points on the nature of forgiveness in two parables of Jesus.**
• **Jesus' teaching on forgiveness and why it was so controversial at that time?**
Students should be able to discuss the main teaching on forgiveness in the Sermon on the Plain (Edexcel A/S) and critically evaluate Jesus' teaching. (CCEA A/2)

Notes on Ch. 18: Forgiveness

1. Howard Marshall, (a) op. cit. p. 138.
2. M. Butterworth, DOTTE, Vol.3, p. 81.
3. Philip G. Ryken, The Message of Salvation, BST, IVP, (2001) p.175.*
4. J. Lunde, Article on "Repentance", DJG, IVP, (1992) p.672.
5. M. J. Wilkins, Article on "Sinners", DJG, op. cit. p. 758.*
6. John Nolland, op. cit. p.235.
7. Robert H. Stein, op. cit. p.176.
8. Robert H. Stein, op. cit. p.236.
9. B.H. Young, The Parables: Jewish Tradition and Christian Interpretation, Peabody: Hendrickson (1998) pp.130-157.
10. Darrell L. Bock, Vol. 2, op. cit. p.1143.
11. Craig L. Blomberg, op. cit. p.343.
12. Darrell L. Bock, op. cit. p.1788.
13. Joel Green, op. cit. p.788.
14. Robert H. Stein, op. cit. p.236.
15. Raymond E. Brown, Vol. 1, op. cit. p.607.
16. Darrell Bock, op. cit. p.605.
17. Joseph A. Fitzmyer, op. cit. p.1141.
18. C.S. Lewis, Mere Christianity, Fontana, (1955) p.37.
19. Josephus, Antiquities, 18.41§§ 85-87.
20. H.L.Strack and P. Billerbeck, 6 Vols. K.N.T. on the Talmud and Midrash, Munich: Beck, (1922-61), 2:193-197.
21. Charles H. Talbert, op. cit. p.145.
22. Howard Marshall, (a) op. cit. p.555.
23. Joseph A. Fitzmyer, op. cit. p.1004.
24. Paul Achtemeier, Joel Green and Meyer Thompson, op. cit. p.163.
25. Hans Conzelmann, op. cit. p.91.
26. Howard Marshall, (a) op. cit. p.194.
27. Howard Marshall, (ibid.)
28. Hans Conzelmann, op. cit. pp.91-93.
29. Howard Marshall, (ibid.)
30. E. Lohmeyer, Gospel of Mark, Gottingen, (1959) p.115.
31. Mark Meynell, Cross-Examined, IVP, (2002) p.194.
32. Kenneth Bailey, op. cit. pp.130-157.
33. Joachim Jeremais, op. cit. p.114.
* This book and article are highly recommended.

Edexcel A/S and A2 (2007ff)

> **Targets:**
> • Identify events in Luke's Gospel in which Jesus had controversies with the Pharisees.
> • Recognise how and why did Jesus' attitude to the Jews differ at that time.
> • Identify Jewish attitudes and teaching about the Sabbath.
> • Recogise the following concepts relating to the Sabbath: the Pharisees, the Essenes, fasting, legal, moral, eschatological, synagogue, Mishnah and Sadducees.

Sabbath Controversies with the Religious Authorities

Introduction

The incidents of Jesus healing on the Sabbath and the disciples breaking the Jewish Sabbath rules produced major controversies raising the question of Jesus' authority to act and interpret. Jesus claims authority over holy time and God's calendar with a promise based upon the commandments (6:1-11; Mk.2:23-26; Matt.12:1-14). On the Sabbath, Jesus preaches in Nazareth and meets with opposition. He regularly attended the synagogue on the Sabbath which was His custom and read and expounded the Scriptures (4:15). Jesus had no qualms about healing on the Sabbath. The people brought the sick to Him, waiting until the Sabbath was over "as the sun was setting." (5:40-41) This will become an issue later in Jesus' ministry.

A) Systematising the views of the Pharisees in first-century Judaism (Carson)

1) The traditional view (Guttmann) **(1)**
The Pharisees were adaptable to the Torah by fine-tuning their interpretation and explanation about the legal requirements designed to make life easier and clarify the right conduct. The views of the Pharisees developed later into the Mishnah (A.D.200). Guttmann argued that they were more effective than the O.T. prophets.

2) A huge gap existed between the rabbinic views in the Mishnah and pre-A.D.70 Pharisaism. The Pharisees influenced the life style of pre-A.D. 70 Judaism extending purity rituals of the Temple to the daily life of every Jew. (Neusner) **(2)**

3) The Pharisees were post-Maccabean (160 B.C.) and theological, revolutionary men of great learning and very persuasive. They developed the oral law, codified it later in the Mishnah and had forsaken their O.T. roots. However, they did not have separatistic tendencies and their influence was pervasive. In this view there was little difference between the Pharisees and the Sadducees. (Rivkin) **(3)**

4) There is a clear distinction between the Pharisees (the perushim/"the separatists") and the Rabbis ("the great ones") behind the Mishnah. In Jesus' time the rabbis were not officially ordained: Jesus is called "rabbi" in three Gospels though not in Luke (Matt.26:49; Mk.9:5; Jn.1:38). Jesus belonged to a class of "proto rabbis" who were the forerunners of the ordained rabbis of the Mishnaic period. The Pharisees were extremists who died out after A.D.70 and left no trace. (Sigal) **(4)**They thought that God would bring in the Kingdom in His own good time (17:20). This was the Jewish view in the first-century (Acts 1:6). [See p. 262.]

B) Carson's comments on the views

• All four views are right in what they affirm but wrong in what they deny. There is no simple equation between a Pharisee and a Mishnaic rabbi. However, it is unlikely that the Pharisees were so separatistic that they did not accept the "proto rabbis." (Carson) **(5)**

• Jesus' messianic claims cannot be dismissed. (Carson) **(6)**

• The Gospels speak about three main religious groups Sadducees, priests and scribes but say nothing about "proto rabbis" who were the main group after A.D. 70. The fact that the Sadducees disappeared after A.D.70 is not surprising because much of their life and influence depended upon the Temple which was destroyed by the Romans.

• Jesus cannot be reduced to a "proto rabbi" training His followers to respect His legal decisions. To onlookers He appeared as a prophet (20:1-8).

• The Pharisees adopted the laws to the times and were effective leaders. (Guttmann) **(7)**

• They made ritual distinctions more difficult and morality too easy. (Carson) **(8)**

• The Pharisees had a wide influence in the nation. It is hard to see them as a separatistic group (Sigal) or exclusively concerned about ritual purity.

• The Pharisees were a non-priestly group of uncertain origin, learned, committed to oral law.

• They were included in the Sanhedrin even though most of the Sanhedrin leaders were Sadducees (20:1-8). References to the "chief priests, scribes and elders" of the people coming to Jesus probably refers to the Sanhedrin (20:1). (Carson) **(9)**

C) The Sabbath in first-century Judaism

In first-century Judaism the Sabbath was a joyous occasion, a sign of the covenant, an ordinance of creation, a reminder of divine creation in six days, a promise of the joys of the world to come and, if the rules were kept, a means of gaining merit for Israel (Mek. Ex.20:16; 23:15; 26:13; b. Shabbath 10b). By Jesus' time the Sabbath separated pious Jews from "sinners."
(10) The Mishnah tractate, Shabbath, is concerned with what is and what is not lawful for the Sabbath and contains many of the oral laws and traditions that Jesus encountered. The Mishnah was an oral law meaning "repetition." In Luke's Gospel the Pharisees are depicted as "having rejected God's purpose for themselves (7:30)."

When they appear with the scribes they are presented as Jesus' adversaries (5:17, 21,30; 6:7; 7:30; 11:53; 14:3; 15:2). Luke portrayed the Pharisees as "lovers of money" and desiring high status by serving as wealthy benefactors to those in need (16:14). They are also presented as self-promoting. They like seats of honour and to receive first greetings in the marketplace (11:43). The scribes appear to have a negative influence on others (11:46).

[1] The controversy with the Pharisees regarding fasting (Read 5:33-39; Matt.9:14-17.)

This is not a Sabbath controversy but one with the religious authorities. It is the third controversy in Mark and Luke's sequence regarding the disciples' lack of fasting. Jesus' disciples do not fast (and drink)(5:30). The tradition of the Pharisees was one of fasting twice a week (18:12) (L). In Judaism fasting was linked with key holidays as on the Day of Atonement and to commemorate the fall of Jerusalem (Lev. 16:29; Zech.7:3).

[2] The controversy with the Pharisees regarding washing before a meal (11:37-41)[Ch.16 pp. 128, 240-41.]

[3] The hypocrisy of the Pharisees who were lovers of money (16:14) [Ch.17]

[4] Four Sabbath controversies

A) Dispute over the disciples plucking the ears of corn on the Sabbath: "Lord of the Sabbath" is Jesus' self-described status. (Read 6:1-5; Mk.2:23-28; Matt. 12:1-8). Who decides what is lawful on the Sabbath?

1) The setting

The disciples are walking through fields on the Sabbath. On their way, they pick from the stalks, rub them in their hands to break down the grain and eat. Their action is innocent enough but in the eyes of the Pharisees it is not appropriate behaviour for the Sabbath as the disciples are about to find out.

2) The teaching of Scripture

The background to the event is rooted in the sacred day of rest, the Sabbath in Judaism (Ex.20:9; Deut. 5:13). The eating of grain from a field was allowed but not on the Sabbath (Ex. 20:8-11; 25:30; 39:36; 40:22-23; Lev 25:5-9; Deut. 23:25).

3) Rabbinic teaching

The disciples were accused of reaping, threshing, winnowing and preparing food from the grain. This action by the disciples was thought by the Pharisees to be a multiple violation of the Sabbath practice. (Sabbat) **(11)** These were four of the thirty-nine kinds of work forbidden on the Sabbath. Food preparation was done one day earlier to honour the Sabbath. Failing to observe such a holy day was regarded as being disrespectful towards the Torah because keeping the Sabbath was one of the ten commandments. The word "Sabbath" is mentioned six times (6:1,2,5,6,7,9) and the question of "lawfulness" three times (6:2,4,9). Matthew notes that the disciples did this out of hunger (12:1) and therefore ate out of necessity. (Kilpatrick) **(12)** Morris says wayfarers were allowed to help themselves to satisfy their hunger (Deut.23:24). **(13)** In later Judaism there was a law which allowed the picking of grain by hand on the Sabbath but did not allow the use of a tool. (b.Shabbath 128 a.b.) **(14)**

4) Legal teaching of the Pharisees

Jesus said that King David was allowed to do something that the law had specifically forbidden. He entered the Temple and ate the consecrated bread giving it to his companions. This bread was for priests only and not for kings and their soldiers (Lev.24:9; 1 Sam.21:1-6; 22: 9-10). All three Gospels show that the bread was for priests only (6: 4b; Matt.12:4; Mk.2:26). Jesus indicates that there are times when a law like the Sabbath could be "broken" as with the consecrated bread. Human need is the point for Jesus: those with Him were hungry. This type of teaching is consistent with concern for one's neighbour. The disciples can pluck the ears of corn for the needy (Deut. 23:25). A Sabbath day's journey was about 1,100 meters (M. Satah 5:3). Why were the disciples not charged with exceeding the Sabbath day limit? In Jesus' time not all the religious authorities were opposed to what the disciples did but the Pharisees did object to the disciples' labour on the Sabbath day.

5) Jesus' reply: who has the authority to interpret the law about the Sabbath

Jesus challenged the custom of the Pharisees. In Judaism Sabbath meals were prepared in advance to avoid the Pharisees' objection (Jub. 2:19). **(15)** In Luke and Matt. ("Q") Jesus says that "the Son of Man is lord of the Sabbath." (6:5) This claim is Messianic. "It allows the Son of Man to handle the Sabbath law any way He wills, or to supersede it in the same way that the Temple requirements superseded the usual restrictions." (Hooker) **(16)** To be lord of a divine ordinance is to have a very high place indeed. (Morris) **(17)** While this is not a remark about humanity's authority over the Sabbath, it does however show Jesus' personal claim of authority over the sacred day constituted by God (Ex.20:8-11). Jesus' substitution of Himself for the groom and the claim to forgive sins, links Jesus with Yahweh (5:34). Jesus argues that His actions help to define who He is. His attitude to the Sabbath shows how different His way is from current practice. Luke's account is the shorter as he makes the basic point about the identity of the One who reigns over even the Sabbath. Jesus' actions help to define who He is. It is no accident that this incident follows that of the "new wineskins" where some Jews did not want any change; this became the basis for opposition to Jesus, "The old is good (5:39)(L)."

Jesus, when faced with formalism, which was the error of the Pharisees, vindicated His healing on the Sabbath by saying, "My Father works until now, and I work (Jn.5:17)." Jesus is not saying that the Sabbath has been removed or abrogated: "the Sabbath rest is not one of inactivity, unemployment but employment of a different sort from that of the six days." (Murray) **(18)** It is an ordinance of creation for everyone and for everyone's good (Gen.2:2-3).

6) Eschatological teaching

This Sabbath law was not designed to be an obstacle for people. The person who is the Son of Man and who has received eschatological judging authority from God, possesses such a right. Jesus is the key figure who brings the new era. This is an eschatological claim which serves as a clinching argument alongside an illustration which allows an exception. Sabbath law was not designed to be an obstacle for people. Jesus' argument operates at many levels: scripture, legal, relationships and eschatological. The right of the disciples to take a grain on the Sabbath as they travel should have been allowed. The "new" way leads to controversy with the "old" practice. Jesus, in fact, honours the relational desire that God had, that mercy be shown and the Sabbath was given for people's good (Gen.2:2-3). The Son of Man, the representative human being, has received authority from God even over the Sabbath. The controversies force a choice about who is Jesus. Sanders sees this incident of the disciples plucking the ears of corn as far-fetched. (Sanders) **(19)** Witherington notes that the controversy is about the disciples and not Jesus, "the disciples plucked the ears of corn (6:1)". [See p. 206.]

B) A synagogue Sabbath healing: the man with the withered hand (Read 6:6-11; Mk.3:1-6; Matt.12:9-14)

Who decides what is lawful on the Sabbath? This is another combined controversy and healing account. There is no attention given to the man's healed hand or to the crowd's reaction. For this controversy it is Jesus versus the Jewish leadership.

1) Setting: A man with a withered hand enters the synagogue. His condition would have prevented him from working. In normal circumstances people would have viewed this kind of healing with greater respect (1 Kgs, 13:6; Testament of Simeon 2.12-13). The Pharisees are "watching" to see if Jesus will heal on the Sabbath. Jesus' opponents are seeking to accuse him; "they are lying in wait for Jesus. (BAGD)" **(20)**

2) Rabbinic teaching

The later Mishnah did discuss what could and could not be done on the Sabbath. For many medicine could be given only if the life was in danger or some other urgent need (m.Yoma 8:6). A broken bone could not be set **(21)** although attempts to get round this restriction existed, especially if the medicine had been prepared before the Sabbath. (m.Sabbat) **(22)** The Essenes were even stricter; they forbade any significant activity on the Sabbath (CD) **(23)**: one is not allowed to pasture an animal beyond a length of 1,000 cubits. (Keener) **(24)**

3) The healing [See p. 188.]

Jesus tells the man to come to him, "Come and stand here (6:8)." Jesus says to do good on the Sabbath is lawful (Gk. exestin). He presses the issue, "Is it lawful on the Sabbath to do good or do harm, to save a life or to destroy it (6:9)?" The Pharisees are trying to see if they can catch Jesus to make an accusation against Him. Jesus will restore a person to complete health. Jesus acts and tells the man to stretch out his hand (6:10). The man shows the evidence that his hand has been healed. In the previous incident the disciples took the initiative to act on the Sabbath. Here there is a display of authority that seemingly proved that God acts on Jesus' behalf. The Pharisees react by discussing what "they might do to Jesus (6:11)."

4) Who decides what is lawful on the Sabbath?

Jesus puts the options very clearly: to do good or harm on the Sabbath, to save or destroy. For Jesus God's purpose is to "save life." Luke use two terms for save (1) (Gk.sozo) save/heal (6:9; 1:47, 2:11) and (2)(Gk. apokathistemi) "to restore as in restoring the man's hand." In the LXX it is used for the restoration of Israel (Is 52:8-10) and in this event "his hand was restored (6:10)." This word expresses Jesus' meditation of God's eschatological redemption. (Green) **(23)** Salvation is available to those who need it today on the Sabbath. Jesus' ministry restores to the Sabbath commandment its profound significance: the restoration of human beings in their integrity as part of God's creation. (Muller) **(26)** Jesus' opponents show their objection to His claim to authority. They show their feelings which is more than anger (Gk.anoia). They are at their wits' end (6:11). The Pharisees discuss among themselves what they might do to Jesus. They plot against Jesus and how they might destroy Him (Matt.12:4). It is better to err on the side of "goodness" than on that of heartless adherence to regulations (Hosea 6:6). (France) **(27)**

5) Relationships

Jesus' Sabbath activity is a key turning point in the dispute with the Pharisees. He brings "new" ways but those who like the "old" ways do not want the reforms. The last two controversies in Luke and Mark (the fourth and fifth) show that the question of the Sabbath controversies were the last straw that led to a heightening of opposition to Jesus.

C) Sabbath healing of a crippled woman (Read 13:10-17.)(L) [See pp. 129, 206 Figure 19.]

Jesus gives this additional opportunity to the Jews. He had told a parable of the unfruitful fig tree in the vineyard (13:1-9) which gave Israel another opportunity. The woman had suffered for eighteen years from a spirit induced condition of being bent over. This combined malady is not uncommon in Judaism (1 Qap). **(28)**

1) The Healing [See p. 206.]

Jesus initiates the healing and declares she is healed. She straightens up immediately. Luke often highlights how quickly the healing takes place (13:13). Jesus heals by touch. The only other occasion He does so is in the late evening when the Sabbath had passed (4:40). His "Sabbath labour" consists of His announcement and the laying on of hands. Her ability to straighten up shows her immediate healing. The reaction of the synagogue leader is to complain, "There are six days on which it is necessary to work (13:16)." The healing should have taken place on one of those days. Jesus calls the leader a hypocrite;

noting that if an ox or donkey were in distress on the Sabbath, one would rescue it or lead it to water. It is better to do good on the Sabbath rather than do nothing. The woman is freed (Gk. apoluo) from the effects of the disease (13:12).

2) Rabbinic teaching
The Mishnah discusses such rules about feeding, handling and rescuing animals on the Sabbath (m.Sabbat) **(29)**.

3) Legalism
The synagogue leader acts like a scribe or Pharisee in monitoring Jesus' actions on the Sabbath (5:17-26). The leader goes directly to the people and not to Jesus with his concern, challenging Jesus' authority as a teacher, reasserting himself as the authorised interpreter of Scripture. Sabbath observance became important during the Second Temple as a central means of nourishing Jewish identity (6:1-11). The leader does not argue on the basis of an interpretation of Deut. 5:13; Ex.20:9 but rather asserts what he believes everyone of real faith will affirm. His basis of argument is what "ought to be done" that is in the divine will (13:14): there are six days in which work ought to be done. Come on those days to be cured. "Do not desecrate the Sabbath by this healing." (13:14-15) This is a Christological issue as Jesus faces the Pharisee. (Green) **(30)** Luke presents Jesus as "Lord", and then One with authority to interpret God's plan of salvation. Both Jesus and the leader use O.T. Scripture.

4) Jesus' use of O.T. Scripture
Jesus returns to Deut.5:14: the prohibition to work on the Sabbath and extends the law not just to humans but to oxen and donkeys. If this is so why then do people untie their animals, and why can the animals not be allowed to walk to the trough for water? On a day set aside to honour God, it is especially appropriate that a daughter of Abraham be freed from Satan's binding power. Jesus' remark divides the crowd from the leaders and their followers as the opponents are shamed and the crowd are delighted at the "wonderful things" that Jesus was doing (13:17). Jesus says that the woman "ought" to be freed from Satanic bondage on the Sabbath. He argues from the lesser to the greater, for example if animals, how much more a daughter of Abraham? He exposes the leader of the synagogue and those like him, "You hypocrites!"

5) Eschatological teaching
The leader of the synagogue separated the needy woman from God's help. Jesus regarded the Sabbath as a right day for God's redemptive purpose to be realised. Here is liberation and restoration for a woman of lowly status. Jesus sees the act of healing as an act of liberation from Satan's bondage. She is set free (13:12). This is "the good news for the poor", the "bringing of release" (4:18-19) and "Satan's kingdom is plundered (13:16; 11:14ff)." God's eschatological purpose has come to fruition (11:20). The O.T. Scriptures are not nullified by this healing and God's grace is extended to surprising people. Luke shows Jesus as the authoritative teacher who is recognised by the "wonderful things He was doing (13:17)." (Green) **(31)** Jesus comments upon the healing by referring to two parables based upon Palestinian peasant life that of the mustard seed and the yeast (13:18-21). The yeast of the Kingdom is unleashed in the heartland of the yeast of the Pharisees: the healing took place in the synagogue (13:10). This healing miracle is a warning about the yeast of the Pharisees (13:15a;12:1,56). [See Ch.12: Parables.] Messianic promises are being fulfilled (13:17; Is.45:16).(Marshall) **(32)**; (Fitzmyer) **(33)** The miracle is also a sign that the Kingdom of God will take over the world: in the same way as a mustard seed becomes a tree, so God's Kingdom will grow (13:18-19) and will gain more followers even though they may start out as an insignificant little flock (12:32).

6) Relationships
The leadership had learned nothing from God's activity or Jesus' teaching. They are not taking advantage of the extra chance (Bock). **(34)** The woman has as much right to be one of God's people as the Pharisee. She is a "daughter of Abraham." (13:16) She deserves to "be untied" on the Sabbath just like a "thirsty animal." (13:15-16) Jesus uses the same word "untie" (13:15 and 16) for the Pharisees the Sabbath was turned into a symbol of the bondage in which they kept the people rather than being set free from slavery in Egypt (Deut.15:5).

D) The man with the dropsy: what is appropriate action on the Sabbath? (Read 14:1-6) (L) [See pp. 129, 207.]

1) The setting
Jesus is enjoying a Sabbath day's hospitality following on from the synagogue service. This is a rare healing in this section of Luke's Gospel which is mainly given over to teaching (13:10-17; 17:11-15; 18:35-43). Jesus' custom was to observe the Sabbath (4:16). [See Ch.7: Structure.]

2) Relationships
He is really inviting his "table friends" to share in the redemption which God has made available. Jesus is at the home of a Jewish "leader," a Pharisee, one of the socially elite for whom the good news means low status. At the table are other Pharisees, those of high status in society. Meals reinforce the social hierarchy. Jesus answers the action or the thoughts of His opponents (14:3). Jesus asks the lawyers and Pharisees, "Is it lawful to heal on the Sabbath, or not ?" (14:3) The question of appropriate Sabbath behaviour was important as it identified Jewish faithfulness during the Second Temple period and enforced socio-religious sanctions relating to one's status in society. Jesus has warned Israel about rejection, yet He continues to minister to Israel. Now He declares judgement on Israel as a nation. Jesus has another meal (14:1-24) again at the house of a Pharisee. This incident takes place at the house of a synagogue leader. The host is one of the "ruling" (Gk. archonton) and could have been a member of the Sanhedrin. Luke often depicts the Pharisees as watchdogs of the faith or

"undercover agents" as they looked for some theological flaw to appear in Jesus' teaching (14:1-3; 5:17; 6:7). This could be interpreted as the fulfilment of Mary's Song with the Pharisees being "brought down (1:52)."(Green) **(35)**

3) Rabbinic teaching

Dropsy could have been regarded as a curse for sin by Jews (Lev.13:2; Num.5:11-27). It was associated in later Judaism with unclean immorality (Midras Rabbah, Leviticus). **(36)** A more lenient view of the Sabbath appears later in the Talmud (A.D. 500) plus a harsher law. (SBK)**(37)** This source allowed for exceptions for pulling animals out of a pit. The harsh view said all one can do is place food in the pit for the animal until the Sabbath is over. Jesus takes the initiative by asking, "Is it lawful to heal on the Sabbath or not?" Their silence allows Jesus to continue (14:4). Nothing in Scripture forbade this healing.

4) The healing on the Sabbath [See p. 207.]

"There in front of Jesus" was a man with dropsy. He could have been planted there to test Jesus. The Pharisees were "watching" Jesus, which means they were carefully watching Him. Jesus does not hesitate to show compassion. Dropsy is a disease in which the limbs are swollen with excessive body fluid. Jesus heals the man by touch mirroring previous Sabbath healings (14:3; 6:6-11; 13:10-17). Jesus notes that they would offer help to a son or even an ox that fell into a ditch on the Sabbath. Again Jesus illustrates the healing by an example of a son or an ox falling into a well and being rescued on the Sabbath. At Qumran **(38)** a distinction would have been made. A person could be rescued; an animal could not be rescued. The Essenes went as far as to say that it was wrong to "assist a beast in giving birth on the Sabbath day," much more to pull it out of a pit (CD) **(39)**. Again Jesus' illustration meets with silence by the leaders (14:4). They could not respond (14:6). The Jewish leaders have learnt nothing from previous Sabbath healings. God's grace is still revealed in the presence of Jesus and despite Jesus' warnings regarding judgement, God still shows Himself. However, closed eyes cannot see the evidence of God's power. Jesus addresses the Pharisee's guests by saying that the disciples are to do good not expecting a future reward but to act unselfishly. God will remember and reward them (14:12-14). Jesus uses the word "release" (Gk. apeluse) from illness, "Jesus took him, healed and released him (14:4)(NRSV)." Jesus' question in (14:3-4) was not designed to oppose the law but to query the conventional wisdom regarding its interpretation. Someone with dropsy could incite pity, because his condition was not life threatening, it did not merit breaking the Sabbath law "to rest."

5) Eschatological teaching

There will be a resurrection of the righteous and the wicked (Dan.12:2; Acts 24:15; Rev.20:4-5). This is the context for Jesus' parable of the Great Banquet. Jesus, in declaring the eschatological Jubilee (4:18-19), has made even the Sabbath day "today" (4:21), the day of God's gracious gift to the needy. Here again is liberation (Gk. apoluo) and restoration for the man. God's eschatological purpose has again come to fruition (14:4; 11:20). Jesus invites those who sit at table with him to share in the redemption God has made available on the Sabbath. The healing of the man with dropsy is an embodiment of "good news to the poor (4:18-19)." (Green) **(40)**

6) Jesus the authoritative teacher

The silence of Jesus' table companions shows that Jesus can determine what is acceptable behaviour by way of Sabbath observance. This prepares the way for further instruction by Jesus as an authoritative teacher (14:7-24). Jesus does not subvert the law but queries the conventional interpretation. He says that deeds of mercy are permissible on the Sabbath.

[5] Another controversy with the religious authorities regarding Jesus' authority (20:1-8; Matt.21:23; Mk.11:28).

Jesus' authority and His work as a teacher and prophet require validation. "By what authority are you doing these things?" (20:2) Luke emphasises Jesus' role as a teacher. He also mentions the people (Gk. laos) who are always receptive to His message in Luke (19:45-48), "they hung on His words." (19:48) Luke distinguishes between the "people" who accepted Jesus, and their leaders and the "crowds" (Gk.ochloi) who did not receive Jesus.

Conclusion

- Teaching in the synagogue on the Sabbath day was the expected behaviour for Jesus (4:14-15,16,31,44).
- The healing of the man with the withered hand confirms Jesus' remark that "the Son of Man is lord of the Sabbath."
- Jesus says that deeds of mercy are permissible on the Sabbath: the Sabbath is a day for doing good rather than nothing.
- Was there a set Jewish tradition about the Sabbath? Meier **(41)** says that no such tradition existed. However the Essenes at Qumran were very strict regarding the Sabbath; animals in difficulty could not be helped on the Sabbath (CD) **(42)**. The Pharisees and Sadducees (Sabbat) **(43)** allowed animals to be helped (except on feast days) as no life or death situation existed. The move to heal could wait a day (13:14). Jesus said that a day given over to contemplating God was the best day for such a healing. Again the Sabbath is a day for doing good rather than nothing.
- "The Pharisees in the time of Jesus were not to be thought of as police but were self-appointed guardians of the Jewish culture." Wright **(44)** argues from Philo's special laws (2,46. Par.253), Jesus' kingdom claims and the prophetic nature of His ministry, all help to make the situation of Mk.3:1-6; Lk. 6:6-11 different in significance from the general practice of those who lived in Galilee. The Pharisees would have paid attention to Jesus. As soon as Jesus was not seen as an ordinary Jew but as a threat, His actions would have been carefully watched.

What do the Sabbath incidents tell us about Jesus?

- They show that Jesus was more than a teacher or prophet. Jesus is either a law breaker or one who stands above the law and uses it to fit His mission and the new situation that results from that mission. (Witherington) **(45)**
- These incidents underscore Jesus' claim to authority even more. Who has the authority to judge over the commands

the Torah? They also highlight His compassion and the nature of the opposition He faced.

• Although part of Jesus' answer in their dispute looks to the legal-ethical issues of the scope of the law in the face of compassion or need, His claim to be lord of the Sabbath" is not the innocent remark of a prophet but His claim to restore the kingdom's presence of God and divine authority over how God's commands operate in that rule. It is like Jesus' claim that the Son of Man has authority to forgive sins (5:27-36; 7:35-50).

• From a Jewish viewpoint, Jesus was a false prophet who, through His teaching, signs and wonders, tried to divert Israel from their authority and their interpretation of God's purpose sanctioned by the Jewish authorities in Jerusalem (AGT). **(46)** "Have you not read..?" This suggests that the Pharisees had read but had not understood the real meaning (6:3).

Pupil's Activity:One

a) Analyse the relationship between Jesus and the Religious Authorities as presented in Luke's Gospel.
(Edexcel A2) (2002)   [12 marks]
b) Explain the teaching of Jesus concerning Prayer and the Sabbath in Luke's Gospel.
(Edexcel A2) (2002)   [12 marks] (See also Ch. 7: Characteristics-prayer.)
c) To what extent were these teachings a departure from traditional Judaism at that time. Examine and evaluate this claim.
(Edexcel A2) (2002/2004/2005)   [8 marks]

> **Outcomes**
> Students should be able to examine and analyse:
> • the significant aspects of Jesus' teaching about the Sabbath.
> • the events in Luke's Gospel in which Jesus had controversies with the Pharisees.
> • how and why did Jesus' attitude to the Jews differed at that time and Jewish attitudes and teaching about the Sabbath.
> • the following concepts relating to the Sabbath: the Pharisees, the Essenes, fasting, legal, moral, eschatological, synagogue and Mishnah.

Notes on Ch.19: the Sabbath

1. Alexander Guttmann, Rabbinic Judaism in the Making, Detroit: Wayne State University, (1970).
2. Jacob Neusner, The Rabbinic Tradition of the Pharisees, (Leiden: Brill). (1971)
3. Ellis Rivkin, A Hidden Revolution: The Pharisee's search for the Kingdom Within, (Nashville: Abingdon) (1978).
4. Philip Sigal, Halakah; The Emergence of Contemporary Judaism, (Pittsburgh: Pickwick), 1980.
5. Donald Carson, Matthew, The Expositor's Bible Commentary, Vol. 8 Zondervan, (1984) p.33.
6. Donald Carson, op. cit. p.33.
7. Alexander Guttmann, (ibid.)
8. Donald Carson, op. cit.p.34.
9. Donald Carson, op. cit.p.34.
10. Mek. Ex.20:16; 23:15; 26:13; b. Shabbath 10b.
11. Sabbat.7.2.
12. G.D.Kilpatrick, According to Mark, p.116 cited by Carson, "regarding the disciples eating the grain, this was included as part of the story; why else would the disciples pick a little grain?" p.279.
13. Leon Morris, op. cit.p.122.
14. b. Shabbath 128 a.b.
15. Jub. 2:19.
16. Morna Hooker, Son of Man, op. cit 100ff. cited in Carson p.283.
17. Leon Morris, op. cit p.122.
18. John Murray, Principles of Conduct, Tyndale Press, (1957) p.33.
19. Sanders, Jesus and Judaism pp.264-267. Contra Witherington (111), n. 8) See also Bock [3] pp.607-609.
20. BAGD, 662.
21. 'Eduyyet 2,5; M. Shabbath 6:3; Mek. Ex.22:2; 23:13.
22 m. Sabbat, 14.4; 19:2.
23. Qumran, CD, 11.5-18: one is not allowed to pasture an animal beyond a length of 1,000 cubits.
24. Craig Keener, Matthew, NAC,22, Nashville: Broadman, (1992) pp.197-199 "Some Jews did at least allow prayer for the sick on the Sabbath. (t. Sabbat 16.22)
25. Joel Green, op. cit. p.256.
26. Paul–Gerd Muller, EDNT 1:129-130.
27. Richard T. France, TNTC, Matthew, IVP, (1985) p.205.
28. 1 Qap Gen.20:16-29.
29. m. Sabbat.15,2; m 'Erubin, 2,1-4.
30. Joel Green, op. cit. 520.
31. Joel Green, op. cit. p.525.
32. Howard Marshall, op. cit p.559.
33. Joseph Fitzmyer, op. cit. p.1014.
34. Darrell Bock, op. cit. p.274.
35. Joel Green, op. cit. p.546.
36 Midras Rabbah, Leviticus 15:2; SB 1926:2:203 van de Loos, (1965): 504-6.
37 SBK 1:629; Sabbat 128b.
38. Qumran, CD, 11:13-14.
39. CD 11.13-17, (15)
40. Joel Green, op. cit. p.541.
41. John Meier, A Marginal Jew, Rethinking the historical Jesus, New York: Doubleday (1996-2001) 2.681-85, says that no such tradition existed. However the Essenes at Qumran were very strict regarding the Sabbath–animals in difficulty could not be helped on the Sabbath.
42. Qumran, CD, 11:13-14.
43. Sabbat 18:3.
44. N. Tom Wright, Jesus and the Victory of God, Fortress Press, (1996) pp.390-6.
45. Ben Witherington (111), The Christology of Jesus, Fortress Press, (1990) p.69.
46. AGT, op. cit. p. 241.